MARKETING MANAGEMENT

Philip Kotler

Northwestern University

MARKETING

PRENTICE-HALL, INC., ENGLEWOOD CLIFFS, NEW JERSEY

THIRD EDITION

MANAGEMENT

Analysis, planning, and control

Library of Congress Cataloging in Publication Data

KOTLER, PHILIP (date)
  Marketing management.

  Includes bibliographical references.
  1. Marketing management.
HF5415.13.K64 1975   658.8
ISBN 0–13–557959–7   75-20278

TO NANCY

MARKETING MANAGEMENT

Analysis, planning, and control

Third Edition

Philip Kotler

10 9 8 7 6 5 4 3 2 1

PRENTICE-HALL INTERNATIONAL, INC., *London*
PRENTICE-HALL OF AUSTRALIA, PTY. LTD., *Sydney*
PRENTICE-HALL OF CANADA, LTD., *Toronto*
PRENTICE-HALL OF INDIA PRIVATE LIMITED, *New Delhi*
PRENTICE-HALL OF JAPAN, INC., *Tokyo*
PRENTICE-HALL OF SOUTHEAST ASIA (PTE.) LTD., *Singapore*

CONTENTS

v

VII BROADENING MARKETING 465

21
International marketing 467

22
Marketing in the contemporary environment 482

VIII CASES IN MARKETING 499

INDICES 517

PREFACE

The "quiet life" is not for marketers. In recent years, marketing executives have had to cope with (1) high and persistent worldwide inflation; (2) material and energy shortages; (3) economic stagnation; (4) consumerism; (5) environmentalism; (6) increased government regulation; (7) changing consumer life styles; and (8) undermarketed public sector needs. Marketers have had to find solutions to these problems that reconcile corporate profitability, customer satisfaction, and social responsibility.

Properly viewed, these problems are also opportunities. Marketing is the link between a society's needs and its industrial activities. It is the function that adjusts the organization's offerings to the ever-changing needs of the marketplace. It is the external sensors of the organization that provide for its adaptation and growth.

This third edition has been written with four objectives:

1 to update the discussion of marketing problems, practices, and principles;

2 to deepen the discussion of marketing topics of increased importance, such as product concept development and testing, product positioning, product life cycle, consumer buying behavior, marketing control, and new marketing philosophies;

3 to shorten the text so that it can be used with maximum profit in a one-quarter or one-semester course; and

4 to add cases that will provide an opportunity to apply marketing thinking to real marketing situations.

Otherwise, the book remains true to its original principles. These principles are:

1 *A managerial orientation.* This book focuses on the major decisions facing marketing executives in their attempt to harmonize the objectives and resources of the organization with the opportunities found in the marketplace.

2 *An analytical approach.* This book does not provide pat answers so much as ways of thinking about and analyzing recurrent marketing problems. Descriptive material is held to a minimum in order to permit the greatest latitude in developing the analytical content of marketing.

3 *A reliance on basic disciplines.* This book draws heavily on the basic disciplines of economics, behavioral science, and mathematics. *Economics* provides the fundamental tools and concepts for seeking optimal results in the use of scarce resources. *Behavioral science* provides fundamental concepts and findings for the interpretation of consumer and organizational buying behavior. *Mathematics* provides the means of developing explicit statements about the relationships among variables in a problem.

4 *A universal approach.* This book develops marketing thinking for the broadest of contexts. Marketing is treated as relevant to industrial as well as consumer markets, service industries as well as goods industries, small companies as well as large ones, nonprofit organizations as well as profit companies, and buyers as well as sellers.

Marketing remains one of the most difficult areas of analysis and decision-making for the company. Marketing problems do not exhibit the neat quantitative properties of many of the problems in production, accounting, or finance. Psychological variables play a large role; marketing expenditures affect demand and costs simultaneously; marketing plans shape and interact with other corporate plans. Marketing decisions must be made in the face of insufficient information about processes that are dynamic, nonlinear, lagged, stochastic, interactive, and downright difficult. However, this is not taken as a case for intuitive decision-making; rather it suggests the need for improved theoretical frameworks and sharper tools for analysis.

The book is organized into eight parts. *Part I* develops the conceptual and strategic underpinnings of marketing. *Part II* presents concepts and tools for analyzing any market and marketing environment to discern opportunities. *Part III* presents principles for selecting target markets and planning effective marketing programs. *Part IV* deals with the formulation of product strategy over the product life cycle. *Part V* deals with assembling the specific elements of the marketing mix based on their unique contributions. *Part VI* develops the administrative side of marketing: organization, information handling, and control. *Part VII* broadens the discussion of marketing to cover international and contemporary issues. *Part VIII* provides several realistic marketing cases for marketing analysis and decision-making.

Acknowledgments

This book bears the imprint of many persons. My present and former colleagues in the marketing department at Northwestern University made an important mark through their zest in blending marketing theory with administrative practice: Fred C. Allvine, Ira D. Anderson, Harper W. Boyd, Jr., Steuart H. Britt, Philip C. Burger, Richard M. Clewett, Vernon Fryburger, James R. Hawkinson, Sidney J. Levy, Robert M. Olsen, Stanley F. Stasch, Louis W. Stern, Brian Sternthal, Lynn H. Stockman, Eugene Webb, Ralph Westfall, and Gerald Zaltman. Donald P. Jacobs, Dean of the Graduate School of Management, provided constant encouragement. The secretarial staff, Edith Bass, Marion Davis, and Sabra Van Cleef, provided invaluable help in manuscript preparation for the third edition.

I am indebted to colleagues at other universities who reviewed this or previous editions and provided insightful suggestions: Professors Robert Brooks (University of Baltimore), Ronald E. Frank (University of Pennsylvania), Fred W. Kniffin (Pennsylvania State University), Joseph W. Newman (University of Michigan), Mitchell Owens (University of Baltimore), and James Patterson (Indiana University).

My overriding debt is to my wife, Nancy, to whom this book is dedicated.

Philip Kotler
Northwestern University
Evanston, Illinois

CONCEPTUALIZING MARKETING MANAGEMENT

1

TASKS AND PHILOSOPHIES OF MARKETING MANAGEMENT

Marketing is so basic that it cannot be considered a separate function. . . . It is the whole business seen from the point of view of its final result, that is, from the customer's point of view.

PETER DRUCKER

As human history moves toward the year 2000, with its awe-inspiring problems and opportunities, the subject of marketing is attracting increasing attention from companies, institutions, and nations. Marketing has evolved from its early origins in distribution and selling into a comprehensive philosophy for relating any organization dynamically to its markets. Marketing is a cornerstone of policy and practice in such giant concerns as General Electric, Procter & Gamble, Sears, and IBM. Large and small business firms everywhere are beginning to appreciate the difference between selling and marketing and are organizing to do the latter. Nonprofit organizations such as museums, universities, churches, and government agencies are seeing marketing as a new way of looking at their relations with their publics. Developing nations are examining marketing principles to see how their domestic distribution system can be improved and how they can compete more effectively in world markets. Socialist nations are beginning to study how they could use marketing research, advertising, and pricing to increase their effectiveness in planning and distributing their goods.

The intensifying interest in marketing is paradoxical because while marketing is one of man's newest action disciplines, it is also one of the world's oldest professions. From the time of *simple barter* through the stage of a *money economy* to today's modern *complex marketing system, exchanges* have been taking place. But marketing—the study of exchange processes and relationships—made its formal appearance only in the early part of the twentieth century out of questions and issues neglected by its mother science, economics.

In this short time, marketing has achieved the image of society's savior in the minds of many, and society's corrupter in the minds of others. Marketing's good deeds have been described in various ways:

> Aggressive marketing policies and practices have been largely responsible for the high material standard of living in America. Today through mass low-cost marketing we enjoy products which were once considered luxuries and which are still so classified in many foreign countries.[1]

> Advertising nourishes the consuming power of men. It creates wants for a better standard of living. It sets up before a man the goal of a better home, better clothing, better food for himself and his family. It spurs individual exertion and greater production. It brings together in fertile union those things which otherwise would not have met.[2]

Others take a dimmer view of marketing's contribution to society:

> For the past 6,000 years the field of marketing has been thought of as made up of fast-buck artists, con-men, wheeler-dealers, and shoddy-goods distributors. Too many of us have been "taken" by the tout or con-man; and all of us at times have been prodded into buying all sorts of "things" we really did not need, and which we found later on we did not even want.[3]

> What does a man need—really need? A few pounds of food each day, heat and shelter, six feet to lie down in—and some form of working activity that will yield a sense of accomplishment. That's all—in a material sense. And we know it. But we are brainwashed by our economic system until we end up in a tomb beneath a pyramid of time payments, mortgages, preposterous gadgetry, playthings that divert our attention from the sheer idiocy of the charade.[4]

It is clear that various social commentators have vastly different views on the meaning and social worth of marketing. This leads us to the major purpose of the first chapter. The purpose is to define the nature of *marketing*, the tasks of *marketing management*, and alternative *philosophies* of marketing management.

MARKETING

Various definitions of marketing have appeared through time:

> It has been described by one person or another as a business activity; as a group of related business activities; as a trade phenomenon; as a frame of mind; as a coordinative, integrative function in policy making; as a sense of business pur-

---

[1]William J. Stanton, *Fundamentals of Marketing* (New York: McGraw-Hill Book Company, 1964), pp. 4–5.

[2]Sir Winston Churchill.

[3]Richard N. Farmer, "Would You Want Your Daughter to Marry a Marketing Man?" *Journal of Marketing,* January 1967, p. 1.

[4]Sterling Hayden, *Wanderer* (New York: Alfred A. Knopf, Inc., 1963).

pose; as an economic process; as a structure of institutions; as the process of exchanging or transferring ownership of products; as a process of concentration, equalization, and dispersion; as the creation of time, place, and possession utilities; as a process of demand and supply adjustment; and as many other things.[5]

All of these definitions provide useful but partial perspectives on the nature of marketing. We would like to propose a definition of marketing that is rooted in the logic of human nature and behavior. Our definition is:

Marketing is human activity directed at satisfying needs and wants through exchange processes.

Human needs and wants

The starting point for the discipline of marketing lies in *human needs and wants.* Mankind needs food, air, water, clothing, and shelter to survive. Beyond this, people have a strong desire for recreation, education, and other services. They have strong preferences for particular versions of basic goods and services.

Whatever the case, there is no doubt that modern man's needs and wants are staggering. In one year, in the United States alone, Americans purchased 67 billion eggs, 250 million chickens, 5.5 million hair dryers, 133 billion domestic air travel passenger miles, and over 20 million lectures by college English professors. These consumer goods and services led to a derived demand for more fundamental inputs such as 150 million tons of steel and 3.7 billion tons of cotton. These are a few of the wants and needs that get expressed in a $1.3 trillion economy.

Products

The existence of human needs and wants gives rise to the concept of products. Our definition of product is:

A *product* is something that is viewed as capable of satisfying a want.

A product is really nothing more than a tool for solving a problem.

A want describes a state of felt deprivation in a person. This deprivation produces discomfort and a wish to act to relieve this discomfort. The want energizes the person—puts him into an active state—and gives him direction. The person will perceive certain things outside of himself that would satisfy his want. These things can be called products. They take on value to the individual because of their capacity to satisfy his wants.

It is important not to limit our concept of product to physical objects. The key thing about a product is the service that it renders. A physical good is simply a physical means of packaging a service. A tube of lipstick is not bought for its own sake but rather in the hope of producing beauty. A drill bit is not bought for its own sake but rather to produce a needed hole. A product is really nothing more than a tool for solving a problem.

Anything capable of rendering a service, that is, satisfying a need, can be called a product. This includes *persons, places, organizations,* and *ideas.* Consumers make a decision among different entertainers to watch on television, different places to go on a vacation, different organizations to contribute to, and different ideas to support. These are alternative products from the point of view of a consumer. If the term *product* seems unnatural at times, we may

[5]Marketing Staff of the Ohio State University, "A Statement of Marketing Philosophy," *Journal of Marketing,* January 1965, p. 43.

substitute the term *resource* or *offering*. All of these terms describe something of value to someone.

Exchange

The fact that man has needs and wants and there are products capable of satisfying them is necessary but not sufficient to define marketing. Marketing exists when man decides to satisfy his needs and wants in a certain way that we shall call exchange. Exchange is one of four alternative options available to man to obtain a product capable of satisfying a particular need he has.

His first option is *self-production*. A hungry man can relieve his hunger through his own efforts at hunting, fishing, or fruit gathering. He does not have to interact with anyone else. In this case there is no market and no marketing.

His second option is *coercion*. The hungry man can forcibly take food from another person or steal it. He offers no benefit to the other party except the chance not to be harmed.

His third option is *supplication*. The hungry man can approach someone and plead for food as a gesture of charity. He has nothing tangible to offer except his gratitude.

His fourth option is *exchange*. The hungry man can approach someone who has food and offer some resource in exchange for the food. He may offer money, some good, or some service of value to the owner.

Marketing centers on the last approach, that of exchange, to the acquisition of products to satisfy human wants and needs. Exchange requires the following conditions:

1 There are two parties.
2 Each party has something that may be of value to the other.
3 Each party is capable of communication and delivery.
4 Each party is free to accept or reject the offer.

If these conditions exist, there is a potential for exchange. Whether exchange actually takes place depends upon whether the two parties can find *terms of exchange* that leave them both better off (or at least not worse off) than before the exchange. This is the sense in which exchange is described as a value-creating process, that is, an act of free exchange normally increases the value felt by both parties.

Market

The concept of exchange leads naturally into the concept of a market. Our definition of market is:

A *market* is an arena for potential exchanges.

An example will illustrate this concept. Suppose an artist spends three weeks creating a beautiful sculpture. He has in mind a particular price. The question he faces is whether there is anyone who will exchange this amount of money for the sculpture. If there is at least one such person, we can say there is a market. The *size of the market* will vary with the price. The artist may ask for so high a price that there will be no market for his sculpture. As he brings the price down, normally the market size increases because more people can afford the sculpture. The size of the market depends upon the number of persons who have both (1) an interest in the object and (2) a willingness to offer the resources required to obtain it.

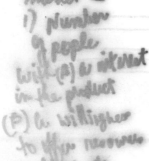

Size of
market =
1) Number
of people
with (P) an interest
in the product
(P) a willingness
to offer resources
to obtain it

Wherever there is a potential for trade, there is a market. The term "market" is often used in conjunction with some qualifying term that describes a *human need* or *product type* or *demographic group* or *geographical location*. An example of a *need market* is the relaxation market, which exists because people are willing to exchange money for lessons on yoga, transcendental meditation, and bio-feedback control. An example of a *product market* is the shoe market, so defined because people are willing to exchange money for objects called shoes. An example of a *demographic market* is the youth market, so defined because young people possess purchasing power that they are willing to exchange for such products as education, bikinis, motorcycles, and stereophonic equipment. An example of a *geographic market* is the French market, so defined because French citizens are a locus of potential transactions for a wide variety of goods and services.

The concept of a market also covers exchanges of resources not necessarily involving money. The political candidate offers promises of good government to a *voter market* in exchange for their votes. The lobbyist offers services to a *legislative market* in exchange for votes for his cause. A university cultivates the *mass-media market* when it wines and dines editors in exchange for more and better publicity. A museum cultivates the *donor market* when it offers special privileges to contributors in exchange for their financial support.

Marketing

The concept of markets finally brings us full circle to the concept of **marketing**. *Marketing* means working with *markets,* which in turn means attempting to actualize *potential exchanges* for the purpose of *satisfying human needs and wants.* Thus we return to our definition of *marketing* as *human activity directed at satisfying needs and wants through exchange processes.*

MARKETING MANAGEMENT

Coping with exchange processes calls for a considerable amount of work and skill. *Individuals* become fairly adroit at buying to meet their household needs. Occasionally, they also undertake selling—selling their car, selling personal services. *Organizations* are more professional in handling exchange processes. They must attract resources from one set of markets, convert them into useful products, and trade them in another set of markets. *Whole nations* also plan and manage exchange relations with others. They search for mutually beneficial trade relations and exchanges with other nations. In this book we will primarily take the perspective of *organizational marketing* rather than that of personal or national marketing.

Our position is that *marketing management* takes place when at least one party to a potential exchange gives thought to his objectives and means of achieving desired responses from other parties. Our formal definition of marketing management is:

> **Marketing management** is the analysis, planning, implementation, and control of programs designed to bring about desired exchanges with target markets for the purpose of achieving organizational objectives. It relies heavily on designing the organization's offering in terms of the target market's needs and desires and using effective pricing, communication, and distribution to inform, motivate, and service the market.

Although various managers in a company deal with markets of different types, marketing management is historically identified with the specialized job of dealing with the customer market for the final products of the firm. We shall adopt this same convention, although everything that we shall say about marketing principles applies with equal force to all market managers.

Formal marketing work is carried out in companies by sales managers, salesmen, advertising managers, marketing research managers, customer service managers, product managers, and the marketing vice-president. Each of these job positions goes along with well-defined missions and responsibilities. Many of these job positions center around the management of a particular marketing resource such as advertising, sales force, or marketing research. On the other hand, product managers, market managers, and the marketing vice-president manage programs. *Their job is to analyze, plan, and implement programs that will produce a desired level of transactions with specified target markets.*

Marketing-management tasks

Marketing management is demand management.

The popular image of the marketing manager is that of someone whose task is primarily to stimulate demand for the company's products. However, this is too limited a view of the range of marketing tasks carried out by marketing managers. *Marketing management is the task of regulating the level, timing, and character of demand in a way that will help the organization achieve its objectives.* Simply put, marketing management is demand management.

The organization forms an idea of a *desired level of transactions* with a market. At any point in time, the *actual demand level* may be below, equal to, or above the *desired demand level.* This leads to the eight distinguishable demand states listed in Table 1-1. The marketing task and the formal name of each task is shown next to each demand state.

Conversional marketing   Conversional marketing grows out of the state of negative demand. *Negative demand* is *a state in which all or most of the important segments of the potential market dislike the product or service and in fact might conceivably pay a price to avoid it.*

Negative demand, far from being a rare condition, applies to many products and services. Vegetarians feel negative demand for meats of all kinds. Numerous Americans feel negative demand for kidneys and sweetbreads. People

Table 1-1

The basic marketing tasks

Demand state	Marketing task	Formal name
I. Negative demand	Disabuse demand	Conversional marketing
II. No demand	Create demand	Stimulational marketing
III. Latent demand	Develop demand	Developmental marketing
IV. Faltering demand	Revitalize demand	Remarketing
V. Irregular demand	Synchronize demand	Synchromarketing
VI. Full demand	Maintain demand	Maintenance marketing
VII. Overfull demand	Reduce demand	Demarketing
VIII. Unwholesome demand	Destroy demand	Countermarketing

have a negative demand for vaccinations, dental work, vasectomies, and gall bladder operations. Many travelers have a negative demand for air travel; others have a negative demand for rail travel. Places such as the North Pole and the desert wastelands are in negative demand by tourists. Atheism, ex-convicts, military service, and even work are in negative demand by certain groups.

The challenge of negative demand to marketing management, especially in the face of a positive supply, is to develop a plan that will cause demand to rise from negative to positive and eventually equal the positive supply level. We call this marketing task *conversional marketing.*

Stimulational marketing   There is a whole range of products and services for which there is no demand. Instead of people having negative or positive feelings toward the offering, they are indifferent or uninterested. *No demand is a state in which all or important segments of a potential market are uninterested in or indifferent to a particular offering.*

Three different categories of offerings are characterized by no demand. First, there are those familiar objects that are perceived as having no value. Examples would be urban junk such as disposable coke bottles, old barbed wire, and political buttons right after an election. Second, there are those familiar objects that are recognized to have value but not in the particular market. Examples would include boats in areas not near any water, snow-mobiles in areas where it never snows, and burglar alarms in areas where there is no crime. Third, there are those unfamiliar objects that are innovated and face a situation of no demand because the relevant market has no knowledge of the object. Examples would include trinkets of all kinds that people might buy if exposed to but would not normally think about or desire.

The task of converting no demand into positive demand is called *stimulational marketing.* Stimulational marketing is a tough task because the marketer does not even start with a semblance of latent demand for the offering. He can proceed in three ways. The first is to try to connect the product or service with some existing need in the marketplace. Thus antique dealers can attempt to stimulate interest in old barbed wire on the part of those who have a general need to collect things. The second is to alter the environment so that the offering becomes valued in that environment. Thus sellers of motorboats can attempt to stimulate interest in boats in a lakeless community by building an artificial lake. The third is to distribute information or the object itself in more places in the hope that people's lack of demand is really only a lack of exposure.

Developmental marketing   Developmental marketing is associated with a state known as latent demand. A state of *latent demand* exists *when a substantial number of people share a strong need for something that does not exist in the form of an actual product or service.* The latent demand represents an opportunity for the marketing innovator to develop the product or service that people have been wanting.

Examples of products and services in latent demand abound. Many cigarette smokers would like a good-tasting cigarette that does not yield nicotine and tars damaging to health. Such a product breakthrough would be an instant success, just as the first filter-tip cigarette won a sizable share of the market. Many people would like a car that promised substantially more safety and substantially less pollution than existing cars. There is a strong latent demand for fast city roads, efficient trains, uncrowded national parks, unpolluted major cities, safe streets, and good television programs.

The process of effectively converting latent demand into actual demand is that of *developmental marketing*. The marketer must be an expert in identifying those prospects who have the strongest latent demand and in coordinating all the marketing functions to develop the market in an orderly way.

Remarketing   All kinds of products, services, places, organizations, and ideas eventually experience declining or *faltering demand. Faltering demand* is *a state in which the demand for a product or service is less than its former level and where further decline is expected in the absence of remedial efforts to revise the target market, offering, and/or marketing effort.*

For example, railway travel has been a service in steady decline for a number of years, and it is badly in need of imaginative remarketing. Many churches have seen their membership thin out in the face of competition from secular recreations and activities. The downtown areas of many large cities are in need of remarketing. Many popular entertainers and political candidates lose their following and badly need remarketing.

The challenge of faltering demand is revitalization, and the marketing task involved is *remarketing*. Remarketing is based on the premise that it is possible in many cases to start a new life cycle for a declining product or service. Remarketing is the search for new marketing propositions for relating the offering to its potential market.

Synchromarketing   Very often an organization might be satisfied with the average level of demand but quite dissatisfied with its temporal pattern. Some seasons are marked by demand surging far beyond the supply capacity of the organization, and other seasons are marked by a wasteful underutilization of the organization's supply capacity. *Irregular demand* is defined as *a state in which the current timing pattern of demand is marked by seasonal or volatile fluctuations that depart from the timing pattern of supply.*

Many examples of irregular demand can be cited. In mass transit much of the equipment is idle during the off-hours and in insufficient supply during the peak hours. Hotels in Miami Beach are insufficiently booked during the summer and overbooked in the winter. Hospital operating facilities are over-booked at the beginning of the week and underutilized toward the end of the week to meet physician preferences.

The marketing task of trying to resolve irregular demand is called *synchro-marketing* because the effort is to bring the movements of demand and supply into better synchronization. Many marketing steps can be taken to alter the pattern of demand. For example, a museum that is undervisited on weekdays and overvisited on weekends could (a) shift most of the optional events to week-days instead of weekends, (b) advertise only its weekday programs, (c) charge a higher admission price during the weekends. In some cases a pattern of demand can be readily reshaped through simple switches in incentives or promotion; in other cases the reshaping may be achieved only after years of patient effort to alter habits and desires.

Maintenance marketing   The most desirable situation that a seller faces is that of full demand. *Full demand* is *a state in which the current level and timing of demand is equal to the desired level and timing of demand.* Various products and services achieve this state from time to time. However, it is not a time for resting on one's laurels and doing perfunctory marketing. Market demand is subject to two erosive forces. One force is changing needs and tastes in the marketplace. The demand for barber services, as well as the demand for mass magazines and college educations, has undergone an unexpected decline because of changing market preferences. The other force is active competition. When a product is doing well, competitors quickly move in and attempt to attract away some of the demand.

The task of the marketer facing full demand is *maintenance marketing*. Maintenance marketing calls for maintaining efficiency in the carrying out of day-to-day marketing activities and eternal vigilance in spotting new forces that threaten to erode demand. The maintenance marketer is primarily concerned with tactical issues such as keeping the price right, keeping the sales force and dealers motivated, and keeping tight control over costs.

Demarketing Sometimes the demand for a product or service substantially begins to outpace the supply. Known as *overfull demand*, it is defined as *a state in which demand exceeds the level at which the marketer feels able or motivated to supply it.*

The problem may be due to *temporary shortages,* as when producers suddenly find themselves facing an unexpected surge in demand or unexpected interruptions of supply. Or the problem may be due to *chronic overpopularity.* For example, the state of Oregon felt that too many people were moving to Oregon and spoiling its natural environment; and the city of San Francisco felt that too many motorists were using the Golden Gate bridge and weakening its structure.

The task of reducing overfull demand is called *demarketing. Demarketing deals with attempts to discourage customers in general or a certain class of customers in particular on either a temporary or a permanent basis.* Demarketing largely calls for marketing in reverse. Instead of encouraging customers, it calls for the art of discouraging them. Prices may be raised and product quality, service, promotion, and convenience may be reduced. The demarketer must have a thick skin because he is not going to be popular with certain groups.

Countermarketing There are many products or services for which the demand may be judged unwholesome from the viewpoint of the consumer's welfare, the public's welfare, or the supplier's welfare. *Unwholesome demand is a state in which any demand is felt to be excessive because of undesirable qualities associated with the offering.* Classic examples of unselling efforts have revolved around the so-called vice products: alcohol, cigarettes, and hard drugs.

The task of trying to destroy the demand for something is called *countermarketing*, or *unselling.* Whereas demarketing tries to reduce the demand without impugning the product itself, countermarketing is an attempt to designate the product as intrinsically unwholesome. The offering may be the organization's own product which it wishes to phase out, a competitor's product, or a third party's product which is regarded as socially undesirable.[6]

---

[6]For further reading of marketing management tasks and accompanying strategies, see the author's "The Major Tasks of Marketing Management," *Journal of Marketing,* October 1973, pp. 42–49.

MARKETING-MANAGEMENT PHILOSOPHIES

We have described marketing management as the conscious effort to achieve desired exchange outcomes with target markets. Now the question arises, What is the philosophy that guides these marketing efforts? What is the relative weight given to serving the interests of the *organization,* the *customers,* and *society?* Very often these conflict. It is desirable that marketing activities be carried out under a clear concept of responsive and responsible marketing.

There are four alternative concepts under which business and other organizations can conduct their marketing activity.

The product concept

The product concept is the oldest concept guiding producers.

> The ***product concept*** is a management orientation that assumes that consumers will respond favorably to good products that are reasonably priced and that little company marketing effort is required to achieve satisfactory sales and profits.

The implicit premises of the product concept are:

1   The company should concentrate its attention on the task of producing good products that are fairly priced.
2   Consumers are interested in buying products rather than solving particular problems.
3   Consumers know the available competing brands.
4   Consumers choose among competing brands on the basis of their quality in relation to their price.

The best-known example of the product concept is the manufacturer who built a better mousetrap.[7] He followed Emerson's advice: "If a man . . . makes a better mousetrap . . . the world will beat a path to his door." But to his surprise, he found few customers panting at his door. People do not automatically learn about new and improved products, believe that they are really superior, or show a willingness to pay a higher price. The inventor of a better mousetrap will get nowhere unless he takes positive steps to design, package, and price his new product attractively, place it into convenient distribution channels, bring it to the attention of persons concerned with rodent problems, and convince them that it has superior qualities.

Companies can be found in all fields that tend to operate on a product concept. Railroad management was so sure that it had a superior form of transportation that it underserved the customers and overlooked the emerging challenge of the airlines, buses, trucks, and automobiles. The story is told of an office-file manufacturer who complained to his sales manager that his files should be selling better. "Our files are the best in the world. They can be dropped from a four-story building and not be damaged." "Yes," agreed his

---
[7]See "So We Made a Better Mousetrap," *The President's Forum,* Fall 1962, pp. 26–27.

sales manager, "but our customers aren't planning to push their files out of four-story buildings."

Nonprofit organizations also frequently exhibit a product orientation. Opera companies assume that the public will want the standard fare of Mozart, Verdi, and Puccini year after year. Colleges and universities assume that high school graduates will continue to want their product. Churches, police departments, the post office, and many other nonprofit organizations feel that they are offering the public the right product and that the public should be grateful. Obviously, this concentration on the purity and immutability of the product eventually gets these organizations into deep trouble, as many are finding out.

The selling concept

The selling concept is a second hallowed way in which producers have sought to guide their exchange activity.

> The *selling concept* is a management orientation that assumes that consumers will normally not buy enough of the company's products unless they are approached with a substantial selling and promotion effort.

The implicit premises of the selling concept are:

1 The main task of the company is to get sufficient sales for its products.
2 Consumers will not normally buy enough on their own.
3 The consumers can be induced to buy through various sales-stimulating devices.
4 The customers will probably buy again, and even if they don't, there are many other consumers out there.

Companies practicing the selling concept typically assume their goods are "sold, not bought." For example, insurance salesmen hold that people do not feel a strong need for insurance and do not beat a path to their door; therefore, it is necessary to aggressively search out potential customers and hard-sell them on the benefits of insurance. The same philosophy guides the thinking of encyclopedia and bible companies, land developers, and home repair contractors.

A prime practitioner of the selling concept is the American automobile industry. From the moment the customer walks into the showroom, some car salesmen will put on an act for the customer, which includes "psyching him out," exaggerating, baiting, and occasionally lying.[8] The new model is described as an excellent car. If the customer likes the floor model, he may be told that there is another customer about to buy it and that he should therefore make up his mind as fast as possible. If the customer balks at the price (which is artificially high to begin with), the salesman says he will talk to the manager to get a special concession only for him. The customer waits ten minutes and the salesman returns with "the boss doesn't like it but I got him to agree." The aim is "work up the customer" so that he is ready to sign then and there. If he walks out of the showroom without buying, he may be lost forever.

Obviously, there are great risks in practicing the selling concept, especially in its hard-driving form where customer satisfaction is considered secondary to getting the sale. It would seem to be a practice that would spoil the market for

---

[8]See Irwin J. Rein, *Rudy's Red Wagon: Communication Strategies in Contemporary Society* (Glenview, Ill.: Scott, Foresman & Company, 1972).

this seller; he would eventually find no more customers who would trust him. For the selling concept to work for an extended period of time, the following circumstances would have to be present:

1 Many of the customers come in knowing that the dealers are hard sellers and feel they can handle the situation.
2 Customers who are dissatisfied soon forget their dissatisfaction.
3 Dissatisfied customers do not talk very much to other customers.
4 Dissatisfied customers probably will not complain to consumer organizations.
5 There are a great number of potential customers out there; the company does not have to depend upon repeat business.

Although we have used business organizations to illustrate the selling concept, it is frequently practiced by nonprofit organizations as well. A perfect example is the political party seeking votes for its candidate. Having chosen a candidate on whatever grounds, it is stuck with him and must vigorously sell him to the voters as a fantastic person for the job.[9] The candidate and his supporters stomp through voting precincts from early morning to late evening shaking hands, kissing babies, meeting power brokers, making breezy speeches. Countless dollars are spent on radio and television advertising, posters, leaflets, and so on. Any flaws in the man are shielded from the public because the aim is to get the sale, not worry about postpurchase satisfaction. After he is elected, the new official continues to take a sales-oriented view toward the citizens. There is little measurement of what the public wants and a lot of selling effort to get the public to accept policies that a few want.

The marketing concept

The marketing concept is a rather new idea in the history of exchange relations.[10]

> The *marketing concept* is a management orientation that holds that the key task of the organization is to determine the needs, wants, and values of a target market and to adapt the organization to delivering the desired satisfactions more effectively and efficiently than its competitors.

The underlying premises of the marketing concept are:

1 The organization conceives of its mission in terms of satisfying a defined set of wants of a defined group of customers.
2 The organization recognizes that satisfying wants requires an active program of marketing research to learn of these wants.
3 The organization recognizes that all customer-impinging company activities must be placed under integrated marketing control.

---

[9]See Joseph McGinness, *The Selling of the President* (New York: Trident Press, 1969).
[10]See John B. McKitterick, "What Is the Marketing Management Concept?" *The Frontiers of Marketing Thought and Action* (Chicago: American Marketing Association, 1957), pp. 71–82; Fred J. Borch, "The Marketing Philosophy as a Way of Business Life," *The Marketing Concept: Its Meaning to Management,* Marketing Series, No. 99 (New York: American Management Association, 1957), pp. 3–5. Also see the statement by a former president of Pillsbury: Robert J. Keith, "The Marketing Revolution," *Journal of Marketing,* January 1960, pp. 35–38.

4 The organization believes that doing a good job of satisfying customers wins their loyalty, repeat business, and favorable word of mouth, all of these being crucial in satisfying the organization's goals.

The selling concept and the marketing concept are frequently confused by the public and many businessmen. Levitt offers the following contrast between these two orientations:

> Selling focuses on the needs of the seller; marketing on the needs of the buyer. Selling is preoccupied with the seller's need to convert his product into cash; marketing with the idea of satisfying the needs of the customer by means of the product and the whole cluster of things associated with creating, delivering and finally consuming it.[11]

The marketing concept replaces and reverses the logic of the selling concept. The two concepts are contrasted in Figure 1-1. The selling concept starts with the firm's existing products and considers the task as one of using selling and promotion to stimulate a profitable volume of sales. The marketing concept starts with the firm's existing and potential customers and their needs; it plans a coordinated set of products and programs to serve these needs; and it derives profits through creating customer satisfaction. In essence:

> The *marketing concept* is a *customer orientation* backed by *integrated marketing* aimed at generating *customer satisfaction* as the key to satisfying *organizational goals*.

Drucker makes the contrast even more extreme:

> Indeed, selling and marketing are antithetical rather than synonymous or even complementary. There will always, one can assume, be need for some selling.

---

[11]Theodore Levitt, "Marketing Myopia," *Harvard Business Review,* July–August 1960, pp. 45–56.

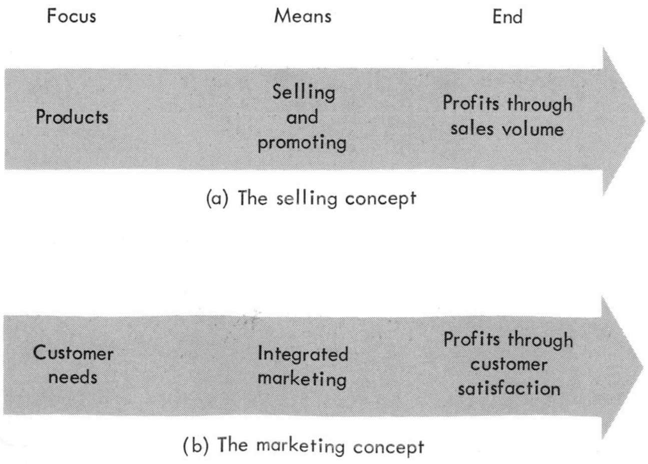

Focus	Means	End
Products	Selling and promoting	Profits through sales volume

(a) The selling concept

Figure 1-1
The sales and marketing concepts contrasted

Customer needs	Integrated marketing	Profits through customer satisfaction

(b) The marketing concept

But the aim of marketing is to make selling superfluous. The aim of marketing is to know and understand the customer so well that the product or service fits him and sells itself. Ideally, marketing should result in a customer who is ready to buy. All that should be needed then is to make the product or service available, i.e., logistics rather than salesmanship, and statistical distribution rather than promotion.[12] (Italics added.)

The marketing concept is the company's commitment to the time-honored concept in economic theory known as *consumer sovereignty.* The determination of what is to be produced should not be in the hands of the companies or in the hands of government but in the hands of consumers. The companies produce what the consumers want, and in this way maximize consumer welfare and earn their profits.

A prime practitioner of the marketing concept is McDonald's, the fast-food franchise chain, which in its first fifteen years served Americans and citizens in several other countries over 15 billion hamburgers. This organization is successful because it determined through research what consumers wanted in the way of fast-food product and service and adapted its organization to delivering them efficiently.

The marketing concept is also relevant to nonprofit organizations. Most nonprofit organizations start out as product oriented. When they begin to suffer declines in support or membership, they resort to selling tactics. Thus many colleges facing declining enrollments are now investing heavily in advertising and recruitment activities. But these selling steps turn out to be only stopgap measures. These organizations begin to realize the need to define their target markets more carefully; research their needs, wants, and values; modernize their products and programs; and communicate more effectively. Such organizations turn from selling to marketing.

**The societal
marketing concept**

In recent years people have begun to raise a number of questions about the marketing concept. One of the major questions is whether the marketing concept is really being practiced by American business firms, or only given lip service. The marketing concept has such a nice-sounding rhetoric when used by businessmen in their speeches. They may even mean what they say. But there is a great deal to do between the utterance and the deed. Establishing the marketing concept in an organization is an extremely difficult task, and it takes considerable planning, persuasion, education, and reorganization.[13] Consequently, a great number of companies really do not practice the marketing concept even though they may espouse it. Drucker considers *consumerism* to be evidence of this:

> That after twenty years of marketing rhetoric consumerism could become a powerful popular movement proves that not much marketing has been practiced. Consumerism is the "shame of marketing."[14]

---

[12]Peter F. Drucker, *Management: Tasks, Responsibilities, Practices* (New York: Harper & Row, Publishers, 1973), pp. 64–65.

[13]See Edward McKay, *The Marketing Mystique* (New York: American Management Association, 1972), pp. 22–30.

[14]Drucker, *op. cit.,* p. 64.

[Handwritten margin note:] "These organizations begin to realize the need to define their target markets more carefully; research their needs, wants + values; modernize their products and programs, + communicate more effectively. Such organizations turn from selling to marketing."*

There is a second, more disturbing question about the marketing concept, one that questions its validity rather than its practice. Recent articles have appeared with such titles as "The Faltering Marketing Concept" and "Societal Adaptation: A New Challenge for Marketing."[15] These articles essentially raise the question of whether the marketing concept is any longer an appropriate organizational goal in an age of environmental deterioration, resource shortages, explosive population growth, worldwide inflation, and neglected social services. The question is whether the firm that does an excellent job of sensing, serving, and satisfying consumer wants is necessarily acting in the best long-run interests of consumers and society. The marketing concept overlooks the conflict between individual want satisfaction and long-run public interest.

As a concrete instance, consider once again McDonald's. It is doing an excellent job of meeting the wants of the American people for quick, inexpensive, tasty food in attractive surroundings. But is it really serving their long-run interests? Here are two recent criticisms that have been leveled against it by consumer and environmental groups:

1 McDonald's serves tasty but not necessarily nutritious food. The hamburgers have a lot of fat in them. McDonald's promotes fries and pies, two products that are dear to American taste but are high in starch and fat.

2 McDonald's uses up a great amount of paper in providing its food. The hamburgers are first wrapped in tissue paper and then placed in paper boxes, presumably to keep them warm. This results in substantial paper wastage and cost to the consumer.

Thus in the effort of a company to serve consumers' wants, questions can be raised about the uncovered social costs. The same thing occurs in many other instances:

1 The American auto industry has catered to the American demand for large automobiles, but the meeting of this desire results in high fuel consumption, heavy pollution, more fatal accidents to those in small cars, and higher auto purchase and repair costs.

2 The soft-drink industry has catered to the American demand for convenience by increasing the share of one-way disposable bottles. The one-way bottle presents a great waste of resources in that approximately seventeen containers are necessary where one two-way bottle would have made seventeen trips before it could no longer be used; many one-way bottles are not biodegradable; and these bottles often are a littering element.

3 The detergent industry has catered to the American passion for whiter clothes by offering a product that at the same time pollutes rivers and streams, killing fish and injuring the recreational possibilities.

These situations have led in recent years to the call for a new concept to revise or replace the marketing concept. Among the proposals are "the human concept," "the intelligent consumption concept," and "the ecological imperative

---

[15]Martin L. Bell and C. William Emery, "The Faltering Marketing Concept," *Journal of Marketing*, October 1971, pp. 37–42; and Laurence P. Feldman, "Societal Adaptation: A New Challenge for Marketing," *Journal of Marketing*, July 1971, pp. 54–60.

concept,"[16] all of which get at different aspects of the same problem. We would like to propose "the societal marketing concept" as an answer to the dilemmas in the simple marketing concept. Our definition of societal marketing concept is:

> The *societal marketing concept* is a management orientation aimed at generating customer satisfaction and long-run consumer and public welfare as the key to satisfying organizational goals and responsibilities.

The underlying premises of the societal marketing concept are:

1   The main mission of the organization is to create satisfied and healthy customers and to contribute to the quality of life.
2   The organization constantly searches for better products defined in terms of appeal and benefit to consumers. It is ready to promote benefits that are in the consumers' interest even if not in his mind.
3   The organization eschews those products that are not in the best interests of the customer.
4   Consumers will sense and patronize those organizations that demonstrate concern for their satisfaction and welfare.

The societal marketing concept differs from the simple marketing concept by adding the consideration "long-run consumer and public welfare." It calls for a shift of the organization's perspective to include more marketing participants and longer-run effects. Societally responsible marketing calls for including four considerations in marketing decision making: *consumer wants, consumer interests, company requirements,* and *societal welfare.*

SUMMARY

Marketing has its origins in the fact that man is a creature of needs and wants. Needs and wants create a state of discomfort in persons, which is resolved through acquiring objects to satisfy these needs and wants. These objects—called products—are obtainable in several ways: self-production, coercion, supplication, and exchange. Most human society works on the principle of exchange, which means that persons specialize in the production of particular commodities and trade these commodities for the other things they need. A market is any arena for potential exchanges—there are need markets, product markets, demographic markets, and geographic markets. Marketing encompasses all those activities that represent working through markets, that is, trying to actualize potential exchanges.

Marketing management is the conscious effort to achieve desired exchange outcomes with target markets. We will consider marketing management primarily from the point of view of organizations acting as sellers, although the various concepts in marketing apply to all markets and marketers.

---

[16]Leslie M. Dawson, "The Human Concept: New Philosophy for Business," *Business Horizons,* December 1969, pp. 29–38; James T. Rothe and Lissa Benson, "Intelligent Consumption: An Attractive Alternative to the Marketing Concept," *MSU Business Topics,* Winter 1974, pp. 29–34; and George Fisk, "Criteria for a Theory of Responsible Consumption," *Journal of Marketing,* April 1973, pp. 24–31.

The marketer's basic skill lies in regulating the level, timing, and character of demand for a product, service, organization, place, person, or idea. The marketer faces up to eight different types of demand situations. If demand is negative, it must be disabused (conversional marketing); if nonexistent, it must be created (stimulational marketing); if latent, it must be developed (developmental marketing); if faltering, it must be revitalized (remarketing); if irregular, it must be synchronized (synchromarketing); if full, it must be maintained (maintenance marketing); if overfull, it must be reduced (demarketing); and if unwholesome, it must be destroyed (countermarketing).

Four alternative philosophies can guide organizations in carrying out their exchange activity. The product concept assumes that consumers will respond favorably to good products that are reasonably priced and therefore little marketing effort is required. The selling concept assumes that consumers will normally not buy enough of the company's products unless they are reached with a substantial selling and promotion effort. The marketing concept holds that the main task of the company is to determine what a chosen set of customers' needs, wants, and values are and to adapt the whole company to delivering the desired satisfactions. The societal marketing concept holds that the main task of the company is to generate customer satisfaction and long-run consumer and public welfare as the key to satisfying organizational goals and responsibilities.

**QUESTIONS
AND PROBLEMS**

1 There are several different approaches to the study of marketing phenomena. A *managerial* approach is one of them. Name some other approaches.

2 Trading is one of several ways of acquiring things. Propose some hypotheses explaining how trade or exchange may have begun.

3 The term *market* has many different usages. What does market mean to a stockbroker, produce merchant, sales manager, economist, and marketer?

4 Is there a contradiction between marketing something to people that is negatively demanded and practicing the marketing concept?

5 In the face of a long-term energy shortage, many public utilities have sought to reduce their customers' use of electricity. Propose a demarketing plan that will bring down the level of demand and help utilities avoid "brownouts."

6 McDonald's faces two alternatives with respect to adopting the societal marketing concept. It can argue that its present practices are sound and in the public's interest. Or it can make some adjustments that will bring it closer to the societal marketing concept. Develop each possibility.

7 Is the purpose of the marketing concept to maximize the customers' satisfaction or to maximize the company's long-run profitability?

8 Do you think the railroad passenger business is doomed? Why or why not? Could the passenger business be remarketed and made profitable through adoption of the marketing concept? Give illustrations.

9 Airlines seem to practice the marketing concept. They show a concern for passenger satisfaction, as exemplified by attractive stewardesses, complementary flight meals, and other amenities. Would you agree that they deserve a high rating for their marketing orientation?

10 Do you think the marketing concept should provide the major orientation for every company? Could you cite companies which do not particularly need this orientation? Which companies need it most?

11 "Marketing is not simply the job of a group of men in the company who are responsible for selling the company's products. Every member of the firm should know how to function as a marketer when needed." What does it mean for a company recruiter, for example, to function like a marketer?

2

THE MARKETING SYSTEM AND ENVIRONMENT

*No substantial part of the universe is so simple that
it can be grasped and controlled without abstraction.
Abstraction consists in replacing the part of the
universe under consideration by a model of similar
but simple structure. Models . . . are thus a central
necessity of scientific procedure.*

ARTURO ROSENBLUETH and NORBERT WIENER

The exchanges that take place between two parties occur in a larger framework
known as the marketing system. The effectiveness with which sellers and buyers
perform their marketing tasks depends on how thoroughly they understand the
major components, operating characteristics, and relationships making up the
marketing system.

OVERVIEW OF THE MARKETING SYSTEM

A marketing system is an abstraction of selected elements from a large set of
possibilities. Our definition of marketing system is:

> A *marketing system* is the set of significant institutions and flows that con-
> nect an organization to its markets.

We shall begin by assuming an organization that produces a single product for a single final market. It could be the Polaroid Company when it first
innovated its instant picture camera; Volkswagen when it offered one automobile; or Northwestern Mutual Life when it offered one insurance policy.

21

The two basic elements of a marketing system, a company and a market, are shown in Figure 2-1. These two elements are connected by four major flows. The company dispatches (1) goods and services and (2) communications to the market; in return it receives (3) dollars and (4) information. The inner loop shows an exchange of money for goods; the outer loop shows an exchange of meanings.

The simple marketing system in Figure 2-1 can be generalized to cover noncommercial transactions as well. The Denver police department produces protective services for the public; in return it receives taxes and the public's cooperation. The American Cancer Society produces research, information, and treatment of cancer; in return it receives donations and volunteer time from members of the public.

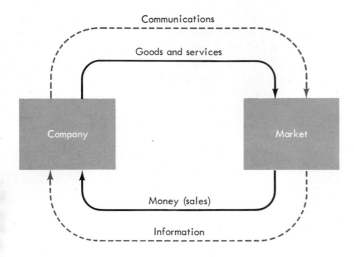

Figure 2-1
A simple marketing system

A marketing system contains more elements than simply the organization and its key consuming market. These additional elements affect the way and success with which the organization serves its markets. They must all be considered by management in developing its marketing plans. These elements are shown in Figure 2-2. First, there is the *core marketing system* consisting of a set of suppliers whose heterogeneous inputs are transformed by a company and its competitors into valued outputs that pass through marketing intermediaries to reach the final market. Second, there is an environment of several *publics* which individually and collectively affect the performance of the core marketing system. These publics include the financial community, independent press, government agencies and legislators, interest groups, and the general public. Finally, there are broad forces in the *macroenvironment*—demography, economics, law and politics, technology, and culture—that exercise a profound influence on the core marketing system directly and through the various publics. This chapter will examine the characteristics, role, and interrelationships of these different elements of the total marketing system.

THE CORE MARKETING SYSTEM

The core marketing system describes the network of key institutions that interact to supply final markets with needed goods and services. Two of the components—the company and the final market—have already been discussed. Here we will describe the other three core components—marketing intermediaries, suppliers, and competitors.

Marketing intermediaries

Marketing intermediaries are institutions that facilitate the flow of goods and services between the company and its final markets. They include resellers (wholesalers and retailers), agents and brokers, transportation companies and warehouses, credit companies, and advertising agencies. These institutions come into being to facilitate the work of consummating exchanges.

Marketing intermediaries carry on at least four functions. First, there is the work of *market search.* Sellers must search for potential buyers and buyers for potential sellers. They can be helped in this by marketing intermediaries. For example, Hewlett-Packard developed a small advanced electronic calculator priced at $395. The company recognized that most people are not in the market for this type of calculator, and it therefore hired a marketing research firm to pinpoint the best prospects. Then it went to a mailing list firm and bought mailing lists of engineers, architects, and mathematicians. Thus its market search was aided by intermediary firms.

The second function is *physical distribution.* Transactions require the delivery of the values being exchanged. Involved in this are three subfunctions: *stocking locations, storage, and transportation.* These functions are borne partly by the seller, partly by the buyer, and partly by specialized intermediaries such

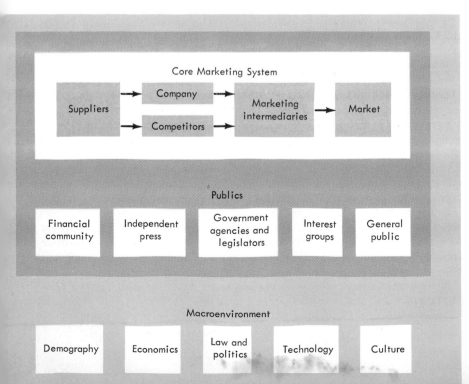

Core Marketing System

Suppliers → Company → Marketing intermediaries → Market

Suppliers → Competitors → Marketing intermediaries

Publics

Financial community | Independent press | Government agencies and legislators | Interest groups | General public

Macroenvironment

Demography | Economics | Law and politics | Technology | Culture

Figure 2-2
Elements of the company marketing system and environment

as warehouses, transportation carriers, wholesalers and retailers, and physical distribution consulting firms. Services also require some physical distribution work. The H&R Block company, for example, provides income-tax assistance to households for a fee. The service is available through franchised outlets operating in different U.S. cities. H&R Block has to decide on the number of outlets, where they should be located, and how much service to stock at each outlet (i.e., the number of tax consultants in each office to place against the expected demand).

Communication is a third function performed by marketing intermediaries. For exchanges to occur, the parties must be able to receive and send information. The seller wants to find efficient ways of informing potential buyers about his product. Among the communication channels are newspapers and magazines, television and radio stations, and billboards. Institutions that assist sellers in using the communication channels effectively are advertising agencies, public relations firms, and sales promotion firms.

The fourth channel function is *negotiation and title transfer*. Intermediaries that assist in the negotiation and title transfer process include credit institutions, legal institutions, merchant middlemen, and agent middlemen. *Merchant middlemen* are intermediaries who buy the goods and take title in order to resell them, that is, they are resellers. *Agent middlemen* are intermediaries such as manufacturers' representatives, manufacturers' agents, and brokers who assist the seller in finding buyers, negotiating, and title transfer, without taking title to the goods themselves.

In addition to these functions, some other work is usually performed in marketing channels to facilitate exchange. *Standardization and grading* establishes quality levels and sorts goods so that buyers can recognize value differences. *Branding* distinguishes one seller's goods from similar goods of other sellers. Some *risk taking* is undertaken by insurance companies and credit firms to share in the seller's risks.

Thus there is a great deal of work in bringing about transactions between buyers and sellers. This work is shared by buyers, sellers, and marketing intermediaries. How this work is split varies from situation to situation and provides some of the great opportunities for the enterprising firm. The buyer would like to see most of the work carried on by the seller and marketing intermediaries. But this would raise his price because the price would have to reflect all the work done by others. To the extent that the buyer accepts part of the work, such as search, travel, and communication, his cost outlay will be less. His final cost, however, depends upon the value he places on his time and how much more efficiently the seller and marketing intermediaries could perform these tasks through large-scale distribution activities.

Suppliers

Suppliers are another key component in the core marketing system. The company is essentially a resource-conversion machine that converts material, machines, labor, and funds into useful products. The necessary resources are obtained from suppliers through market search, physical distribution, communication, and negotiation and title transfer. How well the company buys depends on how well it grasps the workings of the various supply markets and how well it applies marketing principles in conducting its relations with suppliers.

During 1974 companies could not get enough plastic, fuel, paper, aluminum, copper, textiles, and glass. These companies were put on allocation by their regular suppliers, and they had to scramble for additional suppliers to make up for the shortages. They had to carry out market search, offer higher prices, accept fewer services, and persuade the suppliers of their intense needs. The buyers became marketers.

Suppliers, producers, marketing intermediaries, and final customers make up the *total marketing channel.* The channel begins with heterogeneous raw materials found in nature, which are converted by successive processes into final meaningful products that bring form, place, time, and possession utility to final buyers. The value of viewing the total marketing channel is that it leads the market participants to appreciate their opportunities and vulnerabilities. Too often organizations in a given channel stage consider only their relationship to the immediate preceding and succeeding stage. Nylon manufacturers see their customers as textile manufacturers; textile manufacturers see their customers as clothing manufacturers; clothing manufacturers see their customers as retail stores; only the retail stores see their customers as clothes buyers. Yet the reason for the existence of the whole set of interlocked markets starts with the clothes buyer and his needs. All of these organizations have a stake in the buying preferences and plans of the clothes buyer. Each organization has an opportunity to interpret and even influence the clothes buyer's needs and intentions. The long view of channels is the best defense against suddenly finding intermediate customers ceasing to place orders for the company's products.

Competitors

The final component of the core marketing system consists of competitors. They are part of the core marketing system because they actively influence the company's choice of target markets, marketing intermediaries, suppliers, product mix, and marketing mix.

Three different forms of competition can be distinguished. The first is *generic competition,* which comes from other product categories that might satisfy the same consumer need. Generic competition is always present whether or not there are active competitors offering the same product. For example, generic competition to the Schwinn bicycle company would include motorcycles, automobiles, buses, trains, and even walking. The second is *product-form competition,* which refers to specific versions of the product that may be competitive with each other. Product-form competition in the bicycle industry includes two-speed, five-speed, and ten-speed bikes. The third is *enterprise competition,* which refers to specific organizations that are competitive producers of the same product or service. The enterprise competitors in the bicycle industry are Schwinn, Raleigh, Sears, Ward, Murray, and so on.

The implication of this is that the company must strive to understand what it is essentially selling to the customer, or better yet, what the customer is essentially buying. The customer is looking for particular utilities. Existing products are only a current way of packaging these utilities. The company must be aware of all the ways in which the customer can gain the sought satisfaction. These define his competition.

An example of a company marketing system

A company marketing system should be mapped in detail to grasp its structure and functioning.[1] We shall map the marketing system of a leading manufacturer of a popular soft-centered chocolate-covered candy bar.

---

[1]This section is adapted from the author's "Corporate Models: Better Marketing Plans," *Harvard Business Review,* July–August 1970, pp. 135–49.

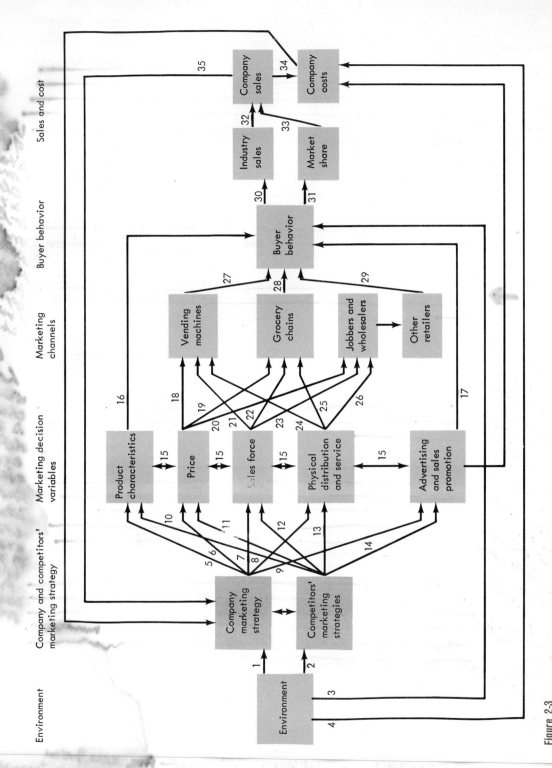

Environment   Company and competitors' marketing strategy   Marketing decision variables   Marketing channels   Buyer behavior   Sales and cost

Figure 2-3
Comprehensive marketing system map: Candy Company

Figure 2-3 shows the major entities and flows in the candy company marketing system. The diagram is divided into six elements.

1 The *environment*, or, more precisely, those forces in the environment that affect candy demand and supply, such as population growth, per capita income, attitudes toward candy, and raw material availability and cost.

2 The *company and competitors' marketing strategies.*

3 The major *marketing decision variables* in this market—product characteristics, price, sales force, physical distribution and service, and advertising and sales promotion.

4 The major *marketing channels* that the company uses for this product.

5 The *buyer behavior model,* which shows customer response to the activities of the manufacturers and the distribution channels, as well as to the environment.

6 The total *industry sales, company sales, and company costs.*

The various arrows show key flows in the marketing system. Flow "5," for example, would refer to a detailed diagram and description showing types of product characteristics decisions, the inputs that influence each of these decisions, and the sources of data for each of the inputs.

Let us select one element in Figure 2-3, the *company marketing strategy* box, and list on the right side of this box all the major marketing decisions made by the company (see Figure 2-4). There are two major types of decisions, trade

Figure 2-4
Input-output map of company marketing decisions: Candy Company

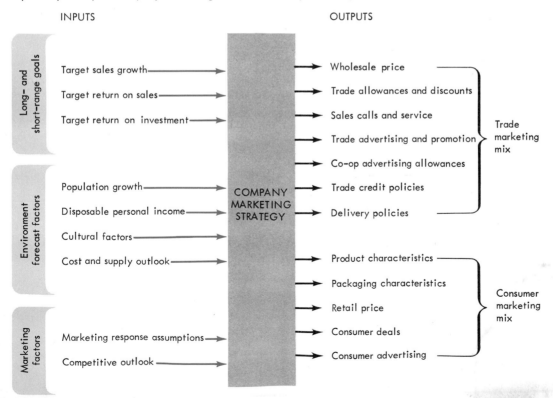

decisions and consumer decisions. To influence the trade, the company uses the wholesale price, trade allowances, sales calls and service, trade advertising, co-op advertising allowances, credit policy, and delivery policy. To influence the consumer, the company uses product characteristics, packaging characteristics, retail price, consumer deals, and consumer advertising.

The next step is to list the various inputs and influences on these decisions, which fall into one of three groups:

1 The company's long- and short-range goals for sales growth, return on sales, and return on investment.
2 Forecastable factors in the environment, such as population growth, disposable personal income, cultural factors, and the cost and supply outlook.
3 Assumptions about the sales effectiveness of different marketing instruments as well as expectations concerning competition.

Any input can be elaborated further. For example, it is possible to isolate three cultural factors that will have a significant effect on future candy consumption:

Weight-consciousness—if there is any relaxation of the pressures in American society toward the idea that "slimness is beautiful," this will lead to a substantial increase in the sales of candy.

Cavity-consciousness—as better dentrifices are developed, people will worry less about the negative effects of sugar on their teeth, and this will reduce their inhibitions against eating candy; on the other hand, some companies will see cavity-consciousness as an opportunity to develop a tasty, sugarless candy.

Cigarette consumption—if people reduce their cigarette consumption, we can expect candy, gum, and other "oral" gratifiers to replace cigarettes.

We can now proceed to trace how the various outputs feed into other parts of the system. Consider the output described as the trade marketing mix. This output becomes input into each of the distributor channels—for example, the grocery-chain model (see Figure 2-5). The trade marketing mix becomes the "handle" that the manufacturer uses to influence the retailer to provide

Figure 2-5
Input-output map of grocery-chain decisions: Candy Company

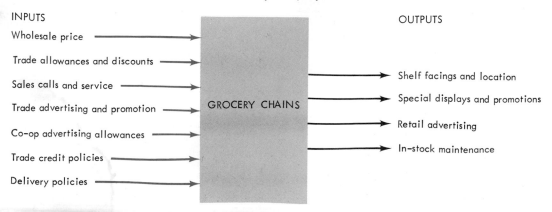

INPUTS

Wholesale price

Trade allowances and discounts

Sales calls and service

Trade advertising and promotion

Co-op advertising allowances

Trade credit policies

Delivery policies

GROCERY CHAINS

OUTPUTS

Shelf facings and location

Special displays and promotions

Retail advertising

In-stock maintenance

favorable shelf facings and location, special displays and promotions, advertising, and in-stock maintenance.

The influence of the dealers' decisions on the final consumers is shown in Figure 2-6, along with influences coming from other parts of the marketing system. The various influences are classified into product and promotion factors (outputs coming from the company marketing decision model), distribution factors (outputs coming from the channels of distribution models), and environmental factors (outputs coming from the environmental model). These factors influence consumers' buying behavior to bring about a certain level of industry sales and brand share sales of candy bars.

At some point it is necessary to estimate the quantitative relationships between various key elements. Figure 2-7 shows the estimated effect of chocolate weight percentage—a product characteristic—on candy bar sales. The company would like to keep this percentage down because chocolate is an expensive ingredient compared with the ingredients that make up the soft center. However, consumer tests reveal that as the chocolate content of the bar is reduced, preference and sales decline. The soft center begins to appear through the chocolate and leads the average consumer to feel that the bar is poorly made. Furthermore, his palate desires more chocolate to offset the soft center. When the layer of chocolate gets too thick (above 35 percent of the weight of the bar), consumer preference for the bar also falls, but for a different reason. The consumer begins to think of this not as a soft-centered bar but as a chocolate bar

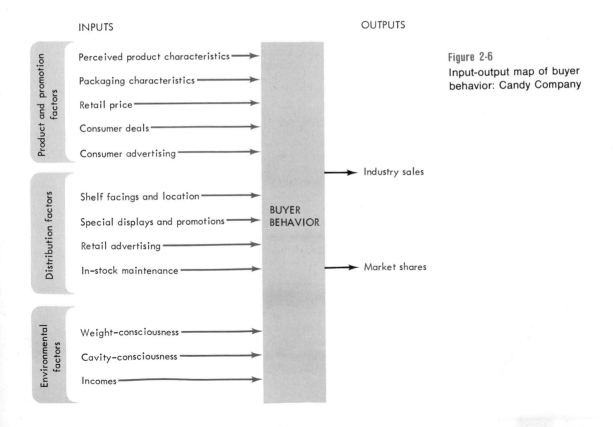

Figure 2-6
Input-output map of buyer
behavior: Candy Company

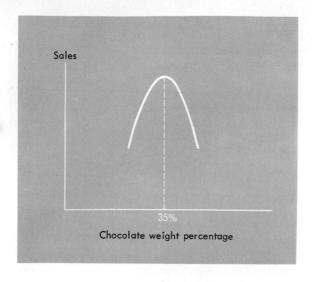

Sales

35%

Chocolate weight percentage

Figure 2-7

Functional relationship map: Candy Company

with "some stuff in it." He compares this bar with pure chocolate bars and it suffers by comparison. To the best of management's knowledge, sales have the curvilinear relationship to percentage chocolate weight that is shown in Figure 2-7.

Given this functional relationship, what is the optimum level of chocolate? If the company wishes to maximize sales, then chocolate should constitute 35 percent of the candy bar's weight. However, since the company is primarily interested in maximizing profit, management needs the ingredient-cost functions, as well as the sales-response function, to determine the profit-maximizing amount of chocolate.

Other functional relationships should be studied—the relationship between the amount spent on advertising and the resulting sales, the number of salesmen and the resulting sales, and so on. In advanced marketing model building, the various functional relationships can be put together in a computer model of the company's marketing system to allow management to explore the implications of alternative marketing programs.

PUBLICS

Making good decisions with respect to the core marketing system is difficult enough. The task is complicated by the presence of many publics in the company's environment whose interest and influence cannot be ignored. We define public in the following way:

A *public* is any distinct group that has an actual or potential interest or impact on an organization.

A company faces three types of publics. A *mutual public* is a public that is interested in the company and the company is interested in it. The financial community is a mutual public of a company. A *sought public* is a public that

30

the company is interested in but that is not necessarily interested in the company. The mass media are a sought public to the extent that the company would like press coverage of its activities but is commonly ignored by the press. Finally, an *unwelcome public* is a public that is interested in the company but the company is not interested in it. Consumer boycotters who are badmouthing the company would be an unwelcome public.

The various publics influence not only the company but also other publics and members of the core marketing system. Ralph Nader's investigations of the safety of General Motors automobiles reverberated throughout the financial, governmental, supplier, and other communities. A company no longer worries only about how its customers feel. It has to worry about how consumer advocates, legislators, stock analysts, and others view its activities.

From the company's point of view, it should seek to cultivate mutually enhancing relations with its key publics based on an exchange of services. The company has to consider what benefits to offer each of its valued publics in exchange for their valued resources and support. Once a company begins to think systematically about cultivating the support of a public, it is beginning to think of that public as a market, that is, a distinct group that has resources that it might be willing to exchange for distinct benefits.

Here we shall note some of the more important publics of a company.

Financial community

The financial community consists of all those publics who supply or influence the company's ability to obtain funds. Banks, investment houses, stock brokerage firms, and stockholders are among the key financial publics of the company. Company management tries to cultivate the goodwill of the financial community, often developing concrete marketing plans to achieve desired responses from different key financial publics.

This is also true of nonprofit organizations, such as universities, museums, and churches. They must mount a major marketing campaign every year to "sell" financial and donor markets on supporting them generously. Often this is a greater marketing challenge than the other problem of attracting and serving final customers for their services.

Independent press

The independent press describes mass and trade media that carry news, features, and editorial opinion. Companies are acutely sensitive to the role played by the press in affecting their capacity to achieve their marketing objectives.

There are two issues of concern to the company. The first is *how much coverage* the press *volunteers* to the company's activities and products. Small companies in particular are hungry for news attention and free publicity. This substitutes for paid advertising that the company would need to achieve the same level of awareness in the marketplace. Large companies, too, like to see more space devoted to their activities. Getting more coverage from the press is a marketing problem for the company.

The second issue is *what* the press *says* about the company's activities and products. There is nothing more valuable to a company than favorable publicity, nor more damaging than unfavorable publicity. When the Mazda automobile (with the Wankel engine) was first introduced in the United States, it received extensive and favorable coverage as a car of the future. The American public read many stories about how well the Wankel engine performed from a driving and pollution control point of view. This boosted U.S. sales considerably. After the gasoline shortage struck in late 1973, the Environmental Protection Agency published the tested mileages of different automobiles. The Mazda was cited as giving about ten miles per gallon in city driving, which is extremely low for a small automobile. This publicity caused a collapse of sales that completely upset Mazda's planned exports level and marketing program. Thus the press can carry news that boosts or destroys the sales possibilities of a major product.

The potential impact of the press on a company's fortunes leads most companies to establish a public relations department with a major responsibility for press relations. The press relations manager is the market manager for this particular public. His job is to anticipate bad news and try to cancel it or present the other side of the story. He must also sense opportunities for favorable publicity and arrange stories and visits with reporters. The effective press relations manager knows most of the editors in the major media and systematically develops a mutually beneficial relation with them. He does not approach them with threats or with supplications. He offers them valuable services such as interesting news items, informational material, and quick access to top management; in return, the media reporters respect his needs for receiving favorable coverage, being informed of things, and being given a chance to submit the company's viewpoint.

Government agencies and legislators

Marketing executives are increasingly finding it necessary to take government developments into account when they formulate their marketing plans and policies. In the past they were relatively free to set their main marketing-mix variables—product features, packaging, price, advertising, sales promotion—at any level; they only had to worry about their consumers and their competitors. In recent years there has been a major and probably irreversible trend toward more government regulation and intervention in these marketing decisions. Manufacturers of drugs, toys, automobiles, appliances, and food items must carefully consider product safety and ecology in designing their products. Company pricing came under price controls for a while and might return at any time. Companies have to be careful about "truth in advertising" or face a suit by the Federal Trade Commission.

Growing government regulation has led to three responses. The first is to increase the company's *legal staff* to advise marketing managers as to what they can and cannot do. An understaffed legal department might hopelessly delay company decisions on advertising messages, price changes, and packaging moves. The second is to establish a larger *government relations department*. The manager of government relations must know the various agencies at the local, state, and national levels, as well as the key legislators. He must anticipate unfavorable developments, visit the right people, express the company's interests, and rally support. The company lobbyist is essentially the company's marketing man in charge of the legislative market. He must know how to segment the legislative market; analyze legislators' needs and motives; know how a bill is passed, defeated, and influenced; and make personal calls and presentations. The third company response is to join with other companies in *trade associations* to lobby for the interests of their industry.

Interest groups

The company's marketing decisions are increasingly being affected by consumer organizations, environmental groups, minority organizations, neighborhood associations, and other vocal interest groups.

One morning in 1972 a major Philadelphia bank found thirty senior citizens at its door demanding to talk to the bank's president. They called themselves the Gray Panthers and presented the bank's president with a list of ten nonnegotiable demands for citizens over sixty-five, including free checking, free safety deposit box, and reduced interest rates. The bank president did his best to handle the situation diplomatically and in the end offered a few "senior citizen bank privileges." This kind of occurrence is becoming increasingly frequent and is facing all organizations, from business firms to universities to churches.

Companies would be foolish to attack or ignore these expressions of consumer interest. Progressive companies have made three responses to the reality of interest groups. First, they are training their decision makers to introduce social criteria into their decision making, to strike a better balance between the needs of consumers, citizens, and stockholders. Second, they have established a community relations or public affairs department to stay in touch with these groups to learn their interests and to express the companies' goals and activities to these groups. Third, these companies will hold conferences with other companies on judicious ways to deal with these groups. Some companies have staked out a leadership role by identifying their interests with these groups and playing the role of leader and model company in furthering social causes.

General public

The company is ultimately concerned with the attitude of the general public toward its products and activities. The general public does not act in an organized way toward the company, as interest groups do. But the members of the general public do carry around images of the company and these lead to a certain level of patronage.

The company undertakes many activities to improve its public image. It supports good causes through lending officers to community fund drives and makes substantial contributions to charities. It sets up systems to respond to consumer grievances. It resorts to institutional advertising to describe what it is doing in the social field. In recent years the telephone company has run a campaign on "How to Save on Long-Distance Calls," the electrical utilities have run a campaign on "How to Conserve Electricity," and the Ford Motor Company has distributed tens of thousands of booklets on "How to Purchase a Car." These steps are designed to help the public become more intelligent consumers and users of the company's products.

MACROENVIRONMENT

We now turn to the most general level of forces that affect the structure, conduct, and performance of company marketing systems. These forces make up the macroenvironment. They have a great impact on the company, while the reverse cannot be said. They are the "uncontrollables" to which companies adapt through setting the "controllable" factors, their marketing mix.

The key point about the macroenvironment is that it keeps changing, and what is even more important, it seems to be changing at an accelerating rate. Toffler has documented how key technological, economic, and social forces show an "accelerative thrust." He quotes a study showing that the average span between introduction and peak production of appliances introduced in the United States before 1920 was thirty-four years; for a group of appliances that appeared between 1939 and 1959, the span was only eight years. Many products that have appeared since 1959 have even had shorter spans.[2] Other forces, such as consumer life-styles and government legislation, also show accelerated change.

The key implication for company marketing is that the company must invest more to keep abreast of significant social changes and be prepared to adapt faster than before. The company that survives is the company that is fine tuned to its environment. Unfortunately, the rate of change in the environment appears to be outstripping the average company's capacity to change. A *passive firm* faces extinction; an *adaptive firm* will survive and probably enjoy modest growth; an *innovative firm* will prosper and even contribute to the changes that are taking place in the external environment.

The concept of a business ecosystem

Every organization and industry is in a delicate balance with the forces in its environment. Consider the auto industry. This industry is central to a vast *business ecosystem* consisting of rubber, glass, and steel plants, petroleum refineries, gasoline stations, superhighways, the economy of Detroit, and the incomes of millions of people. The auto ecosystem has normally gone on year after year in a basically balanced way to which many other ecosystems have adapted, including part of the political system, the American value system, and so on. Disturbances do occur, such as inflation, recessions, safety legislation, and gas shortages. These are taken in stride by the automobile ecosystem through built-in homeostatic mechanisms such as layoffs, budgetary tightening, and product redesign. However, a major disturbance would pose a serious threat to the automobile manufacturers and all the ecosystemic relations that have been built up. Consider the consequences of the successful development of an efficient electric automobile. The petroleum industry and the familiar gas station would be threatened with near extinction. People would use their discretionary incomes to purchase the electric cars, and this would ruin the current holdings of used-car dealers and hurt other industries selling major consumer durables such as boats, small planes, and kitchen appliances. On the other hand, it would forge a new interdependency of automobile manufacturers and electric power companies. It would lead to cleaner air, less need for outdoor painting, and lower mortality rates. Such a major innovation, through its "creative destruction" of the present ecosystem, would pose a tremendous threat to many and a tremendous opportunity to others.

The concept of environmental threat

We now define the concept of environmental threat:

> An *environmental threat* is a challenge posed by an unfavorable trend or specific disturbance in the environment which would lead, in the absence of purposeful marketing action, to the stagnation or demise of a company, product, or brand.

As the environment changes, it calls for a creative adaptation or response on the part of the organisms interacting with it. Too often these organisms are rigid in their ways. They have learned a set of behavioral patterns which marked an efficient and effective adaptation to the environment as it was constituted but

---

[2]See Alvin Toffler, *Future Shock* (New York: Bantam Books, 1970), p. 28.

which grows increasingly inappropriate to the environment as it is moving. Nations (Assyria), species (dinosaurs), industries (horse carriages), and companies (Studebaker) have collapsed because they failed to meet environmental challenges with creative responses.

History is filled with specific products—Packard, *Life*, Ipana—that, in spite of their momentous size, eventually became casualties.[3] Here are examples of two industries currently facing extinction:

Home diaper delivery service. Ever since modern means of transportation and commercial laundering came about, the home diaper delivery service has been a mainstay and boon to mothers. Recently it has been facing three formidable environmental threats. A technological threat is posed by the development of effective disposable paper diapers such as Pampers, which have caught on rapidly. An economic threat is posed by the rising costs of labor, which threaten to push way up the charges for home diaper delivery service. A demographic threat is posed by the slowdown in the birthrate, which is affecting all companies that depend heavily on the infant market.

Night clubs. Nightclubs used to be a healthy industry catering to the nightlife entertainment needs of an urban population and tourist business. Many clubs, however, have gone out of business due to a number of environmental threats, including (1) rising blight and crime in their areas, (2) heavy competition from television and the movies, (3) rising entertainers' fees due to competitive pay levels on television and the movies, and (4) the changing tastes of young people. When added to this is the occurrence of a business recession, nightclubs are particularly hard hit. Their problem is to find a more viable principle for attracting people and reducing nightclub costs.

Given the seriousness and the suddenness of environmental changes, an organization should carry on a program of continuous *threat analysis*, consisting of identifying, appraising, and reacting to threats. Threat identification calls for two steps:[4]

1 The company establishes a well-designed program of general intelligence activity. This includes defining environmental areas of particular interest to management and establishing special groups charged with scanning these areas.

2 Top management sets up mechanisms and incentives to encourage the upward flow of information. Too often, important information is screened out at lower levels because top management is not thought to be "future minded," the information is not deemed to be important, or the information is expected to be embarrassing or threatening to the lower level. Managers tend to become more concerned with short-run minor threats to present products than long-run major threats.

Appraising the threat is largely a matter of forecasting the character and estimating the rate of progress of the expected trend or development. This often involves technological, political, or cultural forecasting, all quite imperfect sciences.

---

[3]*Product casualty* refers to an established product that eventually did not survive. *Product failure* refers to a new product that never became successful.

[4]Arnold C. Cooper, "Identifying, Appraising, and Reacting to Major Technological Change," in *Changing Marketing Systems . . . Consumer, Corporate and Government Interfaces,* ed. Reed Moyer (Chicago: American Marketing Association, 1968), pp. 93–97.

The company may react to a threat in several ways. It may do nothing if it is convinced that the threat is phony or short lived. It may decide to watch the environment carefully but not react just yet. It may seek to improve its products or lower its costs. It may try to fight, restrain, or reverse the development through legal or public relations action. It may increase its flexibility through contingency planning, shortened commitments, and increased liquidity. It may diversify its markets and products. It may decide that the threat is really a veiled opportunity and want to participate in the new development.

We now examine five major components of the marketing macroenvironment and their threat and opportunity implications for marketing-system management.

Demography

Demography refers to the study of the major characteristics of the world's human population. Demographers are interested in the size of the world's population, its geographical distribution and density, its age distribution, its racial composition, and trends in the birth, marriage, and death rates.

Perhaps the major fact about the world population is its "explosive" growth:

> In 1650 the population numbered about 0.5 billion, and it was growing at a rate of approximately 0.3 percent per year. That corresponds to a doubling time of nearly 250 years. In 1970 the population totaled 3.6 billion and the rate of growth was 2.1 percent per year. The doubling time at this growth rate is 33 years. Thus, not only has the population been growing exponentially, but the rate of growth has also been growing.[5]

The world population explosion has been a major concern of many governments and groups throughout the world. Two factors underlie this concern. The first is the possible finiteness of the earth's resources to support this much human life, particularly at levels of living that represent the aspiration of most people. The famous eighteenth century economist, Thomas Malthus, was concerned in his time about the population explosion. He saw the population growing at a geometric rate while the world's food supply grew at an arithmetic rate. To him, this spelled unavoidable disaster for mankind. If mankind could not regulate its own rate of growth, then natural and other forces such as famine, disease, and war would intervene to keep population down to the available food supply. The Malthusian specter has been resurrected many times since—most recently in the tour de force called *The Limits to Growth.*[6] This book presents an impressive array of evidence that unchecked population growth and consumption must eventually result in insufficient food supply, depletion of key minerals, overcrowdedness, pollution, and an overall deterioration in the quality of life.

The second cause for concern is that the rate of population growth is not equal everywhere but is highest in the countries and communities that can least afford it. In many developing nations the death rate has been falling due to modern medical advances while the birthrate has remained fairly stable. The ability of these countries to feed, clothe, and educate their new citizens and

---

[5]Donella H. Meadows, Dennis L. Meadows, Jorgen Randers, and William W. Behrens III, *The Limits to Growth* (New York: New American Library, 1972), p. 41.
    [6]*Ibid.*

provide a rising standard of living for their present citizens is out of the question. Furthermore, the poor families have the most children, and this reinforces the cycle of poverty.

These concerns have led to worldwide cooperation in birth control and family planning. The role of family-planning organizations is twofold: to encourage people to have fewer children, and to provide the education and means for birth control. Many children are born not out of intention but out of lack of birth control knowledge or precaution. The family-planning movement has been effective in certain parts of the world, particularly where the tools of *social marketing* have been applied.[7] It deserves part credit for the recent slowdown in the birthrate in several countries. Other factors include, of course, the continuous shift of people from rural to urban areas and the rising incomes in some parts of the world.

The rate of increase of the world's population has great import for business, although business's views are somewhat mixed. A growing population means growing human needs. It means growing markets if there is sufficient purchasing power. On the other hand, if the growing population presses too hard against the available food supply and resources, it will shoot up costs and not necessarily lead to higher profits.

Individual enterprises are affected differentially by the rate of population increase. The Gerber Company for years advertised "Babies are our business—our *only* business." It quietly dropped this slogan a few years ago as the U.S. fertility rate declined to a record low of 1.9 children per family. The declining birthrate in the United States has sent a chill down the backs of other companies manufacturing children's toys, clothing, furniture, and food. Some—like Johnson & Johnson—are trying to interest grown-ups in using their baby powder and baby hair shampoo. Abbott Laboratories has added a geriatric food to its lines of infant formulas. And Gerber has carried its baby food to other parts of the world where the birthrate is still high.[8]

All organizations that sell to a particular age group must watch what is happening to its size and behavior. Colleges, which have already experienced enrollment declines, will face more trouble because the number of high school graduates is increasing at a decreasing rate and will peak in 1979; by 1982 the number of high school graduates will be 3.8 percent less than the number in 1979.[9] Colleges will have to think about recruiting new groups for the college campus, including housewives and the elderly. Other organizations are concerned about the marital plans of young people. There has been a slowdown in the marriage rate, and some observers predict there will be far fewer marriages in the 1980s. This will severely dampen the sales of life insurance, engagement and wedding rings, furniture, and houses.

Medium-range demographic forecasts are fairly reliable. There is little excuse for a company to be suddenly surprised by a demographic development. The alert firm will have plenty of advance notice and can start searching for new-product lines and better markets when it reads the writing on the wall.

---

[7]See Eduardo L. Roberto, "Social Marketing Strategies for Diffusing the Adoption of Family Planning," *Social Science Quarterly,* June 1972, pp. 33–51.

[8]"Thinking Old," *Newsweek,* May 6, 1974.

[9]*Intellect,* 102, February 1972, pp. 318–36.

We stressed that markets require not only people but purchasing power. Total purchasing power is a function of four major factors: savings, current income, prices, and credit availability.

Savings and wealth have been growing, but at uneven rates in different countries. In 1971, 84 percent of American spending units held some liquid assets, the median amount being $700. Savings have been growing in Arab countries at a tremendous rate but are concentrated in the hands of a few people. The level and the distribution of savings in a country make a great difference as to how much spending occurs for capital goods, consumers' luxury goods, and consumer staples.

Current income is the major source of current expenditure for most people. Current income has shown a substantial rate of growth over the years. In recent years, however, the rate of growth in national income has slowed down in many countries. According to a 1974 consumer survey:

> Today, 65 percent of the American people believe that they are personally worse off than they were 5 years ago. Still more striking is the fact that 40 percent believe they will be even worse off 5 years from now.[10]

If pessimism begins to replace the traditional optimism of the American people, their willingness to spend will be greatly restrained and will affect the basic opportunities for American marketers.

Of course, the pessimism is not based on the current level of income by itself but on the prospects for the level of real income. In recent years prices have escalated in most parts of the world faster than current incomes. Consumers are forced to rethink their consumption priorities, and business cannot count on a continuation of past buying behavior. For example, will a rapid inflation lead consumers to spend less money or more money on consumer durables? Since durables are usually postponable purchases, we might argue that consumers will cut down on durable purchases. On the other hand, many consumers know that by postponing a durable purchase, they might have to pay 10 percent more for it next year. This is like a 10 percent tax and exceeds what they normally earn on their savings. From this point of view, consumers might be expected to increase their durable purchases. On other questions, there is more certainty. For example, rapid inflation is likely to lead consumers to substitute low-priced brands for high-priced brands. A survey by *Better Homes and Gardens* indicated that 72 percent of the respondents were buying more store brands to save money.[11] Store brands (also called private label merchandise) are thought to sell for as much as 10 percent less than national manufacturers' brands. This means that companies must try to respond to the consumers' growing desire for economy brands.

Another key economic variable is the cost and availability of consumer credit. What a consumer can spend is a matter not only of what he earns (income) and what he owns (savings) but also of what he can borrow (credit). The growth of consumer credit in the United States has been a major factor in the rapid economic growth of the nation. It permitted people to buy more than

---

[10]Quoted in *The Cambridge Report* (Cambridge, Mass.), 1974, p. 1.
[11]Reported in *Grey Matter,* "Private Brands Seek Growth in Faltering Economy," June 1974, p. 1.

their current income permitted, and this created more jobs and still more income and more demand. By 1974, outstanding consumer credit (exclusive of home mortgages) stood at close to $178 billion, or $2,600 for every American household. Many economies in other parts of the world have also increased the availability of consumer credit, and this has accelerated their economic growth. In recent years, however, the mounting inflation has pushed up the cost of consumer credit, adversely affecting the housing market and other durable goods markets which depend heavily on credit. Businessmen must pay close attention to what is happening to the cost and availability of credit in laying their plans.

Law and politics

The law, public opinion, and public policy constitute a set of environmental factors that are increasingly affecting decisions on the marketing of goods and services. Most of the nations of the world are becoming *regulated economies*. Government regulation of business occurs for one of three purposes. The first is to protect businessmen from each other. Businessmen all praise competition in the abstract but try to neutralize it when it touches them. If threatened, they show their teeth:

> In 1973, a federal judge handed down the largest antitrust judgment in history, a whopping $352.5 million against giant IBM (later modified to $259.5) to be paid to Telex and some other small peripheral equipment manufacturers. What was found objectionable was IBM's effort to suppress competition rather than respond to it with superior technology. It was charged with using predatory pricing and long-term leasing to stem the growth of its peripheral equipment competitors.[12]

So laws are passed to define and prevent unfair competition. These laws are enforced by the Federal Trade Commission and the Antitrust Division of the attorney general's office. Sometimes, unfortunately, the laws end up protecting the inefficient rather than promoting the efficient. Some students of business regulation go so far as to charge that "judges and the Federal Trade Commission have remade the law into a body of rules of which a large portion impair competition and the ability of the economy to operate efficiently."[13] But, by and large, regulations are needed to keep businessmen fearful about overstepping the line in trying to neutralize or harm competitors. It is hard to imagine that the economy would be more efficient if competition were not supervised by some regulatory agencies.

The second purpose of government regulation is to protect consumers from businessmen. A few disreputable businessmen are ready to adulterate their products, mislead through their advertising, deceive through their packaging, and bait through their prices. Unfair consumer practices must be defined and agencies established to protect consumers. Many businessmen see purple with each new consumer law, and yet a few have said that "consumerism may be the best thing that has happened . . . in the past 20 years."[14]

---

[12]For details, see Louis Berman, "IBM's Travails in Lilliput," *Fortune*, November 1973, pp. 148–64.

[13]See Yale Brozen, "Antitrust Out of Hand," *The Conference Board Record*, March 1974, pp. 14–19.

[14]Leo Greenland, "Advertisers Must Stop Conning Consumers," *Harvard Business Review*, July–August 1974, p. 18.

The third purpose of government regulation is to protect the larger interests of society against unbridled business behavior. The nation has become painfully aware in the last ten years that gross national product is accompanied by gross national pollution. Gross national product might be rising, and yet the quality of life might be deteriorating. Most firms are not charged with the social costs of their production or products. Their prices are artificially low and their sales artificially high until agencies such as the Environmental Protection Agency shift the social costs back to these firms and their customers. As the environment continues to deteriorate, new laws and their enforcement will continue or increase. Businessmen have to watch these developments in planning their products and marketing systems.

The marketing executive cannot plan intelligently without a good working knowledge of the major laws and regulations that exist to protect competition, consumers, and the larger interests of society. The laws are numerous; only the key ones can be listed here. Table 2-1 lists the main federal laws that concern the marketing executive. He should know why these laws were passed, and how they are currently being interpreted in the courts. He should know the many state and local laws affecting the conduct of his marketing activity, and the many consumer organizations that have a potential impact on his activities.

Technology

The most dramatic force shaping man's destiny is his technology. Technology has released such wonders as penicillin, open-heart surgery, and the birth control pill. It has released such horrors as the hydrogen bomb, nerve gas, and the

---

Table 2-1
Milestone U.S. legislation affecting marketing

Sherman Antitrust Act (1890)

Prohibited (a) "monopolies or attempts to monopolize" and (b) "contracts, combinations, or conspiracies in restraint of trade."

Federal Food and Drug Act (1906)

Forbade the manufacture, sale, or transport of adulterated or fraudulently labeled foods and drugs in interstate commerce. (Supplanted by the Food, Drug, and Cosmetic Act, 1938; amended by Food Additives Act, 1958.)

Meat Inspection Act (1906)

Provided for the enforcement of sanitary regulations in meat-packing establishments, and for federal inspection of all companies selling meats in interstate commerce.

Federal Trade Commission Act (1914)

Established the commission, a body of specialists with broad powers to investigate and to issue cease and desist orders to enforce Section 5, which declared that "unfair methods of competition in commerce are unlawful." (Amended by Wheeler-Lea Act, 1938, which added the phrase "and unfair or deceptive acts or practices.")

Table 2-1 (continued)

Clayton Act (1914)

Supplemented the Sherman Act by prohibiting certain specific practices (certain types of price discrimination, tying clauses and exclusive dealing, intercorporate stockholdings, and interlocking directorates) "where the effect . . . may be to substantially lessen competition or tend to create a monopoly in any line of commerce." Provided that violating corporate officials could be held individually responsible; exempted labor and agricultural organizations from its provisions.

Robinson-Patman Act (1936)

Amended the Clayton Act. Added the phrase "to injure, destroy, or prevent competition." Defined price discrimination as unlawful (subject to certain defenses) and provided the FTC with the right to establish limits on quantity discounts, to forbid brokerage allowances except to independent brokers, and to prohibit promotional allowances or the furnishing of services or facilities except where made available to all "on proportionately equal terms."

Miller-Tydings Act (1937)

Amended the Sherman Act to exempt interstate fair-trade (price fixing) agreements from antitrust prosecution. (The McGuire Act, 1952, reinstated the legality of the nonsigner clause.)

Antimerger Act (1950)

Amended Section 7 of the Clayton Act by broadening the power to prevent intercorporate acquisitions where the acquisition may have a substantially adverse effect on competition.

Automobile Information Disclosure Act (1958)
National Traffic and Safety Act (1966)
Fair Packaging and Labeling Act (1966)
Federal Cigarette Labeling and Advertising Act (1967)
Consumer Credit Protection Act (1968)
Toy Safety Act (1969)
National Environmental Policy Act (1969)

Various laws establishing new patterns of consumer and environmental protection.

submachine gun. It has released such mixed blessings as the automobile, television sets, and white bread. Depending upon whether one is more enthralled with the wonders or the horrors determines one's attitude toward technology.

Every new technology may potentially spawn a major industry. One only has to think of transistors, xerography, computers, and antibiotics. These industries not only create but destroy. Transistors hurt the vacuum-tube industry and xerography hurt the carbon-paper business. The auto hurt the railroads and television hurt the movies. Schumpeter saw technology as a force for "creative destruction." Every enterprise must watch what is new in the environment, for this might eventually destroy it. If it has the imagination, the new might save it. It is discouraging that no phonograph company entered the radio field, no wagon manufacturer entered the automobile business, and no steam locomotive company entered the diesel locomotive business.

The growth rate of the economy is intimately tied to how many *major* new technologies will be discovered in the coming years. Unfortunately, technological discoveries do not arise evenly through time—the railroad industry created a lot of investment and then there was a dearth until the auto industry; later radio created a lot of investment and there was a dearth until television. In the absence of major innovations that open up great markets and opportunities, an economy can stagnate. Some scientists do not foresee promising innovations of the magnitude of the invention of the automobile or television. Others see great new innovations on the horizon, such as electric cars, small flying cars, household computer systems, practical desalinization systems, and regular flights to the moon.

In the meantime there are sure to be small innovations filling the gaps. Freeze-dried coffee probably made no one happier and antiperspirant deodorants probably made no one wiser, but they create some daily drama that fights boredom and generates hope in a few. Most large companies are actually in the innovation business. They have set up R&D departments which search for new features, materials, and styles to make their company's products better or at least different. Today, R&D expenditures in the nation stand at $32 billion, or over 2 percent of GNP.

Some people question the value of this expenditure, and some see technology as the enemy of man. Technology has made man's life dependent on machines for his pleasures, whereas he used to get his pleasures from nature and other people. The antitechnologists would ride bikes instead of cars, eat organic food rather than synthetic food, and unplug their television sets. Their call for a return to simpler times may win a growing following, and this will have great implications for business.[15] On the other hand, most Americans are enthralled by technology and every new product. Their faith in technology is boundless. Talk of *limits to growth* is rebuffed with the argument that technology will find solutions to all of our problems.

The marketer must understand the technological environment and the nuances of technology. He must work closely with the R&D people in his organization. He has a fundamental responsibility to try to disenchant them with technology for technology's sake. Some technologists are not interested in the consumer and his problems but in the product and its possibilities. Left unchecked, they will create products that have no markets. Or they will design them in ways that fail to convey their real utility to the buyer.

Culture

The last component of the macroenvironment is the sociocultural milieu. Each man grows up in a particular human culture that defines his relation to other men, himself, nature, and the cosmos. His culture can get very specific and enable him to do, like, and feel things very differently from persons in other cultures. Most Americans know how to speak English, handle money, turn on a television set, tie a shoelace, shake hands, write letters, dance a waltz, hold

[15]Theodore Roszak, *The Making of a Counter Culture: Reflections on the Technocratic Society and Its Youthful Opposition* (Garden City, N.Y.: Anchor Books, Doubleday & Company, Inc., 1969).

a fork, pay income tax, shop in a supermarket, and drive a car. These seem easy and natural. Yet people from another culture would be confused by these customs, just as we would be confused if we saw them rub noses, pierce lips, fast regularly, eat insects, and speak in squeals.

Even within a culture, different patterns of behavior and different value systems may be simultaneously present. Take a modern American family. The grandparents are conservative in their tastes and careful in their expenditures; the parents work hard and play hard and purchase many things on credit; their eighteen-year-old son might show little interest in work or consumption. Recently a ten-year-old boy was told by his mother to behave more like his fourteen-year-old brother, to which he retorted: "Mom, he's from a different generation." Culture used to change slowly, but today every few years brings into focus a new set of ideas, desires, and behaviors.

Even some of the most basic values of a people undergo observable shifts through time. The connection between the Founding Fathers of this country and the present generation of Americans is at best tenuous. Consider the following major shifts in American values:

Self-reliance	Government reliance
"Hard work"	The "easy life"
Religious convictions	Secular convictions
Husband-dominated home	Wife-dominated home
Parent-centered household	Child-centered household
Respect for individual	Dislike of individual differences
Postponed gratification	Immediate gratification
Saving	Spending
Sexual chastity	Sexual freedom
Parental values	Peer-group values
Independence	Security

SUMMARY

A marketing system is the set of significant institutions and flows that connect an organization to its markets. A core marketing system describes all the key institutions that interact to supply final markets with needed goods and services. These institutions are the seller, final buyers, marketing intermediaries, suppliers, and competitors. The participants in the core marketing system perform such functions as market search, physical distribution, communication, and negotiation and title transfer. The particular structures that succeed are those that perform these functions efficiently and effectively.

The core marketing system is surrounded by publics, that is, distinct groups that have actual or potential interest or impacts on the organization. Among the key publics are the financial community, independent press, government agencies and legislators, interest groups, and general public. To the extent that the organization seeks to attract the resources of these publics by offering distinct benefits, it engages in marketing to these publics.

The components of the core marketing system and the surrounding publics are all affected by macroenvironmental forces, the major ones being demography, economics, law and politics, technology, and culture. These forces are the uncontrollables and they appear to be changing at an increasing rate, outstripping the typical organization's capacity to adapt. The passive firm is doomed; the adaptive firm may survive; the innovative firm should succeed.

QUESTIONS AND PROBLEMS

1 Develop a comprehensive marketing system map of some company of your choice. Be sure to show the marketing mix elements and the channels of distribution.

2 Develop an input-output map for the advertising submodel in Figure 2-3.

3 Develop a functional relationship map which shows the relationship between (a) retail price and candy bar sales; (b) advertising and candy bar sales.

4 List as many specific marketing actions to stimulate sales as you can think of available to (a) supermarkets; (b) airlines.

5 Develop a diagram showing the major publics of a privately owned hospital.

6 "I hold strongly that marketing men should confine themselves to the marketing field. I don't think most marketing oriented persons have the experience, aptitude, or approach for sound public relations." Do you agree?

7 The text distinguishes three types of competition: generic, product form, and enterprise. Illustrate the three types of competition for a firm in the copy-duplicating machine industry.

8 What is the generic product of the computer industry that helps define its competition?

9 Name two major threats and two major opportunities facing each of the following industries: (a) automobiles; (b) beer; (c) steel.

10 Indicate some of the ecological consequences of television on courtship, automobile demand, eating habits, and housing.

11 Would you support or not support each of the following new legislative proposals (give your reasoning): (a) a bill to require companies in concentrated industries to go through federal hearings before each price boost; (b) a bill to allow auto makers to prevent dealers from selling outside their territories; (c) a bill to require manufacturers to grant wholesalers a bigger discount than they give to large retail chains; (d) a bill to protect independent retailers from price competition by a manufacturer who does retailing of his own?

12 Do you agree that the cultural trends cited in this chapter are taking place? Does it follow that firms should move with majority values?

3

STRATEGIC MARKETING

We are all continually faced with a series of great
opportunities brilliantly disguised as insoluble problems.

JOHN W. GARDNER

The preceding chapter outlined the anatomy of the marketing system but not
its functioning. The task now is to show how the management process acts to
convert resources found in nature into meaningful want-satisfying products
and services. We shall examine the concrete steps that company management
takes to translate market needs into marketing opportunities and marketing
responses.

A marketer's work starts long before a company product is produced and
continues long after its sale is consummated. The professional marketer is involved in studying consumer needs and desires, developing product concepts
aimed at satisfying unfulfilled needs, testing the validity of these product concepts, designing product features, developing packaging and a brand name,
pricing the product to recover a reasonable return on investment, arranging for
regional, national, and international distribution, creating effective marketing
communications to let the public know about the product's availability, purchasing the most efficient media for the commercial messages, auditing sales,
monitoring customer satisfaction, and revising marketing plans in the light
of results. The marketer is a marketing researcher, a psychologist, a sociologist,
an economist, a communicator, and a lawyer all rolled into one.

There is a larger context for these specific activities, which we would like
to consider in this chapter. We view *strategic marketing* as a process of analyzing

45

Figure 3-1
Steps in the strategic marketing process

opportunities, choosing *objectives,* developing *strategy,* formulating *plans,* and carrying out *implementation* and *control.* This process is depicted in Figure 3-1, and the various steps are described in the rest of this chapter. These steps constitute an overview of the remainder of this book as well.

ANALYZING OPPORTUNITIES

There is an unresolved debate in the management literature as to whether the first step in the strategic-marketing process is to identify opportunities or to set objectives. Those who argue in favor of looking at opportunities offer the following reasons:

1 Many organizations get their start because they recognize an important opportunity. They echo Sir Edmund Hillary's reason for climbing Mount Everest: "Because it is there."
2 Many organizations do not have well-stated objectives. It is difficult for them to state what they really want. But they do recognize good opportunities.
3 Many organizations change their objectives as their opportunities change. Thus the March of Dimes was set up to raise money to conquer the dreaded disease of polio. The development of the Salk vaccine in the early 1950s left the organization without a cause. It looked for new opportunities and recommitted its resources to the problem of birth defects.

On the other hand, there are those who argue that objectives should precede opportunity analysis:

1 Many organizations start with an overriding objective, such as to make high profits, and look for the opportunities that will achieve this objective.
2 A company cannot simply look for opportunities without a directing set of objectives. The world is too full of opportunities.
3 Many organizations make conscious changes in their objectives; and when they do, the new objectives lead them to search for a different set of opportunities.

We have to conclude that both sides have merit. It is possible to start the strategic-marketing process by looking either at opportunities or at objectives. The arguments show that there is a dynamic tension between them, and both

46

**The concept of
marketing opportunity**

must be considered simultaneously. We might even add that the company's resources often provide still a third starting point. This having been said, we shall start with the concept of a company's opportunities.

It is important to distinguish between *environmental opportunities* and *company opportunities*. There are countless environmental opportunities available in any economy as long as there are unsatisfied needs. Currently there are great opportunities to develop new sources of energy, new food products, improved agricultural methods, improved forms of transportation, new forms of leisure, and improved teaching technology. There are opportunities in refuse disposal, lower-cost legal services, containerization, prefab housing, water purification, day-care centers, and biomedical instruments. But none of these necessarily represent opportunities for any specific company. Day-care centers are probably not an opportunity for U.S. Steel, nor are biomedical instruments an opportunity for Kentucky Fried Chicken.

We define company marketing opportunity in the following way:

A *company marketing opportunity* is an arena of relevant marketing action
in which a particular company is likely to enjoy a differential advantage.

The key to a company marketing opportunity lies in the question of whether the specific company can bring more to this environmental opportunity than its potential competitors can. We make the following assumptions:

1 Every environmental opportunity has certain *success requirements.*
2 Every company has certain *distinctive competences,* that is, things that it can do especially well. **(STRENGTHS)**
3 A company is likely to enjoy a *differential advantage* in an area of environmental opportunity if its distinctive competences match the success requirements of the environmental opportunity better than its potential competition.

To illustrate this, suppose it becomes practical to develop and market an electric car. Suppose General Motors, General Electric, and Sears are considering the opportunity. Which firm would enjoy the greatest differential advantage in this market? First we consider the success requirements. The success requirements would include (1) having good relations with suppliers of metal, rubber, plastic, glass, and other materials needed to produce an automobile, (2) having skill at mass production and mass assembly of complicated pieces of equipment, (3) having a great distribution capacity to store, show, and deliver automobiles to the American public, and (4) having the confidence of buyers that the company is able to produce and service a good auto product. Now General Motors has distinctive competences in all four of these areas. General Electric has distinctive competences in (1) supply and (2) production but not in (3) distribution or (4) automobile reputation. It does have great know-how in electrical technology, but General Motors is probably as knowledgeable. Sears's major distinctive competence is its extensive distribution and retailing system, but it would have to acquire the other competences through perhaps joint venturing. All said, General Motors would enjoy a major differential advantage in the production and marketing of electric cars.

The set of all marketing opportunities available to a company can be called the *company opportunity set*. The opportunity set defines the company's possibilities. If the set is small and poor, the company has a poor future; if the set is large and rich, the company can have a great future.

Our view is that a company should continuously develop a well-thought-out set of opportunities. The economy is marked by shortening life spans of new products, intensifying competition, and rapid changes in the macroenvironment; no firm can safely rest its future on its present products and markets. Yet many companies do nothing to generate a well-developed pool of opportunity ideas. They are busy trying to solve day-to-day problems. Occasionally they chance on an interesting venture idea, and if it meets certain conditions, they may pursue it.

Other companies are aware of the need for a well-developed pool of opportunities. To develop them, they often resort to brainstorming sessions or collecting ideas of various company managers. But all this does is produce a set of miscellaneous ideas of tenuous connection with the real dynamics of the firm. A systematic opportunity-generating procedure is needed that starts with the present nature of the company's business and moves out from it. We shall propose a framework and apply it to the following company case.

Musicale Corporation (name disguised) is a leading phonograph-records company that has had a good growth record. At present, along with other companies in the industry, it faces some basic issues and uncertainties with respect to the industry's future. The costs and competition for top recording artists have been escalating. An alternative form of packaging music, tape cassettes, has been making rapid inroads. Channels of distribution have been shifting in favor of mass-merchandise outlets over small retailers. Larger promotion budgets are becoming necessary for launching new releases.

Musicale has not been sitting idly by in the face of these challenges. It acquired a magnetic-tape producing company and proceeded to market its music in cassette form with some success. Because its tape-manufacturing capacity exceeded its music-business needs, it formed a division to market magnetic tape to computer manufacturers and users. However, if it continues in this new business, it must invest in tape quality improvement to meet the higher specifications required by third-generation computers. The company also tried its hand at manufacturing a complete line of phonographs under its own name; it later withdrew because their marketing required more resources than the company chose to risk. Still later Musicale entered the electronics business but withdrew within a few years.

Although Musicale has been willing to venture away from the recording business, it has not done this with any great success. It does not show much patience with its new ventures because of their initial unprofitability. Its various ventures, while all related in a loose way to its major business, represented a set of ad hoc responses to fortuitous opportunities rather than the working out of a well-designed master plan for company growth. This is the most serious criticism of its venturing. Musicale, sorely aware of its aimless growth history, is seeking a more systematic procedure for generating valid marketing opportunities.

Alternative growth opportunities can be generated for a company by mapping its core marketing system and then moving to three levels of analysis. The first level of analysis discerns those opportunities present in the current product-market activity of the company; we call these *intensive growth opportunities.* The second level discerns those opportunities present in other parts of the core marketing system; we call these *integrative growth opportunities.* The third level discerns those opportunities present completely outside of the core marketing system; we call these *diversification growth opportunities.* Table 3-1 lists the specific possibilities latent in each of these broad opportunity classes.

Table 3-1
Major classes of growth opportunities

I. INTENSIVE GROWTH	II. INTEGRATIVE GROWTH	III. DIVERSIFICATION GROWTH
A. Market Penetration	A. Backward Integration	A. Concentric Diversification
B. Market Development	B. Forward Integration	B. Horizontal Diversification
C. Product Development	C. Horizontal Integration	C. Conglomerate Diversification

Intensive growth   Intensive growth makes sense for a company if it has not fully exploited the opportunities latent in its present products and markets. Ansoff has proposed a useful classification of intensive growth opportunities based on a product-market expansion matrix.[1] The matrix is shown in Figure 3-2, and the three major types of intensive growth opportunities are described below:

1   *Market penetration. Market penetration consists of the company's seeking increased sales for its present products in its present markets through more aggressive marketing effort.* This includes three possibilities: (a) The company can try to stimulate customers to

---

[1]H. Igor Ansoff, "Strategies for Diversification," *Harvard Business Review,* September–October 1957, pp. 113–24. Also see his *Corporate Strategy* (New York: McGraw-Hill Book Company, 1965).

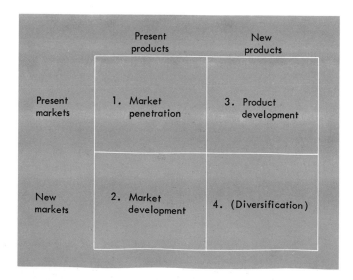

Figure 3-2
Four intensive growth opportunities

increase their present rate of usage. Such steps might be taken as increasing the unit of purchase, increasing the rate of product improvement or obsolescence, suggesting new uses for the product, and offering price incentives for increased use. (b) The company can increase its efforts to attract competitors' customers. Such steps might be taken as improving brand differentiation and stepping up promotion. (c) The company can increase its efforts to attract nonusers. Such steps might be taken as increasing product trial through offering samples and incentives, pricing up or down, and advertising new uses. In the case of Musicale, there is a substantial potential in increasing record purchases by present record buyers and gaining on present competitors.

2 *Market development. Market development consists of the company's seeking increased sales by taking its present products into new markets.* This includes two possibilities: (a) The company can open additional geographical markets through regional, national, or international expansion. (b) The company can try to attract other market segments through developing product versions that appeal to these segments, entering other channels of distribution, or advertising in other media. In the case of Musicale, the company is underrepresented in certain U.S. cities and is only doing an average job of participating in the growing international market. Also, the company is not well represented in the preteen segment of the market.

3 *Product development. Product development consists of the company's seeking increased sales by developing improved products for its present markets.* This includes three possibilities: (a) The company can develop new product features through attempting to adapt, modify, magnify, minify, substitute, rearrange, reverse, or combine existing features.[2] (b) The company can create different quality versions of the product. (c) The company can develop additional models and sizes. For example, Musicale might research and develop a new type of record that carries more sound track or better quality. It might produce all-plastic sheet records, such as those that are increasingly being inserted in magazines. It might produce new program content, such as a do-it-yourself series or a basic education series.

Integrative growth   Integrative growth makes sense for a company if (a) the basic industry has a strong growth future and/or (b) the company can increase its profitability, efficiency, or control by moving backward, forward, or horizontally within the industry. Figure 3-3 shows the core marketing system for Musicale. The three integrative growth possibilities are discussed below:

1 *Backward integration. Backward integration consists of a company's seeking ownership or increased control of its supply systems.* Musicale relies heavily on plastic-material producers and recording equipment manufacturers. Musicale might see an advantage in backward integration if any of these suppliers is facing or enjoying

---

[2]See Alex F. Osborn, *Applied Imagination,* 3rd ed. (New York: Charles Scribner's Sons, 1963), pp. 286–87.

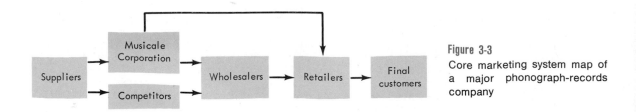

Figure 3-3

Core marketing system map of a major phonograph-records company

high growth or profits, or if there is some uncertainty over the availability or cost of future supplies.

2 *Forward integration. Forward integration consists of a company's seeking ownership or increased control of its distribution systems.* Musicale sells to records wholesalers, and to certain large records retailers. Musicale might see an advantage in forward integration if any of these marketing intermediaries is facing or enjoying high growth or profits, or if Musicale is not getting satisfactory treatment or service from some of these merchants. It might also start a direct mail-order records club to reduce its dependence on middlemen.

3 *Horizontal integration. Horizontal integration consists of a company's seeking ownership or increased control of some of its competitors.* Musicale has witnessed several new smaller companies enjoy phenomenal growth in a short time based on a sharp ability to spot new recording talent. These companies could be an attractive target for takeover if they would provide Musicale with new management talent and some new stars. Musicale would have to be sure that the acquisition would not be challenged by the government as "tending substantially to lessen competition."

Diversification growth Diversification growth makes sense for a company (a) if the core marketing system does not show much additional opportunity for growth or profit, or (b) if the opportunities outside of the present core marketing system are superior. Diversification does not mean that the company will take up any opportunity however unrelated to its present distinctive competences or needs. On the contrary, the company would attempt to identify fields that make use of its distinctive competences or help it overcome a particular problem. There are three broad types of diversification moves:

1 *Concentric diversification. Concentric diversification consists of the company's seeking to add new products that have technological and/or marketing synergies with the existing product line; these products will normally appeal to new classes of customers.* In the case of Musicale, it would search for other products that make use of its ability to work with plastics, to work with sound recording, or to work with artistically talented performers. One intriguing idea is for the company to go into other businesses with the talent it has under contract (such as name franchising) and manage other classes of talent (teachers, businessmen, writers, and so on).

2 *Horizontal diversification. Horizontal diversification consists of the company's seeking to add new products that could appeal to its present customers though technologically unrelated to its present product line.* The products might appeal to the company's ultimate customers or its intermediate customers. For example, Musicale might go into publishing a teenage magazine or making teenage clothing because of its great understanding of teenage tastes and life-styles. Or it might go into the manufacturing of other products that are carried by record retailers, such as phonographs or tape recorders. However, we saw that these horizontal diversification moves did not work out well for Musicale, primarily because it did not have the other competences making up the success requirements in these businesses.

3 *Conglomerate diversification. Conglomerate diversification consists of the company's seeking to add new products for new classes of customers because this (a) promises to offset some deficiency or (b) represents a great environmental opportunity; in either case, these products have no relationship to the company's current technology, products, or markets.* Most companies experience seasonal or cyclical fluctuations which are costly in terms of manpower, inventory carrying costs, or cash-flow management. Musicale has high sales in certain seasons, such as Christmas and Easter, and low sales during business recessions. These factors might lead it to look for a business opportunity

that has a different seasonal or cyclical pattern. Or companies like Musicale may be attracted to environmental opportunities such as pollution control or health sciences simply because they may be very attractive. It might feel that it could acquire whatever competences were necessary to make a success in the new business area. This often proves, however, to be very naive.

Thus we see that through application of a marketing systems framework, looking first at current product-market opportunities, then at opportunities in other parts of the core marketing system, and finally at relevant opportunities outside of the core system, a company can systematically generate a set of opportunities.

SETTING COMPANY OBJECTIVES

We now turn to the role played by company objectives. A company cannot go after all of its opportunities—first, because some of them are inconsistent with each other; second, because it never has enough resources to pursue all of its opportunities; and third, because all the opportunities are not equally attractive. We can imagine the company eliminating those opportunities for which it lacks sufficient resources or synergistic possibilities. Synergy exists when two or more things in combination are worth more than their separate merits; it is often expressed as the condition $2 + 2 = 5$. We shall assume that the company will eliminate those opportunities for which it lacks synergy or differential advantage.

Company purpose and mission

How does a company decide which opportunities to pursue out of the set that remain? The answer is tied up with the question of whether the company has developed a clear sense of its purpose and mission. If it has, the answer is easy; if it has not, the company must struggle to define itself first.

The company's purpose and mission answers the questions, What is our business? and What should it be?[3] These sound like simple questions but are in fact among the most difficult questions the company will ever have to answer. Too many companies like to answer, To make a profit. But this is not an answer; it provides no guidance whatsoever. Profit is necessary to provide the wherewithal for carrying out the corporate mission. Profits are more the result of carrying out a successful corporate purpose than the goal.

The company purpose and mission must be defined in terms of meeting some need in the external environment. It should normally not be stated in terms of delivering some product. A company's purpose is not to produce cars or telephones or computers. These are only hardware. Certain companies see their business mission in more *generic-need* terms:

Volkswagen's mission is to provide an economic means of private transportation.

American Telephone and Telegraph's mission is to provide quick and efficient communication capabilities.

IBM's mission is to meet the problem-solving needs of business.

Shell Oil's mission is to meet the energy needs of mankind.

---

[3]See Peter F. Drucker, *Management: Tasks, Responsibilities, Practices* (New York: Harper & Row, Publishers, 1973), Chap. 7.

International Minerals and Chemical Corporation's mission is to increase agricultural productivity to feed the world's hungry.

Once a company arrives at a strong sense of corporate mission, it finds it easier to scan the environment for opportunities and easier to evaluate the contribution of different opportunities to corporate purpose. At the same time, corporate purpose itself is subject to revision as new opportunities arise and old solutions no longer work.

The company's basic purpose and mission must be translated into more specific areas of endeavor. Consider IMC's mission to improve agricultural productivity. There are many ways in which this can be done: improving seeds, fertilizers, insecticides, farm equipment, and so on. IMC cannot be good at all these things and does not have a differential advantage in all things. So it must make choices and develop suitable sub-missions, such as concentrating on improving plant nutrition and animal health nutrition.

Company objectives

The company's basic purpose and mission must be translated into specific objectives to guide the organization to what it should try to accomplish with various activities in the external environment. Most management analysts underscore the importance of "management by objectives." Objectives serve the following purposes in an organization:

> Objectives provide the people in an organization with a specific sense of their role in the organization.
>
> Objectives provide for consistency in decision making among a great number of different managers.
>
> Objectives provide the basis for specific planning.
>
> Objectives stimulate exertion and accomplishment.
>
> Objectives provide the basis for corrective actions and control.

Company objectives must have certain qualities if they are to serve the purposes just mentioned. In particular, they should be hierarchical, quantitative, realistic, and consistent.

Hierarchical   A company is always pursuing a large number of objectives, not all equally important. When possible, major objectives should be arranged in a hierarchical fashion showing which are the most important, which are derived, and how they are derived.[4] An excellent example of hierarchically arranged objectives is provided by Interstate Telephone Company (name disguised).[5] The company has not been earning the allowed rate of 7.5 percent in recent years, giving various "stakeholders"[6] a real cause for concern. One of management's major objectives is to increase its return on investment to 7.5 percent. Starting from this objective, a whole hierarchy of further objectives can be derived, as shown in Figure 3-4.

---

[4]Charles H. Granger, "The Hierarchy of Objectives," *Harvard Business Review,* May–June 1964, pp. 63–74.

[5]Leon Winer, "Are You Really Planning Your Marketing?" *Journal of Marketing,* January 1965, pp. 1–8.

[6]"Stakeholders" are stockholders and all the other parties who have a "stake" in the firm, such as bankers and managers.

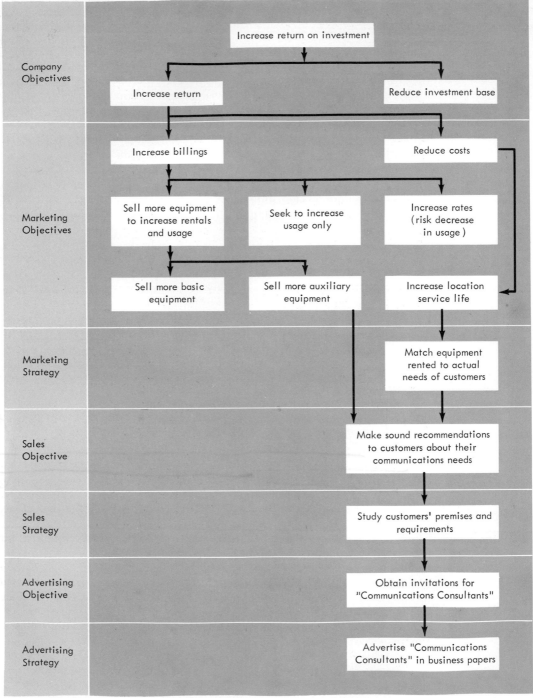

Company Objectives	Increase return on investment Increase return Reduce investment base
Marketing Objectives	Increase billings Reduce costs Sell more equipment to increase rentals and usage Seek to increase usage only Increase rates (risk decrease in usage) Sell more basic equipment Sell more auxiliary equipment Increase location service life
Marketing Strategy	Match equipment rented to actual needs of customers
Sales Objective	Make sound recommendations to customers about their communications needs
Sales Strategy	Study customers' premises and requirements
Advertising Objective	Obtain invitations for "Communications Consultants"
Advertising Strategy	Advertise "Communications Consultants" in business papers

SOURCE: Leon Winer, "Are You Really Planning Your Marketing?" *Journal of Marketing,* January 1965, pp. 1–8, here p. 3.

Figure 3-4
Hierarchy of objectives for the Interstate Telephone Company

There are only two ways to increase the return on investment: increase the total return or reduce the investment base. The company is not about to do the latter. To increase its return, there are two possibilities: the company should increase its billings and/or reduce its costs. Each of these can become an objective. To increase its billings, the company can (1) sell more equipment to increase rentals and usage, (2) seek to increase usage of present equipment, and (3) increase its rates, providing this does not reduce customer usage. (The last possibility is eliminated because the rate commission will not allow higher rates unless the telephone company's rate of return is below 5.5 percent.) As for reducing costs, this could be accomplished by increasing the location service life of telephone equipment, which in turn suggests doing a better job of matching rented equipment to the actual needs of customers.

To the extent that the company tries to increase its billings, this requires setting subsidiary objectives for sales force, advertising, and other elements of the marketing mix. For example, each sales district will be assigned a sales quota based on its potential. Each sales district quota in turn will be broken down and assigned to individual salesmen. In this way the broad objective of the company is ultimately translated into specific objectives and work assignments.

Quantitative   To the extent possible, objectives should be stated in quantitative or operational terms. The objective "increase the return on investment" is not very satisfactory. The objective "increase the return on investment to 7.5 percent" is an improved statement. The objective "increase the return on investment to 7.5 percent by the end of the second year" is a still better statement. The more specifically the objective is stated in terms of magnitudes, time, and place, the more useful it is for developing plans and implementing controls.

Realistic   The telephone company has to be careful in choosing the target rate of return. Not any rate will do. It wants to set the highest rate that is reasonable to seek. This should come out of an analysis of its opportunities and resources, not out of wishful thinking.

Consistent   The company is likely to pursue at any time a number of important objectives rather than one. For example, Kraftco Corporation states that it seeks to

> provide a *quality* product that will *maximize customer satisfaction*, provide an *adequate return*, and *increase* the company's total *market share*.

These are admirable objectives but raise the question of whether they are all consistent. Sometimes the objectives are clearly inconsistent, as when management says that it wants "to maximize sales and profits," or wants "to achieve the greatest sales at the least cost," or wants "to design the best possible product in the shortest possible time." It must be recognized that these objectives are in a trade-off relationship. It is not possible to maximize simultaneously sales and profits. One can increase sales by lowering price, improving product quality, and increasing marketing effort, although these steps, beyond a point, are likely to reduce profit. A statement involving two basic objectives in a trade-off relationship is of no help as a management guide without further specification.

Robert Weinberg has identified eight basic strategic trade-offs facing any firm:

1　Short-term profits vs. long-term growth.
2　Profit margin vs. competitive position.
3　Direct sales effort vs. market development effort.
4　Penetration of existing markets vs. the development of new markets.
5　Related vs. nonrelated new opportunities as a source of long-term growth.
6　Profit vs. nonprofit goals [that is, social responsibilities].
7　Growth vs. stability.
8　"Riskless" environment vs. high-risk environment.[7]

A company has to determine the relative emphasis to give to these conflicting objectives. Consider the following choices made by some chemical companies during the period 1955–64:

> . . . Du Pont and Union Carbide followed a strategy that maintained their profit margins at a level significantly above that of the industry as a whole. To maintain this position, however, the companies had to be highly selective in their choices of markets, resulting in a significantly below-average nine-year average growth rate. Allied Chemical appears to have followed a strategy that would allow the company to improve its below-average profit rate. To do this the company also sacrificed growth.[8]

DEVELOPING MARKETING STRATEGY

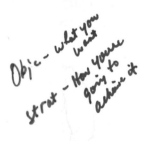

Objectives are a statement of where a company wants to go; strategy is a grand design for getting there. Strategy is a battle plan fused out of marketing, financial, and manufacturing elements; here we will emphasize the marketing elements.

We will use the following situation in the heavy-equipment industrial marketing area to illustrate the concept of strategy.

> International Harvester (IH) is a major manufacturer of trucks, agricultural equipment, and earth-moving equipment, with worldwide sales of $4 billion. In the earth-moving industry, the company competes with the giant of the industry, Caterpillar, as well as with Allis-Chalmers, Massey-Ferguson, and a few other major companies. IH feels that the earth-moving industry will continue to have high growth in the coming years. The need for oil in the United States has led to the approval of the building of a huge pipeline from Alaska. Coal shortages and tougher federal regulations on underground mines have increased the need for equipment for strip mining in Appalachia and elsewhere. Worldwide demand for electrical power means construction equipment will be needed to build dams, prepare sites for power, and mine the power-generating fuels of coal and uranium. The developing nations are building highways and housing, all of which needs construction equipment.
>
> Thus IH sees a major opportunity in further intensive growth in this industry. Let us assume that it adopts the objective "to reach a position of shared leadership with Caterpillar in the earth-moving industry by 1982."

---

[7]Presented in a seminar, "Developing Management Strategies for Short-Term Profits and Long-Term Growth," sponsored by Advanced Management Research, Inc., Regency Hotel, New York City, September 29, 1969.
[8]*Ibid.*

This is an ambitious objective. Caterpillar today commands the major share of the market. Its name and familiar yellow-colored equipment is known and respected the world over. Its quality is so well regarded that equipment buyers are willing to pay a premium of 5 to 10 percent more than for comparable equipment. Its service is considered the best in the industry. Its distribution system is so extensive that it can guarantee parts delivery within twenty-four hours anywhere in the world; this is extremely important to owners of earth-moving equipment who have work crews tied up in remote areas who depend on the machines' continuing to function. A Caterpillar distributor has a net worth of $4 million to $5 million as compared with $1 million of an IH dealer. The greater-size Caterpillar dealer can afford to stock more parts, buy more testing equipment, and do more machine leasing. Caterpillar makes the most complete line in its class, and therefore its dealers can prosper by selling Caterpillar products exclusively. Dealers for IH and Allis-Chalmers cannot survive without other franchises from competing equipment makers. Altogether, it seems that the Caterpillar fortress is invincible and IH's thoughts of catching up are quixotic and misplaced.

We now turn to five strategic concepts that form the basis for a marketing strategy.

Market segmentation

Market segmentation is the basic recognition that every market is made up of distinguishable segments consisting of buyers with different needs, buying styles, and responses to offer variations. No one offer or approach to the market will satisfy all buyers. Each segment of the market represents a somewhat different opportunity. The firm will want to study the opportunities in different parts of the market before taking a position.

There is no unique way to segment a market.[9] The fortunate firm is often the one that has found a creative new way to segment the market. Let us examine some ways that IH can segment the construction equipment buying market.

The first principle is that of *geographical segmentation.* Although Caterpillar operates worldwide, it cannot possibly be equally strong everywhere. There is a great amount of new construction occurring in Latin America, Africa, and Asia. For example, Brazil is building two-thousand-plus miles of the Trans-Amazon Highway. IH's job is to study the construction budgets and growth rates of different regions and nations, find out where Caterpillar is relatively weak but the growth strong, and give top consideration to these markets.

Another way to break down the construction equipment market is by *end uses.* Construction arises in connection with residential housing, business and institutional building, road and highway development, pipeline laying, dam construction, and urban renewal. Each end use calls for different types and mixes of equipment as well as different types of customers. An analysis must be made of the character, growth, and potential profitability of these different segments of the market.

The construction market can also be analyzed by *buyer description variables.* One would be *types of buyers*—for example, construction equipment is purchased or rented by private contractors, business firms, and federal, state, and local government units. Another would be *customer size*—IH could decide to concentrate on large, medium, or small customers. Still another would be *customer class*—customers can be classified by their buying motive (economy, quality,

---

[9]Chapter 7 is devoted to a full discussion of market segmentation methods.

service, etc.) or some other variable. There are a host of alternative parts of the market that IH could concentrate on.

The market can also be segmented by *specific products*, such as track-type tractors, heavy-duty off-highway wheeled tractors, loaders, pipelayers, and motor graders. IH can attempt to manufacture and market the best version of those pieces of equipment that will experience the most rapid growth in demand.

Market positioning

The second principle of marketing strategy is to select a specific pattern of market concentration that will afford the maximum opportunity to the company to achieve its leadership objective. The company cannot be everywhere. It must go after viable positions. It must follow the principle of target marketing.

What makes any part of the market an attractive one for a particular company to go after? A maximally attractive market segment would have four characteristics:

1 The market segment is of sufficient current size.
2 The market segment has the potential for further growth.
3 The market segment is not "owned" or overoccupied by existing competition.
4 The market segment has some relative unsatisfied needs that the particular company can serve well.

If the company decides to seek a leadership position in only one market segment, this is called a strategy of *single segment concentration*. This would happen if IH decided to concentrate strictly on the pipeline construction market. Normally we would expect a company like IH to go after a mix of market segments that hopefully have synergistic relations, that is, where strength in one market segment gives the company an advantage in the other market segments. This strategy would be called *multiple segment concentration*. The company's chosen pattern of market concentration sets the die. It determines the products the company will produce, the customers the company will serve, and the competitors the company will face.

Market entry strategy

The third element of marketing strategy is to determine how to enter a target market segment. The company can proceed through acquisition, internal development, or collaboration with other companies.

Acquisition of an existing product or company is the easiest and quickest way to enter a new market. Acquisition obviates the costly and time-consuming process of attempting to build up internally the knowledge, resources, and reputation necessary to become an effective participant in that part of the market. In fact, the following factors would favor acquisition:

1 The acquiring company has very little knowledge of the industry.
2 There is a strong advantage in entering the new market as soon as possible.
3 The company would face several barriers to entry through internal development, such as patents, substantial economies of scale, closed or difficult-to-enter channels of distribution, costly advertising requirements, or lack of raw materials or other supplies.

Some companies prefer to achieve most of their growth through *internal development*. They may feel that true leadership is only achieved by running their own research and development laboratories. They may feel that acquiring a company will raise the brows of antitrust people. They may feel that the companies around to acquire are not very good or are asking for too much. Or there may be no companies around to acquire.

Entry into a new market or market segment may also be accomplished by *collaboration* with others to jointly exploit the new opportunity. A major advantage is that the risk is shared, and therefore reduced, for each of the participating companies. Another advantage may be that each company brings specific skills or resources whose lack makes it impossible for either company to venture by itself. In the best joint-venturing combinations, there is not only complementarity but synergy.

We would suggest that IH would rely primarily on internal development to secure its target market position; but for certain positions, it might move quickly to acquire, and in a few cases, might jointly venture with another company.

Marketing-mix strategy

A further element in marketing strategy is for the company to determine how it will profile its offering to the particular market segment. The key concept here is *marketing mix:*

> **Marketing mix** is the set of controllable variables that the firm can use to influence the buyers' responses.

Many variables qualify as marketing-mix variables. McCarthy popularized a four-factor classification which he called the "four *P*'s": *product, place, promotion, and price*.[10] This says that buyers are influenced by variables related to the product, the place, promotion, and price. A list of the particular variables under each *P* is provided in Table 3-2.

To show how marketing mix functions as a strategic concept, let us assume that IH wants to increase its penetration in the small-equipment private contractor market to gain the number one position. Consider its options with just two marketing-mix variables, product quality and price, each of which can be set at a high, medium, or low level. Nine different marketing-mix strategies can be generated (see Figure 3-5). A "premium strategy" consists of offering a high-quality product at a premium price. This is Caterpillar's traditional strategy. An "average-quality strategy" consists of offering an average product at an average price. IH might prefer to adopt a "penetration strategy," which calls for offering a superior-quality product at a medium price. If potential buyers can be convinced that IH's product is of comparable quality to Caterpillar's but

---

[10]E. Jerome McCarthy, *Basic Marketing: A Managerial Approach*, 4th ed. (Homewood, Ill.: Richard D. Irwin, Inc., 1971), p. 44 (1st ed., 1960). Two alternative classifications are worth noting. Frey proposed that all marketing decision variables could be divided into two factors: (1) *the offering* (product, packaging, brand, price, and service), and (2) *methods and tools* (distribution channels, personal selling, advertising, sales promotion, and publicity). See Albert W. Frey, *Advertising*, 3rd ed. (New York: The Ronald Press Company, 1961), p. 30. Lazer and Kelley proposed a three-factor classification: (1) *goods and service mix*, (2) *distribution mix*, and (3) *communications mix*. See William Lazer and Eugene J. Kelley, *Managerial Marketing: Perspectives and Viewpoints*, rev. ed. (Homewood, Ill.: Richard D. Irwin, Inc., 1962), p. 413.

Table 3-2
Elaboration of the "four P's"

Product	*Place*	*Promotion*	*Price*
Quality Features and options Style Brand name Packaging Product line Warranty Service level Other services	Distribution channels Distribution coverage Outlet locations Sales territories Inventory levels and locations Transportation carriers	Advertising Personal selling Sales promotion Publicity	Level Discounts and allowances Payment terms

priced at 10 to 15 percent less, they might make their purchase decision in favor of IH.

But certain conditions have to be checked first before IH can confidently select this strategy. First, potential buyers must really be convinced that IH's product possesses the same high quality and performance characteristics as Caterpillar's. This may not be easy to demonstrate and may be suspect because many buyers judge a piece of equipment by its price. Second, potential buyers must feel that the other elements of the marketing mix—such as service and

Product Quality	Price: High	Price: Medium	Price: Low
High	Premium strategy	Penetration strategy	Superbargain strategy
Medium	Overpricing strategy	Average-quality strategy	Bargain strategy
Low	Hit-and-run strategy	Shoddy-goods strategy	Cheap-goods strategy

Figure 3-5
Nine marketing-mix strategies

optional equipment—are comparable for IH and its competitors. If Caterpillar can repair equipment in less than twenty-four hours anywhere in the world and IH can only guarantee repairs in less than forty-eight hours, this may cancel the price savings in the buyers' minds. Third, IH must be sure that Caterpillar will not react to IH's penetration strategy by lowering its prices. This is a real and very likely possibility. In this case IH will neither gain any market share nor recoup an adequate return on its investment. Finally, IH must check that any proposed marketing-mix strategy is compatible with its other departments' resources and competences. The company must be sure that it can develop the quality equipment, achieve the necessary manufacturing economies of scale, and handle the necessary cash flows called for by a penetration strategy.

Timing strategy

The final element of strategy is that of timing. Just because a company has spotted a good opportunity, set an objective, and developed a marketing strategy does not mean it should immediately move in. It may lose by moving in too soon or too late. The proper sequencing and timing of its moves are a key component of strategy.

Let us return to the case where IH has decided that it would like to increase its penetration of the small-construction-equipment market through a penetration pricing strategy. First, it must visualize the sequence of activities that it would have to initiate to launch this strategy. New equipment would have to be designed and tested with a sample of potential buyers, a plant would have to be constructed, dealers would have to be alerted and trained, some new dealerships would have to be established, and promotion would have to be prepared. These activities would have to be time estimated and sequenced so that management could know how long it would be before it could launch its actual competitive attack.

There is also the question of whether this is an opportune time to begin the activities in the strategic sequence. Is the nation headed for recession or prosperity? Is the major competitor getting back-ordered or is he hungry and ready for a fight? These and other questions must be faced in trying to determine the best moment to strike.

FORMULATING PLANS

Much of what we have described up to now can be called strategic planning. The only thing missing is the development of written plans in the form of specific targets, budgets, and work assignments. These things spell out the tactics of accomplishing the given objectives.

The marketing objectives and targets form the backbone of the corporate plan. A commitment is made to achieve a certain level of sales, and then all of the resource decisions on marketing, manufacturing, finance, and personnel are made. Here we shall concentrate on the major concepts used in developing marketing plans and budgets.

Sales targets

The marketing plan begins with a statement of sales targets for each of the company's divisions and products. A sales target does not represent an arbitrary choice of a sales volume but instead emerges from an analysis of the profitability of different possible marketing strategies. The sales target is allocated to the performing units of the company, such as sales regions, sales districts, and finally individual salesmen. They often go under the name of sales quotas and are based on the past performance and estimated potential facing each of these units.

Total marketing budget

To enable the various marketing tasks to be carried out, the company develops a total marketing budget. Normally, the company sets the total marketing budget at some conventional percentage of the sales target. For example, a breakfast cereal company would set its marketing budget at about 35 percent of sales. A fertilizer company would set its marketing budget at much less, say at 15 percent of sales. Companies entering a new market are especially interested in learning what the *marketing budget-to-sales ratio* is in the typical company, although this information is highly confidential and not easy to obtain. A particular company may spend more than the normal ratio in the hope of achieving a higher market share. Ultimately, the company should analyze the marketing work that has to be done to attain a given sales volume or market share and then price this work; the result is the desired marketing budget.

Marketing-mix allocation

The company has to decide how to allocate the total market budget for a product to the various marketing-mix tools, such as advertising, sales promotion, and personal selling. Presumably the question of the relative emphasis of the tools is settled earlier in the forming of a marketing strategy. There may still be conflict among those in different parts of the marketing operation as to how much money they need for their job. The sales manager usually feels that hiring one extra salesman for $20,000 a year will do more good than placing a one-page ad in *Time* magazine each year. The marketing research manager usually feels that spending $20,000 to get some basic information about customer needs is worth more than either of the other two uses of the money.

Pricing

Pricing is the fundamental revenue-producing element in the marketing plan. The rough pricing zone would be considered earlier as a matter of marketing strategy, but the plan requires a specific level of price to be set within that zone. The planned realized price as well as the list price before discounts and allowances must be determined. The marketing department must carefully consider the three elements of demand, cost, and competition in setting the planned price.

Marketing budget allocation to products

Most modern companies are multiproduct firms. The multiproduct firm must resolve each year how much money to allocate to each of the products in its line. The product line consists of a mixed bag of new products that are fairly small but have bright futures; important products that have been around for a while and face continued strong demand; and other products, both large and small, that are the tired breadwinners of the past and are just limping along. The company has to make a basic determination of which products call for increased marketing budgets, which call for harvesting, and which call for reduced marketing budgets.

For example, General Electric Company, a prime practitioner of strategic planning, recently decided to put the maximum company resources into such products as medical systems, aircraft engines, and engineering plastics—based on their highly leveraged total earnings growth in recent years. It decided on a level of steady reinvestment in such product areas as major appliances, steam and gas turbines, and lamps. It decided to disinvest in some smaller appliances such as blenders, fans, heaters, humidifiers, and vacuum cleaners. Finally, it decided to put a lot of money into new venture opportunities such as the "10-ton" aircraft engine, the man-made diamond, and micro-wave cooking.[11]

These plan decisions—on sales targets, total marketing budget, marketing mix allocation, pricing, and marketing budget allocation to products—constitute the key components of *marketing programming*.

IMPLEMENTATION AND CONTROL

A plan is nothing, according to Drucker, "unless it *degenerates into work*."[12] The plan is a blueprint for work and accomplishments. The good plan spells out what is supposed to be accomplished each period along the way. Thus sales targets are stated not only in total and by performing units but also by periods, such as months or quarters. The same is true of marketing budgets.

One of the major jobs of managers, besides planning, supervising, and doing, is controlling. Each manager knows what to watch. The district sales manager scans each period the sales volumes and expenses of each salesman against individual quotas and budgets. He gets on the phone and asks questions of the salesmen who are lagging behind. His approach is constructive rather than critical, trying to pinpoint the trouble and how he can help correct it. In the meantime the regional sales manager scans the actual sales of this district sales manager and the other district sales managers under him, also getting on the phone when he notes deviations from targets. Even the president of the company gets on the phone when he looks at total sales for the period and they are off.

This is only one aspect of control we call *annual plan control*. Management also exercises *profitability control* by examining the real profitability of its various products, markets, and territories and different marketing channels. Finally, there is the major issue of *strategic control*, that is, whether the company's products, resources, and objectives are properly matched to the right markets. In times of rapid change, a company's marketing strategy can easily become inappropriate to its opportunities and threats. The job of a marketing auditor is essentially to evaluate the final and ultimate question of strategic control.

SUMMARY

Management is the catalytic agent that interprets market needs and translates them into meaningful products and services. To do this, management goes through a strategic-marketing process consisting of analyzing opportunities, choosing objectives, developing strategy, formulating plans, and carrying out implementation and control.

---

[11]"Strategic Planning: Three New Slants," *General Electric Monogram*, November–December 1973, p. 4.

[12]Drucker, *op. cit.*, p. 128.

A company's opportunities are not simply the general opportunities in the environment but that subset for which a particular company would enjoy a differential advantage in carrying out marketing action. It must have a set of distinctive competences that match well the success requirements for effectiveness in that area. The company can generate a systematic picture of its relevant opportunities by first considering intensive growth opportunities within its present product-market scope (such as market penetration, market development, and product development), then considering integrative growth opportunities within its core marketing system (such as backward, forward, and horizontal integration), and finally considering diversification growth opportunities outside of its core marketing system (such as concentric, horizontal, and conglomerate diversification).

To choose among opportunities, a company must refer to its basic purpose and mission, which should be defined in terms of meeting generic needs, not producing particular products. For any opportunity, it must develop a well-integrated set of objectives that are hierarchical, quantitative, realistic, and consistent.

Whereas objectives are a statement of where a company wants to go, strategy is a grand design for getting there. The major elements in formulating marketing strategy are five: market segmentation, market positioning, market entry strategy, marketing-mix strategy, and timing strategy.

A strategy must be translated into a concrete documented plan that specifies sales targets, budgets, and work assignments. The key marketing decisions made in the plan are sales targets, total marketing budget, marketing-mix allocation, pricing, and marketing budget allocation to products.

Finally, the work specified in the plan must be implemented and controlled. A good plan provides for periodic checking and corrective action by different levels of management. In addition to annual plan marketing, management must carry out profitability control and strategic control.

**QUESTIONS
AND PROBLEMS**

1   Many companies have defined the food industry as a major area of opportunity. Cite some trends and opportunities that characterize the food industry's future.

2   An automotive parts manufacturer produces three products: mufflers, filters, and silencers. The company is seeking new growth opportunities. Develop a product-market matrix showing some potential expansion opportunities for this manufacturer.

3   Comment on the following statements made about the appropriate marketing strategy of smaller firms: (a) "The smaller firm should concentrate on pulling away the larger firm's customers, while the larger firm should concentrate on stimulating new customers to enter the market." (b) "Larger firms should pioneer new products and the smaller ones stick to copying them."

4   What is the major distinctive competence of (a) Sears; (b) Polaroid Company; (c) Procter & Gamble; (d) Ford Foundation?

5   Develop some propositions of the form "if . . . then" indicating whether a company should pursue an intensive, integrative, or diversification strategy.

6 Many people have noted a similarity between business strategy and military strategy. There are the gasoline "price wars," the "border clashes" and "skirmishes" of the major computer manufacturers, the "escalating arms budgets" of the soap companies, "guerilla warfare" by Purex against the soap giants, the "sabotaging" and "spying" of test markets by competitors, and so on. Without denying the usefulness of military insights and principles, name some limitations of the analogy between business and military competition.

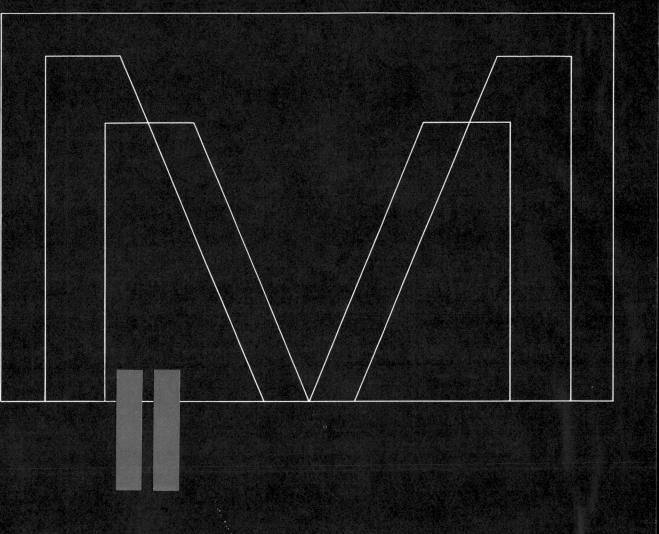

ANALYZING MARKETING OPPORTUNITIES

4

CONSUMER MARKETS
AND BUYER BEHAVIOR

Instead of trying to market what is easiest for us to
make, we must find out much more about what the
consumer is willing to buy . . . we must apply our
creativeness more intelligently to people, *and their*
wants and needs, rather than to products.

CHARLES G. MORTIMER

The preceding chapters examined the nature of marketing, marketing management, the marketing system, and strategic marketing. With this overview, we are
now ready to move to a deeper understanding of *markets,* which are the starting
point for all marketing planning and control.

Markets exhibit vast differences. There would appear to be little in common in the buying and selling of soap, steel, automobiles, jets, haircuts, mental
health, and legal services. One can well wonder whether the person who has
marketed soap successfully would be effective in marketing computers; whether
he will even be effective in marketing soap in a foreign country; or whether he
could effectively market a new soap designed especially for the geriatric market.
A large number of special and unique practices cluster around particular markets, and the marketer has to spend time mastering each new market.

We believe, however, that the well-trained marketer can learn the *special*
qualities of any market with time. He approaches a new market with a method,
not a dogma. Recently two men left positions in a soap marketing company to
head up marketing in two different banks. One marketer brought along the
habits of thought he had learned in mass-consumer marketing and wanted the
bank to increase its advertising and promotional expenditure and sell money
in the same way as soap. The other marketer thought of marketing primarily
as a discipline for analyzing the needs of buyers, creating the products and

services that would satisfy the buyers competitively, and communicating the offer effectively. In the end he developed a marketing program appropriate to the banking industry rather than one that had worked well in another industry.

To understand a particular market, one should first have a working knowledge of the important institutional characteristics of five types of markets: *consumer market, producer market, reseller market, government market,* and *international market.* The consumer market will occupy our attention in this chapter; the other markets will be examined in the next chapter and Chapter 21. These markets are essentially distinguished on the basis of the *buyers' role and motives* rather than the characteristics of the purchased product.[1] Consumers are individuals and households buying for personal use; producers are individuals and organizations buying for the purpose of producing; resellers are individuals and organizations buying for the purpose of reselling; governments are governmental units buying for the purpose of carrying out governmental functions; finally, international markets include all of the foregoing types, as they perform outside of the United States.

The four O's and P's

Because markets are complex, we need to develop some common framework for grasping a market's essentials. The marketer should approach the study of a new market by asking four questions that we shall call the four *O*'s of any market:

1. What does the market buy? — *Objects* of purchase
2. Why does it buy? — *Objectives* of purchase
3. Who buys? — *Organization* for purchasing
4. How does it buy? — *Operations* of purchasing organization

Just as the letter *O* precedes the letter *P,* the four *O*'s of a market should be grasped before one contemplates the four *P*'s of the marketing mix. For example, the fact that price and service are the most important marketing variables in selling steel, and advertising and sales promotion are the most important variables in selling soap, traces back to the substantial differences in these markets regarding the products (objects), the market's motives (objectives), buyers (organization), and the buying process and influences (operations).

Two further questions of a more descriptive nature can also be asked of a market:

5. When does it buy? — *Occasions* for purchase
6. Where does it buy? — *Outlets* for purchase

We now turn to the consumer market, the subject of this chapter.

---

[1]Products cannot be used to distinguish markets, because many products are consumed in several types of markets. For example, fertilizer is sold to the consumer, producer, reseller, government, and international markets. Other examples of multiple-market products are light bulbs, carpets, and typewriters.

GENERAL CHARACTERISTICS OF THE CONSUMER MARKET

The consumer market is the market for products and services that are purchased or hired by individuals and households for personal (nonbusiness) use. The American consumer market consists of 210 million persons who yearly consume $1.3 trillion worth of products and service—the equivalent of $6,200 worth for every man, woman, and child. Each year this market grows by another 2 million persons and another $100 billion, representing one of the most lucrative consumer markets in the world.

Important consumer submarkets

American consumers vary tremendously in their ages, incomes, educational levels, mobility patterns, and tastes. Marketers have found it worthwhile to distinguish different groups in the marketplace and develop products and services tailored to their needs. If a market segment is large and lucrative, some companies may concentrate exclusively in catering to it. Consider three important submarkets:

> *Youth market.* Half of all Americans are under the age of twenty-eight. Within this group are important submarkets: the *infant market* (baby foods, infant wear, diapers), the *teenage market* (records, hair styles, clothing, sporting goods), and the *college market* (books, clothing, beer, travel). The college market alone consists of over 7 million persons who account for direct spending of $45 billion annually and who influence $145 billion of adult purchasing decisions. Companies have been formed for the explicit purpose of creating channels to the student market through a network of student campus representatives working on commissions and selling directly to students, through retailers, and through dormitories.[2]
>
> *Senior-citizen market.* At the other end of the age spectrum are 20 million Americans over the age of sixty-five. This market has specific tastes and needs in the way of food, housing, clothing, recreation, and medical attention. Marketers must be attuned to senior citizens' special needs for economy, small package sizes, and so on.
>
> *Black market.* Comprising an important group in the United States are the 23 million blacks with a spending power of $35 billion. Blacks are especially good consumers—out of proportion to their numbers—of such products as soft drinks, clothing, and canned luncheon meats, making special marketing effort desirable on the part of those manufacturers. Furthermore, the rise in black "class consciousness" suggests the desirability of applying more differentiated marketing effort in terms of selling appeals, ad copy, ad media, and packaging.[3]

Geographical dimensions of the consumer market

Profitable marketing requires observing not only who the consumers are but also where they live. The 210 million Americans are scattered unevenly over an area of 3.6 million square miles. Their concentration is heaviest in the North Atlantic States, along the Great Lakes, and along the California seaboard, where the largest American cities are found.

There is nothing static about the geographical distribution of the American population. Americans are a mobile people; it is estimated that one out

---

[2]"Getting Across to the Young," *Business Week*, October 18, 1969, pp. 89–90.
[3]For an overview, see the special April 1970 issue of *Journal of Advertising Research.*

of every five Americans moves each year, or 42 million Americans.[4] Nor are their movements random. States such as Florida, Nevada, and Arizona have attracted decennial population increases of the order of 35 to 70 percent, while states such as North Dakota and West Virginia have suffered decennial population decreases of the order of 2 to 6 percent. These regional shifts in population are of special interest to marketers because of marked differences in regional expenditure patterns and consumer behavior. Consumers in the West, for example, spend relatively less on food and relatively more on automobiles than their counterparts in the Northeast.

Another geographical movement of considerable marketing significance is the continuous migration from rural to urban areas. This movement has been going on for over a century. In 1880 approximately 70 percent of the nation's population lived in rural areas; now approximately 70 percent live in urban areas.

Urban areas themselves are far from homogeneous. Larger cities are characterized by a faster pace of living, more commuting, typically higher incomes, and a greater variety of goods and services than the small towns that dot America. The largest cities, such as New York, Chicago, and San Francisco, account for most of the sales of expensive furs, perfumes, luggage, and works of art, and they still boast most of what there is of opera, theater, and other forms of "high culture," although some dispersion of the arts is taking place. Each major metropolitan area constitutes a complex market, and profitable marketing often requires expert knowledge of the metropolitan area's unique characteristics.

Also significant is the movement from the city to the suburbs. Many persons have moved far away from their places of work, owing largely to the development of automobiles, major highways, and rapid rail and bus transit. Cities have become surrounded by suburbs, and these suburbs in turn by "exurbs." The U.S. Census Bureau has created a separate population classification for sprawling urban concentrations, called Standard Metropolitan Statistical Areas (SMSA).[5] Over 63 percent of the nation's entire population (and 95 percent of the nation's urban population) are estimated to live in the 212 recognized Standard Metropolitan Statistical Areas, and it is the SMSAs rather than the cities proper that constitute the primary market focus of firms.

Firms normally distinguish between the city and the suburban segments of the metropolitan areas. About 50 percent of the total metropolitan population now live in suburbs, and it is estimated that this may reach 60 percent by 1980. Suburban areas are frequently marked by a style of living different from that in the cities. Suburbs tend to be characterized by casual, outdoor living, greater neighbor interaction, higher incomes, and younger families. Suburban dwellers are the source of much of the demand for station wagons, home workshop equipment, garden furniture, lawn and gardening tools and supplies, and outdoor cooking equipment. Retailers have recognized the importance of convenience and have brought their goods out to the suburbs through the development of branch department stores and suburban shopping centers.

---

[4]Alvin Toffler, *Future Shock* (New York: Bantam Books, 1970), p. 78.

[5]An SMSA consists of the counties of an integrated economic area with a large volume of daily travel and communication between a central city of fifty thousand inhabitants or more and the outlying parts of the area.

Given the size, segmentation, and geographical characteristics of the American consumer market, it is now appropriate to consider the four O's of this market.

OBJECTS IN THE CONSUMER MARKET

Available to the 210 million American consumers is a variety of products and services that mankind until recently never dreamed was possible. The modern housewife presently confronts an average of 6,800 grocery products when she visits her supermarket. Each week that passes sees manufacturers trying to place 150 to 250 new products on the grocery shelves. The modern department store and mail-order catalog offer products in the tens of thousands.

Our interest is in finding some basis for classifying the vast number of consumer products. Two different classifications will be considered.

**Durable goods,
nondurable goods,
and services**

The first classification distinguishes three categories of goods on the basis of their rate of consumption and tangibility:

Durable goods: tangible goods which normally survive many uses (examples: refrigerators, clothing).

Nondurable goods: tangible goods which normally are consumed in one or a few uses (examples: meat, soap).

Services: activities, benefits, or satisfactions which are offered for sale (examples: haircuts, repairs).[6]

These distinctions have implications for marketing strategy. Products that are consumed fast and purchased frequently (nondurables and services) are likely to be made available in many locations, command a small margin, and develop strong brand loyalty. Durable products, on the other hand, are likely to need more personal selling and service, command a higher margin, and require more seller guarantees.

**Convenience, shopping,
and specialty goods**

A second goods classification, based not on the product's characteristics but on the consumer's shopping habits, distinguishes three types of goods:

Convenience goods: those consumers' goods which the customer usually purchases frequently, immediately, and with the minimum of effort in comparison and buying (examples: tobacco products, soap, newspapers).

Shopping goods: those consumers' goods which the customer, in the process of selection and purchase, characteristically compares on such bases as suitability, quality, price, and style (examples: furniture, dress goods, used automobiles, and major appliances).

---

[6]The definitions are taken from *Marketing Definitions: A Glossary of Marketing Terms,* compiled by the Committee on Definitions of the American Marketing Association, Ralph S. Alexander, Chairman (Chicago: American Marketing Association, 1960).

Specialty goods: those consumers' goods with unique characteristics and/or brand identification for which a significant group of buyers are habitually willing to make a special purchasing effort (examples: specific brands and types of fancy goods, hi-fi components, photographic equipment, and men's suits).[7]

The first two categories constitute opposite ends of a pole describing how much effort the consumer puts forth to select and obtain the goods. Convenience goods can be further subdivided into impulse items (for which the consumer puts forth no search effort) and staple items. Shopping goods may require search effort covering anywhere from one to several stores to find the appropriate item. Specialty goods do not involve shopping effort (since the consumer knows what he wants) but only shopping time to reach the outlets that carry these goods.[8]

OBJECTIVES SOUGHT BY CONSUMER BUYERS

Considering the amazing variety of products that consumers seek, it is not possible to cite any simple and single motive that they are trying to satisfy. Whereas the industrial markets buy goods and services primarily for the purpose of earning a profit, the consumer market buys products and services to attain a variety of need-satisfactions. Each consumer good offers a bundle of utilities. There may be a primary utility and several secondary utilities. A person buys toothpaste primarily to maintain clean teeth but may seek additional utilities such as anticavity protection, good taste, and breath freshening. Likewise, a person eats a breakfast cereal primarily to satisfy hunger but may seek additional utilities such as good taste and nutrition.

A marketer needs to understand what buyers are really seeking in their purchase of products and services. For this we turn to five models of the determinants of human needs and motivations as they relate to product desire and purchasing.

Learning model

Classic psychologists interpret man's needs as coming about through the interplay of drives, stimuli, cues, responses, and reinforcement.[9]

Every organism has innate physiological drives connected with survival. Psychologists distinguish between *primary drives* (such as hunger, thirst, sex, and pain avoidance) and *learned drives* (such as fear, guilt, pride, and acquisitiveness). The latter are learned through experience in trying to satisfy primary drives.

A *drive* is a strong internal stimulus impelling action. A drive becomes a *motive* when it is directed toward a particular drive-reducing object. A person

---

[7]*Ibid.*

[8]For further readings on the classification of goods, see Richard H. Holton, "The Distinction between Convenience Goods, Shopping Goods, and Specialty Goods," *Journal of Marketing,* July 1958, pp. 53–56; Louis P. Bucklin, "Retail Strategy and the Classification of Consumer Goods," *Journal of Marketing,* January 1963, pp. 50–55; Leo V. Aspinwall, "The Characteristics of Goods Theory," in *Managerial Marketing: Perspectives and Viewpoints,* rev. ed., ed. William Lazer and Eugene J. Kelley (Homewood, Ill.: Richard D. Irwin, Inc., 1962), pp. 633–43; and Gordon E. Miracle, "Product Characteristics and Marketing Strategy," *Journal of Marketing,* January 1965, pp. 18–24.

[9]See John Dollard and Neal E. Miller, *Personality and Psychotherapy* (New York: McGraw-Hill Book Company, 1950), Chap. 3.

may reach for a soft drink to satisfy his thirst or a candy bar to satisfy his hunger. These objects are *stimuli* in that they are capable of arousing and satisfying his drives.

The particular response of a person to a stimulus is influenced by the configuration of *cues*. Cues are minor stimuli that determine when, where, and how the person responds. In satisfying a thirst, a person is cued by the time of day, the cost and availability of different beverages, and so on.

The *response* is the organism's reaction to the configuration of stimuli and cues. If the response is rewarding, the probability of a similar response next time to the same cue configuration is *reinforced*. If a response is not rewarding, the probability of a similar response is diminished. Forgetting also affects response in that learned responses will weaken because of nonuse, aside from lack of reinforcement.

Cue configurations are constantly changing. For example, the shopper's favorite brand may be out of stock or he may see another brand on sale. He will shift to similar stimuli because learned responses are *generalized*.

A countertendency to generalization is *discrimination*. When a person tries two similar brands and finds one more rewarding, his ability to discriminate between similar cue configurations improves. Discrimination increases the specificity of the cue-response connection, while generalization decreases the specificity.

The practical import of learning theory for marketers is that they can build up demand for a product by associating it with strong drives, providing motivating cue configurations, and providing positive reinforcement. A new company can enter the market by appealing to the same drives as competitors and providing similar cue configurations because buyers are more likely to transfer loyalty to similar brands than to dissimilar brands (generalization). Or it may aim its brand to appeal to a different set of strong drives and offer cue inducements to switch.

Psychoanalytic model

A second model of motivation—the psychoanalytic—claims that man's needs operate at various levels of consciousness that are not readily observable and can only be identified by special methods of probing.

According to Freud, a child enters the world with instinctual drives which he tries to gratify through blatant means such as grabbing or crying. Very quickly and painfully he realizes that he cannot instantly gratify his needs. His repeated frustration leads him to perfect more subtle means for gratification.

As he grows older, his psyche grows more complex. A part, his id, remains the reservoir of his strong drives and urges. Another part, the ego, becomes his conscious planning center for finding outlets for his drives. And a third part, his superego, channels his instinctive drives into socially approved outlets to avoid the pain of guilt or shame.

The guilt or shame that man feels toward some of his urges, especially his sexual urges, causes him to repress them from his consciousness. Through such defense mechanisms as rationalization and sublimation, these urges are denied or become transmuted into socially acceptable expressions. Yet these urges are never eliminated or under perfect control; they emerge in dreams, in slips of the tongue, in neurotic and obsessional behavior, or ultimately in mental breakdowns when the ego can no longer maintain the delicate balance between the impulsive power of the id and the oppressive power of the superego.

The individual's behavior, therefore, is never simple. His motivational wellsprings are not obvious to a casual observer or deeply understood by himself. If he is asked why he purchases an expensive foreign sports car, he may reply that he likes its maneuverability and its looks. At a deeper level he may have purchased the car to impress others or to feel young again. At a still deeper level, he may have purchased the sports car to achieve substitute gratification for unsatisfied sexual strivings.

The most important marketing implication of this model is that buyers are motivated by *symbolic* as well as *functional* product concerns. The change of a bar of soap from a square to a round shape may be more important in its sexual than in its functional connotations. A cake mix that is advertised as involving almost no labor may alienate housewives because the easy life may evoke a sense of guilt.

Motivation research has produced some interesting and occasionally bizarre hypotheses about what may be in the buyer's mind regarding certain purchases. It has been suggested that

> Some businessmen don't fly because of a fear of posthumous guilt—if they crashed, their wives would think them stupid for not taking trains.
>
> Men want their cigars to be odoriferous in order to prove their masculinity.
>
> Consumers prefer vegetable shortening because animal fats stimulate a sense of sin.
>
> Men who wear suspenders are reacting to an unresolved castration complex.

There are admitted difficulties in proving these assertions. Two prominent motivation researchers, Ernest Dichter and James Vicary, were hired by the prune industry to determine why so many people dislike prunes. Dichter found that the prune aroused feelings of old age and insecurity. Vicary found that Americans had an emotional block about prunes' laxative qualities.[10] Which is the more valid interpretation? Or if they are both operative, which motive is found with greater statistical frequency in the population?

Unfortunately, the usual survey techniques of direct observation and interviewing can establish the distribution of characteristics such as age and family size but are not successful in establishing the frequency of mental states that are deeply "buried" within each individual.

Motivation researchers employ projective techniques in the hope of throwing individual "egos" off guard. When carefully administered and interpreted, techniques such as word association, sentence completion, picture interpretation, and role playing can provide clues to deeper human motivations. These findings provide guidance to marketing planners and communicators. Appeals aimed at the buyer's private world of hopes, dreams, and fears can often be more effective than more rationally directed appeals.

Sociological model

A third model of motivation—the sociological—postulates that man's needs and behavior are heavily shaped by social groups and forces. People get their ideas of what they want from their culture, subcultures, social class, and ref-

---

[10]L. Edward Scriven, "Rationality and Irrationality in Motivation Research," in *Motivation and Marketing Behavior*, ed. Robert Ferber and Hugh G. Wales (Homewood, Ill.: Richard D. Irwin, Inc., 1958), pp. 69–70.

erence groups. The challenge to the marketer is to determine the relative influence and content of these different social influence sources.

Culture   Culture is the most fundamental determinant of a person's wants. Whereas the behavior of lower creatures is largely governed by instinct, man's drives are largely learned. His culture provides a pattern of perceptions, values, and behaviors that have been found effective in helping his society adapt to its environment. The individual learns the values of his culture through a process called *socialization.* Various groups and institutions mediate and act to transmit the values of his culture to him.

Culture has a great deal to do with how an individual sees, thinks, and feels. This becomes obvious when one steps into another culture. He suddenly becomes aware of his cultural biases. International marketers in particular must study cultural differences as a prelude to planning their products and marketing programs in different countries.

Subcultures   Each culture contains smaller groups or subcultures, and each of these provides more specific identification and socialization for its members. Four types of subcultures can be distinguished. *Nationality groups* such as the Irish, Polish, Italians, and Puerto Ricans are found within large communities and exhibit distinct ethnic tastes and proclivities. *Religious groups* such as the Catholics, Mormons, Presbyterians, and Jews represent subcultures with specific cultural preferences and taboos. *Racial groups* such as the blacks and orientals have distinct cultural styles and attitudes. *Geographical areas* such as the Deep South, California, and New England are distinct subcultures with characteristic life-styles. Some marketers specialize in the needs of a distinct subcultural group. Major marketers, although their markets are broad, require sensitivity to variations in the needs and preferences of different subcultures.

Social class   Virtually all human societies exhibit social stratification. Stratification may take the form of a caste system where the members of different castes are reared for certain roles and cannot change their caste membership. More frequently, stratification takes the form of social classes. *Social classes are relatively homogeneous and enduring divisions in a society which are ordered with respect to each other and whose members share similar values, life-styles, interests, and behavior.*

Social classes have several characteristics: (1) persons within a given social class tend to behave more alike; (2) persons are ranked as occupying inferior or superior positions according to their social class; (3) social class is not indicated by any single variable but is measured as a weighted function of one's occupation, income, wealth, education, value orientation, and so on; and (4) social class is continuous rather than discrete, with individuals able to move into a higher social class or drop into a lower one.

The American research tradition in social class distinguishes six social classes:[11]

1   *Upper uppers* (less than 1 percent). Upper uppers are the social elite who live on inherited wealth and have a well-known family background. They give large

---

[11]This is based on the discussion of social class in J. F. Engel, D. T. Kollat, and R. D. Blackwell, *Consumer Behavior,* 2nd ed. (New York: Holt, Rinehart & Winston, Inc., 1973), Chap. 5.

sums to charity, run the debutante balls, maintain more than one home, and send their children to the finest schools. They are a market for expensive jewelry, antiques, homes, and vacations. While small as a group, they serve as a reference group for others to the extent that their consumption decisions trickle down and are imitated by the other social classes.

2 *Lower uppers* (about 2 percent). Lower uppers are persons who have earned high income or wealth through exceptional ability in the professions or business. They usually come from the middle class. They tend to be active in social and civic affairs and seek to buy the symbols of status for themselves and their children, such as expensive homes, schools, yachts, swimming pools, and automobiles. They include the *nouveaux riches,* whose pattern of conspicuous consumption is designed to impress those below them. The ambition of lower uppers is to be accepted in the upper-upper stratum, which is more likely to be achieved by their children than themselves.

3 *Upper middles* (12 percent). Upper middles are concerned with "career." They have attained positions as lawyers, physicians, scientists, and college professors. They believe in education and want their children to develop professional or administrative skills so that they do not drop into a lower stratum. This class likes to deal in ideas and "high culture." They are the quality market for good homes, clothes, furniture, and appliances. They seek to run a gracious home entertaining friends and clients. The home, the automobile, and even the wife are used as symbols of the husband's success.

4 *Lower middles* (30 percent). Lower middles are concerned with "respectability." They exhibit conscientious work habits and adhere to culturally defined norms and standards, including going to church and obeying the law. The home is important, and lower middles like to keep it neat and "pretty." They buy conventional home furnishings and do a lot of their own work around the home. The lower-middle-class wife spends a lot of time shopping for the family looking for buys. Although "white collars" make up a large part of this group, so do "gray collars" (mailmen, firemen) and "aristocrat blue collars" (plumbers, factory foremen).

5 *Upper lowers* (35 percent). Upper lowers lead a day-to-day existence of unchanging activities. They live in small houses and apartments in dull areas of the city. The men work at manual jobs and have only a moderate education. The working-class wife spends most of her time in the house cooking, cleaning, and caring for her children. She sees being the mother of her children as her main vocation, and she has little time for organizations and social activity. She tends to buy the same brands from week to week and occasionally buys some items impulsively.

6 *Lower lowers* (20 percent). Lower lowers are at the bottom of society and considered by the other classes as slum dwellers or "riffraff." Some lower lowers try to rise above their class but often fall back and ultimately stop trying. They tend to be poorly educated. They often reject middle-class standards of morality and behavior. They buy more impulsively. They often do not evaluate quality, and they pay too much for products and buy on credit. They are a large market for food, television sets, and used automobiles.

Marketers have found social class a useful variable for segmenting markets. Products, advertising appeals, services, and atmospheres can be designed to appeal to specific social classes. Social classes show distinct differences in their tastes in clothing, home furnishings, leisure activity, automobiles, and so on. There is evidence that social classes differ in their purchase decision processes as well.

Reference groups   An individual is influenced by the many small groups with which he interacts. Some are *primary groups* (family, close friends, neighbors, and fellow workers) and others *secondary groups* (fraternal organizations, professional associations). He is also influenced by groups of which he is not a member, such as sports heroes and movie stars. Groups that interact and influence the attitudes and behavior of an individual are called *reference groups*.

Reference groups function in at least three ways. They expose the person to alternative behaviors and life-styles. They influence the person's attitudes and self-concept because of his desire to "fit in." They create pressures for conformity that may affect his product and brand choices.

Reference group influence affects consumption behavior most strongly in those product and brand categories that are visible and even conspicuous. Bourne found that reference group influence is strong for both product and brand choice in the case of cars and cigarettes; strong in product choice but weak in brand choice for air conditioners, instant coffee, and TV; strong in brand choice but weak in product choice for clothing, furniture, and toilet soap; and weak in both in soap, canned peaches, and radios.[12] The more cohesive the reference group, the more effective its communication process; and the higher the individual esteems it, the more influential it will be in shaping his product and brand choices.

The person   From what has been said, a person's basic motivations are heavily influenced by social learning. The norms and value systems in his culture, subcultures, social class, and reference groups leave an indelible imprint on his needs and wants. These social forces deserve the most careful study by marketers trying to interpret the objectives that might motivate consumer interest in their products and brands.

Economic model

Economists prefer to pass over the question of how human needs are formed or changed. They are more interested in explaining or predicting how a consumer with a given set of needs, tastes, and income will allocate his money over an available set of products at given prices. They postulate that the consumer follows the principle of *utility maximization.* He will act to maximize his satisfaction.

A consumer will not allocate all of his income to any one product because of the principle of *diminishing marginal utility.* No matter how attractive a product, additional units will give him diminishing satisfaction. At some point an additional unit of some other product would give him more satisfaction than more units of the same product. The buyer is assumed to know the relative utility he would derive from different possible bundles of goods. His income allows him to buy only certain bundles, and one of these bundles will give him the greatest total utility. His efficiency in finding that bundle depends on the adequacy of his information. If his information is inadequate, his buying is rational but the results are inefficient.

The economic model suggests useful behavioral hypotheses: (1) The lower the price of a product, the higher its sales. (2) The lower the price of substitute products, the lower the sales of this product. (3) The lower the price of complementary products, the higher the sales of this product. (4) The higher the

---

[12]Foundation for Research on Human Behavior, *Group Influence in Marketing and Public Relations* (Ann Arbor, Mich.: The Foundation, 1956).

real income, the higher the sales of this product, provided that it is not an "inferior" good. (5) The higher the promotional expenditures, the higher the sales.

The validity of these hypotheses does not rest on whether *all* individuals act as economic calculating machines. Some individuals may buy *less* of a product when its price is reduced. They may think that the quality has gone down or that ownership has less status value. If a majority of buyers view price reductions negatively, then sales may fall, contrary to the first hypothesis. But for most products, a price reduction increases the value-to-price ratio and leads to increased sales. This and the other hypotheses describe average effects.

Marketers have usually dismissed the economic model as simplistic. Eva Mueller reported a study where only one-fourth of the consumers purchasing large household appliances bought with any substantial degree of deliberation.[13] One would expect to find even less deliberation in the purchase of smaller items. The economists' answer to this is that information gathering and processing costs money and time, and these costs are included in the consumers' decision making. Furthermore, economists argue that the more important the purchase and the more trained the purchaser—as in industrial purchasing—the more his behavior will conform to a utility maximization model.

Hierarchy of needs model

A person obviously has many needs that vary in importance under different circumstances. Maslow proposed that there are, in fact, five basic needs which are arranged in a hierarchy of importance. They are shown in Table 4-1.[14]

Table 4-1

Maslow's hierarchy of needs

Physical

1. *Physiological*—the fundamentals of survival, including hunger and thirst.
2. *Safety*—concern over physical survival, ordinary prudence, which might be overlooked in striving to satisfy hunger or thirst.

Social

3. *Belongingness and love*—striving to be accepted by intimate members of one's family and to be an important person to them. This striving could also include others to whom the person feels close.
4. *Esteem and status*—striving to achieve a high standing relative to others, including desire for mastery, reputation, and prestige.

Self

5. *Self-actualization*—a desire to know, understand, systematize, organize, and construct a system of values.

[13]Eva Mueller, "A Study of Purchase Decisions: The Sample Survey," in *Consumer Behavior: The Dynamics of Consumer Reaction,* ed. Lincoln H. Clark (New York: New York University Press, 1954), pp. 36–87.

[14]Abraham H. Maslow, *Motivation and Personality* (New York: Harper & Row, Publishers, 1954).

According to Maslow, the first need dominates a person's behavior until it is satisfied; then the second need becomes prepotent until it is satisfied; and so on. Thus a starving man (need 1) is not likely to be interested in the latest doings in the art world (need 5), nor even in how he is seen or esteemed by others (need 3 or 4), nor even in whether he is breathing clean air (need 2). As the lower-order needs are satisfied, the higher-order needs take over.

In affluent societies, marketers endow their products with attributes suggesting their ability to satisfy these higher-order needs. Thus a bar of soap is sold on the basis of satisfying belongingness and love; an American car, on the basis of providing esteem and status.

Maslow's framework provides the marketer with a useful system for identifying the possible needs that a consumer might be seeking to satisfy through a product purchase and explaining why these needs change through time.

ORGANIZATION FOR CONSUMER BUYING

Having considered what the consumer market buys and why it buys, we are now ready to consider who does the buying. The consumer market is made up of *families* who do most of the buying. At present, 54 million families in the United States are the purchasing organizations for a vast amount of food, clothing, and shelter for their members.

Identifying the decision-making unit

A major task facing marketers is to identify the decision-making unit involved in the purchase of their product.

> A *decision-making unit* is an individual or a group of individuals in a decision-making process, who share a common goal or goals which the decision will hopefully help them to achieve, and who share the risks arising from the decision.[15]

For some products and services, it is relatively easy to identify the decision-making unit. For example, men are normally the decision-making unit for pipe tobacco, and women are the decision-making unit for pantyhose. On the other hand, the decision-making unit for a family automobile or vacation is likely to consist of husband, wife, and older children. In these cases the marketer must identify the roles and relative influence of the various family members so that he can effectively target his communications and product features.

Buying roles

There are up to five different roles that a person can play in a purchase decision:

Initiator. The initiator is the person who first suggested or thought of the idea to purchase the particular product.

Influencer. An influencer is a person who explicitly or implicitly carries some influence on the final decision.

Decider. The decider is a person who ultimately determines any part or the whole of the purchase decision: whether to buy, what to buy, how to buy, when to buy, or where to buy.

[15]This definition is taken from R. D. Buzzell, R. E. M. Nourse, J. B. Matthews, Jr., and T. Levitt, *Marketing: A Contemporary Analysis*, 2nd ed. (New York: McGraw-Hill Book Company, 1972), p. 62.

Purchaser. The purchaser is the person who makes the actual purchase.

User. The user is the person(s) who consumes or uses the product or service.

In the decision to buy a new automobile, the suggestion might have been initiated by the oldest child. Each member of the family may exert some influence on the decision or some component part, and even neighbors may have some influence. The husband and wife may make the final decision and act as the purchasing unit. The wife may be the prime user of the car.

Marketers conduct studies to determine the roles and relative influence of different members of the decision-making unit. They interview past buyers, asking whether the husband or the wife had more or equal influence on various component decisions. For example, Davis found that the decision of "when to buy an automobile" was influenced primarily by the husband in 68 percent of the cases, primarily by the wife in 3 percent of the cases, and equally in 29 percent of the cases. On the other hand, the decision of "what color of automobile to buy" was influenced primarily by the husband in 25 percent of the cases, by the wife in 25 percent of the cases, and equally in 50 percent of the cases.[16]

Marketers have to rely on the husband's or the wife's perception of his or her respective influence; they sometimes get conflicting reports from the two sources. Influence can be very subtle. A husband may report that he had the major influence on choosing the make of the car, although in reality his wife may have exerted a determining influence. Her influence could be:

Verbal, explicit:	"We must buy a sports car." (Demand)
	"Buy a sports car or I'll be unhappy." (Threat)
	"I hope you will buy a sports car." (Request)
	"A sports car would be best." (Advice)
Verbal, implicit:	"Let's have a 'fun' car this time." (Hint)
Nonverbal:	She stands around the sports car beaming. (Enthusiasm)
	She stands around the sedan sulking. (Despondency)

The same range of influences can be exercised by a child on his mother when he wants a particular cereal. The child may be highly verbal and explicit about his preference, or he may be nonverbal and refuse to eat a cereal he does not like. Berey and Pollay investigated the hypothesis that the child's influence will be greatest, the more assertive he is, and the more child-centered the mother is.[17] In fact, they found that the child's degree of assertiveness had little effect, and that child-centered mothers submitted less, rather than more, to their child's wishes. They concluded that the child-centered mother, in addition to wanting to please the child, also wants to do what is best for him. Her "gatekeeper effect" is often stronger than her desire to please. They concluded that a lot of advertising could be well directed at the mother.

---

[16]Harry L. Davis, "Dimensions of Marital Roles in Consumer Decision-Making," *Journal of Marketing Research,* May 1970, pp. 168–77.

[17]Lewis A. Berey and Richard W. Pollay, "The Influencing Role of the Child in Family Decision Making," *Journal of Marketing Research,* February 1968, pp. 70–72.

Family characteristics   Marketers have considered various family characteristics that might provide a clue to the relative influence of different family members in the purchase process.

One characteristic is the *locus of family authority*. Herbst has observed four types of families: (1) *autonomic*, where an equal number of separate decisions is made by each partner; (2) *husband-dominance*, the husband dominates; (3) *wife-dominance*, the wife dominates; and (4) *syncratic*, where most decisions are made jointly.[18] All types of families may be found at any time, although the relative proportions may be changing over time. With rising education and income, families are moving away from a husband-dominance model toward a syncratic model, and this has important implications for marketers in their target marketing.

Another important characteristic is the family's *culture and social class* background. Ethnic groups show distinct variations in family member task specialization. Furthermore, the relative influence of different family members tends to be related to self-concepts associated with their social class background.

Another useful characteristic is the stage of the *family life cycle*. Seven stages can be distinguished:

1   *The bachelor stage:* Young, single people
2   *Newly married couples:* Young, no children
3   *The full nest I:* Young married couples with youngest child under six
4   *The full nest II:* Young married couples with youngest child six or over
5   *The full nest III:* Older married couples with dependent children
6   *The empty nest:* Older married couples with no children living with them
7   *The solitary survivors:* Older single people

Each life-cycle group has certain distinguishable needs and interests. The full nest I group is very much in the market for washers and dryers, TV, baby food, and toys, whereas the full nest III group is in the market for nonnecessary appliances, boats, dental services, and magazines. The patterns of task specialization, authority, and relative influence may vary for different life-cycle groups.

OPERATIONS IN CONSUMER BUYING

We are now ready to consider how consumer decision-making units go about their purchasing of goods and services and what factors—particularly marketing factors—influence them.

Types of consumer-buying situations   The number and complexity of operations carried out by consumer buyers will vary with the type of purchase involved. There is a great difference between the buying of a can of beans, a shirt, and a new car. Howard has suggested that

---

[18]P. G. Herbst, "Conceptual Framework for Studying the Family," in *Social Structure and Personality in a City,* ed. O. A. Oeser and S. B. Hammond (London: Routledge & Kegan Paul Ltd., 1954), Chap. 10.

consumer buying can be viewed as problem-solving activity and has distinguished three classes of buying situations.[19]

Routinized response behavior   The simplest type of buying behavior occurs in the purchase of low-cost, frequently purchased items. The buyer is well acquainted with the product class, is aware of the major brands and their attributes, and has a fairly well defined preference order among the brands. He does not always buy the same brand because the choice can be influenced by stockouts, specials, and so on. But, in general, the buyer's operations are routinized, and he or she is not likely to give much thought, search, or time to the purchase.

The marketer's task in this situation is twofold. With respect to present customers, he will want his brand to provide positive reinforcement. He must keep up its expected quality, stock level, and value. With respect to noncustomers, his task is to break their normal buying routines by cues that call attention to his brand and its value in relation to the buyers' preferred brands. These cues include new features or benefits, point-of-purchase displays, price specials, and premiums.

Limited problem solving   Buying is more complex when the buyer confronts an unfamiliar brand in a familiar product class that leads him to gather some information about it before making his purchase choice. For example, a person buying a tennis racket may know the brands except for a new one. He may ask questions and look at ads to learn the new brand concept before choosing. This is described as limited problem solving because the buyer is fully aware of the product class and the qualities he wants but is not familiar with all the brand concepts.

The marketer recognizes that the consumer is trying to reduce risk through information gathering. The marketer must design a communication program that will increase the buyer's brand comprehension and confidence.

Extensive problem solving   Buying reaches its greatest complexity when the buyer faces an unfamiliar product class and does not know the criteria to use. For example, a person may decide to buy an expensive camera for the first time. He has heard brand names such as Leica, Nikon, and Minolta but lacks clear brand concepts. He does not even know what product-class attributes to consider in choosing a fine camera. He is in a state of extensive problem solving.

The marketer of products in this class must understand the information-gathering and evaluation activities of the would-be buyers. His task is to facilitate the buyer's learning of the attributes of the product class, their relative importance, and the high standing of his product on the more important attributes.

**Structure of the
purchase decision**

Whatever the type of buying situation, the purchase decision is really a collection of decisions. Each purchase decision has a structure of up to seven components. They are described below in connection with the purchase of a small radio.

---

[19]John A. Howard, "The Structure of Buyer Behavior," in *Consumer Behavior: Theory and Application,* ed. J. U. Farley, J. A. Howard, and L. W. Ring (Boston: Allyn & Bacon, Inc., 1974), Chap. 1, pp. 13–27.

1   *A product-class decision.* The consumer decides whether he will purchase a radio or use the money for another purpose. *The marketer is interested in the types of persons who get interested in buying radios and the other alternatives they are considering.*

2   *A product-form decision.* The consumer decides on the type of radio to buy. He has to make decisions on its size, sound quality, style, and so on. *The marketer conducts marketing research to learn the product-form preferences of potential radio buyers in order to maximize the attractiveness of his brand.*

3   *A brand decision.* The consumer has to decide which brand to buy. Various brands exhibit small or large differences. *The marketer is interested in how the consumer reaches a brand choice.*

4   *A vendor decision.* The consumer has to decide where to purchase the radio. He chooses a *type of retailer* (department stores, discount stores, radio specialty stores) and then a *specific retailer* (Radio Shack, Pacific Stereo, Allied). *Manufacturers, wholesalers, and retailers are all interested in how the consumer forms vendor preferences.*

5   *A quantity decision.* The consumer decides on how much to buy on the specific purchase occasion. He may buy more than one radio. In the case of certain products, consumers are classified as heavy, medium, or light buyers. *The marketer tries to prepare product sizes to match the ideal purchase amounts of different buyers. He will often target a disproportionate marketing effort at the heavy buyers.*

6   *A timing decision.* The consumer decides when to execute his purchase intention. He may have a well-formed purchase intention to buy a radio but want to exercise it when he receives his next paycheck or just before a holiday. *The marketer is interested in the factors that affect the consumer's timing decision so that he can better schedule his production and marketing effort.*

7   *A payment-method decision.* The consumer decides on a method of paying for the product. He may pay cash, use a credit card, borrow money from a bank, and so on. His payment-method decision may affect his vendor decision and his quantity decision. *Marketers are interested in studying and responding to the payment-method preferences of different buyers.*

These decisions are not necessarily executed in the order shown. In extensive problem solving, the consumer may start with a vendor decision because he relies on a particular vendor to help him define differences among product forms and brands. He may have decided on a timing and quantity decision even earlier. The marketer's task is to grasp the total structure and sequencing possibilities of the buyer's decision tree. This will suggest the critical points where he can facilitate and influence the buyer's choices.

**Stages in the
buying process**

The marketer can begin the task of mapping the consumers' buying process by sampling a number of people who bought the product or brand. These consumers can be asked to describe how they were first aroused, how they gathered information, what problems they tried to resolve, how they made their final choice, and how they felt afterward. These *consumer buying protocols* provide rich information for modeling the significant stages in the buying process.

Table 4-2 shows a consumer protocol of a car buyer. He first got the idea when he saw his neighbor's new car. He then developed reasons for possibly purchasing one. A few days later he saw an ad for a Ford. Two weeks later he stopped in a Ford showroom just to browse. He liked the car and the salesman, found that he could afford financing it, and purchased it. He picked it up a few days later and drove away. The car did not satisfy him completely, but an ad for a competitive brand made him feel that he still bought the best make. He was annoyed a few days later when his salesman did not seem very cooperative in answering some of his questions.

Table 4-2

Consumer protocol of a car buyer

3/17	My neighbor just bought a new car. He says he likes it. It would be nice to buy a new car. My present car is getting ready to fall apart. New cars are safer.
3/19	There's an ad for a new Ford. It looks nice.
4/2	I don't have any plans this evening. I'll go over to the Ford showroom. The cars are nice, especially that deluxe model with air conditioning. Here comes a salesman. He's very helpful. I'm pleased that he is not trying to pressure me. I don't think I can afford the car. How much would it cost a month to finance? I can afford it. My wife has been nagging me for a new car. I'll buy it.
4/5	The car is ready. I wish I had driven it before buying. It seems a little stiff. It is hard to get in and out.
4/6	There's the new Chevy advertised. It doesn't look as good as my car.
4/8	My other neighbor wants to buy a car. I told him the good and bad points about the Ford.
4/11	I phoned the auto salesman for some information. He wasn't helpful. He told me to call the service department.

Through collecting protocols, the marketer gains insight into the stages through which the buyer passes in considering purchase or nonpurchase of a product. Each stage is subject to influence by the marketer. Figure 4-1 presents a buying stages model that we will use to analyze the purchase decision-making process. The model shows the buyer passing through five stages: need arousal, information search, evaluation behavior, purchase decision, and postpurchase feelings.[20] This model emphasizes that purchase decision making starts long before the actual purchase and has consequences long after the purchase. It encourages the marketer to focus on the process rather than the sale.

---

[20]This model underlies many of the more complex models in the literature. The most notable models are John A. Howard and Jagdish N. Sheth, *The Theory of Buyer Behavior* (New York: John Wiley & Sons, Inc., 1969); Alan R. Andreasen, "Attitudes and Customer Behavior: A Decision Model," in *New Research in Marketing,* ed. Lee E. Preston (Berkeley: University of California Institute of Business and Economic Research, 1965), pp. 1–16; Francesco M. Nicosia, *Consumer Decision Processes* (Englewood Cliffs, N.J.: Prentice-Hall, Inc., 1966); James F. Engel, David T. Kollat, and Roger D. Blackwell, *Consumer Behavior,* 2nd ed. (New York: Holt, Rinehart & Winston, Inc., 1973), Chap. 3; and Arnold E. Amstutz, *Computer Simulation of Competitive Market Response* (Cambridge, Mass.: The M.I.T. Press, 1967), Chap. 8.

Figure 4-1
Stages in the buying process

Need arousal   The starting point of the buying process is need arousal. A need can be activated through internal or external stimuli. In the first case, one of the person's normal drives—hunger, thirst, sex—rises to a threshold level. The individual has learned to cope with his drives from previous experience and is motivated toward certain classes of objects that he knows will be drive reducing.

Or a need can be aroused by an external stimulus, or *triggering cue.* A person passes a bakery and the sight of freshly baked bread stimulates his hunger; he admires a neighbor's new boat; he watches a television commercial for a Jamaican vacation; his car fails to start and he is aroused to think about buying a new car.

We can imagine his need exhibiting a certain level of intensity and lasting for a certain length of time. The more intense the need and the longer it lasts, the stronger will be the individual's drive to reduce it through undertaking search behavior and finally acquiring an object that will satisfy his need. A person at midday may feel a small desire to eat, but it may not be sufficiently strong to lead him to walk to a distant vending machine in the building. As time passes, his hunger may subside as his mind becomes preoccupied with more salient needs, such as finishing a report and making some calls. The hunger need will reappear and grow in intensity. Finally it will tend to push out or dominate his other needs until he is driven to take concrete steps to satisfy his hunger.

Some needs are aroused and linger for a long time without reaching a level of intensity sufficient to drive the person into action. A person's car may start fitfully and each time he thinks of replacing it. He may begin to watch car ads more carefully, notice new cars purchased by friends, and discuss the possibility with his wife. But the need intensity fluctuates from day to day below that level that would drive him to a showroom to look at available cars and prices.

The significance of the need arousal stage to the marketer is twofold. First, he must understand the drives that might actually or potentially connect to his product class and brand. An auto marketer recognizes that cars satisfy a need for mobility; they also can satisfy the need for status, power, excitement. To the extent that a car can satisfy several drives simultaneously, it becomes a more intensely wanted object.

Second, the concept of need arousal helps the marketer recognize that need levels for his product fluctuate over time and are triggered by different cues. He can try to plan his cues to conform better to the natural rhythms and timing of need arousal.

Information search   If an aroused need (1) is intense (2) and the gratification object is well defined and (3) near at hand, the person is likely to gratify his need right then. The hungry person who sees a candy bar will probably buy it and consume it immediately. In most cases, however, an aroused need is not gratified immediately. One or more of the above conditions is missing. The need enters the memory's register as an agenda item for future gratification.

Depending on the intensity of the stored need, the need produces one of two states in the individual. The first state is called *heightened attention.* The individual becomes alert to information bearing on the need and its gratification. He does not search actively for information but is simply more receptive. The person who has thought of buying a new car pays more attention to car ads, cars on the street, and remarks made about cars by friends.

Under conditions of more intense need, the individual enters a state of active *information search.* The amount of information he needs depends upon whether he is facing limited problem solving or extensive problem solving. In the latter case he may need information about the key attributes of the product class, about the qualities of the various brands, and about the outlets at which they are available.

Of key interest to the marketer are the various information sources that the consumer will turn to and the relative influence they will have on his choice behavior. *Consumer information sources* fall into four groups:

1   *Personal sources* (family, friends, neighbors, acquaintances)
2   *Commercial sources* (advertising, salesmen, dealers, packaging, displays)
3   *Public sources* (mass media, consumer rating organizations)
4   *Experiential sources* (handling, examining, using the product)

The relative influence of these information sources varies with the product category and the personal characteristics of the consumer, such as his financial status and information-seeking style. Generally speaking, the consumer receives the most information exposures about a product from commercial, that is, marketer-dominated sources. On the other hand, the most effective exposures tend to come from personal sources. Each type of source may perform a somewhat different function in influencing the buying decision. Commercial information normally performs an *informing* function, and personal sources perform a *legitimizing* or an *evaluation* function. For example, physicians normally learn of new drugs from commercial sources but turn to other doctors for evaluation information.

The marketer will find it worthwhile to study the consumers' information sources whenever (1) a substantial percentage of the target market engages in overt search and (2) the target market shows some stable patterns of using the respective information sources. Identifying the information sources and their respective roles and importance calls for interviewing consumers and asking them how they happened to hear about the product, what sources of information they turned to, and which sources of information were decisive. The marketer can use the findings to plan marketer-dominated sources of information and stimulate personal sources of information.

Evaluation behavior   As the individual receives information, he uses it to clarify his alternatives and their relative attractiveness. A key understanding needed by the marketer is how potential consumers process the information to arrive at their product and brand attitudes and purchasing intentions.

Unfortunately there is not a simple and single information process used by all consumers to arrive at a product attitude or judgment. There are alternative processes, and much recent research has been directed to studying them. Certain basic concepts help in the understanding of consumer evaluation processes.

The first concept is that of *product-class attributes*. The consumer tends to view a product as a multiattribute object, that is, as a bundle of attributes. He is not just interested in hearing that it is a "good product" or a "bad product" but is also interested in learning how it stands on particular attributes that are salient to him regarding the product class. The attributes of normal interest to buyers in some representative product classes are:

Toothpaste:	Anticavity protection, whitening power, taste, breath freshening
Aspirin:	Speed of relief, reliability, side effects, cost
Tires:	Tread life, safety, ride quality, cost
Air travel:	Departure time, speed, aircraft, preflight service, in-flight service

Not all buyers are interested in all the attributes of a product class. The market for a product can often be segmented according to the set of attributes or benefits of most interest to different buyers. A key task is to determine these attribute sets, or at least the relative importance of different attributes.

Second, the consumer is likely to develop a set of *brand beliefs,* that is, where each brand stands on each attribute. The conjunction of his beliefs about a particular brand is his *brand concept.*

Third, the consumer is likely to have a *utility function* for each attribute. The utility function describes how he expects product satisfaction to vary with alternative levels of each attribute. For example, an auto buyer may expect his satisfaction to increase linearly with gas economy; he may expect his satisfaction to peak with an intermediate-size car as opposed to a subcompact or a very large car; he may feel more utility for a red car than a green car. If we combine the attribute levels where his utility is highest, they make up his ideal car or *ideal point.* This should not be confused with his fantasy car but rather the car he would most like to obtain if it were available and affordable.

Fourth, the consumer arrives at an attitude (judgment, preference) toward the brand alternatives through some *evaluation procedure* (also called composition rule, decision rule). Starting with a set of brands he considers (the *evoked set*), he compares them using some procedure and emerges with an order of preferences.

Consumers have been found to apply various evaluation procedures to make a choice among multiattribute objects. The major evaluation procedures will be described and illustrated. Suppose Mr. Smith feels a need to buy a new car and has paid attention to ads and has visited some dealer showrooms. Table 4-3 summarizes his current information. The rows show four brands in his evoked set. The columns show five product-class attributes of interest to him. The numbers in the cells describe his brand beliefs. The first three attributes are objectively measured and perceived, and the last two are subjective measurements on a scale from 1 to 10.

The problem is to predict which car Mr. Smith will buy. Much depends upon his utility function for the various attributes. We will assume that Smith prefers less cost to more cost, more gas mileage to less gas mileage, a car length

Table 4-3

A buyer's brand beliefs about alternative brands

			Product-Class Attributes			
	Car	*Price*	*Gas mileage (miles/gal)*	*Car length (inches)*	*Style**	*Handling**
	1	$6,000	10	220	10	10
Evoked	2	5,000	16	190	9	10
set	3	4,000	14	210	5	6
	4	3,500	20	180	4	9

*A score of 10 represents the highest rating.

ideally of 180 inches, more style to less style, and better handling to poorer handling. The utility function can be further specified as to its actual shape, but we will assume linearity. His choice is still not determinant. In fact, at least six alternative models can explain how consumers form a preference ordering of objects.[21]

DOMINANCE MODEL   Suppose one car was priced lowest, gave the highest mileage, and had the ideal length and the highest-rated style and handling. This car would be the buyer's choice. No car in the evoked set has this clear superiority. Dominance can be used, however, to remove a car that is inferior in all respects to some other car in the set. We can imagine a brand that the consumer dropped from consideration because it was exactly like brand 4 in the first four attributes and its handling was inferior. Dominance is a useful procedure to reduce or simplify the brand alternatives in the evoked set.

CONJUNCTIVE MODEL   Mr. Smith can sort the cars in his evoked set into two classes, acceptable and unacceptable, so that he can drop some cars from further consideration. To do this, he may establish a conjunction of minimum attribute levels that cars must possess. He may only consider cars costing less than $5,500, giving gas mileage of more than fifteen miles per gallon, not longer than 195 inches, with a rated style of at least 4 and a handling of at least 6. These cutoffs eliminate brands 1 and 3 from further consideration. Conjunctive evaluation in the extreme may eliminate all brands if the cutoffs are too stringent. Thus we find the consumer who does not make a purchase in a product class because no current brand meets his minimal requirements. Note that conjunctive evaluation does not pay attention to how high an attribute level may be as long as it exceeds the minimum. A high score on one attribute does not compensate for a below-minimum score on another attribute. Conjunctive evaluation is noncompensatory.

DISJUNCTIVE MODEL   A related evaluation procedure arises when Mr. Smith decides that he will only consider cars that are superior on one or more attributes and specifies these levels. Mediocre performance on other attributes

[21]Excellent discussions can be found in Paul E. Green and Yoram Wind, *Multiattribute Decisions in Marketing: A Measurement Approach* (Hinsdale, Ill.: The Dryden Press, 1973), Chap. 2; and Peter L. Wright, "Use of Consumer Judgment Models in Promotion Planning," *Journal of Marketing,* October 1973, pp. 27–33.

does not bother him. Mr. Smith might decide that he will only consider cars that have superior styling (≥ 9) *or* handling (≥ 9). Applied to the evoked set in Table 4-3, Mr. Smith is left with cars 1, 2, and 4 as choices. The model is noncompensatory in that high scores on other variables have no bearing on keeping them in the acceptable set.

LEXICOGRAPHIC MODEL   Another noncompensatory process occurs when the consumer arranges the attributes in order of importance and compares the brands on the first important attribute. If one brand is superior on the most important attribute, it becomes his choice. If two or more brands are tied on this attribute, Mr. Smith considers the second most important attribute; he continues this until one brand remains. Suppose Mr. Smith "prioritizes" the attributes in the following order: handling, style, gas mileage, car length, and cost. He looks at handling and finds cars 1 and 2 to be superior and equal to each other. He eliminates cars 3 and 4 from further consideration. Then he considers style and finds car 1 to be superior to car 2. At this point he has determined that car 1 is the preferred automobile.

EXPECTANCY-VALUE MODEL   A quite different model of evaluation states that the consumer gives weight to every brand belief and its attribute importance in arriving at a global attitude toward each brand. The attribute levels possessed by a brand are believed to be compensatory. The expectancy-value model takes the following general form:[22]

$$A_{jk} = \sum_{i=1}^{n} W_{ik}B_{ijk} \qquad (4\text{-}1)$$

where:

A_{jk} = consumer k's attitude score for brand j
W_{ik} = the importance weight given attribute i by consumer k
B_{ijk} = consumer k's belief as to the extent to which attribute i is offered by brand j
n = the number of attributes important in the selection of a given brand

To illustrate the formula, suppose Mr. Smith feels that only two attributes, style and handling, are important to him in the selection of a car (the other three attributes have a zero weight). Furthermore, he feels that style is three times as important as handling. We would predict his attitude toward the four cars shown in Table 4-3 to be:[23]

---

[22]The model also goes under other names (linear compensatory model, multiattribute attitude model). This model was originally proposed by Milton J. Rosenberg, "Cognitive Structure and Attitudinal Affect," *Journal of Abnormal and Social Psychology,* November 1956, pp. 367–72; and Martin Fishbein, "A Behavior Theory Approach to the Relations between Beliefs about an Object and the Attitude toward the Object," in *Readings in Attitude Theory and Measurement,* ed. M. Fishbein (New York: John Wiley & Sons, 1967), pp. 389–99. Various researchers in marketing have applied and reinterpreted this model. For an excellent review, see William L. Wilkie and Edgar A. Pessemier, "Issues in Marketing's Use of Multi-Attribute Attitude Models," *Journal of Marketing Research,* November 1973, pp. 428–41.

[23]If more attributes were included from Table 4-3, it would be necessary to scale them all on, say, a 1 to 10 scale before applying this formula. It should be recognized that what is meaningful is not the absolute attitude values but their relative values because there is arbitrariness in the metric scaling of the importance weights and beliefs.

$$A_1 = 3(10) + 1(10) = 40$$
$$A_2 = 3(9) + 1(10) \; = 37$$
$$A_3 = 3(5) + 1(6) \; \; = 21$$
$$A_4 = 3(4) + 1(9) \; \; = 21$$

Thus expectancy-value processing says that Mr. Smith gives some weight to every belief and attribute that counts. Note that although cars 3 and 4 differ greatly in their style and handling, they emerge with the same level of overall attractiveness ($=21$) because of compensatory attributes.

IDEAL POINT MODEL   This model introduces a slight variation in the preceding model in not assuming that the utility of every attribute increases with its amount. For example, Mr. Smith does not necessarily get more satisfaction, the longer the car. His ideal-length car is 180 inches. Also assume that his ideal car mileage is fifteen miles per gallon because he knows that he sacrifices power if he gets higher mileage, and sacrifices gas if he gets lower mileage. Suppose car length and gas mileage are the only two attributes he considers. Formula (4-1) can be modified to read:

$$D_{jk} = \sum_{i=1}^{n} W_{ik}|B_{ijk} - I_{ik}| \qquad (4\text{-}2)$$

where D_{jk} is consumer k's *dissatisfaction* with brand j, and I_{ik} is consumer k's *ideal level* of attribute i. Other terms remain the same. The lower the D, the more favorable consumer k's attitude toward brand j. For example, if there were a brand whose attributes were all at the ideal levels, the term $|B_{ijk} - I_{jk}|$ would disappear and the dissatisfaction would be zero.

The ideal point model is illustrated graphically in Figure 4-2. The four brands are shown as points where the consumer perceives them (perception

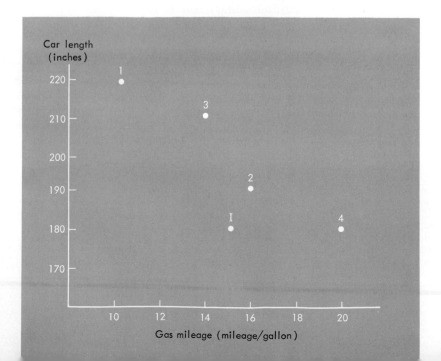

Figure 4-2
Brand space map showing brand perceptions and ideal point

mapping), and the ideal point is also shown (preference mapping). The closer a car is to the consumer's ideal point, the more favorable his attitude will be. Car 2 shows up best. The model is very suggestive of marketer strategies. The marketer can think of (1) designing a product closer to the consumer's ideal point, (2) altering the consumer's perception of his brand's location, (3) altering the consumer's perception of his competitors' brand locations, (4) shifting the consumer's ideal point closer to his brand, (5) altering the importance weights of the attributes, and (6) introducing new attributes favorable to his brand. This strategic analysis is called *brand positioning*.

MARKETING IMPLICATIONS   The important thing for the marketer is to recognize that consumers adopt simplifying strategies for dealing with the available information. They limit the size of their evoked set; they eliminate certain product attributes; they use an evaluation procedure to condense the information. The marketer must carefully identify the evaluation procedure used by his target consumers. If he believes consumers use a compensatory model, he may try to enhance all their beliefs related to his brand. If they proceed disjunctively looking at only a few attributes, then the marketer will try to improve his brand's standing on these critical attributes.

Purchase decision   The evaluation stage leads the consumer to form a set of preferences among the alternative objects in his evoked set. Normally, the brand that he likes most would become the one he intends to purchase. That is, *purchase intention* is a function of *affect* (or attitude). However, two other factors shape his purchase intention.[24]

The first is *social factors*. Suppose the consumer prefers a Cadillac but his wife thinks a Cadillac is pretentious. His overall favorable attitude toward the Cadillac is consequently reduced. The extent to which a social factor will reduce a favorable attitude depends upon two things: (1) the intensity of the source's negative attitude, and (2) the consumer's motivation to comply with the source's feelings.[25] The more intense the other person's negativism, and the closer the other person is to the consumer, the more the consumer will revise downward his purchase intention.

The other factor affecting purchase intention is *anticipated situational factors*. The consumer forms his purchase intention on the basis of his known income, expected dealer terms, expected product availability, and so on.

But a purchase intention may not result in the actual purchase of the intended object. *Purchase behavior* is a function of the *purchase intention* and the *nonpredictable situational factors*. Between the time the consumer forms a purchase intention and the time of its execution, he may learn that the economy is slowing down, he may lose his job, and he may be miffed by the salesman, find some problem with the car, or find the particular car unavailable.

Thus attitudes and even purchasing intentions are not completely reliable predictors of actual buying behavior. They give direction to purchase behavior but fail to include a number of additional factors that may intervene.

The decision of an individual to modify, postpone, or avoid a purchase decision is heavily influenced by *perceived risk*. Marketers have devoted a lot of

---

[24]See Jagdish N. Sheth, "An Investigation of Relationships among Evaluative Beliefs, Affect, Behavioral Intention, and Behavior," in Farley *et al., op. cit.,* pp. 89–114.

[25]See Martin Fishbein, "Attitude and Prediction of Behavior," in Fishbein, *op. cit.,* pp. 477–92.

effort to understand buying behavior as *risk taking*.[26] Consumers cannot be certain about the performance and psychosocial consequences of their purchase decision. This produces anxiety. The amount of perceived risk varies with the amount of money at stake, the amount of attribute uncertainty, and the amount of consumer self-confidence. A consumer develops certain routines for reducing risk, such as decision avoidance, information gathering from friends, and preference for national brand names and warranties. The marketer must understand the factors that provoke a feeling of risk in the consumer and attempt to provide information and buying aids that will help reduce this risk.

Postpurchase feelings   The brand purchase has an important feedback effect on subsequent brand preference. Behavior influences attitudes as well as the reverse. If the purchased brand fails to deliver the expected satisfaction to the buyer, the buyer will revise downward his attitude toward the brand and may even eliminate it from his evoked set. On the other hand, a satisfying experience will tend to strengthen his brand preference.

The reinforcement effect of past brand choices on subsequent brand preferences has been expressed in a brand learning model developed by Kuehn.[27] This model postulates the existence of a pair of "learning operators" that explicitly alter current brand purchase probabilities on the basis of the last brand choice. This model has been fitted for some consumer staples (such as beer, coffee, frozen orange juice). For example, Kuehn found that the probability of rebuying Snow Crop frozen orange juice was .33 with one past (last) purchase of this brand and .806 with four past purchases of this brand.

Brand purchase probabilities are less likely to be strengthened for product classes that are expensive and risky. In part, the consumer carries over uncertainty from the prepurchase period when he was having trouble deciding among the different possible choices. If the product was a car, each brand had attractive and unattractive qualities. Presumably he selected the brand with the most attractive qualities, but this does not resolve his doubts about the unattractive qualities of the brand he purchased or the attractive qualities of the brands he rejected.

Negative feelings may also arise after the purchase. The purchaser may hear information that reflects badly on his choice; a rumor that the product is being discontinued; an awareness that he could have purchased the product for less. Negative feelings may arise through using the product and finding its performance disappointing or encountering unanticipated trouble.

The occurrence of postpurchase anxiety is explained by *cognitive dissonance*.[28] There is often a dissonance, or lack of harmony, among the buyer's various cognitions about the product purchased and the forgone alternatives. "The magnitude of post-decision dissonance is an increasing function of the

[26]The concept of perceived risk was introduced in 1960 by Raymond A. Bauer in "Consumer Behavior as Risk Taking" and is reprinted along with many subsequent studies in Donald F. Cox, *Risk Taking and Information Handling in Consumer Behavior* (Boston: Division of Research, Harvard Business School, 1967). For an excellent review, see James W. Taylor, "The Role of Risk in Consumer Behavior," *Journal of Marketing,* April 1974, pp. 54–60.

[27]Alfred A. Kuehn, "Consumer Brand Choice—A Learning Process?" in *Quantitative Techniques in Marketing Analysis,* ed. R. E. Frank, A. A. Kuehn, and W. F. Massy (Homewood, Ill.: Richard D. Irwin, Inc., 1962), pp. 390–403.

[28]Leon Festinger, *A Theory of Cognitive Dissonance* (Stanford, Calif.: Stanford University Press, 1957).

general importance of the decision and of the relative attractiveness of the un-chosen alternatives."[29] For these reasons, dissonance is common among pur-chasers of homes, automobiles, and major appliances, and among businessmen who have just made a major business investment.

The tension introduced by dissonance leads the buyer to seek its reduction. Festinger postulates a drive in the human organism "to establish internal har-mony, consistency, or congruity among his opinions, knowledge, and values."[30] This drive leads the dissonant purchaser to one of two courses of action. He may try to exercise the dissonant cognition by *removing* the product, returning it for a credit where this is possible or selling it to someone else; or he may try to alleviate the dissonant cognition by *confirming* the product, seeking information that might establish its superiority.

The marketer tries to help the consumer find confirmation for his choice. One step is to direct communications to recent buyers. If they are in a dissonant state, they will be looking for supportive communications. The auto manufac-turer may build assurances into the information brochures that accompany his product. He can also run ads showing recent purchasers expressing satisfaction with their choice. Unless the seller dispels the dissonance by some positive ef-forts, he may lose customers unnecessarily.

Exogenous variables in consumer buying behavior

In describing the stages in the buying process, we focused on the universal char-acter of the process rather than on individual consumer differences. Individual consumers will handle these stages in different ways under the influence of exog-enous variables. These variables are exogenous because the marketer is not interested in explaining them so much as tracing their influence on buying behavior. The influence goes primarily from these exogenous variables to the buyers with little return influence.

The Howard-Sheth buyer behavior model identifies the following seven exogenous variables:[31]

1 *Importance of purchase.* The consumer will attach different degrees of importance to the purchase of various products. The importance will influence his amount of information search, the size of the evoked set, the number of buying attributes, and other variables.

2 *Personality traits.* The consumer's personality traits (such as his self-confidence, venturesomeness, extroversion) will influence his buying motives, overt search, evaluation procedures, and purchase satisfaction.

3 *Financial status.* The consumer's financial status as measured by his current and expected income and savings will influence his buying motives, evaluation cri-teria, purchase timing, and the amount he buys.

4 *Time pressure.* The consumer will allot a certain amount of time for information search and evaluation. The greater the time pressure, the smaller his evoked set, the fewer the product attributes rated, and the greater the simplifying strategies for evaluation.

5 *Social and organizational setting.* The consumer's immediate social and organiza-tional setting will influence his buying motives, overt search, and evaluation behavior.

[29]*Ibid.,* p. 262.
[30]*Ibid.,* p. 260.
[31]Howard and Sheth, *op. cit.,* Chap. 4.

6   *Social class.* The consumer's buying motives and buying process are influenced by his social class background.

7   *Culture.* At the deepest level, the consumer's culture and subculture identifications greatly influence his needs and buying processes.

SUMMARY

Markets have to be understood before marketing can be planned. Any market can be analyzed by asking about its four *O's—objects, objectives, organization,* and *operations.*

The consumer market is the ultimate market for which economic activities are organized. Objects in the consumer market can be classified in two ways: durables, nondurables, and services; convenience, shopping, and specialty goods.

The objectives of consumers are to satisfy a hierarchy of needs—physiological, safety, belongingness, status, and self-actualization. These consumer objectives are shaped through learning, psychic development, social forces, and economic factors.

The organizational context of consumer buying is the family. Marketers have to identify the roles and relative influence of different members of the family decision-making unit. Buying roles include initiating, influencing, deciding, buying, and using. Such family characteristics as the locus of authority, culture and social class background, and stage of the family life cycle influence buying roles.

The buying operations of consumers vary with the type of buying situation: routinized response behavior, limited problem solving, extensive problem solving. Buying is not a single act but a multicomponent act consisting of decisions on the product class, product form, brand, vendor, quantity, timing, and method of payment. The buyer goes through a process consisting of need arousal, information search, evaluation behavior, purchase decision, and postpurchase feelings. Individual differences are influenced by the individual's view of the importance of the purchase and his personality traits, financial status, time pressure, social and organizational setting, social class, and culture. The marketer must study the buying stages and influences as a prelude to planning the four *P's* of his marketing mix.

**QUESTIONS
AND PROBLEMS**

1   The text mentioned two studies by motivational researchers on the attitudes of Americans toward prunes. Name some attitudes that you or others have expressed about prunes. Suggest some strategies and appeals that might overcome negative attitudes toward prunes.

2   Purchasing furniture is an uneasy experience for most families, one involving high perceived risk. Recommend a marketing approach that will help meet the buyer's concerns.

3   Recall some recent important purchase you made and construct a consumer buying protocol of what took place.

4   A grooming aid company has just developed a cologne product available in towel-ettes, that is, flat miniature packages with presoaked cloth that are handy to carry around and open when needed. Develop a map showing the structure of purchase decisions facing a buyer and the decision route he must follow to end up purchasing the new product and becoming a loyal customer.

5   Jim Beam, a brand of whisky, is advertised "Coffee, Tea, or Beam." What is the advertiser trying to accomplish?

6   A friend of yours is planning to buy a new car. He has a preference for foreign makes and his choice has narrowed down to Volkswagen, Opel, and Volvo. He is looking for three things in a car: economy, quality, and roominess, and he values them at .5, .3, and .2, respectively. He would rate Volkswagen as standing at .8, .8, and .2 on the three attributes; Opel, .3, .5, and .9; and Volvo, .5, .8, and .7. Predict the cars he is most likely to buy and least likely to buy if he evaluates cars according to the expectancy value model.

7   "A person will tend to buy the brand in the product class whose image is most congruent with his self-image." Is a person's self-image a highly reliable prediction of his brand choice?

8   Develop a map showing the structure of purchase decisions as they may be made by potential buyers of paint. Indicate how a paint company such as Du Pont can determine points at which advertising might favorably affect Du Pont's share of the market.

5

PRODUCER, RESELLER, AND GOVERNMENT MARKETS

*Companies don't make purchases; they
establish relationships.*

CHARLES S. GOODMAN

In the preceding chapter we examined the objects, objectives, organization, and operations of the consumer market. The consumer market is of prime importance both because of its absolute size and because it provides the major rationale for the existence of the other markets. These other markets—producer, reseller, and government—nevertheless are also large ones and challenging to the marketer. In fact, more dollar sales transactions occur outside the consumer market than inside, because for every product that reaches the final buyer, many transactions among producers and resellers had to take place to bring together the factors necessary to produce and place the final goods within easy reach of the consumers.

These important markets have characteristics and ways of functioning that should be differentiated from those of the consumer market. This chapter will examine the four *O*'s of the producer, reseller, and government markets, respectively. (International markets, which combine the more basic types of markets, will be examined in Chapter 21.)

PRODUCER MARKET

The producer market (also called the industrial or business market) is the market consisting of individuals and organizations who acquire goods and services to be used in the production of further products or services for sale or rental to others.

A partial list of the major types of firms in the producer segment of the economy would include (1) manufacturing establishments, (2) agricultural producers, (3) public utilities, (4) transportation agencies, (5) construction industries, (6) extractive industries, (7) nonprofit institutions, and (8) service industries. There are over 9 million different producer units (leaving out resellers and government), and each is a market for specific types of goods and services. They employ over 52 million workers, generate an annual national income of $705 billion, and constitute the selling environment for most firms.

Compared to ultimate consumers, producers tend to be concentrated geographically, both nationally and regionally. The seven states of New York, California, Pennsylvania, Illinois, Ohio, New Jersey, and Michigan contain within their borders over half of the nation's manufacturing firms. Particular manufacturing industries, such as petroleum, rubber, and steel, show even greater geographic concentration. Most agricultural output comes from a relatively small number of states, and specific commodities, such as tobacco and citrus fruit, are grown in even fewer states. All of this geographical concentration of producers helps to reduce the costs of selling to them. Industrial marketers will want to watch any pronounced tendencies toward or away from further geographic concentration.

More dollars are involved in sales to business buyers than to consumers. To bring a simple pair of shoes into existence, hide dealers (mainly meat packers) must sell the hides to tanners, who sell the leather to shoe manufacturers, who sell the shoes to wholesalers, who in turn sell the shoes to retailers. Each party in the chain of production and distribution pays more than the previous party. The transactions based on one pair of finished shoes selling for $15 may have been $7 (tanner to hide dealer), $9 (shoe manufacturer to tanner), $11 (wholesaler to shoe manufacturer), and $13 (retailer to wholesaler), making a total of $40, whereas the transaction to the consumer involved but $15. More industrial marketing goes on than consumer marketing, although many people have the opposite impression.

In spite of the importance of the producer market, its characteristics and marketing systems have tended to be relatively neglected by marketing writers. According to Corey:

> Any careful survey of marketing literature will disclose that a relatively small amount of it is devoted to the problems and techniques of marketing industrial goods . . . before the Second World War, marketing as a management function was not so highly developed in companies making and selling industrial goods as it had been in the consumer goods field . . . the marketing function tended in many cases to be shared by, and possibly overshadowed by, managers of other functions (the engineers in the organization, for example). . . . Finally, industrial products are very often highly technical products, and perhaps those who would study and write about the problems involved in marketing industrial products have been deterred to some extent because of their technical character.[1]

Industrial marketers are discouraged by the heavy emphasis on consumer marketing principles, because many of them believe that producer marketing is essentially different. The primary difference, according to Ames, lies in the marketing-mix variables that are featured:

---

[1] E. R. Corey, *Industrial Marketing: Cases and Concepts* (Englewood Cliffs, N.J.: Prentice-Hall, Inc., 1962), p. v.

Changes in marketing strategy (in industrial markets) are likely to be based on product design, cost, or service innovations. Contrast this with a consumer goods company, where advertising, promotion, and merchandising are generally the core elements of the marketing plan.[2]

While product design, cost, and service do tend to loom larger in industrial marketing than advertising, promotion, and merchandising, one must avoid blind spots with respect to the importance and creative use of all of the elements of the marketing mix in any marketing situation. For example, industrial marketers of a new breed are calling upon their management to "go consumer"— that is, to build more advertising, promotion, and merchandising into their marketing programs.[3] The industrial firm of Black & Decker has had a lot of success selling its line of industrial power tools through a modern advertising campaign (complete with a pretty bikinied girl posing with a hand power tool) and a wide range of incentive programs, specialty promotions, and trade-in offers.[4] Digital Equipment Company has achieved good results in the selling of computer equipment through the use of "specials"—that is, price reductions on particular machines in particular months. Other industrial marketers are experts in the use of such promotional tools as exhibitions, shows, films, merchandising schemes, giveaways, point-of-sale displays, sales literature, demonstration literature, and posters and showcards. Their activity belies the image of a stodgy, industrial marketer whose marketing decisions are limited to product design, price, and service.

Conversely, it is misleading to imply that consumer marketers generally do not pay much attention to product design, price, and service. Product design is a very important consideration in consumer durable-goods marketing; in fact it is a major influence in the brand selection of automobiles, refrigerators, television, and so on. So, too, are price and service of particular importance in selling consumer durable goods. So we return to our major point, that all the marketing-mix variables deserve consideration in the marketing planning of any product. Often the most spectacular marketing successes occur when a firm begins to push a particular marketing instrument that hitherto was relatively neglected in its industry.

Objects in the producer market

The producer market, like the consumer market, features a vast variety of products and services. An industrial-goods classification would help us understand the varying marketing practices in the producer market. It is not particularly appropriate to base the goods classification on the *shopping habits of the producers,* as we did in the consumer-goods classification, because producers do not shop in the same sense. More often vendors seek them out. Producer goods are more usefully classified in terms of *how they enter the production process and cost structure of the producers.* These considerations determine who in the buying firm is involved in the buying process (organization) and what marketing factors

---

[2]B. Charles Ames, "Marketing Planning for Industrial Products," *Harvard Business Review,* September–October 1968, p. 102.

[3]See Fred C. Alexander, "Is Industrial Marketing Ready to 'Go Consumer'?" *Industrial Marketing,* December 1964, pp. 74–77.

[4]Richard V. Dempster, "Black & Decker Cuts through Industrial Marketing Myths," *Marketing Insights,* October 7, 1968, pp. 15–17.

affect the buying decision (operations). When we use these principles, producer goods fall into the three classes shown in Table 5-1.

Each type of producer good, as a result of its physical characteristics and use pattern in production, has acquired particular patterns of marketing effort and mix. Here are two examples:

> *Steel.* Steel serves as an important component material in a large part of the producer market, especially in durable-goods manufacture and construction. There are different grades and alloys of steel, but within any category most steel is identical. Therefore steel is basically a commodity, and the only product variables that might count are (1) consistency of quality and (2) extent of the steelmaker's product line. The buyer's main concern is price, and a seller who offers his product for even a fraction of a cent less has the best chance of getting the order. The price reduction can come off the basic price or indirectly through volume discounts, freight absorption allowances, or more generous credit terms. Therefore these instruments figure importantly in steel marketing.

Table 5-1
Goods classification for producer market

   I. Goods entering the product completely—materials and parts

     A. Raw materials
        1. Farm products (examples: wheat, cotton, livestock, fruits and vegetables)
        2. Natural products (examples: fish, lumber, crude petroleum, iron ore)
     B. Manufactured materials and parts
        1. Component materials (examples: steel, cement, wire, textiles)
        2. Component parts (examples: small motors, tires, castings)

   II. Goods entering the product partly—capital items

     A. Installations
        1. Buildings and land rights (examples: factories, offices)
        2. Fixed equipment (examples: generators, drill presses, computers, elevators)
     B. Accessory equipment
        1. Portable or light factory equipment and tools (examples: hand tools, lift trucks)
        2. Office equipment (examples: typewriters, desks)

   III. Goods not entering the product—supplies and services

     A. Supplies
        1. Operating supplies (examples: lubricants, coal, typing paper, pencils)
        2. Maintenance and repair items (examples: paint, nails, brooms)
     B. Business services
        1. Maintenance and repair services (examples: window cleaning, typewriter repair)
        2. Business advisory services (examples: legal, management consulting, advertising)

But because most sellers tend to offer similar terms, competition also takes place on a nonprice front. An important variable is the seller's delivery reliability, because the buyer's production operation is geared to the continuous receipt of steel or its emergency ordering. Therefore the steel seller who is located nearest to the buyer, or who pays particular attention to meeting promised delivery dates, has a comparative advantage. As for company salesmen, they cannot make much of a difference if their company's price or delivery reliability is not right, but can make a contribution otherwise by making contacts and being in the right place at the right time. Advertising plays only a small role; usually it takes the form of either corporate advertising to build the steelmaker's image for quality and reliability or new-product advertising to promote a new steel alloy. In this kind of business, where a commodity is involved, it is very hard for a company to discover a marketing angle that helps it substantially increase its market share without competitors' being able to retaliate effectively with the same or some other tactic.

Electric forklift trucks. The marketing mix for equipment such as forklift trucks differs from that for steel, because such trucks can be engineered in many variations to perform different tasks. The buyer seeks a truck that meets certain desiderata of size, lifting capacity, operating cost, features, and price. Thus the seller's product design capability is an important factor in his getting business. If the seller charges a higher price than competitors, this premium must be associated with better performance or extra features. Some buyers, because they view themselves as progressive, may be willing to pay more for factors such as the seller's reputation, extra styling, or comfort. But most buyers operate within narrow budgets and must buy strictly on value, so that their decisions are not challenged within their firm. Some will buy strictly on price, not caring for extra features or styling. This variation in buyer desires leads to a wide variety of possible forklift trucks, with each seller making the decision of how wide a line he wishes to offer.

Another important marketing variable is the seller's backup for the purchase—particularly delivery times, parts availability, and service. Some of these things are in the hands of channel middlemen through whom the manufacturer sells. Most manufacturers do not own their own channels, so they are somewhat restricted in setting certain parts of the marketing mix to the final buyer. As for advertising, its role is limited. Mass-media advertising of forklift trucks is ruled out by the necessity of reaching small, specific market segments at a reasonable cost. Much of the promotional budget goes into specification sheets, catalogs, training films, trade shows, and salesmen contests.

These vignettes show the modal marketing mixes in two quite different industrial markets. Particular firms in each industry may depart from the modal mix in order to be distinctive or to appeal to certain segments of the larger market.

Objectives sought by producer buyers

Products and services are purchased by industrial buyers because they are required in the production process and for the making of profit. Whereas the consumer might contemplate whether to order a frankfurter or a hamburger for lunch, the industrial purchasing agent cannot be indifferent to ordering steel or copper as the material for a new appliance. He is concerned with finding the material that performs the function at the least cost. Any personal preferences felt by the buyer toward one material or another are largely irrelevant. Thus the demand for producer goods is *derived* rather than *primary*.

The degree to which the industrial buyer will be competent in producing profits for his company will rest on his knowledgeability, analytical capacity, and negotiating ability. He needs to be fully informed about competing vendors, products, and terms. He has to have intellectual command of formal cost evaluation models. For example, when choosing which computer to buy, where they vary in calculation speeds, reliability, and prices, he has to know how to place an overall value on these attributes; when evaluating the replacement of an old generator with a new one, he has to know how to use payout-period and rate-of-return analysis; and when considering different ways in which some function can be performed in an appliance, he must know value analysis.[5]

Value analysis, which originated in General Electric in 1948, is *an approach to cost reduction, through the careful study of which components can be redesigned or standardized or made by cheaper methods of production.* The purchasing agent who is a value analyst will carefully examine the high-cost components in a given product—usually 20 percent of the parts will comprise about 80 percent of the costs. The examination proceeds through five steps:

1   Analyze a part's function to determine whether a standardized shelf item could be used.
2   See whether a nonstandardized part could be slightly redesigned into a standardized part. If so, competitive bidding could be solicited, and this generally leads to lower prices.
3   See whether two or more parts could be combined into one.
4   See whether cheaper substitute materials could be used. If so, there may be savings not only in the materials but also in the costs of molds and dies.
5   Contact suppliers and discuss whether certain parts could be made for less by improvements in tooling, by grouping similar work, or by increasing quantities.

In a survey conducted by *Sales Management,* 48 percent of the purchasing agents claimed to use value analysis.

Finally, the industrial buyer must have the knack of getting the vendors to compete for his business and have the negotiating skill to win the most favorable terms.

> . . . A good example of a cagey buyer is [the] vice president in charge of purchasing for Rheingold's big New York brewery. . . . Using the leverage of hundreds of millions of cans a year, like many other buyers, he takes punitive action when one company slips in quality or fails to deliver. "At one point American started talking about a price rise," he recalls, "Continental kept its mouth shut. . . . American never did put the price rise into effect, but anyway, I punished them for talking about it." For a three-month period he cut the percentage of cans he bought from American.[6]

Most descriptions of the industrial buyer portray him as a rational and dedicated servant of the organization, seeking to secure the best terms considering such factors as cost, quality, dependability, and service. Other studies have emphasized personal motives and influences in the industrial buyer's behavior. A recent detailed study of ten large companies concluded:

---

[5]See "What Purchasing Agents Will Demand Tomorrow," *Sales Management,* October 19, 1962, pp. 79–80.
[6]Walter Guzzardi, Jr., "The Fight for 9/10 of a Cent," *Fortune,* April 1961, p. 152.

Corporate decision-makers remain human after they enter the office. They respond to "image"; they buy from companies to which they feel "close"; they favor suppliers who show them respect and personal considerations, and who do extra things for them; they "over-react" to real or imagined slights, tending to reject companies which fail to respond to such items as reader service cards bound into magazines, or which delay in submitting requested bids. . . . Advertising and promotional materials are key factors in establishing a "good image." Good image qualities are said to include being "well known," being considered "big" or a "leader in the field," and having a reputation for providing good service.[7]

In truth, the buyer is guided by both personal and rational goals. Where there is substantial similarity in what suppliers offer in the way of products, price, and service, the industrial buyer has less basis for rational choice. Since he can satisfy his organizational obligations with any one of a number of suppliers, he can be swayed by personal motives. On the other hand, where there are pronounced differences among the competing vendors' products, the industrial buyer is held more accountable for his choice and probably pays more attention to rational factors. Short-run personal gain becomes less motivating than the long-run gain that comes from serving his organization well.

Organization for producer buying

Who does the buying of the hundreds of billions of dollars of products and services needed by the producer market? The buying organizations vary tremendously, from small firms with one or a few men in the purchasing function to huge corporations with a large centralized purchasing department headed by a vice-president of purchasing. Furthermore, in some cases those who do the purchasing make the entire decision as to product specifications and vendor, in other cases they are responsible for vendor choice, and in still other cases they make neither decision but simply place the order. The purchasing agent's authority varies among organizations and for different product categories. He usually makes the decisions regarding smaller items and carries out the wishes of others regarding major capital items.

To understand industrial buying, it is essential to recall that up to five roles may be played in any buying situation, that of *initiator, influencer* (including advisers and approvers), *decider, purchaser,* and *user.* In simple purchases, say of pencils, there may only be two roles, those of users and of buyers. Usually the buyer is also the decider, although feedback from the users on the product's adequacy may lead him to decide next time on another supplier. In more significant purchase decisions, such as replacing one component with a different one, there may be several influencers, and the final decision may have to receive the assent of all or a majority of them. The product-use expectancies of different persons in the buying organization may vary considerably:

The production manager of the buying organization may view a new component under consideration in terms of its effects on assembly cost and reliability of supply. Quality control may be concerned with the uncertainties introduced by the proposed change itself. Purchasing personnel are concerned with relative costs and the risks associated with shifting to a supplier whose performance is unknown. The sales manager is concerned with the effect of modification on the

---

[7]The study was conducted by Motivational Programmers, Inc., a market research firm. and was reported in "Who Makes the Purchasing Decision," *Marketing Insights,* October 31, 1966, pp. 16–18. For similar findings, see Theodore Levitt, *Industrial Purchasing Behavior: A Study of Communications Effects* (Boston: Division of Research, Harvard Business School, 1965).

attractiveness and suitability of the changed end product for his customers and thus the effect of the specification change on sales. Customer service is concerned with expected breakdown rates, possible misuse by customer personnel, the costs of adding new items to the repair parts inventories and of additional training of maintenance, repair and service personnel. Thus each possible buying influence employs his own criteria in evaluating the worth of the salesman's offer.[8]

Thus a key fact about much industrial purchasing is that often several persons participate in some way in the purchasing decision process. The number of multiple buying influences in a typical purchase has been estimated as anywhere from three to twelve persons.[9] Yet it has also been estimated that the salesman generally contacts only one or two persons in a buying organization. What is more discouraging, he often misconceives who is "important" in the buying organization. Functional responsibilities and job titles are not perfectly matched. A study of industrial buying practices concluded:

> Suppliers have significant misconceptions about who in their customers' companies initiates purchases, selects a supplier "pool" and actually approves the final supplier. The role of middle management in these three functions is underestimated, particularly in regard to initiation and conclusion of a purchase, while the importance of top management and the purchasing department is correspondingly inflated.[10]

So the challenge to the industrial marketer is to make a careful assessment of the customer's buying organization, influences, and procedures, and then determine the most effective way to reach the influential parties.

Operations in producer buying

How do producers carry out their purchasing operations? Since this varies considerably between companies and for different goods required within each company, some framework is necessary for distinguishing major classes and phases of buying operations.

A useful analytical framework is shown in Figure 5-1.[11] The grid distinguishes *among* three types of buying situations, or *buy classes*. The *new task* represents the most complex buying situation, involving the largest number of company decision makers and buying influences. The magnitude of the problem-solving challenge, information requirements, and number of alternatives will be at a maximum. Here is where the vendor's salesman faces his greatest opportunity and challenge: to the extent he can pass on useful information, offer a comprehensive solution, or reduce the apparent risk, he will receive more attention from the buyer. At the opposite end is the *straight-rebuy* situation, which is usually handled on a routine basis by the purchasing department. The company chooses from suppliers already on its "list," giving much weight to its past buying experience with the various suppliers. Salesmen from new companies have a hard time breaking into this situation. The salesman's main hope is to convince the buyer that new features, terms, or opportunities justify converting the straight-rebuy situation into a modified-rebuy situation. The

---

[8]See Charles S. Goodman, *Management of the Personal Selling Function* (New York: Holt, Rinehart & Winston, Inc., 1971), p. 204.

[9]See "Finding the Industrial Buying Influence," *Marketing Insights*, April 15, 1968, pp. 14–16.

[10]*Ibid.*, p. 14.

[11]See Patrick J. Robinson, Charles W. Faris, and Yoram Wind, *Industrial Buying and Creative Marketing* (Boston: Allyn & Bacon, Inc., 1967).

	BUY CLASSES		
BUY PHASES	NEW TASK	MODIFIED REBUY	STRAIGHT REBUY
1. Anticipation or recognition of a problem (need) and a general solution			
2. Determination of characteristics and quantity of needed item			
3. Description of characteristics and quantity of needed item			
4. Search for and qualification of potential sources			
5. Acquisition and analysis of proposals			
6. Evaluation of proposals and selection of supplier(s)			
7. Selection of an order routine			
8. Performance feedback and evaluation			

Figure 5-1

The buy-grid analytic framework for industrial buying situations

SOURCE: Redrawn from Patrick J. Robinson, Charles W. Faris, and Yoram Wind, *Industrial Buying and Creative Marketing* (Boston: Allyn & Bacon, Inc., 1967), p. 14.

modified-rebuy situation stands between the two others in terms of problem newness, information requirements, and number of alternatives. Since the buyer faces some new requirement, this creates a small opportunity for suppliers to vie for different shares of the business.

The other kernel idea in the buy grid is the *buy phase*—the notion that there are different stages in the industrial buying process. Eight buy phases are distinguished: (1) recognition of a problem, (2) determination of needed item, (3) description of needed item, (4) search for potential sources, (5) proposal acquisition and analysis, (6) supplier selection, (7) order routine selection, and (8) performance evaluation. As each phase is completed, there is "creeping commitment" and less chance of new vendors' gaining access to the buying situation. The buy phases are usually passed through rapidly and routinely in the straight-rebuy situation, less rapidly in the modified-rebuy situation, and least rapidly in the new-task situation.

A new-task situation involving a computer purchase was studied by Motivational Programmers, Inc. They developed the special map shown in Figure 5-2 to exhibit the flows of influences and events that took place in this situation. The map shows eight different company personnel (represented by desk symbols) who were involved in this buying decision process at one time or another. Three suppliers also were involved, as well as other outside influences (shown in diamond-shaped figures). Finally, fifteen different events (shown as circles) led up to the placing of the order ultimately with supplier C.

All said, industrial buying is complex in its objects, objectives, organization, and operations. The most important lesson for industrial marketers

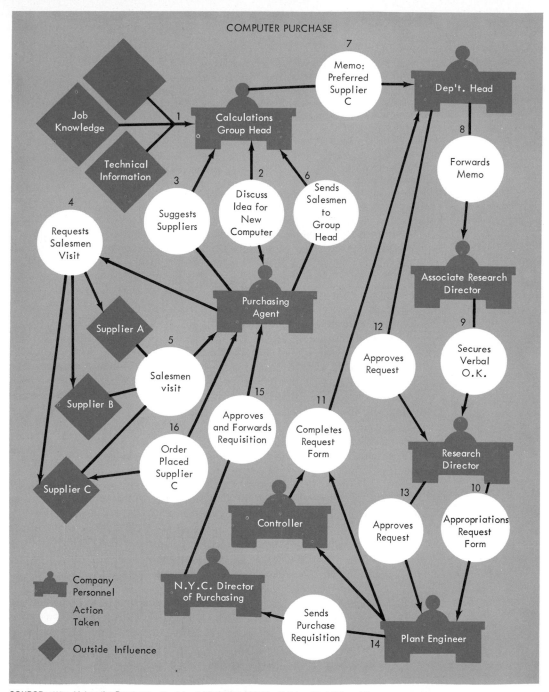

COMPUTER PURCHASE

SOURCE: "Who Makes the Purchasing Decision," *Marketing Insights,* October 31, 1966, p. 18.

Figure 5-2
Map of company events in the purchase of a computer

is that the seller's marketing effort should be based on a thorough understanding of organizational buyer behavior processes. Even if the seller is the preferred supplier, he must keep up his effort and information. For example, for years Kodak's strategy for selling X-ray film to hospitals was to sell through lab technicians. They did not notice that the decision was increasingly being made by professional administrators. As its sales declined, it finally grasped the change in buying practices and hurriedly changed its marketing strategy.

RESELLER MARKET

The reseller market is the market consisting of individuals and organizations who acquire goods for the purpose of reselling or renting them to others at a profit. The reseller market includes over five hundred thousand wholesalers employing 4 million persons, and 2 million retailers employing 12 million persons; both sectors account for over 14 percent of the national income. Resellers are more dispersed geographically than producers but more concentrated geographically than consumers.

Objects in the reseller market

Resellers purchase (1) goods for resale and (2) goods and services for conducting their operations. The latter are bought by resellers in their role as "producers," so we shall confine the discussion here to the goods they purchase for resale.

Resellers handle a vast variety of products for resale, indeed everything produced except the few classes of goods that producers choose to sell direct to final customers. The excluded class would include heavy or complex machinery, customized products, and products sold on a direct-mail or a door-to-door basis. With these exceptions, most products are not marketed directly but travel to the final buyer through one or more selling intermediaries.

Each selling intermediary faces the problem of determining its unique *assortment*—the combination of products and services that it will offer to the marketplace. The wholesaler or retailer can choose one of four assortment strategies:

1 *Exclusive assortment:* representing the line of one manufacturer only.
2 *Deep assortment:* representing a given homogeneous product family in depth, drawing on many producers' outputs.
3 *Broad assortment:* representing a wide range of product lines that still fall within the natural coverage of the reseller's type of business.
4 *Scrambled assortment:* representing many unrelated product families.

Thus a camera store can decide to sell only Kodak cameras (exclusive assortment), many brands of cameras (deep assortment), cameras, tape recorders, radios, and stereophonic equipment (broad assortment), or the last plus stoves and refrigerators (scrambled assortment). The assortment the reseller ultimately chooses will influence its customer mix, marketing mix, and supplier mix.

Objectives sought by reseller buyers

The reseller, like the producer, is in business to make a profit. He and his buyers must be adept at buying goods "cheap" and selling them "dear." This means the reseller must know the various sources of supply, be able to negotiate, and be able to set services, prices, and promotional expenditures at levels that will generate a high level of revenue in relation to his costs of doing business. He must master principles of demand forecasting, merchandise selection, stock control, space allocation, and display, not to mention the careful management of money and personnel resources. He must learn to measure his return on a profit-per-cubic-foot basis rather than on a product-by-product basis.[12] In many retail lines the profit margin on sales is so low (for example, 1 to 2 percent in supermarkets) that a sudden decline in demand will drive profit into the red. Those who complain about middlemen profits overlook the enormous work and risk that must be borne by middlemen in their effort to create assortments that meet the wants and needs of final buyers.

Resellers tend to develop different buying styles to carry out their work. Dickenson has distinguished the following buyer types:

1 *Loyal buyer.* This type remains loyal to a resource, or group of resources, year after year, for reasons other than that he obtains the best deal.
2 *Opportunistic buyer.* This type selects mainly from a preselected list of those vendors who will further his long-term interests. Within his preselected list, he will pursue the best arrangement possible.
3 *Best-deal buyer.* This type looks for and selects the best deal available to him in the market at a given point in time.
4 *Creative buyer.* This type tries not to accept the marketing mixes offered by any of the vendors. He attempts to sell his offers to the market. This may or may not involve a change in the physical product.
5 *Advertising buyer.* This type attempts primarily to obtain advertising moneys; advertising moneys must be a part of every deal and are the prime target of each negotiation.
6 *The chiseler.* This type of buyer constantly negotiates extra concessions in price at the time of the offering. He tends to accept the vendor offer carrying the greatest discount from the price he feels that other accounts might pay.
7 *Nuts-and-bolts buyer.* This buyer selects merchandise that is the best constructed, assuming that the merchandise policies of the vendor are acceptable within a very broad range. He is more interested in the thread count than in the number that will sell.[13]

Organization for reseller buying

Who does the deciding and buying for wholesale and retail organizations? In the smaller ones, the merchandise selection and buying functions may be carried out by persons who also carry out several other functions in the firm. In the larger distributor organizations, buying is a specialist function and often a full-time job. It is carried on in different ways by department stores, supermarkets, drug wholesalers, and so on, and differences can even be found within each type of distributive enterprise.

Much of the flavor of reseller buying practices can be sensed by examining the particular case of supermarket chains and the respective roles played by corporate-headquarter buyers, storewide buying committees, and the individual store managers. In the corporate headquarters of a supermarket chain there will be specialist buyers (sometimes called merchandise managers) for different

---

[12]See Robert D. Buzzell, *Product Profitability Measurement and Merchandising Decisions* (Boston: Harvard University Press, 1965).

[13]Roger A. Dickinson, *Buyer Decision Making* (Berkeley, Calif.: Institute of Business and Economic Research, 1967), pp. 14–17.

product lines carried by the supermarket. These buyers have the responsibility for developing brand assortments and listening to presentations by the salesmen of new brands. In some chains these buyers have great latitude with respect to accepting or rejecting new items. In many chains, however, their latitude is limited to screening "obvious rejects" (and sometimes "obvious accepts"); otherwise they must bring most of the new-item proposals to the chain's buying committee at one of the weekly meetings. The chain's buying committee(s) consists of divisional managers, assistant divisional managers, other buyers, and so on. They listen to the buyer present the case for or against each item (note that the salesman is barred from making a presentation), they sample the item if edible, ask for information about the manufacturer's planned promotion, whether any deals are available, and so on. A typical discussion goes like this:

Buyer: I think this item is a winner.

Member: Why?

Buyer: The brand name is good; the manufacturer has ads in *Good Housekeeping* and *McCall's* and will start TV advertising in the fall.

Division Manager: What does it cost?

Buyer: There are twenty-four units packed and offered for $10.60. The recommended retail is 59¢.

Member: What about the other brand we carry?

Buyer: This one has it beat all over.

Division Manager: Okay, let's put it in.

This fragment raises the important question of whether the store buying committee is really the decisive factor regarding which new products enter the chain's assortment. There is some evidence that buying committees serve a "checking" function rather than an actual decision-making function. Borden found that the buyer's recommendation is highly important and influential to the committee decision;[14] the buyer decides what to communicate to the committee, thus exerting considerable influence on the decision. The committees exerted some important indirect effects on product evaluations and decisions. By serving as a "buffer" between buyers and salesmen, committees provide buyers with an excuse for rejecting a seller's proposition.

 Even if an item is accepted by a chain-store buying committee, it will not necessarily appear in a large number of the chain's outlets. According to one supermarket chain executive: "No matter what the salesmen sell or buyers buy, the man who has the greatest influence on the final sale of the new item is the store manager assisted by his crew." In the nation's chain and independent supermarkets, two-thirds of the new items accepted at the warehouse are ordered on the individual store manager's own decision, and only one-third represent forced distribution.[15]

This picture of the reseller organization's buying procedure for new items points to the formidable problem faced by the producers of new items. Industry

14Neil H. Borden, Jr., *Acceptance of New Food Products by Supermarkets* (Boston: Division of Research, Graduate School of Business Administration, Harvard University, 1968).

15Robert W. Mueller and Franklin H. Graf, "New Items in the Food Industry, Their Problems and Opportunities," a special report to the Annual Convention of the Supermarket Institute, Cleveland, Ohio, May 20, 1968, p. 2.

offers the nation's supermarkets between 150 and 250 new items each week, of which store space does not permit more than 10 percent to be accepted.[16] So intense is the battle for shelf space that the Mafia shot two A&P executives and destroyed several stores because A&P refused to stock their brand of detergent.[17] For those sellers who do not wish to go this far, their need is to understand the buying process just described and to understand the criteria used to make the final decision.

Several studies have attempted to rank the major criteria used by buyers, buying committees, and store managers. A. C. Nielsen Company carried out a study in which store managers were asked to rank on a three-point scale the importance of different elements in swaying their decision to accept a new item.[18] The final ranking showed:

Evidence of consumer acceptance	2.5
Advertising/promotion	2.2
Introductory terms and allowances	2.0
Why item was developed	1.9
Merchandising recommendations	1.8

The first three items are reported to be the most important criteria in other studies also.[19] Yet it appears that whatever criteria are used in deliberations, they are rarely reduced to explicit directives or used with formal weightings by the buyer. Nevertheless, they suggest to the seller that he stands the best chance when he can report strong test-market evidence indicating consumer acceptance, a well-designed and extensive introductory advertising and promotions plan, and deals (primarily margin and allowances) to incentivize the retailer.

These respective roles of chain buyers, chain buying committee, and store manager characterize, with some variation, the buying organizations of other distributive enterprises. Large department stores or chains rely on buyers for merchandise lines, and usually they have a lot of authority and latitude. They may report to buying committees. The buyers are aided by assistant buyers, who carry out preliminary search as well as clerical tasks involved in ordering. The buyers may perform other functions such as demand forecasting, stock control, and merchandising. Individual store managers or their staff may have some freedom with respect to which goods to order and display prominently.

**Operations in
reseller buying**

The manner in which the reseller carries on his buying operations varies with the type of buying situation, of which three general classes can be distinguished. The *new-item situation* describes the case where the reseller has been offered a new

---

[16]E. B. Weiss, *Winning Chain-Store Distributors for New Products* (New York: Doyle-Dane-Bernbach, 1956), pp. 4–38.

[17]*Wall Street Journal,* June 14, 1969, back page.

[18]Mueller and Graf, *op. cit.,* p. 5.

[19]"Merchandising New Items at Retail: The Payoff at Point of Purchase," *Progressive Grocer,* June 1968; also Borden, *op. cit.,* p. 203. Also see David B. Montgomery, *New Product Distribution: An Analysis of Supermarket Buyer Decisions* (Cambridge, Mass.: Marketing Science Institute, March 1973). Montgomery found the two most important variables to be company reputation and the perceived newness of the product.

item. The new-item situation differs from the new-task situation faced by producers in that it is a "go-no" opportunity presented to the buyer, while the new task means that the buyer is confronted with a new problem arising in the manufacturing process and must initiate research and evaluation of solutions and vendors.

The *best-vendor situation* faces the reseller when he knows what he needs but must determine the best supplier(s). This occurs in two situations: (1) when the reseller can carry only a subset of the available brands offered because of space constraints; (2) when the reseller wants to sponsor his own private brand and is seeking a willing and qualified producer. Resellers such as Sears and the A&P resell a substantial number of items under their own name; therefore much of their buying operation consists of vendor selection.

The *better-terms situation* arises when the reseller wants to obtain a better set of terms from his present suppliers. He is not eager to change his supplier, but he does want more advantageous treatment. Legally, sellers are prevented, under the Robinson-Patman Act, from giving discriminating terms to different resellers in the same reseller class unless these reflect corresponding cost differences, distress sales, or a few other special conditions. Nevertheless, individual resellers and classes of resellers (discounters, large outlets, and the like) do press their suppliers for better individual or class treatment, and this can take many forms, such as more supplier services, easier credit terms, and better volume discounts.

Buying procedures in all three situations can be expected to grow more sophisticated over time, as better-trained persons are hired for these jobs, receive more extensive data to work with, and learn how to use more analytical methods. Major changes in purchasing operations are being made possible by advances in computers and telecommunications. Computers are finding increased application in keeping current inventory figures, computing economic order quantities, preparing purchasing orders, developing requests for vendor quotations or expediting of orders, and generating printouts of dollars spent by vendors and by products. Through telecommunications, the buyer can feed prepunched cards describing items and quantities needed into his transmitter, which is linked to the supplier's receiving equipment. The supplier's equipment prepares cards or tapes, which become the input for mechanized preparation of shipping tickets, invoices, and other documents. Many resellers are going over to stockless purchasing of certain items, which means that the supplier inventories the items and supplies them to the buyer on short notice.

GOVERNMENT MARKET

The government market is the market consisting of governmental units of all types—federal, state, and local—who purchase or rent goods for carrying out the main functions of government. The government market has been expanding in size every year since the founding of the Republic—with no abatement, alas, in sight. It now purchases $277 billion of products and services, or 21 percent of the gross national product, making it the nation's largest customer. The federal government accounts for approximately 65 percent of the total spent by government at all levels.[20]

---

[20]*Statistical Abstract of the United States,* 1974, p. 374.

Although substantial government purchasing takes place in Washington, D.C., state capitals, and major cities, it takes place also in every county and village as well. The federal government itself operates an elaborate set of geographically dispersed buying information offices. Local products and services may be bought by local government offices, army posts, and so on. As one example, the naval complex at Hampton Roads, Virginia, paid local Virginia firms $500,000 in one year just for ice cream.[21]

Objects in the government market

What else does government buy, besides ice cream? Practically everything. Governmental units buy bombers, sculpture, chalkboards, furniture, toiletries, clothing, materials-handling equipment, fire engines, mobile equipment, fuel, and so on. All government spent approximately $79 billion for defense, $70 billion for education, $19 billion for highways, $17 billion for health and hospitals, $24 billion for public welfare, $14 billion for natural resources, and smaller sums for postal service, space research, housing and urban renewal, and so on. The mix of expenditures varied considerably with the particular type of governmental unit, with defense looming large in the federal budget (70 percent) and education looming large in the state and local budgets (39 percent).[22] No matter how one feels about government marketing, it represents a tremendous market for any producer or reseller.

Objectives sought by government buyers

Government buying is guided by a different fundamental objective than found in the other sectors of the economy. Government does not pursue a personal consumption or a profit-making standard; rather it buys a level and mix of products and services that it or the voters establish as necessary for the maintenance of the society. Adam Smith pointed out that all governments must carry on at least three functions: defense, justice, and public works. A modern government also pays attention to other objectives in its purchasing activities, such as those affecting the location of business (in favor of depressed areas and more general dispersal), the state of competition in an industry (in favor of promoting small business and helping the weaker firms), and the hiring standards in industry (in refusing contracts to companies that practice racial or sex discrimination).

Organization of government buying

Who in the government does the buying of the $277 billion of goods and services? Every government agency has some buying influence or authority. Each of them represents a potential target for the seller.

Government buying organizations are found on the federal, state, and local levels. The federal level is the largest, and its buying units can be subclassified into the civilian and military sectors. The *federal civilian buying* establishment consists of seven categories: departments (Commerce), administration (General Services Administration), agencies (Federal Aviation Agency), boards (Railroad Retirement Board), commissions (Federal Communications Commission), the executive office (Bureau of the Budget), and miscellaneous (Tennessee Valley Authority). "No single federal agency contracts for all the government's requirements and no single buyer in any agency purchases all that agency's needs for any single item of supplies, equipment or services."[23] Many agencies

---

[21]"Defense Marketing: Finding the Buyer," *Marketing Insights,* November 25, 1968, pp. 12–13.

[22]*Statistical Abstract of the United States,* 1974, p. 252.

[23]Stanley E. Cohen, "Looking in the U.S. Government Market," *Industrial Marketing,* September 1964, pp. 129–38.

control a substantial percentage of their own buying, particularly for industrial products and specialized equipment. At the same time, the General Services Administration plays a main role in attempting to centralize the procurement of the items most commonly used by the civilian section (office furniture and equipment, vehicles, fuels, and so on) and to promote standardized buying procedures for the other agencies. It acts in the capacity of a wholesaler on its own account, and as a reseller and an agent middleman for other government agencies.

Federal military buying is carried out by the Defense Department largely through the Defense Supply Agency and the three military departments of the Army, Navy, and Air Force. The Defense Supply Agency was set up in 1961 by Defense Secretary McNamara to procure and distribute supplies used in common by all military services in an effort to reduce costly duplication (thus it is the equivalent of the General Services Administration in the civilian sector). It operates six supply centers, which specialize in construction, electronics, fuel, personnel support, industrial, and general supplies. The trend has been toward "single managers" for major product classifications. Each individual service branch procures equipment and supplies in line with its own mission; for example, the Army Department operates special branches for acquiring its own material, vehicles, medical supplies and services, and weaponry.

State and local buying agencies include school districts, highway departments, hospitals, housing agencies, and many others.

Operations in government buying

Government buying practices appear complex to the uninitiated supplier because of the many agencies and procedures that characterize the government market. Yet most of this can be mastered in a short time, and the government is generally very helpful in diffusing information about its buying needs and procedures. In fact, government is often as anxious to attract new suppliers as the suppliers are to find customers. For example, the Small Business Administration prints a useful booklet "U.S. Government Purchasing, Specifications, and Sales Directory" listing thousands of items most frequently purchased by government and cross-referenced by the agencies most frequently using them. The Government Printing Office prints "Commerce Business Daily," which lists current proposed defense procurements estimated to exceed $10,000 and civilian agency procurements expected to exceed $5,000, as well as information about recent contract awards that can provide leads to subcontracting markets. The General Services Administration operates Business Service Centers in several major cities, whose staff is set up to provide a complete education on the way it and other agencies buy and the steps that the supplier should follow. Various trade magazines and associations provide information on how to reach schools, hospitals, highway departments, and so on.

Government buying procedures can be classified into two major types: the *open bid* and the *negotiated contract*. In both cases the emphasis is on competitive procurement. Open-bid buying means that the government procuring office invites bids from qualified suppliers for carefully described items, generally awarding a contract to the lowest bidder. Specifically, the interested supplier fills out an application requesting to be placed on the bidders' lists. He then receives mailings of "invitations for bids," which carefully specify the item and quantity needed. The specifications include a description of the materials, dimensions, quality, reliability, packing and crating requirements, and so on, as well as the terms of the contract that will be awarded to the successful bidder.

The supplier must carefully consider whether he can meet the specifications and likes the terms. For commodities and standard items, such as fuel or school supplies, the specifications are not a hurdle. However, specifications may constitute a hurdle for nonstandard items, although the government unit is barred from issuing such narrow specifications that only one existing seller can meet them. Furthermore, the government procurement office is usually—but not always—required to award the contract to the lowest bidder on a winner-take-all basis. In some cases allowance can be made for the supplier's superior product or reputation for completing contracts. A more recent development is to ask for bids, particularly on equipment, to cover its life-cycle maintenance as well as initial price. The award will go to the firm submitting the lowest life-cycle bid, rather than bid for the original equipment only. This practice was started by the Defense Department in recognition that it might spend up to ten times the original purchase price to own and operate the equipment.[24]

In negotiated-contract buying, the agency works with one or a few companies and directly negotiates a contract with one of them covering the project and terms. This occurs primarily in connection with complex projects, often involving major research and development cost and risk and/or where there is little effective competition. Contracts can have countless variations, such as cost-plus pricing, fixed-pricing, and fixed price-and-incentive (the supplier earns more if he decreases his costs). Contract performance is open to review and renegotiation if the supplier's profits appear excessive.

Government contracts won by large companies give rise to substantial subcontracting opportunities, as much as 50 percent, for small companies. Thus government purchasing activity in turn creates derived demand in the producer market. Subcontracting firms, however, must go after this business with a willingness to place performance bonds with the prime contractor, thereby assuming some of the risk.

By and large, major companies or company divisions that have primarily served the government market have not until recently manifested much of a marketing orientation[25]—for a number of reasons. Total government spending is determined by elected officials rather than by marketing effort to develop this market. The government's procurement policies have emphasized price, leading the suppliers to invest all their effort in a technological orientation to bring their costs down. Where the product's characteristics are carefully specified, product differentiation is not a marketing factor. Nor is advertising and personal selling of much consequence in winning bids on an open-bid basis. Therefore suppliers in the past did not recognize a need for a marketing orientation and department. The situation was a little more favorable to marketing in the negotiated-contract case, where product design, personal salesmanship, and company image could count for more.

In general, there is now a strong trend toward the establishment of marketing departments by suppliers to guide government-directed marketing effort. There is greater activity to coordinate bids and prepare them more scientifically, to propose projects to meet government needs rather than just to respond to government invitations, to gather competitive intelligence, to prepare better-coordinated communication programs to tell the story of the company's com-

---

[24]"Picking the Winners with a New System," *Business Week*, May 13, 1967, pp. 62–67.

[25]Salvatore F. Divita, "Government Marketing: An Appraisal," in *Marketing for Tomorrow: Today*, ed. M. S. Moyer and R. E. Vosburgh (Chicago: American Marketing Association, 1968).

petence, and so on. Government suppliers are recognizing the importance of studying the huge opportunities and needs of this market and responding creatively with products and systems. And they are also recognizing the need to understand the value of market coverage not only of the procurement offices but also of the government users—educators, chemists, plant managers, army personnel, and others—who can exercise a great influence on what will be bought.

SUMMARY

Marketing opportunity abounds not only in the consumer market but also in three other major markets—the producer, reseller, and government markets.

The producer market consists of all the business firms engaged in the production of goods and services for sale or rental to others. They are a market for raw and manufactured materials and parts, installations and accessory equipment, and supplies and services. Producer buyers tend to differ from household buyers in being oriented toward profit rather than satisfaction, showing more skill in buying, being larger and more concentrated geographically, and being more influenced by the level of economic activity. A key fact about industrial purchasing is that often several persons participate in the purchasing decision process. The purchasing operations vary according to the buy classes and buy phases involved in a purchasing situation.

The reseller market consists of individuals and organizations who acquire and resell goods produced by others. Producers must apply modern marketing concepts and techniques in approaching resellers, because their buying organizations, needs, styles, and operations vary considerably.

The government market is a vast one that annually purchases $277 billion of products and services—for the pursuit of defense, justice, and public welfare. Government buying practices are highly specialized and specified, with open bidding and/or negotiated contracts characterizing most of the buying. Until recently most firms selling to the government took quite a narrow view of the marketing process, but this view is changing.

QUESTIONS AND PROBLEMS

1   Describe some of the major characteristics of commercial services firms (finance, insurance, and real estate) as a market for goods and services.

2   There are several important institutional markets: hospitals, educational institutions, welfare organizations, etc. Discuss the characteristic buying needs and buying organization for, say, educational institutions.

3   Are industrial buyers more "rational" than household buyers?

4   Cessna Aircraft Company is interested in expanding its sales of small aircraft to business firms. Its marketing research analyst decides to study the buying process using the paradigm: (a) need arousal; (b) information search; (c) evaluation behavior; (d) purchase decision; and (e) postpurchase feelings. List factors under each that affect the potential industrial buyer of a private aircraft.

5   The location of buying authority in a company will vary with the level of the *product's complexity* and with the level of the *commercial investment*. Given two levels (low, high) for each variable, predict who will make the buying decision in each of the four possible cases.

6

DEMAND MEASUREMENT AND FORECASTING

Forecasting is like trying to drive a car blindfolded and following directions given by a person who is looking out of the back window.

ANONYMOUS

Marketing planning requires the conversion of the various qualitative understandings of a market into quantitative estimates of specific demand by product, territory, and type of customer. Furthermore, estimates must be made of the future course of market demand. These tasks are called demand measurement and demand forecasting. Demand estimates are essential in carrying out three important management functions—the *analysis* of market opportunities, the *planning* of marketing effort, and the *control* of marketing performance.

MAJOR CONCEPTS IN DEMAND MEASUREMENT

Demand measurement describes the activity of developing quantitative estimates of demand. Figure 6-1 shows *ninety* different types of demand measurement! Demand can be measured for six different *product levels* (product item, product class, product line, company sales, industry sales, national sales), five different *space levels* (customer, territory, region, U.S.A., world), and three different *time levels* (short-range, medium-range, and long-range).

Each type of demand measurement serves a specific purpose. Thus a company might make a short-range forecast of the total demand for a particular

117

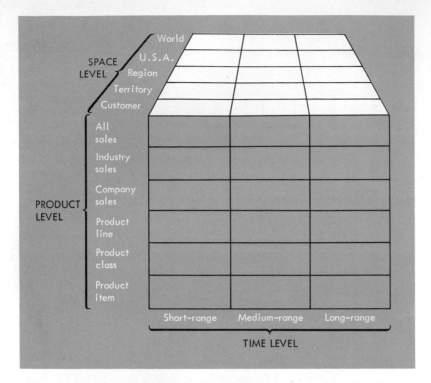

Figure 6-1
Ninety types of demand measurement (6 × 5 × 3)

product item to provide a basis for ordering raw materials, planning production, and scheduling short-run financing. Or it might make a long-range forecast of regional demand for its major product line to provide a basis for considering market expansion.

The field of demand measurement is filled with a confusing number of terms. Company executives talk of forecasts, predictions, potentials, estimates, projections, goals, targets, quotas, and budgets. Many of these terms are redundant. The major concepts in demand measurement are *market demand* and *company demand*. Within each, we distinguish between a *demand function*, a *potential*, and a *forecast*. The six terms are shown in Figure 6-2.

Market demand

In evaluating marketing opportunities, the firm usually starts with the notion of market demand. It is not a simple concept, as the following definition makes clear:

> *Market demand* for a *product* is the *total volume* that would be *bought* by a defined *customer group* in a defined *geographical area* in a defined *time period* in a defined *marketing environment* under a defined *marketing program.*

There are eight elements in this definition.

PRODUCT   Market demand measurement requires a careful definition of the scope of the product class. The seller of tin cans has to define whether his market is all metal-can users or all container users. This depends on how the seller views his opportunities for penetrating adjacent markets.

118

TOTAL VOLUME   Market demand can be measured in terms of physical volume, dollar volume, or relative volume. The U.S. market demand for automobiles may be described as 10 million cars or $50 billion. The market demand for automobiles in Greater Chicago can be expressed as 3 percent of the nation's total demand.

BOUGHT   In measuring market demand, it is important to define whether "bought" means the volume ordered, shipped, paid for, received, or consumed. For example, a forecast of new housing for the next year usually means the number of units that will be ordered, not completed (called housing starts).

CUSTOMER GROUP   Market demand may be measured for the whole market or for any segment(s). Thus a steel producer may estimate the volume to be bought separately by the construction industry and the transportation industry.

GEOGRAPHICAL AREA   Market demand should be measured with reference to well-defined geographical boundaries. A forecast of next year's passenger automobile sales will vary depending upon whether the boundaries are limited to the United States or include Canada and/or Mexico.

TIME PERIOD   Market demand should be measured with reference to a stated period of time. One can talk about the market demand for the next calendar year, for the coming five years, or for 1984. The longer the forecasting interval, the more tenuous the forecast. Every forecast is based on a set of assumptions about environmental and marketing conditions, and the chance that some of these assumptions will not be fulfilled increases with the length of the forecast period.

MARKETING ENVIRONMENT   Market demand is affected by a host of uncontrollable factors. Every forecast of demand should explicitly list the assumptions made about the demographic, economic, technological, political, and cultural environment.[1] Demographic and economic forecasting are well developed, technological forecasting is coming into its own,[2] but political and cul-

---

[1]See, for example, Gerald A. Busch, "Prudent Manager Forecasting," *Harvard Business Review,* May–June 1961, pp. 57–64.

[2]See James R. Bright, *Technological Forecasting* (Englewood Cliffs, N.J.: Prentice-Hall, Inc., 1968).

	Market	Company
Demand	Market demand	Company demand function
Potential	Market potential	Company sales potential
Forecast	Market forecast	Company sales forecast

Figure 6-2
Major concepts in demand measurement

tural forecasting are still in their infancy. Much interest in the whole subject of predicting future environments is being stimulated by futurists such as Kahn and Weiner.[3] At the same time, Levitt has cautioned: "The easiest kind of expert to be is the specialist who predicts the future. It takes only two things: imagination and a good command of the active verb."[4]

MARKETING PROGRAM   Market demand is also affected by controllable factors, particularly marketing programs developed by the sellers. Demand in most markets will show some elasticity with respect to industry price, promotion, product improvements, and distribution effort. Thus a market demand forecast requires assumptions about future industry prices and marketing outlays. We shall use the term *marketing effort* to describe the sum of the company's demand-stimulating expenditures. Marketing effort has three dimensions that make a difference in its impact: (1) *marketing mix,* the amounts and kinds of marketing variables the company is using at a particular time, (2) *marketing allocation,* the company's division of its marketing effort over its sales areas, and (3) *marketing effectiveness,* the efficiency with which the company employs its marketing funds.

The most important thing to realize about market demand is that it is not a single number, but a function. For this reason it is also called the *market demand function* or *market response function.* The functional nature of market demand is shown in Figure 6-3(a). Market demand is shown on the vertical axis, industry marketing effort on the horizontal axis. The market demand function is shown as a curve that rises with higher levels of industry marketing effort. The curve is defined for a given marketing environment.

The shape of the curve has to be determined for each market. The curve in the illustration has the familiar S shape, suggesting that market demand shows first increasing, then diminishing, sales response to increased industry marketing effort. Some base sales, the *market minimum,* would take place without any demand-stimulating marketing expenditures by the industry. Positive marketing expenditures will yield increasing, then decreasing, returns. Still higher marketing expenditures would not stimulate much further demand, thus suggesting an upper limit to market demand, called the *market potential.*

The distance between the market minimum and the market potential shows the overall *marketing sensitivity of demand* in that industry. We can think of two extreme types of markets, the *expansible* and the *nonexpansible.* The expansible market, epitomized by markets for new products, is quite affected in its total size by the level of marketing expenditures. In terms of Figure 6-3(a) the distance between M_0 and M_1 is relatively large. The nonexpansible market, epitomized by cigarettes or drugs, is not much affected by the level of marketing expenditures; the distance between M_0 and M_1 is relatively small. The firm selling in a nonexpansible market can take the market's size for granted and concentrate its marketing resources on getting a good share of the market.

It is important to emphasize that the *market demand function* is *not* a picture of market demand *over time.* Rather, the curve shows alternative forecasts of market demand associated with alternative levels of industry marketing effort.

---

[3]Herman Kahn and Anthony J. Weiner, *The Year 2000* (New York: The Macmillan Company, 1967).

[4]Theodore Levitt, "The New Markets—Think before You Leap," *Harvard Business Review,* May–June 1969, pp. 53–68, here p. 53.

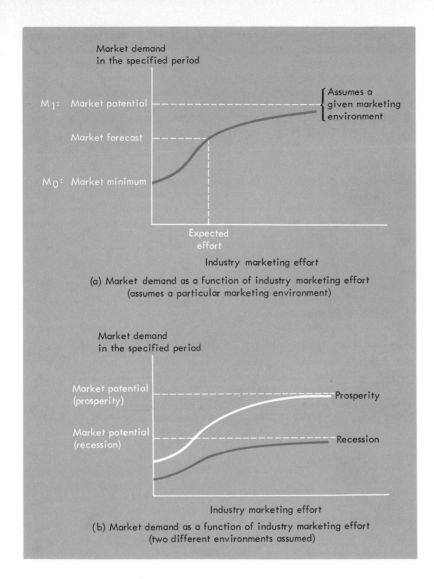

(a) Market demand as a function of industry marketing effort
(assumes a particular marketing environment)

(b) Market demand as a function of industry marketing effort
(two different environments assumed)

Figure 6-3
Market demand

Market forecast

Only one of the many possible levels of industry marketing effort will actually occur. The market demand corresponding to the expected effort is called the *market forecast*. The market forecast shows the expected level of market demand for the expected level of industry marketing effort and the given environment.

Market potential

The market forecast shows the expected market demand, not the highest possible market demand. For the latter, we have to visualize the level of market demand for a very "high" level of industry marketing effort, where further increases in marketing effort would have little effect in stimulating further demand. *Market potential is the limit approached by market demand as industry marketing effort goes to infinity, for a given environment.*

The phrase "for a given environment" is crucial in the concept of market potential. Consider the market potential for automobiles in a period of recession versus a period of prosperity. The market potential is higher during prosperity. The dependence of market potential on the environment is illustrated in Figure 6-3(b). Thus the analyst distinguishes between the position of the market demand function and movement along it. The sellers cannot do anything about the position of the market demand function; this is the result of a given marketing environment. The sellers influence their particular location on the function, however, in deciding how much to spend on marketing.

Company demand

We are now ready to define company demand. *Company demand is the company's share of market demand.* In symbols:

$$Q_i = s_i Q \qquad \text{(6-1)}$$

where:

Q_i = company i's demand
s_i = company i's market share
Q = total market demand

Company demand, like market demand, is a function—called the *company demand function* or *sales response function*—and is subject to all the determinants of market demand *plus whatever influences company market share.*

The most popular theory is that the *market shares* of various competitors will be proportional to their *marketing-effort shares.* This normal expectation can be called *the fundamental theorem of market-share determination* and is expressed:

$$s_i = \frac{M_i}{\Sigma M_i} \qquad \text{(6-2)}$$

where M_i = company i's marketing effort.

For example, consider the simple case where two identical firms are selling the same product but spending different amounts on marketing: $60,000 and $40,000 respectively. Using equation (6-2), company one's market share is predicted to be 60 percent:

$$s_1 = \frac{\$60,000}{\$60,000 + \$40,000} = .60$$

If company one is not enjoying a .60 market share, additional factors must be brought in. Suppose the companies also differ in the *effectiveness* with which they spend marketing dollars. Then equation (6-2) can be revised to read:

$$s_i = \frac{\alpha_i M_i}{\Sigma \alpha_i M_i} \qquad \text{(6-3)}$$

where:

α_i = marketing effectiveness of a dollar spent by company i (with $\alpha = 1.00$ for average effectiveness)

$\alpha_i M_i$ = company i's effective marketing effort

Suppose that company one spends its marketing funds less effectively than company two, with $\alpha_1 = .90$ and $\alpha_2 = 1.20$. Then company one's market share would be forecast to be 53 percent:

$$s_1 = \frac{.90(\$60,000)}{.90(\$60,000) + 1.20(\$40,000)} \cong .53$$

Equation (6-3) assumes a strict proportionality between market share and effective effort share. Yet, if there are grounds for expecting diminishing returns as one firm's effective effort increases relative to the industry's effective effort, equation (6-3) should be modified to reflect this. One way to reflect diminishing returns is through the use of a marketing-effort elasticity exponent that is less than unity:

$$s_i = \frac{(\alpha_i M_i)^{e_m}}{\Sigma(\alpha_i M_i)^{e_m}}, \qquad \text{where } 0 < e_m < 1 \tag{6-4}$$

where:

e_m = elasticity of market share with respect to effective marketing effort

Assume that the marketing-effort elasticity is .8 in the previous example. As a result, company one's market share would be

$$s_i = \frac{[(.90)(\$60,000)]^{.8}}{[(.90)(\$60,000)]^{.8} + [(1.20)(\$40,000)]^{.8}} \cong .50$$

Thus company one's estimated market share is revised to take into account diminishing returns. Although company one is spending 60 percent of the marketing funds in the industry, its market share is only 50 percent, because of both a lower spending efficiency than its competition *and* diminishing returns.

A further improvement in the formulation of market-share determination can be introduced by breaking up each company's marketing effort into its major components and separately expressing the effectiveness and elasticity of each type of marketing effort. The equation becomes:

$$s_{it} = \frac{R_{it}^{e_{Ri}} P_{it}^{-e_{Pi}} (a_{it} A_{it})^{e_{Ai}} (d_{it} D_{it})^{e_{Di}}}{\Sigma[R_{it}^{e_{Ri}} P_{it}^{-e_{Pi}} (a_{it} A_{it})^{e_{Ai}} (d_{it} D_{it})^{e_{Di}}]} \tag{6-5}$$

where:

s_{it} = company i's estimated market share at time t

R_{it} = quality rating of company i's product in year t

P_{it} = price of company i's product in year t

A_{it} = advertising and promotion costs of company i in year t
D_{it} = distribution and sales-force costs of company i in year t
a_{it} = advertising-effectiveness index for company i at time t
d_{it} = distribution-effectiveness index for company i at time t
$\left. \begin{array}{l} e_{Ri}, e_{Pi} \\ e_{Ai}, e_{Di} \end{array} \right\}$ = elasticities of quality, price, advertising, and distribution, respectively, of company i

Thus equation (6-5) is a flexible way to take account of four major influences on a company's market share: *marketing expenditures, marketing mix, marketing effectiveness,* and *marketing elasticity.* Although this would seem to be a great deal, the expression could be further refined (we shall not do so here) to take into account (1) *marketing allocation to territories,* (2) *carry-over effects of past marketing expenditures,* and (3) *synergistic effects of marketing decision variables.*[5]

Company forecast

Company demand describes estimated company sales at alternative levels of company marketing effort. It remains for management to choose one of the levels.[6] The chosen level of marketing effort implies a particular level of sales, which may be called the company sales forecast:

> The *company sales forecast* is the expected level of company sales based on a chosen marketing plan and assumed marketing environment.

The company sales forecast is represented graphically in the same way as the market forecast was in Figure 6-3(a); substitute company sales for the vertical axis and company marketing effort for the horizontal axis.

Too often the sequential relationship between the company forecast and the company marketing plan is confused. One frequently hears that the company should plan its marketing effort on the basis of its sales forecast. The forecast-to-plan sequence is valid if "forecast" means an estimate of national economic activity or if market demand is nonexpansible. The sequence is not valid, however, where market demand is expansible, nor where "forecast" means an estimate of company sales. The company sales forecast does not establish a basis for deciding on the amount and composition of marketing effort; quite the contrary, it is the *result* of an assumed blueprint for marketing action. The sales forecast must be viewed as a dependent variable that is affected, among other things, by the planned marketing activity of the firm.

Two other concepts are worth mentioning in relation to the company forecast.

> A *sales quota* is defined as the sales goal set for a product line, company division, or company agent. It is primarily a managerial device for defining and stimulating sales effort.

The sales quota set by management is arrived at through a joint consideration of the company forecast and the psychology of stimulating its achievement.

---

[5]For further development, see the author's *Marketing Decision Making: A Model-Building Approach* (New York: Holt, Rinehart & Winston, Inc., 1971).

[6]The theory of choosing the best level of marketing effort is described in Chapter 8, pp. 170–72.

The latter consideration generally leads to setting sales quotas that total to a slightly higher figure than the estimated sales forecast.

The other concept is a *sales budget.*

> A *sales budget* is defined as a conservative estimate of the expected volume of sales and is used primarily for making current purchasing, production, and cash-flow decisions.

The sales budget is arrived at through a joint consideration of the sales forecast and of the need to avoid excessive investment in case the forecast is not realized. The latter consideration generally leads to setting a sales budget slightly lower than the company forecast.

Company potential

Company sales potential is *the limit approached by company demand as company marketing effort increases relative to competitors.* The absolute limit of company demand is, of course, the market potential. The two would be equal if the company achieved 100 percent of the market—that is, if the company became a monopolist. In most cases, company sales potential is less than market potential, even when company marketing expenditures increase considerably over those of competitors. The reason is that each competitor has a hard core of loyal buyers who are not very responsive to other companies' efforts to woo them away.

METHODS OF ESTIMATING CURRENT DEMAND

We are now ready to consider practical methods of estimating current demand. There are two types of current demand estimates in which a seller might be interested: total market potential and territorial potential. Total market potential is of interest whenever a seller is facing a decision to introduce a new product or drop an existing one. He wants to know whether the market is sufficient in total size to justify the product.

One method of estimating market potential is known as the *chain ratio method.* Suppose a brewery is interested in estimating the market potential for a new dietetic beer. An initial estimate can be made by the following calculation:[7]

$$\text{Demand for the new dietetic beer} = \left\{ \begin{array}{l} \text{Population} \times \text{personal discretionary income per capita} \\ \times \text{ average percentage of discretionary income spent on} \\ \text{food} \times \text{ average percentage of amount spent on food} \\ \text{that is spent on beverages} \times \text{average percentage of amount} \\ \text{spent on beverages that is spent on alcoholic beverages} \\ \times \text{ average percentage of amount spent on alcoholic beverages that is spent on beer} \times \text{expected percentage of} \\ \text{amount spent on beer that will be spent on dietetic beer.} \end{array} \right.$$

Other methods of estimating total demand are discussed in subsequent sections.

[7]See Russell L. Ackoff, *A Concept of Corporate Planning* (New York: Wiley-Interscience, 1970), pp. 36–37.

All companies are concerned with (1) selecting the markets to sell in, (2) allocating their marketing budget optimally among these markets, and (3) evaluating their performance in the different markets. The basis for these decisions lies in competent estimation of the market potential of different territories. Two major methods are available. The first, or *market-buildup method*, is used primarily by industrial-goods firms. The second, or *index-of-buying-power method*, is used mainly by consumer-goods firms.

Market-buildup method The market-buildup method calls for identifying all the potential buyers for the product in each market and adding up the estimated potential purchases of each. The market-buildup method is straightforward if one has available a list of all potential buyers *and* a good estimate of what each will buy. Unfortunately, one if not both is usually lacking.

Consider the market-measurement problem faced by a machine tool manufacturer. Suppose he wants to estimate territorial market potentials for one of his machines, a medium-size wood lathe. Let us focus on one of his markets, the Greater Boston area.

The first step is to identify all potential buyers of lathes in the Boston area. Household buyers can be excluded, because the lathe is too large for home-workshop purchase. The lathe is of no purchase interest to many other types of buyers, such as hospitals, retailers, and farmers. The market for this lathe is found primarily in manufacturing establishments. Even here, the lathe is of interest only to manufacturing establishments that have to shape or ream wood as part of their operation.

The company could go through a directory of all manufacturing establishments in the greater Boston area and list those that might do woodwork. Then it might estimate the number of lathes each might purchase, based on some ratio of the number of lathes per thousand employees or the number of lathes per $1 million of sales. This would be an arduous task, especially considering that the task would have to be repeated for every other market.

A more efficient method of estimating territorial market potentials makes use of the Standard Industrial Classification System (S.I.C.) The system was developed by the federal government in connection with taking its Census of Manufacturers. The classification is based on the *product produced* or *operation performed*. The S.I.C. System classifies all manufacturing into twenty major industry groups, each having a two-digit code. Thus, #25 is Furniture and Fixtures and #35 is Machinery, except electrical. Each major industry group is further subdivided into about 150 industry groups designated by a three-digit code (#251 is household furniture and #252 is office furniture). Each industry is further subdivided into approximately 450 product categories designated by a four-digit code (#2521 is wood office furniture and #2522 is metal office furniture).

For each four-digit S.I.C. number, the Census of Manufacturers provides the number of establishments subclassified by location, number of employees, annual sales, and net worth.

To use the S.I.C. System, the lathe manufacturer first must determine the four-digit S.I.C. codes that represent products whose manufacture is likely to require lathe machines. For example, lathes will be used by manufacturers in S.I.C. #2511 (wood household furniture), #2521 (wood office furniture), and so on. To get a full picture of all four-digit S.I.C. industries that might use lathes, he can use three methods. (1)He can look at his past sales and determine the S.I.C. codes of his past customers. (2)He can go through the S.I.C. manual and check off all the four-digit industries that his judgment leads him to believe would have an interest in lathes. (3)He can mail questionnaires to a wide range of companies to inquire about their interest in wood lathes.

Once the lathe manufacturer identifies the S.I.C. classifications relevant to his product, his next step is to determine an appropriate base for estimating the likely number of lathes that will be used in each industry. Suppose his experience leads him to believe that the customer industry sales are the most appropriate base. For example, in S.I.C. #2511, ten lathes may be used for every $1 million worth of sales; in S.I.C. #2521, five lathes for every $1 million sales. Once the lathe manufacturer is able to establish the rate of lathe ownership relative to the customer industry's sales (or number of employees, net worth, or whatever), he can turn to the Census of Manufacturers data and compute the market potential.

Table 6-1 shows a hypothetical computation for the Boston area involving two S.I.C. codes. In #2511 (wood household furniture) there are six establishments with annual sales of $1 million and two establishments with annual sales of $5 million. Furthermore, it is estimated that ten lathes can be sold in this S.I.C. code per every $1 million customer sales. Since there are six establishments with annual sales of $1 million, they account for $6 million of sales, which is a potential of 60 lathes (6 × 10). The other figures in the table are similarly computed. Adding up the estimated sales for each S.I.C. code, it appears that there is a market potential for 200 lathes in the Greater Boston area.

In a similar way, the company can estimate the market potential for every other territory in the country. Suppose the market potentials for all the markets sum to two thousand lathes. In this case the company concludes that the Boston market contains 10 percent of the total market potential. Without further qualification, this might warrant the company's investing 10 percent of its marketing effort (sales force, advertising, and so on) in the Boston market. In practice, the lathe manufacturer should determine additional things about each market, such as the extent of market saturation, the number of competi-

Table 6-1

**Market-buildup method using S.I.C. codes
(hypothetical lathe manufacturer—Boston area)**

S.I.C.	1 Annual sales (in millions $)	2 Number of establishments	3 Potential number of lathe sales per $1 million customer sales	4 Market potential (1 × 2 × 3)
2511	$1	6	10	60
	$5	2	10	100
2521	$1	3	5	15
	$5	1	5	25
				200

tors, and the market growth rate, before actually deciding on the amount of resources to allocate to each market.

Index-of-buying-power method   Consumer companies also face the problem of estimating territorial market potentials. Because their final customers are typically so numerous, they cannot list every potential customer and estimate his buying requirements. Nor is there such a thing as a Standard Household Classification that classifies households by types and provides the number of households of each type in each location. Therefore, the company that sells to household buyers has to resort to a different solution.

The method most commonly used is a straightforward *index method.* Suppose our manufacturer is a drug company. He may make the assumption that the market potential for drugs is directly related to a single factor, such as population. For example, if the state of Virginia has 2.28 percent of the U.S. population, the company might readily assume that Virginia would be a market for 2.28 percent of total drugs sold.

A single factor, however, is rarely a complete indicator of sales opportunity. Obviously, regional drug sales are also influenced by such factors as per capita income and the number of physicians per, say, ten thousand people. This leads to the desirability of developing a multiple-factor index, each factor being assigned a specific weight in the index.

One of the best-known, general-purpose, multiple-factor indices of area demand is published in the "Annual Survey of Buying Power" of *Sales Management* magazine. The index purports to reflect the relative buying power in the different counties and cities of the nation. *Sales Management's* index of the relative buying power of an area is given by

$$B_i = .5y_i + .3r_i + .2p_i \tag{6-6}$$

where:

B_i = percentage of total national buying power found in area i
y_i = percentage of national disposable personal income originating in area i
r_i = percentage of national retail sales in area i
p_i = percentage of national population located in area i

For example, suppose Virginia has 2.00 percent of the U.S. disposable personal income, 1.96 percent of U.S. retail sales, and 2.28 percent of U.S. population. The buying-power index for Virginia would be:

$$.5(2.00) + .3(1.96) + .2(2.28) = 2.04$$

That is, 2.04 percent of the nation's drug sales might be expected to take place in Virginia. *Sales Management* holds that these weights reflect market potential for many consumer goods that are neither low-priced staples nor high-valued luxury goods. The weights, however, are not validated, and certainly vary in appropriateness for different products. Multiple regression has been used at times to find index weights.

It should be understood that area market-potential estimates, no matter how developed, reflect relative industry opportunities rather than relative company opportunities. The individual company would have to adjust the market-potential estimates by factors left out of the index. The firm must consider the intensity of competition and its own facilities and competitive advantages in each market in developing its marketing targets and marketing plans.

METHODS OF ESTIMATING FUTURE DEMAND

We are now ready to examine the problem of forecasting the future demand for a product. Very few products or services lend themselves to easy forecasting. The few cases generally involve a product whose absolute level or trend is fairly constant and where competitive relations are nonexistent (public utilities) or stable (pure oligopolies). In the vast majority of markets, market demand and especially company demand are not stable from one year to the next, and good forecasting becomes a central factor in company success. The more unstable the demand, the more important is forecast accuracy and the more elaborate is forecasting procedure.

Forecasting methods range from the crude to the highly sophisticated. Many technical aspects fall in the province of experts. Yet there are compelling reasons for marketing management to possess some familiarity with the major alternative forecasting methods. This familiarity is necessary in order to understand the limitations of the current methods as well as whether better methods are available. Furthermore, forecasting is influenced by marketing planning, requiring a continuous dialogue between marketing management and company forecasters. This dialogue is aided considerably when marketing management understands the basic forecasting techniques.

Six major methods of forecasting demand are discussed below.[8] The proliferation of forecasting methods should not be surprising, given the diversity of products, the variations in the availability, reliability, and types of information, and the variety of forecast objectives. Although six methods are discussed, there are actually only three information bases for building a forecast. The investigator can build his forecast on the basis of *what people say, what people do,* or *what people have done.*

The first basis—*what people say*—involves systematic determination of the opinions of buyers or of those close to them, such as salesmen or outside experts. It encompasses three methods: (1) surveys of buyer intentions, (2) composites of sales-force opinions, and (3) expert opinion. Building a forecast on *what people do* involves another method: (4) putting the product to a market test to provide indications of future buyer response. The final basis—*what people have done*—involves analyzing, with mathematical and statistical tools, records of past buying behavior, using either (5) time-series analysis or (6) statistical demand analysis.

Surveys of buyer intentions

Forecasting is essentially the art of anticipating what buyers are likely to do under a given set of conditions. This immediately suggests that a most useful source of information would be the buyers themselves. Ideally, a list of all potential buyers would be drawn up; each buyer would be approached, preferably

[8]For other classifications and discussions of forecasting methods, see *Forecasting Sales,* National Industrial Conference Board, Business Policy Study No. 106, 1963; and Harry Deane Wolfe, *Business Forecasting Methods* (New York: Holt, Rinehart & Winston, Inc., 1966).

on a face-to-face basis, and asked how much he plans to buy of the stated product in the defined future time period under stated conditions. He would also be asked to state what proportion of his total requirements he intends to buy from the particular firm—or at least what factors would influence his choice among suppliers. With this information, the firm would have an ideal basis for forecasting its sales.

Unfortunately, this method has a number of limitations in practice. Let us accept for the moment that the buyers could be identified and could and would convey valid information about their intentions. Would the value of this information be worth the cost of gathering it? In the case of consumer convenience goods, such as soda beverages, it would be prohibitively expensive to pay a personal call on every buyer. This objection is answered in part by taking a probability sample instead of a census. The cost can also be reduced by substituting telephone or mail interviewing for personal interviewing.

Would the buyers freely report their intentions? In many situations buyers would not confide their buying intentions. A Defense Department official would not reveal how many atomic weapons will be purchased.

The value of this method would depend ultimately on the extent to which the buyers have clearly formulated intentions and then carry them out. The two areas where buyer-intention surveys have proved to be of some value are major consumer durable goods and industrial goods.

In regard to *major consumer durables,* such as automobiles, new housing, furniture, and appliances, several sampling services regularly produce reports on consumer buying intentions.[9] They ask some form of the question whether the consumer intends to buy within a stated period each of several different durables. In the past the question was usually worded:

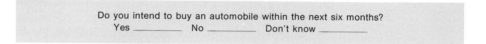

Do you intend to buy an automobile within the next six months?
Yes _____ No _____ Don't know _____

While the proportion of automobile buyers tended to be higher for those reporting a purchase intention than those who did not, the forecasting performance was far from satisfactory. It was believed that two problems were associated with the simple intention-to-buy (0, 1) scale: (1) some consumers who said they didn't intend to buy had a finite, though small, probability of buying, and (2) the "don't know" category had too many responses. Juster suggested the use of a *purchase-probability scale,* such as

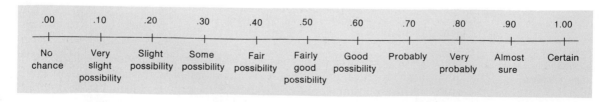

[9]The consumer pollsters include the Survey Research Center at the University of Michigan, Sindlinger & Company of Norwood, Pa., The Conference Board, Inc., and the Commercial Credit Corporation. For a discussion, see "How Good Are Consumer Pollsters?" *Business Week,* November 9, 1969, pp. 108–10.

Juster showed, on the basis of a random sampling of eight hundred households, that the purchase-probability approach explained approximately twice the actual purchase variance for automobiles as the intention-to-buy approach.[10] In addition to this improvement of the basic question, the various surveys also inquire into the consumer's present and future personal finances, and his expectations about the economy. The various bits of information are combined into a *consumer sentiment measure* (Survey Research Center) or a *consumer confidence measure* (Sindlinger). Consumer durable-goods producers subscribe to these indices in the hope of learning in advance of major shifts in consumer buying intentions so that they can adjust their production and marketing plans accordingly. These surveys of consumer buying intentions have proved useful, though not completely accurate, for short-range consumer-durable sales forecasting.

In the realm of *industrial buying*, intention surveys regarding plant, equipment, and materials have been carried out by various agencies. The two best-known capital-expenditures surveys are the one conducted by the U.S. Department of Commerce in collaboration with the Securities and Exchange Commission and the one conducted annually in the late fall by McGraw-Hill through its publication *Business Week*. Most of the estimates have been within a 10 percent error band of the actual outcomes. This is a good record, considering that the business investment component of national income is highly variable.

Various industrial firms find it useful to carry on their own survey of customer buying intentions:

> National Lead's marketing research personnel periodically visit a carefully selected sample of one hundred companies and interview the manufacturer's technical research director, sales manager, and purchasing director, in that order. The technical research director is asked about the rate of incorporation of titanium in the manufacturer's various products; the sales manager is questioned about the sales outlook for the company's products that incorporate titanium; and the purchasing director is queried about the total amount of titanium his company plans to purchase in relation to past purchases. On the basis of these interviews and supplementary information, National's marketing research department estimates the market demand for titanium and prepares a "most favorable" forecast and a "least favorable" forecast.[11] There are also indirect benefits. National Lead's analysts learn of new developments and modes of thinking that would not be apparent through published information. Their visits also promote National's image as a company that is concerned about buyers' needs. Another advantage of this method is that it yields subestimates for various industries and territories in the process of building an aggregate estimate.

In summary, the appropriateness of the buyers'-intentions survey method increases to the extent that (1) the buyers are few, (2) the cost of effectively reaching them is small, (3) they have clear intentions, (4) they follow out their original intentions, and (5) they are willing to disclose their intentions. As a result, it is of value for industrial products, for consumer durables, for product purchases where advanced planning is required, and for new products where past data do not exist.

---

[10]F. Thomas Juster, *Consumer Buying Intentions and Purchase Probability, An Experiment in Survey Design*, National Bureau of Economic Research, Occasional Paper No. 99 (New York: Columbia University Press, 1966).

[11]Adapted from *Forecasting Sales*, pp. 31–32.

Where it is impractical to make direct buyer inquiries, the company may decide to ask its salesmen for estimates. An example is the Pennsalt Chemicals Corporation:

> In August, the field sales personnel are provided with tabulating cards to prepare their sales forecasts for the coming year. Individual cards are prepared for each product sold to each major customer, showing the quantity shipped to the customer in the previous six months. Each card also provides space in which the field salesmen post their forecasts for the coming year. Additional tab cards are also supplied for those customers who were not sold in the current six-month period but who were customers in the prior year; and finally, blank cards are provided for submitting forecasts of sales to new customers. Salesmen fill in their forecasts (on the basis of current prices) using their own informed judgment; in some divisions, they are also in a position to substantiate their forecasts by obtaining purchase estimates from their customers.[12]

Few companies use their salesmen's estimates without some adjustments. In the first place, salesmen can be biased observers. A salesman may be congenitally pessimistic or optimistic, or he may go to one extreme or another because of a recent sales setback or success. Furthermore, he is often unaware of larger economic developments and of company marketing plans that will shape future sales in his territory. He may understate demand so that the company will set a low sales quota. He may not have the time or concern to prepare careful estimates.

In the light of these contaminating factors, why are salesmen's estimates used at all? There is the possibility that the over-and-under errors may cancel out, leaving a good aggregate forecast. Or a consistent bias in the forecast of individual salesmen may be recognized and a correction made for each salesman before aggregating their sales forecasts.

The company may supply certain aids or incentives to the salesmen to encourage better estimating. Each salesman may receive a record of his past forecast compared with his actual sales, and also a set of company assumptions on the business outlook. Some companies will summarize individual forecasting records and distribute them to all salesmen. A tendency for salesmen to produce ultraconservative estimates to keep down their sales quota can be countered by basing territorial advertising and promotional expenditures on the salesmen's estimates.

Assuming these biasing tendencies can be countered, a number of benefits can be gained by involving the sales force in forecasting. Being closest to the customers, salesmen may have more knowledge or better insight into developing trends than any other single group. This is especially likely where the product is fairly technical and subject to a changing technology. Second, because of their participation in the forecasting process, the salesmen may have greater confidence in the derived sales quotas, and this may increase their incentive to achieve them. Finally, a "grass roots" forecasting procedure results in estimates broken down by product, territory, customer, and salesman.

In summary, the appropriateness of the composite of sales-force opinion method increases to the extent that (1) the salesmen are likely to be the most

---

[12]*Ibid.*, p. 25.

knowledgeable source of information, (2) the salesmen are cooperative, (3) the salesmen are unbiased or their biases can be corrected, and (4) there are some side benefits from the salesmen's participation in the procedure.

Expert opinion

Another method of forecasting involves tapping the opinion of well-informed persons other than buyers or company salesmen, such as distributors or outside experts.

The automobile companies solicit estimates of sales directly from their dealers. These estimates are subject to the same strengths and weaknesses as salesmen estimates; like salesmen, distributors may not give the necessary attention to careful estimating; their perspective concerning future business conditions may be too narrow; and they may supply biased estimates to gain some immediate advantage.

Firms also tap outside experts for assessments of future demand. This happens when a firm uses or buys general economic forecasts or special industry forecasts prepared outside of the firm. This also happens when the firm convenes a set of experts to estimate a probabilistic event, such as a new technology or a change in business conditions. There are at least three ways to extract the collective wisdom of a group of experts. They may meet as a committee and come up with a group estimate (*group discussion method*). They may supply their separate estimates to a project leader who merges them into a single estimate (*pooled individual estimates method*). They may supply individual estimates and assumptions that are reviewed by the project leader, revised, and followed by a second round of individual estimation, a third round, and so forth (*Delphi method*). The third method is becoming increasingly popular for developing market and new-product estimates.[13]

An interesting variant of the expert opinion method is used by Lockheed Aircraft Corporation. A group of Lockheed executives pose as different major customers; in a hardheaded way they evaluate Lockheed's offering in relation to its competitors' offerings. A decision on what and where to buy is made for each customer. The purchases from Lockheed are totaled and reconciled with an independent statistical forecast to become Lockheed's sales forecast.

The use of expert opinion has the following advantages: (1) forecasts can be made relatively quickly and inexpensively, (2) different points of view are brought out and balanced in the process, and (3) there may be no alternative if basic data are sparse or lacking. The main disadvantages are: (1) opinions are generally less satisfactory than hard facts, (2) responsibility is dispersed, and good and bad estimates are given equal weight, and (3) the method usually is more reliable for aggregate forecasting than for developing reliable breakdowns by territory, customer group, or product.

Market-test method

The usefulness of opinions, whether those of buyers, salesmen, or other experts, depends upon the cost, availability, and reliability of this type of information. In cases where buyers do not plan their purchases carefully or are very erratic in carrying out their intentions or where experts are not very good guessers, a more direct market test of likely behavior is desirable. A direct market test is especially desirable in forecasting the sales of a new product or the likely sales

---

[13]See Roger J. Best, "An Experiment in Delphi Estimation in Marketing Decision Making," *Journal of Marketing Research*, November 1974, pp. 447–52.

of an established product in a new channel of distribution or territory. Where a short-run forecast of likely buyer response is desired, a small-scale market test is usually an ideal answer.[14]

Time-series analysis

As an alternative to costly surveys or market tests, some firms prepare their forecasts on the basis of a statistical-mathematical analysis of past data. The underlying logic is that past data are an expression of enduring causal relations that can be uncovered through quantitative analysis. They can be used to predict future sales. Thus forecasting becomes an exercise in adroit backcasting.

A time series of past sales of a product can be analyzed into four major temporal components.

The first component, *trend* (T), is the result of basic developments in population, capital formation, and technology. If the trend turns out to be statistically significant—that is, if it has enough consistency to dispel the notion that it is a random artifact—then it becomes central in the preparation of a long-range forecast.

The second component, *cycle* (C), is seen in the wavelike movement of sales. Properly speaking, a cycle exists when the time series shows an undulation of a fairly constant amplitude and periodicity. Few if any business series exhibit pure cyclical behavior in this sense. Some, such as housing construction, hog sales, and pig-iron sales, exhibit approximate cyclical behavior. Many sales series are affected by swings in the level of general economic activity, which tends to be somewhat periodic. Isolation of the cyclical component can be useful in intermediate-range forecasting.[15]

The third component, *season* (S), refers to a consistent pattern of sales movements within the year. Although the term "season" suggests a distinct quarterly pattern induced by changes in the weather, it is used more broadly to describe any recurrent hourly, weekly, monthly, or quarterly sales pattern. The seasonal component may be related to weather factors, holidays, and/or trade customs. The seasonal pattern provides the investigator with a norm for forecasting short-range sales.

The fourth component, *erratic events* (E), includes strikes, blizzards, fads, riots, fires, war scares, price wars, and other disturbances. These erratic components have the effect of obscuring the more systematic components, and the problem becomes one of starting with the original "noisy" time series and separating the underlying systematic forces from the erratic.

Classical time-series analysis involves procedures for decomposing the original sales series (Y) into the components, T, C, S, and E. According to one model, these components interact linearly—that is, $Y = T + C + S + E$; according to another model, they interact multiplicatively—that is, $Y = T \times C \times S \times E$. The multiplicative model makes the more realistic assumption that the seasonal and cyclical effects are proportional to the trend level of sales. T is stated in absolute values and C, S, and E are stated as percentages.

---

[14]Test marketing is discussed in Chapter 10, pp. 218–220.

[15]The most careful methodology for isolating and studying cyclical movements is that developed by the National Bureau of Economic Research. Arthur F. Burns and Wesley C. Mitchell, *Measuring Business Cycles* (New York: National Bureau of Economic Research, 1946).

This is not the place to describe the methodology for decomposing a time series. The procedures are outlined in elementary business statistics textbooks.[16] The main caution is against mechanical extrapolation. The forecast is not simply a matter of putting together systematic components, but rather a creative and further act in itself. The systematic forces underlying past sales may not remain unchanged. Any one of the three components can take on a different form starting tomorrow; the past trend can be altered by the appearance of a competitive product; the cyclical pattern can be altered by new countercyclical government policies; the seasonal pattern can be altered by new counterseasonal company policies. A mechanical extrapolation ignores marketing plans, the effect of which has to be built into the final forecast. The impact of possible erratic forces can be conveyed by preparing an optimistic, pessimistic, and most likely forecast. The size of the forecast error band conveys to management a sense of how much confidence it can repose in the most likely forecast.

For a company with hundreds of items in its product line that wants to produce efficient and economical short-run forecasts, a newer time-series technique called *exponential smoothing* is available. In its simplest form, exponential smoothing requires only three pieces of information: this period's actual sales, Q_t; this period's smoothed sales, $\overline{Q}_t$; and a smoothing parameter, a. The sales forecast for next period's sales is given by

$$\overline{Q}_{t+1} = aQ_t + (1 - a)\overline{Q}_t \qquad (6\text{-}7)$$

where:

$\overline{Q}_{t+1}$ = sales forecast for next period
a = the smoothing constant, where $0 \le a \le 1$
Q_t = current sales
$\overline{Q}_t$ = smoothed sales

Suppose the smoothing constant is .4, current sales are \$50,000, and smoothed sales are \$40,000. Then the sales forecast is

$$\overline{Q}_{t+1} = .4(\$50,000) + .6(\$40,000) = \$44,000$$

In other words, the sales forecast is always between (or at an extreme of) current sales and smoothed sales. The relative influence of current and smoothed sales depends on the smoothing constant, here .4. Thus the sales forecast "tracks" actual sales.

For each of its products, the company determines an initial level of smoothed sales and a smoothing constant. The initial level of smoothed sales can be simply average sales for the last few periods. The smoothing constant,

---

[16]See F. E. Croxton and D. J. Cowden, *Practical Business Statistics*, 3rd ed. (Englewood Cliffs, N.J.: Prentice-Hall, Inc., 1960), Chaps. 28–31. For computer programs, see Julius Shiskin, *Electronic Computers and Business Indicators* (New York: National Bureau of Economic Research, 1957). For an application, see Robert L. McLaughlin, "The Breakthrough in Sales Forecasting," *Journal of Marketing*, April 1963, pp. 46–54.

on the other hand, is derived by trial-and-error testing of different smoothing constants between zero and one to find the one that produces the best fit of past sales. The method can be refined to reflect seasonal and trend factors by adding two more constants.[17]

Statistical demand analysis

Time-series analysis treats past and future sales as a function of time, rather than of any real demand factors. Its main use is in markets where the underlying demand factors remain stable over time. Where this is not the case, it is much more desirable to try to discover the direct relationship between sales and real demand factors.

Numerous real factors, of course, affect the sales of any product. Statistical demand analysis is an attempt not to derive a complete set of factors but rather to discover the most important factors in the hope that they will explain a significant amount of the variations in sales. The factors most commonly analyzed are prices, income, population, and promotion.

The procedure consists of expressing sales (Y) as a dependent variable and trying to explain sales variation as a result of variation in a number of independent demand variables $X_1, X_2, \ldots, X_n$; that is,

$$Y = f(X_1, X_2, \ldots, X_n) \qquad (6\text{-}8)$$

For example, Palda found that the following demand equation gave a fairly good fit to the historical sales of Lydia Pinkham's Vegetable Compound between the years 1908 and 1960:[18]

$$Y = -3649 + .665X_1 + 1180 \log X_2 + 774X_3 + 32X_4 - 2.83X_5$$

where:

Y = yearly sales in thousands of dollars
X_1 = yearly sales (lagged one year) in thousands of dollars
X_2 = yearly advertising expenditures in thousands of dollars
X_3 = a dummy variable, taking on the value 1 between 1908–1925 and 0 from 1926 on
X_4 = year (1908 = 0, 1909 = 1, and so on)
X_5 = disposable personal income in billions of current dollars

The five independent variables on the right helped account for 94 percent of the yearly variation in the sale of Lydia Pinkham's Vegetable Compound between 1908 and 1960. To use it as a sales-forecasting equation for 1961, it would be necessary to insert figures for the five independent variables. Sales in 1960 should be put in X_1, the log of the company's planned advertising expenditures for 1961 should be put in X_2, 0 should be put in X_3, the numbered year corresponding to 1961 should be put in X_4, and estimated 1961 disposable personal income should be put in X_5. The result of multiplying these numbers by the

---

[17]See Peter R. Winters, "Forecasting Sales by Exponentially Weighted Moving Averages," *Management Science*, April 1960, pp. 324–42; or Robert G. Brown, *Smoothing Forecasting, and Prediction of Discrete Time Series* (Englewood Cliffs, N.J.: Prentice-Hall, Inc., 1963).

[18]Kristian S. Palda, *The Measurement of Cumulative Advertising Effects* (Englewood Cliffs, N.J.: Prentice-Hall, Inc., 1964), pp. 67–68.

respective coefficients and summing them gives a sales forecast (Y) for 1961.

Basically, demand equations are derived by trying to fit the "best" equation to historical or cross-sectional data. The coefficients of the equation are estimated according to the *least squares* criterion. According to this criterion, the best equation is one that *minimizes the sum of the squared deviations of the actual from the predicted observations.* The equation can be derived through the use of standard formulas. The closer the fit, the more useful the equation, all other things being equal.

With the advent of high-speed computers, statistical demand analysis is becoming an increasingly popular approach to forecasting. The user, however, should be wary of five problems that might diminish the validity or usefulness of any statistical demand equation: (1) too few observations, (2) too much correlation among the independent variables, (3) violation of normal distribution assumptions, (4) two-way causation, and (5) emergence of new factors not accounted for.[19]

SUMMARY

No firm can conduct its business successfully without trying to measure the actual size of markets, present and future. Quantitative measurements are essential for the analysis of market opportunity, the planning of marketing programs, and the control of marketing effort. The firm may make many measures of demand, varying in the level of product aggregation, the time dimension, and the space dimension. In all its studies, however, the company should be clear about its demand measurement concepts, particularly the distinction between market demand and company demand, and the corollary concepts of forecasts and potentials.

Current demand may be estimated for the market as a whole or for various territories. In the latter case, the market-buildup method is commonly used for industrial goods and the index of buying power is commonly used for consumer goods. For estimating future demand, the company may use one or any combination of at least six different forecasting methods: surveys of buyer intentions, sales-force estimates, expert opinions, market tests, time-series analysis, or statistical demand analysis. These methods vary in their appropriateness with the purpose of the forecast, the type of product, and the availability and reliability of data.[20]

QUESTIONS AND PROBLEMS

1 Two forecasters working for the same automobile manufacturer arrived at substantially different estimates of next year's demand. Does this variance imply that forecasting is largely guesswork?

2 A manufacturer of printing equipment makes estimates of sales by first asking the district sales managers for district forecasts. Describe how these initial forecasts may be refined at higher company levels to arrive at a final companywide forecast.

---

[19]For further discussion, see the author's *Marketing Decision Making: A Model-Building Approach* (New York: Holt, Rinehart & Winston, Inc., 1971), pp. 596–602.

[20]For further reading into contemporary methods of demand analysis, see G. David Hughes, *Demand Analysis for Marketing Decisions* (Homewood, Ill.: Richard D. Irwin, Inc., 1973).

3 A beverage company wants to use multiple regression to determine what factors explain state-to-state variations in the consumption of soft drinks. (a) What independent variables should be tested? (b) If the fitted regression equation "explains" most of the state-to-state variation in sales, does it follow that it is a good device for indicating relative market potential by state?

4 A manufacturer of women's hair products (home permanents, hair rinses, shampoos, etc.) wanted to determine the relative market potential for its products in each county of the United States. What three or four factors are most likely to belong in a weighted index of potential?

5 A marketing researcher sought a multiple regression equation to explain past sales in an industry. Good industry data on the dependent and independent variables only went back five years. He fitted the following equation:

$$Y = 5{,}241 + 31X_1 + 12X_2 + 50X_3$$

where:

Y = yearly sales in thousands of dollars
X_1 = U.S. disposable personal income in billions of dollars
X_2 = U.S. population in millions of households
X_3 = time, in years (1960 = 0)

He was pleased to find that this equation accounted for 98 percent of the yearly variations in industry sales. List any reservations you would have about using this equation in forecasting future industry sales.

6 A chemical company wants to estimate the demand for sulphur next year. One of the many uses of sulphur is the manufacture of sulphuric acid. One of the many end uses of sulphuric acid is its application in polishing new cars. Automaker C is a customer of this manufacturer. Suggest the ratios that have to be linked to go from automaker C's new car production to its impact on the company's sulphur sales.

7 Suppose a company's past sales are: 10, 12, 15, 12, 11, 13, 18, 20. The company forecaster uses an exponential smoothing equation with $a = .4$ and initial $\bar{Q}_t = 10$. Estimate the exponentially smoothed sales that would have been predicted for the third period on.

8 An automotive manufacturer is attempting to develop a sales forecast for next year. The company forecaster has estimated demand for six different environment-strategy combinations:

	Sales forecasts		
	High marketing budget	*Medium marketing budget*	*Low marketing budget*
Recession	15	12	10
Normal	20	16	14

He believes that there is a .20 probability of recession and an .80 probability of normal times. He also believes the probabilities of a low, medium, and high company marketing budget are .30, .50, and .20, respectively. How might he arrive at a single point forecast? What assumptions are being made?

PLANNING MARKETING PROGRAMS

7
MARKET SEGMENTATION AND TARGETING

Never follow the crowd.

BERNARD M. BARUCH

The analysis of market segments lies at the heart of marketing strategy. For marketing strategy involves two basic ideas. The first is the selection of *target markets*. This problem will be considered in this chapter. The second is the development of effective *marketing programs* to win these target markets. This will be considered in the following chapter.

RATIONALE FOR MARKET SEGMENTATION

Every organization must make a determination not only of *what* needs to serve but also *whose* needs. Most markets are too large for an organization to provide all the products and services needed by all the buyers in that market. Some delimitation of the market is necessary for the sake of efficiency and because of limited resources. This is the problem of *selecting target markets*.

Markets vary in their degree of heterogeneity. At one extreme, there are markets made up of buyers who are very similar in their wants, product requirements, and responses to marketing influences. For example, suppose all buyers of salt wanted to buy the same amount per month and wanted the simplest packaging and the lowest price. Such a market would be homogeneous, and selling to it would be fairly straightforward. The market offers of competitors would probably be very similar.

141

At the other extreme are markets made up of buyers seeking substantially different product qualities and/or quantities. For example, furniture buyers are looking for different styles, sizes, colors, materials, and prices. Such a market is heterogeneous. It is made up of customer groups with different buying needs and interests. These groups are called market segments.

In a heterogeneous market, the marketer has three targeting options:

1 He can introduce only one product, hoping to get as many people to want and buy it as possible. We call this *undifferentiated marketing*.
2 He can go after one particular market segment and develop the ideal product for them. We call this *concentrated marketing*.
3 He can introduce several product versions, each appealing to a different group. We call this *differentiated marketing*.

Thus the determination of market segments and the determination of market targets are separate questions. *Market segmentation* is the process of identifying groups of buyers with different buying desires or requirements. *Market targeting* is the firm's decision regarding which market segments to serve.

To illustrate, suppose a company wants to enter a particular market that seems attractive on the basis of demand measurement and forecasting. The company interviews a sample of consumers and asks them to state the attributes (such as quality, price, style, service) they consider important in buying the product. Suppose they name two attributes, X and Y. Each consumer is also asked to state where he would like his ideal or preferred brand to be on the two attributes. The resulting preferences can be plotted as points in product space. They will be distributed according to one of three basic patterns shown in Figure 7-1.

1 *Homogeneous preferences.* Figure 7-1A shows a market where all the consumers have roughly the same preference. The market shows no *natural segments,* at least as far as the two attributes are concerned. We would predict that existing brands would be similar and located in the center of the preferences.
2 *Diffused preferences.* At the other extreme, consumer preferences may be scattered fairly evenly throughout the space with no concentration (Figure 7-1B). Consumers simply differ a great deal in what they want from the product. If one brand exists in the market, it is likely to be positioned in the center because then it would appeal to the most people. A brand in the center minimizes the sum of total consumer dissatisfaction. If a competitor came into the market, he could

Figure 7-1
Basic market preference patterns

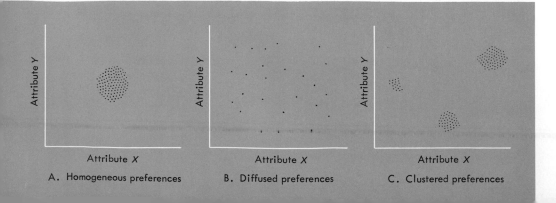

A. Homogeneous preferences   B. Diffused preferences   C. Clustered preferences

locate next to the first brand and engage in an all-out battle for market share. This is the typical situation in a political market where the two candidates both go middle-of-the-road to gain the greatest following. The other choice is for the competitor to locate in some corner to gain the real loyalty of a customer group that is not satisfied with the centered brand. If there are several brands in the market, they are likely to eventually position themselves fairly evenly throughout the space and show real differences to match consumer preference differences.

3 *Clustered preferences.* An intermediate possibility is the appearance of distinct preference clusters (Figure 7-1C). They may be called natural market segments. The first firm to enter this market has three options. (1) It might position itself in the center hoping to appeal to all the groups (undifferentiated marketing). (2) It might position itself in the largest market segment (concentrated marketing). (3) It might develop several brands, each positioned in a different segment (differentiated marketing). Clearly, if it developed only one brand, competition would come in and introduce brands in the other segments.

Thus when a company considers entering a market, it must carry out the following steps. First, it must determine those attributes along which to identify the possible existence of distinct market segments. Second, it must determine the size and value of the various market segments. Third, it must determine how the existing brands are positioned in the market. Fourth, it must look for opportunities consisting of market segments that are not being served or inadequately being served by existing brands. Fifth, it must determine correlated characteristics of attractive segments, such as their geographic, demographic, and psychographic characteristics, because they suggest efficient methods of access to these segments.

Requirements for effective segmentation

We still have to define attractive segments. The mere fact that a market segment is not being served, or is being served poorly, is not sufficient. Three additional conditions must be considered.

The first condition is *measurability,* the degree to which information exists or is obtainable on the particular buyer characteristic. Unfortunately, many suggestive characteristics are not susceptible to easy measurement. Thus it is hard to measure the respective number of automobile buyers who are motivated primarily by considerations of economy versus status versus quality.

The second condition is *accessibility,* the degree to which the firm can effectively focus its marketing efforts on chosen segments. This is not possible with all segmentation variables. It would be nice if advertising could be directed mainly to opinion leaders, but their media habits are not always distinct from those of opinion followers.

The third condition is *substantiality,* the degree to which the segments are large and/or profitable enough to be worth considering for separate marketing cultivation. A segment should be the smallest unit for which it is practical to tailor a separate marketing program. Segmental marketing is expensive, as we shall shortly see. It would not pay, for example, for an automobile manufacturer to develop special cars for midgets.

Benefits of segmentation

Segmentation is a relatively recent and revolutionary concept in marketing thinking. In earlier years many business firms saw the key to profits as being in the development of a single brand that was mass produced, mass distributed, and mass communicated. This would lead to the lowest costs and prices and hence create the largest potential market. The firm would not recognize preference variations and would try to get everyone in the market to want what it produced.

As competition intensified, prices dropped and sellers' earnings declined. Sellers did not have much control over price because of the similarity of their products. At this stage, some sellers began to recognize the potential value of *product differentiation*—that is, the introduction of differential features, quality, style, or image in their brands as a basis for commanding a premium. This led to a proliferation of sizes, models, options, and other characteristics. It is important to recognize, however, that the product variations were not based on an analysis of natural market segments.

Market segmentation, the most recent idea for guiding marketing strategy, starts not with distinguishing product possibilities, but rather with distinguishing customer groups. *Market segmentation is the subdividing of a market into distinct subsets of customers, where any subset may conceivably be selected as a market target to be reached with a distinct marketing mix.* The power of this concept is that in an age of intense competition for the mass market, individual sellers may prosper through developing brands for specific market segments whose needs are imperfectly satisfied by the mass-market offerings.

The seller who is alert to the needs of different market segments may gain in three ways. First, *he is in a better position to spot and compare marketing opportunities.* He can examine the needs of each segment against the current competitive offerings and determine the extent of current satisfaction. Segments with relatively low levels of satisfaction from current offerings may represent excellent marketing opportunities.

Second, *the seller can make finer adjustments of his product and marketing appeals.* Instead of one marketing program aimed to draw in all potential buyers (the "shotgun" approach), the seller can create separate marketing programs aimed to meet the needs of different buyers (the "rifle" approach).

Third, *the seller can develop marketing programs and budgets based on a clearer idea of the response characteristics of specific market segments.* He can allocate funds more efficiently to achieve the desired effects in different parts of the market.

BASES FOR SEGMENTING MARKETS

In our earlier illustration we used differences in buyer preferences or responses as the basis for market segmentation. This is a highly market-oriented basis for segmentation because it is addressed to differences in customer wants. There is still the question of access to any particular segment. Under the best circumstances, the buyer segment is distinguished not only by clear preferences but also by associated demographics and media habits. Thus if the people who want to buy large expensive automobiles are also those in the higher income and age brackets, their numbers, locations, and media habits can be more readily identified.

Under many circumstances, however, marketers divide markets into segments based directly on geographic, demographic, or psychographic variables. One company may decide to produce clothes for teenagers; another, for young adults. Age is used as the segmenting variable, although underlying age is difference in clothes preferences. Another company may decide to produce beer that will appeal to heavy drinkers. Product usage rate thus becomes the segmenting variable, although the company's success with the heavy-user market will depend on identifying some basic uniformities among heavy beer drinkers to which to appeal.

Good segmentation usually involves dividing the market by a succession of variables. Suppose an airline is interested in attracting nonflyers (segmentation variable: *user status*). Nonflyers consist of those who fear flying, those who are indifferent, and those who are positive toward flying (segmentation variable: *attitude*). Among those who feel positive are people with higher incomes and have the ability to afford flying (segmentation variable: *income*). The airline may decide to target those higher-income persons who are positive about flying but simply have not been sufficiently motivated to travel by air.

Table 7-1 lists most of the important variables used in segmenting consumer markets. Industrial markets are generally segmented according to such variables as end users, user needs, usage rate, marketing factor sensitivity, and geographical location. One must always be open to the possibility of finding new segmentation variables and combinations that will reveal fresh marketing opportunities.

Geographic segmentation

In geographic segmentation, the market is divided into different locations, such as nations, states, counties, cities, or neighborhoods. The organization recognizes that market potentials and costs vary with market location. It determines those geographical markets that it could serve best. Thus the Coors brewery until recently served primarily the Denver and surrounding market. The Smithsonian Institution in Washington recently decided to actively solicit members from all parts of the country, instead of only the Washington, D.C., area.

Demographic segmentation

In demographic segmentation, the market is subdivided into different parts on the basis of demographic variables such as age, sex, family size, income, occupation, education, family life cycle, religion, nationality, or social class. Demographic variables have long been the most popular bases for distinguishing significant groupings in the marketplace. One reason is that consumer wants or usage rates are often highly associated with demographic variables; another is that demographic variables are easier to measure than most other types of variables.

For example, a furniture manufacturer may be interested in segmenting his market. Suppose that the company's marketing research reveals three important demographic variables: age of head of household, size of family, and level of income. Figure 7-2 shows a joint segmentation of the market according to these variables. Each variable is subdivided into the number of levels deemed useful for analysis; the result is 36 (4 × 3 × 3) distinct segments. Every family belongs to one of these 36 segments. Having conceptualized the market in this way, management can proceed to determine the profit potential of each segment. This involves estimating for each segment the number of families, the average purchase rate, and the extent of competition. These pieces of information can be combined to estimate the value of each segment.

A seller must be careful in his use of demographics because their influence on consumer product interest does not always operate in the expected direction. For example, the Ford Motor Company used buyers' age in developing its

Table 7-1

Major segmentation variables and their typical breakdowns

Variables	Typical breakdowns
Geographic	
Region	Pacific, Mountain, West North Central, West South Central, East North Central, East South Central, South Atlantic, Middle Atlantic, New England
County size	A, B, C, D
City or SMSA size	Under 5,000, 5,000–19,999, 20,000–49,999, 50,000–99,999, 100,000–249,999; 250,000–499,999, 500,000–999,999, 1,000,000–3,999,999, 4,000,000 or over
Density	Urban, suburban, rural
Climate	Northern, southern
Demographic	
Age	Under 6, 6–11, 12–17, 18–34, 35–49, 50–64, 65+
Sex	Male, female
Family size	1–2, 3–4, 5+
Family life cycle	Young, single; young, married, no children; young, married, youngest child under six; young, married, youngest child six or over; older, married, with children; older, married, no children under 18; older, single; other
Income	Under $5,000, $5,000–$7,999, $8,000–$9,999, over $10,000
Occupation	Professional and technical; managers, officials and proprietors; clerical, sales; craftsmen, foremen; operatives; farmers; retired; students; housewives; unemployed
Education	Grade school or less; some high school; graduated high school; some college; graduated college
Religion	Catholic, Protestant, Jewish, other
Race	White, black, Oriental
Nationality	American, British, French, German, Eastern European, Scandinavian, Italian, Latin American, Middle Eastern, Japanese
Social class	Lower-lower, upper-lower, lower-middle, middle-middle, upper-middle, lower-upper, upper-upper
Psychographic	
Life-style	Swinger, status seeker, plain Joe
Personality	Compulsive, gregarious, authoritarian, ambitious
Benefits sought	Economy, convenience, prestige
User status	Nonuser, ex-user, potential user, first-time user, regular user
Usage rate	Light user, medium user, heavy user
Loyalty status	None; medium; strong; absolute
Readiness stage	Unaware, aware, informed, interested, desirous, intending to buy
Marketing-factor sensitivity	Quality, price, service, advertising, sales promotion

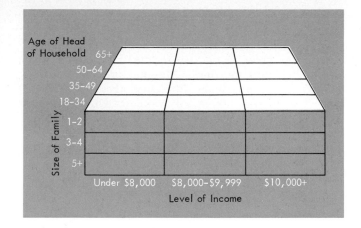

Figure 7-2
Segmentation of the furniture market by three demographic variables

target market for its Mustang automobile; the car was designed to appeal to young people who wanted an inexpensive sporty automobile. Ford found, to its surprise, that the car was being purchased by all age groups. It then realized that its target market was not the chronologically young but those who were psychologically young.

Income is another demographic variable that can be deceptive. One would think that working-class families would buy Chevrolets and managerial-class families would buy Cadillacs. Yet many Chevrolets are bought by middle-income people (often as a second car), and some Cadillacs are bought by working-class families (such as high-paid plumbers and carpenters). Expensive television sets and small boats often sell well to working-class families. Coleman suggested that a distinction should be drawn between the "underprivileged" segments and the "overprivileged" segments of each social class.[1] The cheapest, most economic cars are not bought by the really poor, but rather by "those who think of themselves as poor relative to their status aspirations and to their needs for a certain level of clothing, furniture, and housing which they could not afford if they bought a more expensive car." On the other hand, medium-priced and expensive cars tend to be purchased by the overprivileged segments of each social class.

Psychographic segmentation

The third category of segmentation variables is the psychographic. Psychographic variables tend to refer to the individual and such aspects as his life-style, personality, buying motives, and product knowledge and use. People within the same demographic group can exhibit vastly different traits.

Life-style   Life-style refers to the distinctive mode of orientation an individual or a group has toward consumption, work, and play. Such terms as hippies, swingers, straights, and jet-setters are all descriptive of different life-styles. Marketers are increasingly being drawn to life-style segmentation.[2] They

[1]Richard P. Coleman, "The Significance of Social Stratification in Selling," in *Marketing: A Maturing Discipline,* ed. Martin L. Bell (Chicago: American Marketing Association, 1961), pp. 171–84.

[2]See Mark Hanan, *Life-Styled Marketing* (New York: American Management Association, 1972).

are targeting versions of their products to life-style groups and studying new-product opportunities arising out of life-style analysis. Volkswagen, for example, is introducing life-styled automobiles: there will be a car for "the good citizen" emphasizing economy, safety, and ecology; and a car for the "car freak" empha-sizing handling, maneuverability, and sportiness. Manufacturers of women's clothing have followed Du Pont's advice to design different clothes for the "plain woman," the "fashionable woman," and the "manly woman." Cigarette com-panies develop brands for the "defiant smoker," the "casual smoker," and the "careful smoker." Companies making cosmetics, alcoholic beverages, and furniture are seeing increasing opportunities in life-style segmentation. At the same time, some companies have not found this variable to always work; for example, Nestlé introduced a special brand of decaffeinated coffee for "late nighters" and it failed.

Personality   Marketers have used personality variables to segment the market. They try to endow their products with *brand personalities* (brand image, brand concept) designed to appeal to corresponding *consumer personalities* (self-images, self-concepts). In the late fifties, Fords and Chevrolets were promoted as having different personalities. Ford buyers were thought to be "independent, impulsive, masculine, alert to change, and self-confident, while Chevrolet owners are conservative, thrifty, prestige-conscious, less masculine, and seeking to avoid extremes."[3] Evans investigated whether this was true by subjecting Ford and Chevrolet owners to the Edwards Personal Preference test, which measured needs for achievement, dominance, change, aggression, and so on. Except for a slightly higher score on dominance, Ford owners did not score significantly differently from Chevrolet owners, and Evans concluded that "the distributions of scores for all needs overlap to such an extent that [person-ality] discrimination is virtually impossible." Work subsequent to Evans on a wide variety of products and brands has occasionally turned up personality differences but more often has not. Westfall found some evidence of personality differences between the owners of convertibles and nonconvertibles, the former appearing to be more active, impulsive, and sociable.[4] Gottlieb found compul-sive people to be heavier users of aspirin.[5] Tucker and Painter found some statistically significant but weak personality correlations for nine products in their study.[6]

Benefits sought   Buyers are drawn to products with different buying motives. In the case of toothpaste, there are customers who seek decay preven-tion, bright teeth, good taste, or low price. An attempt is made to determine the demographic or psychographic characteristics associated with each benefit segment. Haley has characterized those seeking decay prevention as worriers, bright teeth as sociables, good taste as sensories, and low price as independents.[7]

---

[3]Quoted in Franklin B. Evans, "Psychological and Objective Factors in the Prediction of Brand Choice; Ford versus Chevrolet," *Journal of Business,* October 1959, pp. 340–69.

[4]Ralph Westfall, "Psychological Factors in Predicting Product Choice," *Journal of Marketing,* April 1962, pp. 34–40.

[5]Maurice J. Gottlieb, "Segmentation by Personality Types," in *Advancing Marketing Efficiency,* ed. Lynn H. Stockman (Chicago: American Marketing Association, 1959), p. 154.

[6]W. T. Tucker and John J. Painter, "Personality and Product Use," *Journal of Applied Psychology,* October 1961, pp. 325–29.

[7]Russell J. Haley, "Benefit Segmentation: A Decision-Oriented Research Tool," *Journal of Marketing,* July 1968, pp. 30–35.

Further characteristics of each group may be found, such as that consumers concerned with decay prevention have larger families and those interested in bright teeth are often tobacco users or single people. Media habits may even vary with each group. The company can choose the benefit it wants to emphasize, create a product that delivers it, and direct a message to the group seeking that benefit.

Choosing a benefit group to market to has some difficulties. First, it is usually difficult to estimate the size of different benefit groups in the total population. It depends on the ease with which persons can cite one benefit as dominating their interest in the product. Yankelovich found that people could do this with watches: as of 1962, "approximately 23 percent of the buyers bought [watches] for lowest price, another 46 percent bought for durability and general product quality, and 31 percent bought watches as symbols of some important occasion."[8] Second, the cited benefit might cover up something deeper; favoring the lowest-price watch may be a form of "sensibility snobbery." Finally, some buyers are interested in a particular benefit bundle rather than in a single benefit; this means the marketers may have to segment by benefit bundle groups.[9]

User status   Many markets can be segmented into nonusers, ex-users, potential users, first-time users, and regular users of a product. High-market-share companies such as Kodak (in the film market) are particularly interested in going after potential users, whereas a small film competitor will concentrate on trying to attract regular users to its brand. Potential users and regular users require different kinds of communication and marketing efforts. In the social marketing area, agencies such as antidrug agencies pay close attention to user status. They direct most of their effort at young people who might be potential users and try to immunize them from an interest in hard drugs. They sponsor rehabilitation programs to help regular users who want to quit their habit. They utilize ex-users to lend credibility to various programs.

Usage rate   Many markets can be segmented into light-, medium-, and heavy-user groups of the product (called volume segmentation). Heavy users may constitute only a small percentage of the numerical size of the market but a major percentage of the unit volume consumed. For example, 50 percent of the beer drinkers account for 88 percent of beer consumption.[10] Naturally, beer companies will want to go after the "heavy half" of the market, because every heavy drinker drinking their brand is worth several light drinkers. Unfortunately, when all the companies go after the same heavy drinkers, their campaigns look alike and cancel each other.

The hope is that the heavy users of a product have certain common demographics, personal characteristics, and media habits. One research company found that the "frequent beer drinker" earns less than $10,000 a year, is married (with two and a half children), and has simple manly tastes. He likes TV and

---

[8]See Daniel Yankelovich, "New Criteria for Market Segmentation," *Harvard Business Review,* March–April 1964, pp. 83–90, here p. 85.

[9]See Paul E. Green, Yoram Wind, and Arun K. Jain, "Benefit Bundle Analysis," *Journal of Advertising Research,* April 1972, pp. 31–36.

[10]See Dik Warren Twedt, "How Important to Marketing Strategy Is the 'Heavy User'?" *Journal of Marketing,* January 1964, pp. 71–72.

he likes to watch sports.[11] Profiles like this are obviously helpful to the marketer in developing pricing, message, and media strategies.

In the area of social marketing campaigns, agencies often face a heavy-user dilemma. The heavy users are often the most resistant to the selling proposition. A family-planning agency, for example, would normally target its marketing effort to those families who would have the most children; but these families are also the most resistant to birth control messages. The National Safety Council should target its marketing effort primarily to the unsafe drivers; but these drivers are also the most resistant to safe-driving appeals. The agencies must consider whether to use their limited budget to go after a few heavy users who are highly resistant or many light users who are less resistant.

Loyalty status   Loyalty status describes the amount of loyalty that users have to a particular object. The amount of loyalty can range from zero to absolute. We find buyers who are absolutely loyal to a brand (such as Budweiser beer), to an organization (such as the Republican party), to a place (such as New England), and so on.

Companies try to identify the characteristics of their hard-core loyals so that they can target their market effort to similar people in the population. Frank found some brand-loyal customers in the consumer-staples category but concluded that they "were not identifiable by socioeconomic or personality characteristics, did not have different average demand levels from nonloyal customers, and did not differ in sensitivity to promotion."[12] In this case, brand loyalty did not appear to be a useful basis for market segmentation.

Furthermore, the concept of brand loyalty has some ambiguities. What may appear to be brand loyalty may be explainable in other ways. Suppose a shopper purchased brand B on the last seven shopping occasions. The purchase pattern BBBBBBB would seem to reflect intrinsic preference for the product but may really reflect *habit, indifference,* a *lower price,* or the *nonavailability of substitutes.* The pattern BBBBAAA for another shopper would seem to indicate a switch in loyalty but may only reflect the fact that the store dropped brand B, or that she switched stores, or that she switched to brand A because of a price promotion. Marked brand continuity in brand-purchase sequences is not necessarily evidence that individual brand loyalty exists or is strong.

Stages of readiness   At any point of time, there is a distribution of people in various stages of readiness toward buying the product. Some members of the potential market are unaware of the product; some are aware; some are informed; some are interested; some are desirous; and some intend to buy. The particular distribution of people over stages of readiness makes a big difference in designing the marketing program. Suppose a health agency wants to attract women to take an annual Pap test to detect cervical cancer. At the beginning, most of the potential market is unaware of the concept. The marketing effort should go into high-reach advertising and publicity using a simple message. If successful, more of the market will be aware of the Pap test and the advertising should be changed to dramatizing the benefits of taking an annual examination

---

[11]See Norton Garfinkle, "A Marketing Approach to Media Selection," *Journal of Advertising Research,* December 1963, pp. 7–14.

[12]Ronald E. Frank, "Is Brand Loyalty a Useful Basis for Market Segmentation?" *Journal of Advertising Research,* June 1967, pp. 27–33, here pp. 27–28.

and the risks of not taking it, so as to move more people into a stage of desire. Facilities should also be readied for handling the large number of women who may be motivated to take the examination. In general, the marketing program must be adjusted to the changing distribution of readiness.

Marketing factors   Markets can often be segmented into groups responsive to different marketing factors such as price and price deals, product quality, and service. This information can help the company in allocating its marketing resources.[13] The marketing variables are usually proxies for particular benefits sought by buyers. A company that specializes in a certain marketing factor will build up hard-core loyals seeking that factor or benefit. Thus Avon, which sells cosmetics on a door-to-door basis, appeals to women who like a lot of personal service.

· · ·

The main conclusion from this discussion of market segmentation is that the seller may segment his market in many different ways. His goal is to determine the *most decisive mode of segmentation*—that is, the differences among buyers that may be the most consequential in choosing among them or marketing to them.

MARKET TARGETING

We mentioned earlier that a firm can choose one of three target market strategies in the face of market heterogeneity. Here we amplify on the respective rationale of these strategies.

Undifferentiated marketing

In undifferentiated marketing, the firm chooses not to recognize the different market segments making up the market. It treats the market as an aggregate, focusing on what is common in the needs of people rather than on what is different. It tries to design a product and a marketing program that appeal to the broadest number of buyers. It relies on mass channels, mass advertising media, and universal themes. It aims to endow the product with a superior image in people's minds, whether or not this is based on any real difference.[14] An excellent example of undifferentiated marketing is the Coca-Cola Company's earlier production of only one bottle-size drink in one taste to suit all.

Undifferentiated marketing is primarily defended on the grounds of cost economies. It is thought to be "the marketing counterpart to standardization and mass production in manufacturing."[15] The fact that the product line is kept narrow minimizes production, inventory, and transportation costs. The undifferentiated advertising program enables the firm to enjoy media discounts

---

[13]This approach is investigated in Henry J. Claycamp and William F. Massy, "A Theory of Market Segmentation," *Journal of Marketing Research,* November 1968, pp. 388–94. Also see Ronald Frank, William Massy, and Yoram Wind, *Market Segmentation* (Englewood Cliffs, N.J.: Prentice-Hall, Inc., 1972), Part IV.

[14]This strategy has also gone under other names, such as "product differentiation" or "market aggregation." See Wendell R. Smith, "Product Differentiation and Market Segmentation as Alternative Marketing Strategies," *Journal of Marketing,* July 1956, pp. 3–8; and Alan A. Roberts, "Applying the Strategy of Market Segmentation," *Business Horizons,* Fall 1961, pp. 65–72.

[15]Smith, *op. cit.,* p. 4.

through large usage. The absence of segmental marketing research and planning lowers the costs of marketing research and product management. On the whole, undifferentiated marketing results in keeping down several costs of doing business.

Nevertheless, an increasing number of marketers have expressed strong doubts about the optimality of this strategy. Gardner and Levy, for example, admitted that "some brands have very skillfully built up reputations of being suitable for a wide variety of people" but added:

> In most areas audience groupings will differ, if only because there are deviants who refuse to consume the same way other people do. . . . It is not easy for a brand to appeal to stable lower middle-class people and at the same time to be interesting to sophisticated, intellectual upper middle-class buyers. . . . It is rarely possible for a product or brand to be all things to all people.[16]

The firm practicing undifferentiated marketing typically develops a product and marketing program aimed at the largest segment of the market. When several firms in the industry do this, the result is hypercompetition for the largest segment(s) and undersatisfaction of the smaller ones. Thus the American auto industry for a long time produced only large automobiles, while foreign firms capitalized on the smaller segments. The "majority fallacy," as this has been called by Kuehn and Day, describes the fact that the larger segments may be less profitable because they attract disproportionately heavy competition.[17] The recognition of this fallacy has led many firms to reevaluate the opportunities latent in the smaller segments of the market.

Differentiated marketing

Under differentiated marketing, a firm decides to operate in two or more segments of the market but designs separate product and/or marketing programs for each. Thus General Motors tries to produce a car for every "purse, purpose, and personality." By offering product and marketing variations, it hopes to attain higher sales and a deeper position within each market segment. It hopes that a deep position in several segments will strengthen the customers' overall identification of the company with the product field. Furthermore, it hopes for greater loyalty and repeat purchasing, because the firm's offerings have been bent to the customer's desire rather than the other way around.

In recent years an increasing number of firms have moved toward a strategy of differentiated marketing. This is reflected in trends toward multiple product offerings and multiple trade channels and media. Coca-Cola now produces different drinks for different tastes; and International Harvester produces light, medium, and heavy trucks for different market segments.

The net effect of differentiated marketing is to create more total sales than undifferentiated marketing. "It is ordinarily demonstrable that total sales may be increased with a more diversified product line sold through more diversified channels."[18] However, it also tends to be true that differentiated marketing increases the costs of doing business. The following costs are likely to be higher:

---

[16]Burleigh Gardner and Sidney Levy, "The Product and the Brand," *Harvard Business Review*, March–April 1955, p. 37.

[17]Alfred A. Kuehn and Ralph L. Day, "Strategy of Product Quality," *Harvard Business Review*, November–December 1962, pp. 101–2.

[18]Roberts, *op. cit.*, p. 66.

Product modification costs. Modifying a product to meet different market segment requirements usually involves some R&D, engineering, and/or special tooling costs.

Production costs. Generally speaking, it is more expensive to produce *m* units each of *n* differentiated products than *mn* units of one product. This is especially true the longer the production setup time for each product and the smaller sales volume of each product. On the other hand, if each model is sold in sufficiently large volume, the higher costs of setup time may be quite small per unit.

Administrative costs. Under differentiated marketing, the company has to develop separate marketing plans for the separate segments of the market. This requires extra marketing research, forecasting, sales analysis, promotion, planning, and channel management.

Inventory costs. It is generally more costly to manage inventories of differentiated products than an inventory of only one product. The extra costs arise because more records must be kept and more auditing must be done. Furthermore, each product must be carried at a level that reflects basic demand plus a safety factor to cover unexpected variations in demand. The sum of the safety stocks for several products will exceed the safety stock required for one product. Thus carrying differentiated products leads to increased inventory costs.

Promotion costs. Differentiated marketing involves trying to reach different segments of the market through advertising media most appropriate to each case. This leads to lower usage rates of individual media and the consequent forfeiture of quantity discounts. Furthermore, since each segment may require separate creative advertising planning, promotion costs are increased.

Since differentiated marketing leads to higher sales and higher costs, nothing can be said a priori regarding the optimality of this strategy. Some firms are finding, in fact, that they have overdifferentiated their market offers. They would like to manage fewer brands, with each appealing to a broader customer group. Called "reverse line extension" or "broadening the base," they seek a larger volume for each brand. Johnson and Johnson, for example, managed to attract adults to use its baby shampoo. Blue Nun was launched as a white wine equally good for meat and fish courses.

Concentrated marketing   Both differentiated marketing and undifferentiated marketing imply that the firm goes after the whole market. However, many firms see a third possibility, one that is especially appealing when the company's resources are limited. Instead of going after a small share of a large market, the firm goes after a large share of one or a few submarkets. Put another way, instead of spreading itself thin in many parts of the market, it concentrates its forces to gain a good market position in a few areas.

Many examples of concentrated marketing can be cited. Volkswagen has concentrated on the small-car market; Bobbie Brooks, on women's junior sportswear; Gerber, on the baby market; Richard D. Irwin, on the economics and business texts market. Through concentrated marketing the firm achieves a strong market position in the particular segments it serves, owing to its greater knowledge of the segments' needs and the special reputation it acquires. Furthermore, it enjoys many operating economies because of specialization in production, distribution, and promotion. If the segment of the market is well chosen, the firm can earn high rates of return on its investment.

At the same time, concentrated marketing involves higher than normal risks. The particular market segment can suddenly turn sour; for example, when young women suddenly stopped buying sportswear and turned to knit dresses one year, it caused Bobbie Brooks's earnings to go deeply into the red. Or a competitor may decide to enter the same segment. For these reasons, many companies prefer to diversify in several market segments.

Selecting a market targeting strategy

Particular characteristics of the seller, the product, or the market serve to constrain and narrow the actual choice of a market targeting strategy.[19]

The first factor is *company resources*. Where the firm's resources are too limited to permit complete coverage of the market, its only realistic choice is concentrated marketing.

The second factor is *product homogeneity*. Undifferentiated marketing is more suited for homogeneous products such as grapefruit or steel. Products that are capable of great variation, such as cameras and automobiles, are more naturally suited to differentiation or concentration.

The third factor is *product stage in the life cycle*. When a firm introduces a new product into the marketplace it usually finds it practical to introduce one or, at the most, a few product versions. The firm's interest is to develop primary demand, and undifferentiated marketing seems the suitable strategy; or it might concentrate on a particular segment. In the mature stage of the product life cycle, firms tend to pursue a strategy of differentiated marketing.

The fourth factor is *market homogeneity*. If buyers have the same tastes, buy the same amounts per periods, and react in the same way to marketing stimuli, a strategy of undifferentiated marketing is appropriate.

The fifth factor is *competitive marketing strategies*. When competitors are practicing active segmentation, it is hard for a firm to compete through undifferentiated marketing. Conversely, when competitors are practicing undifferentiated marketing, a firm can gain by practicing active segmentation if some of the other factors favor it.

EVALUATING THE WORTH OF DIFFERENT MARKET SEGMENTS

The problem facing all firms that segment their market is how to estimate the value of operating in each of the segments. The firm that pursues differentiated marketing must know this in order to allocate its marketing effort over the various segments. The firm that pursues concentrated marketing must know this in order to decide which segments offer the best opportunities.

A useful analytical approach is illustrated in Figure 7-3.[20] The market is one for the mechanical line of a steel fabricating company. Stage 1 shows a segmentation of this market, using as two variables the customer-prospect mix and the product-service mix. The customer-prospect mix consists of contractors in the electrical, general, and plumbing line, respectively. The product-service mix consists of three products sold to these contractors: pipe hangers, concrete

---

[19]R. William Kotrba, "The Strategy Selection Chart," *Journal of Marketing*, July 1966, pp. 22–25.

[20]The approach was developed in William J. Crissy and Robert M. Kaplan, "Matrix Models for Marketing Planning," *Business Topics*, Summer 1963, pp. 48–66. The illustration was developed by Rhett W. Butler in an unpublished paper, Northwestern University, 1964.

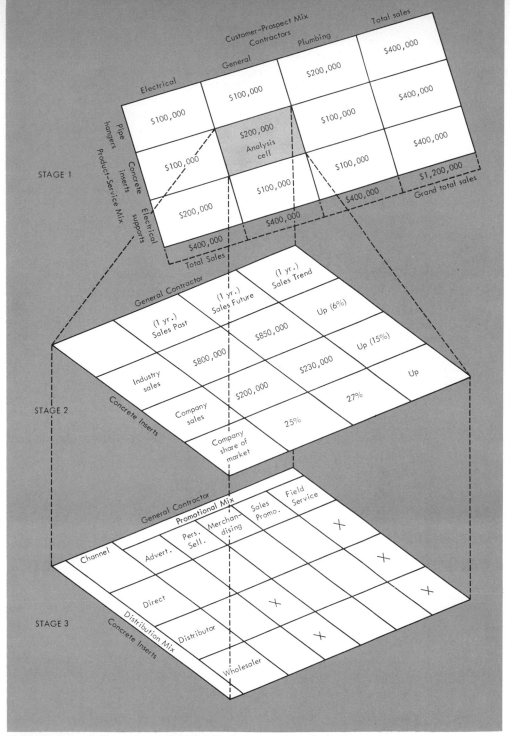

SOURCE: From an unpublished paper by Rhett W. Butler, Northwestern University, 1964.

Figure 7-3
Analyzing the worth of different market segments for steel fabricated products

inserts, and electrical supports. Nine cells result from this joint segmentation of the market. Each cell represents a distinct submarket, or product-market segment. A dollar figure is placed in each cell, representing the company's sales in that submarket.

Relative company sales in the nine submarkets provide no indication of their relative profit potential as segments. The latter depends upon market demand, company costs, and competitive trends in each submarket. Stages 2 and 3 show how a particular product submarket, the general-contractor market for concrete inserts, can be analyzed in depth.

Stage 2 appraises present and future sales in the selected submarket. The vertical axis accommodates estimates of industry sales, company sales, and company market share. The horizontal axis is used to project future sales in these categories and market share. The company sold in this submarket last year $200,000 worth of goods, or one-fourth of total estimated industry sales. Looking ahead, the company expects industry sales in this submarket to rise by 6 percent and its own sales to rise by 15 percent.

Stage 3 probes deeper into the marketing thinking behind the sales forecasts of Stage 2. The horizontal axis shows the promotional mix that the company is using or plans to use to stimulate the sales of concrete inserts to general contractors. The vertical axis shows the distribution mix that the company is using or plans to use to move concrete inserts into the hands of general contractors. The actual promotion-distribution mix could be detailed by placing budget figures (funds and men) in the relevant cells. The company will use all three types of distribution and rely mainly on personal selling and field service for stimulating sales to general contractors.

By carrying out this analysis, the seller is led to think systematically about each segment as a distinct opportunity. His analysis of the profit potential of each segment, in conjunction with objectives, will help him decide on a segmentation strategy.

SUMMARY

The opportunities present in a market increase when the marketer recognizes that it is made up of customer groups with varying preferences, not all of whom are likely to be receiving complete satisfaction from the current offerings of sellers.

Markets can be segmented on geographic, demographic, and psychographic variables. To be ultimately useful, the segments should be measurable, accessible, and substantial.

Firms have shown different targeting strategies toward the existence of market segments, some ignoring them (undifferentiated marketing), some developing a variety of products and marketing programs to meet different needs (differentiated marketing), and some going after only a few segments (concentrated marketing). No particular strategy is superior to the others in all circumstances. Much depends on company resources, product homogeneity, product stage in the life cycle, market homogeneity, and competitive marketing strategies. The firm must analyze the attractiveness of the different market segments as a prelude to selecting its target markets.

1 Market segments can be developed by cross-classifying different variables deemed to be important in the market. What are the problems that arise in trying to cross-classify more than a few variables?

2 Suggest a useful way to segment the markets for each of the following products: (a) household detergents; (b) animal feeds; (c) household coffee; (d) automobile tires.

3 A camera manufacturer is interested in developing a benefit segmentation of the camera market. Could you suggest some major benefit segments?

4 One critic has suggested that most segmentation is unnecessary. Buyers want variety and they switch around. The firm should produce various products, and it will catch those people who switch. Do you agree?

5 The Quaker Oats Company produces a dry breakfast cereal called *Life*. Life's brand manager is interested in ranking different market target groups for the cereal. The groups are to be formed by using age of housewife, family size, and size of city. Propose a list of market target groups ranging from extremely important to extremely unimportant.

6 A shaving cream manufacturer is planning to introduce a new after-shave lotion. Research indicates that light blue is the favored color by a strong margin. Does it follow that light blue should be adopted?

7 There are certain product markets where brand loyalty is weak and cannot be used as a segmentation variable. What are the characteristics of product markets where brand loyalty is weak?

8 It is claimed that some markets are oversegmented, that is, the market segments are too small to be served profitably. Some companies are beginning to think of "desegmentation," that is, putting out fewer products, each designed to satisfy a larger group. How would you view this development?

8
MARKETING PLANNING AND BUDGETING

Make no little plans: they have no magic to stir men's blood.

DANIEL H. BURNHAM

After a company selects its target markets, it must develop appropriate products for them, set volume and profit goals, develop marketing programs, implement them, monitor the results, and take corrective actions when necessary. In this chapter we shall examine the process of annual planning to achieve the company's marketing goals. We shall emphasize the tasks that individual product managers face in developing goals, strategies, and budgets for their products in the context of overall corporate goals.

OVERVIEW OF THE ANNUAL MARKETING-PLANNING PROCESS

Three different styles of annual planning are found in the corporate world. The first is *top-down planning*, so called because top management sets *goals* as well as *plans* for all the lower levels of management. This model is taken from military organizations where the generals do the planning and the troops carry it out. In commercial organizations this goes along with a Theory X view of employees, that they dislike work and responsibility and prefer to be directed.[1]

---

[1]Douglas McGregor, *The Human Side of Enterprise* (New York: McGraw-Hill Book Company, 1960).

The second style is known as *bottom-up planning,* so called because the various units of the organization prepare their own goals and plans based on the best they think they can do, and they send them to upper management for approval. This style is based on Theory Y thinking about human nature, that employees like work and responsibility and are more creative and committed if they participate in the planning and running of the enterprise.

Most companies use a third style known as *goals down–plans up* planning. Here top management takes a broad look at the company's opportunities and requirements and sets corporate goals for the year. The various units of the company are responsible for developing plans designed to help the company reach these goals. These plans, when approved by top management, become the official annual plan. A typical example is afforded by the Celanese Company:

> The annual planning process starts in late August, with top management receiving marketing research reports and sending out a guidance letter stating overall volume and profit goals. During September and October, product planning managers develop overall marketing plans in consultation with the field sales manager and the marketing vice president. In the middle of October, the marketing vice president reviews and approves the plans and submits them to the president for final approval. In the meantime, the field sales manager works with his regional sales managers and salesmen to develop field sales plans. Finally, in the fourth week in October, the controller prepares an operating budget; it goes, in early November, to top management for final approval. Thus, three months after the planning process started, a completed plan and budget are ready to be put into operation.[2]

We shall first examine how top management sets the company's annual goals and budgets. Following this, we shall examine how product managers prepare their marketing plans within the framework of the annual goals set by top management.

SETTING CORPORATE GOALS AND BUDGETS

Top management bases its annual setting of goals on the four categories of factors shown on the left in Figure 8-1. The starting point is the company's long-run goals, G_L. These goals include a target sales growth, a target profit on sales, and a target return on investment. (We shall ignore the company's long-run qualitative goals, such as to be the industry leader, etc.) Suppose that the company strives to average over the years:

1 An annual increase in sales of 10 percent
2 An annual pretax profit on sales of 20 percent
3 An annual pretax profit on investment of 25 percent

This can be expressed compactly as

$$G_L = (R_t/R_{t-1}, Z_t/R_t, Z_t/I_t) = (1.10, .20, .25), \qquad (8\text{-}1)$$

[2]*The Development of Marketing Objectives and Plans: A Symposium* (New York: The Conference Board, 1963), p. 38.

where:

$$G_L = \text{long-run goal vector}$$
$$R_t = \text{sales revenue goal at time } t$$
$$Z_t = \text{profit goal at time } t$$
$$I_t = \text{investment goal at time } t$$

These long-run goals are not necessarily realizable in any particular year. Management considers three other factors. First, it considers its recent results. If sales and profits have been poor in recent years, management will view the challenge differently than if normal sales and profits have been achieved. Second, management considers the current outlook. If an improved economic outlook is seen, management may set this year's sales growth target at more than 10 percent. Third, management considers the pressures and expectations of important publics. If the stockholders are in a near state of rebellion, the company will want to set a higher profit goal for the coming year. Top management considers all of these factors and then announces a set of goals, G_A, for the year. For additional guidance, it also announces a common set of assumptions about the economy and industry to be used by lower levels of management in their planning.

Figure 8-1
Factors influencing the annual goals set by top management

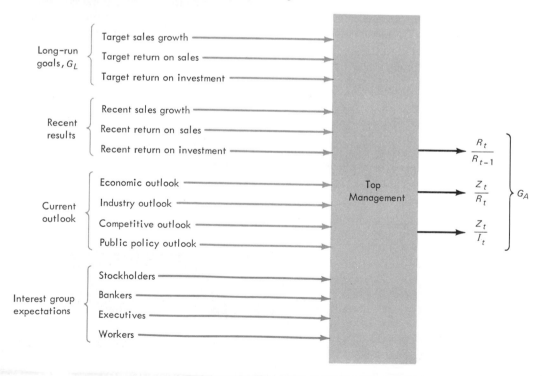

The following case provides an abbreviated example of the goal-setting and budgeting process used in one company.[3]

A wholesale paper company has a present net worth of $300,000. To serve its customers well, top management estimates that the company will have to increase its capitalization to at least $500,000 within the next five or six years. It could bridge this $200,000 gap by earning a net income each year at least equal to 10 percent of the beginning net worth each year. For the coming year, this means attempting to earn an average after-tax profit of $30,000. Since the company's tax rate is approximately .423, this means earning a pretax profit of $52,000.

On the assumption of continuing the present marketing strategy, top management estimates gross sales for the coming year to be $1,720,000. Variable costs tend to run around 80 percent of sales; this would leave a gross profit on sales of $344,000. The salesmen receive a commission of 30 percent on gross profit; this would leave a gross profit after commissions of $240,800. Fixed costs for facilities, marketing, administration, and interest are estimated at $205,800. This would leave a pretax profit of $35,000, which falls $17,000 short of the target pretax profits.

Management will have to take a closer look at costs to see if there are any areas of possible saving or increased efficiency. If not, it will have to examine the accuracy of the demand estimate. If this proves sound, it will have to consider an alternative marketing plan or reduce its profit goal. It will first try the former.

Management needs a way to estimate the sales that would yield pretax profits of $52,000. These "breakeven" sales (R) can be estimated through the following relationship. We know that

$$\frac{\text{Sales}}{\text{revenue}} = \frac{\text{Variable}}{\text{costs}} + \frac{\text{Sales}}{\text{commissions}} + \frac{\text{Fixed}}{\text{costs}} + \frac{\text{Pretax}}{\text{profits}}$$

This can be translated into the following equation:

$$R = cR + b(R - cR) + F + Z \qquad (8\text{-}2)$$

where:

R = sales revenue
c = variable costs as a percentage of sales (in the example, $c = .8$)
b = commission rate on gross profit (in the example, $b = .3$)
F = fixed costs
Z = profit

Combining and rearranging the terms in equation (8-2), we obtain the following result:

$$R = \frac{F + Z}{1 - c - b + bc} = \frac{205,800 + 52,000}{1 - .8 - .3 + (.8)\,(.3)} = \frac{257,800}{.14} = \$1,841,428 \qquad (8\text{-}3)$$

---

[3]Adapted from an example in Allen B. Koltun, "The Profit Approach to Budgeting," *Management Services*, September–October, 1965, pp. 54–59.

Thus the firm's task is to find a marketing plan that will produce $1,841,428 in sales with the specified level of costs.

Product planning

After top management sets the annual sales and profit goals, these goals are communicated to the various product and brand managers. The latter proceed to develop their own product goals and plans in a way that will help the company realize its annual goals. Managers of stronger products are expected to set product goals that exceed those for the company as a whole. This is to compensate for the weaker products that can make less of a contribution to the company's goals. When these plans are finalized, they are reviewed by the marketing vice-president and sent back for further revision if he thinks higher sales goals or lower budgets are warranted. In the 3M Company,

> in early December, each of these managers appears before the executive committee to present and "sell" his plan and budget. He is cross-examined in a friendly but searching manner. He sweats out the next few days waiting to hear whether his budget is approved.[4]

In the past, product marketing plans were developed with little depth or consistency. Each manager had his own format for the plan; the plans contained a lot of statistical detail but little rationale; and they did not spell out strategic alternatives so much as miscellaneous tactics. The product managers often used them as ploys to obtain as much marketing budget as possible. The results at the end of the year rarely matched the targets set.

In recent years good product planning has picked up certain earmarks:

1 A common format is used by all product managers to facilitate understanding and comparison of plans by top management.
2 The plans are increasingly based on a financial framework rather than a sales volume framework. Product managers are required to think in terms of contribution margin, cash flow, and rate of return on manageable assets.
3 Computer programs are available to product managers to help them estimate the impact of alternative marketing plans and environmental assumptions on sales and profit.
4 The product managers are developing contingency plans as well as main plans. Given the high uncertainty, managers are required to think out alternative plans to put into operation if the goals are not met.

Although marketing plan formats vary from company to company, good plans contain at least four components:

1 Product background
2 Sales and profit projections
3 Strategy development
4 Action plan and controls

The rest of this chapter will examine how each of these plan components is developed.

---

[4]"How a Corporate Giant Draws Up Its Forecasts of 1966 Sales, Spending," *Wall Street Journal,* December 20, 1965, pp. 1, 6.

PRODUCT BACKGROUND

The first section of a product plan must provide a review of where the product has been and where it stands. This does not mean citing all the statistics bearing on the product and market for all the past years. Rather it means a selective display of key statistics together with comments as to the causal factors at work. Higher levels of management will want to review the past trends in appraising the new plan.

Table 8-1 provides an example of some of the key statistics to be displayed in the first section of the plan.[5] Five years of past data are shown. Row 1 shows that the market volume is growing at 200,000 units a year. Row 2 shows that the company's brand rose from a 6 percent share to a fairly stable 10 percent share. Row 3 shows that the product's price of $2 has been increasing recently. Row 4 shows that variable cost per unit originally declined but has been increasing recently. Row 5 shows that the gross contribution margin per unit—the difference between price (row 3) and unit variable cost (row 4)—first increased and then decreased in the most recent year. Rows 6 and 7 show sales volume in both units and dollars, and row 8 shows the total gross contribution margin. Row 9 shows a stable and then rising level of overhead. Row 10 shows net contribution margin, that is, gross contribution margin less overhead. Rows 11 and 12 show advertising and distribution expenses, respectively. Finally, row

Table 8-1
Historical Product Data

		1971	1972	1973	1974	1975
1. Market—total units		1,000,000	1,200,000	1,400,000	1,600,000	1,800,000
2. Share		.06	.08	.10	.10	.10
3. Price per unit $		2.00	2.00	2.00	2.20	2.40
4. Variable cost per unit $		1.20	1.10	1.10	1.30	1.55
5. Gross contribution margin per unit $	$(3 - 4)$	.80	.90	.90	.90	.85
6. Sales volume in units	(1×2)	60,000	96,000	140,000	160,000	180,000
7. Sales $	(3×6)	120,000	192,000	280,000	352,000	432,000
8. Gross contribution margin $	(5×6)	48,000	86,400	126,000	144,000	153,000
9. Overhead $		20,000	20,000	20,000	30,000	30,000
10. Net contribution margin $	$(8 - 9)$	28,000	66,400	106,000	114,000	123,000
11. Advertising $		8,000	12,000	15,000	18,000	20,000
12. Distribution $		4,000	8,000	15,000	15,000	20,000
13. Net operating profit $	$(10 - 11 - 12)$	16,000	46,400	76,000	81,000	83,000

---

[5]For another example, see the case "Concorn Kitchens," in Harper W. Boyd, Jr., and Robert T. Davis, *Marketing Management Casebook* (Homewood, Ill.: Richard D. Irwin, Inc., 1971), pp. 125–36.

13 shows net operating profit after marketing expenses. The picture is one of growing sales, with profits, however, growing at a slower rate.

In addition to this information, the first part of the plan should contain information on the main competitors and their prices, variable costs, market shares, and marketing expenditures, to the extent that these are known.

SALES AND PROFIT PROJECTIONS

The second step calls for product managers to make projections of future sales and profits. Two different projection bases are desirable.

The first type of projection assumes that there is a continuation of the (1) *recent environment* and (2) *recent marketing strategy*. This projection is accomplished by extrapolating the past time series in a straight-line or curvilinear manner, whichever is appropriate for each series. For example, market volume for the next year can be forecast at 2 million units, on the assumption that the 200,000 annual increase continues. Market share can be assumed to stay at 10 percent. Prices can be expected to rise by, say, 20 cents, and so forth. By extrapolating the key underlying time series, net operating profits can be estimated.

Suppose the product manager does not believe the same environment will continue. Top management may have laid out some new assumptions about the economic picture; a new technology may promise to bring down variable costs; and so on. In this case the product manager alters the previous baseline projection in the light of the new expected environment but preserving the same marketing strategy. This will enable him to estimate whether continuing the same strategy is likely to produce satisfactory sales and profits.

An example of sales and profit projection

Product managers can use the computer to project sales and profits several years into the future on the basis of their plans and assumed environment. Table 8-2 shows the printout from one such computer program for a ready-to-eat cereal product.

The first line shows that this projection is for a seven-year planning horizon. Details then appear on the undepreciated value of plant and equipment devoted to this product, current opportunity cost, working capital, and expected terminal salvage value.

The rest of the printout shows the expected or planned year-to-year levels of important variables that ultimately affect the internal rate of return. Column 1 shows the retail price per unit, which is expected to rise from $.58 to $.70 in the course of seven years. Column 2 shows that the retail margin for this product (18 percent) is not expected to change. Column 3 shows the resulting wholesale prices. Since this company will sell direct to the retailers, there is no wholesale margin (column 4), and the factory price (column 5) is the same as the wholesale price.

Column 6 shows estimated variable manufacturing costs, and they too are expected to rise over the period, from a present level of $.19 to $.23 in 1982. The ratio of variable manufacturing costs to factory prices is shown in column 7, followed by the planned ratio of variable marketing costs to factory prices (column 8). Subtracting variable manufacturing and marketing costs per unit from the price, the result is the contribution to fixed costs and profits, which is shown in dollar and percentage form in columns 9 and 10 respectively.

Table 8-2
Sample printout from computer system

```
                TIME HORIZON = 7                      YEARS

REMAINING UNDEPR. P&E INVEST. AT BEGIN. YR. 1 = 900000    DOLLARS
REMAINING NO. OF YEARS OF P&E DEPRECIATION   = 3         YEARS
REMAINING UNDEP. BLDG. INVEST. AT BEGIN. YR. 1 = 210000   DOLLARS
REMAINING NO. OF YEARS OF BLDG. DEPRECIATION = 21        YEARS

  DEPRECIATION HORIZON FOR P&E INVESTMENTS   = 10        YEARS
  DEPRECIATION HORIZON FOR BLDG. INVESTMENTS = 30        YEARS

  OPPORTUNITY COST (AT BEGINNING OF PERIOD)  = 2.E+06    DOLLARS
                      WORKING CAPITAL        = 13        PCNT SALES
           SALVAGE VALUE (AT END OF PERIOD)  = 10        X EARNINGS
```

	1	2	3	4
YEAR	RET.PRICE($)	RET.MAR.(PCNT)	WHOLE.PRICE($)	WHOLE.MAR.(PCNT)
1976	.577	18	.473	0
1977	.602	18	.494	0
1978	.621	18	.509	0
1979	.639	18	.524	0
1980	.659	18	.54	0
1981	.675	18	.554	0
1982	.698	18	.572	0

	5	6	7	8
YEAR	FACTORY PRICE($)	VARIABLE MAN. COST($)	VARIABLE MAN. COST(PCNT)	VARIABLE MKTG COST(PCNT)
1976	.473	.191	40.4	5
1977	.494	.196	39.7	5
1978	.509	.202	39.7	5
1979	.524	.208	39.7	5
1980	.54	.214	39.6	5
1981	.554	.221	39.9	5
1982	.572	.227	39.7	5

	9	10	11	12
YEAR	CONTRIB. TO FIXED COSTS AND PROFIT ($)	(PCNT)	FIXED MAN. COST($)	FIXED MKTG. COST($)
1976	.258	54.6	915000	4.25E+06
1977	.273	55.3	971000	4.9E+06
1978	.282	55.3	1.028E+06	5.5E+06
1979	.29	55.3	1.31E+06	5.75E+06
1980	.299	55.4	1.386E+06	6.25E+06
1981	.305	55.1	1.471E+06	6.85E+06
1982	.317	55.3	1.824E+06	7.6E+06

	13	14	15
YEAR	P&E INVEST.	BLDG. INVEST.	DEPREC. EXPENSE
1975	850000	0	
1976	0	0	395000
1977	0	0	395000
1978	850000	1.E+06	395000
1979	0	0	213333
1980	0	0	213333
1981	850000	1.E+06	213333
1982	0	0	331666

	16	17	18	19
YEAR	INDEX OF COMPANY SALES	COMPANY SLS(UNITS)	INDUSTRY SLS(UNITS)	MARKET SHARE
1976	1	3.E+07	1.166E+09	2.6
1977	1.1	3.3E+07	1.182E+09	2.8
1978	1.2	3.6E+07	1.198E+09	3
1979	1.3	3.9E+07	1.215E+09	3.2
1980	1.4	4.2E+07	1.23E+09	3.4
1981	1.5	4.5E+07	1.247E+09	3.6
1982	1.6	4.8E+07	1.265E+09	3.8

	20	21	22	23
YEAR	MKTG. EXP. (PCNT SLS)	P.A.T.(PCNT SLS)	P.A.T.($)	CSH FLOW(A.T.)
1975				-2.85E+06
1976	34.9	7.7	1.097245E+06	-353001
1977	35.1	8.4	1.370807E+06	1.493337E+06
1978	35	8.8	1.610162E+06	-110272
1979	33.1	9.9	2.014062E+06	1.953967E+06
1980	32.5	10.4	2.361914E+06	2.281351E+06
1981	32.5	10.4	2.591395E+06	667228
1982	32.7	9.9	2.723974E+06	2.722089E+06

```
        CALCULATED INTERNAL RATE OF RETURN (AFTER TAXES) = 45        PCNT
```

SOURCE: Case material of the Harvard University Graduate School of Business Administration, prepared by Professors Derek Abell and Ralph Sultan, used by permission.

The next step calls for estimating fixed manufacturing costs and fixed marketing costs over the next seven years, which are shown in columns 11 and 12. The symbol $E + 06$ is computer printout shorthand and means that the reader should move the decimal place, in the associated number, six places to the right. Thus $\$1.028E + 06$ means $\$1,028,000$. Columns 13 and 14 show the anticipated investments in plant, equipment, and building over the next seven years, and column 15 shows the estimated total depreciation expense.

We now arrive at the estimated sales and profits. Columns 16 and 17 show management's estimates of sales (in percentage and in unit terms, respectively) over the next seven years. The figures indicate that management expects company sales (in units) to rise at the rate of about 10 percent a year, on the basis of its planned levels of marketing expenditures. Column 18 presents management's estimates of industry sales for the next seven years.

The figures in column 19, market share, are derived by dividing estimated company sales (column 17) by estimated industry sales (column 18). We see that management expects market share to grow from 2.6 percent to 3.8 percent over a seven-year period. Column 20 expresses total marketing expenditures (columns 8 and 12) as a percent of sales, and this percentage is expected to fall. Examining this more closely, we see that management expects sales to rise faster than marketing expenditures; hence it is assuming an increase in marketing productivity.

Columns 21 and 22 are a derivation of the implied yearly profits after taxes in percentage and dollar terms. The computer program uses the following formula to calculate dollar profits after taxes:

$$Z = (1 - t)(mQ - F - D) \tag{8-4}$$

where:

$Z =$ profits after taxes
$t =$ tax rate
$m =$ contribution margin to fixed costs and profit
$Q =$ sales in units
$F =$ fixed manufacturing and marketing costs
$D =$ depreciation

For example, the profits after taxes for 1976 are

$$(1 - .4967)[(\$.258)(30,000,000) - \$5,165,000 - \$395,000] = \$1,097,245$$

Column 23 shows the results of the conversion of *profits after taxes* to *cash flow after taxes*. The formula for cash flow is

$$L = Z + D - W - I \tag{8-5}$$

where:

$L =$ cash flow after taxes
$Z =$ profits after taxes
$D =$ depreciation

$W =$ working capital in dollars (that is, working capital as a percent
of sales, times wholesale price, times sales in units)

$I =$ new investment expenditure

For example, the cash flow after taxes for 1976 is

$$\$1,097,245 + \$395,000 - [.13(\$.473)(30,000,000)] - 0 = -\$353,001$$

The computer now calculates the internal rate of return implicit in the cash flow in column 23. This is found by taking the opportunity cost at the beginning of the period and searching for the interest rate that would discount the future cash flows so that the sum of the discounted cash flows is equal to the initial opportunity cost; this rate turns out to be 45 percent.

Thus computer programs enable the product manager to determine the financial consequences implied by a particular strategy, environment, and set of costs. He can easily calculate the impact on profit of any alterations in his data or assumptions.

STRATEGY DEVELOPMENT

Very often the product manager will not be able to continue the current marketing strategy. He may find (1) this strategy does not lead to satisfactory sales and profit projections; (2) this strategy is no longer maintainable because of competitors' changes in strategy or a changed economic environment; or (3) there are untried strategies that might greatly improve the profit picture. All of these warrant the product manager's giving serious thought to alternative marketing strategies.

Unfortunately, product managers tend to avoid thinking deeply about alternative strategies. In a study reported by Ames:

> In company after company, we were surprised to see how many planners had tunnel vision in thinking about how the business should be run. In fact, so many plans were based on nothing more than straight-line extrapolation of the past and on repetition of prior programs. . . . In one company when each planner was asked by top management to outline alternative strategies . . . the request drew a complete blank. The planners were so locked into their accustomed way of thinking about their markets that they could not conceive of a different approach that made any commercial sense at all.[6]

Product management needs to think more in strategic terms and should know how to generate alternative strategies. Marketing strategies can be formed around four key dimensions: (1) product positioning, (2) marketing expenditure levels, (3) marketing mix, and (4) marketing budget allocation to target markets.

Product positioning

The first thing a product manager should consider is whether his product continues to be effectively positioned in the market. At least three things can happen in the course of a year to call for fresh positioning thinking:

---

[6]B. Charles Ames, "Marketing Planning for Industrial Products," *Harvard Business Review,* September–October 1968, p. 103.

1 A competitor may have placed a brand right next to his brand, thus cutting into his market share in that segment.
2 Customer preferences may have shifted, leaving his brand less in the center of a preference cluster.
3 New customer preference clusters may have formed that represent attractive opportunities.

The manager can consider two brand strategies to meet these changes.

Repositioning   If it appears that the firm's brand is no longer optimally positioned, the product manager will want to consider repositioning alternatives. The problem and method of analysis can be illustrated in connection with Hamm's position in the beer market. Figure 8-2 shows the distribution of beer brand perceptions and taste preferences on two attributes: lightness and mildness. The dots represent the perceived positions of the various brands, and the circles represent preference clusters. The larger circles represent more-intense densities of preference. This information would reveal that Hamm no longer meets the preferences of any distinct segment.

To remedy this, Hamm's task is to identify the best preference cluster in which to reposition Hamm. Preference cluster #1 would not be a good choice because Schlitz and Budweiser are well entrenched. Preference cluster #2 seems like a good choice because of its size and the presence of only one competitor, Miller. Preference cluster #9 would be another possibility, although it is relatively small. Hamm can also think about a long-shot repositioning toward the supercluster #3, #5, and #8 or the supercluster #4 and #6.

Management must weigh two factors in making its choice. The first is the *cost* of shifting the brand to that segment. The cost includes changing the product's qualities, packaging, advertising, and so on. In general, the repositioning cost *rises* with the repositioning distance. The more radical the brand image change that is contemplated, the greater the investment required to alter people's images. Hamm would need more money to reposition its brand in segment #8 than segment #2. It might be better for Hamm to create a new brand for segment #8 than to reposition its present brand.

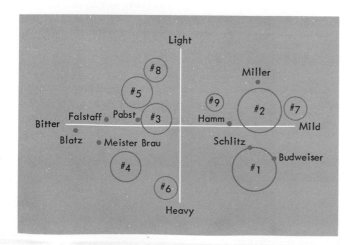

Figure 8-2

Distribution of perceptions and preferences in the beer market

SOURCE: Richard M. Johnson, "Market Segmentation: A Strategic Management Tool," *Journal of Marketing Research,* February 1971, p. 16.

The other factor is the *revenue* that would be earned by the brand in the new position. The revenue depends upon (1) the number of consumers in the preference segment, (2) their average purchase rate, (3) the number and strength of competitors already in that segment or intending to enter it, and (4) the price normally charged for brands selling to that segment.

Brand extension Management can respond to new preference segments in the marketplace by multiplying its brands rather than shifting an existing brand to a more profitable segment or trying to widen its appeal.

Procter & Gamble is a master practitioner of brand extension strategy. Before entering a market (such as mouthwashes or paper tissues), it studies the major preference clusters and competitors' brand positions. It prefers to enter markets where there is only one major competitor. It positions its first brand not in the major competitor's segment but in a neglected segment. Then it creates additional brands for other neglected segments. Each entry creates its own loyal following and takes some business away from the major competitor. Soon the major competitor is surrounded, his revenue is weakened, and he is in no position to launch a counteroffensive of new brands in outlying segments. P&G, in a moment of final triumph, then launches a brand against the major segment.

Heublein, Inc., illustrates another interesting use of brand extension strategy. Its Smirnoff's brand enjoyed 23 percent of the vodka market and was attacked by another brand, Wolfschmidt, priced at one dollar less a bottle. Instead of Heublein lowering the price of its Smirnoff by one dollar to meet the competition, it raised the price by one dollar and put the increased revenue into its advertising. At the same time, Heublein introduced a new brand, Relska, to compete with Wolfschmidt and also introduced Popov, a low-priced vodka. This strategy effectively bracketed Wolfschmidt and gave Smirnoff an even more elite image.

Marketing expenditure level

A second strategic variable is the planned level of total marketing expenditure on behalf of a product. Product managers often say that they could do wonders for their product if they had a larger budget. There is no doubt that sales volume can be increased through higher marketing expenditures, although there is frequent disagreement as to how much.

Given the uncertainty, marketing management tends to set the marketing budget on the basis of a conventional percentage to sales, recent or expected. This percentage is based on what competitors may be spending or what the company feels it can afford. The percentage may be increased slightly during good times to take advantage of market growth, or it may be cut during bad times to conserve on cash.

The correct concept for setting marketing expenditures is on the basis of their expected impact on sales. A conventional percentage approach is not appropriate because the impact varies with the amount spent. The expected impact of marketing expenditures on sales in represented by a *sales-response function* (see Chapter 6, pp. 122–24).

If the product manager has a good estimate of the sales-response function, he can proceed to find the optimum level of marketing expenditures. The analysis is shown in Figure 8-3. The sales-response function here is S-shaped, although other forms may apply, such as linear and quadratic. The product

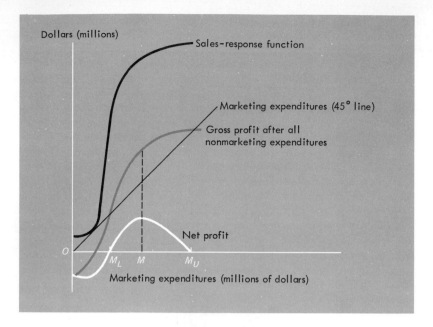

Figure 8-3
Relationship between sales, marketing expenditures, and profits

manager subtracts all nonmarketing costs from the *sales-response function* to derive the *gross-profit curve.* Next, marketing expenditures are drawn in such a way that a dollar on one axis is projected as a dollar on the other axis. This amounts to a 45° line when the axes are scaled in identical dollar intervals. The *marketing-expenditures curve* is then subtracted from the *gross-profit curve* to derive the *net-profit curve.* The net-profit curve shows positive net profits with marketing expenditures between M_L and M_U, which could be defined as the rational range of marketing expenditure. The net-profit curve reaches a maximum at M. Therefore the marketing expenditure that would maximize net profit is $\$M$.

This illustrates the main idea for marketing expenditure optimization, although the analysis has to be refined in actual use. The actual impact of marketing expenditures on sales must take into account competitors' marketing expenditures, marketing expenditure efficiency, marketing mix, and marketing allocation.

Marketing mix   Marketing mix is the third key dimension of marketing programming strategy. Without changing the marketing expenditure level, it may be possible to increase sales by altering the marketing mix. As the marketplace changes, so does the productivity of different marketing tools. For example, products entering the mature stage of the product life cycle may benefit from a switching of some funds out of advertising into sales promotion.

The product manager faces three tasks in considering marketing-mix changes. First, he has to generate a set of plausible marketing-mix alternatives. Second, he has to estimate expected sales associated with each marketing mix. Third, he must determine the optimal marketing mix. We shall describe the underlying theory and then present a numerical example.

Theory of the optimal marketing mix   The first step in identifying the optimal marketing mix calls for identifying the major components of the marketing mix for selling in that market. Although the four *P*'s are the major components, the specific budget items have to be spelled out. Some of these items, such as product quality, may not be variable in the short run. Others, such as trade shows, might be too small to consider.

Let us assume that the product manager has identified advertising dollars and personal selling (distribution) dollars as the two major components of his marketing budget. In principle, there are an infinite number of combinations of spending on these two items. If there are no constraints on the levels of advertising and personal-selling spending, then every point in the *A–D* plane shown in Figure 8-4 is a possible marketing mix. An arbitrary line drawn from the origin, called a "constant-mix line," shows the set of all marketing mixes where the two tools are in a fixed ratio, but where the budget varies. Another arbitrary line, called a "constant-budget line," shows a set of varying mixes that would be affordable with a fixed marketing budget.

Associated with every possible marketing mix is a resulting sales level. Three sales levels are shown in Figure 8-4. The marketing mix (A_1, D_1)—calling for a small budget and a rough equality between advertising and personal selling—is expected to produce sales of Q_1. The marketing mix (A_2, D_2) involves selling; this is expected to produce slightly higher sales, Q_2. The mix (A_3, D_3) calls for a larger budget but a relatively equal splitting between advertising and personal selling, and with a sales estimate of Q_3. Given these and the many other possible marketing mixes, the analyst's job is to find the sales-response function that describes the *Q*'s.

For a given marketing budget, the money should be divided among the various marketing tools in a way that gives the same marginal profit on the marginal dollar spent on each tool. A geometrical version of the solution is shown in Figure 8-5. Here we are looking down at the *A–D* plane shown in

Figure 8-4
The sales-response function associated with two marketing tools

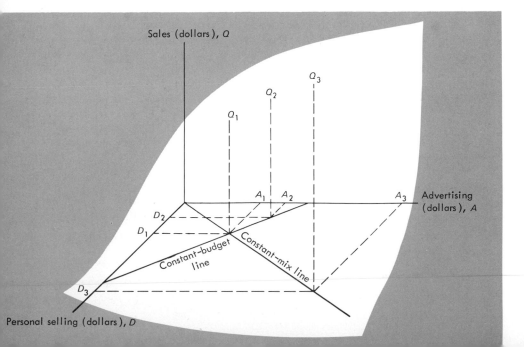

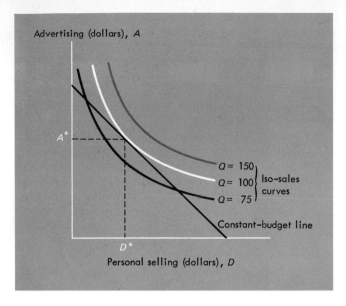

Advertising (dollars), A

A^*

$Q = 150$
$Q = 100$ } Iso-sales curves
$Q = 75$

Constant-budget line

D^*

Personal selling (dollars), D

Figure 8-5
Finding the optimal marketing mix for a given marketing budget

Figure 8-4. A constant-budget line is shown, indicating all the alternative marketing mixes that could be achieved with this budget. The curved lines are called *iso-sales curves.* An iso-sales curve shows the different mixes of advertising and personal selling that would produce a given level of sales. It is a projection into the *A–D* plane of the set of points resulting from horizontal slicing of the sales-response function shown in Figure 8-4 at a given level of sales. Figure 8-5 shows iso-sales curves for three different sales levels: 75, 100, and 150 units. Given the budget line, it is not possible to attain sales of more than 100 units. The optimum marketing mix is shown at the point of tangency between the budget line and the last-touching iso-sales curve above it. Consequently, the marketing mix (A^*, D^*), which calls for somewhat more advertising than personal selling, is the sales-maximizing (and in this case profit-maximizing) marketing mix.

This analysis could be generalized to more than two marketing tools. Dorfman and Steiner proved that the marketing mix of price, promotion, and product quality would be optimized when the following side conditions were met:[7]

Price elasticity of demand = Marginal value product of promotion = Quality elasticity of demand times price markup over average cost of production

Ferber and Verdoorn stated the rule more intuitively:

> In an optimum position the additional sales obtained by a small increase in unit costs are the same for all non-price instruments and at the same time equal to additional sales accompanying a corresponding decrease in unit prices.[8]

[7]Robert Dorfman and Peter O. Steiner, "Optimal Advertising and Optimal Quality," *American Economic Review,* December 1954, pp. 826–36.

[8]Robert Ferber and P. J. Verdoorn, *Research Methods in Economics and Business* (New York: The Macmillan Company, 1962), p. 535.

A numerical example   A product manager has been selling his product for some years using a low-price, low-promotion strategy. His current price is $16, and he is spending $10,000 on advertising and another $10,000 on distribution. Sales are around 12,000 units, and profits around $14,000. His superiors consider this unimpressive. He is anxious to find a better strategy to increase profits.

His first step is to generate a set of alternative marketing-mix strategies. He generates the eight strategies shown in the first three columns of Table 8-3. (The first strategy is his old one). They were formed by assuming a high and a low level for each of the marketing variables and elaborating all the combinations ($2^3 = 8$).

Table 8-3

Marketing mixes and estimated sales

	(1)	(2) Marketing Mix	(3)	(4)
	P	A	D	Q
1.	$16	$10,000	$10,000	12,400
2.	16	10,000	50,000	18,500
3.	16	50,000	10,000	15,100
4.	16	50,000	50,000	22,600
5.	24	10,000	10,000	5,500
6.	24	10,000	50,000	8,200
7.	24	50,000	10,000	6,700
8.	24	50,000	50,000	10,000

His next step is to estimate the likely sales that would be attained with each alternative mix. These estimates are unlikely to be forthcoming through fitting past historical data or through conducting marketing-mix experiments. The best approach is to rely on subjective expert estimation, which if handled carefully, can produce useful information.[9] Suppose this method yields the sales estimates shown in the last column of Table 8-3.

The final step calls for determining which marketing mix maximizes profits, assuming the sales estimates are reliable. This calls for introducing a profit equation and inserting the different marketing mixes into this equation to see which maximizes profits.

The profit equation is developed in the following way. Profits (Z) by definition are equal to the product's revenue (R) less its costs (C):

$$Z = R - C \qquad (8\text{-}6)$$

Revenue is equal to the product's net price (P') times its unit sales (Q):

$$R = P'Q \qquad (8\text{-}7)$$

---

[9]See the author's "A Guide to Gathering Expert Estimates," *Business Horizons,* October 1970, pp. 79–87.

But the product's net price (P') is equal to its list price (P) less any allowance per unit (k) representing freight allowances, commissions, and discounts:

$$P' = P - k \qquad (8\text{-}8)$$

The product's costs can be conveniently classified into unit variable nonmarketing costs (c), fixed nonmarketing costs (F), and marketing costs (M):

$$C = cQ + F + M \qquad (8\text{-}9)$$

Marketing costs in turn are of two kinds, advertising (A) and distribution (D):

$$M - A + D \qquad (8\text{-}10)$$

Substituting equations (8-7), (8-8), (8-9) and (8-10) into (8-6) and simplifying, we obtain the following profit-planning equation:

$$Z = [(P - k) - c]Q - F - A - D \qquad (8\text{-}11)$$

where:

> $Z =$ total profits
> $P =$ list price
> $k =$ allowance per unit (such as freight allowances, commissions, discounts)
> $c =$ production and distribution variable cost (such as labor costs, delivery costs)
> $Q =$ number of units sold
> $F =$ fixed nonmarketing costs (such as salaries, rent, electricity)
> $A =$ advertising cost
> $D =$ distribution cost

The expression $[(P - k) - c]$ is the *gross contribution margin per unit*—the amount the company realizes on the average unit after deducting allowances and the variable costs of producing and distributing the average unit. The expression $[(P - k) - c]Q$ is the *gross contribution margin*—the net revenue available to cover the fixed costs, profits, and discretionary marketing expenditures.

This equation highlights several marketing decision variables available to the marketing planner for influencing sales and profits. Sales are influenced by the list price, allowances, variable cost (to the extent that higher variable costs reflect improved product quality, delivery time, customer service, and so on), advertising, and distribution:

$$Q = f(P,k,c,A,D) \qquad (8\text{-}12)$$

The argument (P,k,c,A,D) is called the *marketing mix,* and equation (8-12) is the *sales-response function.*

The product manager now has a profit equation (8-11) that shows the profit associated with every feasible marketing mix. Suppose fixed costs, F, are \$38,000; unit variable costs, c, are \$10; and the contemplated allowance off list price, k, is \$0. Then profit equation (8-11) reads:

$$Z = (P - 10)Q - 38{,}000 - A - D \qquad (8\text{-}13)$$

Profits are now strictly a function of the chosen price and the advertising and distribution budgets.

At this point the manager can introduce each marketing mix and estimated sales level (from Table 8-3) into this equation. The resulting profits are #1(\$16,400), #2(\$13,000), #3(−\$7,400), #4(−\$2,400), #5(\$19,000), #6(\$16,800), #7(−4,200), and #8(\$2,000). Marketing mix #5, calling for a price of \$24, advertising of \$10,000, and distribution of \$10,000, promises to yield the highest profits (\$19,000).

There is one more step the product manager can take. Some marketing mix not shown might yield a still higher profit. To determine this, the product manager can fit a sales-response function to the data shown in Table 8-3. The sales estimates in the table can be viewed as a sample from a larger universe of expert judgments concerning the sales-response function $Q = f(P,A,D)$. A plausible mathematical form for a sales-response function is the multiple exponential:

$$Q = bP^{p}A^{a}D^{d} \qquad (8\text{-}14)$$

where:

$b =$ a scale factor
$p,a,d =$ price, advertising, and distribution elasticity, respectively

Using least-squares regression estimation, the fitted sales-response function turns out to be:

$$Q = 100{,}000P^{-2}A^{1/8}D^{1/4} \qquad (8\text{-}15)$$

This fits the sales estimates in Table 8-3 extremely well. Price has an elasticity of -2, that is, a 1 percent reduction in price, other things equal, tends to increase unit sales by 2 percent. Advertising has an elasticity of $\frac{1}{8}$, and distribution has an elasticity of $\frac{1}{4}$. The coefficient 100,000 is a scale factor that translates the dollar magnitudes into sales volume in units.

The product manager now substitutes this sales-response function into the Q term in profit equation (8-13). This yields, when simplified:

$$Z = 100{,}000\,A^{1/8}D^{1/4}\,[P^{-1} - 10P^{-2}] - 38{,}000 - A - D \qquad (8\text{-}16)$$

Profits are strictly a function of the chosen marketing mix. The manager can insert any marketing mix (including those not shown in Table 8-3) and derive an estimate of profits. To find the profit-maximizing marketing mix, he applies standard calculus.[10] The optimal marketing mix (P,A,D) is (\$20, \$12,947,

---

[10]The derivation is shown in the Appendix of the author's "Marketing Mix Decisions for New Products," *Journal of Marketing Research,* February 1964, pp. 43–49.

$25,894). Twice as much is spent on distribution over advertising because its elasticity is twice as great. The product manager would forecast a sales volume of 10,358 units and profits of $26,735. While other marketing mixes can produce higher sales, no other marketing mix can produce higher profits. Using this equation, the product manager has solved not only the optimum marketing mix but also the optimum marketing budget ($A + D = \$38,841$).

**Marketing allocation
to target markets**

The fourth dimension of marketing strategy is marketing allocation to the various *target markets* (*TM*'s). *TM*'s include different sales territories, customer groups, and so on. With a given product positioning, marketing budget, and marketing mix, it may still be possible to increase sales and profits by shifting funds among different markets.

Most product managers allocate their marketing budget to the various *TM*'s on the basis of some percentage to actual or expected sales. Consider the following example:[11]

> The Guardian Oil Company (name disguised) estimates its total gasoline sales volume (which combines regular and premium gasoline) and adds premium sales volume back to this figure to yield "profit gallons" (thus double weight is given to premium gasoline sales). The company then takes the ratio of the advertising budget to the profit gallons to establish a figure for advertising dollars per profit gallon. It calls this the prime multiplier. Each market receives an advertising budget equal to its previous year's profit gallons sold multiplied by the prime multiplier. Thus the advertising budget is allocated largely on the basis of last year's company sales in the territory.

Unfortunately, size rules for allocating funds lead to inefficient allocations. They confuse "average" and "marginal" sales response. Figure 8-6 shows the difference between the two and the fact that there is no reason to assume they are correlated. The two dots in the figure show current marketing expenditures and company sales in two *TM*'s. The company spends $3,000 on marketing in both *TM*'s. Company sales are $40,000 in *TM* 1 and $20,000 in *TM* 2.

---

[11]Donald C. Marschner, "Theory versus Practice in Allocating Advertising Money," *Journal of Business,* July 1967, pp. 286–302.

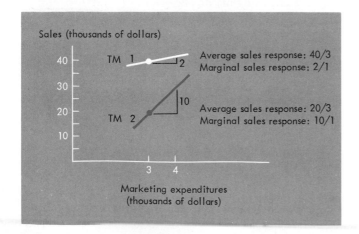

Figure 8-6
Average and marginal sales response in two target markets (*TM*'s)

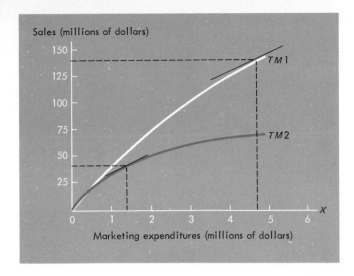

Sales (millions of dollars)

Marketing expenditures (millions of dollars)

Figure 8-7
Sales-response functions in two target markets
(*TM's*)

The average sales response to a dollar of marketing effort is thus greater in *TM* 1 than in *TM* 2; it is $\frac{40}{3}$ as opposed to $\frac{20}{3}$, respectively. It might therefore seem desirable to shift funds out of *TM* 2 into *TM* 1, where the average response is greater. Yet the real issue is one of the marginal response. The marginal response is represented by the *slope* of the sales function through the points. A higher slope has been drawn for *TM* 2 than for *TM* 1. The respective slopes show that another $1,000 of marketing expenditure would produce a $10,000 sales increase in *TM* 2 and only a $2,000 sales increase in *TM* 1. Clearly, marginal response, not average response, should guide the allocation of marketing funds.

Marginal response is indicated along the sales-response function for each territory. We will assume that a company is able to estimate *TM* sales-response functions through statistical regression or expert-estimation techniques. Suppose the sales-response functions for two *TM*'s are those shown in Figure 8-7. The company wishes to allocate a budget of *B* dollars between the two *TM*'s to maximize profits. When costs are identical for the two *TM*'s, then the allocation that will maximize profits is the one that will maximize sales. The funds are optimally allocated when (1) they exhaust the budget and (2) the marginal sales response is the same in both *TM*'s. Geometrically, this means that the slopes of the tangents to the two sales-response functions at the optimal allocations will be equal. Figure 8-7 shows that a budget of $6 million would be allocated in the amounts of approximately $4.6 million to *TM* 1 and $1.4 million to *TM* 2 to produce maximum sales of approximately $180 million. The marginal sales response would be the same in both *TM*'s.[12]

Example   A major oil company had been locating its service stations in every major U.S. city.[13] In many markets, it operated only a small percentage of the total stations. Company management began to question whether this was

---

[12]For an algebraic discussion, see the author's *Marketing Decision Making: A Model Building Approach* (New York: Holt, Rinehart & Winston, Inc., 1971), Chap. 6.

[13]See John J. Cardwell, "Marketing and Management Science—A Marriage on the Rocks?" *California Management Review,* Summer 1968, pp. 3–12.

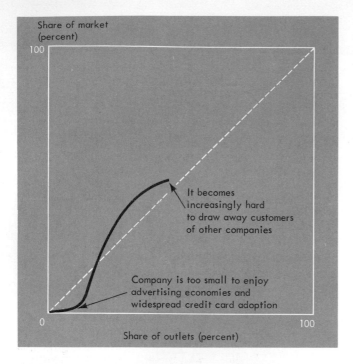

Share of market (percent)

100

It becomes increasingly hard to draw away customers of other companies

Company is too small to enjoy advertising economies and widespread credit card adoption

0

100

Share of outlets (percent)

Figure 8-8
Share of market as a function of share of outlets

wise. It decided to estimate how the company's city market share varied with its percentage share of marketing expenditures in each city (as measured by the share of outlets). A curve was fitted through observations of the share of outlets and share of markets in different cities in its system. The resulting curve was S-shaped (see Figure 8-8). This meant that having a low percentage of stations in a city yielded an even lower percentage of market volume. The practical implication was clear: the company should either withdraw from its weak markets or build them up to, say, having at least 15 percent of the competitive outlets. Instead of an allocation strategy of locating a few outlets in each of many cities, the oil company should set up a greater number of outlets in a more limited number of cities.

ACTION PLAN AND CONTROLS

The purpose of strategy development is to consider alternative strategies that might improve the sales and profit projection over that arrived at by straight-forward continuation of the present strategy. When the product manager is finally satisfied with a new strategy or with continuing the old one, he is ready to finalize the detailed marketing plan for the coming year.

Before developing the actual detail, he will want to discuss the overall strategy with others whose cooperation will make the difference between plan failure and success. In particular, he will see the purchasing and manufacturing people to make sure that they are able to buy enough material and produce enough goods to meet the planned sales volume levels. He will talk with the sales manager to make sure that he can obtain the planned sales-force support.

He may check with important dealers to make sure that they will cooperate. He will discuss the strategy with his immediate superior to see if the latter can spot any flaws.

Now he is ready to spell out a detailed expenditure and work plan for the calendar year. It is one thing to propose spending, say, $3 million on advertising and another to indicate how much will be spent each month and in what media. Similarly, he must indicate how and when, say, $1 million on sales promotion will be spent.

His work plan takes the form of a matrix, with the twelve months (or fifty-two weeks) of the year serving as columns and various marketing activities serving as rows. He enters the dates when various activities or expenditures will be started, reviewed, and terminated. This work plan is subject to change during the year as new problems and opportunities arise, but it serves as a general implementation framework for tactics.

The work plan makes it possible to estimate expected sales and profit levels on a quarterly or other basis. These numbers will serve as his controls. As each period ends, he will compare actual sales against expected sales, and actual expenditures against budgeted expenditures, to see whether his plan is working. If expected sales are not materializing or costs are too high, he will be alerted to the need for corrective action.

The product manager does not put all of this detail into his plan for final presentation and approval by top management. He puts in a description of the product's background, its current situation and opportunities, his recommended strategy and rationale for it, the planned expenditure levels by quarter, the expected sales by quarter, and the planned profits.

SUMMARY

Companies manage their target markets by setting annual sales and profit goals and developing marketing plans and budgets. Most companies use a *goals down–plans up* model of planning. Top management reviews its long-run goals, recent results, current outlook, and interest group expectations and announces a set of sales and profit targets to be used by product managers to develop their particular plans. These plans, when finished, are sent up to top management for approval.

Product managers go through four steps in preparing their individual plans. First they review key statistics showing where their product has been and where it stands. Then they project sales and profit on the basis of assumed continuation of the environment and/or recent marketing strategy. If the projections are not attractive, the product managers evaluate alternative strategies, which come from considering alternative product positionings, marketing expenditure levels, marketing mixes, and marketing allocations to target markets. When they find a satisfactory strategy, they turn it into a detailed expenditure and work plan to be used for implementation and control.

QUESTIONS AND PROBLEMS

1 What kinds of suboptimizing practices often take place in (a) setting sales targets; (b) setting departmental budgets?

2 A marketing decision maker evaluates two alternative marketing strategies and estimates their expected rates of return to be 8 percent and 12 percent, respectively.

Which strategy should be chosen if this decision is to be made many times? Which strategy should be chosen if this decision is to be made only once?

3 Suppose the quantity sold (Q) of an item depends upon the price charged (P), the level of advertising expenditure (A), and the level of distribution expenditure (D). Develop a sales response equation (a) where the marginal effect of each marketing variable is uninfluenced by the level of the other marketing variables; (b) where the marginal effect of each marketing variable is influenced by the level of the other variables.

4 A firm is trying to decide how much quality to build into a new machine tool. Illustrate diagrammatically the logic of determining the optimal quality level.

5 How many different marketing mixes could be formulated given a dozen marketing activities that could each be performed at five different levels?

6 Suggest four improvements in the computer program shown in Table 8-2 for projecting sales and profits.

7 Suggest some equation forms that might be used to represent (a) a sales response function when sales increase at a decreasing rate with marketing expenditures; (b) a sales response function where sales increase at an increasing and then decreasing rate.

8 The product manager in charge of a well-established dry breakfast cereal has the following margin and expense statement:

Net Sales		100%
Manufacturing and shipping costs		
Fixed	12.9	
Variable	39.6	
Total		52.5
All other expenses (excluding advertising and merchandising expenses)		
Distribution and delivery expenses	5.4	
Administrative and general expenses	4.0	
Salesmen's expenses	3.5	
Market research	.5	
Total		13.4
Available for advertising and merchandising and profit		34.1

Name several options he has in trying to increase profits.

IV

FORMULATING PRODUCT STRATEGY

9
PRODUCT-MIX AND BRAND STRATEGY

*In the factory we make cosmetics, and in the drugstore
we sell hope.*

CHARLES REVSON

In the preceding chapter we described how product managers develop their product plans within the context of the annual goals set by top management. However, a company's product-mix and brand strategy is more than the sum of a set of plans by individual product managers. Top management has to take a look at the total product mix and decide whether it is balanced in terms of profit, risk, and growth. Management has to make important decisions on brand policy that affect more than one brand. The development of the product mix and brands is thus another key element of marketing strategy.

THE CONCEPT OF A PRODUCT

Before getting into product-mix and brand issues, the concept of a product will first be clarified. The term will be used broadly:

A *product* is anything that can be offered to a market for attention, acquisition, or consumption; it includes physical objects, services, personalities, places, organizations, and ideas.

183

The character of the product may be seen differently by the buyer and the seller. It is useful to distinguish three concepts of a product: formal product, core product, and augmented product.

The *formal product* is the physical object or service that is offered to the target market. It is what is readily recognized as the offer. Lipsticks, computers, educational seminars, political candidates, are all formal products. If it is a physical object, it may be recognized by the market as having up to five characteristics: a *quality level, features, styling,* a *brand name,* and *packaging.* If it is a service, it may have some or all of these facets in an analogous manner. We can say that the U.S. Income Tax Advisory Service exhibits a certain quality level in that government tax advisers have a certain degree of competence. The service has certain features, such as being offered at no charge and usually requiring some waiting time. The service has a certain styling, such as being brief, cursory, and impersonal. The service has a certain formal name, that of "Federal Income Tax Advisory Service." Finally, the service is packaged within branch offices located in various cities.

At the next level, we can talk about the *core product,* the essential utility or benefit that is being offered to, or sought by, the buyer. The woman purchasing lipstick is not buying a set of chemical and physical attributes for their own sake; she is buying beauty. The person buying a camera is not buying a mechanical box for its own sake; he is buying pleasure, nostalgia, a form of immortality. The formal product is simply the packaging of a core product or benefit. The marketer's job is to sell *benefits,* not *features.* He must find ways to "benefitize" his product.

Finally, the *augmented product* is the totality of benefits that the person receives or experiences in obtaining the formal product. The augmented product of IBM is not only the computer but a whole set of accompanying services, including instruction, canned software programs, programming services, maintenance and repairs, guarantees, and so on. IBM's outstanding position in the computer field is due in part to its early recognition that the customer wants all of these things when he buys a computer. This recognition leads to the notion of *systems selling:* the company is selling a system, not just a computer.[1] It leads the sellers to look at the buyer's total *consumption system*—"the way a purchaser of a product performs the total task of whatever it is that he or she is trying to accomplish when using the product."[2] As a result, sellers are able to recognize many opportunities for augmenting their product offering as a competitive maneuver. According to Levitt, the *new competition* is not between what companies produce in their factories, but between *what they add to their factory output in the form of packaging, services, advertising, customer advice, financing, delivery arrangements, warehousing, and other things that people value.*[3] The firm that develops the right augmented product will thrive in this competition.

---

[1]Systems selling really originated as systems buying, to describe government procurement practices in buying a major weapons or communication system. Instead of purchasing and putting all the components together, the government would solicit bids from prime contractors who would be willing to assemble the package or system. The winning prime contractor would then buy or bid for the subcomponents. Sellers have increasingly recognized that buyers like to purchase in this way and have responded with extended product offerings.

[2]See Harper W. Boyd, Jr., and Sidney J. Levy, "New Dimensions in Consumer Analysis," *Harvard Business Review,* November–December 1963, pp. 129–40.

[3]Theodore Levitt, *The Marketing Mode* (New York: McGraw-Hill Book Company, 1969), p. 2.

PRODUCT-MIX STRATEGY

We are now ready to consider company decisions on its product mix. Most companies, whether in manufacturing, wholesaling, or retailing, handle a number of products. The average supermarket handles 6,800 items, the American Optical Company manufacturers over 30,000 different items, and General Electric handles over 250,000 items.

Items, lines, and the product mix

The large number of products within the typical company means that product-policy decisions are made at three different levels of product aggregation:

> *Product item:* a specific version of a product that has a separate designation in the seller's list.
>
> *Product line:* a group of products that are closely related either because they satisfy a class of need, are used together, are sold to the same customer groups, are marketed through the same types of outlets, or fall within given price ranges.
>
> *Product mix:* the composite of products offered for sale by a firm or a business unit.[4]

For example, the Kodak Instamatic is a product item; Eastman Kodak's cameras are a product line; Eastman Kodak's cameras, photographic supplies, chemicals, plastics, and fibers are its product mix.

Width, depth, and consistency of the product mix

The product mix of a company can be described as having a certain width, depth, and consistency. The *width* of the product mix refers to *how many different product lines are found within the company.* The Bissell Company at one time produced only one product line, carpet sweepers. General Electric, on the other hand, produces transformers, light bulbs, toasters, radios, jet engines, and scores of other product lines. The width of the product mix depends on the definitions established for product-line boundaries.

The *depth* of the product mix refers to the *average number of items offered by the company within each product line.* The Toni Company produces its Home Permanent Waves in nine versions to accommodate different hair types and styles and produces its Deep Magic Skin Creme in two versions to accommodate regular and dry skin. These and other product-line depths can be averaged to indicate the typical depth of the company's product mix.

The *consistency* of the product mix refers to *how closely related the various product lines are in end use, production requirements, distribution channels, or in some other way.* Contrast the product mixes of General Electric and Hunt Foods & Industries, Inc. In spite of the large number of General Electric's lines, there is an overall consistency in that most products involve electricity in one way or another. Hunt, on the other hand, produces tomato products, paint, matches, magazines, metal and glass containers, and steel.

---

[4]The last two definitions are taken from *Marketing Definitions: A Glossary of Marketing Terms,* compiled by the Committee on Definitions of the American Marketing Association, Ralph S. Alexander, Chairman (Chicago: American Marketing Association, 1960).

All three dimensions of the product mix have a market rationale. Through increasing the width of the product mix, the company hopes to capitalize on its good reputation and skills in present markets. Through increasing the depth of its product mix, the company hopes to entice the patronage of buyers of widely differing tastes and needs. Through increasing the consistency of its product mix, the company hopes to acquire an unparalleled reputation in a particular area of endeavor.

The concepts of width, depth, and consistency are related to those of product item, lines, and mix. Figure 9-1 illustrates these relationships for a hypothetical company's product mix. The mix consists of four different lines of products with an average depth of three products to a line.

The figure helps clarify the major issues in product policy. Product policy at the level of the product item involves the issues of whether to modify, add, or drop product items. Product policy at the level of the product line involves the issue of whether to deepen or shorten an existing line. Product policy at the level of the product mix involves the issue of which markets to be in.

Alternative product-mix strategies

A company has several options with respect to the width, depth, and consistency of its product mix. The number of possible combinations is revealed by considering the options available to a company in the hydraulic fluid power industry. At least six product strategies are available:[5]

1 *Full-line, all-market strategy.* This strategy describes the intention to be all things to all people. To implement it one must serve all market segments and offer a full choice of products within the standard range and design of the industry.
2 *Market specialist.* This strategy calls for offering a full line of all types of products required by a particular market segment. A few aerospace-products manufacturers fall into this category.
3 *Product-line specialist.* Here a manufacturer specializes in products of a single type and sells these items to all markets. A few valve companies fit this description.

---

[5]Theodore J. Andrews, "Hydraulic Fluid Power Marketing," unpublished paper.

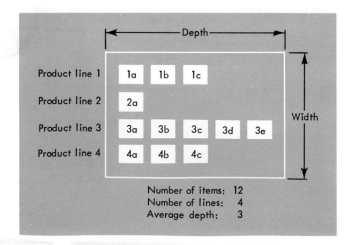

Figure 9-1
Conceptual representation of a product mix

4 *Limited product-line specialist.* Companies in this category offer a particular design of a single type of product, which usually, by virtue of its design, is intended for only one market segment. The industry has numerous examples of small companies of this type.

5 *Specific-product specialist.* This strategy involves picking a particular product and marketing it according to the opportunity available. Usually, because of its singular character, one or only a few market segments are involved.

6 *Special-situation specialist.* A company with this strategy seeks to meet special situation needs with its own special capabilities, perhaps in design engineering, low-cost manufacturing techniques, or job-shop flexibility. The markets for companies in this category are usually limited in size, heterogeneous, and often protected from major competitors.

The concept of an optimal product mix

Given the firm's basic product-mix strategy, it must still review from time to time whether the specific product items and lines in the mix represent a good balance in terms of future sales growth, sales stability, and profitability. Markets are continuously changing in their needs and preferences; competitors keep entering and altering their marketing mixes; and the environment keeps changing. All of these changes favor certain of the company's products and hurt others. Some of its products will just begin to show a profit, others will continue to produce good profits, and still others will be slipping badly.

This is dramatized in Figure 9-2. The company shown produces three products—*A, B,* and *C.* Projected product earnings for the next six years are shown. *A* produces about 60 percent of the company's total profits, *B* about 30 percent, and *C* the remaining 10 percent. Typically, a small percentage of a firm's products account for a large percentage of its earnings. Looking ahead,

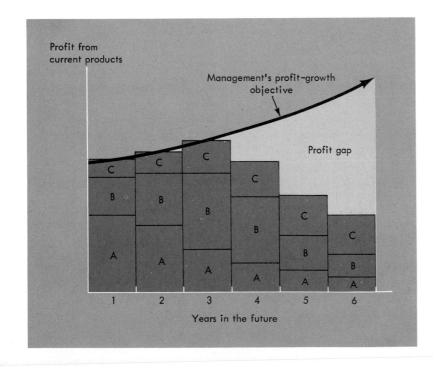

Figure 9-2
Projected profit growth from current products

the company expects *A*'s earnings to decline, *B*'s earnings to grow and then decline, and *C*'s earnings to grow. By the sixth year, *C* will be contributing most of the profit, followed by *B* and *A*. The disturbing development is that the three products will not in total earn enough to sustain the company's desired profit-growth rate. The shaded area in the figure shows a profit gap that must be made up by new-product development or acquisition.

Sound product-mix strategy calls for the continuous addition of new products and the continuous elimination of old products. Drucker described how every company's product mix reveals the potential for future sales growth through the proportions of its products in each of the six following categories:

1   *Tomorrow's breadwinners*—new products or today's breadwinners modified and improved.
2   *Today's breadwinners*—the innovations of yesterday.
3   *Products capable of becoming net contributors if something drastic is done.*
4   *Yesterday's breadwinners*—typically products with high volume, but badly fragmented into "specials," small orders, and the like.
5   *The "also rans"*—typically the high hopes of yesterday that, while they did not work out well, nevertheless did not become outright failures.
6   *The failures.*[6]

If the firm neglects either the new-product development function or the product-pruning function, or both, it will wake up one day to find a very unbalanced and unhealthy product mix.

One way for the company to appraise the soundness of its current product mix is to classify each of its products along three dimensions—*sales growth, market share,* and *profitability.* If each dimension is divided further into two regions, high and low, we have the eight possible product situations shown in Figure 9-3.

This product-mix classification technique has four benefits:

1   It indicates whether the company's rate of new-product development or acquisition is sufficient.
2   It indicates whether the company's rate of product pruning is sufficient and which products are candidates for product pruning.
3   It indicates which objectives might be set for each product, that is, whether the product's market share, sales growth, or profitability should be stressed.
4   It indicates how resources should be allocated to the different products.

The product strategy implications of products in the first four cells has been commented on by the Boston Consulting Group:[7]

1   *Cell 1 products*—showing high growth and high share—will be the company's high dollar earners. The company should spend enough to maintain the high market share and not be tempted to extract extra-high profits now at the expense of market share.

---

[6]Peter Drucker, "Managing for Business Effectiveness," *Harvard Business Review,* May–June 1963, p. 59.
[7]Patrick Conley, *Experience Curves as a Planning Tool: A Special Commentary* (Boston: The Boston Consulting Group, Inc., 1970), pp. 1–17.

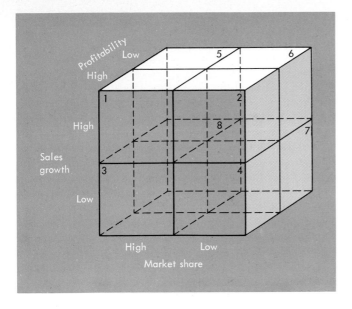

Figure 9-3
Classification of current products by sales growth, market share, and profitability

2 *Cell 2 products*—showing high growth but low share—require extra-heavy spending to build up market share before growth slows down. The company cannot manage too many products like this and should consider withdrawing a product that it cannot move into a high market-share position.

3 *Cell 3 products*—showing low growth but high share—are major sources of earnings. They justify enough investment to maximize cash flow consistent with maintaining market share but not more.

4 *Cell 4 products*—showing low growth and low share—are candidates for product milking or pruning. They do not justify much investment or attention.

General Electric is a prime user of this type of thinking. It has sorted its products into five groups:[8]

1 *High-growth products deserving the highest investment support*—engineering plastics, medical systems, transportation

2 *Steady reinvestment products deserving high and steady investment*—major appliances, steam and gas turbines, lamps

3 *Support products deserving steady investment support*—meters, specialty transformers

4 *Selective pruning or rejuvenation products deserving reduced investment*

5 *Venture products deserving heavy R&D investment*—"10-ton aircraft engine," microwave ovens, man-made diamonds

In the search for new products to add to the product mix, a company is guided by specific criteria, such as seeking products that are compatible with its technological or marketing strengths or products whose sales behave countercyclically or counterseasonally. Considering the last point, the company tries to avoid high sales variability because this means periodic excess capacity,

---

[8]"GE Growth Plans Outline by Jones," *Bridgeport Telegram*, November 8, 1974.

employee layoffs, and so on. It would be a mistake to add new products whose sales correlate closely with current sales so that they aggravate the fluctuations. Even a new product whose sales are stable will not dampen sales fluctuations. The company's main hope is to find new products whose sales are negatively correlated with the sales time pattern of current products.

We still have not defined product-mix optimality. The static product-mix optimization problem is defined as follows: given n product possibilities, choose m of them (when $m < n$) such that profit is maximized subject to a given level of risk and other constraints. This problem is found in a number of situations. Retailers and wholesalers typically have to ration scarce shelf space among a large competing set of products; candy manufacturers have to decide on the best mix of candies to produce and package; and companies facing equipment, labor, or material shortages have to decide which products to produce. The problem may be solvable through mathematical programming, the most important condition being the absence of strong demand and cost interactions among the various products being considered.

The dynamic product-mix optimization problem is the problem of timing deletions and additions to the product mix in response to changing opportunities and resources so that the product mix remains optimal through time. Although little work has been done on this problem, computer simulation offers the greatest hope of some breakthrough. Management is interested in what will happen to profits, sales stability, and sales growth as the product mix is changed. A logical approach would be to simulate possible sequences and timings of planned product deletions and additions over some future time period. The computer's contribution would be to present management with the profit, stability, and growth characteristics of the different possible transformations of the product mix through time.[9]

BRAND STRATEGY

Brand strategy is intimately tied up with the question of product-mix strategy. A marketer faces three difficult decisions on brand strategy. The first is whether, and to what extent, he should put brand names on his products (brands versus no brands). His second is whether the brand names should be those of his firm or of the distributors (manufacturers' versus distributors' brands). His third is whether his own brands should go under one, a few, or many individual names (family brands versus individual brands).

Before we turn to these issues, a few definitions are in order. A *brand* is "a name, term, sign, symbol, or design, or a combination of them which is intended to identify the goods or services of one seller or group of sellers and to differentiate them from those of competitors."[10] A *brand name* is "that part of a brand which can be vocalized—the utterable." Well-known brand names include Oldsmobile, Coke, and Del Monte.

---

[9]For the mathematics of product-mix strategy, see the author's *Marketing Decision Making: A Model Building Approach* (New York: Holt, Rinehart & Winston, Inc. 1971), Chap. 7.

[10]This and the following definitions are taken from *Marketing Definitions: A Glossary of Marketing Terms, op. cit.*

A *brand mark* is that part of a brand which can be recognized, but is not utterable, such as a symbol, design, or distinctive coloring or lettering. Well-known brand marks include the Playboy bunny and the Metro-Goldwyn-Mayer lion. Finally, a *trademark* is "a brand or part of a brand that is given legal protection because it is capable of exclusive appropriation. . . ." Thus a trademark is essentially a legal term protecting the seller's exclusive rights to use the brand name and/or brand mark. *Branding* will be used as a general term describing the establishing of brand names, marks, or trade names for a product.

Brands versus no brands

Probably the earliest examples of branding occurred in art. In the ancient world such sculptors as Phidias and playwrights as Aristophanes put their names on their products. During the Renaissance Cellini, Michelangelo, and Rubens continued this tradition. Other artistic works, particularly handicrafts such as oriental rugs and Chinese carvings, still go without producer identification. Small wonder that common products—sugar, salt, bacon, and cloth—for most of history went without branding. The producer would ship his goods to the distributor who would sell them out of barrels, bins, or cases, without either the mark of the manufacturer or a mark of his own.

A change began in the 1890s with the growth of national firms and national advertising media. The growth of brand names has been so dramatic that today, in the United States, hardly anything is sold unbranded. Salt is packaged in distinctive manufacturers' containers, oranges are stamped, common nuts and bolts are packaged in cellophane with a distributors' label, and various parts of an automobile—spark plugs, tires, filters—bear visible brand names different from that of the automobile.

Why should a producer rush into branding when it clearly involves a cost—packaging, stamping, legal protection—and a risk, if the product should prove unsatisfying to the user? At least four purposes may move him:

1 He may want a brand mark for identification purposes to simplify handling or tracing.
2 He may want a legal trademark and patent to protect unique features of his product from imitation.
3 He may want to connote a certain quality that he is offering so that satisfied buyers might easily obtain his product again through brand recognition.
4 He may see the brand name as an opportunity for endowing his product with a unique story and character that may create the basis for price differentiation.

Sometimes the pressure for branding comes not from the purchaser but from the distributor or ultimate buyer. Distributors may want brand names as a means of making the product easier to handle, identifying suppliers, holding production to certain quality standards, and increasing buyer preference. Ultimate buyers may want brand names to help them identify the products they want without close inspection.[11] The brand name has informational value to the buyer; without it, how could he shop in the modern supermarket with its 6,800 items?

---

[11]Until recently, Soviet factories did not brand their products but put identification marks indicating the factory. Because of the variable quality, consumers began to buy the products produced at the better-known factories. Before long, state-sponsored advertising agencies emerged to tell consumers about the quality of the various factories.

In branding his products, the producer may use his own name(s) (manufacturers' brands), the names of his distributors (distributors' brands), or follow a mixed brand policy, producing some output under his own name(s) and some output under distributors' names.[12] For example, such companies as Kellogg's, International Harvester, and IBM produce virtually all of their output under their own brand names. A manufacturer such as Warwick Electronics produces virtually all of its output under various distributors' names. Whirlpool produces output both under its own name and under distributors' names.

Historically, manufacturers' brands have dominated the American scene. Consider such well-known brands as Campbell's soup and Heinz ketchup. In recent times, however, large retailers and wholesalers have seen an advantage in developing and offering their own brands. The distributor may be able to obtain and sell the products at lower prices than the manufacturers' brand (because private brands do not bear the manufacturers' promotional expenses and because of volume purchasing), passing on some of these cost savings and still realizing a higher profit margin. Having his own brand gives a distributor more control over pricing and also some measure of control over the producing company because the distributor can threaten to change his sources of supply.

Because of these and other advantages, distributors' brands have become an important factor in brand competition. Consider that over 90 percent of Sears's products are under its own label, and that 25 percent of A&P's products are under its own label. More and more distributors, department stores, service stations, clothiers, drugstores, and appliance dealers are responding to these advantages by initiating their own brands.

The competition between manufacturers' and distributors' brands has been labeled the "battle of the brands." In this confrontation, the distributor has many advantages on his side. Retail shelf space is scarce, and many manufacturers, especially newer and smaller ones, cannot introduce products into distribution under their own name. The distributors take special care to maintain the quality of their brands, building consumers' confidence. Many buyers know that the private label is often manufactured by one of the big manufacturers anyway. The distributors' brands are often priced lower than comparable manufacturers' brands, thus appealing to budget-conscious shoppers, especially in times of inflation. The distributors give more prominent display to their own brands and make sure they are better stocked. For these and other reasons, the former dominance of the manufacturers' brands is ending. Indeed, some marketing commentators predict that distributors' brands will eventually knock out most manufacturers' brands.

Manufacturers of national brands are in a very trying situation. Their instinct is to spend a lot of money on consumer-directed advertising and promotion to maintain strong brand preference. Their price has to be somewhat higher to cover this promotion. At the same time, the mass distributors put strong pressures on them to put more of their promotional money toward trade allowances and deals if they want adequate shelf space. Once manufacturers

---

[12]*Manufacturers' brands* also go under such names as national brands, regional brands, and advertising brands, none of which is a completely defensible term. *Distributors' brands* also go under a variety of names: private brands, store brands, dealer brands, house brands, ghost brands, and so on. For a discussion of terminology, see Thomas F. Schutte, "The Semantics of Branding," *Journal of Marketing*, April 1969, pp. 5–11.

start giving in, they have less to spend on consumer promotion and their brand demand starts deteriorating. This is the national brand manufacturers' dilemma.[13]

Family brands versus individual brands

Manufacturers who choose to produce most of their output under their own name still face several choices. At least four brand name strategies can be distinguished:

1 *Individual brand names.* This policy is followed by such companies as Procter & Gamble (Tide, Bold, Dash, Cheer, Gain, Oxydol, Duz) and Genesco, Inc. (Jarman, Mademoiselle, Johnson & Murphy, and Cover Girl).

2 *A blanket family name for all products.* This policy is followed by such companies as Heinz and General Electric.

3 *Separate family names for all products.* This policy is followed by Sears (Kenmore for appliances, Kerrybrook for women's clothing, and Homart for major home installations).

4 *Company trade name combined with individual product names.* This policy is followed by Kellogg's (Kellogg's Rice Krispies and Kellogg's Raisin Bran).

Competitors within the same industry may adopt quite different brand strategies. In the soap industry, for example, Procter & Gamble prefers individual brand names. It will associate the name P&G with each of its new products during the first six weeks of television promotion and then gradually deemphasize its name. It wants each product to make it on its own. Colgate, on the other hand, makes much use of the phrase "the Colgate family" to help its individual products along.

What are the advantages of an individual-brand-names strategy? A major advantage is that the company does not tie its reputation to the product's acceptance. If the product fails, it is not a bad mark for the manufacturer. Or if the new product is of lower quality, the company does not dilute its reputation. The manufacturer of a line of expensive watches or high-quality food products can introduce lower-quality lines without using its own name. On the positive side the individual-brand-names strategy permits the firm to search for the best name for each new product. Another advantage is that a new name permits the building of new excitement and conviction.

The opposite policy, that of using a blanket family name for all products, also has some advantages if the manufacturer is willing to maintain quality for all items in the line. The cost of introducing the product will be less, because there is no need for "name" research, or for expensive advertising to create brand name recognition and preference. Furthermore, sales will be strong if the manufacturer's name is good. Thus Campbell's is able to introduce new soups under its brand name with extreme simplicity and instant response.

Where a company produces or sells quite different types of products, it may not be appropriate to use one blanket family name. Thus Swift and Company, in producing both hams and fertilizers, developed separate family names (Premium and Vigoro). When Mead Johnson developed a diet supplement for *gaining* weight, it created a new family name, Nutriment, to avoid confusion

---

[13]For an excellent example of decision theory applied to a national bakery facing this dilemma, see Robert D. Buzzell and Charles C. Slater, "Decision Theory and Marketing Management," *Journal of Marketing,* July 1962, pp. 7–16.

with its family brand for weight-*reducing* products, Metrecal. Companies will often invent different family brand names for different quality lines within the same product class. Thus A&P sells a primary, secondary, and tertiary set of brands—Ann Page, Sultana, Iona, respectively.

Finally, some manufacturers will want to associate their company name along with an individual brand for each product. In these cases, the company name legitimizes, and the individual name individualizes, the new product. Thus the Quaker Oats in *Quaker Oats Cap'n Crunch* allows the new product to benefit from the company's reputation in the breakfast-cereal field and Cap'n Crunch allows room to individualize and dramatize the product.

In the present discussion two particular strategies deserve mention: brand-extension strategies and multibrand strategies.

Brand-extension strategy   A brand-extension strategy is any effort to use a successful brand name to launch product modifications or additional products. In the case of product modifications, it is commonplace in the detergent industry to talk about brand X, then the new improved brand X, then the new brand X with additives. Brand extension also covers the introduction of new package sizes, flavors, models, and so on. More interesting is the use of a successful brand name to launch new products. After Quaker Oats' success with Cap'n Crunch dry breakfast cereal, it used the brand name and cartoon character to launch a line of ice-cream bars, T-shirts, and other products. Brand extension has also been used by Armour Dial soap to cover a variety of new products that could not easily find distribution without the strength of the Dial name.[14]

Another kind of brand extension occurs when manufacturers of consumer and producer durables add stripped-down models to the lower end of their line to permit advertising their brand as starting at a low price. Thus Sears may advertise room air conditioners as "starting at $129" and General Motors may advertise a new Chevrolet for sale at $2,900. In both cases, these "fighter" or "promotional" models are used to draw in customers on a price basis who, upon seeing the better models, usually decide to trade up. This is a common strategy but must be used carefully. The "promotional" brand, although stripped, must be up to the line's quality standards. The seller must be sure to have the promotional product in stock when it is advertised. Consumers must not get the feeling they were "taken," or else they may terminate their future business with the seller.

Multibrand strategy   A multibrand strategy is the development by a particular seller of two or more brands that compete with each other. Procter & Gamble deserves credit for pioneering this strategy. Following the phenomenal success of its Tide detergent brand introduced after World War II, it introduced another brand, Cheer, in 1950. Cheer took some sales away from Tide, but the combined sales volume was larger than if P&G had sold only Tide. P&G subsequently introduced other brands of detergents, each launched with a claim of somewhat different performance and ingredients. Other manufacturers in the soap and other fields began to follow a multibrand strategy.

---

[14]See Theodore R. Gamble, "Brand Extension," in *Plotting Marketing Strategy*, ed. Lee Adler (New York: Simon and Schuster, Inc., 1967), pp. 170–71.

There are several reasons why manufacturers turn to multibrand strategy. First, there is the severe battle for shelf space in the nation's supermarkets. Each brand that the distributors accept gets some allocation of shelf space. By introducing several brands, a manufacturer ties up more of the available shelf space, leaving less for competitors.

Second, few consumers are really so loyal to a brand that they won't, under the right circumstances, try another. They respond to cents-off deals, gifts, and new-product entries that claim superior performance. Thus the manufacturer who never introduces another brand entry will almost inevitably face a declining market share. The only way to capture the "brand switchers" is to be on the offering end of a new brand.

Third, creating new brands develops excitement and efficiency within the manufacturer's organization. Companies such as General Motors and P&G see their individual brands and managers in internal competition that keeps everyone on his toes.

Fourth, a multibrand strategy enables the company to take advantage of different market segments. Consumers respond to various appeals, and even marginal differences between brands can win a large following.

In deciding whether to introduce another brand, the manufacturer should consider such questions as

Can a unique story be built for the new brand?

Will the unique story be believable?

How much will the new brand cannibalize the sales of the manufacturer's other brands versus the sales of his competitors' brands?

Will the cost of product development and promotion be justified by the estimated return of investment?

A major pitfall to avoid is introducing a number of multibrand entries, each of which obtains only a small share of the market and none of which is particularly profitable. In this case, the company has dissipated its resources over several partially successful brands instead of concentrating on a few brands and building each one up to highly profitable levels. Such companies should weed out the weaker products and establish tighter screening procedures for choosing new brands to introduce.[15]

SUMMARY

A key element of marketing strategy is the development of a viable set of company products and brands.

By a product, we mean anything that might be offered to a market for attention, acquisition, or consumption. Each product has a formal, a core, and an augmented character.

The sum of the product items and lines constitutes the firm's product mix. This product mix will have a certain width, depth, and consistency. It will express the company's positioning strategy, whether to be full line or specialize by

---

[15]For an excellent discussion of multibrand strategies, see Robert W. Young, "Multibrand Entries," in Adler, *op. cit.,* pp. 143–64.

market, product line, or situation. The company must periodically review its product mix to see if it will yield the desired profit and sales growth over time. Current products can be classified by their sales growth, market share, and profitability. The analysis often reveals the need for stepped-up new-product development as well as product pruning. Management-science techniques offer an opportunity to determine the optimal product mix for a given set of management objectives.

Companies also develop a set of brand policies concerning whether to sell their products under their own name, distributors' names, or both, and whether to develop family or individual brands. Many manufacturers of consumer goods employ brand-extension and multibrand strategies.

QUESTIONS AND PROBLEMS

1 Define the primary want-satisfying purpose(s) of the following goods: (a) cars; (b) bread; (c) oil; (d) pillows; (e) pens; (f) novels; (g) textbooks; (h) uniforms; (i) watches; (j) detergents.

2 Offer a definition of the basic business of each of the following large companies: (a) General Motors; (b) Bayer's (maker of aspirins); (c) Massachusetts Investors Trust (a mutual fund); (d) Sears; and (e) *Time* magazine.

3 Most firms prefer to develop a diversified product line to avoid overdependence on a single product. Yet there are certain advantages that accrue to the firm that produces and sells one product. Name them.

4 "As a firm increases the number of its products arithmetically, management's problems tend to increase geometrically." Do you agree?

5 Does the ranking of a company's products according to their relative profit contribution indicate the best way to allocate the marketing budget to these products? If yes, how should the budget be allocated to the products? If no, why?

10
NEW-PRODUCT DEVELOPMENT STRATEGY

*Don't keep forever on the public road, going only where
others have gone. Leave the beaten track occasionally
and dive into the woods. You will be certain to find
something you have never seen before. Of course, it will
be a little thing, but do not ignore it. Follow it up,
explore all around it; one discovery will lead to another,
and before you know it you will have something worth
thinking about.*

ALEXANDER GRAHAM BELL

Business firms are increasingly recognizing that the key to their survival and
growth lies in the continuous development of new and improved products.
Gone is the confidence that established products will maintain strong market
positions indefinitely. There are too many competitors with fast-moving research laboratories, sophisticated marketing strategies, and large budgets standing ready to woo away customers.

"New products" for our purposes will mean "products new to the company." This definition embraces original products, major modifications of
existing products, duplications of competitors' products, and product-line
acquisitions, all of which involve assimilation of something "new" into the
product mix. Newness can also be defined from the viewpoint of the customer,
which we shall consider later.

THE NEW-PRODUCT DEVELOPMENT DILEMMA

Under modern conditions of competition, it is becoming increasingly risky not
to innovate. Consumers and industrial customers want and expect a stream of
new and improved products. Competition will certainly do its best to meet these

desires. Continuous innovation seems to be the only way to avert obsolescence of the company's product line.

At the same time, successful new-product development is becoming increasingly hard to achieve. There are several reasons for this.

Shortage of important new-product ideas

Some technologists think there is a shortage of fundamentally new technologies —on the order of the automobile, television, computers, xerography, and wonder drugs. Although there are many minor new products emerging, the nation needs major innovations to avoid economic stagnation.

Fragmented markets

Keen competition is leading to increasingly fragmented markets. A new product is aimed at capturing a large share of a small market segment rather than the mass market. This means smaller sales and profits, although the company may maintain its position longer.

Growing social and governmental constraints

New products have to increasingly satisfy public criteria in addition to promising reasonable profits. They must be designed with consideration given to consumer safety and ecological compatibility. Government requirements have slowed down the rate of innovation in the drug industry and have considerably complicated product design and advertising decisions in such industries as cosmetics, automobiles, small appliances, and toys.

Costliness of new-product development process

A company typically has to develop a great number of new-product ideas in order to finish with a few good ones. Booz, Allen & Hamilton studied this question for fifty-one companies and summarized its findings in the form of a decay curve of new-product ideas. (See Figure 10-1).[1] Of every fifty-eight-odd ideas, about 12 pass the initial screening test, which shows them to be compatible with company objectives and resources. Of these, some seven remain after a thorough evaluation of their profit potential. About three survive the product-

[1]*Management of New Products,* 4th ed. (New York: Booz, Allen & Hamilton, Inc., 1968), p. 9.

Figure 10-1
Decay curve of new-product ideas (51 companies)

SOURCE: Redrawn from *Management of New Products,* 4th ed. (New York: Booz, Allen & Hamilton, Inc., 1968), p. 9.

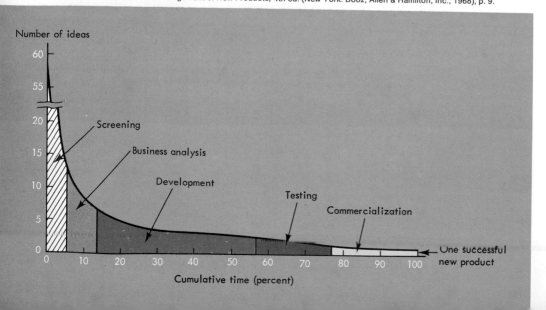

development stage, two survive the test-marketing stage, and only one is commercially successful. Thus, about fifty-eight new ideas must be generated to find one good one. This one successful idea must be priced at a profitable enough level to cover all the money lost by the company in researching fifty-seven other ideas that failed.

**High rate of
product failure**

A recent survey of 125 companies indicated that the median percentage of major new products and services whose performance fell short of expectations was slightly more than 20 percent: the breakdown was 20 percent for industrial product manufacturers, around 18 percent for service industries, and approximately 40 percent for consumer product manufacturers.[2] The last rate is particularly discouraging and very costly to the consumer product manufacturers who miss the mark.

**Shorter life spans
of successful products**

Even when a new product turns out to be a commercial success, rivals are so quick to follow suit that the new product is typically fated for only a short happy life. As told by Fred J. Borch of General Electric:

> The honeymoon cycle of a new product is becoming shorter. We introduced the GE automatic toothbrush just two years ago. There are now 52 competitors. Our slicing knife, a product that we introduced approximately one year ago, now competes with seven others and at least that many more manufacturers are preparing to enter the marketplace.[3]

The race to be first on the market sometimes assumes grotesque proportions. Alberto-Culver was so eager to beat a new Procter & Gamble shampoo to the market that it developed a name and filmed a TV commercial before it even developed its own product.[4]

Being first on the market does not guarantee good profits. Monsanto offered the first soap for automatic washers but decided to withdraw in the face of the tremendous promotion budgets of the soapmakers. Lestoil introduced the first liquid cleaner and almost had to withdraw when Lever Brothers, Procter & Gamble, and Colgate jumped in.

Thus management finds itself in a dilemma: it must develop new products, yet the odds weigh heavily against their success. The answer still must lie in new-product development, but conducted in a way that reduces the risk of failure. Two needs stand out: the need for effective organizational arrangements and the need for improved techniques at each stage of the new-product development process.

EFFECTIVE ORGANIZATIONAL ARRANGEMENTS

Companies use five different organizational arrangements for handling the development of new products:

---

[2]David S. Hopkins and Earl L. Bailey, "New Product Pressures," *The Conference Board Record,* June 1971, pp. 16–24.

[3]Fred J. Borch, "Tomorrow's Customers," Speech at the Sales Executive Club of New York, September 15, 1964.

[4]This illustration and some of the following ones were reported in *Time,* March 29, 1963, p. 83.

1 *Product managers.* Many companies leave new-product development up to their product managers. In practice, this system has several faults. The product managers are usually too busy managing their product lines to give much thought to new products other than brand modification or extension; they also lack the specific skills and knowledge needed to successfully develop new products.

2 *New-product managers.* General Foods and Johnson and Johnson have established positions of new-product managers (also called product planners) who report to group product managers. This position adds professionalization to the new-product function; on the other hand, new-product managers tend to think in terms of product modifications and line extensions limited to their product market. The position often does not have sufficient authority or top-level support.

3 *New-product committees.* Most companies have a high-level management committee charged with reviewing new-product proposals. Consisting of representatives from marketing, manufacturing, finance, engineering, accounting, and other functional areas, its function is not actual development work or coordination of development work so much as the reviewing and approving of new-product plans. These committees tend to be conservative; their members are very busy and too far removed from the actual details of the new-product areas. They are not a total solution to the new-product development problem.

4 *New-product departments.* Large companies often establish a new-product department headed by an officer who is given substantial authority and access to top management. He normally reports to the chief executive, or marketing vice-president, or research and development vice-president. The department's major responsibilities include generating and screening new ideas, directing and coordinating research and development work, and carrying out field testing and pre-commercialization work.

5 *New-product venture teams.* Dow, Westinghouse, Monsanto, and General Mills have entrusted new-product development to venture teams. A venture team is a group specifically brought together from various operating departments and charged with the responsibility of bringing a specific product to market or a specific new business into being. Hanan sees them as a regenesis of the entrepreneurial spirit. "By incorporating a small business-minded group of zealous men around a common objective, venture teaming reproduces in spirit and substance what is largely a more modern version of the Founding Fathers' bicycle shop."[5] Venture teams bring together a good mix of expertise and enthusiasm. The membership of the venture team changes as the venture passes through the different stages of development. When the new product has been successfully established, it may be taken over by the regular marketing organization and the venture team passes out of existence.

The fact that highly formal arrangements for new-product development still allow a high rate of new-product failure means that certain *organizational factors* operate and must be understood.[6] Most new-product ideas do not get anywhere in an organization without a *product champion*, a self-appointed person who tries to convince everyone else in the organization that the idea is great. In his enthusiasm for the idea, he is sometimes blind to its weaknesses; furthermore, he accepts the support of others even if it means compromising the idea somewhat. The marketing research department presses for a certain new re-

---

[5]Mark Hanan, "Corporate Growth through Venture Management," *Harvard Business Review,* January–February 1969, p. 45.

[6]This discussion is based on the excellent analysis of organizational factors in Volney Stefflre's "New Products and New Enterprises" (unpublished manuscript, March 31, 1971).

search method that it is interested in; the packaging department presses for a packaging concept that reflects its own interests; the purchasing department argues that a cheaper ingredient should be used. When the product finally emerges, it is a sad version of nothing because every department turned the project to its own ends as a condition for support. Stefflre calls this the problem of *coalition formation*.

In venture-team organizations, a different problem arises. At some point the venture team must surrender control of the project to the new-product department for final market research and testing; later control is passed to line-operating management for a national rollout. These transfers of controls of the product from its originators to developers to managers may be fatal because each group adds new wrinkles to satisfy its own goals. The product emerges with little resemblance to its original conception. Stefflre calls this the problem of *discontinuous jumps*.

A company has to seek organizational arrangements that do not lead to fatal compromising and diffusion of responsibility with various departments meeting their own needs rather than the new product's needs.

IDEA GENERATION

We are now ready to look at the successive stages of the new-product development process with an eye toward examining the techniques that would improve the chances of developing good products and eliminating poor product ideas as early as possible. Seven stages are involved: idea generation, screening, concept development and testing, business analysis, product development, test marketing, and commercialization.

Idea generation calls for procedures that will help the organization develop a large and interesting pool of possible product ideas. A large number of ideas must be generated to find a few good ones; and the greater the number of ideas generated, the better the best ones are likely to be.

Many companies do nothing formally about generating product ideas. They rely on the spontaneous emergence of ideas from various sources inside and outside of the company. But an increasing number of companies are turning to more systematic idea search procedures. A management team in a major appliance company, for example, went on a weekend retreat and returned with sixty exciting ideas for new appliances and appliance modifications.

Sources of
new-product ideas

The major sources of new-product ideas are customers, scientists, competitors, company salesmen and dealers, and top management.

Customers The marketing concept would suggest that customers' needs and wants should be the starting point in the search for new-product ideas. Companies can identify customers' needs and wants in several ways: (1) direct customer surveys, (2) projective tests, (3) focused group discussions, (4) suggestion systems and letters received from customers, and (5) perceptual and preference mapping of the current product space to discern new opportunities.

Scientists Many companies search for product ideas in research labs. Basic research into solid-state physics has yielded television and transistors, new forms of packaging, and synthetic fibers for clothing. Du Pont and Bell

Laboratories are particularly noted for basic research, whereas most other companies are content to exploit the basic technologies and to search for minor modifications of existing products.

Competitors Companies must watch the new products being developed by their competitors. Marketing intelligence can come from distributors, suppliers, and salesmen. The sales performance of these new products can be audited through research services.

Company salesmen and dealers Company salesmen and dealers are a particularly good source of product ideas. They have firsthand experience of customers' unsatisfied needs and complaints. They are often the first to learn of competitive developments. An increasing number of companies are developing more systematic procedures to tap the ideas of salesmen and dealers.

Top management Top management can help by defining those product-market areas of greatest interest in which new-product ideas should be sought. They may be areas that tap company strengths or would help overcome company weaknesses.

Idea-generating devices

Really good ideas come out of a combination of inspiration, perspiration, and method. Several "scientific" techniques have been developed over the years to help individuals and groups generate better ideas.

Attribute listing This technique involves listing the attributes of an object and then modifying different attributes in the search for a new combination that will improve the object. Consider a screwdriver.[7] Its attributes are a round, steel shank; a wooden handle, manually operated; and torque provided by twisting action. Now imagine changing attributes to improve preference or appeal. The round shank could be changed to a hexagonal shank so that a wrench could be applied to increase the torque; electric power could replace manual power; the torque could be produced by pushing. Osborn suggested the following helpful list of questions to stimulate ideas for changing attributes:

Put to other uses?	New ways to use as is? Other uses if modified?
Adapt?	What else is this like? What other idea does this suggest? Does past offer parallel? What could I copy? Whom could I emulate?
Modify?	New twist? Changing meaning, color, motion, sound, odor, form, shape? Other changes?
Magnify?	What to add? More time? Greater frequency? Stronger? Higher? Longer? Thicker? Extra value? Plus ingredient? Duplicate? Multiply? Exaggerate?
Minify?	What to subtract? Smaller? Condensed? Miniature? Lower? Shorter? Lighter? Omit? Streamline? Split up? Understate?
Substitute?	Who else instead? What else instead? Other ingredient? Other material? Other process? Other power? Other place? Other approach? Other tone of voice?

[7]See John E. Arnold, "Useful Creative Techniques," in *Source Book for Creative Thinking*, ed. Sidney J. Parnes and Harold F. Harding (New York: Charles Scribner's Sons, 1962), p. 255.

Rearrange?	Interchange components? Other pattern? Other layout? Other sequence? Transpose cause and effect? Change pace? Change schedule?
Reverse?	Transpose positive and negative? How about opposites? Turn it backward? Turn it upside down? Reverse roles? Change shoes? Turn tables? Turn other cheek?
Combine?	How about a blend, an alloy, an assortment, an ensemble? Combine units? Combine purposes? Combine appeals? Combine ideas?[8]

Forced relationships This technique relies upon listing a lot of ideas and then considering each one in relation to every other one as a means of sparking new ideas. A manufacturer of office equipment might list separate items he manufactures, such as a desk, bookcase, filing cabinet, and chair.[9] This may lead him to visualize designing a desk with a built-in bookcase. Then he may get the idea of replacing two desk drawers by a filing cabinet drawer. He goes systematically through the list considering all the combinations.

Morphological analysis This method consists of singling out the most important dimensions of a problem and then examining all the relationships between them. Suppose the problem is described as that of "getting something from one place to another via a powered vehicle."[10] The important dimensions are the type of vehicle to use (cart, chair, sling, bed); the medium in which the vehicle operates (air, water, oil, hard surface, rollers, rails); the power source (pressed air, internal combustion, engine, electric motor, steam, magnetic fields, moving cables, moving belt). The next step is to let the imagination loose on every combination. A cart-type vehicle powered by an internal-combustion engine and moving over hard surfaces is the automobile. The hope is that some other combinations will turn out to be quite novel and appealing.

Brainstorming Persons can also be stimulated to greater creativity through certain forms of organized group exercise. One well-known technique is *brainstorming*, whose principles were developed by Alex Osborn. A brainstorming session is held for the sole purpose of producing a lot of ideas. Generally the group size is limited to between six and ten. It is not a good idea to include too many experts in the group, because they tend to have a stereotyped way of looking at a problem. The problem should be made as specific as possible, and there should be no more than one problem. The sessions should last about an hour, and may be held at almost any time of the day, although the morning is often the most effective time.

As the system works in Osborn's advertising agency, BBD&O, almost every field office contains one or more brainstorming groups.[11] When a client brings in a problem, the chairman notifies the members of the brainstorming group of the problem, in brief and specific terms, and schedules a meeting to take place in the next day or two. The purpose of outlining the problem before

[8]See Alex F. Osborn, *Applied Imagination,* 3rd ed. (New York: Charles Scribner's Sons, 1963), pp. 286–87.

[9]*Ibid.,* pp. 213–14.

[10]Arnold, *op. cit.,* pp. 256–57.

[11]This account is adapted from Arnold, *op. cit.,* pp. 260–62.

the meeting is to stimulate some preparation and idea incubation. When the meeting takes place, the chairman starts with "Remember now, we want as many ideas as possible—the wilder the better, and remember, no *evaluation.*" The ideas start to flow, one idea sparks another, and within the hour over a hundred or more new ideas may find their way into the tape recorder. For the conference to be maximally effective, Osborn believes the following four rules must be observed:

1 *Criticism is ruled out.* Adverse judgment of ideas must be withheld until later.
2 *Free-wheeling is welcomed.* The wilder the idea, the better; it is easier to tame down than to think up.
3 *Quantity is wanted.* The greater the number of ideas, the more the likelihood of useful ideas.
4 *Combination and improvement are sought.* In addition to contributing ideas of their own, participants should suggest how ideas of others can be joined into still another idea.[12]

Freewheeling brainstorming sessions are highly productive of new-product ideas. Within forty minutes, one group of twelve men and women produced 136 ideas.[13]

Operational creativity An alternative technique, called "synectics," was developed by William J. J. Gordon. Gordon felt that the main weakness of the Osborn brainstorming session was that it produced solutions too quickly before a sufficient number of perspectives had been developed. Gordon decided that instead of defining the problem specifically, he would define it so broadly that the men would have no inkling of the specific problem.

One of the problems, for example, required designing a vaporproof method of closing vaporproof suits worn by workers who handled high-powered fuels.[14] Gordon kept the specific problem a secret and sparked a discussion of the general notion "closure." This led to images of different closure mechanisms such as bird nests, mouths, or thread. As the group exhausted the initial perspectives, Gordon gradually interjected facts that further defined the problem. Only when Gordon sensed that the group was close to a good solution would he describe the exact nature of the problem. Then the group would start to refine the solution. These sessions would last a minimum of three hours, and often longer, for Gordon believed that fatigue played an important role in unlocking ideas.

Gordon described five themes that guided these idea-conception conferences:

1 *Deferment.* Look first for viewpoints rather than solutions.
2 *Autonomy of object.* Let the problem take on a life of its own.
3 *Use of the commonplace.* Take advantage of the familiar as a springboard to the strange.

---

[12]Osborn, *op. cit.,* p. 156.
[13]*Ibid.,* p. 174.
[14]John W. Lincoln, "Defining a Creativeness in People," in Parnes and Harding, *op. cit.,* pp. 274–75.

4 *Involvement/detachment.* Alternate between entering into the particulars of the problem and standing back from them, in order to see them as instances of a universal.

5 *Use of metaphor.* Let apparently irrelevant, accidental things suggest analogies which are sources of new viewpoints.[15]

SCREENING

The main purpose of the first stage in the new-product development process is to increase the number of good ideas. The main purpose of all the succeeding stages is to *reduce* the number of ideas. The company is not likely to have the resources or the inclination to develop all of the new-product ideas, even if they were all good. And they will not all be equally good. Evaluation and decision now enter the picture. The first idea-pruning stage is screening.

In the screening stage, the company must seek to avoid two types of errors. A *DROP-error* occurs when the company dismisses an otherwise good idea because of a lack of vision of its potentialities. Some companies still shudder when they think of some of the ideas they dismissed:

> Xerox saw the novel promise of Chester Carlson's copying machine; IBM and Eastman Kodak did not see it at all. RCA was able to envision the innovative opportunity of radio; the Victor Talking Machine Company could not. Henry Ford recognized the promise of the automobile; yet only General Motors realized the need to segment the automobile market into price and performance categories, with a model for every classification, if the promise was to be fully achieved. Marshal Field understood the unique market development possibilities of installment buying; Endicott Johnson did not, calling it "the vilest system yet devised to create trouble." And so it has gone.[16]

If a company makes too many DROP-errors, its standards are obviously too conservative.

A *GO-error* occurs when the company lets a poor idea proceed to development and commercialization. We can distinguish at least three types of product failures that ensue. An *absolute product failure* loses money and its sales do not cover variable costs; a *partial product failure* loses money but its sales cover all the variable costs and some of the fixed costs; and a *relative product failure* yields a profit that is less than the company's normal rate of return. Poor screening cannot be held responsible for all product failures; many subsequent factors often cause a bad performance in spite of an essentially good idea. Ford's loss of a whopping $350 million on the Edsel was the result not of a poor idea (to introduce a good car midway between the Ford and Lincoln lines) but of poor execution.[17] Nevertheless, overly lax screening procedures could let too many poor ideas go through, causing GO-errors.

---

[15]*Ibid.,* p. 274.
[16]Hanan, *op. cit.,* p. 44.
[17]For two interesting accounts, see John Brooks, *The Fate of the Edsel and Other Business Adventures* (New York: Harper & Row, Publishers, 1963); and William H. Reynolds, "The Edsel Ten Years Later," *Business Horizons,* Fall 1967, pp. 39–46.

An increasing number of companies are using some sort of formal device for rating and screening product ideas. Checklists are a favorite method.[18]

An example of such a checklist is shown in Table 10-1. The first column lists factors required for successful launching of the product in the marketplace.

Table 10-1
Product-idea rating device

Product success requirements	(A) Relative weight	(B) Company competence level											Rating (A × B)
		.0	.1	.2	.3	.4	.5	.6	.7	.8	.9	1.0	
Company personality and goodwill	.20							√					.120
Marketing	.20										√		.180
Research and development	.20								√				.140
Personnel	.15							√					.090
Finance	.10										√		.090
Production	.05									√			.040
Location and facilities	.05				√								.015
Purchasing and supplies	.05										√		.045
Total	1.00												.720*

Adapted with modifications from Barry M. Richman, "A Rating Scale for Product Innovation," *Business Horizons,* Summer 1962, pp. 37–44.

*Rating scale: .00–.40 poor; .41–.75 fair; .76–1.00 good. Present minimum acceptance rate: .70.

In the next column, management allocates weights to these factors according to their importance. Thus management believes marketing competence will be very important (.20), and purchasing and supplies competence will be of minor importance (.05). The next task is to rate the company's degree of competence on each factor on a scale from .0 to 1.0. Here management feels that its marketing competence is very high (.9) and its location and facilities competence is low (.3). The final step is to multiply the relative importance of the success requirements by the corresponding levels of company competence to obtain a single overall rating of the company's fitness to carry this product successfully into the market. Thus, if marketing is an important success requirement, and this company is very good at marketing, this will increase the overall rating of the product idea. In the example, the product idea scored .72, which, in the company's experience, places it at the high end of the "fair idea" level.

This basic rating device is capable of additional refinements; whether it is advisable to introduce them is largely a matter of how much more would be

[18]For examples, see Charles H. Kline, "The Strategy of Product Policy," *Harvard Business Review,* July–August 1955, pp. 91–100; Barry M. Richman, "A Rating Scale for Product Innovation," *Business Horizons,* Summer 1962, pp. 37–44; John T. O'Meara, Jr., "Selecting Profitable Products," *Harvard Business Review,* January–February 1961, pp. 83–89; and Marshall Freimer and Leonard S. Simon, "Screening New Product Ideas," in *Marketing and the New Science of Planning,* ed. Robert L. King (Chicago: American Marketing Association, 1968), pp. 99–104.

gained. The purpose of the product-screening stage might be missed if the devices became too elaborate. It costs a company money and valuable executive time to review product proposals. Since over half of the proposals are likely to be eliminated at this stage, the company has an interest in rapidly screening out ideas that do not have prima facie appeal. The checklist serves as a means of promoting systematic evaluation and discussion of the product idea among management—it is not designed to make the decision for them.

CONCEPT DEVELOPMENT AND TESTING

Those ideas that survive screening must undergo further development into fully mature product concepts. It is important to distinguish between a product idea, a product concept, and a product image. A *product idea* is a possible product, described in objective functional terms, that the company can see itself offering to the market. A *product concept* is a particular subjective consumer meaning that the company tries to build into the product idea. A *product image* is the particular subjective picture consumers actually acquire of the product.

Concept development

Assume that a large food processor gets the idea to produce a powder that consumers could add to milk to increase the nutritional level and taste of milk. This is a product idea. Consumers, however, do not buy product ideas; they buy product concepts.

A product idea can be turned into a large number of alternative product concepts. First, the question can be asked, Who is to use this product? The powder can be aimed at infants, children, teenagers, adults, senior citizens, or some combination. Second, What primary benefit should be built into this product? Taste, nutrition, refreshment, energy? Third, What is the primary occasion for this drink? Breakfast, midmorning, lunch, midafternoon, dinner, late evening? By asking these questions, many alternative product concepts can be formed for the powder. One is an *instant breakfast drink* aimed at adults who want a quick way to get nutrition at breakfast without preparing a breakfast. Another is a *health supplement* aimed at senior citizens as a nighttime beverage; still another is a *tasty snack drink* designed for children for midday refreshment.

The company must narrow down the choice to one of these concepts. Here it introduces criteria that it wants to achieve with this new product: good rate of return, high sales volume, rounding out of product line, utilization of idle capacity. The criteria could be listed as rows of a matrix, and the alternative product concepts as columns. In each cell a number between 1 and 10 can be placed to indicate how high that product concept stands on that criterion. Certain concepts will profile very poorly on the set of criteria: the market is not large enough, the concept is too novel, and so forth. More data are then collected on the remaining concepts until one is finally chosen as the core product concept.

Product and
brand positioning

Once the core product concept is chosen, it defines the character of the product space in which the new product has to be positioned. An *instant breakfast drink* means that this product will compete against bacon and eggs, breakfast cereals, coffee and pastry, and other solutions to the breakfast problem. A *tasty snack drink* means that this product will compete against soft drinks, ovaltine, and other tasty thirst quenchers. Thus the product concept, and not the product idea, defines the product's competition.

Assume that the instant breakfast drink concept is selected. Figure 10-2A is a *product-positioning map* showing where an instant breakfast drink stands in relation to other breakfast products, using the two dimensions of cost and speed of preparation. An instant breakfast drink stands in a distinctive part of the market, offering the buyer low cost and quick preparation. Its nearest competitor is cold cereal; its most distant competitor is bacon and eggs. This should be kept in mind and utilized in communicating the concept to the market.

If the company is entering a market that has already been formed, then it also has to develop a *brand-positioning map*. Suppose companies A, B, and C have already introduced brands of instant breakfast drinks which are positioned as shown in Figure 10-2B. The new company must decide on how much to charge and how calorific to make its drink, assuming these are salient attributes used by buyers. One possibility is to position the new brand in the medium-price, medium-calorie part of the market; another is to position it in the low-price, low-calorie end of the market. Both would give the new brand distinctiveness, as opposed to positioning the brand right next to another brand and fighting intensely for share-of-market. This decision requires researching the size of alternative preference segments of the market.

Concept testing

Through these steps, the company will arrive at some viable product or brand concepts. Concept testing calls for showing these concepts to a group of target consumers and getting their reactions. The concepts may be presented sym-

Figure 10-2
Product and brand positioning

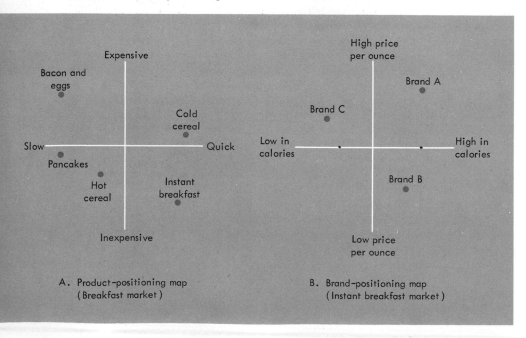

A. Product-positioning map
(Breakfast market)

B. Brand-positioning map
(Instant breakfast market)

bolically or physically. The consumers may be offered a word description such as the following:

> A powdered product that is added to milk to make an instant breakfast that gives the person all the breakfast nutrition he needs, along with good taste and high convenience. The product would be offered in three flavors, chocolate, vanilla, strawberry, and would come in individual packets, six to a box, at seventy-nine cents a box.

The consumers will be asked to react to the total concept and several of its specific attributes. The concept test should include the following questions:[19]

1 *Is the concept clear and easy to understand?* (Often the concept test reveals that people are not really grasping the concept.)

2 *Do you see some distinct benefits of this product over competing offerings?* (The respondents must recognize distinct benefits of this product over its near substitutes.)

3 *Do you like this product better than that of its major competitors?* (The respondents report whether they really prefer this product.)

4 *Would you buy this product?* (The company must find out if there is a sufficient percentage of respondents with an actual intention to buy this product.)

5 *Would this product meet a real need of yours?* (If consumers do not feel a real need for the product, they may buy it only once for curiosity; this will not make it a successful product.)

6 *What improvements can you suggest in various attributes of the product?* (This enables the company to bring about further improvements in form, features, pricing, quality, and so on.)

The contributions of the concept testing will be to help the company enrich the concepts and choose the best among them.

We have focused on a particular example in describing concept development and testing. But the methodology applies to any product, service, or idea, such as an electric car, a new banking service, a new type of museum, or a new health plan. Too many companies think their job is done when they get a product idea. They do not mature it into a full concept and subject it to adequate concept testing. Later the product encounters all kinds of problems in the marketplace which would have been avoided if the company had done a good job of concept development and testing.

BUSINESS ANALYSIS

The purpose of this stage is to project the future sales, profits, and rate of return for the proposed new product, and to determine whether these meet the company's objectives. If they do, the company will develop the new product. Business analysis occurs not only at this stage but throughout the development process as new information is accumulated about the product and the market.

---

[19]For a good discussion, see Edward M. Tauber, "Reduce New Product Failures: Measure Needs as Well as Purchase Intention," *Journal of Marketing*, July 1973, pp. 61–64.

Companies resort to a variety of methods for carrying out the business analysis, such as breakeven analysis, earnings flow discounting, Bayesian decision theory, and risk analysis.[20]

Estimating future sales

The key to whether a product should be developed is whether it will find early and sufficient market acceptance to return a satisfactory profit to the firm. There is no way to estimate future sales with certainty, although one can obtain some helpful benchmarks by carefully examining the history of previous (analogous) products and surveying market opinion. At the very least, management finds it helpful to have estimates of minimum and maximum sales to provide some indication of the risk involved. Unfortunately, the range is sometimes so broad that there is a lot of room for manipulating the figures to draw the desired conclusions. An executive in a small tools company complained that if the salespeople wanted a new product added to the line, they would create a market-potential estimate that would justify it.

Nevertheless, most managers seek a reliable model for sales estimation. Models differ depending upon whether they are designed to estimate the sales of a one-time purchased product, an infrequently purchased product, or a frequently purchased product.[21] Figure 10-3(a) illustrates the life-cycle sales

[20]See Edgar A. Pessemier, *New-Product Decisions: An Analytical Approach* (New York: McGraw-Hill Book Company, 1966).

[21]Among the most promising new-product sales forecasting models are: Frank M. Bass, "A New Product Growth Model for Consumer Durables," *Management Science,* January 1969, pp. 215–27; David B. Learner, "Profit Maximization through New Product Marketing Planning and Control," in *Applications of the Sciences in Marketing Management,* ed. Frank M. Bass, Charles W. King, and Edgar A. Pessemier (New York: John Wiley & Sons, Inc., 1968), pp. 151–67; William F. Massy, "Forecasting the Demand for New Convenience Products," *Journal of Marketing Research,* November 1969, pp. 405–13; J. H. Parfitt and B. J. K. Collins, "The Use of Consumer Panels for Brand Share Prediction," *Journal of Marketing Research,* May 1968, pp. 131–46; Glen L. Urban, "A New Product Analysis and Decision Model," *Management Science,* April 1968, pp. 490–517. These various models are described in detail in Philip Kotler, *Marketing Decision Making: A Model-Building Approach* (New York: Holt, Rinehart & Winston, Inc., 1971), Chap. 17.

Figure 10-3
Sales life cycle for three types of products

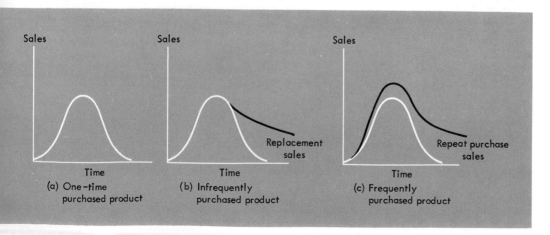

that can be expected for one-time purchased products. They rise at the beginning and later fall toward zero, stopping when no buyers are left. If new buyers keep entering the market, the curve will not go down quite to zero.

Products that are purchased infrequently are exemplified by many durable goods, such as automobiles, toasters, and industrial equipment. These goods exhibit replacement cycles, dictated either by their physical wearing out or their obsolescence associated with changing styles, features, and tastes. Most sales forecasting for this category of products consists of separately estimating new sales to first-time buyers and expected replacement sales (see Figure 10-3(b)).

New products that are repurchased frequently, such as consumer and industrial nondurables, have a sales life cycle resembling Figure 10-3(c). The number of persons buying the product for the first time first increases and then decreases as there are fewer left (assuming a fixed population). Repeat-purchase sales occur soon, providing that the product satisfies some fraction of people who become steady customers. The sales curve eventually falls to a plateau level representing a level of steady repeat-purchase volume; by this time the product is no longer in the class of new products.

Estimating first-time sales   The first task, regardless of the type of product, is to estimate first-time purchases of the new product in each period. There are different ways to do this. Three examples will be described here.

MEDICAL EQUIPMENT   A medical-equipment manufacturer developed a new instrument for rapidly analyzing blood specimens for various potential illness indicators. It could handle a higher volume of blood samples and make a quicker, more accurate analysis than competitive products. The instrument was expensive and likely to be purchased at the rate of one per customer and not replaced for many years.

To estimate market potential, the company first defined the various market segments—they included hospitals, clinics, and unaffiliated laboratories. For each segment, management defined the minimum-size facility that would still be a potential customer for the instrument. Then it turned to data indicating the number of such units in each segment. It reduced the number by the estimated purchase probability, which varied from segment to segment. It then cumulated the number of remaining potential customers over the segments and called this the *market potential.*

The *rate of market penetration* was then estimated. The company saw this as depending on the amount of advertising and personal selling effort per period, the rate of favorable word of mouth, the price set on the machine, and the activity of competitors. This led to an estimate of how much penetration of the remaining market potential could be expected in each period, and this was easily translated into company sales.

ROOM AIR CONDITIONERS   A number of investigators have proposed that models of epidemics (sometimes called contagion models) provide a useful analogy to the new-product diffusion process. They argue that the passage of a message, an idea, or a product from a knower (company or adopter) to a nonknower (potential adopter) is like passage of a germ from an infective to a susceptible. Admittedly, catching a contagious disease lacks the human elements of cognition and volition, which figure prominently in the adoption process. On the other hand, these human mechanisms may not be so important in the case of some new-product introductions; furthermore, modifications of the model may be possible to take these higher-order processes into account.

Bass has used an equation based on an epidemic model to forecast future sales of major appliances, including room air conditioners, electric refrigerators, home freezers, black-and-white television, and power lawn mowers.[22] In each case he used sales data for only the first few years of product introduction to estimate sales for the subsequent years, until replacement demand became a big factor. For example, for one of the new products, room air conditioners, his sales projection fit the pattern of actual sales with a coefficient of determination, $R^2 = .92$. The predicted time of peak was 8.6 years as against an actual time of peak of 7.0 years, and the predicted magnitude of peak was 1.9 million as against an actual peak of 1.8 million. This prediction is close, and the Bass model gave reasonably good fits to several of the other eleven innovations studied.

CONSUMER NONDURABLES   Fourt and Woodlock developed a useful first-time sales model that they tested against several new consumer nondurable products.[23] Their observation of new-product market penetration rates showed that (1) cumulative sales approached a limiting penetration level of less than 100 percent of all households, frequently far less, and (2) the successive increments of gain declined. Their equation is

$$q_t = r\overline{q}(1 - r)^{t-1} \tag{10-1}$$

where:

q_t = percentage of total U.S. households expected to try the product in period t

r = rate of penetration of untapped potential

$\overline{q}$ = percentage of total U.S. households expected to eventually try the new product

t = time period

Assume that a new product is about to be introduced where it is estimated that 40 percent of all households will eventually try the new product ($\overline{q} = .4$). Furthermore it is believed that in each period 30 percent of the remaining new-buyer potential is penetrated ($r = .3$). Therefore the percentage of U.S. households trying the product in each of the first four periods will be

$$q_1 = r\overline{q}(1 - r)^{1-1} = (.3)(.4)(.7^0) = .120$$

$$q_2 = r\overline{q}(1 - r)^{2-1} = (.3)(.4)(.7^1) = .084$$

$$q_3 = r\overline{q}(1 - r)^{3-1} = (.3)(.4)(.7^2) = .059$$

$$q_4 = r\overline{q}(1 - r)^{4-1} = (.3)(.4)(.7^3) = .041$$

As time goes to infinity, the incremental trial percentage goes to zero. To estimate dollar sales from new triers in any period, the estimated trial rate for the

[22]Bass, *op. cit.*

[23]Louis A. Fourt and Joseph N. Woodlock, "Early Prediction of Market Success for New Grocery Products," *Journal of Marketing*, October 1960, pp. 31–38.

period given by equation (10-1) is multiplied by the total number of U.S. households times the expected first purchase expenditures per household on the product.

The analyst who wishes to use equation (10-1) first estimates $\bar{q}$ using market surveys. He then estimates r on the basis of how fast potential buyers are likely to learn about the product and seek to purchase it. Once the product has been introduced, and two periods have passed, the analyst can update his estimate of r by observing what occurs.

Estimating replacement or repeat sales If the product is expected to have replacement sales, they are estimated and added to the estimate of first-time sales. The company has to guess at the *survival-age distribution* of the product it has designed. The lower end of the age distribution will indicate when the first replacement sales will take place. The actual dates of replacement will also be influenced by how much discretion the buyers have with respect to replacing the product, new-product alternatives, the state of the economy, and other factors. Needless to say, replacement sales are difficult to estimate before the product is in actual use, and some manufacturers prefer to rest the case for the new product solely on the basis of first-time sales.

As for frequently purchased products, the seller has to estimate repeat as well as first-time sales. This is because the unit value of frequently purchased products is low, and repeat purchases take place soon after the introduction. A high rate of repeat purchasing means buyer satisfaction with the product; sales are likely to remain high even after all first-time purchases take place. The seller should note the percentage of repeat purchases that take place in each *repeat-purchase class:* those who buy once, twice, three times, and so on. Some products and brands are bought a few times and then dropped. It is important to estimate whether the repeat-purchase ratio is likely to rise or fall, and at what rate, with deeper repeat-purchase classes.[24]

Estimating future costs and profits

Most companies treat costs as something to consider after the sales have been estimated. This is because many costs, particularly labor and raw material, vary with the level of output. Marketing costs are also often treated in the same way because of a budgeting approach to setting them. However, this treatment of marketing costs is illogical, because it is in the nature of promotional expenditures to influence both sales and cost simultaneously. The dual role of marketing effort as both a cost and a sales stimulant must be simultaneously considered in the analysis.

The ideal way to plan marketing costs is to seek an expression that relates sales and profits to alternative marketing programs and costs. We start with the *profit equation:*

$$Z_t = (P_t - c_t)Q_t - F_t - M_t \qquad (10\text{-}2)$$

where:

Z_t = profits in year t
P_t = average price in year t

---
[24]See *ibid.*

c_t = variable cost per unit in year t
Q_t = number of units demanded in year t
F_t = fixed cost of manufacturing and selling in year t
M_t = marketing costs in year t

Next suppose we estimate a total demand forecasting equation:[25]

$$Q_t = Q_0(1 + g)^t \left(\frac{P_0}{P_t} \right)^{e_P} \left[\frac{M_t}{M_0(1 + g)^t} \right]^{e_M} \left(\frac{Y_t}{Y_0} \right)^{e_Y} \tag{10-3}$$

where:

Q = total market demand
g = annual growth rate of demand
P = average industry price (each brand's price weighted by its market share)
M = total marketing expenditure for industry
Y = average income per capita
e = elasticity parameter
t = time subscript for year
0 = time subscript for year 0

According to this equation, total market demand is expected to be responsive to both environmental and marketing factors. Starting with a specific demand level in the base year, Q_0, demand grows through time at the constant annual rate g. A separate environmental influence on demand is wielded by the current level of national income in relation to the base level of national income, its magnitude of response being given by e_Y, the income elasticity. Demand is also influenced by two marketing variables, price and marketing expenditure. As current price rises above the base price, demand is depressed to an extent governed by the price elasticity of demand. As current marketing expenditures rise above the base level modified by normal growth, demand is stimulated to an extent governed by the promotional elasticity of demand.

Finally, assume that the company's market share will be determined by its marketing effort relative to competitors, as given by a market-share equation such as equation (6-5), p. 123. This market-share equation predicts that the company's market share will be related to the settings of its marketing instruments relative to the average settings of competition. The marketing expenditure items are adjusted for their effectiveness indices, as well as their elasticities.

Given the profit equation, total-demand equation, and market-share equation, management has a framework for studying the profit impact of different possible marketing programs. In principle, the last two equations can be substituted into the profit equation, and calculus can be used to find the profit-maximizing marketing program. If the equation is too intractable to be solved for an optimum, then simulation methodology can be used.[26]

[25]This demand equation is adapted from Alfred A. Kuehn and Doyle L. Weiss, "Marketing Analysis Training Exercise," *Behavioral Science,* January 1965, pp. 51–57, esp. p. 55.

[26]For example, see the author's "Competitive Strategies for New Product Marketing over the Life Cycle," *Management Science,* December 1965, pp. 104–19.

PRODUCT DEVELOPMENT

Product ideas appearing sound from a business point of view can now be turned over to the research and development department. This is an important step in at least three ways. It marks the first attempt to develop the product in a "concrete" form. Up to now, it has existed only as an idea, or perhaps as a drawing, or a very crude mock-up. Second, it represents a very large investment, which is likely to dwarf the idea-evaluation costs incurred in the earlier stages. Much time and many dollars go into trying to develop a technically feasible product. And finally, it provides an answer as to whether the product idea can be translated into a technically and commercially feasible product. If not, the company's investment up to now is lost except for any by-product information gained in the process.

Three steps are involved in the product-development stage: prototype development and consumer testing, branding, and packaging.

Prototype development and consumer testing

The first task is for the research and development department to build a physical prototype that realizes the attributes specified in the product concept and is trouble-free and economical to manufacture. For example, the Maxwell House Division of General Foods discovered, through consumer research, a strong preference for a brand of coffee that would strike the consumer as "bold, vigorous, deep tasting." Its laboratory technicians spent over four months working with various coffee blends and flavors to formulate a corresponding taste. Even then it turned out to be very expensive to produce, and the company took steps to "cost reduce" the blend.[27] All too often the technicians produce a prototype that compromises the original product concept, and this contributes to subsequent product failure.

The experience of the Bissell Company is also enlightening. The company designers and engineers developed a prototype for a combination electric vacuum and floor scrubber:

> . . . four were left with the research and development department for continued tests on such things as water lift, motor lift, effectiveness in cleaning, and dust bag design. The other eight were sent to the company's advertising agency for test by a panel of fifty housewives. The research and development department found some serious problems in their further tests of the product. The life of the motor was not sufficiently long, the filter bag did not fit properly, and the scrubber foot was not correct. Similarly, the consumer tests brought in many consumer dissatisfactions that had not been anticipated: the unit was too heavy, the vacuum did not glide easily enough, and the scrubber left some residue on the floor after use.[28]

Consumer testing goes hand in hand with prototype development. Various methods have been proposed for the testing of consumer preferences among a set

---

[27]See "Maxwell House Division (A)" (Soldiers Field, Boston: Intercollegiate Case Clearing House, ICH 13M83, 1970).

[28]Ralph Westfall and Harper W. Boyd, Jr., *Cases in Marketing Management* (Homewood, Ill.: Richard D. Irwin, Inc., 1961), p. 365.

of prototype alternatives, such as paired comparisons, multiple choices, and ranking procedures. Consumers are normally asked to sample the alternative products in a laboratory or home setting, and the testing organization exercises the normal controls to avoid biased results. The company examines the results and decides on the prototype model that seems most promising on the overall criteria.

Brand naming

The brand name should not be a casual afterthought but an integral part or reinforcer of the product concept. Among the desirable qualities for a brand name are:

1   *It should suggest something about the product's benefits.* Examples: Coldspot, Beautyrest, Craftsman, Accutron.
2   *It should suggest product qualities such as action, color, or whatever.* Examples: Duz, Sunkist, Spic and Span, Firebird.
3   *It should be easy to pronounce, recognize, and remember.* Short names help. Examples: Tide, Crest.
4   *It should be distinctive.* Examples: Mustang, Kodak.

Some marketing research firms have developed elaborate name-research procedures including *association tests* (what images come to mind), *learning tests* (how easily is the name pronounced), *memory tests* (how well is the name remembered), and *preference tests* (which names are preferred).

The goal of many firms is to build a unique brand name that will eventually become identified with the generic product. Such brand names as Frigidaire, Kleenex, Levis, Jello, Scotch tape, and Fiberglas have succeeded in this way. However, their very success has threatened some of the companies with the loss of exclusive rights to the name. Cellophane and shredded wheat are now names in the common domain. Because of legal action, Du Pont has to describe its product as Du Pont Cellophane and Nabisco has to describe its product as Nabisco Shredded Wheat.

Packaging

Until recently, packaging has been considered a minor element in the marketing mix for a product. The two traditional packaging concerns of manufacturers are product *protection* and *economy*. A third packaging objective, which comes closer to considering the consumer, is *convenience*. This means such things as size options and packages that are easy to open. Over the years a fourth packaging objective has received increasing recognition from manufacturers, particularly those in the consumers' goods field. This is the *promotional* function. Various factors account for the growing recognition of packaging as an independent and potent selling tool:

Self-service. An increasing number of products are sold on a self-service basis as a result of the spread of supermarkets and discount houses. The package must now perform many of the sales tasks. It must attract attention, describe the product's features, give the consumer confidence, and make a favorable overall impression.

Consumer affluence. The steady rise in American incomes has caused consumers to attach increasing importance to nonprice features. They are willing to pay a little more for convenience, appearance, dependability, and prestige. Packaging is an important vehicle for projecting these qualities.

Integrated marketing concept. Companies are increasingly trying to endow their brands with distinctive personalities. These personalities are conveyed through the general company image, through advertising messages and media, through the choice of brand name, and through packaging.

Innovational opportunity. Packaging is an area where innovation per se can bring large sales gains. One has only to think of pop-top and aerosol cans, boil-a-pak dinners, and plastic-animal bubble-bath containers.

Developing the package for a new product requires a large number of decisions. The first task is to establish the *packaging concept.* The packaging concept is a definition of what the package should basically *be* or *do* for the particular product. Should the main function(s) of the package be to offer superior product protection, introduce a novel dispensing method, suggest certain qualities about the product or the company, or something else?

> General Foods developed a new dog-food product in the form of meatlike patties. Management decided that the unique and palatable appearance of these patties demanded the maximum visibility. Visibility was defined as the basic packaging concept, and management considered alternatives in this light. It finally narrowed down the choice to a tray with a film covering.[29]

A host of further decisions must be made on the component elements of the package design—*size, shape, materials, color, text,* and *brand mark.* Decisions must be made between much text or little text, between cellophane and other transparent films, a plastic or a laminate tray, and so on. Each packaging element must be harmonized with the other packaging elements; size suggests certain things about materials, materials suggest certain things about colors, and so forth. The packaging elements also must be guided by decisions on pricing, advertising, and other marketing elements.

After the package is designed, companies put it through a number of tests before it is finalized. *Engineering tests* are conducted to ensure that the packaging stands up under normal conditions; *visual tests,* to ensure that the script is legible and the colors harmonious; *dealer tests,* to ensure that dealers find the packages attractive and easy to handle; and *consumer tests,* to ensure favorable consumer reaction.

In spite of these precautions, a packaging design occasionally gets through with some basic flaw that is discovered belatedly:

> Sizzl-Spray, a pressurized can of barbecue sauce developed by Heublein, . . . had a potential packaging disaster that was discovered in the market tests. . . . "We thought we had a good can, but fortunately we first test marketed the product in stores in Texas and California. It appears as soon as the cans got warm they began to explode. Because we hadn't gotten into national distribution, our loss was only $150,000 instead of a couple of million."[30]

[29]See "General Foods—Post Division (B)," Case M-102, Harvard Business School, 1964.

[30]"Product Tryouts: Sales Tests in Selected Cities Help Trim Risks of National Marketings," *Wall Street Journal,* August 10, 1962, p. 1.

By now it becomes clear why developing a packaging for a new product may cost a few hundred thousand dollars and take from six months to a year to finalize. According to a traditional view of the functions of packaging, it may seem an excessive amount. But to those who recognize the promotional potency of packaging, it is a very small investment.

TEST MARKETING

Up to this time the reaction of potential buyers to the new product has not been tested under normal marketing conditions. Potential customers have been asked to react to one or more product features and to comment on the packaging and advertising appeals. Test marketing is the stage where the entire product and marketing program is tried out for the first time in a small number of well-chosen and authentic sales environments.

Not all companies choose the route of test marketing. A company officer of Revlon, Inc., stated:

> In our field—primarily higher-priced cosmetics not geared for mass distribution—it would be unnecessary for us to market test. When we develop a new product, say an improved liquid makeup, we know it's going to sell because we're familiar with the field. And we've got 1,500 demonstrators in department stores to promote it.[31]

The decision to test-market is related to the degree of confidence the manufacturer has in the new product. In Bayesian language, it is a matter of comparing the "expected value of immediate action" and the "expected value of first sampling and then acting." Suppose, in a particular case, it is estimated that test marketing would cost $100,000. Suppose the company has estimated that it may lose at most $2 million if the product fails. If management felt the odds of this product's failing were one in 100, then its expected loss for going national would only be $20,000 (2,000,000 × 1/100). Thus the expected loss from immediately going national is only one-fifth of the sure loss of $100,000 if the company pays for a market test.

If management thought the product had only an even chance of succeeding—and only 50 percent of new products are clear successes, according to the Booz, Allen & Hamilton study—then paying $100,000 for a market test makes good sense. The company is paying a small sum of money to protect its interest in a much larger sum.

Test marketing is more frequently used by consumer companies than industrial companies. Industrial companies get their new-product feedback in more informal ways. When an industrial concern develops a new product, its sales representatives usually take it around to a sample of prospective buyers to learn their reactions. Often they pick up ideas and suggestions that lead the company to rework the product. When the company is finally satisfied that a sufficient number of prospective customers like the product in its latest form, the company adds the product to its catalog and prepares to sell it nationally. Thus "test marketing" in industrial situations amounts in reality to a "market probe."

---

[31]*Ibid.*

The test marketing of new consumer products is a much more organized and grandiose proposition. The normal test costs more than $100,000, mostly in fees for marketing research and advertising. Typically these figures do not include production and physical distribution expenses, since they are expected to be covered by test sales. The test may involve three to six different cities and run from six weeks to as much as two years, depending on how long it takes to establish the repurchase rate.

**Reasons for
test marketing**

Test marketing is expected to yield several benefits. The primary motive for testing is to *improve knowledge of potential product sales.* If product sales fall below breakeven expectations in the test markets, then for a relatively small amount of money, the company has averted the expense and embarrassment of a national product fiasco.

A second motive for test marketing is to *pretest alternative marketing plans.* Some years ago Colgate-Palmolive used a different marketing appeal in each of four cities to test-market a new soap product.[32] The four approaches were:

An average amount of advertising coupled with free samples distributed door to door

Heavy advertising plus samples

An average amount of advertising linked with mailed redeemable coupons

An average amount of advertising with no special introductory offer

Colgate found that the third alternative generated the best sales. Subject to certain qualifications, it gained some evidence on the relative merits of different marketing mixes.

Some other benefits may also be derived from test marketing. The company may discover a product fault that escaped its attention in the product-development stage. The company may pick up valuable clues to distribution-level problems. And the company may gain a richer understanding of the various segments making up the market.

**Procedures for
test marketing**

Test marketing is rapidly approaching the state of a science, or at least a highly developed art. Large companies such as Procter & Gamble and General Foods have accumulated considerable experience, and they generally develop their test plans internally. Companies with less experience generally rely on advertising agencies, specialized consultants, or large marketing service firms such as A. C. Nielsen Company. The major decisions in test marketing concern the number of test cities to use, the selection of the cities, the length of the test run, the type of information to collect, and the action to take on the basis of test results.

How many test cities?

Great variation is found in the number of cities used in market tests. When 102 firms were asked how many test cities they use, almost half used fewer than four cities.[33] Results can be expected to be more representative as the sample size is increased. Additional cities allow the company to set up better experi-

---

[32]*Ibid.*

[33]*Printer's Ink,* April 13, 1962, p. 22. This was a special issue devoted to test marketing. The author has relied on this source for some of the statistics.

mental controls, test more alternative mixes, and probe more carefully for regional differences. But setup and auditing fees increase with the number of cities. The benefits of including an additional city must exceed the cost of including it. In general, a larger number of cities should be used: the greater the maximum possible loss and/or the probability of loss from going national; the greater the number of alternative marketing plans and/or the greater the uncertainty surrounding which is best; the greater the number of regional differences; and the greater the chance of calculated test-market interference by competitors.

Which cities?

No single city in the United States is a perfect replication in miniature of the nation as a whole. Some cities, however, typify aggregate national or regional characteristics better than others and have become popular for test-marketing purposes: Syracuse, New York; Dayton, Ohio; Peoria, Illinios; and Des Moines, Iowa.

Each company develops its own test-city selection criteria. One company restricts its choice of test cities to those with several industries, good media coverage, cooperative chain stores, average competitive activity, and no evidence of being overtested. Additional test-city selection criteria may be introduced because of the special characteristics of the product. For example, Patio Foods wanted to test-market a new line of frozen Mexican dinners; its city selection criteria included the incidence of travel to Mexico, the existence of a Spanish-language press, and the retail sales of prepared chili and frozen Chinese food.

How long should the test run?

Market tests have lasted anywhere from a few months to several years. The test duration is decided in each case by the individual circumstances.

The first factor is the product's *average repurchase period,* that is, the length of time that normally elapses before the purchaser restocks the product. The new product may have gotten into the consumer's hands as a free sample, or on a special deal, or as an impulse purchase. Asking for his opinion after he uses it is not an adequate substitute for observing his next purchase. It is highly desirable to observe a few repurchase periods.

The second factor is the *competitive situation.* A company wants the market test to last long enough to get useful information but not so long that competitors are given a chance to catch up.

The third factor is *cost.* The total costs of test marketing vary directly with the test's duration. The expenses of auditing the sales results and supervising the test continue through the test period. The company also bears the opportunity costs of not introducing the product earlier.

What information should be collected during the test?

The planner must decide what sales and other information is required to evaluate the new product's strengths and weaknesses. He must then make arrangements with the company's marketing research department and outside commercial services to gather this information.

Product-shipments data The most readily available data are product shipments to test markets. Product shipments are made in response to dealers' orders for new stock. But because of reporting lags and inventory-level changes, weekly changes in shipment figures do not necessarily reflect weekly changes in the rate of retail sales.

Store audits To keep abreast of the actual movement of retail sales, it is necessary to arrange for periodic store audits. The company has the option of buying periodic reports from a regular commercial service or arranging for special auditing. One limitation is that sales information gained through store audits does not reveal anything about the characteristics of the buyers, such as the proportion of new buyers to repeat buyers.

Consumer panels Information on buyer characteristics can be obtained from consumer panels. If the company has introduced a new brand of coffee, it can purchase information on the coffee-brand purchase sequences of the sample of households in the test areas. From these data, the firm can estimate how much repeat purchasing of its brand is taking place, from what particular brands it is gaining customers and to what particular brands it is losing customers, what types of customers are showing the most interest in the new brand, and so forth. The firm can process the data into a Markov model for forecasting future market shares on the basis of the early brand-switching and -staying rates.[34]

Buyer surveys The company may also want to obtain direct data on buyer attitudes and reactions to the new product. This involves getting the names of a sample of new buyers and arranging to interview them. The following plan was used by a company that was introducing a new aftershave lotion:

> It was proposed that retailers be induced to procure names and addresses of all purchasers of the new item until names of about 600 purchasers in each city were obtained. This could be done by offering clerks in retail outlets 10¢ for each purchaser's name secured. Six weeks after their purchases, these consumers would be contacted by investigators who would disguise their interest in after-shave lotion through a series of questions concerning other products. During the interview attention would finally be centered on after-shave lotions.[35]

Miscellaneous studies Among other things to study during the test-market period are trade attitudes, retail distribution, and the effectiveness of advertising, promotion, and point-of-sale material. In general, the more information the company collects, the better its chances of making its right decision.[36]

**What action should be
taken after the test?**

The test results will be helpful to management in two ways. First, hopefully they will yield some reliable evidence of the product's sales and profit potential. Table 10-2 shows four possible results for two key measures, *trial rates* and *repurchase rates*. If the test markets show a high trial and high repurchase rate, this suggests the desirability of a Go decision. If the test markets show a high trial rate and a low repurchase rate, then the customers are not satisfied with the

---

[34]See Benjamin Lipstein, "Tests for Test Markets," *Harvard Business Review,* March–April 1961, pp. 74–77; and William D. Barclay, "Probability Model for Early Prediction of New Product Market Success," *Journal of Marketing,* January 1963, pp. 63–68.

[35]Harper W. Boyd, Jr., and Ralph Westfall, *Marketing Research: Text and Cases* (Homewood, Ill.: Richard D. Irwin, Inc., 1956), p. 613.

[36]For a Bayesian approach to deciding what type of market information to gather, see Frank M. Bass, "Marketing Research Expenditures: A Decision Model," *Journal of Business,* January 1963, pp. 77–90.

product and it should be either redesigned or abandoned. If the test markets show a low trial rate and a high repurchase rate, then the product seems good but more people must be influenced to try it earlier: this means increasing advertising and sales promotion. Finally, if the trial and repurchase rates are both low, then the product appears destined to fail.

Table 10-2
Alternative actions following test-market results

Trial rate	Repurchase rate	Action
High	High	Commercialize the product
High	Low	Redesign product or drop it
Low	High	Increase advertising and sales promotion
Low	Low	Drop the product

Even here, some authorities will question the predictive value of test-market results. Achenbaum has listed five concerns:

1. There is the problem of obtaining a set of markets that is reasonably representative of the country as a whole.

2. There is the problem of translating national media plans into local equivalents.

3. There is the problem of estimating what is going to happen next year based on what has happened in this year's competitive environment.

4. There is the problem of competitive knowledge of your test and of deciding whether any local counteractivities are representative of what competition will do nationally at a later date.

5. There is the problem of extraneous and uncontrollable factors such as economic conditions and weather.[37]

Achenbaum contends that market testing's main value lies not in sales forecasting but in learning about unsuspected problems and opportunities connected with the new product. He points to the large number of products that failed after successful test-market results. Some large companies are beginning to skip the test-marketing stage altogether.

COMMERCIALIZATION

What is involved in introducing the product commercially? Among other things, the company must finalize all the attributes of product and package. It must invest in new equipment and facilities to make large-scale production possible. It must train and motivate the sales force and dealers. It must arrange a complete advertising and promotion program with its agency.

---

[37]Alvin A. Achenbaum, "The Purpose of Test Marketing," in *The Marketing Concept in Action,* ed. Robert M. Kaplan (Chicago: American Marketing Association, 1964), p. 582.

All of these steps involve expenditures that rapidly dwarf those incurred up to this stage. To introduce a major new household detergent into the national market may require $10 million for advertising and promotion alone. In the introduction of new food products, marketing expenditures typically represent 57 percent of sales during the first year. This average ratio is 4.1 times as great as the overall advertising-to-sales ratio of the companies introducing these products.[38] The companies cannot expect to operate in the black for the first two years.

The product generally is not introduced all at once on a national scale but is rolled out into the prime markets and regions first.[39] The *rate of planned market expansion* is governed by a number of factors. If the test-market results are very encouraging, the company will try to introduce the product on a full-speed basis, especially if competition is rushing into the same market. A company that is less confident about its new product will move more slowly into new markets. It recognizes that it may be limiting its gain for the sake of being able to limit its loss.

Whether the company introduces its new product swiftly or gradually, it needs to schedule its commercial introduction carefully. The smooth coordination and progression of the hundreds of activities making up the commercialization stage warrant the use of some advanced scheduling technique, such as critical path analysis.[40]

THE CONSUMER-ADOPTION PROCESS

The *consumer-adoption process* begins where the *firm's innovation process* leaves off. It deals with the process by which potential customers come to learn about the new product, try it, and eventually adopt or reject it. It underlies the introduction and rapid growth stages of the product life cycle. The producer's problem is to understand this process so that he can bring about early market awareness and trial usage. The *consumer-adoption process* should be distinguished from the *consumer-loyalty process*, which is the concern of the established producer.

The earliest approach used by new-product marketers for launching a new product was to distribute it widely and inform everyone who might be a potential purchaser. This *mass-market approach*, however, has two drawbacks: (1) it requires heavy marketing expenditures, and (2) it involves a substantial number of wasted exposures to nonpotential buyers. These drawbacks led to a second approach called *heavy-user target marketing*, that of directing the product to the group that tends to account for a substantial share of all purchasing. This makes sense, providing heavy users are identifiable and among the first to try the new product. But it was noticed that even within the heavy-user group, persons differed in how much interest they showed in new products and in how

---

[38]Robert D. Buzzell and Robert E. Nourse, *Product Innovation, the Product Life Cycle, and Competitive Behavior in Selected Food Processing Industries, 1947–1964* (Cambridge, Mass.: Arthur D. Little, Inc., 1966).

[39]For an analysis of the problem of ranking alternative market areas for expansion, see William R. King, "Marketing Expansion—A Statistical Analysis," *Management Science*, July 1963, pp. 563–73.

[40]See Yung Wong, "Critical Path Analysis for New Product Planning," *Journal of Marketing*, October 1964, pp. 53–59.

fast they could be drawn into trying them. Certain persons tended to be earlier adopters than others. The import of this finding is that the new-product marketer ought to direct his marketing effort to those persons who are most likely to adopt the product early. *Early-adopter theory* grew around this view and held that

1 Persons within a target market will differ in the amount of time that passes between their exposure to a new product and their trial of the new product.
2 Early adopters are likely to share some traits in common which differentiate them from late adopters.
3 There exist efficient media for reaching early adopter types.
4 Early adopter types are likely to be high on opinion leadership and therefore helpful in "advertising" the new product to other potential buyers.

The new-product marketer's task, at the time of launching, is to define the best early prospects for his new product. Ideally, the best early prospects would have four characteristics:

1 They would be early-adopter types.
2 They would be heavy users.
3 They would be high on opinion leadership.
4 They would not be too expensive to reach.

We now turn to the theory of innovation diffusion, which provides clues to identifying the best early prospects.

Concepts in innovation diffusion

The central concept is that of an *innovation*, which refers to any good, service, or idea that is *perceived* by someone as new.[41] The idea may have had a long history, but it is still an innovation to the person who sees it as being new.

Innovations are assimilated into the social system over time. *Diffusion process* is the name given to "the spread of a new idea from its source of invention or creation to its ultimate users or adopters."[42] The *adoption process*, on the other hand, focuses on "the mental process through which an individual passes from first hearing about an innovation to final adoption." *Adoption* itself is a decision by an individual to use an innovation regularly.

The differences among individuals in their response to new ideas is called their *innovativeness*. Specifically, innovativeness is "the degree to which an individual is relatively earlier in adopting new ideas than the other members of his social system." On the basis of their innovativeness, individuals can be classified into different *adopter categories*. (See pp. 225–26.)

Individuals also can be classified in terms of their influence on others with respect to innovations. *Opinion leaders* are "those individuals from whom others seek information or advice." Individuals or firms who actively seek to change other people's minds are called *change agents*.

Propositions about the consumer-adoption process

We are now ready to examine the main generalizations drawn from hundreds of studies of how people accept new ideas.

---

[41]This discussion leans heavily on Everett M. Rogers's *Diffusion of Innovations* (New York: The Free Press, 1962).
[42]See *ibid.* for this and following definitions.

Stages in the adoption process The first proposition is that *the individual consumer goes through a series of stages of acceptance in the process of adopting a new product.* The stages are classified by Rogers as follows:

1 *Awareness:* the individual becomes cognizant of the innovation but lacks information about it.
2 *Interest:* the individual is stimulated to seek information about the innovation.
3 *Evaluation:* the individual considers whether it would make sense to try the innovation.
4 *Trial:* the individual tries the innovation on a small scale to improve his estimate of its utility.
5 *Adoption:* the individual decides to make full and regular use of the innovation.[43]

The value of this model of the adoption process is that it requires the innovator to think carefully about new-product acceptance. The manufacturer of electric dishwashers may discover that many housewives are frozen in the interest stage; they cannot jump the gap to the trial stage, because of their uncertainty and the large investment. But these same housewives would be willing to use an electric dishwasher on a trial basis for a small fee. Recognizing this, the manufacturer may institute a trial-use plan with option to buy.

Individual differences in innovativeness The second proposition is that *people differ markedly in their penchant for trying new products.* In each product area, there are apt to be leaders and early adopters. Some women are the first to adopt new clothing fashions or new appliances such as the microwave oven; some doctors are the first to prescribe new medicines;[44] and some farmers are the first to adopt new farming methods.[45]

Other individuals, however, tend to adopt innovations much later. This has led to a classification of people into the adopter categories shown in Figure 10-4.

---

[43]*Ibid.*, pp. 81ff.
[44]See James Coleman, Elihu Katz, and Herbert Menzel, "The Diffusion of an Innovation among Physicians," *Sociometry*, December 1957, pp. 253–70.
[45]See J. Bohlen and G. Beal, *How Farm People Accept New Ideas*, Special Report No. 15 (Ames: Iowa State College Agricultural Extension Service, November 1955).

Figure 10-4
Adopter categorization on the basis of relative time of adoption of innovations

SOURCE: Redrawn from Everett M. Rogers, *Diffusion of Innovations* (New York: The Free Press, 1962), p. 162.

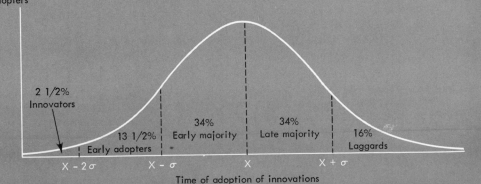

The adoption process is represented as following a normal (or near normal) distribution when plotted over time. After a slow start, an increasing number of people adopt the innovation, the number reaches a peak, and then it diminishes as fewer individuals remain in the nonadopter category.

Convenient breaks in the distribution are used to establish adopter categories. Thus innovators are defined as the first $2\frac{1}{2}$ percent of the individuals to adopt a new idea, the early adopters are the next $13\frac{1}{2}$ percent who adopt the new idea, and so forth. Although this partitioning in terms of unit standard deviations is somewhat arbitrary, the model provides the standardization needed to facilitate comparisons of different studies of product adoption.

Rogers has tried to characterize the five adopter groups in terms of ideational values.[46] The dominant value of innovators is *venturesomeness;* they like to try new ideas, even at some risk, and are cosmopolite in orientation. The dominant value of early adopters is *respect;* they enjoy a position in the community as opinion leaders and adopt new ideas early but with discretion. The dominant value of the early majority is *deliberateness;* these people like to adopt new ideas before the average member of the social system, although they rarely are leaders. The dominant value of the late majority is *skepticism;* they do not adopt an innovation until the weight of majority opinion seems to legitimize its utility. Finally, the dominant value of the laggards is *tradition;* they are suspicious of any changes, mix with other tradition-bound people, and adopt the innovation only because it has now taken on a measure of tradition itself.

The marketing implication of the adopter classification is that an innovating firm should direct its communications to those people who are likely to be early in adopting the innovation; messages reaching late adopters and laggards are wasted.

The identification of early adopters is not easy. So far no one has demonstrated the existence of a general personality factor called innovativeness. Individuals tend to be innovative in certain areas and laggard in others. We can think of a businessman who dresses conservatively but who delights in trying unfamiliar cuisines. The firm's problem is to identify the characteristics of those who are likely to be early adopters in its product area. The probability of being an early adopter may turn out to be related to easily identified economic, educational, social or personality characteristics. For example, studies show that innovative farmers are likely to be better educated and more efficient than noninnovative farmers.[47] Innovative housewives are more gregarious and usually of a higher social status than noninnovative housewives.[48] Certain communities, especially those with higher than average mobility, tend to be more ready to accept new ideas. Drawing on several studies, Rogers offered the following hypotheses about early adopters:

> The relatively earlier adopters in a social system tend to be younger in age, have higher social status, a more favorable financial position, more specialized operations, and a different type of mental ability from later adopters. Earlier adopters utilize information sources that are more impersonal and cosmopolite than later adopters and that are in closer contact with the origin of new ideas. Earlier

[46]*Ibid.,* pp. 168ff.

[47]For a summary of these studies, see Rogers, *op. cit.,* p. 176.

[48]Elihu Katz and Paul F. Lazarsfeld, *Personal Influence* (New York: The Free Press, 1955), pp. 234ff.

adopters utilize a greater number of different information sources than do later adopters. The social relationships of earlier adopters are more cosmopolite than for later adopters, and earlier adopters have more opinion leadership.[49]

Once the characteristics of early adopters are identified, a marketing communications program can be developed for the new product calculated to reach and interest these people. The known media habits of these people can be used to increase the effectiveness of the company's advertising. The company can also supply samples to community leaders and utilize store demonstrations to attract the early adopters.

Role of personal influence   The third proposition is that *personal influence plays a very large role in the adoption of new products.* By *personal influence* is meant the effect of product statements made by one person on another's attitude or probability of purchase. Katz and Lazarsfeld reported:

> About half of the women in our sample reported that they had recently made some change from a product or brand to which they were accustomed to something new. The fact that one third of these changes involved personal influences indicates that there is also considerable traffic in marketing advice. Women consult each other for opinions about new products, about the quality of different brands, about shopping economies and the like. . . .[50]

Although personal influence is an important factor throughout the diffusion process, its significance is greater in some situations and for some individuals than for others. Personal influence seems to be more important in the evaluation stage of the adoption process than in the other stages. It seems to have more influence on the later adopters than the earlier adopters. And it appears to be more important in risky situations than in safe situations.[51]

Recognizing the role of personal influence can make an important contribution to marketing planning. It tempers one's enthusiasm about media advertising messages designed to supply early adopters with ways of verbalizing their opinions to others. It highlights the importance of designing a good product that users will want to talk about to others.

Influence of product characteristics on the rate of adoption   The fourth proposition is that *the character of the innovation itself affects the rate of adoption.* Five characteristics seem to have an especially important influence on the adoption rate.[52] The first is the innovation's *relative advantage,* or the degree to which it appears superior to previous ideas. The greater the perceived relative advantage, whether in terms of higher profitability, reliability, or ease of operation, the more quickly the innovation will be adopted.

---

[49]Rogers, *op. cit.,* p. 192.

[50]Katz and Lazarsfeld, *op. cit.,* p. 234.

[51]Rogers, *op. cit.,* pp. 219–23. For additional hypotheses about personal influence, see Johan Arndt, "Role of Product-Related Conversations in the Diffusion of a New Product," *Journal of Marketing Research,* August 1967, pp. 291–95; and Shlomo I. Lampert, "Word of Mouth Activity during the Introduction of a New Food Product," in *Consumer Behavior: Theory and Application,* ed. J. U. Farley, J. A. Howard, and L. W. Ring (Boston: Allyn & Bacon, Inc., 1974), pp. 67–88.

[52]Lampert, *op. cit.,* Chap. 5.

The second characteristic is the innovation's *compatibility*, or the degree to which it is consistent with the values and experiences of the individuals in the social system.

Third is the innovation's *complexity*, or the degree to which it is relatively difficult to understand or use. The more complex innovations are likely to take a longer time to diffuse, other things being equal.

Fourth is the innovation's *divisibility*, or the degree to which it may be tried on a limited basis. The evidence of many studies indicates that divisibility helps to increase the rate of adoption.

The fifth characteristic is the innovation's *communicability*, or the degree to which the results are observable or describable to others. Innovations that lend themselves to better demonstration or description of advantage will diffuse faster in the social system.

All of these characteristics should be given maximum consideration in developing the new product and its marketing program.

SUMMARY

More and more organizations are recognizing the advantages, indeed the necessity, of developing new products and services. If anything, their current offerings are facing shortening life spans and must be replaced by newer products.

New-product development, however, is not a primrose path. The risks of innovation are as great as the rewards. A large percentage of new products fail in the marketplace, and a still larger number have to be dropped before commercialization. The secret of successful innovation lies in developing sound research and decision procedures.

We have viewed the new-product development process as consisting of seven stages: idea generation, screening, concept development and testing, business analysis, product development, test marketing, and commercialization. The purpose of each successive stage is to decide whether the idea should be further developed or dropped. The company seeks decision criteria for each stage that minimize the chances of poor ideas moving forward and good ideas being rejected. The last stage, commercialization, involves the introduction of the products that have passed the previous tests; it is benefited by marketing planning and strategy based on an understanding of the consumer-adoption process.

QUESTIONS AND PROBLEMS

1 The new-product development process starts with a search for good ideas. Suggest some concepts that define a company's search effort.

2 A candy store chain is seeking ideas for a new sales promotion campaign. Show how morphological analysis might be used to generate a large number of ideas for a campaign.

3 Complained a research executive: "Would fluorocarbon resins, nylon, or polyethylene have come out of a screening formula—or a check list, for that matter? The important things are intuition and judgment. Research is a creative art." Is this a valid argument against formal screening devices? Can you name any advantages of using formal screening devices?

4 (a) Expected profit and risk are two major dimensions for determining whether to introduce a new product nationally. Can you develop a diagram using these two dimensions to show how critical limits might be set up by a firm before a market test to guide its decision after the test? (b) Suppose a firm finds that the test-market results are borderline and concludes that the product would probably yield a below-average return. It has sunk a lot of money into the development of the product. Should it introduce the product nationally or drop it? (c) State the two opposing risks that a firm faces when it bases its new-product decision on test-market results. How can it reduce these risks? (d) In the Colgate test marketing of its new soap (described in the text), the third marketing mix yielded the highest sales. Does this mean that it should be preferred to the other mixes if the product is launched nationally?

5 In 1950, Charles Saunders introduced a store called the Keedozall. The customer would pass a series of closed displays and insert a key into slots for wanted merchandise. He would take a resulting punched tape to a check-out cashier who fed the tape to a register. The amount would be totaled and the assembled merchandise delivered at the check-out point. Do you think this innovation in retailing was successful? Why or why not?

6 General Foods developed a new dog food product, PC-33. Not a canned or dry dog food, this product had a meat formulation and the appearance of hamburgers and could be sold on the regular grocery shelves. It offered a new combination of convenience and nutritional values. Develop four alternative product concepts for this new dog food.

7 A company is concerned about its dismal success record in launching new products. Looking at its past results, it found:

Stage	*Pass ratio*	*Cost per product idea*
1. Idea screening	1:4	$ 1,000
2. Concept test	1:2	20,000
3. Prototype development	1:2	200,000
4. Test marketing	1:2	500,000
5. National launch	1:2	5,000,000

What is the total cost that the company must recoup by a successful product to cover the total cost of the failing products as well?

11
PRODUCT LIFE-CYCLE STRATEGY

Destiny is not a matter of chance,
it is a matter of choice;
it is not a thing
to be waited for,
it is a thing to be achieved.

WILLIAM JENNINGS BRYAN

The *product life cycle* begins where the *new-product development process* leaves off. New products are launched by companies in the hope that they will enjoy a long sweet life of growing sales and profits. Some do, but along the way many more meet all kinds of problems that threaten to end the product's career prematurely. The various stages in a product's life cycle call for constant reprogramming of strategies and resources. In this chapter we shall examine the concept of the product life cycle and consider appropriate strategies during the stages of introduction, growth, maturity, and decline.

THE CONCEPT OF PRODUCT LIFE CYCLE

A product's sales position and profitability can be expected to change over time. The product life cycle is an attempt to recognize *distinct stages* in the *sales history* of the product. Corresponding to these stages are distinct opportunities and problems with respect to marketing strategy and profit potential. By identifying

**Stages in the product
life cycle**

the stage that a product is in, or may be headed toward, better marketing plans can be formulated.[1]

Most discussions of product life cycle (PLC) portray the sales history of a typical product as following the form of an S-shaped sales curve as illustrated in Figure 11-1. This curve is typically divided into four stages known as *introduction, growth, maturity,* and *decline.*[2] *Introduction* is a period of slow growth as the product is introduced in the market. The profit curve in Figure 11-1 shows profits as almost nonexistent in this stage because of the heavy expenses of product introduction. *Growth* is a period of rapid market acceptance and substantial profit improvement. *Maturity* is a period of a slowdown in sales growth because the product has achieved acceptance by most of the potential buyers. Profits peak in this period and start to decline because of increased marketing outlays (not shown) to sustain the product's position against competition. Finally, *decline* is the period when sales continue a strong downward drift and profits erode rapidly toward the zero point.

The designation of the points where these stages begin and end is somewhat arbitrary. Usually, they are based on where the rate of sales growth or decline tend to become pronounced. Polli and Cook proposed a more operational measure based on a normal distribution of percentage changes in real sales from year to year.[3]

Not all products pass through the idealized S-shaped product life cycle shown in Figure 11-1. Some products show a rapid growth from the very beginning, thus skipping the slow sales start implied by the introductory stage. Some other products, instead of going through a rapid-growth stage, go directly from introduction to maturity. Some products move from maturity to a second period

---

[1]For some excellent articles on product life cycle, see Robert D. Buzzell, "Competitive Behavior and Product Life Cycles," in *New Ideas for Successful Marketing,* ed. John S. Wright and Jac L. Goldstucker (Chicago: American Marketing Association, 1966), pp. 46–68; William E. Cox, Jr., "Product Life Cycles as Marketing Models," *Journal of Business,* October 1967, pp. 375–84; Theodore Levitt, "Exploit the Product Life Cycle," *Harvard Business Review,* November–December 1965, pp. 81–94; Rolando Polli and Victor Cook, "Validity of the Product Life Cycle," *Journal of Business,* October 1969, pp. 385–400; and Thomas A. Staudt and Donald A. Taylor, *A Managerial Introduction to Marketing* (Englewood Cliffs, N.J.: Prentice-Hall, Inc., 1970), Chap. 10.

[2]Some authors add *saturation* as a fifth stage between maturity and decline. Maturity ends when sales peak and saturation takes over until a real decline occurs.

[3]Polli and Cook, *op. cit.*

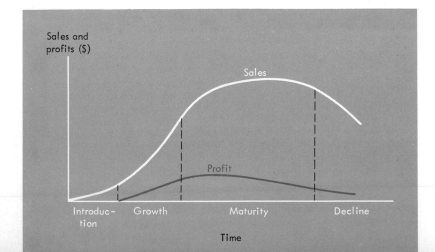

Sales and profits ($)

Sales

Profit

Introduction   Growth   Maturity   Decline

Time

Figure 11-1
Sales and profit life cycles

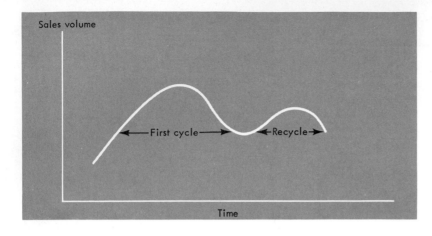

Sales volume

←First cycle→ ←Recycle→

Time

Figure 11-2
The cycle-recycle product life cycle

SOURCE: William E. Cox, Jr., "Product Life Cycles as Marketing Models," *Journal of Business*, October 1967, pp. 375–84, here p. 382.

of rapid growth. Cox studied the product life cycles of 754 ethical-drug products and found six different product life-cycle patterns.[4] The most typical form he found shows a second cycle (see Figure 11-2). Cox explained the second "hump" in sales as being caused by a traditional promotional push in the decline stage.

On the other hand, studies by Buzzell of grocery food products and Polli and Cook of various consumer nondurables showed the PLC concept to hold up well for many product categories. Anyone planning to use this concept must investigate the extent to which the PLC concept holds up for products in his industry. He will learn whether the idealized sequence of stages is typically followed and the typical length of each stage. Cox found that a typical ethical drug that followed the normal PLC cycle spanned an introductory period of one month, a growth stage of six months, a maturity stage of fifteen months, and a decline stage that exceeded the sum of the previous three stages—mainly because of the reluctance of the manufacturer to drop the drug from his catalog.

Before plotting a sales time series to assess its PLC characteristics, the sales data should be adjusted or deflated for changes in such variables as population size, prices, personal income, and supply shortfalls. Early investigators often overlooked these adjustments, and this created PLC pictures that were atypical or incorrect in their portrayal of the length of the various stages.

Product-class, product-form, and brand life cycles

The PLC concept should be defined with respect to whether the product is a product class (cigarettes), a product form (plain filter cigarettes), or a brand (Philip Morris regular nonfilter). (See Figure 11-3.) The PLC concept has a different degree of applicability in these three cases. Product classes have the longest life histories, longer than particular product forms, and certainly longer than most brands. The sales of many product classes can be expected to continue in the mature stage for an indefinite period, since they are highly population related (cars, refrigerators, steel, and so on). Product forms, on the other hand, probably exhibit the standard PLC histories more faithfully than do product classes. Product forms such as "the dial telephone" and "cream deodorants" seem to pass through a regular history of introduction, rapid growth, maturity, and decline. As for brands, an individual brand's sales history is likely to be

---

[4]Cox, *op. cit.*

more erratic than its production history because changing competitive strategies and tactics can produce substantial ups and downs in sales and market shares, even to the extent of causing a mature brand to suddenly enjoy another period of rapid growth.

**Rationale for the
product life cycle**

We have described the product life-cycle curve without offering any underlying explanation in market terms. Support for it lies in the theory of the diffusion and adoption of innovations.[5] When a new product appears, it must overcome the resistance of existing purchasing patterns. Steps must be taken by the company to stimulate awareness, interest, trial, and purchase of the new product. This takes time, and in the introductory stage only a few persons ("innovators") will buy it. If the product is satisfying, larger numbers of buyers ("early adopters") are drawn in. The entry of competitors into the market speeds up the adoption process by increasing the market's awareness and by exerting a downward pressure on prices. More buyers come in ("early majority") as the product is legitimized. Eventually the rate of growth decreases as the proportion of potential new buyers approaches zero. Sales become steady at the replacement purchase rate. Eventually they decline as new-product classes, forms, and brands

---

[5]See Everett Rogers, *The Diffusion of Innovations* (New York: The Free Press, 1962). Also see Chapter 10, pp. 223–28, in this text.

Figure 11-3
PLCs for a product class, product form, and brand

SOURCE: Rolando Polli and Victor Cook, "Validity of the Product Life Cycle," *Journal of Business*, October 1969, p. 389.

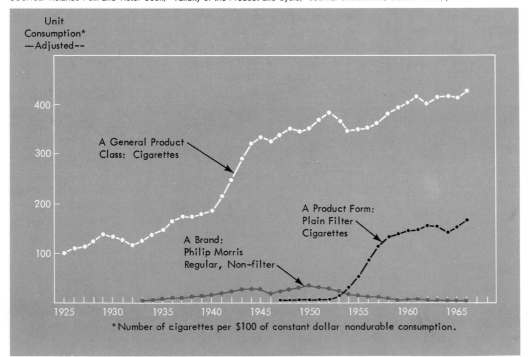

appear and divert the interest of the buyers from the existing product. Thus the product life cycle is closely related to normal developments that can be expected in the diffusion and adoption of any new product.

The PLC concept is useful mainly as a framework for developing effective marketing strategies in different stages of the product life cycle. We now turn to these different stages and their appropriate marketing strategies.

INTRODUCTION STAGE

The introduction stage is marked by a slow growth in sales. Such well-known products as instant coffee, frozen orange juice, and powdered coffee creamers lingered for many years before they entered a stage of rapid growth. Buzzell identified four causes for the slow growth of many processed food products:

1   Delays in the expansion of production capacity.
2   Technical problems ("working out the bugs").
3   Delays in making the product available to customers, especially in obtaining adequate distribution through retail outlets.
4   Customer reluctance to change established behavior patterns.[6]

During this stage there are likely to be only a few firms selling the new product. They tend to put out limited versions of the product, since the market is not ready for product refinements. The firms direct their selling effort to those buyers who are the readiest to buy, usually higher-income groups. Prices tend to be on the high side because "(1) costs are high due to relatively low output rates, (2) technological problems in production may have not yet been fully mastered, and (3) high margins are required to support the heavy promotional expenditures which are necessary to achieve growth."[7]

The heavy promotional expenditures, which are often at their highest ratio to sales during this stage, occur not only because sales are small but "more importantly because of the need for a high level of promotional effort to (1) inform potential consumers of the new and unknown product, (2) induce trial of the product, and (3) secure distribution in retail outlets."[8]

Marketing strategies in the introduction stage

In launching a new product, marketing management can set a high or a low level for each marketing variable such as price, promotion, distribution, and product quality. Working only with price and promotion, the four strategies shown in Figure 11-4 are available to management.

A *high-profile strategy* consists of launching the new product with a high price and a high promotion level. The firm charges a high price in order to recover as much gross profit per unit as possible. At the same time, it spends a lot on promotion to convince the market of the product's merits even at the high-price level. The high promotion serves to accelerate the rate of market penetration. This strategy makes sense under the following assumptions: (1) a large part of the potential market is not aware of the product; (2) those who

---

[6]Buzzell, *op. cit.*, p. 51.
[7]*Ibid.*, p. 52.
[8]*Ibid.*, p. 51.

become aware of the product are eager to have it and pay the asking price; (3) the firm faces potential competition and wants to build up brand preference.

A *selective penetration strategy* consists of launching the new product with a high price and low promotion. The purpose of the high price is to recover as much gross profit per unit as possible; and the purpose of the low promotion is to keep marketing expenses down. This combination is expected to skim a lot of profit from the market. This strategy makes sense under the following assumptions: (1) the market is relatively limited in size; (2) most of the market is aware of the product; (3) those who want the product are prepared to pay a high price; and (4) there is little threat of potential competition.

A *preemptive penetration strategy* consists of launching the product with a low price and heavy promotion. This strategy promises to bring about the fastest rate of market penetration and the largest market share for the company. This strategy makes sense under the following assumptions: (1) the market is large in size; (2) the market is relatively unaware of the product; (3) most buyers are price-sensitive; (4) there is strong potential competition; and (5) the company's unit manufacturing costs fall with the scale of production and accumulated manufacturing experience.

A *low-profile strategy* consists of launching the new product with a low price and low level of promotion. The low price will encourage the market's rapid acceptance of the product; at the same time, the company keeps its promotion costs down in order to realize more net profit. The company firmly believes that market demand is highly price-elastic but minimally promotion-elastic. This strategy makes sense if (1) the market is large; (2) the market is highly aware of the product; (3) the market is price-sensitive; and (4) there is some potential competition.

GROWTH STAGE

If the new product satisfies the market, sales will start climbing substantially. Previous purchasers will continue their purchasing, and new buyers will enter in large numbers. The product attains sales momentum through favorable word of mouth as well as distinctive steps taken by the firm.

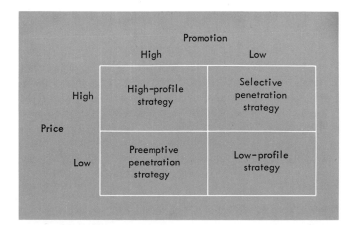

Figure 11-4
Four introductory marketing strategies

In this stage, new competitors enter the market attracted by the promise of a large market with opportunities for large-scale production and profit. The firm begins to add new product features and refinements to move into new parts of the market. The increase in the number of competitors leads to a scramble for available distribution outlets, hopefully on an exclusive basis. More often than not, however, dealers tend to adopt a multibrand policy.[9]

Prices tend to remain where they are or fall only slightly during this period, insofar as demand is managing to increase quite rapidly. Companies maintain their promotion expenditures at the same or at a slightly raised level to meet competition and continue educating the market. Sales rise much faster, causing a decline in the promotion-sales ratio. The falling ratio of promotional expenditures to sales is one of the important contributions to the high profits during this stage.

Marketing strategies in the growth stage

During this stage, the firm tries to sustain rapid market growth as long as possible. This is accomplished through such actions as:

1 The firm undertakes to improve product quality and add new-product features and models.
2 It vigorously searches out new market segments to enter.
3 It keeps its eyes open to new distribution channels to gain additional product exposure.
4 It shifts some advertising from building product awareness to trying to bring about product conviction and purchase.
5 It decides when the time is right to lower prices to attract the next layer of price-sensitive buyers into the market.

The firm that aggressively pursues any or all of these market-expanding activities will increase its competitive position. But this comes at additional cost. The firm in the growth stage thus faces a trade-off between high market share and high current profit. By spending a lot of money on product improvement, promotion, and distribution, it can capture a dominant position; but it forgoes maximum current profit in the hope, presumably, of making up for this in the next stage.

MATURITY STAGE

At some point in the history of every product, its rate of sales growth will slow down and the product will enter a stage of relative maturity. This stage normally lasts much longer than the previous stages, and it poses some of the most formidable challenges to marketing management. *Most products are in the maturity stage of the life cycle, and therefore most of marketing management deals with the mature product.*

The maturity stage can be divided into three phases. The first phase is called *growth maturity.* Here, total sales continue to grow slowly because of some laggard buyers entering the market, although most of the demand comes from present customers. The second phase is *stable maturity* (also called saturation).

---

[9]See Staudt and Taylor, *op. cit.*, pp. 170–74.

Sales now maintain a constant level, consisting almost entirely of replacement demand. The third phase is *decaying maturity*. The absolute level of sales now starts to decline as some of the customers move toward other products and substitutes.

The beginning of a slowdown in the rate of sales growth has the effect of producing some overcapacity in the industry. This overcapacity leads to intensified competition. Competitors engage more frequently in markdowns and off-list pricing. There is a strong increase in promotional budgets, in the form of trade and consumer deals. Other firms increase their research and development budgets to find better versions of the product. All of these steps, to the extent that they do not stimulate adequate sales increases, mean some profit erosion. Some of the weaker competitors start dropping out. The industry eventually consists of a set of well-entrenched competitors whose basic orientation is toward gaining competitive advantage.

Marketing strategies in the mature stage

The product manager whose product has settled into a stage of sales maturity is not content to simply defend its current position. He recognizes that a good offense will provide the best defense of his product. Three basic strategies are available in this stage: market modification, product modification, and marketing-mix modification.

Market modification   The product manager first looks for opportunities to find new buyers for the product. There are several possibilities.

First, the manager looks for *new markets and market segments* that have not yet tried the product. For example, a key to the success of nylon over the years is that Du Pont continued to find new types of customers. Originally, nylon's end uses were primarily military—parachutes, thread, rope. Then it received a big boost when it entered the circular-knit market, particularly women's hosiery. At various later stages the product entered such areas as clothing, tires, and carpeting, each time breaking out of the mature stage into a new growth phase.[10]

Second, the manager looks at ways to stimulate *increased usage* among present customers. A common practice of food manufacturers, for example, is to list several recipes on their packages to broaden the consumers' uses of the product.

Third, the manager may want to consider *repositioning* his brand to achieve larger brand sales, although this will not affect total industry sales. For example, a manufacturer of a chocolate drink mix may find that its heavy users are mostly older people. This firm should give serious consideration to trying to reposition the drink in the youth market, which is experiencing faster growth.

Product modification   Managers also try to break out of a stagnant sales picture by initiating calculated changes in the product's characteristics that will attract new users and/or more usage from current users. The trade term for this is *product relaunch*, and it can take several forms.

A strategy of *quality improvement* aims at increasing the functional performance of the product—such traits as its durability, reliability, speed, and taste. A manufacturer may feel that he can make a real gain on his competition

---

[10]Levitt, *op. cit.,* pp. 88–91.

by launching the "new and improved" automobile, television set, coffee, or cigarette. Grocery manufacturers often call this a "plus" launch and talk about a new additive or advertise the terms "stronger," "bigger," or "better." This strategy is effective to the extent that (1) the product is capable of quality improvement, (2) buyers believe the claims about improved quality, and (3) a sufficient number of buyers are highly responsive to improved quality.

A strategy of *feature improvement* aims at adding new features that expand the product's versatility, safety, or convenience. For example, the introduction of power to hand lawn mowers increased the speed and ease of cutting grass. Manufacturers then worked on the problem of engineering better safety features. Some manufacturers have built in conversion features so that the lawn mower doubles as a snow plow. All of these feature improvements are quite distinguishable from quality improvements on the one hand and styling improvements on the other. Stewart outlines five advantages flowing from a strategy of feature improvement:

1   The development of new functional features is one of the most effective means of building a company image of progressiveness and leadership.
2   Functional features are an extremely flexible competitive tool because they can be adapted quickly, dropped quickly, and often can be made optional at very little expense.
3   Functional features allow the company to gain the intense preference of preselected market segments.
4   Functional features often bring the innovating company free publicity.
5   Functional features generate a great amount of sales-force and distributors' enthusiasm.[11]

The chief disadvantage is that feature improvements are highly imitable; unless there is a permanent gain from being first, the feature investment in innovation may not be justified.

A strategy of *style improvement* aims at increasing the aesthetic appeal of the product in contrast to its functional appeal. The periodic introduction of new car models amounts to style competition rather than quality or feature competition. In the case of packaged food and household products, companies introduce color and texture variations and often put great emphasis on package restyling, treating the package as an extension of the product. The outstanding advantage of a style strategy is that each firm may achieve a unique market identity and secure some durable share of the market on the basis of that identification. Yet styling competition also brings a number of problems. First, it is difficult to predict whether people—and which people—will like a new style. Second, style changes usually mean discontinuing the old style, and the company risks losing some of the customers who liked the old style.

Marketing-mix modification   As a final source of mature product strategy, the product manager considers the possibility of stimulating sales through altering one or more elements of the marketing mix. One strong possibility is to cut *prices* as a way of drawing new segments into the market as well as attracting other brand users. Another is to search for a new and brilliant *advertising* appeal

---

[11]John B. Stewart, "Functional Features in Product Strategy," *Harvard Business Review,* March–April 1959, pp. 65–78.

that wins the consumers' attention and favor. A more direct way to attract other brand users is through aggressive and attractive promotions—trade deals, cents-off, gifts, and contests. The company can also consider moving into higher-volume *market channels,* particularly discount channels, if it is in a growth stage. The company can also offer more services to the buyer as a patronage-building step.

The main problem with relying exclusively on marketing-mix modification is that these steps are highly imitable by competition, especially price reductions, additional services, and mass-distribution penetration. This means that the firm may not gain as much as expected, and, in fact, all firms may pay a price in the form of profit erosion.

The dominant versus the trailing firm

All of the preceding strategies are available to both dominant and smaller firms in an industry, but their situations are different enough to warrant further discussion. In the mature stage there is often one dominant firm that is the acknowledged leader and enjoys the largest market share: examples are General Motors (autos), Coca-Cola (soft drinks), Sears (retailing), and Procter & Gamble (toiletries). There are also trailing firms in second and third place: Ford and Chrysler (autos), Pepsi-Cola and Royal Crown Cola (soft drinks), J. C. Penney and Montgomery Ward (retailing), and Lever Brothers and Colgate (toiletries). Finally, there are additional firms that account for still smaller market shares and tend to be located in special parts of the market. A characteristic of the mature stage is that these firms are relatively locked into their present positions; it is difficult to alter their relative market standings very much. As soon as one firm starts gaining on another, the latter adopts a series of sharp countermeasures that tend to restore it to its former market position.

Yet we may ask, What are the strategic options available to the trailing firms and the dominant firm, respectively? The trailing firms live in the constant hope of capturing the first-place position in an industry. If the trailing firm is not as large as the dominant firm, it will want to avoid a frontal attack through price cutting or increased promotional expenditure. The firm must search for an area in which it can achieve a *differential advantage* over its dominant competition.

The first and most important area to consider is the product. Is there an opportunity to improve upon the product of the dominant competitor? Several second-place companies attained substantial success because they found a better product. Xerox developed a better copying machine; Zenith developed a better television set; Control Data developed a better computer for scientific research; and Avis offered a cleaner car and more personal attention.

The firm should next consider whether there are some profitable segments of the market that the larger firm is failing to cater to. In many cases the large firm gives its attention to the mass market or the large customers and neglects various fringe markets. Consider the success of Ford's Mustang, which was designed as a relatively inexpensive sports car for younger people; and the success of U.S. Time Company's Timex watch, which was designed as a cheap but reliable watch for a segment of the market that was neglected by the major watch companies.

A third competitive strategy for the trailing firm is to find a new way to distribute its goods that offers substantial economies or covers particular segments of the market more efficiently. Examples include Timex, which got its watch into unconventional outlets such as drug stores and discount stores; and Avon Products, which moved into the door-to-door selling of cosmetics.

Another recourse is to try to develop a superior advertising campaign. Consider Philip Morris's "Marlboroman" or Standard Oil's "Tiger in Your Tank." However, too many trailing firms assume erroneously that advertising will be the key to their success, when they should be spending their time searching for real product or distribution advantages backed by good advertising. Behind Avis's notably successful campaign "We're No. 2, We Try Harder" was a solid effort to offer superior car rental service.

Finally, the smaller firm may sometimes try to overtake the larger firm through legal maneuvers. Smaller computer firms have used this weapon several times against IBM.

The quality of life for the dominant firm is not one of wine and roses. Its very success and bigness make it extremely vulnerable. Consider a giant such as Procter & Gamble:

> Colgate can pick and choose where it wants to hit the giant; the giant, by contrast, must defend itself everywhere. It's not unlike the situation in guerilla warfare, where the guerillas, with a lot less to defend, can concentrate their forces on one or two points and take a heavy toll. . . . Procter is fighting on additional fronts at a time when it is under heavy pressure on the home front. . . . "As we [Colgate] continue to put the pressure on at home, Procter will have to make a decision on whether to push back at us in a big way or go deeper into things like paper and coffee. I don't think, big as they are, that they can do it all."[12]

What can the large firms do to discipline or discourage an upstart firm? The relevant concepts, militarily speaking, are "brinkmanship," "massive retaliation" (or threat of), "limited warfare," "graduated response," "diplomacy of violence," "threat systems," and so on. But for our purposes it is important to define specific types of action.

A *strategy of innovation* is the most effective. It means that the dominant firm refuses to be content with the way things are, that it wants to continue to outperform itself and the industry by being the source of new-product ideas, customer services, means of distribution, and cost-cutting discoveries. It is applying the military "principle of the offensive": the commander must exercise initiative, set the pace, and exploit enemy weaknesses.

A *strategy of segmentation and fortification* is also a positive approach to maintaining leadership. Here the company does its best to fortify and extend itself to additional segments. One variant is the *multibrand strategy,* where the company introduces a number of brands competing with each other, the effect being to lock out some of the competition; another variant is the *brand extension strategy,* where the company introduces additional items under its current brand names.[13]

A *confrontation strategy* will most likely be the principal defense of noninnovative firms. The dominant firm can initiate a *promotional war,* engaging in massive promotional expenditures that the smaller firm cannot possibly match. Or it might resort to *price war.* A major steel company makes it clear that it will meet all competitive price cuts, thus discouraging any potential benefits to the would-be cutter. It wants to convince competitors that they have more to gain through followership than through attack.

---

[12]"Colgate vs. P&G," *Forbes,* February 1, 1966, pp. 27–28.
[13]These are discussed in Chapter 9, pp. 194–95.

Finally, the dominant firm sometimes pursues a *persecution strategy,* attempting to wield its power with suppliers, channels, and legislators to restrict the growth of the upstart firm. The persecution strategy is apt to be used by the dominant firm that has grown sluggish, inefficient, or overly content. Having lost the spirit of innovation, it attempts to protect its position through deterrent measures, including direct or implied threats, harassment, and brinkmanship, to would-be competitors.

Table 11-1 summarizes the hierarchy of strategies available to the smaller firm and the dominant firm, respectively. *Innovistic competition* stands highest for both firms as the best means to achieve their objectives. After this the strategy courses differ, with the smaller firm relying on segmentation, or improved distribution or promotion, while the large firm relies on fortification, confrontation, and possibly persecution.

Table 11-1

**Hierarchy of strategies for the smaller firm
and the dominant firm**

Smaller firm	*Dominant firm*
1. Innovation	1. Innovation
2. Segmentation	2. Segmentation and fortification
3. Improved distribution	3. Confrontation
4. Improved promotion	4. Persecution

DECLINE STAGE

Most product forms and brands eventually enter a stage of sustained sales decline. The decline may be slow, as in the case of oatmeal cereal; or rapid, as in the case of the Edsel automobile. Sales may plunge to zero and the product may be withdrawn from the market, or they may petrify at a low level and continue for many years at that level.[14]

As sales of the product decline, a number of firms withdraw from the market in order to invest their resources in more profitable areas. Those remaining in the industry tend to reduce the number of product offerings. They withdraw from selling in the smaller market segments and more marginal trade channels. The promotion budget is reduced. The price may also be reduced to keep demand from falling further.

Unfortunately, most companies have not developed a well-thought-out policy for handling their aging products. Management's attention is riveted on its new products and mature products. Yesteryear's products are a source of embarrassment. There is a reluctance to take up the ax. There is a hope that they will fade away without any action on the part of management.

Companies show an aversion to product abandonment decisions for a number of reasons. Sentiment plays a role:

---

[14]George C. Michael, "Product Petrification: A New Stage in the Life Cycle Theory," *California Management Review,* Fall 1971, pp. 88–91.

"But putting products to death—or letting them die—is a drab business, and often engenders much of the sadness of a final parting with old and tried friends. The portable, six-sided pretzel was the first product The Company ever made. Our line will no longer be our line without it."[15]

Logic also plays a role. Sometimes it is expected, or hoped, that product sales will pick up when economic or market factors become more propitious. Sometimes the fault is thought to lie in the marketing program, which the company plans to revitalize. Management may feel that the solution lies in product modification. When none of these explanations work, a weak product may be retained because of its alleged contribution to the sales of the company's other products. The ultimate argument may be that its sales volume at least covers "out-of-pocket" costs, and the company may temporarily have no better way of keeping its fixed resources employed.

Unless strong retention reasons exist, carrying a weak product is very costly to the firm. The cost of sustaining a weak product is not just the amount of uncovered overhead and profit. No financial accounting can adequately convey all the hidden costs:

The weak product tends to consume a disproportionate amount of management's time.

It often requires frequent price and inventory adjustments.

It generally involves short production runs in spite of expensive setup times.

It requires both advertising and sales-force attention that might better be diverted to making the "healthy" products more profitable.

Its very unfitness can cause customer misgivings and cast a shadow on the company's image.

The biggest cost imposed by carrying weak products may well lie in the future. By not being eliminated at the proper time, these products delay the aggressive search for replacement products; they create a lopsided product mix, long on "yesterday's breadwinners" and short on "tomorrow's breadwinners"; they depress present profitability and weaken the company's foothold on the future.

Marketing strategies in the decline stage

A company faces a number of tasks and decisions to ensure the effective handling of its aging products.

Identifying the weak products The first task is to set up an information system that will spot those products in the line that are truly in a declining stage.

An overall view of such a system is charted in Figure 11-5: (1) A product review committee is appointed with the responsibility for developing a system for periodically reviewing weak products in the company's mix. This committee includes representatives from marketing, manufacturing, and the controller's office. (2) This committee meets and develops a set of objectives and procedures for reviewing weak products. (3) The controller's office fills out data for each product showing industry sales, company sales, unit costs, prices, and other information over the last several years. (4) This information is run against

---

[15]R. S. Alexander, "The Death and Burial of 'Sick' Products," *Journal of Marketing*, April 1964, p. 1.

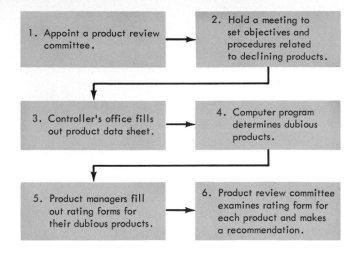

Figure 11-5
Weak-product review system

SOURCE: Adapted from the author's "Phasing Out Weak Products," *Harvard Business Review,* March–April 1965, pp. 107–18.

a computer program that identifies the most dubious products. The criteria include the number of years of sales decline, market-share trends, gross profit margin, and return on investment. (5) Products put on the dubious list are then reported to those managers responsible for them. Each manager fills out a diagnostic and prognostic rating form showing where he thinks sales and profits on dubious products will go with no change in the current marketing program and with his recommended changes in the current program. (6) The product review committee examines the product rating form for each dubious product and makes a recommendation (a) to leave it alone, (b) to modify its marketing strategy, or (c) to drop it.

Determining marketing strategies   In the face of declining sales, some firms will abandon the market earlier than others. The firms that remain enjoy a temporary increase in sales as they pick up the customers of the withdrawing firms. Thus any particular firm faces the issue of whether it should be the one to stay in the market until the end. For example, Procter & Gamble decided to remain in the declining liquid-soap business until the end and made good profits as the others withdrew.

If it decides to stay in the market, the firm faces further strategic choices. The firm could adopt a *continuation strategy,* in which case it continues its past marketing strategy: same market segments, channels, pricing, promotion, and so on. The product simply continues to decline until at last it is dropped from the line. Or the firm could follow a *concentration strategy,* in which case it concentrates its resources only in the strongest markets and channels while phasing out its efforts elsewhere. Finally, it could follow a *milking strategy,* in which case it sharply reduces its marketing expenses to increase its current profits, knowing this will accelerate the rate of sales decline and ultimate demise of the product. In some situations the hard-core loyalty may remain strong enough to allow marketing the product at a greatly reduced level of promotion, and at the old or even a higher price, both of which mean good profits. An interesting example is afforded by Ipana toothpaste:

243

Ipana toothpaste was marketed by Bristol-Myers until 1968, when it was abandoned in favor of promoting new brands. In early 1969, two Minnesota businessmen picked up the Ipana name, concocted a new formula, but packaged the
product in tubes similar to those used by the former marketer. With no promotion, the petrified demand for Ipana turned out to be $250,000 in the first seven
months of operation.[16]

The drop decision   When a product has been singled out for elimination,
the firm faces some further decisions. First, it has the option of selling or transferring the product to someone else or dropping it completely. It will usually
prefer the former because this will bring in some cash and will minimize the
hardship to customers and employees. Second, the organization has to decide
when the product should be terminated. It could be dropped quickly and
decisively so there would be no chance for resistance to build up and reverse
the decision. Or it could be discontinued gradually with a timetable to allow
resources to transfer out in an orderly way and to allow customers to make
other arrangements. Management will also want to provide a stock of replacement parts and service to stretch over the expected life of the most recently
sold units.

SUMMARY

Every new product that is launched enters a product life cycle marked by a
changing set of problems and opportunities. The sales history of the typical
product is commonly thought to follow an S-shaped curve made up of four
stages. The *introduction* stage is marked by slow growth and minimal profits
as the product is pushed into distribution. The company has to decide during
this stage between the four strategies of high-profile marketing, low-profile
marketing, selective penetration, and preemptive penetration. If successful, the
product enters a *growth* stage marked by rapid sales growth and increasing
profits. During this stage, the company attempts to improve the product, enter
new market segments and distribution channels, and reduce its prices slightly.
There follows a *maturity* stage in which sales growth slows down and profits
stabilize. The company seeks innovative strategies to renew sales growth, including market, product, and marketing-mix modification. Finally, the product
enters a stage of *decline* in which little can be done to halt the deterioration of
sales and profits. The company's task during this period is to identify the truly
declining products, develop for each one a strategy of continuation, concentration, or milking, and finally phase out the product in a way that minimizes the
hardship to company profits, employees, and customers.

The PLC concept is of varying usefulness in different types of management
decision making. As a *forecasting* tool, it is of limited usefulness because sales
histories exhibit various shapes in practice and the stages last for varying lengths
of time. As a *planning* tool, the PLC concept is quite useful in characterizing the
main marketing features of each stage and indicating the major alternative
marketing strategies available to the firm in each stage. As a *control* tool, the

---

[16]"Abandoned Trademark Turns a Tidy Profit for Two Minnesotans," *Wall Street Journal*,
October 27, 1969, p. 1.

PLC concept allows the company to roughly gauge how well a product is doing in relation to successful and comparable products that were launched in the past.

1 Beer is a product that appears to be in the mature stage of its life cycle. Can you suggest some steps that can be taken by the industry to boost sales?

2 "In fact, it is this writer's contention that once one has stated that products are 'born' and that most 'die,' most of the usefulness of the life cycle model has been exhausted. It is simply not a very rich model." Do you agree?

3 Develop a long-range plan for marketing a new line of electric can openers, indicating for each stage in the product's life cycle (introductory, growth, maturity, and decline) the major objective and the likely policy on price, quality, advertising, personal selling, and channels.

4 Honda produces the top selling lightweight motorcycle in the United States. Its market dominance came about through designing an excellent low-priced, lightweight machine, getting wide distribution, and creating a distinct image ("You Meet The Nicest People on a Honda"). Recommend a competitive strategy for use by a second place firm to edge Honda out of first place.

5 For each appliance, indicate in which stage of the product life cycle it is found: a) refrigerators; b) room air conditioners; c) wringer-type washing machines; d) compactors.

6 As a product passes through the successive stages of its product life cycle, both its rate of sales growth and its rate-of-return on investment change. Using these two variables as axes, develop a diagram showing the typical trajectory of these variables over the product life cycle.

7 Discuss the changes in the promotion level and mix in the different stages of the product life cycle.

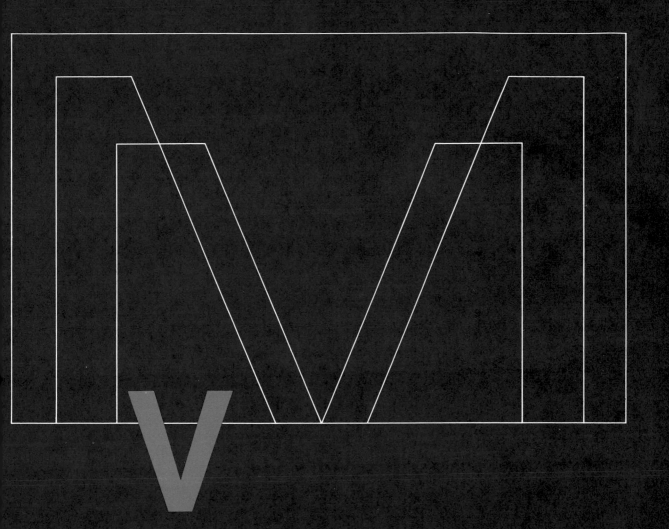

ASSEMBLING
THE MARKETING MIX

12

PRICE DECISIONS

There ain't no brand loyalty that two-cents-off can't overcome.

ANONYMOUS

All profit organizations and many nonprofit organizations face the task of setting a price on their products or services. Price goes by many names: fares, tuitions, rents, assessments, and plain old price. Historically, price had been the single most important decision of the marketer, for it determined the value of his product in the customer's eyes relative to competitors' products. Over time, nonprice factors grew in importance until the point was reached where over half of a sample of company managers "did not *select* pricing as *one of the five most important* policy areas in their firm's marketing success."[1] More recently, because of worldwide inflation, price is again attracting considerable attention.[2]

Pricing is a problem in four general types of situations. It is a problem *when a firm must set a price for the first time.* This happens when the firm develops or acquires a new product, when it introduces its regular product into a new distribution channel or geographical area, or when it regularly enters bids on new contract work. Pricing is a problem *when circumstances lead a firm to consider initiating a price change.* This happens when a firm begins to doubt whether its price is right in relation to its demand and costs. It can be triggered by inflation or shortages. It also happens on a more regular basis in firms that periodically

---

[1]See Jon G. Udell, "How Important Is Pricing in Competitive Strategy?" *Journal of Marketing,* January 1964, pp. 44–48.

[2]See "Pricing Strategy in an Inflation Economy," *Business Week,* April 6, 1974, pp. 43–49.

introduce temporary price deals to stimulate the trade or final buyers. Pricing is a problem *when competition initiates a price change.* The firm has to decide whether to change its own price, and if so, by how much. Finally, pricing is a problem *when the company produces several products that have interrelated demands and/or costs.* The problem is one of determining optimal price relationships for the products in the line.

PRICE SETTING IN THEORY

Theoretical pricing model

Economists have developed a simple yet elegant model of how to set a price. The model has the properties of logical consistency and optimization. There is value in examining it because it provides some fundamental insights into the pricing problem and because its very limitations help bring out the complex issues involved in pricing.

The model assumes a profit-maximizing firm that has knowledge of its demand and cost functions for the product in question. The demand function describes the expected quantity (Q) demanded per period at various prices (P) that might be charged. Suppose the firm is able to determine through statistical demand analysis that its *demand equation* is

$$Q = 1,000 - 4P \qquad (12\text{-}1)$$

This equation expresses the "law of demand," that less will be bought at higher prices.

The cost function describes the expected total cost (C) for alternative quantities per period (Q) that might be produced. It is customary to distinguish between total fixed costs (those that do not vary with output) and total variable costs (those that do vary with output). In the simplest case, the total-cost function can be described by the linear equation $C = F + cQ$ where F is total fixed cost and c is unit variable cost. Suppose the company derived the following *cost equation* for its product:

$$C = 6,000 + 50Q \qquad (12\text{-}2)$$

With the preceding demand and cost equations, the pricing executive is almost in a position to determine the best price. He only needs two more equations, both definitional in nature. First, *total revenue* (R) is defined as equal to price times quantity sold—that is,

$$R = PQ \qquad (12\text{-}3)$$

Second, *total profits* (Z) are defined as the difference between total revenue and total cost—that is,

$$Z = R - C \qquad (12\text{-}4)$$

With these four equations, the pricing executive is in a position to solve for the profit-maximizing price.

The executive is essentially trying to determine the relationship between profits (Z) and price (P). He must solve the four equations simultaneously in order to find the single relationship between Z and P. It is best to start with the profit equation (12-4). The derivation is as follows:

$$
\begin{aligned}
Z &= R - C \\
Z &= PQ - C \\
Z &= PQ - (6{,}000 + 50Q) \\
Z &= P(1{,}000 - 4P) - 6{,}000 - 50\,(1{,}000 - 4P) \\
Z &= 1{,}000P - 4P^2 - 6{,}000 - 50{,}000 + 200P \\
Z &= -56{,}000 + 1{,}200P - 4P^2
\end{aligned}
\tag{12-5}
$$

Total profits turn out to be a quadratic (that is, second-degree) function of price. It is a hatlike figure (a parabola), and profits reach their highest point ($34,000) at a price of $150.[3]

This theoretical model is based on some highly restrictive assumptions which unfortunately limit its applicability to actual pricing problems. Four assumptions will be examined here.

The problem of objectives

The theoretical pricing model assumes a single product for which the seller is trying to determine the price that would maximize current profits. Current profits rather than long-run profits are at issue because of the use of stable demand and cost assumptions. In reality, demand can be expected to change over time (as a result of changes in tastes, population, and income), and cost can be expected to change over time (as a result of changes in technology and input prices). Pricing to maximize long-run profits would have to utilize projections of the likely long-run course of demand and cost. A more sophisticated model would be required to solve the problem of pricing optimally over the product's life cycle.

Another limitation is that the company often pursues a more specific objective in setting its price. At least five different objectives of a more concrete sort can be found in practice.[4]

Market-penetration objective Some companies set a relatively low price in order to stimulate the growth of the market and to capture a large share of it. Any of several conditions might favor setting a low price:[5] (1) The market appears to be highly price-sensitive. (2) The unit costs of production and distribution fall with cumulated output. (3) A low price would discourage actual and potential competition.

---

[3]The profit function is illustrated in Figure 19-3(a), p. 438. The optimal price of $150 can be found through inspection or calculus.

[4]For a documentation of pricing objectives, see the Brookings study by A. D. H. Kaplan, Joel B. Dirlam, and Robert F. Lanzilloti, *Pricing in Big Business* (Washington, D.C.: Brookings Institution, 1958).

[5]See Joel Dean, *Managerial Economics* (Englewood Cliffs, N.J.: Prentice-Hall, Inc., 1951), pp. 420ff.

Market-skimming objective Some firms want to take advantage of the fact that some buyers stand ready to pay a much higher price than others because the product has high present value to them. The objective of skimming pricing is to gain a premium from these buyers and only gradually reduce the price to draw in the more price-elastic segments of the market. It is a form of price discrimination over time rather than over space. It makes good sense when any of the following conditions is present: (1) There are enough buyers whose demand is relatively inelastic. (2) The unit production and distribution costs of producing a smaller volume are not so much higher that they cancel the advantage of charging what some of the traffic will bear. (3) There is little danger that the high price will stimulate the emergence of rival firms. (4) The high price creates an impression of a superior product.

Early-cash-recovery objective Some firms seek to set a price that will lead to a rapid recovery of cash. They may either be strapped for funds or regard the future as too uncertain to justify patient market cultivation.

Satisficing objective Some companies describe their pricing objective as the achievement of a satisfactory rate of return. The implication is that although another price might produce an even larger return over the long run, the firm is satisfied with a return that is conventional for the given level of investment and risk. Target pricing (see pp. 256–57) is an example of this.

Product-line promotion objective Some firms seek to set a price that will enhance the sales of the entire line rather than yield a profit on the product by itself. An example is loss-leader pricing, in which a popular product is priced low to attract a large number of buyers who can be expected to buy the other products of the vendor.

**The problem of
multiple parties**

The theoretical pricing model assumes that the only significant group to consider in the pricing of a product is the firm's customers. But in reality, several parties have to be considered simultaneously.

Intermediate customers The firm must think through its pricing not only for ultimate customers but also for intermediate customers. Some companies set a price for distributors and allow them to set whatever final price they wish. This is done where it is thought that each distributor is in the best position to determine the price suited to local conditions and to set it high enough to provide sufficient selling incentive. The disadvantage is that the manufacturer relinquishes control over the final price. The other approach is for the manufacturer to determine the final price and how much of a distributor's margin is necessary to provide sufficient distributor incentive. The distributors must recognize that the important incentive variable is not the difference between the distributor's and final price (the margin) but rather the margin times the sales volume stimulated by the particular final price.

Rivals The theoretical pricing model does not explicitly consider competitive reactions. It can be argued that whatever assumption is made about competitive reactions can be incorporated in the shape of the demand function, but this treatment of competitive reaction is too implicit and static. The price set by the manufacturer influences the rate of entry of new rivals and the pricing policies of existing rivals. The traditional demand curve is too summary a way to represent the dynamic reactions and counterreactions occasioned by a pricing policy.

Suppliers The company's suppliers of materials, funds, and labor also must be considered. Many suppliers interpret the product's price as indicating the level of the firm's revenues (and profits) from the product. Labor unions will act as if a high price, or price increase, constitutes grounds for higher wages. Farmers believe they deserve higher cattle prices if retail meat prices are high. The firm's bank often feels uneasy if the firm's price is on the low side. Thus the firm may have to consider various supplier groups in setting a price.

Government Another price-interested party is the government. Under the Robinson-Patman Act, the seller cannot charge different prices to comparable customers unless the price differences are based strictly on cost differences. Under the Miller-Tydings Act, the seller may or may not be able to require retailers to sell his branded product at a uniform list price, depending upon the state laws. Public utilities must justify their rates before regulatory commissions. At various times, pricing in the steel, auto, meat, drug, and heavy-equipment industries has been subject to government pressure. The prices of agricultural goods and of imported goods are affected by agricultural and tariff legislation, respectively. And various state and local governmental units pass legislation and rulings affecting the prices that can be set by sellers.

Other company executives Price is a concern of different parties within the company. The sales manager wants a low price so that his salesmen can "talk price" to customers. The controller likes to see a price leading to an early payout. The price makes an important difference in copy and media tactics to the advertising manager. The production scheduling manager is interested because the price will affect the rate of sales. These and other executives in the organization can be expected to have strong views on where to set the price.

The problem of marketing-mix interaction

The theoretical pricing model assumes that other marketing variables are held at some constant level while the effect of price on sales is being examined. This is evident in the usual treatment of the demand function as a relationship only between quantity demanded (Q) and price (P). But this begs the whole question of how optimal values can be set on advertising, personal selling, product quality, and other marketing variables before price is set. As emphasized throughout this book, the several marketing variables have to all be considered simultaneously to arrive at the optimal mix. This task is missing or assumed away in the theoretical pricing model.

The problem of estimating demand and cost functions

Grave statistical problems handicap the determination of actual demand and cost functions. In the case of a new product, there is no experience upon which to base these estimates. Unless data are available on a similar, established product, estimates are likely to take the form of soft facts and guesses rather than hard facts. Data on established products are usually not much more satisfactory.

Johnston has described the major econometric techniques for estimating cost functions from existing data.[6] Demand functions are more difficult to determine because several of the variables are not quantifiable; they are typically highly intercorrelated; both demand and cost have been shifting during the period; and the random errors tend to be large. Because some of the "independent" variables are also dependent (sales depends on advertising, and advertising depends upon sales), a system of simultaneous equations rather than a single equation estimate of demand seems to be required. Finally, even were these hurdles to be overcome, there are always lingering doubts about whether the relationships measured from historical data apply to today's situation.

Since the demand and cost equations are estimated with an unknown degree of error, the criterion of maximizing profits may have to be replaced with the criterion of maximizing *expected* profits (where probability distributions are put on the estimated functions) or the criterion of maximizing the minimum possible gain. In any situation of risk and uncertainty, the pricing executive will want to see how sensitive the theoretically calculated price is to revisions in the estimated data.

PRICE SETTING IN PRACTICE

The fault with the economist's pricing model is not one of illogic but of oversimplification. The pricing models used in practice also for the most part tend to be based on a limited view of the pricing problem. They tend to emphasize one of the factors, such as cost, demand, or competition, to the neglect of the other factors. Nevertheless they meet some of the more practical requirements for price determination in the presence of imperfect information and multiple parties. We shall examine cost-oriented, demand-oriented, and competition-oriented pricing.

Cost-oriented pricing

A great number of firms set their prices largely or even wholly on the basis of their costs. Typically, all costs are included, including a usually arbitrary allocation of overhead made on the basis of expected operating levels.

Markup pricing   The most elementary examples of this are markup pricing and cost-plus pricing. They are similar in that the price is determined by adding some fixed percentage to the unit cost. Markup pricing is most commonly found in the retail trades (groceries, furniture, clothing, jewelry, and so forth) where the retailer adds predetermined but different markups to various goods he carries. Cost-plus pricing is most often used to describe the pricing of jobs that are nonroutine and difficult to "cost" in advance, such as construction and military-weapon development.

Markups vary considerably among different goods. Some common markups on the retail price in department stores are 20 percent for tobacco goods, 28 percent for cameras, 34 percent for books, 41 percent for dresses, 46 percent for costume jewelry, and 50 percent for millinery.[7] In the retail grocery industry,

---

[6]See Jack Johnston, *Statistical Cost Analysis* (New York: McGraw-Hill Book Company, 1960).
[7]*Departmental Merchandising and Operating Results of 1965* (New York: National Retail Merchants Association, 1965).

items like coffee, canned milk, and sugar tend to have low average markups, while items like frozen foods, jellies, and some canned products have high average markups. In addition, quite a lot of dispersion is found around the averages. Within the category of frozen foods, for example, one study showed the markups on retail price to range from a low of 13 percent to a high of 53 percent.[8]

Many hypotheses have been advanced to explain the variations in markups within selected product groups. Preston conducted a detailed study to examine how much of the markup variance within common grocery-product groups could be explained by three commonly used rules of thumb:

> Markups should vary inversely with unit costs.
> Markups should vary inversely with turnover.
> Markups should be higher and prices lower on reseller's (private) brands than on manufacturer's brands.[9]

In one product group a single rule helped explain 61 percent of the variance in percentage markups, and in two groups a combination of two rules helped explain over 60 percent. But the principal finding was that a large amount of variation remained unexplained in most product categories and was probably due to erratic decisions, random factors, and frequently better adaptations to the current market than could be provided by the rules.

Does the use of a rigid customary markup over cost make logical sense in the pricing of products? Generally, no. Any model that ignores current demand elasticity in setting prices is not likely to lead, except by chance, to the achievement of maximum profits, either in the long run or in the short run. As demand elasticity changes, as it is likely to do seasonally, cyclically, or over the product life cycle, the optimum markup should also change. If markup remains a rigid percentage of cost, then under ordinary conditions it would not lead to maximum profits.

Under special conditions, however, a rigid markup at the right level may lead to optimum profits. The two conditions are that average (unit) costs must be fairly constant over the range of likely outputs and price elasticity must be fairly constant for different points on the demand curve and over time.[10] Both conditions are apt to characterize many retailing situations. This may explain why fairly rigid markups are in widespread use in retailing and why this may not be inconsistent with optimal pricing requirements. In manufacturing, however, it is less likely that the two special conditions obtain, and here fixed-markup pricing is more difficult to justify on logical grounds.

Still, markup pricing remains popular for a number of reasons. First, there is generally less uncertainty about costs than about demand. By pinning the price to unit costs, the seller simplifies his own pricing task considerably; he does not have to make frequent adjustments as demand conditions change. Second, where all firms in the industry use this pricing approach, their prices are likely to be similar if their costs and markups are similar. Price competition

---

[8]See Lee E. Preston, *Profits, Competition, and Rules of Thumb in Retail Food Pricing* (Berkeley: University of California Institute of Business and Economic Research, 1963), p. 31.

[9]*Ibid.*, pp. 29–40.

[10]The argument is developed mathematically in the author's *Marketing Decision Making: A Model-Building Approach* (New York: Holt, Rinehart & Winston, Inc., 1971), mathematical note 12-1, pp. 702–3.

is therefore minimized, which would not be the case if firms paid attention to demand variations when they priced. Third, there is the feeling that cost-markup pricing is socially fairer to both the buyer and the seller. The seller does not take advantage of the buyer when his demand becomes acute; yet the seller earns a fair return on his investment. Thus the popularity of a cost-oriented approach to pricing rests on considerations of administrative simplicity, competitive harmony, and social fairness.

Target pricing A common cost-oriented approach used by manufacturers is known as *target pricing,* in which the firm tries to determine the price that would give it a specified target rate of return on its total costs at an estimated standard volume. This pricing approach has been most closely associated with General Motors, which has publicly stated that it prices its automobiles so as to achieve a long-run average rate of return of 15 to 20 percent on its investment.[11] It is also closely associated with the pricing policies of public utilities, which have a large investment and are constrained by regulatory commissions in view of their monopoly position to seek a fair rate of return on their costs.

The pricing procedures used in target pricing can be illustrated in terms of the breakeven chart in Figure 12-1. Management's first task is to estimate its total costs at various levels of output. The total-cost curve is shown rising at a constant rate until capacity is approached. Management's next task is to estimate the percentage of capacity at which it is likely to operate in the coming period. Suppose the company expects to operate at 80 percent of capacity. This means that it expects to sell 800,000 units if its capacity is 1 million units. The total cost of producing this volume, according to Figure 12-1, is $10 million. Management's third task is to specify a target rate of return. If the company aspires for a 20 percent profit over costs, then it would like absolute profits of $2 million. Therefore one point on its total-revenue curve will have to be $12 million at a volume of 80 percent of capacity. Another point on the total-revenue curve will be $0 at a volume of zero percent of capacity. The rest of the total-revenue curve can be drawn between these two points.

Where does price come in? The slope of the total-revenue curve is price. In this example, the slope is $15 a unit. Thus if the company charges $15 a unit

---

[11]Kaplan *et al., op. cit.,* pp. 48–55, 131–35.

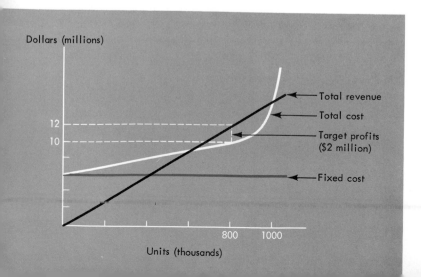

Figure 12-1
Breakeven chart for determining target price

and does manage to sell 800,000 units, it will attain through this price the target rate of return of 20 percent, or $2 million.

Target pricing, however, has a major conceptual flaw. The company used an estimate of sales volume to derive the price, but price is a factor that influences sales volume! A price of $15 may be too high or too low to move 800,000 units. What is missing from the analysis is a demand function, showing how many units the firm could expect to sell at different prices. With an estimate of the demand curve and with the requirement to earn 20 percent on costs, the firm could solve for those prices and volumes that would be compatible with each other. In this way, the firm would avoid setting a price that failed to generate the estimated level of output.

Demand-oriented pricing

Cost-oriented approaches rely on the idea of a standard markup over costs and/or a conventional level of profits. Demand-oriented approaches look instead at the intensity of demand. A high price is charged when or where demand is intense, and a low price is charged when or where demand is weak, even though unit costs may be the same in both cases.

Some pricing experts believe that demand should be the only factor in setting the price. They believe that price should be set not on cost but on the customer's *perceived value* for the product. The customer's perceived value is based on the total performance, psychological, and service characteristics of the seller's offer. The customer's perceived value is estimated, and then a price is set that would leave the customer with a slightly higher *perceived value-to-price ratio* than with any competing offer. This is felt to be a customer-oriented approach to pricing. Cost only comes in if it is too high to leave a profit in selling the product at that price.

Price discrimination A common form of demand-oriented pricing is price discrimination, in which a particular commodity is sold at two or more prices that do not reflect a proportional difference in marginal costs. Price discrimination takes various forms, according to whether the basis is the customer, the product version, the place, or the time.

Pricing that discriminates on a *customer basis* is illustrated in the retail selling of automobiles and major appliances. A car buyer may come into an automobile showroom and pay the list price for the automobile. Later, another car buyer may hold out for a lower price and pay it. The automobile may be identical in both cases, and the marginal cost of the transaction may be identical; yet the seller has managed to extract a higher price from one buyer than from the other. The occurrence of price discrimination among customers may indicate different intensities of demand or variation in consumer knowledge. Charging different prices to different customers raises strong ethical questions and is potentially disruptive of customer goodwill.

Pricing that discriminates on a *product-version basis* occurs when slightly different versions of a product are priced differently but not proportionately to their respective marginal costs. An example would be the sale of an electric dishwasher with a $5 formica top for $180 and the same dishwasher with a $10 wooden top for $220. The higher premium for the latter dishwasher reflects not so much the extra production cost as the extra psychological demand. Manufacturers, however, do not always mark up the more costly version at a disproportionately higher price. In many cases the price discrimination is reversed to encourage the buyer to trade up, thereby increasing total dollar sales.

Pricing that discriminates on a *place basis* is also quite common, since place is a form of utility. The pricing of theater seats is a case in point. Although all seats cost virtually the same to install, theater managements price seats differently because of different intensities of demand for the various locations. Different prices are charged so that each customer pays close to the maximum of what he is willing to pay. The theater is filled, and theater revenue is maximized.

Pricing that discriminates on a *time basis* also takes many forms. The demand for a product is likely to vary in intensity over the business cycle, over the seasons, by the day, and sometimes by the hour. Public utilities, in their pricing to commercial users, typically vary their prices according to the day (weekend versus weekday) and even the time of day. An economist advocated that public transportation services be priced higher at peak hours than at off-hours.[12] Generally speaking, the firm whose costs are largely fixed can gain by varying prices according to temporal variations in demand.

For price discrimination to work, certain conditions must exist. First, the market must be segmentable, and the segments must show different intensities of demand. Second, there should be no chance that the members of the segment paying the lower price could turn around and resell the product to the segment paying the higher price. Third, there should be little chance that competitors will undersell the firm in the segment being charged the higher price. Fourth, the cost of segmenting and policing the market should not exceed the extra revenue derived from price discrimination. Fifth, the practice should not breed customer resentment and turning away.

Competition-oriented pricing

When a company sets its prices chiefly on the basis of what its competitors are charging, its pricing policy can be described as competition-oriented. It is not necessary to charge the same price as competition, although this is a major example of this policy. The competition-oriented-pricing firm may seek to keep its prices lower or higher than competition by a certain percentage. The distinguishing characteristic is that it does *not* seek to maintain a rigid relation between its price and its own costs or demand. Its own costs or demand may change, but the firm maintains its price because competitors maintain their prices. Conversely, the same firm will change its prices when competitors change theirs, even if its own costs or demand have not altered.

Going-rate pricing   The most popular type of competition-oriented pricing is where a firm tries to keep its price at the average level charged by the industry. Called *going-rate pricing,* it is popular for several reasons. Where costs are difficult to measure, it is felt that the going price represents the collective wisdom of the industry concerning the price that would yield a fair return. It is also felt that conforming to a going price would be least disruptive of industry harmony. The difficulty of knowing how buyers and competitors would react to price differentials is still another reason for this pricing.

Going-rate pricing primarily characterizes pricing practice in homogeneous product markets, although the market structure itself may vary from pure competition to pure oligopoly. The firm selling a homogeneous product

---

[12]See George Stigler, *The Theory of Price,* rev. ed. (New York: The Macmillan Company, 1952), pp. 215ff.

in a *highly competitive market* has actually very little choice about the setting of its price. There is apt to be a market-determined price for the product, which is not established by any single firm or clique of firms but through the collective interaction of a multitude of knowledgeable buyers and sellers. The firm daring to charge more than the going rate would attract virtually no customers. The firm need not charge less because it can dispose of its entire output at the going rate. Under highly competitive conditions in a homogeneous product market (such as food, raw materials, and textiles), the firm really has no pricing decision to make. In fact, it hardly has any significant marketing decisions to make. The major challenge facing such a firm is good cost control. Since promotion and personal selling are small elements, the major marketing costs arise in physical distribution, and here is where cost efficiency may be critical.

In *pure oligopoly*, where a few large firms dominate the industry, the firm also tends to charge the same price as competition, although for different reasons. Since there are only a few firms, each firm is quite aware of the others' prices, and so are the buyers. A certain grade of steel is likely to possess the same quality whether it is produced by Inland or Bethlehem, and so the slightest price difference would favor the lower-price firm unless service or contractual relationships are sufficient to overcome this. The observed lack of price competition in these industries has been explained on the basis of the individual oligopolist's demand curve's having a kink in it at the level of the present prices. The demand curve tends to be elastic above the kink because other firms are not likely to follow a raise in prices; the demand curve tends to be inelastic below the kink because other firms are likely to follow a price cut. An oligopolist can gain little by raising his price when demand is elastic or lowering his price when demand is inelastic, and this is held to explain much of the price timidity in these markets.

This does not mean that the going price in an oligopoly market will be perpetuated indefinitely. It cannot, since industry costs and demand change over time. Usually, the industry takes collective action to raise the price, or in rarer cases, to lower the price. This is not done through official channels, for that would be illegal. Typically, one firm assumes the role of price leader. Of the twelve general price increases in the steel industry between World War II and 1960, United States Steel led in eleven cases.

In markets characterized by *product differentiation*, the individual firm has more latitude in its price decision. Product and service differences serve to desensitize the buyer to existing price differentials.[13] Firms try to establish themselves in a pricing zone with respect to their competitors, assuming the role of a high-price firm or a medium-price firm or a low-price firm. Their product and marketing program are made compatible with this chosen pricing zone or vice versa. They respond to competitive changes in price to maintain their pricing zone.

Sealed-bid pricing Competitive-oriented pricing also dominates in those situations where firms compete for jobs on the basis of bids, such as original equipment manufacture and defense contract work. The bid is the firm's offer price, and it is a prime example of pricing based on expectations of how com-

---

[13]See Richard D. Sampson, "Sense and Sensitivity in Pricing." *Harvard Business Review*, November–December 1964, pp. 99–105.

petitors will price rather than on a rigid relation based on the firm's own costs or demand. The objective of the firm in the bidding situation is to get the contract, and this means that it hopes to set its price lower than that set by any of the other bidding firms.

Yet the firm does not ordinarily set its price below a certain level. Even when it is anxious to get a contract in order to keep the plant busy, it cannot quote a price below marginal cost without worsening its position. On the other hand, as it raises its price above marginal cost, it increases its potential profit but reduces its chance of getting the contract.

The net effect of the two opposite pulls can be described in terms of the *expected profit* of the particular bid. Suppose a bid of $9,500 would yield a high chance of getting the contract, say .81, but only a low profit, say $100. The expected profit with this bid is therefore $81. If the firm bid $11,000, its profit would be $1,600, but its chance of getting the contract might be reduced, say to .01. The expected profit would be only $16. Table 12-1 shows these and some other bids and the corresponding expected profits.

Table 12-1

Effect of different bids on expected profit

Company's bid	Company's profit	Probability of getting award with this bid (assumed)	Expected profit
$ 9,500	$ 100	.81	$ 81
10,000	600	.36	216
10,500	1,100	.09	99
11,000	1,600	.01	16

One logical bidding criterion would be to state the bid that would maximize the expected profit. According to Table 12-1, the best bid would be $10,000, for which the expected profit is $216.

The use of the expected-profit criterion makes sense for the large firm that makes many bids and is not dependent on winning any particular contract. In playing the odds, it should achieve maximum profits in the long run. The firm that bids only occasionally and/or may need a particular contract badly will probably not find it advantageous to use the expected-profit criterion. The criterion, for example, does not distinguish between a $1,000 profit with a .10 probability and a $125 profit with an .80 probability. Yet the firm that wants to keep production going is likely to prefer the second contract to the first. In other words, the dollar value of expected profits may not reflect the utility value.

The chief obstacle to the use of formal bidding theory is guessing the probability of getting the contract at various bidding levels. This estimate requires information about what the competitors are likely to bid. Here lies the problem, because competitors keep their intentions as secret as possible. Therefore the company has to rely on conjecture, trade gossip, or past bidding history.

The theory of competitive bidding has received considerable refinement in the hands of applied mathematicians. Not only the standard situation but also special situations have been explored, such as that of a company that wants to bid simultaneously on a number of contracts and yet cannot afford to win them all.[14] The major problem remains that of obtaining reliable data to insert into the model.

INITIATING PRICE CHANGES

Pricing is a challenging decision not only when a price is being set for the first time but also when the firm is about to initiate a price change. The firm may be considering a *price reduction* in order to stimulate demand, to take advantage of lower costs, or to shake out weaker competitors. Or it may be considering a *price increase* in order to take advantage of tight demand or to pass on higher costs. Whether the price is to be moved up or down, the action is sure to affect buyers, competitors, distributors, and suppliers, and may interest government as well. The success of the move depends critically on how the parties respond.

Buyers' reactions to price change

The traditional analysis of buyers' reactions to price change is based on assuming that all buyers learn of the price change and take it at face value. The magnitude of their response to the price change is described by the concept of *price elasticity of demand*.

Price elasticity of demand   This term refers to the ratio of the percentage change in demand (quantity sold per period) caused by a percentage change in price.[15] A price elasticity of -1 means that sales rise (fall) by the same percentage as price falls (rises). In this case, total revenue is left unaffected. A price elasticity greater than -1 means that sales rise (fall) by more than price falls (rises) in percentage terms; in this case, total revenue rises. A price elasticity less than -1 means that sales rise (fall) by less than price falls (rises) in percentage terms; in this case, total revenue falls.

Price elasticity of demand gives more precision to the question of whether the firm's price is too high or too low. From the point of view of maximizing *revenue*, price is too high if demand is elastic and too low if demand is inelastic.

---

[14]See C. W. Churchman, Russell L. Ackoff, and E. Leonard Arnoff, *Introduction to Operations Research* (New York: John Wiley & Sons, Inc., 1957), pp. 559–73.

[15]In symbols,

$$E_{qp} = \frac{\dfrac{Q_1 - Q_0}{Q_0}}{\dfrac{P_1 - P_0}{P_0}} = \frac{relative\ change\ in\ quantity}{relative\ change\ in\ price}$$

where:

E_{qp} = elasticity of quantity sold with respect to a change in price
Q_1 = quantity sold per period after price change
Q_0 = quantity sold per period before price change
P_1 = new price
P_0 = old price

Whether this is also true for maximizing *profits* depends on the behavior of costs.[16]

In practice, price elasticity is extremely difficult to measure. There are definitional as well as statistical hurdles. Definitionally, price elasticity is not an absolute characteristic of the demand facing a seller but rather a conditional one. Price elasticity depends on the magnitude of the contemplated price change. It may be negligible with a small price change (one below the threshold level) and substantial with a large price change. Price elasticity also varies with the original price level. A 5 percent increase over current prices of $1 and $1.20, respectively, may exhibit a quite different elasticity. Finally, long-run price elasticity is apt to be different from short-run elasticity. Buyers may have to continue with the present supplier immediately after his price increase because choosing a new supplier takes time, but they may eventually stop purchasing from him. In this case, demand is more elastic in the long run than in the short run.[17] Or the reverse may happen; buyers drop a supplier in anger after he increases prices but return to him later. The significance of this distinction between short-run and long-run elasticity is that the seller will not know for a while how wise his price change is.

Major statistical estimation problems face the firm wishing to evaluate price elasticity. Different techniques have evolved, none completely appropriate or satisfactory in all circumstances. The whole problem can be brought into focus by considering the following case:

> One of the telephone companies in the Bell chain was considering a rate reduction. After the war, the number of telephone connections climbed rapidly with the housing boom and the increase in incomes, but the rate of new connections then began to taper off. One of the company's important sources of income was the extension (or second) phone which it installed in a home for an extra monthly charge of 75 cents. The company noticed that the percentage of homes with one or more extension phones was approaching a stable level of around 30 percent. The company had been using heavy promotion to sell families on second phones, but the advertising stimulation appeared to be showing diminishing returns. There was some evidence that many families whose dwelling units were large resisted two phones because the 75 cents monthly charge seemed too high to them. The company was wondering how many additional extension phones would be ordered if the charge were reduced to 50 cents.

A telephone company would not have any competitive reactions to worry about in contemplating a price change. The company could proceed directly to the task of estimating the likely reactions of the ultimate customers, using one of four methods.

DIRECT ATTITUDE SURVEY   The company could interview a sample of potential users as to whether they would add another phone if the monthly service charge were lowered to 50 cents. The percentage who said yes could

---

[16]Suppose unit variable costs are higher at reduced production levels and that demand is relatively inelastic. The firm can increase its total revenue by raising its price. But if it does so, sales may decline enough to increase unit costs to the point where the higher total revenue may be more than offset by higher total costs.

[17]Stigler suggests that demand is generally more elastic in the long run because the short run is marked by the difficulty of rapid adjustment, the existence of market imperfections, and the presence of habit. Stigler, *op. cit.*, pp. 45–47.

then be applied against the known total number of potential users (those who lived in apartments or homes with more than three rooms, according to one definition) to find the number of extra extensions this would mean.

STATISTICAL ANALYSIS OF RELATIONSHIP BETWEEN PRICE AND QUANTITY   This could take the form of either a historical or a cross-sectional analysis. A historical analysis consists in observing how extension usage was affected in the past by rate reductions. A cross-sectional analysis consists in observing how extension usage varies with the rates charged by different companies in the Bell System.

MARKET TEST   The company could offer a representative sample of potential users the chance to have an extension phone for 50 cents a month if they acted on the offer within a specified time period. The percentage who took advantage could then be applied against the estimated number of potential users.

ANALYTIC INFERENCE   The company could conjecture how many additional families would be likely to find a second phone worthwhile at the lower price. The issue of a second phone would be one of convenience versus cost. The company could segment the market into dwelling units of different sizes and different income levels. A family in a large home with a good income would tend to be more receptive to a second phone. The company could estimate how many families in this segment were without second phones and apply the probability that they would acquire the phone at the reduced rate. This could be done for all the segments to build up an estimate.

These different approaches to estimating demand elasticity work with different degrees of success in different circumstances, and sometimes two or more of them may be undertaken simultaneously for additional confirmation. In practical situations, the task is not one of estimating the absolute level of elasticity so much as whether it differs substantially from the breakeven level where nothing would be gained through a price change. This level is an elasticity of one if costs are constant. The breakeven level of elasticity can be translated into the actual number of new extensions that would have to be ordered to make up for the loss in revenue from reducing the rate on all existing extensions from 75 to 50 cents a month. Suppose in the Bell case this number was 5,000. If Bell had reason to believe that the rate reduction would easily stimulate at least 5,000 new extension installations, and probably more, then it is academic whether the number is 8,000, 10,000, or some other number.

Perceptual factors in buyers' response   Although economists have tended to ignore perceptual factors, they constitute an important intervening variable in explaining market response to price changes. In the Bell case, this turned out to be particularly true. In a direct attitude survey, potential extension users were asked what they thought the extension service cost. Over 80 percent of the respondents named a price above 75 cents a month, in some cases as high as $2. The amount of price misinformation was profound, and this could have been an important deterrent of purchase. The policy implication is quite interesting. It means that *bringing people closer to an understanding of the correct price would be tantamount to a price reduction.* If a housewife thought the monthly charge was $1 and then learned that it was only 75 cents, this is tantamount to a price reduction *in her mind* of 25 percent. Rather than reducing the monthly rate to 50 cents the company might gain more through an advertising campaign that clarified the current price.

Customers may not always put the most straightforward interpretation on a price change when it occurs.[18] A price reduction may symbolize any number of things:[19]

The item is about to be superseded by a later model.

The item has some fault and is not selling well.

The firm is in financial trouble and may not stay in business to supply future parts.

The price will come down even further and it pays to wait.[20]

The quality has been reduced.

A price increase may also be interpreted in several ways:

The item is very "hot" and may be unobtainable unless it is bought soon.

The item represents an unusually good value and could not yield a profit at the old price.

The seller is greedy and is charging what the traffic will bear.

In a period of rapidly rising prices, the seller is particularly vulnerable to the charge of taking advantage of buyers. Some customers suspect "price pyramiding" where the seller raises his prices by more than his cost increases. The seller risks spoiling the goodwill he has built and driving customers to find substitutes for his product when they feel that his prices have risen too much. It is incumbent on the seller to gain credibility for his price increases, even to the point of showing how much his costs have increased. Alternatively, he may try to keep his prices down by reducing his services or charging for them, and by constantly searching for ways to improve productivity.

Competitors' reactions to price changes

A firm contemplating a price change has to worry about competitors' as well as customers' reactions. Competitors' reactions are important where the number of firms is small, the product offering is homogeneous, and the buyers are discriminating and informed.

How can the firm estimate the likely reaction of its competitors? Let us assume at first that the firm faces only one large competitor. The likely behavior of this competitor can be approached from two quite different starting points. One is to assume that the competitor has a set policy for reacting to price changes. The other is to assume that the competitor treats each price change as a unique challenge and considers afresh his self-interest. Each assumption has quite different research implications.

If the competitor has a set price-reaction policy, there are at least two different ways to fathom it—through inside information and through statistical analysis. Inside information can be obtained in many ways, some quite acceptable and others verging on the cloak-and-dagger. One of the more respect-

---

[18]For an excellent review, see Kent B. Monroe, "Buyers' Subjective Perceptions of Price," *Journal of Marketing Research,* February 1973, pp. 70–80.

[19]See Alfred R. Oxenfeldt, *Pricing for Marketing Executives* (San Francisco: Wadsworth Publishing Company, 1961), p. 28.

[20]Economists use the concept of *elasticity of expectations* to convey this possibility. The elasticity of expectations is the ratio of the future expected percentage change in price to the recent percentage change in price. A positive elasticity means that buyers expect a price reduction (increase) to be followed by another reduction (increase).

able methods is hiring an executive away from a competitor. In this way the firm acquires a rich source of information on the competitor's thought processes and patterns of reaction. It may even pay to set up a unit of former employees whose job is to think like the competitor. Information on the thinking of a competitor can also come through other sources, such as customers, the financial community, suppliers, dealers, and the business community at large.

A set policy toward meeting price changes may be discerned through a statistical analysis of the firm's past price reactions. We can employ the concept "conjectural price variation" (V), defined as the ratio of the competitor's reactive price change to the company's previous price change. In symbols:[21]

$$V_{A,t} = \frac{P_{B,t} - P_{B,t-1}}{P_{A,t} - P_{A,t-1}}$$

where:

$$V_{A,t} = \text{the change in competitor B's price during period } t \text{ as a proportion of company A's price change during period } t$$
$$P_{B,t} - P_{B,t-1} = \text{the change in competitor B's price during period } t$$
$$P_{A,t} - P_{A,t-1} = \text{the change in company A's price during period } t$$

The last-observed $V_{A,t}$ can be used by the company as an estimate of the probable reaction of the competitor. If $V_{A,t} = 0$, then the competitor did not react last time. If $V_{A,t} = 1$, then the competitor fully matched the company's price change. If $V_{A,t} = \frac{1}{2}$, then the competitor only matched half of the company's price change. However, it could be misleading to base the analysis only on the last price reaction. It would be better to average several of the past V terms, giving more weight to the more recent ones because they are reflections of more current policy. A possible estimate of future competitive price reaction ($V_{A,t+1}$) might be

$$V_{A,t+1} = .5V_{A,t} + .3V_{A,t-1} + .2V_{A,t-2}$$

where three past conjectural price-variation terms are combined in a weighted average.

The statistical method makes sense only on the assumption that the competitor has a fairly consistent price-reaction policy. Otherwise it would be better to base the analysis on a quite different assumption, that the competitor decides afresh on each occasion of a price increase what reaction would be in his best interest. If this is so, an analysis must be made of how the competitor perceives his self-interest. His current financial situation should be researched, along with his recent sales and capacity, the basis of his customer appeal, and his corporate objectives. If evidence points to a market-share objective, then the competitor is likely to match the price change. If evidence points to a profit-maximization objective, the competitor may react on some other policy front, such as increasing his advertising or improving his product's quality. The job is to get into the mind of the competitor through inside and outside sources of information.

---

[21]See William Fellner, *Competition among the Few* (New York: Alfred A. Knopf, Inc. 1949); and Richard M. Cyert and James G. March, *A Behavioral Theory of the Firm* (Englewood Cliffs, N.J.: Prentice-Hall, Inc., 1963), Chap. 5, esp. pp. 88–90.

The problem is complicated because each price change occurs under unique circumstances, and the competitor is capable of putting different interpretations on it. His reaction to a price reduction will depend on whether he interprets it to mean:

The company is trying to steal the market from him.

The company is not doing well and is trying to improve its sales.

The company is hoping that the whole industry will reduce its prices in the interests of stimulating total demand.

When there is more than one competitor, the company must estimate each competitor's likely reaction. If all competitors are likely to behave alike, this amounts to analyzing only a typical competitor. If the competitors cannot be expected to react uniformly because of critical differences in size, market shares, or policies, then separate analyses are necessary. If it appears that a few competitors will match the price change, there is good reason to expect the rest will also match it.

Using decision theory for price changes

The following case illustrates how a major chemical company integrated various uncertain factors to analyze a contemplated price reduction.

A large chemical company had been selling a plastic substance to industrial users for several years and enjoyed 40 percent of the market. The management became worried about whether its current price of $1 per pound could be maintained for much longer. The main source of concern was the rapid buildup of capacity by its three competitors and the possible attraction of further-competitors by the present price. Management saw the key to the problem of possible oversupply in further market expansion. The key area for market expansion lay in an important segment of the market that was closely held by a substitute plastic product produced by six firms. This substitute product was not as good, but it was priced lower. Management saw a possible solution in displacing the substitute product in the recalcitrant segment through a price reduction. If it could penetrate this segment, there was a good chance it could also penetrate three other segments which had resisted the displacement.[22]

The first task was to develop a decision structure for the problem in which all components would be related. This meant defining the objectives, policy alternatives, and key uncertainties. It was decided that the objective would be to maximize the present value of future profits over the next five years. Management decided to consider the four alternatives of maintaining the price at $1 or reducing the price to 93, 85, and 80 cents, respectively. The following were considered among the key uncertainties that had to be evaluated:

How much penetration in the key segment would take place without a price reduction?

How would the six firms producing the substitute plastic react to each possible price reduction?

How much penetration in the key segment would take place for every possible price reaction of the suppliers of the substitute plastic?

---

[22]See Paul E. Green, "Bayesian Decision Theory in Pricing Strategy," *Journal of Marketing*, January 1963, pp. 5–14.

How much would penetration into the key segment speed up penetration into the other segments?

If the key segment were not penetrated, what was the probability that the company's competitors would initiate price reductions soon?

What would be the impact of a price reduction on the decision of existing competitors to expand their capacity and/or potential competitors to enter the industry?

The data-gathering phase consisted mainly in asking key sales personnel to place subjective probabilities on the various possible states of the key uncertainties. Meetings were held with the sales personnel to explain the concept of expressing judgments in the form of probabilities. The probabilities were filled out on a long questionnaire. For example, one question asked for the probability that the producers of the substitute product would retaliate if the company reduced its price to 93 cents per pound. On the average, the sales personnel felt that there was only a 5 percent probability of a full match, a 60 percent probability of a half match, and a 35 percent probability of no retaliation. They were also asked for probabilities if price were reduced to 85 and to 80 cents. The sales personnel indicated, as expected, that the probability of retaliation increased with an increase in price reduction.

The next step was to estimate the likely payoffs of different courses of action. A decision-tree analysis revealed that there were over four hundred possible outcomes. For this reason, the estimation of expected payoffs was programmed on a computer. The computer results indicated that in all cases a price reduction had a higher expected payoff than status quo pricing, and, in fact, a price reduction to 80 cents had the highest expected payoff. To check the sensitivity of these results to the original assumptions, the results were recomputed for alternative assumptions about the rate of market growth and the appropriate cost of capital. It was found that the ranking of the strategies was not affected by the change in the assumptions.

The analysis clearly pointed to the desirability of some price reduction in preference to the status quo. The last step belongs to management: to decide on the basis of this analysis, as well as other factors that may have eluded analysis, whether to initiate the price reduction and, if so, by how much.

MEETING PRICE CHANGES

Let us reverse the previous question and ask, How can a firm that has just witnessed a price change by a competitor decide on its best course of action?

In some market situations the firm has no choice but to meet a competitor's price change. This is particularly true when the price is cut in a homogeneous product market. Unless the firm meets the price reduction, most buyers will shift their business to the lowest-price competitor.

When the price is raised by a firm in a homogeneous product market, the other firms may or may not meet it. They will comply if the price increase appears designed to benefit the industry as a whole. But if one firm does not see it that way and thinks that it or the industry would gain more by standing pat on prices, its noncompliance can make the leader and the others rescind any price increases.

In nonhomogeneous product markets, a firm has more latitude in reacting to a competitor's price change. The essential fact is that buyers choose the seller on the basis of a multiplicity of considerations: service, quality, reliability, and other factors. These factors desensitize many buyers to minor price differences. The reacting firm has a number of options: doing nothing and losing few or many customers, depending upon the level of customer loyalty; meeting the price change partly or fully; countering with modifications of other elements in its marketing mix.

The firm's analysis should take the form of estimating the expected payoffs of alternative possible reactions. It should consider the following questions:

Why did the competitor change his price? Is it to steal the market, to meet changing cost conditions, or to evoke a calculated industry-wide price change to take advantage of total demand?

Is the competitor intending to make his price change temporary or permanent?

What will happen to the company's market share (and profits) if it ignores the price change? Are the other companies going to ignore the price change?

What is the competitor's (and other firms') response likely to be to each possible reaction?

Consider the situation of a firm that enjoys a dominant market share whose major competitor has just cut the price in an effort to win market share. The dominant firm has two broad options:

1 *Market-share maintenance.* The firm may choose to lower its price to the competitor's price to avoid losing market share. It may choose this course of action because (a) its costs fall with volume; (b) it believes that the market is very price-sensitive and it will lose a substantial market share; and (c) it believes that it would be hard to rebuild its market share once it is lost.

2 *Margin maintenance.* The firm may choose to maintain its price and therefore its profit margin. It may believe that (a) it would lose too much profit if it reduced its price on all the units it sells; (b) it would not lose much market share; and (c) it would be easy to regain or hold market share by investments to increase the perceived value of its brand.

Between these extremes, the firm could also consider a partial price reduction to limit its market-share loss.

The proper course of action depends upon estimating the price elasticity of demand, the behavior of costs with volume, and the supply capabilities of the competitor. For example, margin maintenance would make good sense where there is low price elasticity (the company has built up high perceived value and has loyal customers), costs are not too sensitive to small-volume losses, and the competitor is small and cannot finance large expansions in capacity.

An extended analysis of company alternatives is not always feasible at the time of a price change. The competitor who initiated the price change may have spent considerable time in preparing for this decision, but the company that must react may have only hours or days before some decisive position must be taken. The analysis and information are necessarily below the standard usually required for determining such an important decision as a price reaction. About the only way to place such decisions on a surer footing is to anticipate their possible occurrence and to prepare an advanced program to guide managers' responses. An example of such a program to meet a possible price cut is shown in Figure 12-2. Reaction programs for meeting price changes are

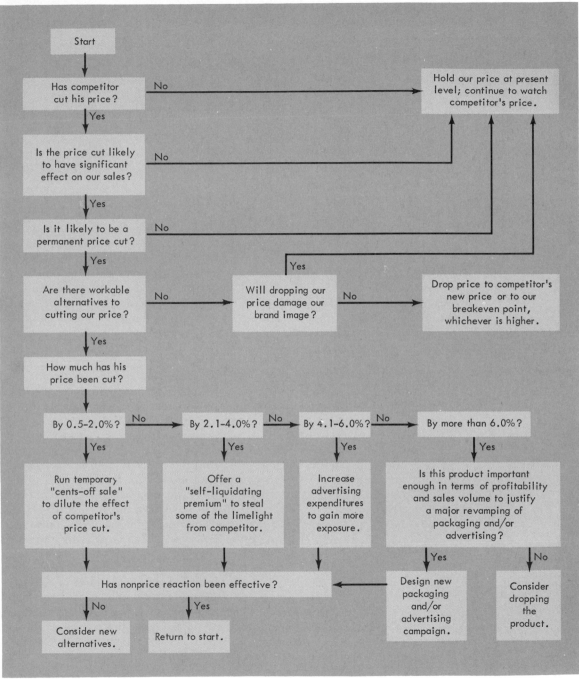

Figure 12-2
Decision program for meeting a competitor's price cut

likely to find their greatest application in industries where price changes occur with some frequency and where it is important to react quickly. Examples could be found in the meat-packing, lumber, and oil industries.[23]

PRODUCT-LINE PRICING

The logic of setting or changing a price on an individual product has to be modified when the product is a member of a product line. In the latter case, the true quest is for a set of mutual prices that maximizes the profits of the line. This quest is made difficult because various company products are interrelated in demand and/or cost and are subject to different degrees of competition.

Interrelated demand

Two products are interrelated in demand when the price (or some other element of the marketing mix) of one affects the demand for the other. Economists use the concept of "cross-elasticity of demand" to express the interaction.[24] A positive cross-elasticity means that two goods are *substitutes,* a negative cross-elasticity means that two goods are *complements,* and a zero (or low) cross-elasticity means that two goods are *unrelated* in demand. If a television manufacturer lowered the price of his color television sets, this would decrease the demand for his black-and-white sets (substitutes), increase the demand for the components of his color sets (complements), and probably would not affect the demand for his pocket radios. Before changing the price of any single item in his line, the seller should consider the various cross-elasticities to determine the overall impact of his move.

Interrelated cost

Two products are interrelated in cost when a change in the production of one affects the cost of the other. By-products and joint products are related in this sense. If the production of ham is cut down, the production of pork will be also. As a result, the unit cost of the pork that is produced will rise because the overhead is spread over fewer units. More generally, any two products using the same production facilities are interrelated on the cost side even if they are not joint products. This is largely because accounting practice requires a full allocation of costs. The significance of all this is that if the company increases the price of A, for example, and causes its sales to fall, the cost of the other products, assuming they are not complementary goods, will be higher. Thus management must examine the cost interactions before it changes the price of a single product in the line.

Effect of competition

Various products in a company line are exposed to different degrees of competition. The seller may have little latitude in pricing products in his line where existing or potential competition is keen, and he will have varying degrees of price discretion in the other cases. Therefore the structure of prices for the products in the line should not simply be proportional to costs, however measured, for this would overlook profit opportunities that are associated with taking advantage of different degrees of competition.

---

[23]See, for example, William M. Morgenroth, "A Method for Understanding Price Determinants," *Journal of Marketing Research,* August 1964, pp. 17–26.

[24]Technically, the cross-elasticity of demand (E_c) is the percentage change in quantity sold of product B associated with a percentage change in price of product A.

In practice, costs have provided the usual starting point for determining the prices of interrelated products in the line. Even here there seems to be considerable disagreement over which costs should be used. The three most popular cost bases are full costs, incremental costs, and conversion costs. The price structures resulting from using these respective cost bases are illustrated for a hypothetical soap manufacturer in Table 12-2.

The soap manufacturer makes two different types of specialty soap. The second soap requires more labor cost but less material cost per bar than the first soap. The second bar also takes more manufacturing support and overhead than the first. The specific costs per bar are shown in Table 12-2(A).

The first pricing principle calls for pricing the soaps proportionately to their full costs. Since both soaps have the same full costs, they will bear the same price (here 42 cents because of a 20 percent markup). The chief criticism against using the full cost is that the allocation of overhead unavoidably involves some arbitrariness. Therefore the resulting prices take on a partly arbitrary character. As a result, the company may be blind to profit opportunities that would exist if the prices of the two soaps were not geared so tightly to the recovery of a somewhat arbitrary overhead burden.

The second pricing principle calls for setting prices that are proportional to incremental costs. The underlying theory is that the company should charge customers proportionately to the extra costs it has to bear in supplying additional units of the two soaps. In the example, supplying an additional unit of soap 2 imposes less additional cost than supplying another unit of soap 1. The net effect of pricing on an incremental cost basis is to shift sales toward the soap that absorbs more company overhead.[25]

Table 12-2

Illustration of alternative product-line pricing principles

(A) *Product-line cost structure*

	Soap 1	Soap 2
1. Labor cost	.10	.15
2. Material cost	.20	.10
3. Overhead cost	.05	.10
Full cost (1 + 2 + 3)	.35	.35
Incremental cost (1 + 2)	.30	.25
Conversion cost (1 + 3)	.15	.25

(B) *Alternative product-line prices*

	Markup	Soap 1	Soap 2
1. Full cost pricing	20%	.42	.42
2. Incremental cost pricing	40%	.42	.35
3. Conversion cost pricing	180%	.42	.70

---

[25]The principle of marking up incremental costs is analyzed and defended for retail pricing in Malcolm P. McNair and Eleanor G. May, "Pricing for Profit, A Revolutionary Approach to Retail Accounting," *Harvard Business Review,* May–June 1957, pp. 105–22.

The third pricing principle calls for setting prices that are proportional to conversion costs. Conversion costs are defined as the labor and company overhead required to convert purchased materials into finished products. Conversion costs thus amount to the "value added" by the firm in the production process; it can be found by subtracting purchased material costs from the allocated full costs. The argument that has been advanced for using conversion costs is that the firm's profits should be based on the value its own operations add to each soap. The net effect of pricing on a conversion cost basis is to shift sales toward the soap that has more material cost. This pricing principle economizes on the use of scarce company resources, such as labor and machines. Other than this, there is no particular economic justification for choosing certain elements of cost to bear the profit markup rather than others; furthermore, this basis again involves arbitrary allocations of overhead.

As stated earlier, costs represent a starting point for developing the pricing structure, but they hardly represent sufficient criteria. Incremental costs provide the lower limit to individual product pricing (except in special circumstances, such as loss leading). But a *uniform* markup over incremental or any other costs is fallacious in that it ignores the different demand intensities, cross-elasticities, competitive conditions, and life-cycle characteristics of each product. Pricing theory still has to progress to a stage where the cost, demand, and competitive factors can be blended to produce a set of determinate prices.

OTHER PROBLEMS

Other pricing problems not treated here are of special concern in certain situations. Clothing retailers regularly mark down the prices of fashion merchandise as the season progresses, and the problem of the appropriate size and timing of the markdown(s) is a question of substantial interest.[26] Other retailers are interested in "sales" or "loss-leader" pricing. Food producers regularly offer price deals (cents-off on branded food products) and are concerned with the problem of seasonal timing and magnitude.[27] The psychology of pricing is of great interest to other sellers, who are concerned with whether sales are really stimulated by prices ending in odd figures, such as $9.95 instead of $10.00.[28] Some manufacturers are concerned with how to price to different distributors and customers and particularly whether a policy of resale price maintenance makes sense. Other manufacturers are concerned with the effectiveness of special pricing methods, such as step-pricing, early-payment pricing, and pricing for separate services.

Pricing is an acute concern in particular industrial situations, such as where there is production overcapacity, where forms of distribution are rapidly

---

[26]A markdown pricing model is described in Cyert and March, *op. cit.*, pp. 140–46. Also see Sterling D. Sessions, "Sales/Stock Ratios: Key to Markdown Timing," in *New Research in Marketing*, ed. Lee E. Preston (Berkeley: University of California Institute of Business and Economic Research, 1965), pp. 57–69.

[27]See Ronald E. Frank and William F. Massy, "Short Term Price and Dealing Effects in Selected Market Segments," *Journal of Marketing Research*, May 1965, pp. 171–85.

[28]Dean reports some evidence that odd prices do not stimulate more sales. See Dean, *op. cit.*, pp. 490–91. For a demand-curve interpretation of odd prices (and other pricing policies), see Edward H. Hawkins, "Price Policies and Theory," *Journal of Marketing*, January 1954, pp. 233–40.

changing, where competition is keen, where costs are rising rapidly, and where jobs must be bid for. In these and other situations, price decisions require skill and experience, and the companies involved would gain from developing pricing specialists within the company.[29] At the same time, prices must be set as part of a total marketing strategy covering channels, promotion, personal selling, and other marketing variables, and pricing executives must make their decisions in this broader context.

SUMMARY

In spite of the increased role of nonprice factors in the modern marketing process, price remains an important element and especially challenging in certain situations.

In setting a price, a firm can draw guidance from the theoretical pricing model of the economists. The model suggests how the firm can find the short-run profit-maximizing price when estimates of demand and cost are available. The model, however, leaves out several factors that have to be considered in actual pricing situations, such as the presence of other objectives, multiple parties, marketing-mix interactions, and uncertainties surrounding the estimates of demand and cost. In practice, companies tend to orient their pricing toward cost (as in markup pricing and target pricing), or demand (as in price discrimination), or competition (as in going rate pricing and bidding).

When a firm considers changing its established price, it must carefully consider customers' and competitors' reactions. The probable reaction of customers is summarized in the concept of price elasticity of demand. There are several ways to estimate price elasticity and some problems in interpreting it, but it is a key input in the determination of how much would be gained by the price change. Competitors' reactions also must be taken into account, and they depend very much on the nature of the market structure and the degree of product homogeneity. Competitors' reactions may be studied on the assumption either that they flow from a set reaction policy or that they flow from a fresh appraisal of the challenge each time. The firm initiating the price change must also consider the probable reactions of suppliers, middlemen, and government.

The firm that witnesses a price change must try to understand the competitor's intent and the likely duration of the change. If swiftness of reaction is desirable, the firm should preplan its reactions to different possible pricing developments.

Pricing is complicated when it is realized that various products in a line typically have important demand and/or cost interrelationships. Then the objective is to develop a set of mutual prices that maximize the profits on the whole line. Most companies develop tentative prices for the products in the line by marking up full costs, or incremental costs, or conversion costs and then modifying these prices by individual demand and competitive factors.

[29]For the main factors determining the size and type of pricing department needed to carry out the pricing function, see Oxenfeldt, *op. cit.*, p. 19.

1 Does an "early cash recovery" pricing objective mean that the firm should set a high rather than low price on its new product?

2 The statement was made that a firm might set a low price on a product to discourage competitors from coming in. Are there any situations (aside from anti-trust reasons) when a firm might deliberately want to attract competitors into a new market and set a high price for this reason?

3 Four different methods of estimating the price elasticity of demand for extension telephones were described in the text. What are the limitations of each method?

4 Xerox developed an office copying machine called the 914. The machine was more expensive than competitive machines but offered the user superior copy and lower variable costs: 1 cent per copy as opposed to between 4 to 9 cents for competing processes. The machine cost around $2,500 to produce, and management was considering pricing it at either $3,500 or $4,500. How could it estimate unit sales at the two alternative price levels?

5 Bell and Howell was the first company to develop an electric-eye camera by combining a regular $70 camera with a $10 electric-eye mechanism. What price do you think might be charged for the new camera?

6 A group of people were asked to choose between two raincoats, one bearing a brand label and a higher price and another bearing a store label and a lower price. The two coats happened to be identical, but the customers were not told this. If customers were completely knowledgeable, (a) what percentage would choose the higher-priced coat, and (b) what percentage do you think actually chose the higher-priced coat?

7 A reduction in price, in principle, is tantamount to an increase in marketing effort. How can the price reduction be monetized into its equivalent in increased marketing effort?

8 The leading manufacturer of a food flavor intensifier has recently watched its market share fall from 100 percent to 85 percent. Its declining share is due to its insistence on maintaining a high price in the face of new competitors who have introduced the same product for substantially less. The company has fought the new competition by increasing its advertising expenditures and dealer promotions. Does this make as much sense as cutting its price?

9 Restate the following prose description of a pricing procedure in either (a) mathematical or (b) logical flow diagram form.

> Given that my competitor is operating at or above his breakeven point with a price equal to mine, then: If I cut my price, my competitor will cut his to match mine providing the price cut is likely to be permanent and the competitor can break even at my new price. If I do not cut my price, my competitor will not cut his either. If I cut my price, and the price cut is not likely to be permanent, my competitor will watch price and volume but will do nothing now. If I cut my price, and if the price cut is likely to be permanent and my competitor cannot break even at my new price, he will cut his price down to his breakeven point.

13
CHANNEL DECISIONS

*The middleman is not a hired link in a chain forged
by a manufacturer, but rather an independent market,
the focus of a large group of customers for whom he
buys. . . . As he grows and builds a following, he may
find his prestige in his market is greater than that of
the supplier whose goods he sells.*

PHILLIP McVEY

In today's economy, most producers do not sell their goods directly to the final
users. Between them and the final users stands a host of marketing intermediaries performing in a variety of functions and bearing a variety of names. Some
middlemen—such as wholesalers and retailers—buy, take title to, and resell the
merchandise; they are called *merchant middlemen*. Others—such as brokers, manufacturers' representatives, and sales agents—search for customers and may negotiate on behalf of the producer but do not take title to the goods; they are called
agent middlemen.

Two aspects of channel decisions place them among the most critical
marketing decisions of management. The first is that *the channels chosen for the
company's products intimately affect every other marketing decision.* The firm's pricing
decisions depend upon whether it seeks a few franchised high-markup dealers
or mass distribution; the firm's advertising decisions are influenced by the
degree of cooperation from channel members; the firm's sales-force decisions
depend upon whether it sells directly to retailers or uses manufacturers' representatives. This does not mean that channel decisions are always made prior
to other decisions, but rather that they exercise a powerful influence on the
rest of the mix.

The second reason for the significance of channel decisions is that *they
involve the firm in relatively long-term commitments to other firms.* When an automobile

275

manufacturer signs up independent franchised dealers to merchandise his automobiles, he cannot easily replace them with company-owned outlets if conditions change. When a drug manufacturer relies heavily on retail druggists for the distribution of most of his products, he must heed them when they object to his merchandising through chain stores. There is a powerful tendency toward status quo in channel arrangements. Therefore management must choose its channels with an eye on tomorrow as well as today.

THE NATURE AND TYPES OF MARKETING CHANNELS AND INTERMEDIARIES

Every producer seeks to link together the set of marketing intermediaries that best fulfill the firm's objectives. This set of marketing intermediaries is called the *marketing channel* (also trade channel, channel of distribution). According to Breyer, "a trading channel exists once the terms of the franchises or agreements spanning the whole gap from producer to consumer are concluded between concerns assumed to possess the necessary marketing capabilities."[1] The relationship among the participating concerns is symbiotic in that they are usually dissimilar but work together for mutual advantage. Cooperation is the dominant theme among the members of a marketing channel, but at times conflict is no less pronounced.

Number of channel levels

Marketing channels can be characterized according to the number of channel levels. Each institution, beginning with the producer, that takes title ownership or selling responsibility constitutes a *level*. The number of levels in the channel make up its *length*. Figure 13-1 illustrates several marketing channels of different lengths.

The shortest marketing channel consists of two levels—a producer selling directly to a consumer. Many examples of *direct marketing* can be found. A manufacturer of cosmetics employs saleswomen to sell to housewives on a door-to-door basis; a manufacturer of heavy machinery solicits business directly from user firms; and an apple orchard invites the public to pick their own apples at a flat price per bushel.

A three-level channel contains one selling intermediary. In consumer markets this intermediary is typically a retailer; in industrial markets he is often a sales agent or a broker.

A four-level channel contains two intermediaries. In consumer markets they are typically a wholesaler and a retailer; in industrial markets they may be a sales agent and a wholesaler.

A five-level channel contains three intermediaries. An example is found in the meat-packing industry, where a jobber usually intervenes between the wholesalers and the retailers. The jobber buys from wholesalers and sells to the smaller retailers, who generally are not serviced by the large wholesalers.

Higher-level marketing channels are also found, but with less frequency. From the producer's point of view the problem of control increases with the number of levels, even though the producer typically deals only with the adjacent level.

---

[1]Ralph F. Breyer, "Some Observations on 'Structural' Formation and the Growth of Marketing Channels," in *Theory in Marketing*, ed. Reavis Cox, Wroe Alderson, and Stanley J. Shapiro (Homewood, Ill.: Richard D. Irwin, Inc., 1964), p. 165.

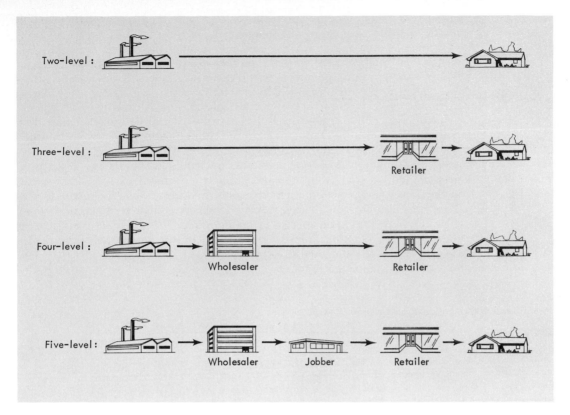

Figure 13-1
Examples of different-level channels

The various institutions that make up a marketing channel are connected by several distinguishable types of flows. The most important are the physical flow, title flow, payment flow, information flow, and promotion flow. These are illustrated in Figure 13-2 for the marketing of forklift trucks.

The *physical flow* describes the actual movement of physical products from raw materials to final customers. In the case of a forklift-truck manufacturer, such as Allis-Chalmers or Clark Equipment, raw materials, subassemblies, parts, and engines flow from suppliers to the company's warehouses. They then travel to the manufacturer's plant(s), which turn them into trucks. The finished trucks are warehoused and later shipped to dealers in response to their orders. The dealers in turn sell and ship them to customers. Large orders may be supplied directly from the company warehouses or even from the plant itself. At each stage of movement, one or more modes of shipment may be used, including railroads, trucks, and air freight.

The *title flow* describes the actual passage of title (of ownership) from one marketing institution to another. In the case of forklift trucks, title to the raw materials and components passes from the suppliers to the manufacturer. The title to the finished trucks passes from the manufacturer to the customer—the

277

dealer only holds the trucks on *consignment*. Otherwise, if he buys and owns the trucks, the title passes to the dealer first.

The *payment flow* shows the customer paying his bill to the dealer, the dealer remitting payment to the manufacturer (less his commission), and the manufacturer making payments to the various suppliers. If the warehouses do not belong to the manufacturer, then some payment will also go to them.

The *information flow* describes how information is exchanged among the institutions in the marketing channel. A two-way information exchange takes place between each successive stage in the channel, and there are several information flows between nonadjacent institutions.

Finally, the *promotion flow* describes directed flows of influence (advertising, personal selling, sales promotion and publicity) from one party to other parties in the system. Suppliers promote their name and products to the manufacturer. They may also promote their name and products to final customers in the hope of influencing the manufacturer to prefer products embodying their parts or materials. A promotion flow is also directed by the manufacturer to dealers (trade promotion) and final customers (end-user promotion).

Figure 13-2
Five different flows in the marketing channel for forklift trucks

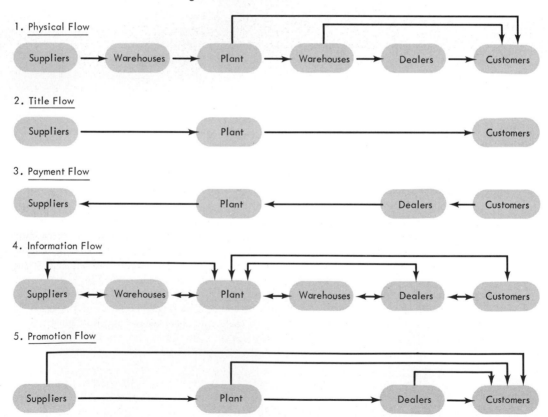

Were all of these flows to be superimposed on one diagram, they would emphasize the tremendous complexity of even simple marketing channels. This complexity goes even further, once we start distinguishing among different suppliers and different final customers.

Why is the producer generally willing to delegate some of the selling job to intermediaries? The delegation usually means the relinquishment of some control over how and to whom the products are sold. The producer appears to be placing the firm's destiny in the hands of intermediaries.

Since producers are free in principle to sell directly to final customers, there must be certain advantages or necessities for using middlemen. Some of the major factors are:

Many producers lack the financial resources to embark on a program of direct marketing. For example, General Motors' new automobiles are marketed by over 18,000 independent dealers; even as the world's largest manufacturing corporation, General Motors would be hard pressed to raise the cash to buy out its dealers.

Direct marketing would require many producers to become middlemen for the complementary products of other producers in order to achieve mass distributional efficiency. For example, the Wm. Wrigley Jr. Company would not find it practical to establish small retail gum shops throughout the country or to sell gum door to door or by mail order. It would have to tie gum in with the sale of many other small products and end up in the drugstore and foodstore business. It is much easier for Wrigley to work through the existing and extensive network of privately owned distribution institutions.

Those producers who have the required capital to develop their own channels often can earn a greater return by increasing their investment in other aspects of their business. If a company is earning a 20 percent rate of return on its production operations and foresees only a 5 percent rate of return on investing in direct marketing, it would not make sense to put money toward vertically integrating its channels.

The use of middlemen largely boils down to their superior efficiency in the performance of basic marketing tasks and functions. Marketing intermediaries, through their experience, their specialization, their contacts, and their scale, offer the producer more than he can usually achieve on his own.

Figure 13-3 shows just one source of the economies effected by the use of middlemen. Part (a) shows three producers using direct marketing to reach each of three customers. This system requires nine different contacts. Part (b) shows the three producers working through one middleman, who in turn contacts the three customers. This system requires only six contacts. In this way the use of middlemen reduces the amount of work that must be done.

From the point of view of the economic system, the basic role of marketing channels is to transform the heterogeneous supplies found in nature into meaningful goods assortments desired by man:

The materials which are useful to man occur in nature in heterogeneous mixtures which might be called conglomerations since these mixtures have only random relationship to human needs and activities. The collection of goods in the possession of a household or an individual also constitutes a heterogeneous supply, but

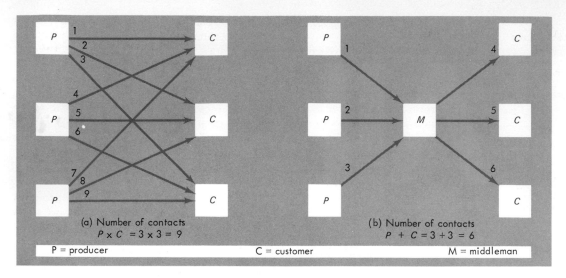

Figure 13-3
How a middleman effects an economy of effort

it might be called an assortment since it is related to anticipated patterns of future behavior. The whole economic process may be described as a series of transformations from meaningless to meaningful heterogeneity.[2]

The chief functions of selling intermediaries are to assemble the lines of many producers into an assortment of potential interest to buyers and to break bulk so as to meet the scale of need of the customer. Alderson has summarized this role in the statement that "the goal of marketing is the matching of segments of supply and demand."[3]

The matching of segments of supply and demand requires the carrying out of a number of specific marketing functions. McGarry identified the following functions:

1 *Contactual*—the searching out of buyers and sellers.
2 *Merchandising*—the fitting of the goods to market requirements.
3 *Pricing*—the selection of a price high enough to make production possible and low enough to induce users to accept the goods.
4 *Propaganda*—the conditioning of the buyers or of the sellers to a favorable attitude toward the product or its sponsor.
5 *Physical distribution*—the transporting and storing of the goods.
6 *Termination*—the consummation of the marketing process.[4]

---

[2]Wroe Alderson, "The Analytical Framework for Marketing," *Proceedings—Conference of Marketing Teachers from Far Western States* (Berkeley: University of California Press, 1958).
[3]Wroe Alderson, *Marketing Behavior and Executive Action: A Functionalist Approach to Marketing Theory* (Homewood, Ill.: Richard D. Irwin, Inc., 1957), p. 199.
[4]Edmund D. McGarry, "Some Functions of Marketing Reconsidered," in *Theory in Marketing*, ed. Reavis Cox and Wroe Alderson (Homewood, Ill.: Richard D. Irwin, Inc., 1950), pp. 269–73.

It is not a question of whether these functions must be performed in order to bridge the gap between producer and customer—they must be—but rather who is to perform them. All of the functions have two things in common: they use up scarce resources, and they can often be performed better through specialization. To the extent that the producer performs them, his costs go up and his prices have to be higher. When some of these tasks are delegated to middlemen, the producer's costs and prices are lower, but the middlemen must add a charge to cover the use of scarce resources. The issue of who should perform various channel tasks is largely one of relative efficiency and effectiveness. To the extent that specialist intermediaries achieve economies through their scale of operation and their knowhow, the producer can gain by transferring some of the channel functions to their charge.[5]

A major point to keep in mind is that marketing functions are more basic than the institutions that at any given time appear to perform them. Changes in the number of channel levels and/or types of selling intermediaries largely reflect the discovery of more efficient ways to combine or separate the economic work that must be carried out if meaningful assortments of goods are to be presented to customers.

CHANGING CHANNEL INSTITUTIONS

Channel institutions, like products, exhibit a life cycle. A particular channel institution may emerge suddenly, enjoy rapid growth, reach a point of relative maturity, and eventually move into a period of slow decline. A major force behind the channel life cycle is the changing economics, which makes new combinations of marketing functions suddenly more efficient than previous ones.

In retailing, totally new institutions have appeared in an industry that a hundred years ago consisted only of small general and specialty stores. *Department stores* first came on the American scene in the 1860s, about a decade after they started in Europe. Shortly thereafter *mail-order houses,* such as Montgomery Ward (1872) and Sears Roebuck (1886), were established. During the 1920s, *chain-store organizations* emerged and entered a period of rapid growth. The principal retailing innovation in the 1930s was the *supermarket.* The late 1940s were marked by the appearance of *planned suburban shopping centers.* The major retailing development in the early 1950s was the *discount house.* The 1950s also produced a rapid expansion of *automatic merchandising,* that is, vending machines. More recent years witnessed the growth of *superstores* and *hypermarkets, convenience stores,* and *boutiques.* None of these retailing forms have passed out of existence, but they show different vitalities depending on their economics and ability to deliver what the consumer wants.

---

[5]Many social critics of the distribution system fail to grasp this point. In observing that a good part of the final price of many products goes to middlemen, they conclude that the middleman is an exploitative entity in the process of moving goods from producer to consumer. They overlook the fact that the economic work performed by middlemen—making contact, stocking goods, shipping goods, and so forth—has to be performed somewhere in the channel. The producer's price is artificially low because he does not perform this work. One of the reasons he doesn't choose to perform this work is that the middlemen, through specialization, may perform it for less. Thus middlemen generally bring down the final cost of goods. Middlemen's charges are close to their costs if there is heavy competition among them. When certain middlemen do begin to cost too much, new channel innovations usually develop to replace them.

The retailing revolution is thus a many-faceted thing. It is a process of "creative destruction." Some of the changes in retail institutions, but not all of them, can be explained by the *wheel of retailing* hypothesis.[6] According to this hypothesis, many new types of retailing institutions first begin as low-status, low-margin, low-price operations. They become effective competitors of more conventional outlets, which have grown "fat" over the years. Their success gradually leads them to upgrade their facilities and offer additional services. This increases their costs and forces price increases until they finally resemble the conventional outlets that they displaced. They, in turn, become vulnerable to still newer types of low-cost, low-margin operations. This wheel pattern explains the success and later troubles of department stores, supermarkets, and, more recently, discount houses. On the other hand, it does not explain the growth of suburban shopping centers and automatic retailing, both of which started out as high-margin and high-cost operations.

Growth of vertical marketing systems

While individual channel forms undergo continuous and occasionally dramatic change, a very significant development is occurring that cuts across many industries. This development is the emergence of *vertical marketing (channel) systems.*[7] To understand them, we should first define *traditional marketing channels.* Traditional channels are "highly fragmented networks in which loosely aligned manufacturers, wholesalers, and retailers have bargained with each other at arm's length, negotiated aggressively over terms of sale, and otherwise behaved autonomously."[8] By contrast, *vertical marketing systems* are "professionally managed and centrally programmed networks, pre-engineered to achieve operating economies and maximum market impact."[9] These systems offer effective competition to individualistic marketing systems because they achieve impressive scale economies through their size, bargaining power, and elimination of duplicated services. In fact, they have emerged in the consumer-goods sector of American economy as the preferred mode of distribution, accounting for as much as 64 percent of the available market.

Corporate system   Three types of vertical marketing systems (VMS) can be distinguished. A *corporate vertical marketing system* has as its distinguishing characteristic the combining of successive stages of production and distribution under a single ownership. As examples:

> . . . Sherwin-Williams currently owns and operates over 2,000 retail outlets . . . Sears reportedly obtains 50 percent of its throughput from manufacturing facilities in which it has an equity interest. . . . Holiday Inns is evolving into a self-supply network that includes a carpet mill, a furniture manufacturing plant, and numerous captive redistribution facilities. In short, these and other organizations are massive, vertically integrated systems. To describe them as "retailers," "manu-

---

[6]Malcolm P. McNair, "Significant Trends and Developments in the Postwar Period," in *Competitive Distribution in a Free, High-Level Economy and Its Implications for the University,* ed. A. B. Smith (Pittsburgh: University of Pittsburgh Press, 1958), pp. 1–25. Also see the critical discussion by Stanley C. Hollander, "The Wheel of Retailing," *Journal of Marketing,* July 1960, pp. 37–42.

[7]The following discussion is indebted to Bert C. McCammon, Jr., "Perspectives for Distribution Programming," in *Vertical Marketing Systems,* ed. Louis P. Bucklin (Glenview, Ill.: Scott, Foresman, Company, 1970), pp. 32–51.

[8]*Ibid.,* p. 43.

[9]*Ibid.*

facturers," or "motel operators" oversimplifies their operating complexities and ignores the realities of the marketplace.[10]

Administered system   An *administered vertical marketing system*, by contrast, achieves coordination of successive stages of production and distribution not through common ownership but through the size and power of one of the parties within the system. Thus, manufacturers of a dominant brand are able to secure strong trade cooperation and support from resellers. Such companies as General Electric, Procter & Gamble, Kraftco, and Campbell Soup are able to command unusual cooperation from their resellers and retailers in connection with displays, shelf space, promotions, and price policies.

Contractual system   A *contractual vertical marketing system* consists of independent firms at different levels of production and distribution integrating their programs on a contractual basis to obtain more economies and/or sales impact than they could alone. Contractual VMSs have expanded the most in recent years and constitute one of the most significant developments in the economy.

Three different types of contractual VMS can be distinguished. The first is the *wholesaler-sponsored voluntary chain*, which originated in the efforts of wholesalers to save the independent retailers they served against the competition of large chain organizations. The wholesaler develops a program in which independent retailers join with him either to standardize their name or practices or to achieve buying economies that enable them to stand as a group against the inroads of the chains.

A second type of contractual VMS is *retailer cooperatives*. Usually they arise through the efforts of a group of retailers to defend themselves against the corporate chains. The retailers organize an entity to carry on the wholesaling process and possibly a production process as well. Members are expected to concentrate their purchases, and profits from the wholesale operation are passed back to members in the form of patronage refunds. Individual retailers may agree to identify as members of a group and carry on cooperative advertising; in many cases, however, they do not, and only use the cooperative facilities as an economical source of supply.

A third type of contractual VMS is the *franchise organizations*. Here several successive stages in the production-distribution process are linked under an agreement with one entity of the system, which is considered the franchiser. Franchising has been the fastest growing and most interesting retailing development in recent years. Although the basic idea is an old one, some forms of franchising are quite new. In fact, three different forms can be distinguished.

The first form is the *manufacturer-sponsored retailer franchise system*, exemplified in the automobile industry. A car manufacturer such as Ford licenses dealers to sell its product, the dealers being independent businessmen who are nevertheless obligated to meet various conditions of sales and service.

The second form is the *manufacturer-sponsored wholesaler franchise system*, which is found in the soft-drink industry. The soft-drink manufacturer licenses bottlers (wholesalers) in various markets who buy its concentrate and then carbonate, bottle, and sell it to retailers in local markets.

---

[10]*Ibid.*, p. 45.

The third form is the *service-firm sponsored retailer franchise system*. Here a service firm organizes a whole system for bringing its service efficiently to consumers. Examples are readily found in the auto rental business (such as Hertz and Avis), restaurant business (McDonald's, Burger King), and motel business (Howard Johnson, Ramada Inn). The motel franchiser, for example, uses his mass-purchasing power to obtain favorable terms from suppliers; in some cases he buys an equity interest or owns them entirely. The motels are standardized so that they can engender standard expectations by travelers, and advantage can be taken of advertising economies of scale. Individual unaffiliated motels and hotels have to compete with this system, and it explains why the individualistic marketing channel is so disadvantaged. It is not surprising that durable and programmed networks of suppliers and retailers are rapidly replacing the "opportunistic and ad hoc linkages" that have historically prevailed in many lines of trade.

To survive, some independents are joining together in their own VMSs. Among those that stay independent, many become specialty-store operators, serving special segments of the market that are not available or attractive to the mass merchandisers. (Even here some mass merchandisers have begun to open boutiques and specialty stores.) Thus there is a polarization in retailing, with large vertical marketing organizations on the one hand and specialty independent stores on the other. This development causes distribution problems for suppliers of national brands as well as bulk products. At present these suppliers are generally aligning themselves with the traditional outlets, which they cannot easily give up. At the same time, they must eventually realign themselves with the high-growth mass-merchandising outlets. When they do, they will probably have to accept poorer terms from these large buying organizations. Vertical marketing systems can always decide to bypass large manufacturers and set up their own production facilities. In general, the new competition in retailing is no longer between independents but rather between whole systems of centrally programmed networks (corporate, administrative, and contractual) competing against each other to achieve the best economies and customer response.

Growth of horizontal marketing systems

Another significant development is the readiness of two or more companies to form alliances to jointly exploit an emerging marketing opportunity. Neither firm is able to amass the capital, know-how, production or marketing facilities to venture alone; or it prefers not to because of the high risk; or it envisions a substantial synergy in the proposed relationship. The companies may set up temporary or permanent arrangements to work with each other, or to create a third entity owned by the two parents. Such developments in horizontal marketing systems have been described by Adler as *symbiotic marketing*.[11] Here are two examples:

> In spite of *Pillsbury Company*'s acceptance in grocery outlets, it lacked the resources to market its new line of refrigerated doughs for biscuits, cookies, and rolls because merchandising these products required special refrigerated display cases. But Kraft Foods Company was expert at selling its cheeses in this manner. Accordingly, the two firms set up an arrangement whereby Pillsbury makes and advertises its dough line while Kraft sells and distributes it.

[11]Lee Adler, "Symbiotic Marketing," *Harvard Business Review*, November–December 1966, pp 59–71.

In the advertising field, *Million Market Newspapers, Inc.*, is the sales company held in common by five newspapers—*St. Louis Post-Dispatch, Washington Star, Boston Globe, Philadelphia Bulletin,* and *Milwaukee Journal-Sentinel.* By selling these five markets in one convenient package, a beneficial synergistic effect is created.

The individual firm's position in the channel

Our discussion of vertical and horizontal marketing-channel systems underscores the dynamic and changing nature of channels. Each firm in an industry has to define its relation to the dominant channel type and pricing policies, advertising, and sales-promotion practices. McCammon has distinguished five types of relationship of an individual firm to the dominant channel.[12] The *insiders* are the members of the dominant channel who enjoy continuous access to preferred sources of supply and high respect in the industry. They have a vested interest in perpetuating the existing channel arrangements and are the main enforcers of the industry code. The *strivers* are those firms who are seeking to become insiders but have not yet arrived. They have discontinuous access to preferred sources of supply, which can disadvantage them in periods of short supply. They adhere to the industry code because of their desire to become insiders. The *complementors* neither are nor seek to be part of the dominant channel. They perform functions not normally performed by others in the channel, or serve smaller segments of the market, or handle smaller quantities of merchandise. They usually benefit from the present system and tend to respect the industry code. The *transients*, like the complementors, are outside of the dominant channel and do not seek membership. They go in and out of the market or move around as opportunities arise, but are really members of another channel. They have short-run expectations and little incentive to adhere to the industry code. Finally, the *outside innovators* are the real challengers and disrupters of the dominant channels. They come with an entirely new system for carrying out the marketing work of the channel; if successful, they cause major structural realignments. They are men like Richard Sears, J. C. Penney, and King Cullen, who doggedly develop a new system to challenge the old.

Channel competition and conflict

The preceding discussion demonstrates that marketing channels undergo a high degree of competition and conflict. *Channel competition* occurs between marketing institutions or entire marketing channel systems that are trying to serve the same target market. Thus various appliance retailers (department stores, discount stores, etc.) are in competition for the consumer's appliance dollar. And there is competition within and between corporate and contractual marketing systems within the motel industry for the consumer's travel dollar.

Channel conflict, on the other hand, describes the opposition of interests that exists between different levels making up the same channel. Many examples can be cited:

1 Auto manufacturers threaten to drop dealers who refuse to comply with the manufacturers' ideas on service, pricing, advertising, and so on.
2 Toy wholesalers boycott toy manufacturers who choose to do some direct selling to large retail discounters.
3 Drug retailers threaten to drop drug manufacturers who put their lines in supermarket outlets.

---

[12]Bert C. McCammon, Jr., "Alternative Explanations of Institutional Change and Channel Evolution," in *Toward Scientific Marketing*, ed. Stephen A. Greyser (Chicago: American Marketing Association, 1963), pp. 477–90.

Channel conflict arises because the members of the channel differ in their goals, roles, perceptions, and power. A strong manufacturer may want his wholesalers to sell at low margin, grant credit to retailers, maintain adequate inventories, provide customer information, push his products aggressively, not carry competing brands, and pay promptly. The wholesalers, on the other hand, may want a wider and deeper line from the manufacturer, lower prices, extensive consumer advertising, exclusive distribution rights, a liberal returns policy, and liberal credit terms. Each channel member typically thinks he is in a "zero-sum game," and hard feelings develop when the strongest member uses his economic power to settle the issue. Some amount of channel conflict is healthy, and the problem is not one of eliminating it but of managing it better. The solution to channel conflict lies in two possible directions.[13] The first is the effort to develop superordinate goals for the system from which everyone would gain. Superordinate goals would include trying to minimize the total cost of moving the product through the system, improving information flows within the system, and cooperating to increase consumer acceptance of the product. The second is to develop administrative mechanisms that increase participation and trust, such as dealer and distributor councils.

CHANNEL-DESIGN DECISIONS

We shall now look at channel decision problems from the point of view of the producer. Although other firms in the marketing system are growing in importance, it is easier to appreciate the major issues in channel design and management by starting from the producer's vantage point and looking toward the market.

Choosing channels or being chosen?

In developing channels of distribution, producers have to struggle with what is ideal and what is available. In the typical case, a new firm starts as a local or regional operation seeking sales in a limited market. Since it has limited capital, it usually utilizes existing middlemen. The number of middlemen in any local market is apt to be limited: a few manufacturers' sales agents, a small number of wholesalers, an established set of retailers, a few trucking companies, and a few warehouses. The best way to market may be a foregone conclusion. The problem may be to convince one or a few available middlemen to handle the line.

If the new company is successful, it may branch out to new markets. Again, the producer will tend to work through the existing intermediaries, although this may mean using different types of marketing channels in different areas. In the smaller markets, the producer may deal directly with the retailers; in the larger markets, he may work only through distributors. In rural areas, he may work with general-goods merchants; in urban areas, he may work with limited-line merchants. In one part of the country he may grant exclusive franchises because the merchants are accustomed to work this way; in another

---

[13]For an excellent discussion, see Louis W. Stern and J. L. Heskett, "Conflict Management in Interorganization Relations: A Conceptual Framework," in *Distribution Channels: Behavioral Dimensions,* ed. Louis W. Stern (Boston: Houghton Mifflin Company, 1969), pp. 288–305.

part of the country he may sell through any and all outlets willing to handle his merchandise. In this way, the producer's channel system evolves as an expedient adaptation to local opportunities and conditions.

The starting point for the effective planning of channels is a determination of which markets are to be reached by the company. In practice, the choice of markets and choice of channels may be interdependent. The company may discover that markets it would like to serve cannot be served profitably with the available channels.

> An example is provided by a producer of gypsum wallboard who defined his market target as all contractors and dry-wall applicators. But this producer could not get lumber yards to handle this product, since existing lumber yards were tied to existing competitors. This led him to change his market target to large tract builders who would prefer to deal directly with him as a producer rather than through lumber yard intermediaries. Thus the choice of market target was redetermined after the consideration of channels.

Each producer shapes his specific channel objectives from major situational constraints stemming from the customers, products, intermediaries, competitors, company policies, and the environment.

Customer characteristics Channel design is greatly influenced by customer characteristics. When the *number* of customers is large, producers tend to use long channels with many middlemen on each level. The importance of the number of buyers is modified somewhat by their degree of *geographical dispersion*. It is less expensive for a producer to sell directly to five hundred customers who are concentrated in a few geographical centers than to sell them if they are scattered over five hundred locations. Even number and geographical dispersion are further qualified by the *purchasing pattern* of these buyers. Where the ultimate customers purchase small quantities on a frequent basis, lengthier marketing channels are desirable. The high cost of filling small and frequent orders leads manufacturers of such products as hardware, tobacco, and drug sundries to rely chiefly on wholesalers. At the same time, these same manufacturers may also bypass their wholesalers and sell direct to certain larger customers (retail chains and cooperative associations) who can place larger and less frequent orders. The buyers' *susceptibilities to different selling methods* also influence channel selection. For example, a growing number of furniture retailers prefer to make selections at trade shows, and this has increased the popularity of this channel.

Product characteristics Product characteristics also influence channel design. *Perishable* products require more direct marketing because of the dangers associated with delays and repeated handling. Products that are *bulky* in relation to their value, such as building materials or soft drinks, usually require channel arrangements that minimize the shipping distance and the number of handlings in the movement from producer to ultimate customers. *Unstandardized* products, such as custom-built machinery and specialized business forms, are usually sold directly by company salesmen because of the difficulty of finding middlemen with the requisite technical knowledge. Products requiring installation and/or maintenance *services* usually are sold and maintained directly by the company or by dealers given exclusive franchises. Products of *high unit value* are often sold through a company sales force rather than through middlemen.

Middleman characteristics Channel design must take into account the strengths and weaknesses of different types of intermediaries in handling various tasks. For example, manufacturers' representatives are able to contact customers at a relatively low cost per customer because the total cost is shared by several clients. But the selling effort per customer during the contact is often less intense than if the company's salesmen were doing the selling. In general, intermediaries differ in their aptitude for performing such functions as transit, advertising, storage, and contact, as well as in their requirements for credit, return privileges, training, and frequency of shipment.

Competitive characteristics The producer's channel design is influenced by the channels competitors use. The producers in some industries want their products to compete in or near the same outlets carrying the competitors' products. Thus food producers want their brands to be displayed next to competitive brands, and this means using the same middlemen. The marketing channels used by competitors sometimes define what the producer wants to avoid rather than imitate. Avon decided not to compete with other cosmetics manufacturers for scarce and inconspicuous positions in retail stores and established instead a profitable door-to-door selling operation.

Company characteristics Company characteristics play an important role in channel selection. The company's overall *size* determines the extent of its markets, the size of its larger accounts, and its ability to secure the cooperation of intermediaries it elects to use. Its *financial strength* sets limits on which marketing tasks it can handle and which ones to delegate to intermediaries. A financially weak company tends to employ commission methods of distribution and tries to enlist intermediaries able and willing to absorb some of the inventory, transit, and customer-financing costs. The company's *product mix* influences its channel pattern. The wider the company's product mix, the greater the ability of the company to deal with its customers directly. The greater the average depth of the company's product mix, the more it is likely to favor exclusive or selective dealers. The more consistent the company's product mix, the greater the homogeneity of its marketing channels. The *past channel experience* of the company affects channel design as well as *present company marketing policies.* A policy of speedy delivery and service to ultimate customers affects the functions the producer wants intermediaries to perform, the number of final-stage outlets and stocking points, and the type of transportation system used. A policy of heavy advertising leads the producer to seek intermediaries willing to handle displays and join in cooperative advertising programs.

Environmental characteristics Channel design is further influenced by environmental factors. Where *economic conditions* are depressed, producers want to move their goods to market in the way that is least expensive for final customers. This often means using shorter channels and dispensing with inessential services that add to the final price of the goods. *Legal regulations and restrictions* also affect channel design. The law has sought to prevent channel arrangements that "may tend to substantially lessen competition or tend to create a monopoly." The most sensitive areas have to do with agreements by manufacturers not to sell to certain types of outlets, attempts by a manufacturer to offer his line to dealers on condition they do not carry competitive lines, attempts by a manufacturer to force his full line through dealers, arbitrary action by a manufacturer in the withdrawal or refusal to renew dealer franchises, and attempts to set up territorial restrictions which substantially lessen competition.

Distinguishing the major channel alternatives

After specifying channel objectives and constraints, the firm should proceed to distinguish the channel alternatives. A channel alternative specifies four elements:

The basic *types of business intermediaries* who will be involved in selling and facilitating the movement of the goods to the market.

The *number of intermediaries* who will be used at each stage of distribution.

The particular *marketing tasks* of the participating intermediaries.

The *terms and mutual responsibilities* of the producer and intermediaries.

Types of intermediaries   The firm should first distinguish the alternative intermediaries available to carry on its channel work. Consider the following case:[14]

A manufacturer of test equipment for public utilities developed a new product that had considerable appeal. The product was an audio device that could help detect poor mechanical connections in any machinery with moving parts. The company executives felt that this product would have a market in all industries where electric, combustion, or steam engines were either used or manufactured. This meant such industries as aviation, automobile, railroad, food canning, construction, and oil. The problem was how to reach these diverse industries in an effective way. The following channel alternatives came out of management discussions:

1   Rely mainly on the present sales force and a heavy program of direct-mail and trade-magazine advertising.

2   Expand the company sales force and assign each salesman to a large industrial center where he is to contact all these industries.

3   Rely mainly on several manufacturers' agents, each of whom specializes in a different industry and a different region of the country.

4   Rely mainly on mill supply houses (wholesalers) who would undertake a limited amount of promotion and carry stocks in their warehouses. The company could gain national coverage by selecting five to fifteen of these supply houses as exclusive distributors.

Not only do conventional channel arrangements suggest themselves, but sometimes more innovative possibilities. This happened when the Conn Organ Company decided to merchandise organs through department and discount stores, thus drawing more attention to them than they ever enjoyed in the small music stores where they had always been merchandised. A daring new channel

---

[14]Adapted from David E. Faville, *Selected Cases in Marketing Management* (Englewood Cliffs, N.J.: Prentice-Hall, Inc., 1961), pp. 98–101, by permission of the Board of Trustees of the Leland Stanford Junior University.

was exploited when a group decided to merchandise books through the mails in the now famous Book-of-the-Month Club. Other sellers, perceiving the success of the Book-of-the-Month Club, developed Record-of-the-Month clubs, Candy-of-the-Month clubs, and dozens of others.

Number of intermediaries   The number of intermediaries to use at each stage is influenced by the degree of *market exposure* sought by the company. Three degrees of market exposure can be distinguished.

INTENSIVE DISTRIBUTION   Producers of convenience goods and common raw materials generally seek *intensive distribution*—that is, the stocking of their product in as many outlets as possible. The dominant factor in the marketing of these goods is their place utility. The producers of cigarettes, for example, try to enlist every possible retail outlet and device to create maximum brand exposure and convenience. This policy has culminated in the use of over 1 million outlets, which is about as intensive as distribution can get.

EXCLUSIVE DISTRIBUTION   Some producers deliberately limit the number of intermediaries handling their products. The extreme form of this is *exclusive distribution,* a policy of granting dealers exclusive rights to distribute the company's products in their respective territories; it often goes along with *exclusive dealing,* where the manufacturer requires the dealers not to carry competing lines. This is found at the retail level with respect to the distribution of new automobiles, some major appliances, and some brands of women's apparel. But why would a manufacturer want to limit his products' market exposure? Obviously, he must be gaining other advantages in giving up some exposure. Through granting exclusive distribution privileges, the producer hopes to gain a more aggressive selling effort and be able to exercise more direct controls over intermediaries' policies on prices, promotion, credit, and various services. Exclusive distribution also tends to enhance the prestige or image of the product and allow higher markups.

SELECTIVE DISTRIBUTION   Between the two extreme policies of intensive distribution and exclusive distribution stands a whole range of intermediate arrangements that have been called *selective distribution*. Selective distribution involves the use of more than one but less than all of the intermediaries who are willing to carry a particular product. It is used both by established companies with good reputations and by new companies seeking to get distributors by promising them selective distribution. The producer does not have to dissipate his efforts over a lot of outlets, many of which would be marginal. He can develop a good working understanding with the selected intermediaries and expect a better than average selling effort. In general, selective distribution enables the producer to gain adequate market coverage with more control and less cost than intensive distribution.

Specific marketing tasks of channel members   Every producer faces a certain set of tasks in moving his goods to the target markets. The role of intermediaries is not to increase the number of these tasks but to perform them more efficiently. Looking at a channel as a sequence of tasks rather than a linkage of business entities makes it immediately apparent that every producer faces a large number of alternatives, even when there is little choice regarding the basic types of intermediaries and the best degree of market exposure.

Assume that the following four tasks have to be performed:

T = transit, the work of transporting the goods toward the target markets

A = advertising, the work of informing and influencing buyers through advertising media

S = storage, the work of carrying an inventory out of which orders are filled

K = contact, the work of searching for and negotiating with buyers over terms

Assume that there are three channel members—producer (P), wholesaler (W), and retailer (R)—and each can perform one or more of these tasks. Consider some possible patterns of task allocation to the various members of the channel. The first one is

$$\frac{P}{TAOO} \longrightarrow \frac{W}{TOSO} \longrightarrow \frac{R}{OAOK}$$

In this channel, the producer limits his marketing work to shipping the goods as they are produced and to advertising the product. (An *O* means the absence of the corresponding task). The inventory is held by the marketing intermediary W, who also takes responsibility for further shipment. W is therefore a warehouse agent (a facilitating intermediary) rather than a full-service wholesaler. The final intermediary R is responsible for further advertising (perhaps on a cooperative basis with the producer) and the contactual work.

A different marketing channel is implied by the pattern

$$\frac{P}{TOSO} \longrightarrow \frac{W}{OOOO} \longrightarrow \frac{R}{OAOK}$$

Here the producer is reduced to a private-brand operator who produces, stocks, and ships on order, the W intermediary is eliminated, and the R intermediary assumes the complete selling function. This is the marketing channel developed by mail-order houses for many of its products.

There are a great number of other possible patterns of task allocation in a marketing channel.[15] Many can be ruled out because they would be uneconomic, unstable, or illegal. Management's task is to identify the feasible alternatives and select the one that promises the highest degree of effectiveness in serving customers relative to competition.

Terms and responsibilities of channel members   In conceiving the tasks to be performed by different types of intermediaries in the channel, the producer must also determine the mix of conditions and responsibilities that must be established among the channel members to get the tasks performed effectively and enthusiastically. The "trade-relations" mix is capable of many variations and introduces a still further dimension of alternatives.

---

[15]The number of possible patterns of task allocation in a marketing channel is given by $(2^n)^m$, where n represents the number of tasks and m represents the number of channel members. In the example, there are $(2^4)^3 = 4,096$ possible task allocations.

The main elements in the trade-relations mix are the *price policies, conditions of sale, territorial rights,* and *the specific services to be performed by each party.*

Price policy is one of the major elements in the trade-relations mix. The producer usually establishes a list price and then allows discounts from it to various types of intermediate customers and possibly for various quantities purchased. In developing his schedule of discounts, the producer must proceed carefully. First, different types of intermediate customers have strong feelings about the discounts they and others are entitled to. For example, small retailers who buy through wholesalers resent a producer who allows the large retail chains to buy direct at the wholesaler's discount; whereas the larger retailers resent not being allowed better terms on the basis of their quantity purchases. Thus the discount schedule is a potential source of channel conflict. Second, the Robinson-Patman Act forbids price discrimination between different buyers of the same goods where the discrimination may tend to lessen competition, except where the price differences are proportional to *bona fide* differences in the costs of selling to the different buyers. Therefore the producer must be able to justify the discounts he offers to different buyers.

Conditions of sale are the second element of the trade-relations mix. The most important conditions relate to the payment terms and to producer guarantees. Most producers grant a discount from the distributor's invoice price for early cash payment. For example, "2 percent in 10 days, net 30" means that the distributor can deduct 2 percent from the invoice price if he pays within ten days, or otherwise the full cash price would be payable within thirty days. The particular terms can play an important role in the producer's costs and distributor's motivation, because they indicate the extent to which the producer will finance the distributor's inventories. The producer may also extend certain guarantees to the distributor regarding defective merchandise or price declines. The offer of a guarantee against price declines may be necessary to induce the distributors to buy in large quantities rather than on a hand-to-mouth basis.

Distributors' territorial rights are a third element in the trade-relations mix. A distributor wants to know where the producer intends to enfranchise other distributors. He also would like to receive full credit for all sales taking place in his territory, whether or not they were stimulated through his own efforts.

Mutual services and responsibilities are a fourth element of the trade-relations mix. These are likely to be comprehensive and well defined in franchised- and exclusive-agency channels where the relation between producer and distributor is close. For example, the Howard Johnson Company provides the restaurant leaseholders with the building, promotional support, a record-keeping system, training, and general administrative and technical assistance. In turn, the leaseholders are supposed to meet company standards regarding physical facilities, comply with new promotional programs, furnish requested information, and buy specified food products. In contrast, where the producer goes after more intensive distribution, he may supply distributors only occasionally with some promotional materials and some technical services. The distributor in turn is less willing to furnish an accounting of his efforts, an analysis of customer buying differences, or cooperation in distributing promotional materials.

Evaluating the major channel alternatives

By this time, the producer will have identified several major channel alternatives for reaching the market. His problem is to decide which of the alternatives would satisfy best the long-run objectives of the firm. For this, he weighs the alternatives against *economic, control,* and *adaptive* criteria.

Economic criteria   Of the three, economic criteria are the most important, since the firm is not pursuing channel control or adaptability as such but is pursuing profits. True, channel control and adaptability have implications for long-run profit, but the more outstanding a channel alternative seems from an economic point of view, the less important seem its potentialities for conflict and rigidity.

To illustrate the economic analysis, a concrete and familiar pair of channel alternatives will be examined—the choice between a company sales force and the use of a manufacturers' sales agency.

> Assume that the company wishes to reach a large number of retailers in a certain region of the country. Suppose an adequate company sales force would require hiring and training ten salesmen who would operate out of a branch office in the region. They would be given a good base pay along with the opportunity for further earnings through a commission plan. The other alternative would be to use a reputable manufacturers' agency in the region who has developed extensive contacts with these retailers through the other lines he carries. The agent has thirty salesmen in his organization and would receive a fixed percentage of the sales price of each unit he sold.

Each alternative will produce a different level of sales and costs. The better system is not the one producing the greater sales or the one producing the lesser cost, but rather the one that produces the best profit.

The analysis should begin with an estimate of *sales* under each system, because some costs will be dependent upon the level of sales. Will more sales be produced through the use of company salesmen or the sales agency? Most marketing managers answer that company salesmen sell more. A company salesman concentrates only on the company products; he is better trained to sell the company's products; he is more aggressive because his future depends on the company; he is more successful with customers because they prefer to deal with company personnel.

But these are abstract arguments. It is conceivable that the sales agent's operation could produce as many as or more sales than a company-sponsored sales effort. In the first place, the producer is considering representation by ten company salesmen versus thirty sales-agency salesmen. The sheer difference in the number of salesmen may lead to more sales through the agency. Second, the agency's salesmen may be just as aggressive as the company salesmen. This depends on how much pay incentive the line offers them in relation to the other lines they represent. Third, it is not unconditionally true that customers prefer to deal with company salesmen over agents. Where the product and terms are standard, the customers may be quite indifferent. They may prefer dealing with the agent who represents a wider assortment of goods instead of dealing with a company salesman representing a single line. Fourth, one of the chief assets of the sales agent is the extensive contacts he has built up over the years, while a company sales force would have to cultivate contacts from scratch. The agency can often produce more sales for the manufacturer, at least in the beginning.

Thus the relative sales levels of a company sales force versus a sales agency require a detailed analysis of the concrete plans for each. The opinion of various managers can be sought, and a field test under actual operating conditions might even be conducted.

Once sales have been estimated, the next step is to estimate the costs of the two channel systems. Only costs that are variable with each particular channel and level of sales should be considered. If the company has been using both types of marketing channels, a fairly good estimate of the respective costs can be made through a standard marketing-cost analysis of existing data. If the company is new, then judgmental estimates have to be made.

The last step consists of bringing together the estimates of sales and costs, in the form of either a *breakeven analysis* or a *rate-of-return analysis.*

A hypothetical *breakeven chart* is shown in Figure 13-4. The costs of each channel vary with the sales level. The fixed costs of engaging a sales agency are obviously lower than those of conducting a branch sales operation. On the other hand, costs rise faster with additional sales through a sales agency than through company salesmen. The reason is that sales agents get a larger fixed percentage of sales than company salesmen, who are only on part commission.

Looking at the chart, there is one sales level (S_B) at which distribution cost would be the same for the two channels. Now suppose there was no reason to believe that either channel was better at producing sales. Then the chart could be read in a straightforward manner. The sales agency would constitute a superior channel at any volume of sales lower than S_B, and the company sales branch would constitute a superior channel at any volume of sales higher than S_B. This analysis accords with common observations of the circumstances under which the two channels have been used. Sales agents tend to be engaged by smaller firms, or by larger firms in their smaller territories, because in both cases the sales volume is too low to justify a fixed investment in a company sales force.

If it cannot be assumed that both channels produce the same sales, it is better to make a straightforward estimate of *return on investment.* One possible measure would be:

$$R_i = \frac{S_i - C_i}{C_i}$$

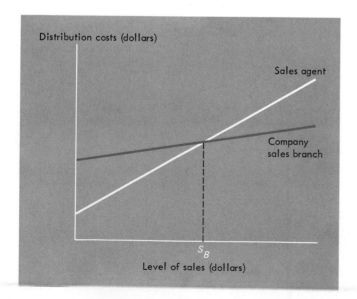

Figure 13-4

Breakeven cost chart for the choice between a sales agency and a company branch

where:

R_i = return on investment associated with marketing channel i
S_i = estimated sales associated with using channel i
C_i = estimated costs associated with using channel i

R_i is an estimate of the return of investment expected on the costs of using channel i. All other things being the same, the channel emerging with the higher R_i is preferred.

Control criteria   The evaluation of the economics of sales agents versus company salesmen provides a rough guide to the probable economic superiority of one channel over the other. The evaluation must now be broadened by a consideration of the motivational, control, and conflict aspects of the two channel alternatives.

The use of sales agents can give rise to a number of control problems. The central fact is that the sales agent is an independent businessman. He is primarily interested in maximizing his own profits. This sometimes can lead to suboptimization from the producer's point of view. The sales agent is more concerned with promoting the image of his organization than his clients'. He often does not cooperate with the client's sales agent in an adjacent territory, although the cooperation may benefit the client. He concentrates his calls on the customers who are most important to him in terms of his total assortment of goods rather than on the customers who are most important to the client. He may not take the time to master the technical details concerning the client's product or show care in using client promotional material. Altogether, the use of sales agents comes at the price of creating certain problems of control.

The control aspects of a channel are broader than suggested in reviewing the sales agent example. Where the producer is considering a complicated channel alternative, the following issues should be evaluated:

VERTICAL RELATIONS IN THE CHANNEL   How will the various levels in the channel interact? Here there are two opposing dangers. At one extreme, the self-interests of two or more levels may be so diametrically opposed that they are always in conflict at the expense of the producer. At the other extreme, the self-interests of two or more channel levels may be so alike that they collude to force concessions from the producer.

HORIZONTAL RELATIONS IN THE CHANNEL   How will the members located at a particular level in the channel interact? At one extreme, their self-interests may clash, as when territorial or business boundaries are not clear. At the other extreme, they may form an association to gain power at the expense of the producer, as the automobile dealers did some years ago.

INTERCHANNEL CONFLICT   Will the different marketing channels established by a producer be in too much conflict? For example, watch manufacturers have a difficult time pleasing both small retailers and discount outlets.

LEGAL CONFLICT   Will the channel contain any questionable features that might involve the company in a legal suit? For example, a producer who plans to set up exclusive distribution should first determine its legal status.

Adaptive criteria   Suppose a particular channel alternative appears superior from an economic point of view and poses no particular problem of control. One other criterion should be considered—that of the producer's freedom to adapt to changing conditions. Each channel alternative involves some duration of commitment and loss of flexibility. A manufacturer who decides to use a sales agent may have to offer a ten-year contract; during this period, other means of selling, such as direct mail, might become more efficient, but he is not free to drop the sales agent.

In general, the less certain the future seems to be, the less favorable are channel alternatives involving long commitments. A channel alternative involving a long commitment must appear to be greatly superior on economic or control grounds in order to be considered.

CHANNEL-MANAGEMENT DECISIONS

After a company has determined its basic channel design, individual middlemen must be *selected*, *motivated*, and periodically *evaluated*.

Selecting channel members

Each producer finds himself somewhere between two extreme positions respecting the recruitment of middlemen for his proposed channel operation. Some producers have no trouble finding specific business establishments to join the channel. Their proposal attracts more than enough middlemen either because of the great prestige enjoyed by the firm or because the specific product (or line) appears to be a good money-maker. For example, Ford had no trouble attracting twelve hundred new dealers for its ill-fated Edsel. In some cases the promise of exclusive or selective distribution will influence a sufficient number of middlemen to join the channel. The main problem for the producer who is fortunate enough to get all the middlemen he needs is one of selection. He must decide on what characteristics of middlemen prospects provide the best indication of their competence.

The other extreme position is where a producer chooses a channel alternative for which he has to work hard to line up the desired number of qualified middlemen. For example, the producer of a new soft drink finds it very hard to get shelf space in food outlets. He may have to accept whatever middlemen he can get, although he should initiate his recruitment effort among the more desirable middlemen. His task is to market his product to intermediate customers. This means he must study how middlemen make their buying decisions; specifically, how much weight they give to gross margin, planned advertising and promotion, return guarantees, and so on. The producer must develop an offer that promises to make a lot of money for the middlemen.

Whether the producer finds it easy or difficult to recruit middlemen, he should determine what characteristics distinguish the better middlemen from the poorer ones. Even where the producer's aim is intensive distribution, he may not want his product associated with weak or faltering middlemen. The producer wants to evaluate the middleman's number of years in business, his growth record, his solvency, his cooperativeness, and his reputation. If the middleman is a sales agent, the producer also wants to evaluate the number and character of other lines he carries, whether he is adequately staffed to give sufficient attention and know-how to the new line, and the turnover record of his salesmen. If the middleman is a department store being considered for exclusive distribution, the producer wants to evaluate the store's location, future growth potential, and type of clientele.

Middlemen must be motivated to do their best job. The factors and terms that led them to join the channel provided some of the motivation, but these must be supplemented by continuous supervision and encouragement from the producer. The producer must sell not only through the middlemen but to them. The question of motivation is a complex one, since there are grounds for both cooperation and conflict between the producer and his distributors.

The job of stimulating channel members to good performance must start with the psychology and behavioral characteristics of the particular middlemen. Many a middleman has been criticized, according to McVey:

> for failure to stress a given brand, or for the poor quality of his salesmen's product knowledge, his disuse of suppliers' advertising materials, his neglect of certain customers (who may be good prospects for individual items but not for the assortment), and even for his unrefined systems of record keeping, in which brand designations may be lost.[16]

However, what are shortcomings from the producer's point of view may be quite understandable from the middleman's point of view. McVey listed the following four propositions to help understand the middlemen:

> The middleman is not a hired link in a chain forged by a manufacturer, but rather an independent market. . . . After some experimentation, he settles upon a method of operation, performing those functions he deems inescapable in the light of his own objectives, forming policies for himself wherever he has freedom to do so. . . .
>
> [The middleman often acts] primarily as a purchasing agent for his customers, and only secondarily as a selling agent for his suppliers. . . . He is interested in selling any product which these customers desire to buy from him. . . .
>
> The middleman attempts to weld all of his offerings into a family of items which he can sell in combination, as a packaged assortment, to individual customers. His selling efforts are directed primarily at obtaining orders for the assortment, rather than for individual items. . . .
>
> Unless given incentive to do so, middlemen will not maintain separate sales records by brands sold. . . . Information that could be used in product development, pricing, packaging, or promotion-planning is buried in nonstandard records of middlemen, and sometimes purposely secreted from suppliers.[17]

These propositions serve as a provocative departure from otherwise stereotyped thinking about the purpose and performance of middlemen. The first step in motivating others is to see the situation from their viewpoint.

The producer must steer a careful course between overmotivating and undermotivating the middlemen. Overmotivation occurs when the producer's terms are more generous than they have to be to secure a particular level of cooperation and effort. The result may be high sales for the producer but low profits. Undermotivation occurs when the producer's terms are too anemic to stimulate more than a token effort by middlemen. The result is low sales and low profits. The producer's problem is to determine the optimal level and kind of motivation to provide the trade.

---

[16]Phillip McVey, "Are Channels of Distribution What the Textbooks Say?" *Journal of Marketing*, January 1960, pp. 61–64.

[17]*Ibid.*

The basic level of motivation is established by the original trade-relations mix. If the middlemen are still undermotivated, the producer has two alternatives. He can improve their margins, extend better credit terms, or do any one of a number of things that alter the trade-relations mix in favor of the middlemen. Or he can stimulate greater middlemen effort by using any of a host of familiar devices, ranging from nagging the middlemen (until they either produce or quit) to pep rallies, sales contests, and increased advertising.

Some producers find it easier to use the stick than the carrot to motivate their middlemen, particularly if they enjoy a great deal of power over them. One of the large toy manufacturers forces slow-moving items on toy retailers if these retailers want to receive enough of the fast-moving items. One of the large soap companies uses sheer market power to get favorable shelf space from its dealers rather than offering trade allowances or other incentives. These policies can breed deep ill will in the channels and someday come back to haunt the manufacturers.

Evaluating channel members

The producer must periodically evaluate the performance of his middlemen. Where a channel member's performance is seriously below standard, it is necessary to determine the underlying causes and to consider the possible remedies. The producer may have to tolerate the unsatisfactory performance if dropping or replacing the middleman would lead to even worse results. But if there are attractive alternatives to the use of this middleman, then the producer should require the middleman to reach a certain level of performance within a stated time or be dropped from the channel.

Much grief can be avoided if standards of performance and sanctions are agreed upon at the very beginning between the producer and the channel members. The areas posing the greatest need for explicit agreement concern sales intensity and coverage, average inventory levels, customer delivery time, treatment of damaged and lost goods, cooperation in company promotional and training programs, and middleman services owed to the customer.

The producer might issue periodic sales quotas to define current performance expectations. Automobile manufacturers and many appliance dealers set quotas not only for total units to be sold but often for types of units. In some cases these quotas are treated only as guides; in others, they represent serious standards. Some producers list the sales of various middlemen after each sales period and send the rankings out. This device is intended to motivate middlemen at the bottom of the list to do better for the sake of self-respect (and continuing the relationship) and middlemen at the top to maintain their performance out of pride.

A simple ranking of the middlemen by level of sales is not necessarily the best measure. Middlemen face varying environments over which they have different degrees of control; the importance of the producer's line in their assortments also varies. One useful measure is to compare each middleman's sales performance against his own performance in the preceding period. The average percentage of improvement (or decline) for the group can be used as the norm. Another useful measure is to compare each middleman's performance against a quota established for him based on an analysis of the sales potential in his territory. After each sales period, middlemen are ranked according to the ratio of their actual sales to their sales potential. Investigatory and motivational effort can then be focused on those middlemen who have underachieved.

CHANNEL-MODIFICATION DECISIONS

A producer must do more than design a good channel system and set it into motion. Every so often the system requires modification to meet new conditions in the marketplace.

This fact struck a large manufacturer of major household appliances who had been marketing exclusively through franchised dealers. A relative loss in market share made the producer take stock of several distributional developments that had taken place since the original channel was designed:

> An increasing share of major brand appliances were being merchandised through discount houses.
>
> An increasing share of major appliances were being sold on a private-brand basis through large department stores.
>
> A new market was developing in the form of volume purchases by tract home builders who preferred to deal directly with the manufacturers.
>
> Door-to-door and direct-mail solicitation of orders was being undertaken by some dealers and competitors.
>
> The only strong independent dealers were those in small towns, and rural families were increasingly making their purchases in large cities.

These and other developments in the ever-changing distribution scene led this manufacturer to undertake a major review of possible channel modifications.

Three different levels of channel change should be distinguished. The change could involve adding or dropping individual channel members; adding or dropping particular market channels; or developing a totally new way to sell goods in all markets.

The decision to add or drop particular middlemen usually requires a straightforward incremental analysis. The economic question is, What would the firm's profits look like with this middleman and without this middleman? The incremental analysis could be complex if the decision would have many repercussions on the rest of the system. An automobile manufacturer's decision to grant another dealer franchise in a city will require taking into account not only that dealer's probable sales but the possible losses or gains in the sales of his other dealers.[18]

Sometimes a producer contemplates dropping not an isolated middleman but all middlemen who fail to bring their unit sales above a certain level within a certain period. This happened when a large manufacturer of motor trucks selling through a network of franchised dealers noted that at least 5 percent of its dealers were selling fewer than three or four trucks a year. According to the controller's calculation, it cost more for the company to service these small dealers than the sale of three or four trucks was worth. If the issue were a matter of dropping a few of these weak dealers, then an incremental analysis would probably indicate that company profits would rise. But the decision to drop

---

[18]See T. E. Hlavac, Jr., and John D. C. Little, "A Geographical Model of an Urban Automobile Market," in *Proceedings of the Fourth International Conference on Operational Research*, ed. David B. Hertz and Jacques Melese (New York: John Wiley & Sons, Inc., 1966), pp. 302–11.

most of these dealers could have such large repercussions on the system as a whole that an incremental analysis would not suffice. Such a decision would raise the unit costs of producing trucks, since the overhead would have to be spread over fewer trucks; some men and equipment would be idled; some business in the markets where the smaller dealers were cut out would go to competitors; and other company dealers might be made insecure by the decision. Nothing short of a detailed, total systems simulation would be adequate for comprehending all the effects.

A producer sometimes faces the question of whether his channel for reaching a particular geographical area or customer type is still optimal. A breakeven or rate-of-return analysis could be made of the present and alternative systems. The most difficult "channel change" decision involves the revision of the overall system of distribution. For example, an automobile manufacturer may consider replacing independent dealers with company-owned dealers; a soft-drink manufacturer may consider replacing local franchised bottlers with centralized bottling and direct sales. These are decisions made at the highest level, decisions that not only change the channels but necessitate a revision of most of the marketing-mix elements and policies to which the firm is accustomed. Such decisions have so many ramifications that any quantitative modeling of the problem can only be a first approximation.

A conceptual approach to the problem of channel modification

In analyzing the desirability of changing a channel, the task is one of determining whether the channel is in equilibrium.[19] A channel is in equilibrium when there is no structural or functional change that would lead to increased profits. A structural change is one involving the addition or elimination of some middleman level in the channel. A functional change is one involving the reallocation of one or more channel tasks among the channel members. A channel is ripe for change when it is in disequilibrium—that is, when it provides an opportunity for gain through a structural or functional modification.

A simple example will convey the concept of channel disequilibrium. Assume there is a channel of the producer-wholesaler-retailer type (P-W-R). (See Figure 13-5.) Each channel member makes a set of decisions on price, advertising, and distribution (P,A,D). For simplicity, assume that these decisions mainly affect the succeeding stage. Thus the producer makes decisions $(P,A,D)_1$, which influence the quantity (Q_1) ordered by the wholesaler. The producer calculates his net profits (Z_1) by subtracting his costs from his revenue from the wholesaler. In the same fashion, each channel member makes an independent

---

[19]This section leans heavily on Stanley Stasch's "A Method of Dynamically Analyzing the Stability of the Economic Structure of Channels of Distribution," (Ph.D. dissertation, School of Business, Northwestern University, 1964).

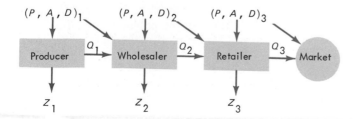

Figure 13-5

Conceptual picture of the profits in a marketing channel

SOURCE: Redrawn, with modifications, from Stanley Stasch, "A Method of Dynamically Analyzing the Stability of the Economic Structure of Channels of Distribution" (Ph.D. dissertation, School of Business, Northwestern University, 1964), p. 63.

set of decisions that influence his revenue and cost and bring about a particular net profit.

Looking at the channel as a whole, a set of independent decisions is made $[(P,A,D)_1, (P,A,D)_2, (P,A,D)_3]$ that results in some total channel profit $(Z_1 + Z_2 + Z_3)$. The concept of channel disequilibrium can now be defined precisely. The channel is in disequilibrium if there exists an alternative set of decisions $[(P,A,D)_1, (P,A,D)_2, (P,A,D)_3]^*$ that would result in a different total channel profit $(Z_1 + Z_2 + Z_3)^*$ that is greater than $(Z_1 + Z_2 + Z_3)$. If this is the case, the channel presents an opportunity for increased profit. But the alternative decisions are not likely to be made as long as the channel members make their decisions independently. The greater the difference between $(Z_1 + Z_2 + Z_3)^*$ and $(Z_1 + Z_2 + Z_3)$, the greater will be the incentive of the channel members to pursue joint planning or for some channel member to absorb one or more of the others to achieve the extra profits from integrated decision making.

SUMMARY

Marketing-channel decisions are among the most complex and challenging facing the firm. Each firm usually confronts a number of alternative ways to reach the market. They vary from direct selling, to using one, two, three, or more intermediaries. The firms making up the marketing channel are connected in different ways by physical, title, payment, information, and promotional flows. Marketing channels do not stay static but are characterized by continuous and sometimes dramatic change. Two of the most significant recent trends are the emergence of vertical marketing systems and horizontal marketing systems. Each channel system has a different potential for creating sales and producing costs. Once a particular marketing channel is chosen, the firm must usually adhere to it for a substantial period. The chosen channel will significantly affect and be affected by the rest of the marketing mix.

Good channel design should proceed with a clarification of channel objectives, alternatives, and likely payoffs. The objectives are conditioned by the particular characteristics of customers, products, middlemen, competitors, and environment. The alternatives are usually many because of the variety of types of intermediaries, the different possible intensities of market coverage, the various ways in which channel tasks can be allocated among channel members, and the many possible trade-relations mixes. Each feasible alternative way to reach the market has to be spelled out and evaluated according to economic, control, and adaptive criteria.

After the basic design of the channel is determined, the firm faces the task of effective channel management. It has to select particular firms to work with or find business firms willing to work with it. It has to supplement the motivations provided to channel members through the trade-relations mix by special incentives and supervision. It has to periodically evaluate the performance of individual channel members against their own past sales, other channel members' sales, and, possibly, sales quotas.

Because markets and the marketing environment are continually changing, the firm must be prepared to make channel revisions: individual members may be dropped or added, the channels in specific markets may be modified, and sometimes the whole channel system may have to be redesigned. Evaluating a proposed channel change may be approached through incremental analysis if only the particular unit or channel is affected; it may require a systems-level analysis if the change is likely to affect other units. In the latter case, system simulation may be the most efficient way to determine the channel's equilibrium. The greater the disequilibrium in a channel, the more apparent it will be to observers that channel modification would lead to increased profits.

QUESTIONS AND PROBLEMS

1 If there are five producers and five customers in a market, how many contacts would have to be made (a) without a middleman? (b) with a middleman? What are the general formulas?

2 Explain how the characteristics of (a) peaches and (b) cement affect the channels for them.

3 Suggest some alternative channels for (a) a small firm which has developed a radically new harvesting machine; (b) a small plastic manufacturer who has developed a picnic pack for keeping bottles and food cold; and (c) a manufacturer of expensive watches.

4 A new manufacturer of FM car radios is searching for an effective channel of distribution. Distinguish four channel alternatives and also list the drawbacks of each.

5 Is the following channel pattern plausible? What kinds of institutions are implied?

$$\frac{P}{OOOK} \longrightarrow \frac{W}{OASO} \longrightarrow \frac{R}{TAOO}$$

6 Produce a checklist of questions for rating prospective applicants for a distributorship.

7 "Discussions of merchandising practices in the oil industry have often proceeded from the premise that the existing distributive channel structure for gasoline is a millstone around the industry's neck." Can you think of innovations for improving the distribution of automobile fuel or for improving the profitability of service stations?

8 Can you think of a radically different way to organize the distribution of (a) automobiles; (b) beer?

14

PHYSICAL-DISTRIBUTION DECISIONS

That's why [physical] distribution is the next—some say possibly the last—place where truly significant savings can be achieved.

BUSINESS WEEK

Throughout the years, the term "marketing" has connoted two different but related processes, the first dealing with the *search for and stimulation of buyers* and the second with the *physical distribution of goods.* With the increased competition for markets, marketing executives have devoted the bulk of their time to the search and stimulation function. Their attention has been given over to developing a mix of products, prices, promotion, and channels that would keep demand high and growing. They have viewed physical distribution, or the logistics of getting goods to the buyers, as a supportive and subsidiary activity.

More recently, several developments have awakened management's interest in the logistics problem and led them to wonder whether they were not overlooking many opportunities, not only for cost saving but also for improved demand stimulation.

One of the alerting factors is the steady climb in the bill for such physical-distribution services as freight, warehousing, and inventory. Freight and warehousing bills are rising as a result of increased labor and equipment costs. The inventory bill is rising because buyers are tending to place smaller orders more frequently, and manufacturers are tending to expand the width and depth of their lines. Many executives have been shocked to learn that the total costs of storing, handling, and moving their products are anywhere between 15 and 30 percent of sales.[1]

Authorities in increasing numbers argue that substantial savings can usually be effected in the physical-distribution area, which has been variously described as "the last frontier for cost economies"[2] and "the economy's dark continent."[3] There is much evidence of uncoordinated physical-distribution decisions resulting in suboptimization. Not enough use is being made of modern decision tools for determining economic levels of inventories, efficient modes of shipment, and sound plant, warehouse, and store locations.

Furthermore, physical distribution is a potent instrument in the demand-stimulation process. Companies can gain by offering more in the way of service or by cutting prices through successfully reducing physical-distribution costs.

THE SCOPE OF PHYSICAL DISTRIBUTION

There is a broad and a narrow view of the scope of physical distribution. In the broad view, physical distribution starts with the location of original materials and labor inputs required in the productive process and stretches to the location of final consumer markets. It becomes coextensive with the basic marketing task, according to Wroe Alderson, of bridging the gap between the un-assorted supplies found in nature and the assortment needs found in man.[4] This perspective is particularly pertinent to the firm planning to enter a new-product market. Having as yet no investment in suppliers, factories, warehouses, middlemen, or final markets, it is in a position to consider all of them as variables in designing its physical-distribution system. Final markets are generally the best starting point for planning the new system. The company selects its final target markets and then works backward to an appropriate set of middlemen, warehouses, and plant locations.

The narrow view of physical distribution assumes that the company is already established in the marketplace and has commitments to a set of factories, suppliers, middlemen, and final markets. The company's problem is to find efficient arrangements for locating, stocking, and shipping its goods to meet the service requirements of the marketplace. This is the point of view we shall take in this book. A useful conception of the component activities of physical distribution is reproduced in Figure 14-1. Eleven different activity "cogs" make up the physical-distribution system. The whole system centers on the inventory-management cog. Inventory is the link between the customers' orders and the company's manufacturing activity. Customers' orders draw down the inventory level, and manufacturing activity builds it up. Manufacturing activity requires an inflow of raw materials into the company, and this involves

---

[1]Richard E. Snyder, "Physical Distribution Costs," *Distribution Age*, December 1963, pp. 35–42.

[2]Donald D. Parker, "Improved Efficiency and Reduced Cost in Marketing," *Journal of Marketing*, April 1962, pp. 15–21.

[3]Peter Drucker, "The Economy's Dark Continent," *Fortune*, April 1962, pp. 103, 265, 268, and 270.

[4]See Chapter 13, pp. 279–80.

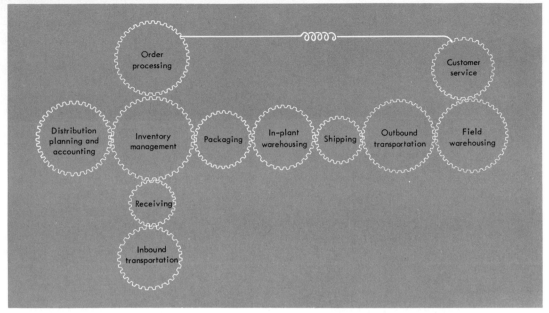

SOURCE: Redrawn from Wendell M. Stewart, "Physical Distribution: Key to Improved Volume and Profits," *Journal of Marketing,* January 1965, p. 66.

Figure 14-1
Activity cogs in a distribution system

inbound freight and receiving operations. Finished goods then flow off the assembly line, involving packaging, in-plant storage, shipping-room activities, outbound transportation, field warehousing, and customer delivery and service.

THE PHYSICAL-DISTRIBUTION OBJECTIVE

Many companies state their physical-distribution objective as *getting the right goods to the right places at the right time for the least cost.* Unfortunately, this provides little actual guidance. No physical-distribution system can simultaneously maximize customer service and minimize distribution cost. Maximum customer service implies such policies as large inventories, premium transportation, and many warehouses, all of which raise distribution cost. Minimum distribution cost implies such policies as slow, cheap transportation, low stocks, and few warehouses.

The physical-distribution objective can be defined more carefully by introducing the notion of an *efficient system.* System efficiency is a matter of the ratio of a system's output to its input. By clarifying what the outputs and inputs are in a physical-distribution system, we can come closer to defining a clear objective for such a system.

305

A basic output of a physical-distribution system is the *level of customer service.* Customer service represents one of the key competitive benefits that a company can offer potential customers in order to attract their business. From the customer's view, customer service takes several forms:

1 The speed of filling and delivering normal orders
2 The supplier's willingness to meet emergency merchandise needs of the customer
3 The care with which merchandise is delivered in good condition
4 The supplier's readiness to take back defective goods and resupply quickly
5 The availability of installation and repair services and parts from the supplier
6 The number of options on shipment loads and carriers
7 The supplier's willingness to carry inventory for the customer
8 The service charges, that is, whether the services are "free" or separately priced

From the supplier's point of view, he sets certain service-level goals. For example, Pillsbury defined its delivery objectives to be "third-morning rail delivery anywhere in the U.S." Some companies define the level of service as the "percentage of customers who should get their orders in *x* days." Others think in terms of a system that holds down backorders to a certain level.[5]

How does the company determine a desirable level of customer service? In many cases it uses the standard set by competitors. If it offers a lower level of service than the prevailing one, it is in danger of losing patronage unless there is some compensatory element in its marketing mix. If it offers a higher level of service than the prevailing one, the competitors may increase their service level in self-defense, and all companies would be stuck with higher costs. Any advantage will be temporary, especially if it is an effective advantage.

The company's decision on the service level must rest ultimately on an analysis of probable customer and competitor response to alternative levels of service. Sometimes a slight increase in customer service can produce a good gain in customer patronage—say 15 percent, whereas a major costly increase may produce only a slightly higher gain—say 20 percent. The value customers place on service is admittedly one of the hardest things to evaluate in marketing. Nevertheless, it can sometimes be measured with a little ingenuity. One investigator was able to estimate how the percentage of returned merchandise to a mail-order house varied with the length of the delay in shipment.[6] Even where the estimates are rough, one can use sensitivity analysis to find out how much difference any estimate would make in the choice between physical-distribution alternatives.

A company bears certain costs, of which freight, inventory, and warehousing are the main ones, in providing its present level of customer service. Often the total bill is not known because companies typically lack centralized management and accounting of their physical-distribution activities. These costs, however, must be measured as a prerequisite for distribution planning and control.

The present system can be said to be efficient if no reorganization of logistical inputs could reduce the costs *while maintaining the present service level.*

---

[5]William B. Saunders, "Designing a Distribution System," *Distribution Age,* January 1965, pp. 32–36.
[6]See Chapter 19, p. 433.

Many companies think their physical-distribution system is efficient because each decision center—inventory, warehousing, and traffic—appears to do a good job of keeping down its own costs. However, this is an area where the sum of distributional costs is not necessarily minimized by a set of uncoordinated efforts to minimize the separate costs. As stated by Parker:

> Pressures are applied by top management which encourage the separate functional units to control and reduce their costs of operation. Cost reduction becomes the primary way for these functional units to call attention to themselves. . . . As a result, when decisions are made about transportation, warehousing, packaging, inventory levels . . . they are based on an analysis of alternatives within that specific function, without regard for the possible effects upon other closely related functions. Functional costs are considered, but the all-important total cost of the related functions is ignored.[7]

Various physical-distribution costs interact, often in an inverse way:

> The traffic manager favors rail shipment over air shipment whenever possible. This reduces the company's freight bill. However, because the railroads are slower, this ties up company capital longer, delays customer payment, and may cause customers to buy from competitors offering more rapid service.

> The shipping department uses cheap containers to minimize shipping costs. This leads to a high damage rate of goods in transit and the loss of customer goodwill.

> The inventory manager favors holding low inventories to reduce total inventory cost. However, this results in many stockouts, backorders, accompanying paperwork, special production runs, and high-cost fast-freight shipments.

The import is that since physical-distribution activities are highly interrelated, decisions must be made on a total system basis.

The objective

We are now ready to define the objective of physical-distribution design. A physical-distribution system consists of a set of decisions on the number, location, and size of warehouses; freight policies; and inventory policies. Each possible physical-distribution system implies a total distribution cost, as given by the expression:

$$D = T + FW + VW + S$$

where

D = total distribution cost of proposed system
T = total freight cost of proposed system
FW = total fixed warehouse cost of proposed system
VW = total variable warehouse costs (including inventory) of proposed system
S = total cost of lost sales due to average delivery delay under proposed system.[8]

---

[7]Parker, *op. cit.*, p. 17.

[8]Adapted from Alfred A. Kuehn and Michael J. Hamburger, "A Heuristic Program for Locating Warehouses," *Management Science*, July 1963, pp. 657–58.

The choice of a physical-distribution system calls for examining the total distribution cost associated with different proposed systems and selecting the system that minimizes total distribution cost.

MAJOR ALTERNATIVES IN PHYSICAL-DISTRIBUTION STRATEGY

A firm faces a large number of alternatives in designing its physical-distribution system. The variety increases in number and complexity as we go from a firm with a single plant serving a single market to a firm with multiple plants and multiple markets.

Single plant, single market

The vast majority of the three hundred thousand manufacturers in the United States are single-plant firms doing business in single markets. The single markets served may be a small city, as in the case of small bakeries and printing firms, or a region, as in the case of local breweries and boat manufacturers.

Does the single-plant firm generally locate in the midst of its market? It often does, for the cost of serving a market increases with the distance. The distant firm has to absorb higher outbound freight costs and is normally at a competitive disadvantage.

Yet in some cases there are offsetting economies in locating a plant at some distance from the market. The higher market transportation cost may be offset by lower costs of land, labor, energy, or raw materials.

> A small pickler serving the Chicago market located his plant in the midst of a cucumber-growing region two hundred miles from Chicago. This gave him better control over crop selection. His labor costs were lower because pickling and packing were done only in certain months, when farmers had surplus time on their hands. Finally, the acreage for his plant cost only a fraction of what it would have cost near the city.

The merits of locating a plant near the market or near its sources depend mainly on relative transfer and processing costs. A substantial change in certain costs could upset the balance of advantages. The firm choosing between two alternative plant sites must carefully weigh not only present alternative costs but expected future alternative costs.

Single plant, multiple markets

The firm having a single plant and selling in a dispersed set of markets has a choice of several physical-distribution strategies. Consider a midwestern manufacturer who wishes to expand his operation into the East. He can serve the eastern market in at least four alternative ways:

> *Direct shipments* to customers on the East Coast from the Midwest plant.
> *Carload shipments to a warehouse* on the East Coast.
> *Fabricated-parts shipments to an assembly plant* on the East Coast.
> *Establishment of a manufacturing plant* on the East Coast.

Direct shipments to customers Any proposed system of physical distribution must be evaluated in terms of customer service and cost. The direct-shipment proposal leaves the impression that it would score poorly on both of these counts. In the first place, direct shipment would seem to imply slower delivery than shipments to the customer from an eastern-based warehouse. Second, direct shipment would seem to imply more cost, because the typical customer order is likely to be smaller than carload size. Carload rates (CL) are often 50 percent lower than less-than-carload rates (LCL).

But whether direct shipment does involve these disadvantages depends upon a number of things. It is conceivable that direct shipment from a distant plant could effect *faster* delivery than shipment from a nearby warehouse. A Kansas City manufacturer of colored, flavored ice-cream cones learned that his customers in the East could receive shipments sooner by air freight direct from Kansas City than by truck shipments out of New York City. Furthermore, direct shipment of less-than-carload orders must be measured against the cost of maintaining warehoused inventories in the East. The decision on whether to use direct shipment depends on such factors as the nature of the product (its unit value, perishability, and seasonality), the required speed and cost of delivery, the size and/or weight of the typical customer order, and the geographical distance and direction.

What is being compared to warehoused inventories in the East is not direct shipment in the abstract, but some particular mode of direct shipment. The cost of direct shipment varies with selection of waterways, railroad, motor carriers, air freight, or some combination. Figure 14-2 shows how the cost of different modes of transportation may be compared. If the company tended to receive eastern orders for shipments weighing less than ten pounds on the average, it could minimize transportation cost by using air freight. If eastern orders averaged between ten and thirty-five pounds, motor freight would be the

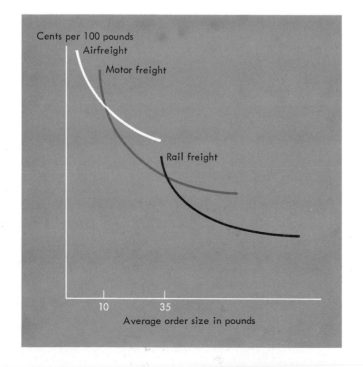

Figure 14-2
Shipping cost as a function of average weight and type of transportation

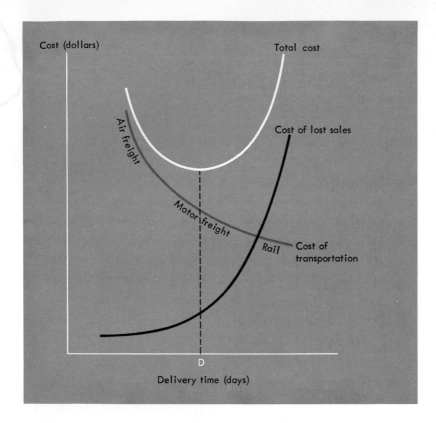

Cost (dollars)

Total cost

Cost of lost sales

Air freight

Motor freight

Rail   Cost of transportation

D

Delivery time (days)

Figure 14-3
Total cost as a function of delivery time

preferred alternative. Finally, if the average-size order exceeded thirty-five pounds, shipment by rail would minimize the freight bill.

    This analysis is incomplete because each transportation alternative implies a different average delivery time. We can assume a higher cost of lost sales for longer delivery delays. Thus the slower modes of transportation cost less freight-wise but more saleswise. These two diverging cost functions of delivery time are shown in Figure 14-3. By adding the two cost curves vertically, we can find a total-cost curve. The total-cost curve tends to be U-shaped, and by projecting its minimum point down to the days-of-delivery axis, we can estimate the optimum delivery delay, D. This delay has the property that the marginal savings in freight from a slightly longer delay would just equal the marginal cost of lost patronage.

    Bulk shipments to a warehouse near the market The firm may find it less expensive to make bulk shipments to a regional warehouse in the East and to fill customer orders from that regional warehouse. The savings would arise mainly because of the substantial difference between carload and less-than-carload shipping rates. Suppose the midwestern manufacturer expects to sell 5,000 units annually in the East, and virtually all of the individual orders call for less-than-carload shipments. Assume that the shipping cost is $8 per unit on a carload basis, and $12 per unit on a less-than-carload basis. The cost of shipping the 5,000 units directly to customers at less-than-carload rates would be $60,000 (5,000 × $12). The cost of shipping carloads to a warehouse would be $40,000 (5,000 × $8). This represents a gross cost saving of $20,000.

From this, we have to subtract the cost of local delivery from the warehouse to the customer and the cost of warehousing. Suppose the typical local delivery charge is $1 a unit; then local delivery charges of $5,000 (5,000 × $1) must be subtracted from the gross savings, leaving savings of $15,000. Suppose the average unit stays in the warehouse one week before shipment and the warehouse charge per unit per week is $2, including handling, insurance, and all other charges. Then the annual warehousing bill would be $10,000 (5,000 × $2), leaving net savings of $5,000. Given these figures, the midwestern manufacturer could save $5,000 a year by making bulk shipments to a warehouse in the East as an alternative to direct shipments to customers.

To this possible freight savings should be added another advantage accruing from the use of a market-located stocking point. A regional warehouse typically makes it possible to make faster deliveries to customers and thereby increase customer patronage. In general, the optimizing rule for adding regional warehouses is simple enough. A regional warehouse should be added *if the freight savings and increased patronage resulting from faster delivery exceed the incremental costs of operating the warehouse.*

Large manufacturers must consider a whole system of regional warehouses, or stocking points, to serve a national market. Maytag, a large manufacturer of home laundry equipment, has over one hundred regional stocking points. Instead of sending small-volume orders of washing machines to over fifteen thousand different dealers, the company sends carload shipments to its various stocking points. In this way it can promise speedier delivery and also save considerably on freight costs.

But an extensive regional warehouse system raises a number of new problems: (1) What is the best number of stocking points?; (2) Where should they be located?; (3) What is the best inventory level to hold at each? Paper-and-pencil analysis is exceedingly inadequate to answer these questions. Companies are increasingly turning to computer models. Gerson and Maffei have described a computer simulation program for evaluating a system of up to forty warehouses, four thousand customers, and ten factories.[9] This program can be used to estimate quickly the cost of alternative arrangements in the existing number and locations of factories and warehouses. Other models are available which use mathematical programming techniques to determine the optimal distribution system.[10]

Fabricated-parts shipments to an assembly plant near the market A third alternative for the midwestern manufacturer is to establish an assembly plant near the market. Parts are shipped in carload quantities to the regional assembly plant at lower freight charges. The presence of a regional plant also stimulates the increased interest of local salesmen, dealers, and the community at large.

---

[9]Martin L. Gerson and Richard B. Maffei, "Technical Characteristics of Distribution Simulators," *Management Science*, October 1963, pp. 62–69.

[10]See Kuehn and Hamburger, *op. cit.*

Against this the company must consider the sunk investment cost in additional facilities.

Establishment of a regional manufacturing plant The midwestern manufacturer's fourth alternative is to establish a regional plant in the East. The decision to build a regional manufacturing plant requires the most detailed factual information and analysis of the local scene. Many factors are involved, including the availability and costs of manpower, energy, land, transportation, and, not the least important, the legal and political environment.

One of the most important factors is the nature of mass-production economies in the industry. In industries requiring a relatively heavy fixed investment, a plant has to be quite large in order to achieve cost economies. If unit costs of manufacture decrease continuously with the scale of plant, then one plant could logically supply the entire company volume at minimum *production* costs. However, it would be fallacious to ignore distribution costs, because they tend to be higher at higher volumes. The two considerations are combined in Figure 14-4. Unit production costs decline steadily as increased volume is produced by a single plant, while unit distribution costs tend to rise as the volume requires direct shipment to more distant markets. When the two curves are summed vertically, total costs may in fact rise as a result of using only one plant location. The company should consider a second plant as an alternative to expanding the size of a single plant much past *V*. It is conceivable in this case that two plants, each involving higher unit production costs, may effect a large enough saving in distribution costs to constitute the better arrangement.

**Multiple plants,
multiple markets**

Many of the large companies that do not require extremely large plants to achieve production economies utilize a physical-distribution system consisting of many plants and many warehouses. These companies face two optimization tasks. The first is to set a factory-to-warehouse shipping pattern that minimizes total freight costs, given the present plant and warehouse locations. The second is to determine the number and location of facilities that will minimize total distribution costs. Here system simulation is a potent technique. A physical-

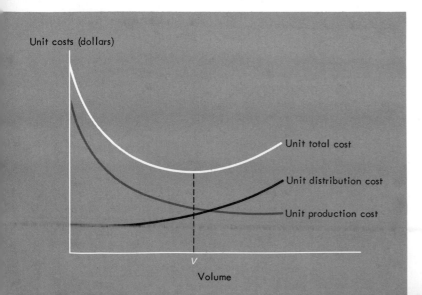

Figure 14-4
Unit production and distribution costs
for a single plant

distribution simulation at General Electric showed how a subsidiary with $50 million sales could save $2.9 million a year through system redesign.[11]

The physical-distribution system must be designed not for maximum economy for the present so much as maximum flexibility for the future, even if present costs must be a little higher in order to gain this flexibility. The company's plans for entering new product markets, for introducing new product styles and models, and for changing the number of distributors all should count in designing the system. The system should be planned with an awareness of environmental developments, particularly in the areas of communications, transportation, and automation. Such innovations as automated warehouses, piggyback freight, electronic hookups between computers in different locations, containerization, and air freight are all factors to consider.

INVENTORY DECISIONS

While marketing management generally does not have control over inventory policy, it is inclined to seek a strong voice in the making of inventory policy. The marketer's chief concern lies in providing a high level of service for his customers. Inventory policy is viewed by him as an instrument in the demand-creation and demand-satisfaction process. He would, if he could, promise his customers that all their orders would be filled immediately and shipped by the most rapid transportation.

However, it is not realistic from a cost point of view for a company to carry the amount of stock that would virtually guarantee no stockouts. A major reason is that *inventory cost increases at an increasing rate as the customer service level approaches 100 percent.* A typical cost relationship is illustrated in Figure 14-5. To be able to fill 85 percent of the total received orders from existing stock, the

---

[11]The Case for 90% Satisfaction," *Business Week*, January 14, 1961.

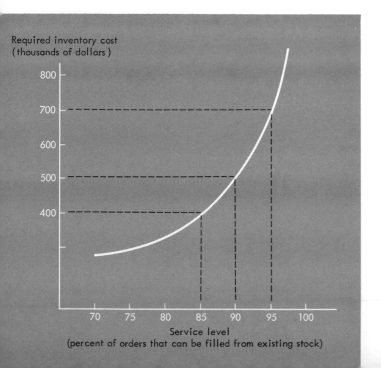

Figure 14-5
How inventory cost rises with the level of customer service

company has to carry an inventory valued at $400,000. To raise the customer service standard by five percentage points, to 90 percent, inventory investment must be increased by $100,000. To raise the customer service standard another five percentage points, to 95 percent, inventory investment must now be increased by $200,000.

This acceleration of inventory cost does not mean that increases in customer service are never warranted. Increases in service spell increases in patronage and sales. But how much do sales increase with service? The graph only tells us that an increase from 90 to 95 percent service requires another $200,000 of inventory investment. We need to know whether sales and profits will increase enough to justify the higher investment.

**Types of inventory
decisions**

Inventories are carried because *producing* and *using* activities typically take place at different times, in different locations, and at different rates. In the case of agricultural food crops, rate of usage is usually even throughout the year, but harvesting occurs at discrete times. In the case of manufacturing output, factories achieve production economies by producing large runs of items infrequently. The savings in producing large runs generally exceed the cost of storing the goods over the period required for their complete sale.

Inventory decision making can be thought of as a two-step decision process: (1) when to order (order point), and (2) how much to order (order quantity).

When to order   The basic characteristic of an inventory is that it is drawn down during the period. This calls for a determination of the level at which the remaining stock justifies the placement of a new order. This level is called the order (or reorder) point. An order point of 20 would mean that when the seller's supply of an item falls to 20 units, he should place an order for more stock.

The determination of the order point depends upon the order lead time, the usage rate, and the service standard. The higher the order lead time, the customer usage rate, and the company service standard, the higher the order point. Furthermore, if the order lead time and customer usage rate are variable, the order point would have to be higher by an amount of *safety stock*. The final order point is set on the basis of balancing the risks of stockouts against the costs of overstock.

How much to order   The decision the firm makes on how much to order (its order quantity) directly influences *how often* it has to order. The larger the quantity ordered, the less often an order has to be placed.

Order-processing costs are somewhat different for the distributor and the manufacturer. The distributor's processing costs consist of whatever materials, machine accounting time, and labor are used up every time an order is placed, received, and inspected. Distributors have variously estimated their order-processing costs anywhere from a few dollars to fifty dollars an order. The figure used makes quite a difference in the final determination of optimal order quantity.

Order-processing costs for a manufacturer consist of setup costs and running costs for the item. If setup costs are very low, the manufacturer can produce the item often and the cost per item is pretty constant and equal to the running costs. However, if setup costs are high, the manufacturer can reduce the average cost per unit by producing a long run and carrying more inventory.

Order-processing costs must be compared with the costs of maintaining the order quantity in inventory, called *carrying costs*. The larger the average stock carried, the higher the inventory carrying costs. These carrying costs fall into four major categories: (1) storage charges, (2) cost of capital, (3) taxes and insurance, and (4) depreciation and obsolescence.

Inventory carrying costs may run as high as 30 percent of the inventory value. This is generally higher than the estimate used by many businessmen, but there is growing recognition that the cost is this high. This means that marketing managers who want their companies to carry larger inventories must be able to convince top management that the higher inventories will yield new sales with an incremental gross profit that would more than cover the incremental inventory carrying costs.

The optimal order quantity can be determined by observing how order-processing costs and inventory carrying costs sum up at different possible order levels. In Figure 14-6 the order-processing cost per unit is shown to fall with the number of units ordered, because the order costs are spread over more units. Inventory carrying charges per unit are shown to rise with the number of units ordered, because each unit remains longer in inventory. The two cost curves

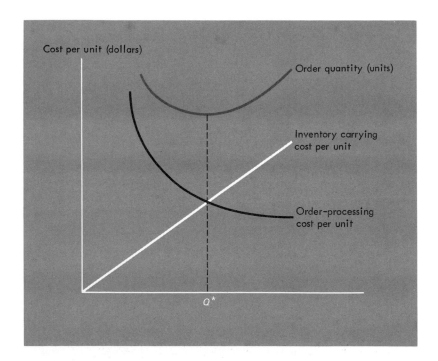

Figure 14-6
Determining optimal order quantity (Q^*)

are summed vertically into a total-cost curve. The lowest point on the total-cost curve is projected down on the horizontal axis to find the optimal order quantity $Q*$.[12]

LOCATION DECISIONS

Marketing management has a keen interest in location decisions made by the firm. Retail outlets must be carefully located near the greatest number of potential customers, because of the importance of shopper convenience in store patronage. Even warehouse locations should be located near the customer concentration points to ensure faster and cheaper delivery to customers.

**Types of
location decisions**

Location decision making can be thought of as a two-step decision process: (1) selecting a general area, and (2) selecting a specific site.

We can illustrate the major issues in retail location by citing the experience of the Rayco Manufacturing Company.[13] Rayco was formed after World War II as a manufacturer of automobile seat covers. Its distribution network consisted of independently financed, franchised dealers who merchandised Rayco products exclusively. By 1955, it had over 150 dealers operating in sixty different cities. Its national retail structure continued to grow, and new lines were taken on, such as convertible tops, automobile replacement parts, and a line of home-furnishing fabrics. But auto seat covers remained its main product.

Selecting the area Rayco's Research Division has the responsibility of evaluating the profit potential of various areas of the country. The areas might be cities, standard metropolitan areas, or some other geographical unit. Suppose a set of n areas $(1, 2, 3, \ldots, i, \ldots, n)$ is to be evaluated. Let Z_i represent the expected profit potential of the ith area. Let X_i be a proposed company dollar investment in developing area i. The expected profit potential will vary with development expenses. That is, $Z_i = f(X_i)$. A larger outlet, a better dealer, or a larger promotion budget invested in a particular area would create higher profits, although the rate of profit increase can be expected to diminish beyond some level of investment.

Rayco's task is to estimate, for each candidate area, how profits would behave at different levels of investment. Once it derives a set of area profit functions, it can allocate its total "new locations" budget to these areas in such a way that the marginal profit is the same in all areas.

---

[12]The optimal order quantity is given mathematically by the formula

$$Q* = \sqrt{\frac{2DS}{IC}}$$

where D = annual demand, S = cost to place one order, and IC = annual carrying cost per unit. Known as the economic-order quantity formula, it assumes a constant ordering cost, a constant cost of carrying an additional unit in inventory, a known demand, and no quantity discounts. For the derivation of this and more complex formulas, see Martin K. Starr and David W. Miller, *Inventory Control: Theory and Practice* (Englewood Cliffs, N.J.: Prentice-Hall, Inc., 1962).

[13]The discussion that follows is adapted from "Rayco Manufacturing Company, Inc.: Pinpointing Store Locations by Electronic Computer," Case 3M38, Intercollegiate Case Clearing House, Harvard Graduate School of Business Administration, Boston, by permission of the author, Charles H. Dufton, Northeastern University, Boston.

Although the area investment problem turns out to be simple to solve in principle, everything hinges on being able to estimate expected profits as a function of investment: $Z_i = f(X_i)$. Area profits are a complex function of area cost and area demand characteristics. The relevant cost characteristics of an area, such as land costs and advertising rates, are fairly easy to determine. It is the area's demand potential that is usually hard to determine.

Rayco initially identified about three hundred variables that could influence area sales. The Research Division examined the logical rationale for each variable and was able to reduce the set to seventy-four. Included were such variables as "average January temperature," "percent of the dwellings that were one-unit detached structures," and an "index for the physical appearance of a store." An equation was fitted to these seventy-four variables based on data from 150 existing outlets. Several of the variables failed to pass tests of statistical significance, and in the final equation, thirty-seven variables were retained, yielding an R^2 of .92. Rayco felt it could now estimate the "market potential" of any new area by inserting thirty-seven characteristics into the formula.

Selecting the site   After determining the areas of high potential, the firm must decide how many outlets to establish and where they should be specifically situated. If San Francisco appeared to be a high-potential market, Rayco could establish, for about the same investment, one large outlet in a central location or a few smaller outlets in separate parts of the city. If consumers behaved as though auto seat covers were specialty goods, they would be willing to travel longer distances, and this would favor one large, centrally located store. If consumers regarded Rayco's products as convenience goods, this would favor Rayco's establishing a few smaller outlets.

A store's trading area or reach is affected by a number of other factors besides the type of merchandise. One is the number of different items carried by the store. Baumol and Ide developed an analysis in which they visualized each consumer as calculating his net gain from patronizing a store with N items at a distance D.[14] They assumed that increases in N more than compensated for increases in D up to a point. Beyond this point, the cost of traveling to the store, and within the store, became dominant. The cost of traveling within a store, which is a function of N, would never reach discouraging proportions in the case of a Rayco outlet but could be a real factor in very large supermarkets and department stores, especially for the shopper who plans to purchase only a few items.

The *utility* expected by a consumer in location i of shopping at an outlet in location j is affected by many variables in addition to N and D. Included are such factors as store image, delivery, credit, service policies, promotion, parking facilities, and air conditioning. If consumer utility as a function of these variables could be measured, the choice of the best site and store size from a list of alternatives is solvable in principle.[15] Suppose there are three alternative proposed sites—1, 2, and 3—offering utilities 40, 30, and 10, respectively, to a

---

[14]See William J. Baumol and Edward A. Ide, "Variety in Retailing," *Management Science*, October 1956, pp. 93–101.

[15]See David L. Huff, "Defining and Estimating a Trading Area," *Journal of Marketing*, July 1964, pp. 34–38.

consumer in location i. The probability that this consumer would shop at site 1 is the ratio of the utility of site 1 to the total utility, in this case .50 ($= 40/80$). If there are 1,000 similar consumers clustered at location i, then half of them, or 500, can be expected to patronize proposed site 1. In a more advanced analysis, it would be desirable to distinguish major socioeconomic types of consumers at location i, because there are strong interactions of consumer type and store type.

In practice, firms vary considerably in how analytically they investigate the trade potential of proposed sites. Small firms rely on population census data and on simple traffic counts. Large firms carry out expensive surveys of consumer shopping habits and make extensive calculations of expected sales volume.

The expanding firm often develops explicit criteria to guide its search for sites and cut down its search time. Goldblatt's, a million-dollar department store chain centered in Chicago, uses the following principles to narrow down its site choices.[16]

The store must be designed to do from $3 to $5 million in annual sales volume.

The store must be located in a one-stop shopping center only.

The store must not be located in a major metropolitan center, but rather in secondary areas, such as are found in most suburban shopping centers.

The store must be in an area of population and consumer income growth potential, not in an area past its peak.

The store must not be located more than two hundred miles from the central Chicago store.

Each store unit property must be leased and not bought.

There must be a minimum trading area of one hundred thousand persons.

While these heuristic principles may lead Goldblatt's to overlook a very good site, they save the company the expense of considering a great number of potentially poor sites.

In undertaking a detailed *trade analysis* for a proposed site, the large firm first prepares area maps indicating density and the location of competitive intercepting facilities. An overlay on this map indicates major arteries to pinpoint traffic flows. Additional information is obtained by surveying the license plates in the parking lots of competitive facilities and through inquiries at noncompeting stores as to customer sources.

The real estate department then determines the availability and cost of potential sites within the general area. The trade potential of each site is then evaluated. A series of circles is drawn around each site at varying distances to indicate the primary trading area, the secondary trading area, and the fringe trading area. The secondary and fringe areas are further away from the new site and closer to competitive sites; they can be expected to contribute a progressively smaller amount of per capita sales. Use can be made of intracity

---

[16]See Ralph Westfall and Harper W. Boyd, Jr., *Cases in Marketing Management* (Homewood, Ill.: Richard D. Irwin, Inc., 1961, pp. 77–83.

versions of Reilly's law, which supplies a means for estimating the sales volume drawn by competing shopping sites as a function of store size and driving time.[17]

The major chains utilize elaborate site-location checklists in their evaluation of sites. Nelson has published a very elaborate checklist containing over thirty factors, each of which has to be rated excellent, good, fair, or poor in evaluating a proposed site.[18] These factors relate to the site's trading area potential, accessibility, growth potential, competitive interception, and site economics. Some of the large chain organizations have gone beyond checklists into elaborate computer models for site location. One very large merchandising organization dropped its location consultant firm when it realized that the methods being used were at the checklist stage and undertook to build its own internal consultancy group for sophisticated location research.

ORGANIZATIONAL RESPONSIBILITY FOR PHYSICAL DISTRIBUTION

Divided authority

By now it should be abundantly clear that decisions on warehousing, transportation, inventory levels, and location require the highest degree of coordination. Yet in the typical company, physical-distribution responsibilities tend to be divided in an ill-coordinated and often arbitrary way among several company departments. Furthermore, each department tends to adopt a narrow view of the company's physical-distribution objective. The *traffic manager* seeks to minimize the freight bill. He prefers less-expensive modes of transportation and infrequent and large shipments. The *sales manager* seeks to maximize the level of customer service. He prefers large inventories and premium transportation.

---

[17]Studies were conducted, starting in 1927, by William J. Reilly and subsequently by Paul D. Converse to measure the retail trade influence of a city. The original "law" developed by Reilly reads like an adaptation of the law of planetary attraction. According to Reilly: "Two cities attract retail trade from any intermediate city or town in the vicinity of the breaking point approximately in direct proportion to the population of the two cities and in inverse proportion to the squares of the distances from these two cities to the intermediate town." Mathematically this can be expressed as

$$\frac{B_a}{B_b} = \left(\frac{P_a}{P_b}\right)^1 \left(\frac{D_b}{D_a}\right)^2$$

where:

B_i = the proportion of retail trade from the intermediate town attracted by city i
P_i = the population of city i
D_i = the distance from the intermediate town to city i
a, b = the particular cities being compared

Subsequent empirical investigations revealed that the exponents may vary because of other variables not explicitly included in the equation. Population and distance are still considered the primary variables, but other variables may warrant different exponents. Among these second-order variables are lines of transportation and communication; business, social, and amusement attractions of the two cities; psychology of distance prevailing in that part of the country; differences in promotional intensity; and parking facilities. For a good exposition of the various laws of retail gravitation, see George Schwartz, *Development of Marketing Theory* (Cincinnati: South-Western Publishing Co., 1963), pp. 9–34.

[18]Richard L. Nelson, *The Selection of Retail Locations* (New York: F. W. Dodge Corporation, 1958), pp. 349–50.

The *inventory control manager* seeks to minimize inventory costs. He prefers small inventories because inventory carrying costs tend to be more tangible than stockout costs. Each manager jealously guards his prerogatives. The result is system suboptimization.

**Organizational
alternatives**

Companies are increasingly recognizing the potential benefits of developing some coordinating mechanism and have generally chosen one of two forms. Many companies have set up a permanent committee, composed of personnel responsible for different physical-distribution activities, that meets periodically to work out policies for increasing the efficiency of the overall distribution system. Other companies have centralized their physical-distribution activities in the hands of a single authority.

The example of the Burroughs Company is particularly illuminating.[19] Burroughs organized the Distribution Services Department to centralize control over its physical-distribution activities. Within two and one-half years following the reorganization, the company claimed savings of over $2 million annually (on $200 million of sales), plus a higher level of service to field branches and customers.

When a company establishes a separate department with responsibility for physical distribution, the major issue is whether the new department should have separate status or be placed within one of the major existing departments. For example, Heinz created a new department of coordinate stature with Marketing and Production which was headed by a vice-president of Distribution. Heinz hoped that this arrangement would guarantee respect for the department, develop a greater degree of professionalism and objectivity, and avoid partisan domination by Marketing or Production.

On the other hand, Burroughs placed its new Distribution Services Department within the Marketing Department. By this move, Burroughs was expressing the great importance it attached to good customer service relative to the costs of providing it. Wherever marketing is the crucial factor in competitive success, physical distribution is usually placed under the marketing department. This is especially true in such competitive industries as soap, food, and cosmetics, where marketing and physical distribution must be coordinated not only to minimize costs but also to harmonize distribution with frequent advertising campaigns and customer and dealer promotions.

But the location of the department, or even its creation, is a secondary concern. The important thing is the recognition by the company that if it does not coordinate the planning and operation of its physical-distribution activities, it is missing the opportunity for often sizable cost savings and service improvements. When this fundamental awareness takes place, each company can then make a determination of what would constitute the most appropriate coordinative mechanism.

SUMMARY

Just as the marketing concept is receiving increasing recognition by business firms, a growing number are beginning to heed the physical-distribution concept. When traffic managers, inventory managers, and warehouse planners

[19]See L. O. Browne, "Total Distribution in an Age of Computers," *Distribution Age,* July 1964, pp. 33–40.

make decisions only with reference to their own framework, they affect each other's costs and demand-creation influences but do not take them into consideration. The physical-distribution concept calls for treating all these decisions within a unified total systems framework. Then the important task becomes that of designing physical-distribution arrangements that minimize the cost of providing a given level of customer service.

The firm can choose from a number of alternative physical-distribution strategies, ranging from direct shipment to field warehousing to local assembly plants to local manufacturing plants. It must develop inventory policies that reconcile the value of a high level of customer service with the need to economize on inventory carrying costs. It must find more accurate ways to evaluate alternative general areas and specific sites for marketing expansion. It must review the whole question of organizational responsibility for physical distribution, particularly how to coordinate the various decisions and where leadership should be located in the organization.

We have deliberately emphasized the planning rather than the operations aspects of physical distribution. Physical distribution is an area where good systems design counts for as much as or more than good operations management. Nevertheless, many of the potential economies come from improved management of the existing system.

**QUESTIONS
AND PROBLEMS**

1   Does it follow that the company offering a high customer service level tends to bear high physical distribution costs in relation to sales?

2   A small midwestern boat company with good sales wants to expand into the eastern part of the country. What physical distribution strategy might it use to bring its boats to the East?

3   A national can manufacturer operates many local plants because cans are a low-cost, low-price product that has a relatively high transportation cost when shipped assembled, being mostly "air." Some of his plants appear uneconomic, and he is considering closing them. Much depends upon whether customers in the affected areas would accept a longer delivery time, switch business to a competitor's local plant, or manufacture their own cans. Develop a flow diagram showing how the company might analyze probable customer reactions to the elimination of a local plant.

4   What are the two inventory-production policy alternatives facing a seasonal producer?

5   Suppose a company's inventory carrying cost is 30 percent. A marketing manager wants the company to increase its inventory investment from $400,000 to $500,000. He believes this would lead to increased sales of $120,000 because of greater customer loyalty and service. The gross profit on sales is 20 percent. Does it pay the company to increase its inventory investment?

6   The text mentioned that Rayco approached the problem of finding the characteristics of good locations through multiple regression. (a) Suggest some of the various ways in which the dependent variable, sales, might be defined. (b) How could the research department further reduce the number of independent variables in the market evaluation formula?

7   Suppose you are the marketing manager of a medium size manufacturing company. The president has just made the following statement: "The distribution activity is not a concern of the marketing department. The function of the marketing department is to sell the product . . . let the rest of the company handle production and distribution." How would you reply to this statement?

15

COMMUNICATION–PROMOTION DECISIONS

People no longer buy shoes to keep their feet warm and dry. They buy them because of the way the shoes make them feel—masculine, feminine, rugged, different, sophisticated, young, glamorous, "in." Buying shoes has become an emotional experience. Our business now is selling excitement rather than shoes.

FRANCIS C. ROONEY

Modern marketing calls for more than developing a good product, pricing it correctly, and making it easily available to the customer. The company that wants more than "walk-in" sales must develop an effective program of communication and promotion. Every company is cast, by the very nature of customers and competition, into the role of a communicator.

Companies have recognized this and have responded by hiring sales forces to carry persuasive messages; advertising agencies to develop attention-getting ads; sales promotion specialists to develop sales campaigns; and public relations firms to enhance the company's image. Not all companies feel good about all of these things, and some positively act as if promotional expenditures were among the least productive made by the firm. Yet they all continue to spend large and growing sums for promotion. For most companies the question is not whether to promote, but how much to spend and in what ways.

Effective promotion for today's firm requires an *integrated marketing communications concept.* It involves the firm in answering an extremely difficult question, What does it want to be? Whether or not the firm answers this question, it *will be* something to the public and to its customers. All of its products and actions communicate. And the only question is what is communicated. The firm that has recognized this sees its relationship to the buyer as a *courtship.* In the best sense, the firm strives to establish an *emotionally satisfying* relationship between itself and its customers. This is not to say that the buyers will pay less attention to quality, value, and price. It is precisely these aspects of the offer that help build the emotional relationship. Wooing the customer with a cheap dinner is not likely to lead to a lasting relationship. And it is the *lasting relationship,* built through offering real values and effective communication, that more and more companies are coming around to seeking with their customers.

MODELS OF THE PERSUASION PROCESS

The modern corporation and its agents are in continuous communication with others: customers, suppliers, bankers, government, the general public. Some of the communication is *casual,* some is designed to be *informative,* and some is designed to be *persuasive.* We are particularly interested in the last: persuasive communication. *Persuasive communication is said to take place when a communicator consciously develops his messages to have a calculated impact on the attitude and/or behavior of a target audience.*

The persuasion process has been of interest to politicians, missionaries, lawyers, educators, reformers, demogogues, negotiators, administrators, marketers, and military men. Each field has developed its own theories and vocabulary to describe the process, and consequently the commonalities have been lost sight of.

Rhetorical model

Three basic models of the persuasion process can be distinguished. The first, or *rhetorical model,* received its original formulation in the hands of Aristotle over twenty centuries ago in his *Rhetoric.* It is a model designed for the situation where a *speaker* is addressing an *audience.* This applies to a politician addressing an assembly, a lawyer addressing a jury, a salesman addressing a potential customer. Rhetoric is the faculty of determining the most effective means of persuasion in a given case. Rhetoric must begin with an analysis of the audience and the desired responses. Aristotle distinguished three modes of persuasion available to a speaker: the use of his *character* to make his speech credible, the excitation of desired *emotion* in the audience, and *proof* or apparent proof. Various modern settings for persuasion in the marketing field still draw on these basic principles. In the advertising world we see ads that build or trade on the character of the company, others designed to stimulate audience emotions, and still others documenting the product's superiority. In the sales field we see salesmen who emphasize their company's reputation, others who stir the customers' emotions, and still others who attempt to demonstrate the technical qualities of their product.

Propagandistic model

The second, or *propagandistic model,* is formulated for the situation where an *institution* (church, state, business organization) is trying to win potential supporters to its cause. Here the persuasion process is seen in much broader terms than simply the use of words. The earliest practitioners were princely and religious leaders who saw the task of winning converts as one of manipulating words (rhetoric), feelings (atmospheres), and experiences (events) in a way that would capture one's devotion. Thus the state and the church made ample use of words, architecture, ceremony, and symbols to develop and fortify loyal feelings. More recently, the modern corporation has begun to compete for the support of various groups and has turned to these same ancient instruments. Rhetoric, the most familiar technique, is consciously crafted in advertising, personal selling, and public relations. *Atmospherics* is rather new for the business firm, and expresses itself in the design of buildings and executive offices, corporate identification symbols, product design and packaging, the "look" of the salesman, and so on. It is a recognition that people derive impressions from every *sign* of the corporation or the product. *Event management* is even newer to the modern corporation; it means the arrangement of "happenings" that are calculated to induce desired feelings in potential supporters. The modern corporation, through its public relations people, creates events to make news. The president makes speeches to various influential groups, new products and new stores are launched with fanfare and ceremony, and so on.

Negotiation model

The third, or *negotiation model*, examines persuasion in the context of a *negotiator* facing another *negotiator*. This model is prominent in labor-management relations, international diplomacy, the legislative process, and sales negotiation. Each negotiator is trying to win the best terms for his constituency; and what he wins, the other loses. A settlement is possible if terms can be found that allow each party to claim a partial victory. The negotiator has two broad persuasion instruments. *Inducements* are positive motivators and concessions offered to the other party; they include flattery, promises, and bribes. *Threats* are negative motivators offered to the other party; they include boycott, exposure, and blandishment. In marketing situations, the modern firm favors an inducement strategy over a threat strategy, although there are still examples of the latter.[1]

THE COMMUNICATION MODEL

A more general model, formulated and researched in recent times, is available for improving communication processes. We shall call it the *communication model*. The model requires thought about (1) who (2) says what (3) in what channel

[1]For a discussion of negotiation tactics, see Gerald I. Nierenberg, *The Art of Negotiation* (New York: Hawthorn Books, Inc., 1968).

Figure 15-1
The communication model

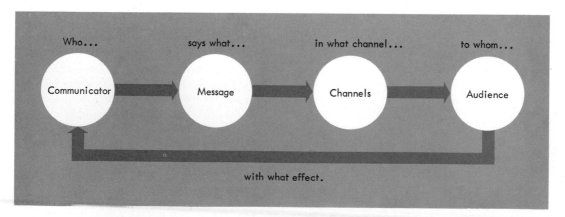

(4) to whom (5) with what effect. The model's basic elements—communicator, message, channels, and audience—are illustrated in Figure 15-1 and can be defined as follows:

> The *communicator* is the sender or the source of the message.
>
> The *message* is the set of meanings being sent and/or received by the audience.
>
> The *channels* are the ways in which messages can be carried or delivered to audiences.
>
> The *audience* is the receiver or the destination of the message.

This model ties together many interesting aspects and findings about the communication process. It provides guidance to marketing communicators on how to arrange effective messages and media for an intended audience.[2] We will discuss the four elements not in the order of the *message flow* (from communicator to audience) but in terms of the *planning flow* (from target audience backward through channels to the communicator).

Audience

The communicator must start with the audience because the audience determines *what* is to be said, *how* it is to be said, *when* it is to be said, *where* it is to be said, and *who* is to say it. The audience will be an individual, a group, a particular public, or the general public.

Audience response models The purpose of the communication is to bring about some response from the audience. The response sought may be at the *cognitive, affective,* or *behavioral level.* Figure 15-2 shows three alternative models of audience response repertoires. The AIDA model shows the buyer as passing through successive stages of awareness, interest, desire, and action. The "hierarchy-of-effects" model shows the buyer as passing through stages of awareness, knowledge, liking, preference, conviction, and purchase. The "innovation-adoption" model shows the buyer as passing through stages of awareness, interest, evaluation, trial, and adoption. Most of these differences are semantic. They all see the buyer as capable of three basic levels of response.

The communicator normally assumes that buyers pass through these stages in succession on the way to purchase. However, there is some evidence that the stages can occur in different orders. Ray has distinguished three plausible response models.[3]

LEARNING RESPONSE MODEL The learning response model is the normal one showing a person passing from cognition to affect to behavior. It is particularly applicable where the buyer feels *involved* and there are *clear differences among alternatives.* It applies, for example, to the purchase of durable goods such as washing machines and computers. For the marketer, it suggests that he must

---

[2]Recent work emphasizes the audience as playing a more active role in the communication process. The audience shows selective attention and perception; the audience may actively seek information; the audience may send signals back to the communicator. The view of communication as a two-way process has been called "transactional" or "phenomenalistic." See Raymond A. Bauer, "The Initiative of the Audience," *Journal of Advertising Research,* June 1963, pp. 2–7. The paradigm in Figure 15-2 does not exclude discussion of the two-way aspects of the communication process, although it focuses on the sender's communication task.

[3]Michael L. Ray, "Marketing Communication and the Hierarchy-of-Effects" (unpublished research paper #180, Stanford University, August 1973).

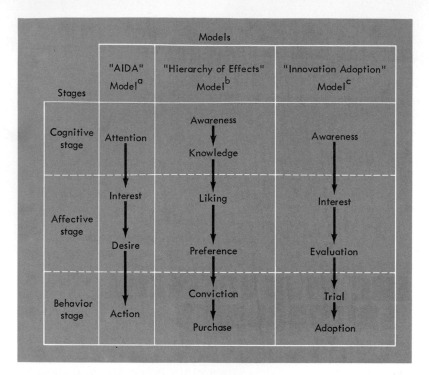

	Models		
Stages	"AIDA" Model[a]	"Hierarchy of Effects" Model[b]	"Innovation Adoption" Model[c]
Cognitive stage	Attention	Awareness ↓ Knowledge	Awareness
Affective stage	Interest ↓ Desire	Liking ↓ Preference	Interest ↓ Evaluation
Behavior stage	Action	Conviction ↓ Purchase	Trial ↓ Adoption

Figure 15-2
Models of buyer readiness stages

SOURCES. (a) E. K. Strong, *The Psychology of Selling* (New York: McGraw-Hill Book Company, 1925), p. 9. (b) Robert J. Lavidge and Gary A. Steiner, "A Model for Predictive Measurements of Advertising Effectiveness," *Journal of Marketing,* October 1961, p. 61. (c) Everett M. Rogers, *Diffusion of Innovations* (New York: The Free Press, 1962), pp. 79–86.

plan a communication campaign to first build product awareness, then comprehension, interest, conviction, and finally motivation to purchase.

DISSONANCE-ATTRIBUTION RESPONSE MODEL   This model describes situations where the buyer goes through a behavioral-affective-cognitive sequence. He buys the product through the recommendation of some nonmedia source, then his attitude changes through experience with the object, and then he learns by paying attention to messages supporting that choice. An example would be the purchase of insurance where a general agent recommends a particular policy and company, the person buys it, then his attitude starts changing, and he watches for messages about this company. His attitude changes after purchase to reduce dissonance, and his learning takes place as he attributes the purchase to his own volition. This model applies to situations where the audience is *involved* but the alternatives are almost *indistinguishable.* For the marketer, it suggests that his main tasks are to induce purchase through effective incentives and to use mass media to reduce dissonance *after* purchase and promote learning.

LOW-INVOLVEMENT RESPONSE MODEL   Here the consumer is thought to pass from cognition to behavior to attitude change. Krugman proposed this sequence for products where there is *low involvement* or *minimal differences* between alternatives (e.g., detergents, flour).[4] Television advertising for these products is a low-involvement learning experience where many messages penetrate the person's normal perceptual defenses (because of his low involvement) and create

---

[4]Herbert E. Krugman, "The Impact of Television Advertising: Learning without Involvement," *Public Opinion Quarterly,* Fall 1965, pp. 349–56.

cognitive shifts such as awareness but not attitude change. In the purchase situation, the consumer recognizes the product, buys it, and a change in attitude occurs after use. According to this model, the function of marketing communication is to build product awareness and to support favorable attitudes after purchase.

Audience characteristics The marketing communicator must ascertain the specific characteristics of his target audience as they relate to achieving the type of response he wants. If the communicator wants to improve audience comprehension of the features of his product, he will want to research the audience's present level of awareness and comprehension, its cognitive capacity, and its media habits. If he wants to improve attitudes toward the product, he will want to research the audience's present attitudes and its persuasibility. If he wants to motivate purchase, he will want to research its present level of interest, its willingness to take risks, and its purchasing power.

The relation of many of these audience characteristics to buying response behavior has been researched. Consider audience persuasibility. If audience persuasibility is high, then attitude-changing communications would be feasible. For example, intelligence is widely thought to be negatively correlated with persuasibility, but the evidence is inconclusive. Women have been found to be more persuasible than men, but men who feel socially inadequate also show this trait.[5] Persons who accept external standards to guide their behavior and who have a weak self-concept appear to be more persuasible. Persons who are low in self-confidence are also thought to be more persuasible. However, research by Cox and Bauer and later by Bell showed a curvilinear relation between self-confidence and persuasibility, with those moderate in self-confidence being the most persuasible.[6] In general, the communicator should consider this research, look for audience traits that correlate with differential persuasibility, and use them to guide his audience targeting and communication.

Audience image One of the most important steps in audience analysis is to assess the audience's currently held image of the company, its products, and its competitors. This helps the company recognize what it must aim for in terms of communication objectives. There are many techniques for measuring audience images, but here we shall describe the popular one known as the *semantic differential.*[7]

Images are the simplified impressions persons hold of an otherwise complex entity. Osgood, Suci, and Tannenbaum suggested that images are built on three factors:

---

[5]I. L. Janis and P. B. Field, "Sex Differences and Personality Factors Related to Personality," in *Personality and Persuasibility,* ed. C. Hovland and I. Janis (New Haven: Yale University Press, 1958), pp. 55–68.

[6]Donald F. Cox and Raymond A. Bauer, "Self-confidence and Persuasibility in Women," *Public Opinion Quarterly,* Fall 1964, pp. 453–66; and Gerald D. Bell, February 1967, pp. 46–53. However, see the attempted refutation by Abe Shuchman and Michael Perry, "Self-confidence and Persuasibility in Marketing: A Reappraisal." *Journal of Marketing Research,* May 1969, pp. 146–54.

[7]For a discussion of various image measurement techniques, see the author's *Marketing for Nonprofit Organizations* (Englewood Cliffs, N.J.: Prentice-Hall, 1975), pp. 131–37. The semantic differential technique was originally developed in C. E. Osgood, C. J. Suci, and P. H. Tannenbaum, *The Measurement of Meaning* (Urbana: University of Illinois Press, 1957).

1 Evaluation (the good-bad qualities of the image)
2 Potency (strong-weak qualities)
3 Activity (active-passive qualities)

To develop a corporate-image profile, subjects are asked to rate a company on various scales made up of polar adjectives reflecting these factors. The ratings of many persons are averaged. Each company will emerge with a certain average standing on each scale. A comparison can be made of its image or "semantic differential" relative to competitors on each scale. Consider the hypothetical scales and results for two companies, A and B, shown below:

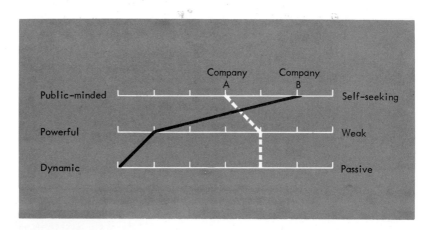

Company A emerges with a profile showing average public-mindedness, and it seems a little weak and possibly passive. Company B strikes the public as highly self-seeking, powerful, and dynamic. A company can take steps to repair the aspects of its image that it regards as weak, largely through advertising, publicity, and corporate-identification programs. Its success, however, depends on how well it also changes the underlying reality that produced the image.

Channels

Once the target audiences are specified, the communicator can think about the best channels for reaching them. Channels of influence are of two broad types, *personal* and *nonpersonal.*

Personal influence channels are means of direct contact with target individuals or groups. Three types can be distinguished. *Advocate channels* consist of salesmen or other company representatives in personal contact with the buyer trying to influence him. *Expert channels* consist of independent persons (consultants, authorities) exercising an influence on the buyer by dint of their expertise. *Social channels* consist of the buyer's associates, neighbors, friends, or family who may exercise an influence on him. This last channel is also known as *word-of-mouth influence,* and it may be the strongest of the three personal channels, especially in the consumer-products area.

Nonpersonal influence channels are media that carry influence without involving direct contact. Three types of nonpersonal media can be distinguished. *Mass and selective media* consist of newspapers, magazines, radio, television, and billboards that people might buy or perceive. Mass media are aimed at large, often undifferentiated audiences; selective media are more specialized in reach and focus. *Atmospheres* are designed environments calculated to create desirable feelings in persons regarding a company or a product. *Events* are designed occurrences.

We shall now look more closely at these various channels of influence.

Personal influence channels   There has been much discussion of the relative effectiveness of personal versus nonpersonal influence in changing attitudes and behavior. Most observers believe that personal influence is generally the more potent of the two. Thus, while nonpersonal media can create awareness and interest in a buyer, it usually takes a salesman to close the sale. Or a favorable reference to a product by a friend may do more to bring about the purchase than a dozen advertising exposures. Personal influence, especially social influence, would appear to be especially potent in two cases:

1   *Where the product is expensive, risky, or purchased infrequently.* In such cases, the buyer is likely to be a high information-seeker. He will probably go beyond mass-media information and seek out the product experiences and opinions of knowledgeable persons.

2   *Where the product has a significantly social, as opposed to private character.* Products such as automobiles, clothing, and even beer and cigarettes have significant brand differentiation that implies something about the status or taste of the individual. Here he is likely to choose brands acceptable to his group.

The more decisive influence of social channels, as against mass media, in creating opinion has been documented in a number of studies. The well-known study by Lazarsfeld, Berelson, and Gaudet of the 1940 presidential campaign found a greater number of persons influenced by political discussions in their primary groups than by mass media.[8] Radio and the printed page appeared to have only a negligible effect on vote, or change in vote decisions. These and subsequent studies led Berelson and Steiner to state:

> Word-of-mouth or personal communication from an immediate and trusted source is typically more influential than media communication from a remote and trusted source, despite the prestige of the latter.[9]

This should normally incline the marketer to favor personal influence channels, especially social channels, over mass media. Unfortunately, the marketer has little direct control over social influence channels. He cannot "hire" neighbors and friends to speak favorably about his product. Ironically what little control he has comes through the mass media! According to Klapper:

> Personal influence may be more effective than persuasive mass communication, but at present mass communications seems the most effective means of stimulating personal influence.[10]

---

[8]P. F. Lazarsfeld, B. Berelson, and H. Gaudet, *The People's Choice*, 2nd ed. (New York: Columbia University Press, 1948).

[9]Bernard Berelson and Gary A. Steiner, *Human Behavior: An Inventory of Scientific Findings* (New York: Harcourt, Brace & World, Inc., 1964), p. 550.

[10]Joseph T. Klapper, *The Effects of Mass Communication* (New York: The Free Press, 1960), p. 72.

Thus the relationship and relative influence of personal influence and mass communication is more complicated than it at first appears. Many observers hold that mass communications affect personal attitudes and behavior through a *two-step flow-of-communication process.* "Ideas often flow from radio and print to opinion leaders and from these to the less active sections of the population."[11]

If true, this hypothesis has several significant implications. First it says that mass media's influence on mass opinion is not as direct, powerful, and automatic as supposed. It is mediated by *opinion leaders,* persons who are members of primary groups and whose opinions tend to be sought out in one or more areas. Opinion leaders are more exposed to mass media than the people they influence. They are the carriers of the messages to people who are less exposed to media, thus extending the influence of the mass media; or they may carry altered or no messages, thus acting as *gatekeepers.*

Second, the hypothesis challenges the notion that persons are influenced in their consumption styles primarily from a "trickle-down" effect from the higher-status classes. Since people primarily interact with others in their own social class, they pick up their fashion and other ideas in this way—from people like themselves who are opinion leaders.

A third implication is that the mass communicator may accomplish his message dissemination more efficiently by using a lower advertising budget and directing it specifically at opinion leaders, letting them carry the message to others. Thus a pharmaceutical firm may direct new drug promotion to influential doctors. In many markets, however, opinion leaders and the people whom they influence are very much alike. It is hard to identify opinion leaders, aim communications specifically at them, and trust that they will say positive things about the product.

Although the two-step flow-of-communication hypothesis opened up some important new understandings about the flow of influence, it also has certain difficulties as a theory, and it could be misleading if interpreted literally. The following qualifications must be made:

1 Opinion leadership is not a dichotomous trait. It is a matter of degree. All group members may have some opinion leadership in certain areas of consumption.
2 Opinion followers do not get their information only from opinion leaders. They too are in touch with mass media, although a little less so.
3 An effective mass-media strategy might be to aim it at everyone and stimulate *opinion seeking;* this is a useful way to use opinion leaders.[12]

Companies can take some steps to stimulate personal influence channels to work on their behalf, even if their actual control is somewhat limited. Among the things they can do are:

1 Observe whether certain individuals or companies seem to stand out as influentials in their groups and devote extra effort to them, either through personal attention, direct mail, or advertising.

---

[11]Lazarsfeld *et al., op. cit.,* p. 151.

[12]For further discussion, see Elihu Katz, "The Two-Step Flow of Communication," *Public Opinion Quarterly,* Spring 1957, pp. 61–78; and Everett M. Rogers, *Modernization among Peasants: The Impact of Communication* (New York: Holt, Rinehart & Winston, Inc., 1969), p. 222.

2 Create opinion leaders out of certain persons, by supplying them with the product on attractive terms, or selecting them as company representatives.

3 Work through community influentials such as disc jockeys, class presidents, presidents of women's organizations.

4 Let the advertising feature interpersonal discussion of products or testimonials by influentials as part of the content.

5 Develop advertising that is high in "conversational value."

6 Choose salesmen who are of the same general social status as their prospects.[13]

Nonpersonal influence channels Nonpersonal influence channels tend to have a less insistent presence than personal influence, which means that audience members can more easily avoid or tune them out. Even during high-saturation campaigns, many members of the audience will not be reached. Three psychological processes, commonly referred to as factors of *perceptual defense*, operate to cut down the reach and impact of mass media. *Selective attention* means that a person notes only a small fraction of all the media vehicles and only a small fraction of their content. *Selective distortion* means that he may perceive the content differently than intended—because it is filtered through his needs and values. *Selective retention* means that he remembers certain things better than others—again because of his needs and values.

These selective processes have led recent writers to minimize the persuasive impact of the mass media, quite contrary to years ago when the mass media was seen as a brainwashing specter with total influence over the mind. The current view is that mass media do not accomplish *persuasion* (in the sense of changing men's minds) so much as *learning* and *reinforcement*.[14]

Message

We have argued that effective communication calls for (1) specifying the target audience and (2) determining the major channels for reaching this audience. The third step is to design product messages that are appropriate to the audience and the channels.

Message design requires the communicator's empathic understanding of the audience. For the *sent message* to be the *received message*, it must be encoded in a way that is meaningful to the receiver. Schramm has shown in Figure 15-3 the ingredients for successful communication.[15] Messages are essen-

---

[13]These and other points are discussed in Thomas S. Robertson, *Innovative Behavior and Communication* (New York: Holt, Rinehart & Winston, Inc., 1971), Chap. 9.

[14]For some development of this view, see Klapper, *op. cit.,* and Raymond Bauer, "The Limits of Persuasion," *Harvard Business Review,* September–October 1958, pp. 105–10.

[15]Wilbur Schramm, "How Communication Works," in *The Process and Effects of Mass Communication,* ed. W. Schramm (Urbana: University of Illinois Press, 1965).

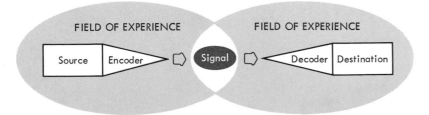

Figure 15-3
Elements affecting shared meaning

SOURCE: Wilbur Schramm, "How Communication Works," in *The Process and Effects of Mass Communication,* ed. W. Schramm (Urbana: University of Illinois Press, 1965), p. 4.

tially signs. The sender should select signs that will be familiar to the receiver. He is better able to do so, the greater the overlap in the field of experience of the two parties. "The source can encode, and the destination can decode, only in terms of the experience each has had."[16] Imagine what this implies for communicators from one stratum of society—advertising executives, teachers, and so on—who are trying to encode meaningful messages for members of another stratum.

A communicator wants to *choose* a message that has ideal stimulus value (message function) and construct the message for maximal impact (message structure). We shall consider each of these aims in turn.

Message function   What can a single message possibly do to a buyer? According to Maloney, not very much. "No single advertisement is likely to produce absolute 'belief' in a product. Rather, each advertisement is likely to make its most significant contribution by 'nudging' the consumer onto and along the path of the adoption process."[17] Most communicators expect to achieve extended effects as a result of a series of messages reaching the buyer at discretely separated intervals.

What effects? Messages can attempt to convey information, alter perceptions, stimulate desires, produce conviction, direct action, and provide reassurance. The choice of message depends largely on the state the audience is in. Each type of message works on a different set of principles.

We shall illustrate this by considering one type of message, the one that intends to stimulate a desire for a product. Suppose a new toothpaste brand is introduced into the marketplace and the manufacturer wants to encourage people to try it. What can he say about the new toothpaste to break through their existing brand choice patterns? Naturally he wants to talk in terms of the new brand's benefits to users, such as cleaner teeth, decay protection, sex appeal. But the other brands make the same claims. The general principle that should guide his message development is to create *cognitive dissonance* in the receiver. Two elements of knowledge are in a dissonant relationship if they contradict or do not square with each other. Dissonance ". . . being psychologically uncomfortable will motivate the person to try to reduce dissonance and achieve consonance."[18] He will try to eliminate the tension in one of several ways, one of which is to buy and try the product.

For example, the toothpaste manufacturer may say a major experiment has proved conclusively that his brand reduces cavities better than any other brand in the market. People using other brands for their presumed effectiveness in fighting tooth decay will now question their brand. "Is the new brand really better?" As they hear this claim repeated, the tension increases, because their present brand *or* the new brand must be better—they cannot both be "best." Their tension heightens their sensitivity to toothpaste advertisements and conversations about brands. They will try to eliminate the tension by either dismissing the claim as an advertising agent's gimmick or buying the brand to see for themselves. The latter step, of course, is what the manufacturer wants.

---

[16]*Ibid.*, p. 4.

[17]John C. Maloney, "Is Advertising Believability Really Important?" *Journal of Marketing.* October 1963, p. 6.

[18]Leon Festinger, *A Theory of Cognitive Dissonance* (New York: Harper & Row, Publishers, 1957), p. 13.

The toothpaste manufacturer may attempt to increase dissonance at a more basic level. He may find that many people are not overly concerned with tooth decay, in which case his claim of better decay-prevention does not get at the real issue. His job is to challenge the complacency people feel about their teeth. He must show that tooth decay is a real and frightening thing. This calls for a fear-building message to create tension and anxiety about one's teeth. The tension generated by the fear appeal will lead the individual to pay more attention to toothbrushing and the proper brand.

The use of fear or threat messages has a long history in marketing, as it has in other realms of human action, such as politics and child rearing. It used to be held that the message's effectiveness increased with the level of fear presented. The more fear-building, the more tension, and the greater the drive to reduce the tension. Then the famous 1953 study of Janis and Feshbach, in which they tested the effectiveness of different fear levels in a dental-hygiene message directed to high school students, indicated that the strong fear appeal was less effective than a moderate one in producing adherence to a recommended dental hygiene program.[19] For a while, this finding became the standard, that neither extremely strong nor weak fear appeals were as effective as moderate ones. Ray and Wilke supported this position by hypothesizing two types of effects as fear increases:

> First, there are the facilitating effects that are most often overlooked in marketing. If fear can heighten drive, there is the possibility of greater attention and interest in the product and message than if no drive were aroused. . . . But fear also brings the important characteristic of inhibition into the picture. . . . If fear levels are too high, there is the possibility of defensive avoidance of the ad, denial of the threat, selective exposure or distortion of the ad's meaning, or a view of the recommendations as being inadequate to deal with so important a fear.[20]

Other researchers have found cases where high fear appeals appear maximally effective. This may mean that the buyers have different tolerances for fear, and the level of the fear message should be set separately for different segments. Further, if the fear message is to be maximally effective, the communication should promise to relieve in a believable and efficient way the fear it arouses; otherwise the buyers will ignore or minimize the threat.[21]

Thus far we have been talking about messages that are effective because they create unpleasant appeals, and thus tension. Does this mean that pleasant messages will be less effective? If a pleasant message has any effect, it must work on a principle other than cognitive dissonance. The theory of the pleasant message is that the recipient is less likely to avoid it and will pick up a pleasant association that he will transfer to the product. Thus a toothpaste ad showing a person enjoying the aftertaste provides a *vicarious model* for the type of response the person can expect when he uses the product. Or a funny toothpaste commercial is expected to carry over good feelings to the product.

[19]Irving L. Janis and Seymour Feshbach, "Effects of Fear-Arousing Communications," *Journal of Abnormal and Social Psychology,* January 1953, pp. 78–92

[20]Michael L. Ray and William L. Wilke, "Fear: The Potential of an Appeal Neglected by Marketing," *Journal of Marketing,* January 1970, pp. 55–56.

[21]See Carl I. Hovland, Irving L. Janis, and Harold H. Kelley, *Communication and Persuasion* (New Haven: Yale University Press, 1953), pp. 87–88.

An unsettled issue is whether high, moderate, or low pleasantness in a message works best. Many observers feel that *intensity* of appeal is more important than the type of appeal, and favor high pleasantness or high unpleasantness over any intermediate levels. Thus the relative effectiveness of unpleasant versus pleasant messages and of levels within them is still in need of more definitive research.

Message structure   The stimulus value of a message is affected not only by the choice and intensity of appeal but also by the manner in which the message is structured. Research started many years ago by Hovland and his associates at Yale shed much light on such classic issues in rhetoric as conclusion drawing, one- versus two-sided arguments, and order of presentation.

Conclusion drawing raises the question of whether the communicator should draw a definite conclusion for the audience or leave it to them. In a laboratory-type experiment, Hovland and Mandell found that more than twice as many persons changed in the direction advocated when the conclusion was stated than when they were left to form their own conclusions.[22] However, other studies produced conflicting results, and it appears that some situations are unfavorable to conclusion drawing:

1   If the communicator is seen as untrustworthy, the audience may resent the attempt to influence them.
2   If the issue is simple, or the audience is intelligent, the audience may be annoyed at the attempt to explain the obvious.
3   If the issue is highly personal, the audience may resent the communicator's interference.

Sometimes drawing too explicit a conclusion, especially in the area of new products, can overly limit the product's acceptance. If the Mustang people had hammered away that the car was for young people, this strong definition might have ruled out the many other age groups who were attracted to it. Some *stimulus ambiguity* can play a definite role in leading to a broader market definition and more spontaneous uses of new products. It permits more people to read their own meaning into the product. Conclusion drawing seems better suited for complex or specialized products where a single and clear use is intended.

One- or two-sided arguments raise the question of whether the communicator should only praise the product or also mention or anticipate some of its short-comings. Intuitively, it would appear that the best effect is gained by a one-sided presentation: this is the predominant approach in sales presentations, political contests, and child rearing. Yet the answer is not so clear-cut. It depends on such things as the initial position of the audience, the audience's level of education, and the audience's exposure to subsequent communication.[23] (1) *One-sided messages tend to work best with audiences that are initially favorably predisposed to the communicator's position, whereas two-sided arguments tend to work best with audiences*

---

[22]Carl I. Hovland and Wallace Mandell, "An Experimental Comparison of Conclusion-Drawing by the Communication and by the Audience," *Journal of Abnormal and Social Psychology,* July 1952, pp. 581–88.

[23]See C. I. Hovland, A. A. Lumsdaine, and F. D. Sheffield, *Experiments on Mass Communication,* Vol. III (Princeton, N.J.: Princeton University Press, 1948), Chap. 8.

who are opposed. A seller of a new brand whose other products are well accepted might think of favorably mentioning the existing products and then going on to praise his new product. (2) *Two-sided messages tend to be more effective with better-educated audiences.* A salesman dealing with engineers might not pretend his product has it all over competing products but mention more factually where it excels and where it lags. (3) *Two-sided messages tend to be more effective with audiences who are likely to be exposed to counterpropaganda.* By mentioning a minor shortcoming in his product, a salesman takes the edge off this mention when it comes from a competitor, much as a small discomforting inoculation now prevents a greater sickness later. But he must be careful to inoculate only enough negative vaccine to make the buyer resistant to counterpropaganda, not to his own product. The success of some products that emphasize minor limitations, such as Benson & Hedges, Volkswagen, and Avis, derives from a two-sided message strategy.

Order of presentation raises the question of whether a communicator should present his strongest arguments first or last. In the case of a one-sided message, presenting the strongest argument first has the advantage of establishing attention and interest. This may be especially important in newspapers and other media where the audience does not attend to all of the message. However, it means an anticlimactic presentation. If the audience is captive, as in a sales presentation or conference, then a climactic presentation may be more effective. Studies have yielded both findings, and we can say only that the strongest arguments do *not* belong in the middle of the message. In the case of a two-sided message, the issue is whether to present the positive argument first (primacy effect) or last (recency effect). If the audience is initially opposed, it would appear that the communicator would be smarter to start with the other side's argument. This will tend to disarm the audience and allow him to conclude with his strongest argument. It does not appear that either the primacy or the recency effect dominates in all or most situations, and more research is needed into the underlying processes.

Communicator

The communicator influences the audience directly through his choice of message and channels and directly through how he is perceived by the audience. The latter is called the *source effect.*

Source credibility Marketers have known for years that messages delivered by highly credible sources will add to the persuasiveness of the message itself. Pharmaceutical companies will use doctors in their commercials to testify to their products' benefits because doctors have high credibility. Antidrug crusaders will use former drug addicts to warn high school students against drugs because ex-addicts have high credibility relative to teachers. Other marketers will hire well-known personalities such as newscasters or athletes to carry their messages.

But what factors underlie source credibility? The three factors most often identified are *expertness, trustworthiness,* and *likability.*[24] Expertness is related to the qualifications the person is perceived to possess for having knowledge of what he is claiming. Doctors, scientists, and professors rank high on expertness.

---

[24]Herbert C. Kelman and Carl I. Hovland, "'Reinstatement' of the Communicator in Delayed Measurement of Opinion Change," *Journal of Abnormal and Social Psychology,* 48 (1953), 327–35.

Trustworthiness is related to how disinterested the source is perceived to be. Friends are perceived to be more trustworthy than strangers or salespeople. Likability is related to how attractive the source is to the audience. Likability is a special affective quality that resides in the personality of the source.

The most highly credible source, then, would be a person who scored high on all three dimensions. If such a message carrier could not be found, it would be helpful to know the relative influence of expertness, trustworthiness, and likability on message acceptance. This will of course vary for different products and situations.

Source credibility plays a critical role during periods of shortages or rapid inflation. In a shortage the seller has to put his customers on allocation and they are suspicious of his fairness. In an inflation the seller has to raise prices which may easily appear excessive. In both cases the seller must strive to make his actions credible to his customers. For example, customers are more inclined to believe the statements of salesmen with whom they have dealt a long time than those of new salesmen. Customers will be more convinced when they hear experts explain the allocations or price increases. The company must seek source enhancement strategies to avoid losing the goodwill and confidence of its customers.

Source incongruity   If a person has a positive attitude toward a source and a message—or a negative attitude toward both—a state of congruity is said to exist. But what happens if he holds one attitude toward the source and the opposite toward the message? Suppose, for example, the person hears a celebrity (whom he likes) praise a brand (that he dislikes). Osgood and Tannenbaum posit that *attitude change will take place in the direction of increasing the amount of congruity between the two evaluations.*[25] In this example, the person will end up respecting the celebrity somewhat less and respecting the brand somewhat more. If this happens on further occasions with other negatively valued brands, he will eventually develop a negative evaluation of the celebrity and maintain his negative attitudes toward the brands. The principle of congruity says that the communicator can use his good image to reduce some negative feelings toward a brand, but in the process may lose some of his trusted standing, especially if he does this often.

THE PROMOTION MODEL

We now turn to the *promotion model*, which describes the array of tools available to the communicator whose major role is persuasive communication. Excluded are the marketing-mix elements of product, price, and place because, while they have some persuasive effects, their major role is not persuasive communication.

Table 15-1 lists the major promotional tools, or *promotools*. Each of these promotools has specific potentialities and complexities that could justify managerial specialization. Yet a company, even a very large one, typically does not have a specialist in each area but only in those areas where the importance

---

[25]C. E. Osgood and P. H. Tannenbaum, "The Principle of Congruity in the Prediction of Attitude Change," *Psychological Review*, 62 (1955), 42–55.

Table 15-1

Examples of promotools

Space advertising	Point-of-sale displays
Loudspeaker advertising	Sales literature
Mailings	Catalogs
Speeches	Films
Sales presentations	Trade exhibits
Demonstrations	Sales conference
Trading stamps	Packaging
Contests	House-organ publications
Premiums	Product publicity
Free samples	Corporate publicity
Price specials	Corporate identification programs
Coupons	Endorsements
Posters and show cards	

and usage frequency of the tool justify specialized competence. Historically, companies first made a separate function out of *personal selling*, later out of *advertising*, and still later out of *publicity*. The other tools in Table 15-1 are employed by the sales manager, advertising manager, or public relations manager as needed. In the early 1950s some large companies began to appoint sales promotion managers to handle or advise on miscellaneous promotion tools that no one cared about. The term *sales promotion* (as distinct from *promotion*) came gradually into wide use to describe a fourth component of the promotion mix. Today the following four components make up the promotion mix:

Advertising: any paid form of nonpersonal presentation and promotion of ideas, goods, or services by an identified sponsor.

Personal selling: oral presentation in a conversation with one or more prospective purchasers for the purpose of making sales.

Publicity: nonpersonal stimulation of demand for a product, service, or business unit by planting commercially significant news about it in a published medium or obtaining favorable presentation of it upon radio, television, or stage that is not paid for by the sponsor.

Sales promotion: those marketing activities, other than personal selling, advertising, and publicity, that stimulate consumer purchasing and dealer effectiveness, such as displays, shows and exhibitions, demonstrations, and various nonrecurrent selling efforts not in the ordinary routine.[26]

Here we will discuss the special qualities of each promotional component.

Advertising

In spite of the tight definition of advertising, it is far from a unitary thing. Advertising involves such varied media as magazine and newspaper space; radio and television; outdoor displays (such as posters, signs, skywriting); direct mail;

---

[26]*Marketing Definitions: A Glossary of Marketing Terms,* compiled by the Committee on Definitions of the American Marketing Association, Ralph S. Alexander, Chairman (Chicago: American Marketing Association, 1960). *Packaging* can be added as a fifth element of the promotion mix or be considered as part of sales promotion.

novelties (matchboxes, blotters, calendars); cards (car, bus); catalogs; directories and references; programs and menus; and circulars. It can be carried out for such diverse purposes as long-term buildup of the company name (institutional advertising), long-term buildup of a particular brand (brand advertising), information dissemination about a sale, service, or event (classified advertising), announcement of a special sale (sales advertising), and so on.

Because of the many forms and uses of advertising, it is hard to advance all-embracing generalizations about its distinctive qualities as a component of the promotional mix. Yet the following qualities can be noted, especially when it comes to brand and institutional advertising:[27]

1 *Public presentation.* Advertising, unlike personal selling, is a highly public mode of communication. Its public nature confers a kind of legitimacy to the product and also suggests a standardized offering. Because many persons receive the same message, buyers know that their motives for purchasing the product will be publicly understood.

2 *Pervasiveness.* Advertising is a pervasive medium that permits the seller to repeat his message many times. It also allows the buyer to receive and compare the messages of various competitors. Large-scale advertising by a seller says something positive about the seller's size, popularity, and success.

3 *Amplified expressiveness.* Advertising provides opportunities for dramatizing the company and its products through the artful use of print, sound, and color. Sometimes the tool's very success at expressiveness may, however, dilute or distract from the message.

4 *Impersonality.* Advertising, in spite of being public, pervasive, and expressive, cannot be as compelling as a personal salesman. The audience does not feel obligated to pay attention or respond. Advertising is only able to carry on a monologue, not a dialogue, with the audience.

Personal selling

Personal selling also takes several forms, such as sales calls by a field representative (field selling), assistance by a salesclerk (retail selling), and a golf invitation from one company president to another (executive selling). It can be used for many purposes, such as creating product awareness, arousing interest, developing product preference, negotiating prices and other terms, closing a sale, and providing posttransactional reinforcement.

Personal selling has certain distinctive qualities as a component of the promotional mix:

1 *Personal confrontation.* Personal selling involves an alive, immediate, and interactive relationship between two or more persons. Each party is able to observe at close hand the characteristics and needs of the other and make immediate adjustments. Each party has the potentiality to help or hurt the other by his interest or lack of it, and this can make the encounter stressful.

2 *Cultivation.* Personal selling permits all kinds of relationships to spring up, ranging from a matter-of-fact selling relationship to a deep personal friendship. In most cases, the salesman will be in a deferential position to the buyer; he must use art

[27]The distinctive qualities of advertising and personal selling, as found in this discussion, are adapted from Sidney J. Levy, "Promotional Behavior," *Managerial Analysis in Marketing,* ed. Frederick D. Sturdivant *et al.* (Glenview, Ill.: Scott, Foresman & Company, 1970), Chap. 8, pp. 418–20.

to woo him. The salesman at times will be tempted to put on pressure or to dis-semble to get an order, but at his best he will keep the customer's long-run interests at heart.

3 *Response.* Personal selling, in contrast with advertising, makes the buyer feel under some obligation for having listened to the sales talk or using up the salesman's time. He has a greater need to attend and respond, even if the response is a polite "thank you."[28]

Publicity

A company and its products can come to the attention of the public through being newsworthy. Here the seller pays nothing for the press he receives. The results of free publicity can sometimes be spectacular. Consider the case of the diet drink Metrecal:

> Almost overnight, Metrecal became part of the American tribal customs, fashions and language. The signs were everywhere. Drugstores served Metrecal across soda fountains. Newspapers printed Metrecal-inspired cartoons. Fashionable luncheon clubs served Metrecal cocktails. Steve Allen and a probate judge in Charleston, South Carolina, wrote songs about Metrecal. Don Wilson, the an-nouncer, danced "The Metrecal Bounce" on television. Overweight football players in Chicago ate at "the Metrecal table."[29]

Because of the sales potential of good publicity, many sellers have geared up to make a deliberate use of publicity, or "free advertising." This means preparing company or product-slanted news stories and features and trying to interest the press in using them. Companies have realized that special skills are required to write good publicity and "reach" the press, and they have turned this job over to professional public relations men. Because of their salaries and cost, however, publicity turns out not to be costless advertising.

Publicity has three distinctive qualities:

1 *High veracity.* News stories and features seem to most readers to be authentic, media-originated reports. Therefore readers are likely to regard news stories about products and companies as having a higher degree of veracity than if they came across as sponsored by a seller.

2 *Off guard.* Publicity can reach many potential buyers who otherwise avoid sales-men and advertisements. This is because the message is packaged in a way that gets to him as news rather than as a sales-directed communication.

3 *Dramatization.* Publicity has, like advertising, a potential for dramatizing a company or product.

Sales promotion

Sales promotion is the catchall for various promotools that are not formally classifiable as advertising, personal selling, or publicity. These tools may be sub-classified into items for *consumer promotion* (e.g., samples, coupons, money-refund offers, prices-off, premiums, contests, trading stamps, demonstrations), *trade*

---

[28]*Ibid.*, pp. 420–22.
[29]Peter Wyden, *The Overweight Society* (New York: William Morrow & Co., Inc., 1965), p. 50.

promotion (e.g., buying allowances, free goods, merchandise allowances, cooperative advertising, push money, dealer sales contests), and *sales-force promotion*
(e.g., bonuses, contests, sales rallies).[30]

The older concept saw sales promotion as an ad hoc collection of sales
tools to be used when necessary as a direct, short-term sales stimulus. With its
professionalization in recent years, sales promotion is increasingly viewed as an
important tool in its own right. It plays a critical role in the introductory and
maturity stages of the product life cycle and also appears to be especially effective during periods of rapid inflation. The level of expenditures on sales promotion has been variously estimated as ranging from 20 to 35 percent of the typical
company's promotion budget, which means that business firms may be spending anywhere between $15 billion and $25 billion annually on sales promotion. The effects of sales promotion are often more immediate and measurable
than those of advertising. Yet there has been insufficient research and decision
modeling devoted to it.[31]

Although sales promotion tools are a motley collection, they have two
distinctive qualities as a class:

1 *Insistent presence.* Many sales promotion tools have an attention-getting, sometimes urgent, quality that can break through habits of buyer inertia toward a
   particular product. They tell the buyer he has a chance that he won't have again
   to get something special. This appeals to a broad spectrum of buyers, although
   particularly to the economy-minded, with the disadvantage that this type of
   buyer tends to be less loyal to any particular brand in the long run.
2 *Product demeaning.* Some of these tools suggest that the seller is anxious for the
   sale. If they are used too frequently or carelessly, they may lead buyers to wonder
   whether the product class or brand is desirable or reasonably priced.

THE PROMOTION MIX

When the firm considers promotion as a whole, it faces two major decisions.
The first is how much total effort to invest in promotion; the second, how much
relative usage should be made of the different promotional tools.

Since promotion is only one of several ways to stimulate company sales,
the company faces the question of whether promotional funds could not be
spent better in marketing research, new-product development, lower prices, or
more customer services. These latter alternatives tend to increase the real value
of the company's offering in the buyer's mind. Buyers, if asked, would probably
want the company to cut down on promotion and use the funds to make the
offering more attractive.

Yet some promotion is essential in order to create customer awareness of
the product's existence and characteristics. Furthermore, promotion can create
positive psychological associations that can enhance the buyer's satisfaction.
In this last sense promotion may be considered to add to the real value of the
company's offering.

---

[30]An excellent discussion is found in John F. Luick and William Lee Ziegler, *Sales Promotion
and Modern Merchandising* (New York: McGraw-Hill Book Company, 1968).

[31]However, see Marketing Science Institute, *Promotional Decisions Using Mathematical Models*
(Boston: Allyn & Bacon, Inc., 1967).

The problem of how much for promotion is not difficult in principle. The total promotional budget should be established at a level where the marginal profit from the marginal promotional dollar just equals the marginal profit from using the dollar in the best nonpromotional alternative. A few generalizations might help indicate whether promotion will be a relatively important or unimportant component of the marketing mix. In general, promotion will be more important in markets where:

1 Products are alike, thus leading manufacturers to try to differentiate them psychologically.
2 Products are in the introductory stage of the life cycle, where awareness and interest must be built, or in the mature stage, where defensive expenditures are required to maintain market shares.
3 Products are sold on a mail-order basis.
4 Products are sold on a self-service basis.

The optimal proportion to use of the various promotion tools is a difficult question. The most striking fact about promotional tools is their substitutability. It is possible to achieve a given sales level by increasing advertising expenditures or personal selling, or by offering a deal to the trade or a deal to consumers. This substitutability explains why marketing departments are increasingly trying to achieve administrative coordination over all the instruments of promotion. The theory of determining the optimal marketing mix has already been reviewed in Chapter 8, pp. 170–76.

The promotion mix in consumer versus industrial marketing

Advertising is widely felt to be the most important promotool in consumer marketing, and personal selling the most important promotool in industrial marketing. Sales promotion is considered of equal, though smaller, importance in both markets. (And publicity is considered to have even smaller, but equal, importance in both markets.) This common view is illustrated in Figure 15-4.

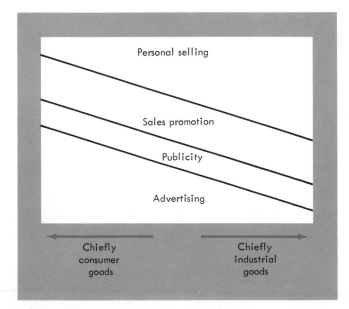

Figure 15-4

The promotional mix related to consumer and industrial goods

SOURCE: Modified from Patrick J. Robinson and Bent Stidsen, *Personal Selling in a Modern Perspective* (Boston: Allyn & Bacon, Inc. 1967), p. 57.

This view leads some marketers to act as if advertising is unimportant in industrial marketing and as if personal selling is unimportant in consumer marketing. Such conclusions are erroneous and can be refuted both in terms of common sense and some recent studies.

The role of advertising in industrial marketing   The industrial marketing situation appears to involve sellers of steel, heavy machinery, and so on confronting highly rational buyers who respond primarily to the quality of the product, its price, and delivery and reliability considerations. It would seem that a sales call would have much more impact than an advertising impression, especially if the product is complex. Yet consider the following functions that can be performed by advertising:

1   *Awareness building.* If the prospect is not aware of the company or product, he may refuse to see the salesman, or the salesman may have to use up a lot of time in introducing himself and his company.
2   *Comprehension building.* If the product represents a new concept, some of the burden of explaining it can be effectively carried on by advertising.
3   *Efficient reminding.* If the prospect knows about the product but is not ready to buy, an advertisement reminding him of the product would be much more economical than a sales call.
4   *Lead generation.* Advertisements carrying return coupons are an effective way to generate leads for salesmen.
5   *Legitimation.* Company salesmen can use tear sheets of the company's advertisements to legitimatize their company and products.
6   *Reassurance.* Advertising can remind customers how to use the product and reassure them about their purchase.

At least two different experiments have confirmed the important role played by advertising in a well-designed promotion program for industrial products. The first studied the effectiveness of four promotional tools—personal selling, advertising, education, and publicity—for introducing new business equipment. The typical sales transaction process was divided into four stages: awareness, comprehension, conviction, and order. About six weeks after the sales campaign began, interviewers contacted target customers to find out each customer's stage of awareness or interest and the types of communication efforts he recalled receiving. The results are summarized in Figure 15-5.

The results show that advertising, along with publicity, plays the most important role in the awareness stage, more than is played by "cold calls" from salesmen. Customer comprehension is primarily affected by education, with advertising and personal selling playing secondary roles, each equal to the other. Customer conviction is influenced most by personal selling followed closely by advertising. Finally, closing the sale is predominantly a function of the sales call. These findings have important practical implications. First, the company could effect promotional economies by cutting back on salesmen's involvement in the early stages of the selling job so that they could concentrate on the vital phase: closing the sale. Second, in relying on advertising to do more of the job, it should take different forms, some addressed to building product awareness and some to creating conviction.

The second study sought to determine the relative roles of the company's reputation (built mainly by advertising) and the company's sales presentation

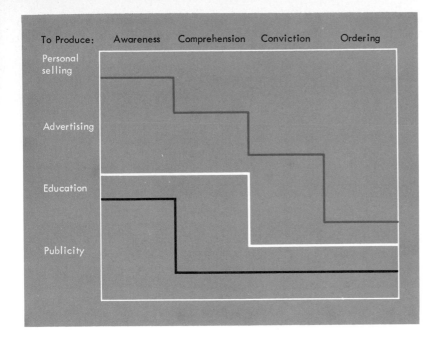

To Produce: Awareness Comprehension Conviction Ordering

Personal selling

Advertising

Education

Publicity

Figure 15-5
Contribution of different promotion instruments over the
sales transaction cycle

(personal selling) in producing sales.[32] The experiment consisted of showing various groups of purchasing agents different filmed sales presentations of a new, but fictitious, technical product for use as an ingredient in making paint. The variables were the quality of the presentation and whether the salesman represented a well-known company, a less known but creditable company, or an unknown company. The reactions and ratings of the purchasing-agent groups were collected after the films and then again five weeks later. The findings were:

1 A company's generalized reputation (the source effect) has a positive influence on sales prospects in improving the chances of (a) getting a favorable first hearing and (b) getting an early adoption of the product. Therefore, to the extent that corporate advertising can build up the company's reputation (other factors also shape its reputation), this will help the company's salesmen.

2 Salesmen from well-known companies have an edge in getting the sale, provided that their sales presentation is up to the expected standard. If, however, a salesman from a lesser-known company makes a highly effective sales presentation, this can overcome his disadvantage. To this extent, smaller companies may find it better to use their limited funds in selecting and training better salesmen rather than in advertising.

3 Company reputations tend to have the most effect where the product is complex, the risk is high, and the purchasing agent is less professionally trained.

In general, the findings confirm the constructive role of both advertising and the source effect in the industrial marketing process.[33] Findings such as

---

[32]Theodore Levitt, *Industrial Purchasing Behavior: A Study in Communications Effects* (Boston: Division of Research, Harvard Business School, 1965).

[33]Also see John E. Morrill, "Industrial Advertising Pays Off," *Harvard Business Review*, March–April 1970, pp. 4ff.

these have been developed by Cyril Freeman into a formal model for apportioning promotional funds between advertising and personal selling on the basis of the selling tasks that each performs more economically.[34]

The role of personal selling in consumer marketing The role of a company's sales force in consumer marketing would appear to be small relative to brand advertising. Many consumer companies use their sales force (or a middleman sales force) mainly to collect weekly orders from dealers and to see that sufficient stocks are held and displayed. The common feeling is that "salesmen put products on shelves and advertising takes them off."

Yet even here, an effectively trained sales force can make three important contributions:

1 *Increased stock position.* Persuasive salesmen can influence dealers to take more stock or devote more shelf space to the company's brand.
2 *Enthusiasm building.* Persuasive salesmen can build dealer enthusiasm for a new product by dramatizing the planned advertising and sales promotion backup.
3 *Missionary selling.* Salesmen are crucial in any effort to sign up more dealers to carry the company's brands.

Within the same consumer industry, companies can be found with quite different relative emphasis on the advertising, personal-selling mix. Nabisco and Kraftco rely very heavily on sales-force "push," while many of their competitors rely more heavily on advertising "pull." Revlon puts most of its promotional money into advertising, while Avon puts most of it into personal selling.

Promotion mix and the marketing organization

Members of the marketing organization have strong and varying feelings about the proper proportions of the company's promotion money to spend on the different promotools. The sales manager finds it hard to understand how the company could get more value by spending $60,000 on a one-minute television commercial than by hiring three or four additional salesmen for a whole year. Public relations also feels that the company can realize more through switching some of the advertising budget into publicity efforts. There is much disagreement on how money should be divided between advertising and sales promotion, and within advertising between institutional and brand advertising, and within sales promotion between consumer and trade deals.

Historically, companies left these decisions to different people. No one was given the responsibility for thinking through the roles of the various promotional tools and coordinating the company's communication and promotion mix. Today companies are moving rapidly toward the concept of *integrated communications*. This concept calls for:

1 Developing a corporate position, such as marketing communications director, who has overall responsibility for the company's persuasive communication efforts.
2 Working out a philosophy of the role and the extent to which the different promotools are to be used.

---

[34]Cyril Freeman, "How to Evaluate Advertising's Contribution," *Harvard Business Review*, July–August 1962, pp. 137–48.

3   Keeping track of all promotional investments by product, promotool, stage of product life cycle, and observed effect, as a basis for improving subsequent effective use of each tool.

4   Coordinating the promotional inputs and their timing when major campaigns take place.

One reason for this organizational integration is that an increasing number of promotional campaigns are multitooled and multibrand. In introducing a new product, the company has to coordinate advertisements in the major media, dealer shipments, trade deals, consumer deals, and publicity. Introduction of the new brand may even be tied to existing brands. All of this takes careful planning, timing, vision, and authority.

Another argument is that normally records are not kept of the different promotional effects tried for various company products. One product manager may be considering a spoon premium to boost sales, unaware that this type of premium bombed for another product manager. By centralizing and analyzing data on promotional efforts for a product over time and across products, the company is in an excellent position to improve its promotional planning.

Finally, integrated management of promotional activities promises more consistency in the company's *meaning* to its buyers and publics. It places a responsibility in someone's hand—where none existed before—to constructively worry about the company's image as it comes through the thousand activities the company carries on. It leads to the determination of a total marketing communications strategy aimed at showing how the company can help customers solve their problems.

SUMMARY

Promotion is one of the four major elements of the company's marketing mix. Promotion is the company's attempt to stimulate sales by directing persuasive communications to the buyers. The instruments of promotion—advertising, personal selling, sales promotion, and publicity—have separate and overlapping capabilities, and their effective coordination requires careful definition of communication goals.

Persuasive communication makes use of three basic models: the rhetorical model with its emphasis on a speaker and audience; the propagandistic model with its emphasis on an institution and potential supporters; and the negotiation model with its emphasis on two negotiators. These models are generalized in the communication model, which attempts to understand the communication process in terms of four major elements: communicator, message, channels, and audience. The communicator's planning proceeds in the reverse order, by first determining audience, then channels, message, and finally the source effect.

The promotion model describes the relative characteristics and properties of the four forms of promotion—advertising, personal selling, publicity, and sales promotion. The firm seeks to blend these elements into an optimal promotion mix. The pure theory calls for using these instruments up to the point where their marginal productivities are equal. Although consumer marketers appear to underplay personal selling and industrial marketers underplay advertising, these instruments have distinct contributions to make in any marketing program that involves the integrated communications concept.

1 Draw up a list of sales situations which can be aided by (a) atmospherics; (b) event management.

2 The dairy industry would like to interest teenagers in drinking more milk. Outline a nationwide promotion campaign using all the promotools and making use of the planning paradigm: audience, channels, message, and communicator.

3 An advertising agency is preparing a cake mix commercial. It is trying to choose between two copy versions. Version A allows the audience to share the entire product experience from the moment of purchase through the act of baking the cake and the family enthusiastically receiving it. Version B stops short of completing the process, hoping to involve the audience in imagining the rest. Which version do you think will be more effective and why?

4 A marketing research agency was asked to find out what consumers thought of the soft drink, Seven-Up. The agency found that most consumers regarded it as a wholesome drink. The company was pleased with this finding. Should they be?

5 A major basketball team has recently experienced a decline in home game attendance. The team's owner decided to hire a marketing man to stimulate attendance. What are some of the steps the marketing man can take?

6 A nationwide trucking company uses a combination of advertising and personal selling to stimulate demand for its services. Can you envision roles for publicity and sales promotion in the promotion of trucking services? What percentages of the total promotion budget should go into advertising, personal selling, publicity, and sales promotion?

7 The various mass media—newspapers, magazines, radio, television, and outdoor media—show striking differences in their capacity for dramatization, credibility, attention getting, and other valued aspects of communication. Describe the special characteristics of each media type.

8 Develop a set of thematic guidelines that laundry soap companies might follow in preparing soap ads aimed at upper-lower and lower-middle-class housewives in the 24–45 age bracket.

16
ADVERTISING DECISIONS

"Is your advertising getting results?"
"It sure is! Last week we advertised for a night
watchman and the next night we were robbed."

ANONYMOUS

Advertising is one of the four major tools by which the firm directs persuasive communications to target buyers and publics. It consists of *nonpersonal forms of communication conducted through paid media under clear sponsorship*. This form of communication runs up a bill of over $20 billion a year in the United States. It is a tool by no means restricted to commercial firms. Advertising is used by the U.S. Army, museums, fund raisers, and various social action organizations to bring messages about their causes and organizations to various target publics.

Within the commercial sector, the top 125 national advertisers account for as much as one-fifth of all national advertising. The top five spenders are Procter & Gamble ($310 million), Sears ($215 million), General Foods ($180 million), General Motors ($158 million), and Warner-Lambert ($141 million). The highest absolute spenders are found in soaps and cleaners, drugs and cosmetics, autos, food, and tobacco. The highest relative advertising spenders (as a percentage of sales) are found in drugs and cosmetics (between 10% and 20%), gum and candy (12%), and soaps (6% to 12%).[1]

Purpose of advertising

People have sought for years to define the purpose of advertising. In his *Madison Avenue, U.S.A.*, Martin Mayer sounded a skeptical note by saying: "Only the very brave or the very ignorant . . . can say exactly what advertis-

---

[1]For this information, see the special issue of *Advertising Age* on the one hundred leading national advertisers, August 26, 1974, esp. p. 28.

ing does in the marketplace." It is fairly clear, however, what advertising is *supposed* to do. In ultimate terms, advertising is undertaken to increase company sales and/or profits over what they otherwise would be. Advertising, however, is rarely able to create sales by itself. Whether the customer buys also depends upon the product, the price, the packaging, the personal selling, the services, the financing, and other aspects of the marketing process.

More specifically, the purpose of advertising is to enhance potential buyers' responses to the organization and its offerings. It seeks to do this by providing information, by trying to channelize desires, and by supplying reasons for preferring the particular organization's offering.

The power of advertising　There is much debate and confusion about the extent of advertising's power to influence buyer behavior. Critics of advertising such as Vance Packard charge that "many of us are being influenced and manipulated, far more than we realize, in the patterns of our everyday lives."[2] Packard believes that the scientific probing into subconscious motives has given advertising agencies unprecedented skill in molding buyer thought processes and purchasing decisions. Others dispute this position. They point to the few messages people really observe out of the thousands they are exposed to. They point to the immunity developed by many Americans to much of the advertising around them. They point to the fact that advertising is only one of several influences on a person's behavior and probably far less important—because it is known to be self-serving—than such influences as peers and personal observation.

It is difficult to know how effective advertising is, except in the more obvious cases. Direct-action advertising, such as mail-order and want ad advertising, purports to stimulate immediate sales. Its effectiveness is therefore directly measurable. Delayed-action advertising purports to build up favorable attitudes. There is little doubt that the brand advertising of such companies as Alberto-Culver and Revlon has been a major factor in their success, but one must remember that these companies also offer good products and have good merchandising and trade coverage. Effective advertising alone would not compensate for bad products or other faults in the marketing program. In fact, it can even hasten the demise of a bad product by accelerating its use and negative word of mouth. If the firm's offering is sound, however, advertising can make a significant contribution in the marketing process.

Various lists have been drawn up of the conditions under which advertising is likely to be a significant factor in the marketing process. The contribution of company advertising is likely to be greater:

> When buyer awareness is minimal.
> When industry sales are rising rather than remaining stable or declining.
> When the product has features normally not observable to the buyer.
> When the opportunities for product differentiation are strong.
> When discretionary incomes are high.

Defining advertising goals　The wide diversity of occasions for the use of advertising makes it essential that management develop a clear conception of what it specifically wants to achieve

---

[2]Vance Packard, *The Hidden Persuaders* (New York: Pocket Books, Inc., 1957), p. 1. For a contrary view, see Raymond A. Bauer, "Limits of Persuasion," *Harvard Business Review*, September-October 1958, pp. 105–10.

through its overall advertising effort as well as through particular advertising campaigns down to specific ads. Defining goals is the key requirement for effective advertising planning and the measurement of results. Yet the failure to define advertising goals is the leading deficiency, according to the two major studies.[3]

The ultimate goal of advertising is to increase the firm's profitability. Because of the difficulty of measuring this, most advertisers settle for more measurable goals. The possible goals, ranked in terms of ease of measurement (though inversely in terms of importance), are:

1 *Exposure.* Advertisers often set the goal of achieving a certain number of exposures per period to a target audience. An exposure means that a target member of the audience was exposed to the medium carrying the ad, not that he actually saw it. If 17 million people read *Time,* placing an ad in an issue of *Time* is considered as achieving 17 million exposures. Advertisers often get more specific and set goals for exposure *reach* and exposure *frequency.*

2 *Awareness.* Advertisers would have more confidence if they knew that the target audience actually heard or saw the ad. They may set a goal of achieving a certain level of audience awareness of the message. The campaign's success can be measured through surveys collecting audience ad recall or recognition.

3 *Attitudes.* A higher-level goal occurs when the advertiser specifies a certain level of favorable attitude he wants the advertising to achieve in the target audience. Attitudes are of course influenced by other things than the advertising, but the advertiser may want to measure as carefully as possible the attitude impact of the advertising campaign.

4 *Sales.* Companies would prefer to set a certain sales goal for their advertising to achieve. While the actual sales impact of advertising is difficult to isolate, some progress in measurement is being made.

Advertising goals should be formulated by advertisers as specifically as possible in order to guide the copy development, media selection, and results measurement. The stated goal "to create brand preference" is much weaker than "to establish 30 percent preference for brand X among Y million housewives by next year." Colley listed as many as fifty-two specific communication goals, including:

Announce a special reason for "buying now" (price, premium, and so on).

Build familiarity and easy recognition of package or trademark.

Place advertiser in position to select preferred distributors and dealers.

Persuade prospect to visit a showroom, ask for a demonstration.

Build morale of company sales force.

Correct false impressions, misinformation and other obstacles to sales.[4]

What are the major advertising decisions?

This chapter will examine the following major decisions called for in the realm of advertising:

How much should be spent for overall company advertising?

What message and mode of presentation should be used?

---

[3]See Russell H. Colley, ed., *Defining Advertising Goals* (New York: Association of National Advertisers, 1961); and H. D. Wolfe, J. K. Brown, and G. C. Thompson, *Measuring Advertising Results,* Studies in Business Policy, No. 102 (New York: The Conference Board, 1962).

[4]Colley, *op. cit.,* pp. 62–68.

What media should be used?

How should the advertising be phased during the year?

What are the best methods for knowing what the advertising is accomplishing?

SIZE OF THE ADVERTISING BUDGET

Common methods
for setting the
advertising budget

Each year the firm must decide how much to spend on advertising. Four of the more common methods in use are described below.[5]

"Affordable" method   Many companies set the advertising budget on the basis of what they think the company can afford. As told by one advertising executive:

> Why it's simple. First I go upstairs to the controller and ask how much they can afford to give us this year. He says a million and a half. Later, the boss comes to me and asks how much we should spend, and I say "Oh, about a million and a half." Then we have an advertising appropriation.[6]

Setting budgets in this manner is tantamount to saying that the relationship between advertising expenditure and sales results is at best tenuous. If the company has enough funds, it should spend them on advertising as a form of insurance.

The basic weakness of the affordable approach is that it leads to a fluctuating advertising budget that makes it difficult to plan for long-range market development.

Percentage-of-sales method   Many companies set their advertising expenditures at a specified percentage of sales (either current or anticipated) or of the sales price. A railroad company executive said:

> We set our appropriation for each year on December 1 of the preceding year. On that date we add our passenger revenue for the next month, and then take 2% of the total for our advertising appropriation for the new year.[7]

Automobile companies typically budget a fixed percentage for advertising based on the planned price for each car, and oil companies tend to set the appropriation as some fraction of a cent for each gallon of gasoline sold under their own label.

A number of advantages are claimed for this method. First, the percentage-of-sales method means that advertising expenditures are likely to vary with what the company can "afford." This pleases the more financial-minded members of top management who feel that expenses of all types should bear a close relation to the movement of corporate income and the business cycle. Second, this method encourages management to think in terms of the relationship

[5]For basic discussions, see Joel Dean, *Managerial Economics* (Englewood Cliffs, N.J.: Prentice-Hall, Inc., 1951), pp. 363–75; and David L. Hurwood and James K. Brown, *Some Guidelines for Advertising Budgeting* (New York: The Conference Board, 1972).

[6]Quoted in Daniel Seligman, "How Much for Advertising?" *Fortune*, December 1956, p. 123.

[7]Albert Wesley Frey, *How Many Dollars for Advertising?* (New York: The Ronald Press Company, 1955), p. 65.

between advertising cost, selling price, and profit per unit. Third, the method encourages competitive stability to the extent that competing firms spend approximately the same percentage of their sales on advertising.

In spite of these advantages, the percentage-of-sales method has little to justify it on theoretical grounds. It uses circular reasoning in viewing sales as the cause of advertising rather than as the result. It leads to an appropriation set by the availability of funds rather than by the opportunities. It discourages experimentation with countercyclical advertising or aggressive spending. The dependence of the advertising budget on year-to-year fluctuations in sales militates against the planning of long-range advertising programs. The method does not provide a logical basis for the choice of a specific percentage, except what has been done in the past, or what competitors are doing, or what the costs will be. Finally, it does not encourage the constructive development of advertising appropriations on a product-by-product and territory-by-territory basis but instead suggests that all allocations be made at the same percentage of sales.

Competitive-parity method   Some companies set their advertising budgets specifically to match competitors' outlays—that is, to maintain competitive parity. This thinking is illustrated by the executive who asked a trade source: "Do you have any figures which other companies in the builders' specialties field have used which would indicate what proportion of gross sales should be given over to advertising?"[8]

Two arguments are advanced for this method. One is that competitors' expenditures represent the collective wisdom of the industry. The other is that maintaining a competitive parity helps to prevent advertising wars.

Neither of these arguments is valid. There are no a priori grounds for believing that competition is using more logical methods for determining outlays. Advertising reputations, resources, opportunities, and objectives are likely to differ so much among companies that their budgets are hardly a guide for another firm to follow. Furthermore, there is no evidence that appropriations based on the pursuit of competitive parity do in fact stabilize industry advertising expenditures.

Knowing what competition is spending on advertising is undoubtedly useful information. But it is one thing to know this and another to follow it blindly.

Objective-and-task method   The objective-and-task method calls upon an advertiser to develop his budget by (1) defining his advertising objectives as specifically as possible, (2) determining the tasks that must be performed to achieve these objectives, and (3) estimating the costs of performing these tasks. The sum of these costs is the proposed advertising budget.

The method has strong appeal and popularity among advertisers. Its major limitation is that it does not indicate how the objectives themselves should be chosen and whether they are worth the cost of attaining them.

Decision models for setting advertising budgets

In recent years various researchers have designed advanced decision models for setting the advertising budget. These models differ in the advertising situation to which they are addressed and the type and number of variables they include. We shall review four of the models here.

---

[8]*Ibid.,* p. 49.

Sales-response and decay models The earliest advertising budgeting models attempted to measure the shape of the advertising sales-response function. Given this function, the profit-maximizing advertising outlay can be determined. As for the shape itself, the evidence is mixed.[9] Many analysts hold that the sales/advertising curve is S-shaped. This curve implies initial advertising economies of scale. According to Joel Dean:

> Larger appropriations may make feasible the use of expert services and more economical media. More important than specialization usually are economies of repetition. Each advertising attack starts from ground that was taken in previous forays, and where no single onslaught can overcome the inertia of existing spending patterns, the hammering of repetition often overcomes skepticism by attrition.[10]

Dean has also spelled out the reasons why diminishing returns to advertising can eventually be expected to set in:

> Presumably the most susceptible prospects are picked off first, and progressively stiffer resistance is encountered from layers of prospects who are more skeptical, more stodgy about their present spending patterns, or more attached to rival sellers. The rise may also be caused by progressive exhaustion of the most vulnerable geographical areas or the most efficient advertising media. Promotional channels that are ideally adapted to the scale and market of the firm are used first.[11]

Other models of the advertising sales-response function assumed that it was concave from the beginning (that is, additional advertising yielded continuously diminishing returns). One of the earliest and best of these models was developed by Vidale and Wolfe.[12] In their model, the change in the *rate of sales* at time t is a function of four factors: the *advertising budget*, the *sales-response constant*, the *saturation level of sales*, and the *sales-decay constant*. Their basic equation is

$$\frac{dS}{dt} = rA\,\frac{M - S}{M} - \lambda S \qquad\qquad (16\text{-}1)$$

where

S = rate of sales at time t

$\dfrac{dS}{dt}$ = change in the rate of sales at time t ⎫ *variables*

A = rate of advertising expenditure at time t ⎭

r = sales-response constant (defined as the sales generated per advertising dollar when $S = 0$)

M = saturation level of sales ⎬ *parameters*

λ = sales decay constant (defined as the fraction of sales lost per time unit when $A = 0$)

[9] For an excellent summary and evaluation of studies bearing on the shape of the sales/advertising curve, see Julian L. Simon, "Are There Economics of Scale in Advertising?" *Journal of Advertising Research,* June 1965, pp. 15–20.

[10] Dean, *op. cit.,* p. 357.

[11] *Ibid.,* p. 358.

[12] M. L. Vidale and H. B. Wolfe, "An Operations-Research Study of Sales Response to Advertising," *Operations Research,* June 1957, pp. 370–81.

The equation says that the change (increase) in the rate of sales will be higher, the higher the sales-response constant, the higher the advertising expenditure, the higher the untapped sales potential, and the lower the decay constant. Suppose, for example, the sales response to advertising dollars is estimated at 4, current sales are $40,000, saturation-level sales are $100,000 and the company loses .1 of its sales per period if no advertising expenditure is made. In this case, by spending $10,000 in advertising, the company can hope to achieve an additional $20,000 of sales:

$$\frac{dS}{dt} = 4(10,000)\frac{100,000 - 40,000}{100,000} - .1(40,000) = \$20,000$$

If the profit margin on $20,000 is better than 50 percent, it pays to spend the $10,000 on advertising.

The Vidale-Wolfe model can be embedded in a long-run profit equation and used to estimate the profit consequences of alternative advertising-budgeting strategies. Its main significance is that it brings together and relates three useful concepts for determining the proper size of the advertising budget.

Some models of sales response to advertising go beyond the Vidale-Wolfe model in the number of factors they postulate. A notable example is Kuehn's model.[13] Here company sales are a function of the percentage of customers with brand loyalty and the rate of decay in this brand loyalty; the percentage of customers not committed to this firm or its main competitor; the size and rate of growth of the total market; the relative influence of product characteristics, price, advertising, and distribution as selling influences; the relative influence of the *interaction* of product characteristics and advertising as a selling influence; and the relative share and effectiveness of this company's advertising expenditure. Using this model to describe company sales for the case of two-firm competition, Kuehn derived an optimal formula for setting advertising expenditures.

Communication-stage models Communication-stage advertising models arrive at an advertising budget by noting its effects on several intermediate variables that link advertising expenditures to ultimate sales. Ule developed an example to show how a manufacturer of a brand new filter-tip cigarette, Sputniks (name fictitious), could establish the necessary advertising budget.[14] The steps are as follows:

1 *Establish the market-share goal.* The advertiser wants 8 percent of the market. There are 50 million cigarette smokers, which means the company wants to attract 4 million regular Sputnik smokers.
2 *Determine the percent of the market that should be reached by Sputnik advertising.* The advertiser hopes to reach 80 percent (40 million smokers) with his advertising.
3 *Determine the percent of aware smokers that should be persuaded to try the brand.* The advertiser would be pleased if 25 percent of aware smokers, or 10 million smokers, tried

[13]Alfred A. Kuehn, "A Model for Budgeting Advertising," in *Mathematical Models and Methods in Marketing,* ed. Frank M. Bass *et al.* (Homewood, Ill.: Richard D. Irwin, Inc., 1961), pp. 302–53.
[14]G. Maxwell Ule, "A Media Plan for 'Sputnik' Cigarettes," *How to Plan Media Strategy,* American Association of Advertising Agencies, 1957 Regional Conventions, pp. 41–52.

Sputnik. This is because he estimates that 40 percent of all triers, or 4 million persons, would become loyal users. This is the market goal.

4 *Determine the number of advertising impressions per one percent trial rate.* The advertiser estimates that 40 advertising impressions (exposures) for every one percent of the population would bring about a 25 percent trial rate.

5 *Determine the number of gross rating points that would have to be purchased.* A gross rating point is one exposure to one percent of the target population. Since the company wants to achieve 40 exposures to 80 percent of the population, it will want to buy 3,200 gross rating points.

6 *Determine the necessary advertising budget on the basis of the average cost of buying a gross rating point.* To expose one percent of the target population to one impression costs an average of $3,277. Therefore 3,200 gross rating points would cost $10,486,400 (= $3,277 × 3,200) in the introductory year.

Ule's method is essentially an implementation of the objective-and-task method. It has the advantage of requiring management to spell out its assumptions about the relations between dollars spent, exposure levels, trial rates, and regular usage. Its major conceptual weakness is that the market-share goal is established at the beginning on the basis of what management wants, rather than as a result derived from a profit-maximizing approach to sales.

This deficiency is made up in a microlinkage advertising model called DEMON.[15] DEMON, an acronym for Decision-Mapping via Optimum GO-NO Networks, was developed under the auspices of the advertising agency of Batten, Barton, Durstine and Osborne. The model is oriented toward new products, and most of its logic deals with finding the profit-maximizing advertising budget. The marketing planning framework is illustrated in Figure 16-1. Three different marketing decision variables are shown to affect the number of triers: advertising, sales promotion, and distribution. Some percentage of triers become users, and their number, usage rate, and the product's price mul-

---

[15]David B. Learner, "Profit Maximization through New-Product Marketing Planning and Control," in *Applications of the Sciences to Marketing Management*, ed. Frank M. Bass, Charles W. King, and Edgar A. Pessemier (New York: John Wiley & Sons, Inc., 1968), pp. 151–67.

Figure 16-1
Marketing planning framework of DEMON

SOURCE: Redrawn from David B. Learner, "Profit Maximization through New-Product Marketing Planning and Control," in *Application of the Sciences to Marketing Management,* ed. Frank M. Bass *et al.* (New York: John Wiley & Sons, Inc., 1968), p. 153.

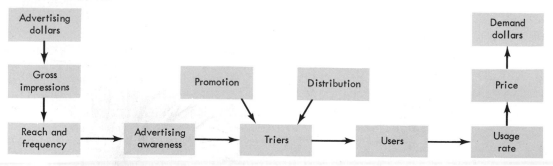

tiply out to the level of demand in dollars. Costs can then be netted against revenue to produce an estimate of expected profits.

The effect of advertising on sales is spelled out in the greatest detail. The company's advertising dollars first produce a certain number of gross impressions or exposures. These gross impressions come in the form of a certain percentage reached of the target market at a certain average frequency. DEMON then translates the advertising reach and frequency into a number of persons who become aware. Ad awareness is defined as "the number of people in the target audience who can recall having seen or heard the message—not merely brand recall, but rather awareness of the advertising message." The given level of ad awareness, along with given levels of sales promotion and distribution, is then expected to create a certain trial rate. The DEMON designers applied least-squares regression techniques to the data for over two hundred packaged goods in sixteen product categories to estimate the functional relationship at each stage. With these functional relationships, they are able to test different marketing-mix plans in search of the best one.

Adaptive-control models Adaptive advertising budgeting models make the assumption that the parameters of the advertising sales-response function are not stable but change through time. If they were stable, it would pay the company to make a big effort to measure the functions as soon and as accurately as possible because the benefits in achieving optimization would extend far into the future. However, there is good reason to believe that the parameters are not stable because of continuously changing competitive activity, advertising copy, product design, and national economic activity. In this case it would not pay to invest heavily in learning the exact parameters of the sales response function in the current period. Suppose the parameters change slowly through time. Then the best research strategy would be to collect some new information each time about the current parameters and combine this with the old information to produce new estimated parameters for the sales-response function on which the current outlay for promotion can be based.

The manner in which the periodic data can be collected and used to determine an optimal advertising expenditure has been described by Little.[16] Advertising expenditures should be set each period in such a way as to yield information about the current levels of the sales-response parameters. Suppose the company has picked an advertising expenditure rate for the coming period on the basis of applying profit-maximization criteria to its most current information on the sales function. It then decides to spend this rate in all markets except a subset of $2n$ of them randomly drawn. In n of the test markets the company will plan to spend a deliberately low amount of dollars, and in the other n it will plan to spend a deliberately high amount of dollars. This experiment will yield information on the average sales created by the low, medium, and high rates of advertising, and this will provide the best estimate of the current sales-response function. In turn, this estimate is used to determine the best promotional rate for the next period. If this procedure is carried out each period, actual advertising expenditures will track closely to the optimal advertising expenditures. Several large companies, including Du Pont and Anheuser-Busch,

---

[16]John D. C. Little, "A Model of Adaptive Control of Promotional Spending," *Operations Research*, November 1966, pp. 1075–97.

are known to set aside matched test markets in which they advertise at substantially higher and lower promotional rates in order to measure the effects of advertising.

Competitive-share models   The preceding models do not explicitly take competitors' expenditures into account. This omission is valid where there are many competitors, none of whom is large; or where it is difficult for companies to know what others are spending for advertising. In many situations, however, firms know what others are spending and try to maintain a competitive parity. In these situations a firm must take competitive reactions into account in determining its own advertising appropriation.

Under certain assumptions, the problem can be treated with some of the techniques of game theory. Friedman has developed some models to show how fixed advertising budgets should be allocated by two duopolists to different territories under the assumption that each is interested in taking maximum advantage of the other's mistakes.[17] He distinguishes between the case where resulting company sales are proportional to the company's share of advertising expenditures and the case where the company with 50-plus percent of the total advertising takes the whole market (as when a single customer is at stake).

Most models incorporate *the fundamental theorem of market-share determination:* that market shares in the long run will tend to equal marketing-effort shares.[18] The idea that market shares approximate effort shares is frequently expressed by businessmen. "To *get* a 10 percent share of market, you have to spend roughly 10 percent of all marketing funds." In many industries the correlation is high— but perhaps the reason is the tendency of companies to set their marketing budgets as a ratio to sales.

Competitive-share determination and interaction is a more dynamic phenomenon than the foregoing discussion suggests. Competitors may adopt a wait-and-see attitude toward the advertising spending level of the firm. If the firm's sales increase significantly, competitors may increase their own expenditures, cut prices, expand their sales force, and so on. Each type of reaction would have a different effect on market share. Finally, even if competitors did react by increasing their advertising expenditures, it makes a difference how they spend the additional funds—whether they develop a new copy approach, move toward broader media coverage, or adopt some other strategy. A game-theoretic approach seems almost too simple to catch the flavor of the uncertainties and issues posed by competition.

MESSAGE DEVELOPMENT

The effect of advertising on sales is not simply a function of *how much* is spent. Even more important may be *how* it is spent—specifically, what is said, how it is said, where it is said, and how often it is said.

Most of the statistical studies of the effect of advertising on sales or attitude have tended to neglect the creative factor. Some analysts rationalize the

---

[17]Lawrence Friedman, "Game-Theory Models in the Allocation of Advertising Expenditures," *Operations Research*, September–October, 1958), pp. 699–709.

[18]This theorem is discussed in Chapter 6, pp. 122–24.

omission of creative factors with the argument that all large advertising agencies are equally creative and therefore differences in individual campaigns tend to "wash out." But it is precisely the differences in individual campaigns that advertisers want to note and exploit. The consequence of leaving out the creative factors is that a substantial part of the movement of market shares remains "unexplained."

One study claims to have overcome the neglect of the creative factor.[19] A five-year study of sixty-seven different television campaigns led to the development of a multiple-regression formula that purportedly "explained" 73 percent of the fluctuations in market shares. What is most interesting is that one of the three independent variables was a measure of the effectiveness of message content. The study's major conclusion is that a campaign's quality is far more important than the number of dollars spent. Whether this is actually so, there is no doubt that differences in creative strategy are very important in advertising success.

Many things can be said about any product. But buyers will neither believe nor remember too many claims. Message focus is needed so that the buyer can learn something distinctive about the product. Every ad or campaign should be built on a central theme (also called motif, idea, appeal, or selling proposition). Advertisers go through three stages to develop their message: message generation, message evaluation and selection, and message execution.

Message generation

Message generation is the problem of finding effective things to say about the product to the target markets. Properly speaking, the message strategy is determined by the prior decisions on the product concept, product positioning, and other elements of the marketing strategy and objectives. If the product has been properly conceived and positioned, the advertising message is almost predetermined.

At the same time, a product faces many new challenges as it passes through its life cycle. There is a constant need to review the attributes of the product and the benefits sought by the market to determine the timeliness of the message. A leading hair-spray company, for example, carries out consumer research annually to determine consumer dissatisfaction with existing brands. If it is the hair-spray's holding power this year, this would be a good appeal, assuming that the company's brand promises good holding power or can be reformulated to meet this claim.

Creative people use different methods to generate possible advertising appeals. Many creative people proceed *inductively*. They talk to consumers, dealers, experts, and competitors to spot ideas. Consumers are by far the most important source of good ideas. Their feelings about the strengths and shortcomings of existing brands provide the most important clues to creative strategy. Even the way customers put their satisfactions and dissatisfactions into words can provide orienting ideas for campaigns. Dealers, suppliers, competitors, and office brainstorming also supply a pool of good ideas.

Today there is increasing interest in *deductive* frameworks for generating advertising appeals. Two such frameworks will be briefly described here. The first is the framework provided by product-positioning theory. The advertiser

---

[19]See "New Study Tells TV Advertisers How Advertising Builds Sales and Share of Market," *Printer's Ink*, May 8, 1964, pp. 27–38.

recognizes that his brand currently occupies a certain perceived position in the product space. To alter the market's behavior toward his brand, he may adopt one or more of six communication strategies:

1 Attempt to shift his brand's perceived location in the product space in a direction closer to the ideal point of his target market.
2 Attempt to shift the ideal point of the target market closer to the present position of his product.[20]
3 Attempt to demonstrate through comparison advertising that competitors' products are further away from the ideal point than commonly supposed.
4 Attempt to alter the relative saliencies of the existing attributes in the buyer's mind.
5 Attempt to introduce new attributes into the product space on which his brand rates strong.
6 Attempt to introduce his brand into new product spaces and target markets.

Viewing the product-positioning opportunities facing a brand provides a rich number of possible communication messages.

Maloney proposed an alternative deductive framework for message generation.[21] He suggested that buyers may be expecting any of four types of reward from an offering: *rational, sensory, social,* or *ego-satisfaction*. And they may visualize these rewards from *results-of-use experience, product-in-use experience,* or *incidental-to-use experience*. Crossing the four types of rewards with the three types of experience gives twelve different modes of buyer evaluation to be found concurrently in the marketplace. The advertiser can generate a theme for each of the twelve cells as possible messages for his product. For example, the appeal "gets clothes cleaner" is a rational reward promise following results-of-use experience; and the appeal "real gusto in a great light beer" is a sensory reward promise connected with product-in-use experience.

Message evaluation and selection

The task of selecting the best message out of a large number of possibilities calls for the introduction of some criteria for judging the market potency of different messages. Twedt has suggested that the contending appeals be rated on three scales: *desirability, exclusiveness,* and *believability*.[22] He believes that the market potency of an appeal is a function of a multiplicative relationship among the three named factors—multiplicative because if any of the three has a low rating, the appeal's market potency will be greatly reduced. The appeal must first say something desirable about the product. This is not enough, however: many brands will be making the same claim. Therefore the statement must also say something exclusive that does not apply to every brand in the product category. Finally, the statement must be either believable or provable. By getting a sample of consumers to rate different product statements on the three scales of *desir-*

---

[20]Strategy 2 is harder to accomplish than strategy 1. The marketing concept advises that it is easier to offer something that matches what buyers want than to attempt to persuade buyers to change their wants.

[21]John C. Maloney, "Marketing Decisions and Attitude Research," in *Effective Marketing Coordination,* ed. George L. Baker, Jr., (Chicago: American Marketing Association, 1961), pp. 595–618.

[22]Dik Warren Twedt, "How to Plan New Products, Improve Old Ones, and Create Better Advertising," *Journal of Marketing,* January 1969, pp. 53–57.

ability, exclusiveness, and *believability,* these statements can be numerically rated and ranked for market potency.[23]

Consumer ratings of ad appeals are not completely reliable however; they reflect opinion and not necessarily behavior. The advertiser should employ some pretest procedure to determine which final appeals are the strongest. For example, the Washington State Apple Commission was trying to decide which of two advertising themes for apples appealed more to housewives.[24] One theme stressed the various *uses* of apples; the other, the *healthful* qualities of apples. An experiment was carried out in seventy-two self-service food stores in six midwestern cities for sixteen weeks. An analysis of the final sales results revealed that the apple use theme was significantly more effective in promoting sales than the health theme.

Message execution

The impact of an advertisement depends not only upon what is said but also upon how it is said. In fact, message execution may be decisive in those industries, such as detergents or cigarettes, where companies use substantially the same appeals.

Message execution calls for decisions on *message structure,* that is, the way in which the major arguments will be phrased and phased to achieve maximal impact. We discussed in the preceding chapter such issues as conclusion drawing, one- versus two-sided arguments, and order of presentation.

Another step in message execution is *copy development,* that is, finding the words, pictures, symbols, colors, and tones that lend potency to the chosen theme. Agencies often provide broad rules to guide their creative personnel. Among the rules are: (1) design the ad to attract attention, (2) tailor the message to the media, (3) keep the message as simple as possible, and (4) use words and images that are relevant and familiar to the audience. Some agencies are more specific. David Ogilvy developed the prescription "To attract women, show babies or women; to attract men, show men." His agency followed this rule in developing the highly successful "The Man in the Hathaway Shirt" and "The Man from Schweppes." Ogilvy also holds that ads should not strive to be funny but should be informative. "People are amused by clowns—they don't buy from them." This is contrary to the widely held view that humor evokes less perceptual defense in the audience and develops pleasant, better-remembered associations with the product.[25]

The *format elements* of the ad—size, color, headlines, and so forth—can make a large difference in its impact, as well as in its cost. In an analysis of business ads, the two most prominent factors affecting the level of readership were pictorial color and size, both of which are mechanical variables rather than content variables in the advertisements.[26]

---

[23]For a good illustration of the method applied to selecting a "birth-defects" theme for a March-of-Dimes fund-raising campaign, see William A. Mindak and H. Malcolm Bybee, "Marketing's Application to Fund Raising," *Journal of Marketing,* July 1971, pp. 13–18.

[24]See Peter L. Henderson, James F. Hind, and Sidney E. Brown, "Sales Effects of Two Campaign Themes," *Journal of Advertising Research,* December 1961, pp. 2–11.

[25]For an insightful analysis of the role of humor in advertising, see Brian Sternthal and C. Samuel Craig, "Humor in Advertising," *Journal of Marketing,* October 1973, pp. 19–26.

[26]Dik Warren Twedt; "A Multiple Factor Analysis of Advertising Readership," *Journal of Applied Psychology,* June 1952, pp. 207–15. Also see Daniel S. Diamond, "A Quantitative Approach to Magazine Advertisement Format Selection," *Journal of Marketing Research,* November 1968, pp. 376–87.

How many advertisements should be created?	The client typically wants the agency to create and test several alternative ideas before making a selection. The more ads created, the higher the probability that the agency will find a first-rate one. Yet the more time it spends creating alternative ads, the higher the costs. Therefore it would seem that there must be some optimal number of alternative ads that an agency should try to create and test for the client.

If the agency were reimbursed by the client for the cost of creating ads, the agency would create the optimal number. Under the present commission system, however, the agency does not like to go to the expense of creating and pretesting many ads. In an ingenious study, Gross concluded that agencies generally create too few advertisement alternatives for their clients.[27] The advertiser does not get a very good ad but only the best (hopefully) of the few that have been created.

Gross estimates that advertising agencies spend from 3 to 5 percent of their media income on creating and testing advertising, whereas he estimates they should be spending closer to 15 percent. He thinks agencies should devote a larger part of their budget to finding the best ad and somewhat less to buying media. He proposed splitting advertising agencies into two types, purely creative agencies and marketing agencies. The company hires a marketing agency, and this agency in turn hires several creative agencies to create advertisements from which the best one is selected.

MEDIA SELECTION

An important part of the advertising job consists of deciding on the best media for carrying the advertising message to the target market. The advertiser is trying to achieve a certain *reach, frequency, impact,* and *continuity* with his advertising budget. He needs to know the target market's media habits and the qualities and costs of different media.

The selection of the major media categories will be examined first and then the selection of specific media vehicles within these categories. The problem of scheduling the advertising will be examined in the next section.

Choosing among major media categories	The extent to which the firm should use television, radio, newspapers, magazines, billboards, and other media depends on at least three factors.

The target audience's *media habits* are the first factor to consider in media category selection. Taking an extreme case, a company producing toys for preschoolers—and believing that the children rather than their parents should be reached—would stay away from newspapers, magazines, and radio. The only medium that reaches preschoolers, and reaches them effectively, is television.

The *product* is another important factor. The major media categories have different potentialities for demonstration, visualization, explanation, believability, and color. A product like Polaroid cameras is best advertised through live demonstrations in the television medium. A product like dresses, where color might be important, is best advertised in a color medium like magazines.

---

[27]Irwin Gross, "An Analytical Approach to the Creative Aspects of Advertising Operations" (Ph.D. Dissertation, Case Institute of Technology, November 1967).

The *cost* of the different media is a third factor. Television is a very expensive medium, whereas newspaper advertising is comparatively inexpensive. Yet what is ultimately important is not the absolute cost differences but audience size and composition in relation to these costs. On a per-thousand cost basis, it may be cheaper to reach buyers through television than through newspapers.

Selecting specific media vehicles

The first stage of analysis should result in a decision on how much to spend in each media category. The decision may be made, for example, to spend approximately $240,000 out of a $1 million advertising budget on magazines. But which magazines? And how many issues of each should be purchased?

At this point the media planner turns to several volumes put out by Standard Rate and Data that provide cost, circulation, and other information on hundreds of magazines. The prices are given for different ad sizes, color options, ad positions, and quantities of insertions. Most magazines offer quantity discounts varying with the number of purchased insertions for the year.

The cost-per-thousand criterion   Media planners try to calculate the *cost per thousand persons* reached by the particular vehicle. If a full-page, four-color advertisement in *Time* costs $50,000 and *Time*'s estimated readership is 10 million persons, then the cost of reaching each one thousand persons is $5. The same advertisement in *Business Week* may cost $15,000 but reach only 2 million persons, at a cost per thousand of $7.50. The media planner would rank the various magazines according to cost per thousand and place advertisements in those magazines with the lowest cost per thousand.

The cost-per-thousand criterion, at least in its simple form, has come under increasing attack. Its major fault is that it uses the figure for the total readership of the magazine instead of weighing the different readership groups by their *exposure value*. For a baby lotion advertisement, the exposure value might be 1 million if all the readers were young mothers and zero if all the readers were old men.

The second weakness has to do with the concept of an exposure. An exposure is said to take place to all readers of *Time* when an advertisement is placed in *Time*. In point of fact, only a fraction of *Time*'s readers will perceive the advertisement, a smaller fraction will grasp the message, and a still smaller fraction will be impressed positively. The ultimately desirable unit would be the number of target readers who both see and are motivated by the advertisement. But this unit is almost impossible to estimate.

A third weakness of cost-per-thousand is that it neglects qualitative differences that might exist in the editorial image and impact of different magazines. Even if two magazines reach the same number of target buyers, an advertisement may take on more believability, prestige, or other qualities in one magazine than the other.

A fourth weakness of cost-per-thousand is that it tends to be used in an average sense rather than in a marginal sense. If a magazine retained its lowest-cost-per-thousand standing independently of how much it is used, then logically the entire magazine budget should be spent on it. In reality, the magazine may quickly lose its cost-per-thousand advantage as more advertisements are placed in it. This is because successive-issue ads are seen largely by the same people, with possibly diminishing impact in relation to what could be achieved by exposing new readers to the advertisement through new magazines.

Computerized media selection   An increasing number of agencies are using a computer program to develop their advertising media plan. At least three different basic types of models are in use.

LINEAR PROGRAMMING   Linear programming seems like a natural format for analyzing the media-selection problem. The method can be used to discover the media mix that will maximize the number of effective exposures subject to a set of constraints—in this case the advertising budget, minimum and maximum media availabilities, and minimum desired exposure rates.

Figure 16-2 shows the linear programming statement of the media-selection problem. In the sample problem, the total advertising budget is $500,000, and at least $250,000 must be spent on medium one. Medium one gives 3,100 (in thousands) effective exposures with each use and costs $15,000. It is possible to buy anywhere between 0 and 52 advertisements in medium one over a year's time. The other values are similarly interpreted. Given these con-

Figure 16-2
Linear programming model for a media selection

Sample statement

Maximize $E = e_1X_1 + e_2X_2 + \ldots + e_nX_n$ } Effectiveness function

$E = 3,100X_1 + 2,000X_2 + \ldots + 2,400X_n$

Subject to $c_1X_1 + c_2X_2 + \ldots + c_nX_n \leq B$ } Budget constraint

$15,000X_1 + 4,000X_2 + \ldots + 5,000X_n \leq 500,000$

$c_1X_1 + c_2X_2 \qquad \leq B_1$ } Media category usage constraint

$15,000X_1 \qquad \geq 250,000$

$X_1 \qquad \geq k_{1L}$

$X_1 \qquad \geq 0$

$X_1 \qquad \leq k_{1U}$

$X_1 \qquad \leq 52$

$X_2 \qquad \geq k_{2L}$

$X_2 \qquad \geq 1$

$X_2 \qquad \leq k_{2U}$ Individual medium usage constraints

$X_2 \qquad \leq 8$

$\vdots$

$X_n \geq k_{nL}$

$X_n \geq 6$

$X_n \leq k_{nU}$

$X_n \leq 12$

where:

E = total exposure value (number of rated exposures)

e_i = exposure value of one ad in medium i

X_i = number of ads placed in medium i

c_i = cost of one ad in medium i

B = total advertising budget

B_1 = part of advertising budget

k_{iL} = minimum number of units to purchase of medium i

k_{iU} = maximum number of units to purchase of medium i

crete values, a mathematical solution technique is used to find the precise optimum solution to the problems as stated.[28]

The problem, as stated, unfortunately contains a number of artificialities. The four most important limitations are: (1) linear programming assumes that repeat exposures have a constant marginal effect; (2) it assumes constant media costs (no discounts); (3) it cannot handle the problem of audience duplication; and (4) it fails to say anything about when the advertisement should be scheduled.

HEURISTIC PROGRAMMING   An alternative technique proceeds with a sequential rather than a simultaneous selection of media. The basic idea is to start with the media available in the first week of the year and select the single best buy. After this selection is made, the remaining media choices are re-evaluated to take into account audience duplication and potential media discounts. A second selection is made for the same week if the *achieved* exposure rate for the week is below the *optimal* rate. The latter is a complex function of several marketing and media variables. This continues until the optimal exposure rate for the week is reached, at which point new media choices are considered for the following week. This cycling process continues until the year's schedule is completed.[29]

The sequential procedure has four advantages: (1) it develops a schedule simultaneously with the selection of media; (2) it handles the audience-duplication problem; (3) it handles the media-discount problem; and (4) it incorporates theoretically important variables such as brand-switching rates and multiple-exposure coefficients.

SIMULATION MODEL   A simulation model does not profess to find the "best" media plan but rather to estimate the exposure value of any given media plan. For example, the Simulmatics media model consists of a sample universe of 2,944 make-believe media users representing a cross section of the American population by sex, age, type of community, employment status, and education. Each individual's media choices are determined probabilistically as a function of his socioeconomic characteristics and location in one of ninety-eight American communities. A particular media schedule is exposed to all the persons in this hypothetical population. The computer tabulates the number and types of people being exposed. Summary graphs and tables are prepared at the end of the hypothetical year's run, and they supply a multidimensional picture of the schedule's probable impact. The advertiser examines these tabulations and decides whether the audience profile and the reach and frequency characteristics of the proposed media schedule are satisfactory.

Simulation complements rather than competes with the preceding models. Its major limitations are: (1) simulation normally does not include an overall effectiveness function; (2) it lacks a procedure for finding better schedules; and (3) the representativeness of the hypothetical population is always suspect.

OTHER MODELS   Current media models have gone beyond these simple ones to incorporate additional variables and complications. Little and Lodish

---

[28]See James F. Engel and Martin R. Warshaw, "Allocating Advertising Dollars by Linear Programming," *Journal of Advertising Research*, September 1964, pp. 41–48.

[29]For an example, see William T. Moran, "Practical Media Decisions and the Computer," *Journal of Marketing*, July 1963, pp. 26–30.

created one of the best models, which they call MEDIAC.[30] MEDIAC handles in an analytical fashion a large number of marketing and advertising facets of the real media problem, such as market segments, sales potentials, exposure probabilities, diminishing marginal response rates, forgetting, seasonality, and cost discounts. It is programmed for on-line access in a conversational mode so that the user can follow the model's logic, supply the requested data, and receive in a matter of minutes an optimal media schedule. The user can easily change the data inputs and note the effect on the media schedule.

Computerized media-selection models should be thought of as an aid rather than a substitute for executive judgment. The computer can produce or "test" in a matter of hours a media plan that formerly might have taken days or weeks. The plan itself must be regarded only as a starting point. This sounds paradoxical, because it may represent the optimum solution to a mathematical programming statement of the media problem. But it must be remembered that the programming statement is somewhat artificial in the weights used and the constraints set up. The media planner will want to bring his judgment to bear on the quality of the plan as a whole as well as on its parts. He may want to revise some of the specifications in the programming statement of the problem. A great advantage of the computer is that new plans can be quickly generated to show the significance of changes made in problem specifications. The final media plan should be the joint product of the machine's ultralogical mind and man's imagination and judgment.

TIMING OF ADVERTISING EXPENDITURES

A major advertising decision involves the timing of advertising expenditures throughout the year. We shall distinguish between the macroscheduling problem and the microscheduling problem.

Macroscheduling problem

The macroscheduling problem involves describing how to allocate advertising expenditures over the year in response to the seasonal pattern of industry sales. Suppose industry sales of a particular product peak in December and slough in March. Any individual seller in this market has three broad options. The firm can vary its advertising expenditures to follow the seasonal pattern; it can vary its advertising expenditures to oppose the seasonal pattern; or it can hold its expenditures constant throughout the year. The vast majority of firms tend to pursue a policy of seasonal rather than constant or counterseasonal advertising. Even here, the firm faces options. It has to decide whether its advertising expenditures should lead or coincide with seasonal sales. It also has to decide whether its advertising expenditures should be more intense, proportional, or less intense than the seasonal amplitude of sales.

Forrester has proposed using his "industrial dynamics" methodology to test alternative seasonal advertising policies.[31] He visualizes advertising as having a lagged impact on consumer awareness; awareness in turn has a lagged impact on factory sales; and factory sales have a lagged impact on advertising

---

[30]John D. C. Little and Leonard M. Lodish, "A Media Planning Calculus," *Operations Research*, January–February 1969, pp. 1–35.

[31]See Jay W. Forrester, "Advertising: A Problem in Industrial Dynamics," *Harvard Business Review*, March–April 1959, pp. 100–110.

expenditures. He suggests that these time relationships be studied for the individual company and formulated mathematically into a digital computer simulation model. The parameters for this model would be estimated from company data supplemented by executive judgment. Alternative timing strategies would be stimulated in an effort to assess their differential impacts on company sales, costs, and profits.

Kuehn developed a model to explore how advertising should be "timed" for frequently purchased, highly seasonal, low-cost grocery products. He adopted the following product and market assumptions for illustrative purposes:

> The long-run demand for the particular product is stable. The product, however, is subject to a seasonal demand. The timing and magnitude of industry advertising expenditures does not affect the seasonal demand. A company's advertising only influences the company's share of industry demand. Advertising has no effect on retailers. There are two dominant competitors who both develop their timing patterns independently of each other, but optimally. The gross margin from sales is constant throughout the year (no price or cost changes). Other brand merchandising variables, such as product characteristics, retail availability, and competing brand prices, maintain a constant relative appeal to consumers throughout the sales cycle.[32]

Kuehn showed that the appropriate timing pattern depends upon the *degree of advertising carry-over* and the *amount of habitual behavior in customer brand choice.* Carry-over refers to the rate at which the effect of an advertising expenditure decays with the passage of time. A carry-over of .75 per month means that the current effect of a past advertising expenditure is 75 percent of its level last month, whereas a carry-over of only .10 per month means that only 10 percent of last month's effect is carried over. Habitual behavior, the other variable, indicates how much brand holdover occurs by reason of habit, inertia, or brand loyalty, independently of the level of advertising. High habitual purchasing, say .90, means that 90 percent of the buyers repeat their purchase of the brand regardless of the marketing stimuli.

Kuehn found that in the case of no advertising carry-over and no habitual purchasing, the decision maker is justified in using a percentage-of-sales rule in budgeting advertising. The optimal timing pattern for advertising expenditures coincides with the expected seasonal pattern of industry sales. But, if there exists any advertising carry-over and/or habitual purchasing, the percentage-of-sales budgeting method is not optimal. In all these cases it would be better to "time" advertising to lead the sales curve. The peak in advertising expenditures should come before the expected peak in sales, and the trough in advertising expenditures should come before the trough in sales. Lead time should be greater, the higher the carry-over. Furthermore, advertising expenditures should be steadier, the greater the extent of habitual purchasing.

Microscheduling problem

The microscheduling problem involves how to allocate a set of advertising exposures over a short period of time to obtain the maximum impact. Suppose the firm has decided to buy thirty radio spot announcements in the month of September.

---

[32]See Alfred A. Kuehn, "How Advertising Performance Depends on Other Marketing Factors," *Journal of Advertising Research*, March 1962, pp. 2–10.

One way to classify the multitude of possible patterns is shown in Figure 16-3. The left side shows that advertising messages for the month can be concentrated in a small part of the month ("burst" advertising), dispersed continuously throughout the month, or dispersed intermittently throughout the month. The top side shows that the advertising messages can be beamed with a level frequency, a rising frequency, a falling frequency, or an alternating frequency. The advertiser's problem is to decide which of these twelve general patterns would represent the most effective phasing of his messages.

The most effective pattern depends upon the advertising communication objectives in relation to the nature of the product, target customers, distribution channels, and other marketing factors. Consider the following cases:

> A *retailer* wants to announce a preseason sale of skiing equipment. He recognizes that only certain people will be interested in the message. Furthermore he recognizes that the target buyers only need to hear the message once or twice to know whether they are interested. His objective is to maximize the *reach* of his message, not the *repetition*. He decides to concentrate the messages on the days of the sale at a level rate, but varying the time of day to avoid the same audiences. He uses pattern (1).

> A *muffler manufacturer-distributor* wants to keep his name before the public. Yet he does not want his advertising to be too continuous because only 3 to 5 percent of the cars on the road need a new muffler at any given time. He has therefore chosen to use intermittent advertising. Furthermore, he recognizes that Fridays are paydays for many potential buyers, and this would influence their interest in replacing a worn-out muffler. So he sponsors a few messages on a midweek day and more messages on Friday. He uses pattern (12).

Figure 16-3
Classification of advertising timing patterns

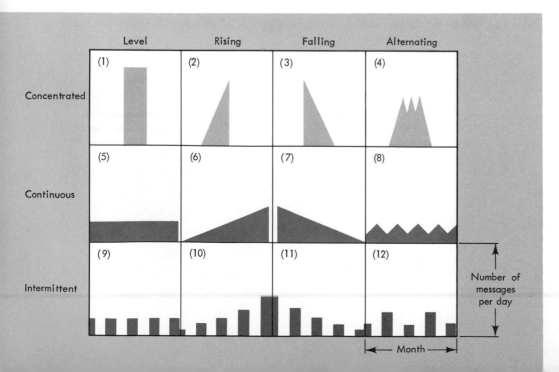

The timing pattern should take into account three general factors. *Buyer turnover* expresses the rate at which new buyers appear in the market; the higher this rate, the more continuous the advertising ought to be to reach these new buyers. *Purchase frequency* is the number of times during the period that the buyer buys the product; the higher the purchase frequency, the more continuous the advertising ought to be to keep the brand on the buyer's mind. The *forgetting rate* is the rate at which the buyer forgets the brand in the absence of stimuli; the higher the forgetting rate, the more continuous the advertising ought to be to keep the brand in the buyer's mind.

There is the question of how much the message should be repeated to a particular buyer group to produce learning and retention. A low number of repetitions may be a waste, according to Lucas and Britt:

> It can be reasoned that introductory advertisements make too weak an impression to initiate much interest in buying. Succeeding advertisements may sometimes be more effective by building up already established weak impressions to the action level.[33]

A high number of repetitions may also be a waste if they do not bring about any further increase in awareness, message familiarity, or positive brand feelings; the number is positively harmful if they bring about boredom or irritation.

In launching a new product, advertisers must make a choice between a campaign based on *flighting* and one based on *continuity*. A budget of five exposures a week could be used up in one day or presented at the rate of one daily exposure for five days. Those who favor flighting feel that the resulting reduction in continuity is more than compensated for by the increased learning that takes place. They cite Ebbinghaus's finding that information learned more quickly is retained better than information learned more slowly.[34] However, the issue requires more research, and the decision model must take into account product, consumer, and competitive factors at the time of product introduction.

MEASURING ADVERTISING EFFECTIVENESS

Good planning and control of advertising depend critically on measures of advertising effectiveness. Yet the amount of fundamental research on advertising effectiveness is appallingly small. According to Forrester:

> I doubt that there is any other function in industry where management bases so much expenditure on such scanty knowledge. The advertising industry spends 2% or 3% of its gross dollar volume on what it calls "research," and even if this were really true research, the small amount would be surprising. However, I estimate that less than a tenth of this amount would be considered research plus development as these terms are defined in the engineering and product research departments of companies . . . probably no more than 1/5 of 1% of total advertising expenditure is used to achieve an enduring understanding of how to spend the other 99.8%.[35]

---

[33]Darrell B. Lucas and Steuart Henderson Britt, *Measuring Advertising Effectiveness* (New York: McGraw-Hill Book Company, 1963), p. 218.

[34]Hermann Ebbinghaus, *Memory* (New York: Columbia University Press, 1913).

[35]Forrester, *op. cit.*, p. 102.

Most of the measurement of advertising effectiveness is of an applied nature, dealing with specific advertisements and campaigns. Of the applied part, most of the money is spent by agencies on *pretesting* the given advertisement or campaign before launching it into national circulation. Relatively less tends to be spent on *posttesting* the effect of given advertisements and campaigns.

The research techniques used to measure advertising effectiveness vary with what the advertiser is trying to accomplish. The behavioral change of ultimate interest to the advertiser is the act of purchase. One would expect to find that research on the "sales effect" of advertising predominates. Actually, sales-effect research tends to be meager in comparison with "commmunication-effect" research—research to determine the effect of given advertising on buyers' knowledge, feelings, and convictions. Many advertisers feel that the links between sales and advertising are too tenuous, complicated, and long-term to permit measuring the direct impact. They feel instead that the more short-term communication effects of given advertisements should be measured.

Communication-effect research

Communication-effect research seeks to discover whether the advertising is achieving the intended communication effects. There are various ways to evaluate the communication effectiveness of, say, an individual ad.[36] Called *copy testing*, it can occur before an ad is put into actual media and after it has been printed or broadcast. The purpose of *ad pretesting* is to make improvements in the advertising copy to the fullest extent possible prior to its release. There are three major methods of ad pretesting:

1 *Direct ratings.* Here a panel of target consumers or advertising experts examine alternative ads and fill out rating questionnaires. Sometimes a single question is raised, such as "Which of these ads do you think would influence you most to buy the product?" Or a more elaborate form consisting of several rating scales may be used, such as the one shown in Figure 16-4. Here the person evaluates the ad's attention strength, read-through strength, cognitive strength, affective strength and behavioral strength, assigning a number of points up to a maximum in each case. The underlying theory is that an effective ad must score high on all of these properties if it is ultimately to stimulate buying action. Too often ads are evaluated only on their attention- or comprehension-creating abilities. At the same time, it must be appreciated that direct rating methods are less reliable than harder evidence of an ad's actual impact on target consumers. Direct rating scales help primarily to screen out poor ads rather than identify great ads.

2 *Portfolio tests.* Here respondents are given a dummy portfolio of ads and asked to take as much time as they want to read them. After putting them down, the respondents are asked to recall the ads they saw—unaided or aided by the interviewer—and to play back as much as they can about each ad. The results are taken to indicate an ad's ability to stand out and its intended message to be understood.

3 *Laboratory tests.* Some researchers assess the potential effect of an ad through measuring physiological reactions—heart beat, blood pressure, pupil dilation, perspiration—through such equipment as galvanometers, tachistoscopes, size-distance tunnels, and pupil dilation measuring equipment. These physiological tests at best measure the attention-getting and arousing power of an ad rather than any higher state of consciousness that the ad might produce.

---

[36]For an excellent survey of research methods, see Lucas and Britt, *op. cit.*

		Maximum points
Attention strength		
How well does the ad catch the reader's attention? (Consider the picture, headline, typography, and layout).	______	(15)
How well does the ad catch the right reader's attention?	______	(5)
Read-through strength		
How well does the ad lead the reader to read further?	______	(20)
Cognitive strength		
How clear is the central message or benefit?	______	(20)
Affective strength		
How well-chosen is the particular appeal among the variety of possible appeals?	______	(10)
How effectively is this appeal presented in terms of arousing the desired emotions?	______	(10)
Behavioral strength		
How well does the ad suggest follow-through action?	______	(10)
How likely is the aroused reader to follow through?	______	(10)
	______	Total

0 - 20	20 - 40	40 - 60	60 - 80	80 - 100
A very poor ad	A mediocre ad	An average ad	A pretty good ad	A very effective ad

Figure 16-4
Rating sheet for ads

There are two popular *ad posttesting* methods, the purpose of which is t assess the actual communication impact of the ad after it has appeared i media:

1 *Recall tests.* Recall tests involve finding persons who are regular users of the media vehicle and asking them to recall advertisers and products contained in the issue under study. They are asked to recall or play back everything they can remember. The administrator may or may not aid them in their recall. Recall scores are prepared on the basis of their responses and are used to indicate the power of the ad to be noticed and retained.

2 *Recognition tests.* Recognition tests call for sampling the readers of a given issue of, say, a magazine, asking them to point out what they recognize as having seen and/or read. For each ad, three different Starch readership scores (named after

Daniel Starch, who provides the leading service) are prepared from the recognition data:

Noted. The percentage of readers of the magazine who say they have previously seen the advertisement in the particular magazine.

Seen/associated. The percentage of readers who say they have seen or read any part of the ad that clearly indicates the names of the product or service of the advertiser.

Read most. The percentage of readers who not only looked at the advertisement, but who say that they read more than half of the total written material in the ad.

The Starch organization also furnishes Adnorms, that is, average scores for each product class for the year, and separately for men and women for each magazine, to enable advertisers to evaluate their ads in relation to competitors' ads.

It should be noted that most of these efforts rate the attention and comprehension effectiveness of the ad and not necessarily its impact on attitude or behavior. The latter are admittedly harder to measure. Too many advertisers and agencies unfortunately stop short of investing the necessary money to really measure what the ad is accomplishing.

Sales-effect research

Communication-effect advertising research undoubtedly helps advertisers improve the quality of message content and presentation, but it reveals very little about how much sales may be affected, if at all. What *sales* conclusion can the advertiser draw in learning that his recent campaign has increased brand awareness by 20 percent and brand comprehension by 10 percent? What has the advertiser learned about the sales productivity of his advertising dollars and therefore how much to spend?

The sales effect of advertising will generally be more difficult to measure than the communication effect. Advertising sales effectiveness is easiest to measure in mail-order situations and hardest to measure in brand or corporate-image-building advertising. Efforts to measure the sales impact of advertising usually follow one of two approaches.

The *historical approach* involves the researcher in fitting past company sales to past company advertising expenditures on a current or lagged basis using least-squares regression. Simple regression usually leads to unsatisfactory or suspect results, and the researcher tries to introduce additional variables that might explain the behavior of past sales. One of the best studies of this type was conducted by Palda to estimate the effect of advertising expenditures on the sales of Lydia Pinkham's Vegetable Compound between 1908 and 1960. Fortunately, the marketing factors in this market were minimal:

The firm spent a very high proportion (40–60 percent) of its sales on advertising. Furthermore, it did not employ many of the customary "parameters" of marketing action: sales force, credit, discounts, frequent changes in package, point of purchase efforts, special offerings, etc. The assumption thus could safely be made that advertising had a measurable effect on Pinkham's sales. The product itself, Lydia Pinkham's Vegetable Compound, had no close substitutes. Competitors' marketing action was not, therefore, a complicating factor to be coped with. By the same token certain allied issues, such as the geographic distribution of

Pinkham's marketing effort, could be ignored. During the detailed examination which followed the decision to delve into the Pinkham case, further factors were discovered which added to the simplicity of the ultimate quantitative analysis. On the whole the conclusion was reached that there was remarkable stability (between 1907–60) in the universe from which the sample observations were obtained.[37]

Using a single equation with five explanatory variables, Palda managed to measure the direct and the lagged effects of advertising expenditures on current sales (see p. 136), which in turn allowed him to calculate short-term and long-term marginal rates of return on the company's invested advertising dollars. Other investigators applying multiple-regression methods to historical data have also produced useful advertising impact-on-sales measures for such items as cigarettes,[38] branded gasoline,[39] coffee,[40] and ethical drugs.[41] In all cases, these investigators have had to cope with the following problems: (1) autocorrelation of annual advertising and sales series, respectively; (2) high intercorrelation among the explanatory variables; (3) confounding of the sales/advertising response coefficient by the fact that many companies set advertising as a percentage-of-sales; and (4) insufficient number of years of data to fit the required number of variables.

These problems have led a growing number of companies to rely on a second method of measuring the sales impact of advertising, that of *experimental design*. Here the company chooses a set of matched markets which normally receive the same advertising/sales expenditure rate. During the experimental period however, the company spends, say, 50 percent more than the normal amount in some areas, 50 percent less in another set of areas, and the normal amount in the remaining set or control areas. At the end of the experimental period, the company determines the average sales gains and losses due to additional versus reduced advertising spending. For example, Du Pont found that above-normal advertising expenditure led to increased sales at a diminishing rate and was especially not profitable when it occurred in cities where Du Pont already had a large market share.[42] Anheuser-Busch is another frequent user of experimental design and has managed to estimate fairly accurately the shape of the sales-response function in different types of territories.[43] An increasing number of companies see experimental design as the best way to determine the impact of advertising dollars on sales.

---

[37]Kristian S. Palda, *The Measurement of Cumulative Advertising Effect* (Englewood Cliffs, N.J.: Prentice-Hall, Inc., 1964), p. 87.

[38]Lester G. Telser, "Advertising and Cigarettes," *Journal of Political Economy*, October 1962, pp. 471–99.

[39]Jean-Jacques Lambin, "A Computer On-Line Marketing Mix Model," *Journal of Marketing Research*, May 1972, pp. 119–26.

[40]William F. Massy and Ronald E. Frank, "Short-Term Price and Dealing Effects in Selecting Market Segments," *Journal of Marketing Research*, May 1965, pp. 171–85.

[41]David B. Montgomery and Alvin J. Silk, "Estimating Dynamic Effects of Market Communications Expenditures," *Management Science*, June 1972, pp. 485–501.

[42]See Robert D. Buzzell, "E. I. Du Pont de Nemours & Co.: Measurement of Effects of Advertising," in his *Mathematical Models and Marketing Management* (Boston: Division of Research, Graduate School of Business Administration, Harvard University, 1964), pp. 157–79.

[43]See Russell L. Ackoff and James R. Emshoff, "Advertising Research at Anheuser-Busch, Inc. (1963–68)," *Sloane Management Review,* Winter 1975, pp. 1–15.

SUMMARY

Advertising—the use of paid media to present the ideas of an explicit sponsor about his products, services, or organization—is a potent promotional tool. American marketers spend over $20 billion annually on advertising. This includes many types of advertising (national, regional, local; consumer, industrial, retail; product, brand, institutional; and so on) designed to achieve a variety of objectives (immediate sales, brand recognition, preference, and so on).

The size of the advertising budget is commonly determined in a number of ways—according to what can be afforded, or as a regular percentage of the company's sales dollar, or to match competitors' expenditures, or by defining the cost of accomplishing specific communication goals. Four types of new decision models for setting the advertising budget are (1) sales-response and decay models, (2) communication-stage models, (3) adaptive-control models, and (4) competitive-share models. The effectiveness of the advertising dollar will also depend upon the development of good message development and execution. The advertising copy must be placed in the most effective media, a problem that is increasingly being assisted by computerized media-selection models. The budget must be set over the business cycle, the seasons, the months, and even the days, with a careful consideration for delays in impact and the psychology of repetition. A continuous effort must be made to research the communication and sales effects of advertising programs before they are run, while they are running, and after they are terminated.

QUESTIONS AND PROBLEMS

1 Consider the following two statements: "The purpose of advertising is to create sales." "The purpose of advertising is to improve the buyers' disposition toward the company's products." Which comes closer to the truth?

2 The advertising manager of a large firm asks the executive committee to approve a $100,000 increase in the advertising budget. He submits that this extra money will probably increase company sales by $500,000 over what they would otherwise be. What other information would you want in order to judge the budget request?

3 A company's advertising expenditures average $5,000 a month. Current sales are $29,000, and the saturation sales level is estimated at $42,000. The sales response constant is $2, and the sales decay constant is 6 percent per month. Use the Vidale-Wolfe formula to estimate the probable sales increase next month.

4 A canned dog food manufacturer is trying to decide between media A and B. Medium A has 10,000,000 readers and charges $20,000 for a full page ad ($2.00 per 1,000). Medium B has 15,000,000 readers and charges $25,000 for a full page ad ($1.67 per 1,000). Is there any other calculation which might be made before assuming that B is the better medium?

5 A large oil company allocates its advertising budget to its territories according to current territorial sales. The advertising manager justifies using a constant advertising-to-sales ratio by saying that the company loses a certain percentage of its customers in each market each year and that advertising's most important job is to get new customers to replace them. What assumptions underlie this reasoning?

6 At one time, executives at Alberto-Culver expressed the following view about the relationship between increased advertising and sales: "We have found an astounding

fact: the more we invest in advertising, the less our advertising-to-sales ratio becomes . . . once we get a brand off the ground, its ability to grow and return profits to the company accelerates at a much greater rate than the increased advertising expenditure." Is this plausible?

7 Hershey Foods for many years had the distinction of no consumer advertising. In spite of this, its candy bar sales continued to grow. Does this suggest that companies with excellent products may need little or no advertising?

8 Suggest some rules for developing effective advertising headlines and copy. Give examples of effective headlines.

9 "The art department in an advertising agency is properly called the creative department. Media is not a creative function." Do you agree?

10 Is industrial advertising harder to measure for its communication effectiveness than consumer advertising?

11 Maloney's deductive scheme for generating advertising messages provides twelve ways to advertise a product. Develop an appeal illustrating each of the twelve types of messages.

17

SALES-FORCE DECISIONS

I don't know who you are.
I don't know your company.
I don't know your company's product.
I don't know what your company stands for.
I don't know your company's customers.
I don't know your company's record.
I don't know your company's reputation.

Now—what was it you wanted to sell me?

MCGRAW-HILL PUBLICATIONS

Personal selling in most economies represents a larger marketing expenditure than advertising. In 1970 American firms spent $32 billion on personal selling compared with $20.7 billion on advertising. Salesmen serve as a unique link with the company's customers. The salesman *is* the company to most of its customers. He provides and tailors the company's offering to the individual customer's needs. He also provides the company with much needed intelligence from the marketplace.

There are probably more stereotypes about salesmen than about any other group. The salesman is likely to conjure up an image of Arthur Miller's pitiable Willy Loman or Meredith Wilson's ebullient Harold Hill—a glib, boisterous character always ready with a glad hand and a racy story. The salesman is typically pictured as a guy who loves sociability—in spite of some recent evidence that many salesmen actually dislike it. He is criticized for aggressively foisting goods on people—in spite of the fact that buyers often search out sales representatives.

   Actually, the term "salesman" covers a broad range of positions in our economy, within which the differences are often greater than the similarities. McMurry offered the following classification of selling positions:

1 Positions where the "salesman's" job is predominantly to deliver the product, e.g., milk, bread, fuel oil.

2 Positions where the salesman is predominantly an inside order-taker, e.g., the haberdashery salesman standing behind the counter.

3 Positions where the salesman is also predominantly an order-taker but works in the field, as the packing house, soap, or spice salesman does.

4 Positions where the salesman is not expected or permitted to take an order but is called on only to build good will or to educate the actual or potential user . . . the distiller's "missionary man" or the medical "detailer" representing an ethical pharmaceutical house.

5 Positions where the major emphasis is place on technical knowledge, e.g., the engineering salesman who is primarily a consultant to the "client" companies.

6 Positions which demand the creative sale of tangible products like vacuum cleaners, refrigerators, siding, and encyclopedias.

7 Positions requiring the creative sale of intangibles, such as insurance, advertising services, or education.[1]

The positions move along a spectrum ranging from the least to the most creative types of selling. The earlier jobs call primarily for maintaining accounts and taking orders, while the latter require hunting down prospects and creating new sales. Most of the following discussion deals with the creative type of salesman.

The buyer-seller relationship

Effective selling is in large part a matter of having the correct attitude toward the customer. *The customer needs help in solving his problems. An effective salesman recognizes his customer's problems and knows how to be of help.* A vice-president of a major food company spent one week watching fifty sales presentations to a busy buyer for a major supermarket chain. Here are some of his experiences:

> I watched a soap company representative come in to the buyer. He had three separate new promotional deals to talk about with six different dates. He had *nothing* in writing. . . . After the salesman left, the buyer looked at me and said, "It will take me 15 minutes to get this straightened out." I watched another salesman walk in to the buyer and say, "Well, I was in the area, and I want you to know that we have a great new promotion coming up next week." The buyer said, "That's fine. What is it?" He said, "I don't know . . . I'm coming in next week to tell you about it." The buyer asked him what he was doing there today. He said, "Well, I was in the area." Another salesman came [and] said, "Well, it's time for us to write that order now . . . getting ready for the summer business." The buyer said, "Well, fine, George, how much did I buy last year in total?" The salesman looked a little dumfounded and said, "Well, I'll be damned if I know. . . ." The majority of salesmen were ill-prepared, unable to answer basic questions, uncertain as to what they wanted to accomplish during the call. They did not think of the call as a studied, professional presentation. They didn't have a real idea of the busy retailer's *needs and wants.*[2]

---

[1]Robert N. McMurry, "The Mystique of Super-Salesmanship," *Harvard Business Review,* March–April 1961, p. 114.

[2]From an address by Donald R. Keough at the 27th Annual Conference of the Super-Market Institute in Chicago, April 26–29, 1964.

Companies are striving to overcome these problems through better selection and training of their sales force. They are wary of "the old drummer type of salesman." Much of the old sales job has been taken over by mass media and nonpersonal retailing. The new breed of salesman is better schooled and able to absorb a vast amount of information about many products and customers. The new salesman is likely to have technical training and be backed by a top-flight team of engineers and market researchers. He knows how to read the needs of customers and recognizes that they are growing more interested in buying systems and services than single products. He goes after the *long-run relationship* rather than the *quick sale*. In the jet age, he is a traveling executive. Even his name has been changed to "field manager" (Ford), or "market specialist" (Wyandotte Chemicals), or "sales engineer" (Burroughs), or "medical service representative" (Parke, Davis). As technology grows more complex and competition more keen, one can expect to see more of this new type of salesman.[3]

A salesman's tasks

Selling is only one of several tasks of the salesman. He may perform as many as six different activities:

1 *Prospecting.* The company does its best to generate leads for the salesman, but he is expected to search for additional prospects.
2 *Communicating.* Much of a salesman's work consists of communicating information to existing and potential buyers about his company's products and services.
3 *Selling.* The salesman engages in the art of salesmanship—approaching, presenting, answering objections, and closing sales.
4 *Servicing.* The salesman provides various services to his customers—consulting on their problems, rendering technical assistance, arranging financing, and expediting delivery.
5 *Information gathering.* The salesman conducts market research and intelligence work for his company and is responsible for supplying regular reports on his call activity and findings.
6 *Allocating.* In times of product scarcity, the salesman helps evaluate customer profitability and advises on customer allocation.

The salesman's actual mix of tasks varies with the character of the purchase decision process, company marketing strategy, and the economy. The nature of the purchase decision process establishes the kinds of activities that the salesman must perform in order to develop and maintain satisfied customers. The sales activities required to handle straight rebuy situations are different from those required to handle new task buying situations.

Company marketing strategy also influences the sales force strategy. In the food industry, many manufacturers use a *pull strategy*, relying on massive consumer advertising to draw customers into the retailers' establishments to ask for their brands. The company salesmen play a servicing role of seeing to it that the retailers carry a sufficient stock, give good shelf exposure, and cooperate in sales promotion programs. Other food manufacturers may use a *push strategy*, placing a primary role on their salesmen's selling the trade on carrying their

---

[3]See Carl Rieser, "The Salesman Isn't Dead—He's Different," *Fortune,* November 1962, pp. 124ff.

brands. Even within the selling task, companies may vary in how much time they want their salesmen to spend on selling present products versus new ones and on visiting present customers versus prospects.

The salesman's mix of tasks also varies with the state of the economy. When widespread product shortages appeared in 1973, salesmen in many industries found themselves with nothing to sell. Some observers jumped to the conclusion that salesmen were redundant and could be dismissed. But this overlooked the other roles of the salesman—allocating the product, counseling unhappy customers, communicating company plans on remedying the shortage, and selling the company's other products that were not in short supply.

SALES-FORCE SIZE

Salesman are among the most productive and expensive assets a company has. Increasing their number will increase both sales and costs. We shall discuss two popular approaches to setting the right sales-force size.

Salesman productivity approach

Semlow proposed a solution to the problem of sales-force size that depended upon measuring the sales productivity of salesmen in different-size territories.[4] He noted that salesmen in territories rated as having higher sales potential produced more sales but that their sales were less than proportionate to the increase in sales potential. Citing a particular company's case, Semlow found that the sales in a territory with 1 percent of total national potential were $160,000 and sales in a territory with 5 percent of total potential were $200,000. In the latter case, there was only $40,000 of sales for every 1 percent of potential.

Now if the company employed one hundred salesmen and wanted them all to work territories of equal potentials, it would create one hundred territories, each with 1 percent of total potential. This means that sales would average $160,000 in each territory, according to the previous analysis. Since there are one hundred men, total company sales would be $16 million.

If the company employed only twenty men, it would create twenty territories, each with 5 percent of the total potential. In this case, sales would average $200,000 in each territory according to the previous analysis. Since there were twenty men, total company sales would be only $4,000,000. Semlow applied the same reasoning to other possible sizes of the sales force. For each size, he projected the total sales volume, based on the estimated productivity of salesmen in different-size territories.

His final step was to convert each sales volume into operating profit on investment. He first estimated the operating profit before variable selling cost on each sales volume. Then he deducted the variable selling cost, specifically the number of men times the cost per salesman. This left an estimate of operating profit on that sales volume. Then he estimated the working capital and plant investment required at alternative sales volumes. Finally, he expressed the estimated operating profit as a ratio to the required investment. In his example, the operating profit on investment was 11.6 percent with one hundred

---

[4]Walter J. Semlow, "How Many Salesmen Do You Need?" *Harvard Business Review,* May–June 1959, pp. 126–32.

men and only 8.7 percent with twenty men. The optimal-size sales force called for sixty-five men, with the estimated rate of return of 22.0 percent.

Semlow's method depends on having a sufficient number of existing territories to allow making a statistical estimate of creating territories of equal sales potential. It also assumes that sales productivity is a function only of territory sales potential, neglecting the variations that might be produced by the mix of accounts in the territory, their geographical dispersion, and other factors.

Salesman workload approach

Talley proposed an approach based on equalizing the workload of salesmen rather than territory sales potential.[5] His method assumes that management has determined the economic number of calls to make on accounts of different sizes. The method consists of the following steps:

1 Customers are grouped into size classes according to their annual sales volume.
2 The desirable call frequencies (number of sales calls on an account per year) are established for each class.
3 The number of accounts in each size class are multiplied by the corresponding call frequency to arrive at the total workload for the country, in sales calls per year.
4 The average number of calls a salesman can make per year is determined.
5 The number of salesmen needed is determined by dividing the total annual calls required by the average annual calls made by a salesman.

Suppose, for example, the company estimates that there are one thousand A-accounts and two thousand B-accounts in the nation; and A-accounts require thirty-six calls a year and B-accounts twelve calls a year. This means the company needs a sales force that can make sixty thousand sales calls a year. Suppose the average salesman can make one thousand calls a year. The company would need sixty full-time salesmen.

SALES-FORCE DESIGN

Sales-force structure

The effectiveness of a sales force depends a great deal on how it is organized. A sales force can be organized around company territories, products, customers, or some mixture of the three.

Territorial-structured sales force In the simplest sales organization each salesman has an exclusive territory in which he represents the company's full line. This sales structure has a number of advantages. First, it results in a very clear definition of the salesman's responsibilities. As the only salesman working the territory, he bears the credit or blame for area sales to the extent that personal selling effort makes a difference. This tends to encourage a high level of effort, especially when management is able to gauge fairly accurately the area's sales potential. Second, his responsibility for a definite territory increases his incentive to cultivate local business and personal ties. These ties tend to

---

[5]Walter J. Talley, "How to Design Sales Territories," *Journal of Marketing*, January 1961, pp. 7–13.

improve the quality of both his selling effectiveness and his personal life. Third, salesman travel expenses are likely to be relatively small, since each salesman's travel takes place within the bounds of a small geographical territory.

The territorial form of sales organization works quite well in companies with a relatively homogeneous set of products and customers. But these same companies, as their products or markets become diversified, find this form increasingly less effective. At the heart of the problem is the fact that to be effective, the salesman must know his products and his customers. But there is a clear limit to how much knowledge a salesman can acquire about different types of products and customers.

Product-structured sales force　The importance of salesmen's knowing their products, together with the desire for product responsibility, has led many companies to structure their sales force along product lines. Specialization of the sales force by product is particularly warranted where the products are (1) technically complex or (2) highly unrelated or (3) very numerous.

The mere existence of different company products, however, is not a sufficient argument for specializing the sales force by product. A major drawback may exist if the company's separate product lines are bought by many of the same customers. For example:

> The *American Hospital Supply Corporation* has four major divisions and several subsidiaries, each with its own sales force. All of these sales forces call on the same hospitals. It is conceivable that as many as seven different salesmen representing the American Hospital Supply Corporation may call on the same hospital on the same day.[6]

This means that company salesmen travel over the same routes, and each uses up valuable time waiting in the outer office to see the customer's purchasing agents. These extra costs must be weighed against the benefits that may result from the higher level of customer service and the more knowledgeable product representation.

Customer-structured sales force　Companies may set up separate sales forces along customer lines. The customers may be differentiated by:

> *Type of industry.* (A large steel-strapping firm uses separate sales forces to sell to the railroad industry, the construction industry, and a miscellaneous category.)
> *Size.* (A manufacturer of aluminum products uses separate sales forces to sell to large customers and small ones.)
> *Channel of distribution.* (A food manufacturer uses separate sales forces to sell to the chains, to wholesalers, and to large independents.)
> *Company.* (An automotive parts manufacturer uses separate sales forces to sell to the Ford account, the Chevrolet account, and so forth.)

The most obvious advantage of customer specialization is that each sales force can become more knowledgeable about specific customer needs. At one

---

[6]See Ralph Westfall and Harper W. Boyd, Jr., *Cases in Marketing Management* (Homewood, Ill.: Richard D. Irwin, Inc., 1961), pp. 376–83.

time General Electric's salesmen specialized in specific products (fan motors, switches, and so forth), but it later changed to specialization in markets, such as the air-conditioning market, because this is how the customer saw the problem of fan motors, switches, and so on. A customer-specialized sales force can also sometimes reduce total sales-force costs. A large pump manufacturer at one time used a single sales force of highly trained sales engineers to sell to both original equipment manufacturers (who needed to deal with technical representatives) and to jobbers (who did not need to deal with technical representatives). Later the company split its sales force and staffed the one selling to jobbers with less highly trained salesmen.

The major disadvantage of customer-structured sales forces arises if the various types of customers are scattered evenly throughout the country. This means an overlapping coverage of territories, which is always more expensive.

Complex sales-force structures When a company sells a wide variety of products to many types of customers over a broad geographical area, it often combines several principles of sales-force structure. Salesmen may be specialized by territory-product, territory-customer, product-customer, or ultimately by territory-product-customer. A salesman may then be responsible to one or more line managers and/or one or more staff managers. Multiple lines of supervision should generally be avoided, however.

The structure of a sales force, no matter how effective it may originally be, is always in danger of antiquation in the course of time. A company should reconsider periodically whether its sales force is organized along the most effective lines. In comparing the existing structure with a proposed alternative, the most detailed analysis of the *economic* and *human* factors is required. Even when the economic advantages seem substantial, the human factor should not be treated lightly. If any reorganization is perceived by all or a substantial part of the sales force as reducing its opportunities, its alleged economic advantages on paper may never be realized in practice.

Territorial design

The great majority of companies assign their salesmen to specific territories whether or not they are further specialized by product or type of customers. The territories are aggregated into larger groupings called *districts*, and in turn these districts may be aggregated into major sales *regions*. Many of the larger companies, for example, utilize an eastern, southern, central, and western regional plan for field operations.

In designing a system of territories, the company generally tries to achieve the following territorial characteristics: the territories are easy to administer; their sales potential is easy to estimate; they keep down total travel time; and they provide a sufficient and equitable workload and sales potential for each salesman. These characteristics are achieved through decisions about the size and shape of territorial units.

Territory size As we saw earlier, there are two competing philosophies on the proper size of territories. One approach calls for forming territories of *equal sales potential*, and the other calls for forming territories of *equal workload*. Each principle offers advantages at the cost of some real dilemmas.

The logic of creating territories of *equal potential* is to provide each salesman with the same income opportunities and to provide the company with a means of evaluating performance. It is thought that under this principle chronic differences in sales yield by territory reflect differences in the ability or effort of individual salesmen. This awareness will encourage salesmen to work at their top capacity.

But because customer geographical density almost always varies, territories with equal potential typically cover vastly different areas. For example, the potential for the sale of large drill presses is as large in Chicago as it is in a number of the western states. A salesman assigned to the Chicago territory can cover the same potential with far less effort than the salesman who sells in the territory spanning the several western states.

The problem is that salesmen assigned to the larger and sparser territories are either going to end up with less sales—and income, where commissions are involved—for equal effort or with equal sales only through extraordinary effort. Is there any way around the problem? One possible adjustment is to pay higher compensation to the western salesman, providing him with incentive and insuring that good men will be attracted to larger territories. But this reduces the profits on sales in the larger territories. An alternative adjustment is to acknowledge that territories differ in attractiveness and assign the better men to the better territories. Transfers to the better territories would be awarded on the basis of seniority and demonstrated ability. But this has several disadvantages. The salesmen are taken out of their territories just when they begin to know them well. Their home life is disrupted by the frequent transfers. Transfer expenses, which may be considerable, must be absorbed by the company. And the men who do not get the better territory may be bitter.

The other leading principle for creating territories is to try to equalize the salesmen's workloads.[7] The objective is to permit each salesman to adequately cover his territory. However, this principle generally results in some variation in territory sales potentials. This is not a concern where salesmen are on straight salary. But where salesmen are compensated partly for their sales, territories definitely vary in their attractiveness even though the workloads are approximately equalized. The same solutions appear. A lower compensation rate can be paid to salesmen in the territories with the higher sales potential, or the territories with the better potential can go to the men with higher ability and/or seniority.

Territory shape   Territories are formed by combining smaller units, such as counties or states, until they add up to a territory of a given potential or workload. They are put together with reference to the location of natural barriers, the compatibility of adjacent areas, the adequacy of transportation, and so forth. Many companies also try to achieve a certain territory shape because this can influence the cost and ease of coverage and the salesman's satisfaction. Three different common territorial shapes are shown in Figure 17-1.

---

[7]A computer-based method that creates territories that are compact and equal in workload is described in Sidney W. Hess and Stuart A. Samuels, "Experiences with a Sales Districting Model: Criteria and Implementation," *Management Science*, December 1971, pp. 41–54.

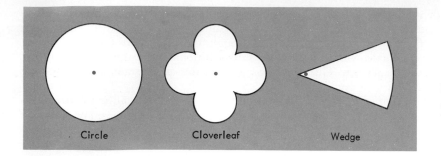

Figure 17-1
Alternative shapes for territories

Circle   Cloverleaf   Wedge

A circular territory with the salesman headquartered in the center offers two advantages. The circle makes it easier for the salesman to prepare a routing plan that requires a minimum of backtracking. In effect, he travels in a circle, and when finished, he returns to his branch location. Furthermore, he is not very far from any of his accounts when special trips have to be made.

A cloverleaf pattern with the salesman headquartered in the center enables the salesman to travel in a series of loops around his territory. If cloverleaves are made the right size, the salesman can start out each Monday and finish a clover section by Friday evening and return home. Furthermore, the cost of special trips is low because the accounts are not far away.

A wedge-shaped territory radiating out from a central metropolitan area is often employed when a metropolitan area is too large for one salesman to handle. It also tends to balance rural and urban calls among salesmen. Its major disadvantage is that it places the salesman quite far from some of his accounts. In making special calls on these accounts, his return to headquarters would represent a lot of "deadheading."

Actual routing costs depend on the geographical location of accounts within the territory as well as the territory's shape. It is not generally obvious which routing through a set of points is the most efficient. An increasing number of companies are subjecting the routing problem to mathematical analysis. By finding computer solutions to the "traveling salesman problem," they can help their salesmen reduce travel time or cost.[8]

RECRUITING AND SELECTING SALESMEN

Importance of careful selection

At the heart of a successful sales-force operation is the selection of good salesmen. The performance level of an average salesman and that of a top salesman are quite different. A survey of over five hundred companies revealed that 27 percent of the salesmen brought in over 52 percent of the sales.[9] Beyond the differences in salesman productivity are the great wastes in hiring the wrong men. Of the sixteen thousand salesmen who were hired by the surveyed companies, only 68.5 percent still worked for their company at the end of the year, and only 50 percent were expected to remain through the following year. The

[8]See John D. C. Little, *et al.*, "An Algorithm for the Traveling Salesman Problem," *Operations Research*, November–December 1963, pp. 972–89.

[9]The survey was conducted by the Sales Executives Club of New York and was reported in *Business Week*, February 1, 1964, p. 52.

cost of recruiting, training, and supervising an individual salesman for one year was estimated at the time at $8,730. As a result, the surveyed companies were expected to lose around $70 million, or half their investment.

The financial loss due to turnover is only part of the total cost. The new salesman who remains with the company receives a direct income averaging around half of the direct selling outlay. If he receives $12,000 a year, another $12,000 may go into fringe benefits, expenses for travel and entertainment, supervision, office space, supplies, and secretarial assistance. Consequently, the new salesman should be capable of creating sales on which the gross margin at least covers his selling expenses of $24,000. If this margin were 10 percent, for example, he would have to sell at least $240,000 of product to constitute a breakeven resource for his company.

What makes a good salesman?

Selecting salesmen would not be so much a problem if one could be sure what characteristics make up an ideal salesman. If ideal salesmen are outgoing, aggressive, and energetic, it would not be too difficult to check for these characteristics in applicants. But a review of the most successful salesmen in any company is likely to reveal a good number who are introverted, mild-mannered, and far from energetic. The successful group will also include men who are tall and short, articulate and inarticulate, well groomed and slovenly.

Nevertheless, the search for the magic combination of traits that spells sure-fire sales ability continues unabated. The number of lists that have been drawn up is countless. Most of them recite the same qualities. One observer with broad experience wrote:

> It is my conviction that the possessor of *effective* sales personality is *a habitual "wooer," an individual who has a compulsive need to win and hold the affection of others.* . . . His wooing, however, is not based on a sincere desire for love because, in my opinion, he is convinced at heart that no one will ever love him. Therefore, his wooing is primarily exploitative . . . his relationships tend to be transient, superficial and evanescent.[10]

McMurry went on to list five traits, in addition to the wooing instinct, that made the supersalesman: a high level of energy, abounding self-confidence, a chronic hunger for money, a well-established habit of industry, and a state of mind that regards each objection, resistance, or obstacle as a challenge.[11]

Mayer and Greenberg offered one of the shortest lists of traits common to good salesmen.[12] Their seven years of fieldwork led them to conclude that the good salesman has at least two basic qualities: (1) *empathy*, the ability to feel as the customer does; and (2) *ego drive*, a strong personal need to make the sale. Using these two traits, they were able to make fairly good predictions of the subsequent performance of applicants for sales positions in three different industries.

It may be true that certain basic traits may make a man a good salesman in any line of selling. From the viewpoint of a particular company, however, these basic traits are rarely enough. Each selling job is characterized by a unique

---

[10]McMurry, *op. cit.*, p. 117.

[11]*Ibid.*, p. 118.

[12]David Mayer and Herbert M. Greenberg, "What Makes a Good Salesman?" *Harvard Business Review*, July–August 1964, pp. 119–25.

set of duties and challenges. One only has to think about insurance selling, computer selling, and automobile selling to realize the different educational, intellectual, and personality requirements that would be sought in the respective salesmen.

How should a company proceed to determine the characteristics its prospective salesmen should "ideally" possess? The particular duties of the job suggest some of the characteristics to look for in applicants. Is there a lot of paperwork? Does the job call for much travel? Will the salesman confront a high proportion of refusals? In addition, the traits of the company's most successful salesmen suggest additional qualities to look for. Some companies compare the standing of their best versus their poorest salesmen to see which characteristics differentiate the two groups of men.

Recruitment procedures

After management develops general criteria for new sales personnel, it has the job of attracting a sufficient number of applicants. The recruiting is turned over to the personnel department, which seeks applicants through various means, including soliciting names from current salesmen, using employment agencies, placing want ads, and contacting college students. As for the college students, companies have not found it easy to sell them on selling. A survey of one thousand male students in 123 colleges indicated that only one in seventeen college men showed an interest in selling.[13] The reluctant ones gave as reasons the fear of insecurity and a dislike of travel and being away from their families. To counter these objections, company recruiters emphasized starting salaries, income opportunities, and the fact that one-quarter of the presidents of large U.S. corporations started out in marketing and sales.

Applicant-rating procedures

Recruitment procedures should lead to the development of more applicants than jobs, and the company's task is to select the better applicants. The selection procedures vary in elaborateness from a single informal interview to highly detailed testing and interviewing, not only of the man but of his wife as well.

An increasing number of companies are giving formal tests to applicants for sales positions. Although test scores are only one information element in a scheme that includes personal characteristics, references, past employment history, and interviewer reactions, they are weighed quite heavily by some companies, such as IBM, Prudential, Procter & Gamble, and Gillette. Gillette claims that the use of tests has resulted in a 42 percent reduction in turnover and that test scores have correlated well with the subsequent progress of new salesmen in the sales organization.

The choice of an appropriate battery of tests is not simple. Standard tests are available to measure intelligence, interests, sales aptitude, personal adjustment, personality characteristics, and social intelligence. There are also tailor-made tests for special selling situations. These tests vary considerably in reliability and validity. Furthermore, many of them are vulnerable to manipulation by the applicant. A man can fake a lower IQ if he thinks this is desirable. He can also spot red-herring questions, such as "Do you prefer golf or reading?" Whyte laid down the following rules for the job applicant who takes company

---

[13]"Youth Continues to Snub Selling," *Sales Management*, January 15, 1965, p. 69.

psychological tests: (1) Give the most conventional answer; (2) show that you like things as they are; (3) indicate that you never worry; and (4) deny any taste for books or music.[14]

TRAINING SALESMEN

Not too long ago many companies sent their salesmen out into the field almost immediately after hiring them. The salesman would be supplied with a pack of samples, order books, and instructions to sell west of the Mississippi. Training programs were considered luxuries. A training program meant large outlays for instructors, materials, and space; the payment of a base salary to a man who is not selling; and lost opportunities because he is not in the field.

Nowadays a new salesman can expect to spend from a few weeks to many months in the limbo state known as training. In industries such as steel or data processing, the new salesman is not on his own for two years! A number of environmental changes have convinced sales management that an extended training period may generate more value than cost. The salesman of today is selling to more cost-conscious and value-conscious buyers. Furthermore, he is selling a host of products, often loosely related, and sometimes technically complex. He is preparing more reports. His company wants him to appear mature and knowledgeable before the customer even though he was recently hired.

During training, companies hope to pass on some mix of the following skills and understandings:

The salesman should know his company and identify with it. Most companies devote the first part of the training program to describing the history and objectives of the company, the organizational setup and lines of authority, the names of the chief officers, the company's financial structure and facilities, and the company's chief products and sales volume.

The salesman should know his products. The sales trainee is shown how the products are produced and how they function in various uses.

The salesman should know customers' and competitors' characteristics. The salesman is introduced to the different types of customers and their needs, buying motives, and buying habits. He learns about his company's and competitors' policies on credit, shipment, and so forth.

The salesman should learn how to make effective sales presentations. Companies explain the major sales arguments for each product, and some go so far as to develop scripts. Part of the training time is used to develop the salesman's personality and provide hints on self-development.

The salesman should be introduced to field procedures and responsibilities. He should know how he is expected to divide his time between active accounts and potential accounts; how to use his expense account, prepare reports, route himself effectively.

New methods of training are continually being sought to speed up and deepen skill development and understanding. Among the instructional ap-

---

[14]William H. Whyte, Jr., *The Organization Man* (New York: Simon and Schuster, Inc., 1956), pp. 405–10.

proaches are role playing, sensitivity training, cassette tapes, videotapes, programmed learning, and films on salesmanship and company products.

The substantial costs of company training programs raise the question whether a company would be better off to hire experienced men away from other companies. The gain is often illusory, however, because the experienced man is brought in at a higher salary, which sometimes may simply represent a capitalization of the equivalent training costs. From a socioeconomic point of view, there is probably a net loss when an industry practices pirating on a large scale. Some of his specific training and company experience is wasted when a man transfers to another company. Within some industries, companies have entered into tacit agreement not to hire men away from each other.

COMPENSATING SALESMEN

The major requirements for building a topflight sales force are (1) attracting good men, (2) motivating them, and (3) keeping them. In all three areas company compensation policies can make the crucial difference.

It is not easy to formulate a compensation plan that can be trusted to attract, motivate, and keep good salesmen. This is because diverse and often incompatible sets of objectives are sought by salesmen and by management. Prospective salesmen would like a plan that offers the following features:

> *Income regularity.* Since sales are influenced by many factors beyond the salesman's control, he wants to be assured of some regular base income regardless of his sales. This minimum income will help him pay his bills and feed his family in periods of declining sales.
>
> *Reward for above-average performance.* Most salesmen think they can sell more than the average salesman and want a compensation plan that provides superior income for superior performance.
>
> *Fairness.* Salesmen want to feel that their pay is about right in relation to their experience and ability, the earnings of co-workers and salesmen working for competitors, and the cost of living.

On the other hand, an ideal compensation plan from management's point of view would emphasize:

> *Control.* Management likes a plan that facilitates its control over how salesmen spend their time.
>
> *Economy.* Management wants to establish a level of pay that is reasonable in relation to the value of the salesman's effort and the cost and value of company products.
>
> *Simplicity.* Management prefers a plan that is simple to administer from a payroll point of view, simple to explain to sales supervisors and salesmen, and simple to change as product situations and business conditions alter.

Management is obviously hard pressed to reconcile all these objectives in one plan. Plans with good control features are generally not simple. Management goals, such as economy, conflict with salesmen's goals, such as financial security. In the light of these and other conflicts, it is understandable why compensation plans exhibit a tremendous variety, not only among industries but among companies within the same industry.

The level of compensation

Management must determine the level, components, and structure of an effective compensation plan. The level must bear some relation to the "going market price" for the type of sales job and abilities required. If the market price for sales manpower is well defined, the individual firm has little choice but to pay the going rate. To pay less would not bring forth the desired quantity or quality of applicants, and to pay more would be unnecessary. More often, however, the market price for sales manpower is not well defined. For one thing, company plans vary in the importance of fixed and variable salary elements, fringe benefits, and expense allowances. And data on the average take-home pay of salesmen working for competitive firms can be misleading because of significant variations in the average seniority and ability levels of the competitors' salesmen. Published comparisons of industry-by-industry salesman compensation levels are infrequent and generally lack sufficient detail.[15]

The theoretical solution to the problem of the optimal compensation level is implicit in the analysis shown earlier in Figure 8-3. Assume a situation where a company is preparing to establish a specialized sales force of ten men to handle a new product. They will be paid on a straight salary. Higher salary levels would allow the company to recruit better men and lead to higher sales volumes. The sales curve can be assumed to be S-shaped with respect to greater total expenditures on the sales force. From the estimated sales curve would be deducted all costs before the total sales-force expenditures to find gross profits. Then total sales-force expenditures would be deducted from gross profits, allowing a projection to be made of net profits. At the point where net profits are highest, the optimal total sales-force expenditure is found. This figure can be divided by the size of the planned sales force, ten men in this case, to find the optimal salary level.

The elements of compensation

After a firm decides on the average pay level, it must determine the appropriate mix of the four basic elements of salesmen's compensation—a fixed amount, a variable amount, expenses, and fringe benefits. The fixed amount, which might be salary or a drawing account, is intended to satisfy the salesman's need for some stability of income. The variable amount, which might be commissions, bonus, or profit sharing, is intended to stimulate and reward greater effort. Expense allowances are intended to stimulate and reward greater effort. Expense allowances are intended to enable the salesman to undertake selling efforts that are considered necessary or desirable. And, fringe benefits, such as paid vacations, sickness or accident benefits, pensions, and life insurance, are intended to provide security and job satisfaction.

Top sales management must decide which elements should be in the compensation plan and their relative importance. A popular rule seems to favor making about 70 percent of the salesman's total income fixed and allocating the remaining 30 percent among the other elements. But the variations around

---

[15]Studies are published by the Dartnell Corporation, The Conference Board, and the American Management Association.

this average are so pronounced that it can hardly serve as a sufficient guide in planning. For example, fixed compensation should have more emphasis in jobs with a high ratio of nonselling duties to selling duties and in jobs where the selling task is technically complex. Variable compensation should have more emphasis in jobs where sales are cyclical and/or depend on the personal initiative of the salesman.

Fixed and variable compensation taken alone give rise to three basic types of salesman compensation plans—straight salary, straight commission, and combination salary and commission.

Straight salary   With this plan, the salesman receives a fixed sum at regular intervals in total payment for his services. Generally he also receives an amount to defray part or all of the expenses he has incurred in performing his duties. Once the most popular plan for salesmen, it has been increasingly modified by the addition of incentive elements, so that today a minority of firms operate exclusively on this basis.

From management's point of view, a number of advantages are secured under a straight salary plan. The primary one is that management is freer to direct and alter salesmen's duties without incurring strong opposition from the men affected. Men on fixed salaries are more ready to go along with requests from management to spend more of their time in activities not associated with immediate sales, such as trying to open new accounts, providing technical services, or filling out longer reports. In addition, straight salary plans are generally less costly to administer and easier to explain. They also simplify the task of projecting the sales payroll for the coming year. Finally, by providing the salesman with security through stability of income, the straight salary plan may lead to a greater evenness in the morale of the salesmen.

The chief weakness of the straight salary plan is that it does not present the salesmen with any direct incentive to do a better than average selling job. This puts a greater supervision burden on management to control, evaluate, and reward the performances of individual salesmen. Other problems posed by straight salary plans are an inflexible selling-expense burden during downswings in business; the danger that during upswings salesmen on fixed salaries do not have sufficient incentive to exploit the increased business potential; thorny questions in salary adjustment for ability, rising living costs, length of service; and the probability that the more hard-driving type of salesman is not easy to attract.

Some of these advantages and disadvantages are reversed under straight commission plans.

Straight commission   This plan pays the salesman some fixed or sliding rate related to his sales or profit volume. The salesman may or may not also receive reimbursement for the expenses he incurs in performing his selling function. Although the general trend is away from straight plans, the straight commission plan is still found in many companies and industries, *especially where there is a need for aggressive selling and the salesman's nonselling duties are relatively minor.* Straight commission plans are particularly prominent in the selling of insurance and investment securities, furniture, office equipment, small office machines, clothing, the textile and shoe industries, and drug and hardware wholesaling.

The straight commission plan offers at least three advantages. The most obvious one is that it provides a maximum financial incentive for the salesman to work to capacity. The earnings of individual salesmen are more likely to reflect their true abilities and efforts under this plan. A second advantage is that a straight commission plan leads to selling expenses more closely related to funds either currently available or becoming available through sales revenues. The company avoids the hazards of bearing fixed selling expenses in the face of declining sales revenues. A third advantage is that commission plans enable management to employ *financial* incentives to direct salesmen in their use of selling time. Higher commission rates can be established for those products or accounts that management wants to emphasize.

These advantages of straight commission plans come at a substantial price, however. The foremost difficulty is that management encounters great resistance when it tries to get salesmen to do things that do not generate immediate sales. Salesmen may neglect to follow up leads, fill out reports, or provide sufficient customer service. Their personal financial involvement in getting the sale may lead them to use high-pressure tactics or price discounting, which in the long run may damage customer goodwill and company profits. Second, straight commission plans are generally more costly to administer. The cost arises in auditing salesmen's reports, applying sliding scales, and making more elaborate calculations. Third, straight commission plans provide little security and could have a deteriorative effect on the morale of salesmen when sales fall through no fault of their own.

In developing a commission plan, management has several options regarding the commission base, the nature of commission rates, and the starting point for commissions. The *commission base* may be gross sales volume, net sales after returns, gross margins, or net profits. The *commission rates* may be identical for all sales or differentiated by customers and/or products; they may be constant with sales volume or vary in a progressive or regressive fashion. The *starting point for commissions* may be the first sale or some sales level above a breakeven point.

Most companies base sales commissions on sales volume because of administrative simplicity and because of sales management's traditional interest in promoting volume. But this base is coming under increasing attack by more profit-conscious sales executives. Sales commissions based on sales volumes may not properly relate selling effort to company profitability. The payment of commissions on *gross margin* has been recommended as a better base and one that is practical to administer.[16] It has been shown mathematically that commissions tied to product gross margins would do a superior job of directing the salesmen to act in a way that would maximize the contribution to company profits.[17]

Combination salary and commission The great majority of firms use a combination of salary and commission features in the hope of achieving the advantages of each while avoiding the disadvantages. The combination plan

[16]See Ralph L. Day and Peter D. Bennett, "Should Salesmen's Compensation Be Geared to Profits?" *Journal of Marketing Research*, May 1964, pp. 39–43.

[17]See John U. Farley, "An Optimal Plan for Salesmen's Compensation," *Journal of Marketing Research*, May 1964, pp. 39–43.

is especially appropriate where sales volume depends upon the salesman's motivation and yet where management wants some control over the amount of nonselling duties performed by the salesman. The plan also means that during downswings the company is not stuck with rigid selling costs but neither does the salesman lose his whole income.

Many companies pay *bonuses* as a supplement or a substitute for commission-type incentives. Bonuses are noncontractual payments for extra effort or merit or for results beyond normal expectations. They are used to reward salesmen for performing tasks that are desirable but not rewardable through commissions, such as preparing prompt reports, supplying useful selling ideas, protecting the customer's inventory interests, and developing unusual product or market knowledgeability. The main problem with bonuses is that managerial judgment enters into their determination, and this can raise questions of fairness in the minds of individual salesmen.

The structure of compensation

Sales management must develop a rational pay structure for the various positions in the sales organization. The simplest sales organization contains sales trainees, junior salesmen, senior salesmen, and sales managers. More complex sales organizations contain separate sales forces differing in ability, type of selling, and so forth. It is necessary to arrive at some overall system of compensation that will be regarded as both fair and motivating to the diverse members of the sales force.

Over the years, *job evaluation* techniques have been refined, and they represent a rational management approach to developing a structure of compensation for an organization.[18] Among a number of existing job evaluation systems, one of the best-known and most widely used is the *point system*. It is based on the identification of job factors, such as responsibility, education, creativeness, experience, and other elements deemed to be important. Each factor is assigned a maximum number of points. The points are assigned to each job, representing the amount of each factor required. Finally all jobs are ranked by point values, and ranges of points are set up as compensation classes.

SUPERVISING SALESMEN

The new salesman is given more than his territory and a salary—he is given supervision. Supervision is the fate of all men who work for someone else. It is the expression of the employer's natural and continuous interest in the activities of his agents. Through supervision, the employer hopes to direct and motivate the salesman to do a better job.

Directing salesmen

Companies differ in the extent to which they try to prescribe to their salesmen what they should be doing. Much depends upon the nature of the selling job and the particular salesmen. Salesmen who are paid largely on commission and who are expected to hunt down their own prospects are generally left on their own. Salesmen who are largely salaried and who must cover a definite set of accounts are likely to receive substantial supervision.

---

[18]See David W. Hall, *Wage and Salary Administration* (Englewood Cliffs, N.J.: Prentice-Hall, Inc., 1958).

The importance of efficiency in making calls is highlighted by figures on the cost of sales calls. The average sales call today costs the company between $40 and $60.

Clearly, the sales manager has a major interest in helping his men manage their time better. Salesmen spend their time in the field in three major activities: traveling, waiting, and selling. In many jobs, they end up spending about one-third of their time in each activity. Although traveling and waiting time is not all a loss, because the time might be used to fill out reports and plan, it is desirable to reduce these to the extent possible. Here the sales manager can help by showing salesmen how to use the phone more effectively, how to route better, and so on. A more important task is to help the salesmen make the right calls in the first place.

Developing customer call norms Most companies classify their customers into a number of types, such as A, B, C, D, reflecting the sales volume or profit potential of the different accounts. They establish a certain desired number of calls per period that their salesman should make to each customer type. Thus A accounts may be assigned to receive twelve calls a year, B accounts six calls, C accounts four calls, and D accounts two calls. The exact levels that are set depend upon competitive call norms and expected account profitability.

These call norms are to be taken as rough guidelines only.[19] The real issue is how much sales volume could be expected from a particular account as a function of the annual number of calls made to that account. In one current computer model for sales call planning, the salesman is asked to estimate sales for each of his accounts for five different possible call levels. The computer then calculates the optimal number of calls he should make on each account, given these subjective sales-response functions, the account profit margins, and the total available sales call time.[20]

It may be possible to determine the sales call response function experimentally. Magee described an experiment where salesmen were asked to vary their call pattern in a particular way to determine what effect this would have on sales.[21] The experiment called first for sorting accounts into major classes. Each account class was then randomly split into three sets. The respective salesmen were asked, for a specified period of time, to spend less than five hours a month with accounts in the first set, five to nine hours a month with the second set, and more than nine hours a month with the third set. The results demonstrated that additional call time increases sales volume, leaving only the question of whether the magnitude of sales increase was sufficient to justify the additional increase.

---

[19]The story is told about a salesman who thought he literally had to make twelve prospect calls a day. At 4:45 P.M. he was still talking with the eleventh prospect, who was getting increasingly interested in the company's products. "Tell me more, young man," said the prospect. "I'm sorry, sir," replied the salesman. "There are only fifteen minutes left, and I must leave to make my last call."

[20]Leonard M. Lodish, "Callplan: An Interactive Salesman's Call Planning System," *Management Science*, December 1971, pp. 25–40.

[21]See John F. Magee, "Determining the Optimum Allocation of Expenditures for Promotional Effort with Operations Research Methods," in *The Frontiers of Marketing Thought and Science*, ed. Frank M. Bass (Chicago: American Marketing Association, 1958), pp. 140–56. See also Arthur A. Brown, Frank T. Hulswit, and John D. Kettelle, "A Study of Sales Operations," *Operations Research*, June 1956, pp. 296–308.

Developing prospect call norms   Companies like to specify to their salesmen how much time to spend prospecting for new accounts. For example, Spector Freight wants its men to spend 25 percent of their time prospecting; and to stop calling on a prospect after three unsuccessful calls.

There are a number of reasons why many companies try to set up a minimum requirement for the canvassing of new accounts. If left alone, many salesmen tend to spend most of their time in the offices of present customers. Present customers are better-known quantities. The salesmen can depend upon them for some business, whereas a prospect may never deliver any business or deliver it only after many months of effort. Unless the salesman receives a bonus for new accounts, he assumes the risks during the courting period. Some companies try to open new accounts by using salaried missionary salesmen exclusively.

The key issue in developing prospect call norms is to have a way to estimate the *value of any given prospect*. This problem is especially acute in situations where there are more prospects than time available for developing them. They must be ranked so that salesmen can concentrate on the best prospects. A useful model can be formulated by looking at the value of an account in terms of investment theory. First the salesman should estimate the value of the prospect's business if the prospect were converted to a customer. The value of the prospect's business may be represented in terms of a discounted income stream lasting so many years. Specifically,

$$Z = \sum_{t=1}^{\bar{t}} \frac{mQ_t - X}{(1 + r)^t} \tag{17-1}$$

where:

Z = present value of the future income from a new customer
m = gross margin on sales
Q_t = expected sales from new customer in year t
X = cost of maintaining customer contact per year
r = company discount rate
t = a subscript for year
$\bar{t}$ = number of years that this new customer is expected to remain a customer

Thus the salesman estimates that this prospect, if converted to a customer, would annually purchase from the company Q_t units with a profit per unit of m less a customer contact cost (X) and that this will last for $\bar{t}$ periods. Future income is discounted at an interest rate r.

The next step is to consider the investment necessary to convert this prospect to a customer. The investment can be described as:

$$I = nc \tag{17-2}$$

where:

I = investment in trying to convert the prospect to a customer
n = number of calls to convert the prospect into a customer
c = cost per call

The number of calls to the prospect will influence the probability of his conversion—that is,

$$p = p(n)$$

$$(17\text{-}3)$$

The value of the prospect's business should be scaled down by this probability. Putting the previous elements together, the following investment formula emerges for the value (V) of a prospect:

$$V = p(n) \sum_{t=1}^{\bar{t}} \frac{mQ_t - X}{(1 + r)^t} - nc \qquad (17\text{-}4)$$

According to this formula, the value of a prospect depends on the difference between the expected present value of the income stream and the investment made in prospect conversion. Both the expected present value and the investment depend in turn on the intended number of calls, n, upon the prospect. The intended number of calls should be the optimal number of calls, and this can be found mathematically if the probability-of-conversion function is known.

The formula could easily be incorporated into a computer program wherein the salesman sits down at a terminal, types in a set of estimates for each prospect regarding the expected volume of his business, maximum probability of conversion, and so on, and receives back a ranking of all the prospects in order of their investment value along with the suggested number of calls to make on each.

Motivating salesmen

A small percentage of salesmen in any sales force can be expected to do their best without any special stimulation from management. To them, selling is the most fascinating job in the world. These men are ambitious, and they are self-starters. But the majority of salesmen on nearly every sales force require personal encouragement and special incentives to work at their best level. This is especially true for creative field selling for the following reasons:

> *The nature of the job.* The selling job is one of frequent frustration. The salesman works alone; his hours are irregular; he does not lead a normal family life; he confronts aggressive competing salesmen; he is in an inferior status relative to the buyer; he sometimes does not have the authority to do what is necessary to win an account.
> *Human nature.* Most men operate below capacity in the absence of special incentive. They won't "kill themselves" without some prospect of financial gain or social recognition.
> *Personal problems.* The salesman, like everyone else, is occasionally preoccupied with personal problems, such as sickness in the family, marital discord, or debt.

Management can affect the morale and performance of the salesmen through its organizational climate, sales quotas, and positive incentives.

Organizational climate Organizational climate describes the feeling that the salesmen get from their company regarding their opportunities, value, and rewards for a good performance. Some companies treat their sales force as being of minor importance. Other companies treat their salesmen as the prime movers and allow unlimited opportunity for income and promotion. The company's attitude toward its salesmen acts as a self-fulfilling prophecy: if they are held in low opinion, there is much turnover and poor performance; if they are held in high opinion, there is little turnover and high performance.

The quality of personal treatment from the salesman's immediate supervisor is an important aspect of the organizational climate. An effective supervisor keeps in touch with the salesman through periodic correspondence and phone calls, personal visits in the field, and evaluation sessions in the home office. At different times he is the salesman's boss, companion, coach, and confessor.

Sales quotas   Many companies set sales quotas for their salesmen specifying what they should sell during the year. Sometimes this is a total dollar figure, sometimes a set of sales figures for different products in the line. Often the compensation system is related to the quota: salesmen selling more than their quota earn a bonus or commission. If salesmen fulfill their quotas on the average, the company will have a profitable year.

Sales quotas are developed each year in the process of developing the annual marketing plan. The company first decides on a sales forecast that is reasonably achievable. This becomes the basis of planning production, workforce size, and financial requirements. Then management establishes sales quotas for all of its territories, which typically add up to more than the sales forecast. Sales quotas are set higher than the sales forecast in order to move the sales managers and salesmen to their best effort. If they fail to make their quotas, the company nevertheless may make its sales forecast.

Each field sales manager takes his quota and divides it up among his salesmen. He too may make the sum of their quotas higher than the territory's actual quota. Actually, there are three schools of thought on quota setting. The *high-quota school* likes to set quotas that are above what most salesmen will achieve but that are possible for all. They are of the opinion that high quotas spur extra effort. The *modest-quota school* likes to set quotas that a majority of salesmen can attain. They feel that the salesmen will accept the quotas as fair, attain them, and gain confidence from attaining them. Finally, the *variable-quota school* thinks that individual differences among salesmen warrant high quotas for some, modest quotas for others. According to Heckert:

> Actual experience with sales quotas, as with all standards, will reveal that sales representatives react to them somewhat differently, particularly at first. Some are stimulated to their highest efficiency, others are discouraged. Some sales executives place considerable emphasis upon this human element in setting their quotas. In general, however, good men will in the long run respond favorably to intelligently devised quotas, particularly when compensation is fairly adjusted to performance.[22]

More formally, the variable-quota school will base quotas for the individual salesman on a number of considerations, including the salesman's sales performance in the previous period, his territory's estimated potential, and a

---
[22]J. B. Heckert, *Business Budgeting and Control* (New York: The Ronald Press Company, 1946), p. 138.

judgment of his aspiration level and reaction to pressure and incentive. Some propositions in this area are:

1   The sales quota for salesman j at time t, Q_{jt}, should generally be set above his sales in the year just ending, $S_{j,t-1}$; that is,

$$Q_{jt} > S_{j,t-1}$$

2   The sales quota for salesman j at time t should be higher, the greater the positive gap between the estimated sales potential of his territory S_{Pjt} and his sales in the year just ending; that is,

$$Q_{jt} \sim (S_{Pjt} - S_{j,t-1})$$

3   The sales quota for salesman j at time t should be higher, the more positively he responds to pressure, E_j; that is,

$$Q_{jt} \sim E_j$$

These three propositions can be combined in an equation for setting a salesman's quota:

$$Q_{jt} = S_{j,t-1} + E_j(S_{Pjt} - S_{j,t-1}) \tag{17-5}$$

Thus, salesman j's quota at time t should be at least equal to his actual sales last period, plus some fraction E_j of the difference between estimated territorial sales potential and his sales last year; the more positively he reacts to pressure, the higher the fraction.

Positive incentives   Companies use a number of positive motivators to stimulate salesmen effort. Periodic *sales meetings* provide a social occasion, a break from routine, a chance to meet and talk with "company brass," a chance to air feelings and to identify with a larger group. Companies also sponsor *sales contests* when they want to spur salesmen to make a special selling effort above what would be reasonably expected. Planning these contests has developed into a real science, and experienced administration is needed for good results.

What is the relative effectiveness of different types of incentives on salesmen? This topic has not been researched experimentally. One of the few studies is a survey of the opinions of sales executives conducted a number of years ago. The sales executives were asked: "Which of the following methods will do the most to stimulate your *average* salesman to *better* his usual or normal performance?" Their assigned rankings were converted into ratings with the results shown in Table 17-1.

In the opinion of sales executives, financial incentives assume the first three positions of importance. They are followed by a succession of more social incentives. Thus in the minds of sales executives, dollar motivation is of prime importance but must be complemented by social sources of motivation.

EVALUATING SALESMEN

We have been describing the *feedforward* aspects of supervision—the efforts of management to communicate to the salesmen what they should be doing and to motivate them to do it. But good feedforward requires good feedback. And good

Table 17-1

Effectiveness of incentives to stimulate average salesmen
to better their usual performance

Factor	Rating
Basic compensation plan	100
Sales contests	58
Bonus payments	55
Friendly, informal supervisors	44
Scientific planning of quotas and territories	34
Honor awards and letters of commendation	23
Sales conventions	18
Profit sharing plan	17
Fringe benefits—retirement, hospitalization, etc.	14
Vacations with pay	11
Suggestion systems	2
Complaint procedures	1

SOURCE: Albert Haring and Robert H. Myers, "Special Incentives for Salesmen," *Journal of Marketing*, October 1953, p. 159.

NOTE: The ratings were derived in the following manner. Executives were asked to select the five most important incentives from the list and to rank them one to five. The answers were weighted by assigning values from five down to one point for the five rankings. The highest total rating went to basic compensation plans, and all other ratings were expressed as a percentage of this figure.

feedback means getting regular information from and about salesmen to evaluate their performance.

Sources of information

Management gains information about its salesmen through a number of channels. Probably the most important source of information is the salesmen's periodic reports. Additional information comes through personal observation, through customers' letters and complaints, and through other salesmen's conversations.

A distinction can be drawn between salesmen reports that represent *plans for future activities* and those that represent *write-ups of completed activities*. The best example of the former is the *salesman's work plan*, which most salesmen are required to submit for a specified future period, usually a week or a month in advance. The plan describes the calls he will make and the routing he will use. This report serves the purposes of encouraging the salesman to plan and schedule his activities, informing management of his whereabouts, and providing a basis for comparing his plans with his accomplishments. The salesman can be evaluated for his ability to "plan his work and work his plan." Occasionally, management contacts the salesman after receiving his plan and suggests improvements.

Companies moving toward annual marketing planning in depth are beginning to require their salesmen to draft an annual *territory marketing plan* in which they outline their program for developing new accounts and increasing business from existing accounts. The formats vary considerably, some asking merely for ideas on territory development and others asking for detailed estimates. This type of report reflects the conception of the salesman as an entrepreneur and as the manager of his territory. The plans are studied by the immediate supervisor and become the bases for rendering constructive suggestions to salesmen and developing branch sales objectives and estimates for higher-level management.

Several forms are used by salesmen to write up their completed activities and accomplishments. Perhaps the best known is the *call report* on which the salesman records pertinent aspects of his dealings with a customer, including competitive brands used, best time for calling, degree and type of resistance, and future account promise. Call reports serve the objectives of keeping management informed of the salesman's activities, indicating the status of the customer's account, and providing information that might be useful in subsequent calls.

Salesmen also report their *expenses* incurred in the performance of selling duties, for which they are partly or wholly reimbursed. The objective from management's standpoint is primarily to exercise control over the type and amount of expenses and secondarily to have the requisite expense data for income-tax purposes. It is also hoped that the salesmen will exercise more care in incurring expenses when they must report them in some detail.

Additional types of reports that some companies require from their salesmen are:

> *A report on new business secured or potential new business.* This alerts management to new accounts and new prospects for which it can formulate special marketing plans in the form of direct mail, team solicitation, and so on. It is also used to evaluate the extent and effectiveness of the salesman's prospecting work.
>
> *A report on lost business.* This report enables the company to keep abreast of competitive efforts, needed product or service improvements, and, not the least important, to evaluate the effectiveness of the individual salesman.
>
> *A periodic report on local business and economic conditions.* This report aids the development of territory norms and sales programs, although it must be recognized that salesmen sometimes distort the local picture to rationalize their own performance.

The reports that companies require their salesmen to submit contain a wealth of information. Salesmen, however, frequently complain that they have to devote too much time to writing when they should be selling and that their reports are not read. Management must guard against these criticisms by thinking carefully through the intended uses of the information. The forms should be brief and easy to fill out. Management should make a point of regularly responding to the information.

Formal evaluation of performance

The salesmen's reports along with other reports from the field and the manager's personal observations supply the raw materials for formally evaluating the salesmen. Formal evaluation procedures lead to at least three benefits. First, they lead management to develop specific and uniform standards for judging salesman performance. Second, they lead management to draw together all its information and impressions about individual salesmen and make more systematic, point-by-point evaluations. Third, they tend to have a constructive effect on the performance of salesmen. The constructive effect comes about because the salesmen know that they will have to sit down one fine morning with their supervisor and explain certain facets of their routing or call decisions or their failure to secure or maintain certain accounts, and the like.

Salesman-to-salesman comparisons One type of evaluation frequently made is to compare a salesman's current performance with that of other company salesmen. Such comparisons, however, can be misleading. Relative sales performances are meaningful only if there are no variations from territory to territory in the market potential, workload, degree of competition, company promotional effort, and so forth. Furthermore, sales are not the best denominator of achievement. Management should be more interested in how much each salesman contributed to net profits. And this cannot be known until the salesman's sales mix and his sales expenses are examined. A possible ranking criterion would be the *salesman's actual contribution to company net profits as a ratio to his territory's potential contribution to company net profits.* A ratio of 1.00 would mean that the salesman did the best job possible in his territory. A ratio of .50 would mean that a salesman earned only 50 percent of what a perfect salesman could have earned in that territory. The lower a salesman's ratio, the more supervision and counseling he needs.

Current-to-past-sales comparisons A second common type of evaluation is to compare a salesman's current performance with his own past performance. This should provide a more direct record of his progress. An example is shown in Table 17-2.

Many things can be learned by the sales manager from the information in this table. One of the first things to note is that Smith's total sales increased every year (line 3). This does not necessarily mean that Smith is doing a better job. The product breakdown shows that he has been able to push further the sales of product B than product A (lines 1 and 2). According to his quotas for the two products (lines 4 and 5), his success in increasing sales of product B may be at the expense of product A. According to gross profits (lines 6 and 7), the company earns about twice as much on A as B. The picture begins to emerge that John Smith may be pushing the higher-volume, lower-margin product at the expense of the more profitable product. In fact, although he increased total sales by $1,100 between 1974 and 1975 (line 3), the gross profits on his total sales actually decreased by $580 (line 8).

Sales expense (line 9) shows a steady increase, although total expense as a percentage of total sales seems to be under control (line 10). The upward trend in Smith's total dollar expense does not seem to be explained by any increase in the number of calls (line 11), although it may be related in part to his success in acquiring new customers (line 14). However, there is a possibility that in prospecting for new customers, he is neglecting present customers, as indicated by an upward trend in the annual number of lost customers (line 15).

The last two lines show the level and trend in Smith's sales per customer and the gross profits on his sales per customer. These figures become more meaningful when they are compared with overall company averages. For example, if John Smith's average gross profit per customer is lower than the company's average, he may be concentrating on the wrong customers or may not be spending enough time with each customer. Looking back at his annual number of calls (line 11), it may be that Smith is making fewer annual calls than the average salesman. If distances in his territory are not much different, this may mean he is not putting in a full workday, he is poor at planning his routing or minimizing his waiting, or he spends too much time with certain accounts.

Table 17-2

Form for evaluating salesman's progress

	Territory: **Midland**	Salesman: **John Smith**		
	1972	*1973*	*1974*	*1975*
1. Net sales product A	$251,300	$253,200	$270,000	$263,100
2. Net sales product B	$423,200	$439,200	$553,900	$561,900
3. Net sales total	$674,500	$692,400	$823,900	$825,000
4. Percent of quota product A	95.6	92.0	88.0	84.7
5. Percent of quota product B	120.4	122.3	134.9	130.8
6. Gross profits product A	$ 50,260	$ 50,640	$ 54,000	$ 52,620
7. Gross profits product B	$ 42,320	$ 43,920	$ 55,390	$ 56,190
8. Gross profits total	$ 92,580	$ 94,560	$109,390	$108,810
9. Sales expense	$ 10,200	$ 11,100	$ 11,600	$ 13,200
10. Sales expense to total sales (%)	1.5	1.6	1.4	1.6
11. Number of calls	1,675	1,700	1,680	1,660
12. Cost per call	$ 6.09	$ 6.53	$ 6.90	$ 7.95
13. Average number of customers	320	324	328	334
14. Number of new customers	13	14	15	20
15. Number of lost customers	8	10	11	14
16. Average sales per customer	$ 2,108	$ 2,137	$ 2,512	$ 2,470
17. Average gross profit per customer	$ 289	$ 292	$ 334	$ 326

Qualitative appraisal of salesmen The appraisal usually includes an evaluation of the salesman's knowledge, personality, and motivation. He can be rated on the extent of his knowledge of his company, products, customers, competitors, territory, and responsibilities. Personality characteristics can be rated, such as his general manner, appearance, speech, and temperament. The supervisor can also consider any problems in motivation or compliance. Since an almost endless number of qualitative factors might be included, each company must decide what would be most useful to know. It also should communicate these criteria to the salesmen so that they are aware of how their performance is judged.

SUMMARY

The great majority of companies utilize salesmen, and many assign them the pivotal role in the creation of sales. Because salesmen are capable of performing a wide variety of tasks, each company must decide exactly what it expects to accomplish through direct selling. The objectives set for the sales force influence the strategies and tactical decisions arising in the management of an effective sales operation.

At the strategic level, the company must decide on the size of its sales force and how it should be organized. In principle, the sales force should be expanded up to the point where an additional salesman would impose more cost on the company than he generates in the way of a gross margin on sales. In practice, sales-force size decisions are made on estimates of salesman productivity in different territories or feasible territory workloads. The effectiveness of the sales force will depend upon whether it is organized along territorial, product, or customer lines and whether sales territories are designed thoughtfully in terms of size and shape.

Salesmen must be continuously recruited and selected on the basis of scientific procedures to hold down the high costs of hiring the wrong men. Salesman training programs are growing more elaborate and require careful thought and planning to justify their costs. Salesmen who emerge from the training program must be assigned to territories in a way that recognizes their varying productivity in different possible assignments. Compensation is probably the most important single element in their motivation and should somehow provide a measure of both incentive and security to be maximally effective. The average salesman needs supervision and continuous encouragement because he must make a large number of decisions and is subject to many frustrations. Periodically his performance must be formally evaluated to help him do a better job.

**QUESTIONS
AND PROBLEMS**

1 A district sales manager voiced the following complaint at a sales meeting. "The average salesman costs our company $20,000 in compensation and expenses. Why can't we buy a few less $20,000 full-page advertisements in *Time* magazine and use the money to hire more men? Surely one man working a full year can sell more products than a one-page ad in one issue of *Time*." Evaluate this argument.

2 The text described some of the characteristics that might be looked for in salesmen. What characteristics should be looked for in selecting district sales managers? What about the top sales manager?

3 (a) Show diagrammatically, in terms of distances traveled, why a product-structured sales force involves more total travel distance than an unspecialized sales force. (b) Show diagrammatically why a customer-structured sales force involves more total travel distance than an unspecialized sales force.

4 The sales manager of a large company would like to determine how many sales calls per month his men should make to average-size accounts. Describe how an experiment might be set up to answer the question.

5 A sales manager is trying to figure out the most that should be spent to win a particular account. This account would produce sales of $10,000 a year, and the company is likely to retain it for at least four years. The company's profit margin on sales is 15 percent. The company wants its various investments to earn 8 percent. What is the most that the company should spend to win this account?

6 Suppose a salesman in a particular industry can make an average of 1,600 calls a year. If he has been writing $420,000 worth of business a year, how many calls can the salesman afford to make to a $10,000-a-year account without diluting his total business written during the year?

7 Describe several types of selling situations where a straight salary plan seems appropriate.

8 A company regularly asks for its salesmen's views on such questions as whether to introduce a new product or to raise the price on one of its products. How unbiased are the salesmen's reactions likely to be?

9 Should individual salesmen participate in the establishment of sales quotas for their territories? What would be the advantages and disadvantages of such participation?

10 Develop a formula showing Talley's method of determining the optimal size sales force.

VI

ADMINISTERING THE MARKETING PROGRAM

18
MARKETING ORGANIZATION

Do your work with your whole heart and you will
succeed—there is so little competition!

ELBERT HUBBARD

We now turn to the administrative side of marketing management to examine how firms organize their marketing department and their marketing activities. In this chapter we shall deal with marketing organization, and in the following chapters with the conduct of marketing research, information, and control activities.

We shall illustrate our discussion of marketing organization mainly in connection with manufacturing companies because it is in these companies that the marketing management function first emerged. The same developments are now taking place in such service industries as retailing, banking, and insurance. The marketing management function is even emerging in large non-profit organizations, such as the U.S. Postal Service, U.S. Army, health maintenance organizations, and mass transit companies.

THE EVOLUTION OF THE MARKETING DEPARTMENT

The modern marketing department is the product of a long evolution from very humble beginnings. Five stages in this evolution can be distinguished. Company examples can currently be found of departments in each of these stages.

405

Simple sales department	All companies start out with three simple functions. Someone must raise and manage capital (finance), produce the product or service (operations), and sell it (sales). The selling function is headed by a sales vice-president who basically manages a sales force and does some selling himself. When the company needs some marketing research or advertising, the sales vice-president also handles these because they fall in the selling area. Nevertheless, he has his heart in the sales force and handles these other assignments halfheartedly.
Sales department with ancillary functions	As the company expands, it finds that it needs marketing research, advertising, and customer service on a more regular basis. The sales vice-president now hires a few specialists who can carry out this work under him. He continues to spend most of his time managing the sales force and may appoint a marketing director to manage the other marketing activities.
Separate marketing department	The continued growth of the company inevitably increases the importance of other marketing functions—marketing research, new-product development, advertising and promotion, customer service—relative to sales force activity. Since the sales vice-president tends to neglect or not have his heart in these other activities, the company president will often take the step of creating a separate marketing department. The company now has a sales vice-president and a marketing vice-president.
Modern marketing department	Although the sales vice-president and the marketing vice-president are supposed to work harmoniously together, their relation is often characterized by rivalry and distrust. The sales vice-president sees a conspiracy to make the sales force less important in the marketing mix; and the marketing vice-president seeks to extend his power over all the customer-impinging functions. The sales vice-president tends to be short-run oriented and preoccupied with achieving current sales. The marketing vice-president tends to be long-run oriented and preoccupied with planning the right products and marketing strategy to meet the customers' long-run needs.

If there is too much conflict, the company president must either (1) eliminate the marketing vice-president's office and place marketing activities back under the sales vice-president or (2) place the marketing vice-president in charge of everything, with the sales department reporting to him. The second solution is eventually chosen in many companies and forms the basis of the modern marketing department, a department headed by a marketing vice-president with subordinates reporting to him from every marketing function, including sales management. |
| Modern marketing company | A company can have a modern marketing department and yet not operate as a modern marketing company. Whether it is the latter depends upon how the officers of the company view the marketing function. If they view marketing as one of the several equal functions in the organization, the company is probably not a modern marketing company. If they view marketing as the hub of the enterprise, and not just one of its spokes, the company has achieved modern marketing stature.

The vice-president of marketing, no matter how well he runs his own department, meets frequent resistance from other vice-presidents as to what he regards as marketing imperatives. The manufacturing vice-president holds |

to the logic of cost minimization and resents interrupting production schedules to please customers. He acts as if the company's assets are centered on the factory floor rather than in the marketplace. The financial vice-president is oriented toward visible and measurable investment returns. He is not sure about the payouts of investments in marketing research, communication, and promotion, and he reacts to sales declines by recommending cuts in market development expenditures. Only a few companies have attained the stature of a genuine marketing company: a few consumer packaged goods firms, a few industrial companies, and so on. There is opposition to bending all of the company functions to the task of producing satisfied customers. Ultimately the answer must lie in increasing the power and authority of the marketing vice-president over the other business functions.

WAYS OF ORGANIZING THE MODERN MARKETING DEPARTMENT

An examination of modern marketing departments reveals innumerable arrangements. All marketing organizations must somehow accommodate to three basic dimensions of marketing activity: *functions, products,* and *markets.*

Functional organization

The earliest and still most common form of marketing organization has various functional marketing specialists reporting to a marketing vice-president who is in charge of coordinating all of their activities. Figure 18-1 shows three such specialists who bear the titles of advertising manager, sales manager, and marketing research manager, respectively. Additional functional specialties (not shown) might also be present in the marketing department, such as merchandising, new products, customer service, sales analysis, and market planning.

If the number of functions reporting to the marketing vice-president becomes large, they may be subgrouped into *operations* functions and *planning* functions. Reporting to the marketing vice-president would be a manager of marketing operations responsible for sales, customer services, and advertising, and a manager of marketing planning responsible for marketing research, sales forecasting, and new-product planning. The marketing vice-president then has two major functions to think about, planning and doing, instead of several specialties.

The main advantage of a functional marketing organization is its administrative simplicity. On the other hand, this organizational form suffers from

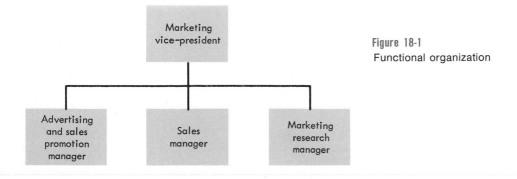

Figure 18-1
Functional organization

certain disadvantages as the company's product line or number of markets increases. First, there is inadequate detailed planning for specific products and markets, since no one is assigned full responsibility for any product or market. Products that are not favorites with various functional specialists tend to get neglected. Second, each functional group develops its own subgoals that include trying to gain importance vis-à-vis the other functions. The marketing vice-president has to constantly sift the claims of competing functional specialists and faces a difficult problem in coordination.

Product management organization

Companies producing a variety of products and/or brands often establish a product management system (also called a brand management system). The product management system does not replace the functional management system but serves as another layer of management (see Figure 18-2). The functional managers are essentially *resource managers,* and the product managers are essentially *program managers.* This type of organization is called a *matrix organization* because each resource manager gets involved with each program manager. The organization can be visualized as a set of rows representing marketing functions and columns representing products.

The decision to establish a product management system is influenced by the extent of product heterogeneity and the sheer number of products. If the company product lines can benefit from specialized marketing programs, or if the sheer number of products is beyond the capacity of a functional marketing organization to handle, a product management organization is a natural recourse.

Product management first made its appearance in the Procter & Gamble Company in 1927. A new company soap, Camay, was not doing well, and one of the young men, Neil H. McElroy (later president of P&G), was assigned to give his exclusive attention to developing and promoting this product. This he did successfully, and the company soon afterward added other product managers. Since then a large number of firms, especially in the food, soap, toiletries,

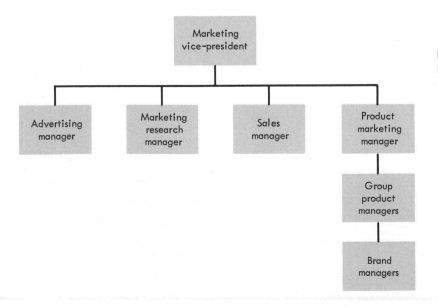

Figure 18-2
Product management organization

and chemical industries, have established product-management systems. General Foods, for example, uses a product-management system in its Post Division. There are separate product group managers in charge of cereals, pet food, and beverages. Within the cereal product group, there are separate product managers for nutritional cereals, children's presweetened cereals, family cereals, and miscellaneous cereals. In turn, the nutritional cereal product manager supervises several brand managers.[1]

The product management system creates a focal point of planning and responsibility for individual products. The product manager's role is to create product strategies and plans, see that they are implemented, monitor the results, and take corrective action. This responsibility breaks down into the following six tasks:

1   Developing a long-range growth and competitive strategy for the product.
2   Preparing an annual marketing plan and sales forecast.
3   Working with advertising and merchandising agencies to develop copy, programs, and campaigns.
4   Stimulating interest in and support of the product among salesmen and distributors.
5   Gathering continuous intelligence on the product's performance, customer and dealer attitudes, and new problems and opportunities.
6   Initiating product improvements to meet changing market needs.

These basic functions are common to both consumer and industrial product managers. Yet there are some important differences in their jobs and emphases.[2] The consumer product manager tends to manage fewer products than his industrial counterpart. He spends considerably more time dealing with advertising and sales promotion. He spends most of his time working with people in his organization and the agency, and little time in direct contact with customers. He tends to be younger and better educated. The industrial product manager, by contrast, thinks more carefully about the technical aspects of his product and possible improvements in design. He spends more time with laboratory and engineering personnel in his company. He is in closer touch with the sales force and key buyers. He tends to pay less attention to advertising, sales promotion, and promotional pricing. He emphasizes rational product factors over emotional ones.

The product management system introduces several advantages in the management of the firm's marketing activity. First, the product manager can balance and harmonize the various functional marketing inputs needed by a product. Second, the product manager is in a position to react quickly to problems in the marketplace without involving several different people in lengthy meetings. Third, smaller brands, because they have a product champion, are not as neglected in this system as they tend to be in functional marketing organizations. Fourth, product management is an excellent training ground for

---

[1]For details, see "General Foods Corporation: Post Division," in E. Raymond Corey and Steven H. Star, *Organization Strategy: A Marketing Approach* (Boston: Division of Research, Graduate School of Business Administration, Harvard University, 1971), pp. 201–30.

[2]See Elmer E. Waters, "Industrial Product Manager . . . Consumer Brand Manager: A Study in Contrast," *Industrial Marketing*, January 1969, pp. 45-49.

promising young executives, for it involves them in every area of company operations—marketing, production, and finance.

But a price is paid for these advantages. First, the product management system introduces many sources of conflict and frustration that might not otherwise be present.[3] The product manager is not given authority commensurate with his responsibility. As a program manager, he has to rely on persuasive methods to gain cooperation from various resource managers. He spends so much time importuning advertising, sales, and manufacturing for special support that he has little time for planning. He has been told by his superiors that he is a mini-president, but he is often treated like a low-level coordinator. He solicits the help of specialists but often does not follow their advice. Sometimes he goes over their heads. He is bogged down by a great amount of "housekeeping" paperwork. If this results in a rapid turnover of product managers, it can damage the sound long-range planning of products.

Second, the product manager becomes an expert in his product but rarely has a chance to become an expert in any of the functions for which he is responsible. He vacillates between posing as an expert and being cowed by real experts. This is particularly unfortunate where the product basically depends on a particular type of expertise, such as advertising; here it would almost make more sense to put it in the hands of an advertising specialist.

Third, the product management system often turns out to be costlier than anticipated. Originally, one man is appointed to manage each important product. Soon, product managers are appointed to manage even minor products. Each product manager, usually overworked, pleads and gets an assistant brand manager. Later, both of them, still overworked, persuade management to give them an assistant. Product managers who supervise the more important company products, in their frustration in having to coax time from advertising, packaging, and other specialists, next pressure to hire their own specialists. In one large brewery, the main brand manager has his own advertising department. With all these personnel, the payroll climbs. In the meantime the company continues to increase its number of functional specialists in copy, packaging, media, promotion, market surveys, statistical analysis, and so on. The company soon finds itself stuck with a costly superstructure of product management people and a superstructure of specialists.

When a company has a product management system that breeds too much conflict or cost, it has four recourses. The first is to try to improve its functioning through better training and procedures. Although P&G managed to achieve over the years a smooth-working product management system, many of its imitators have installed the form without the substance. Pearson and Wilson have suggested five things that will make it work better:

1 *Clearly delineate the limits of the product manager's role and responsibility for the management of a product.* [He is essentially a proposer, not a decider.] . . .

2 *Build a strategy development and review process to provide an agreed-to-framework for the product manager's operations.* [Too many companies allow product managers to get away with shallow marketing plans featuring a lot of statistics but little strategic rationale.] . . .

---

[3]See David J. Luck, "Interfaces of a Product Manager," *Journal of Marketing*, October 1969, pp. 32–36.

3   *Take into account areas of potential conflict between product managers and functional special-*
    ists when defining their respective roles. [Clarify which decisions are to be made by
    the product manager, which by the expert, and which will be shared.] . . .

4   *Set up a formal process that forces to the top all conflict-of-interest situations between product*
    management and functional line management. [Both parties might be expected to
    put all issues in writing and forward them to general management for settle-
    ment.] . . .

5   *Establish a system for measuring results that is consistent with the product manager's re-*
    sponsibilities. [If the product manager is to be held accountable for profit, he
    should be given more control over the factors that affect his profitability.] . . .[4]

A second alternative is to switch from a product manager to a product
team approach. The product is turned over to a team representing different
company areas which is assigned responsibility for the product, with the product
manager as the team leader. Thus the 3M company divided its commercial tape
division into nine business planning teams, with each team further broken down
into a team leader, as well as sales, marketing, laboratory, engineering, accounting, and marketing research members. Instead of a product manager's having
to bear the entire responsibility for a product plan, the responsibility is shared
by representatives from the various key parts of the company, and the opportunity for conflict is lessened.

A third alternative is to eliminate product managers of minor brands and
load two or more brands on the existing product managers. This is feasible
especially where the company products appeal to a similar set of needs. Thus
a cosmetics company does not need separate product managers as much because
cosmetics serve one major need—beauty—whereas a toiletries company needs
a different manager for headache remedies, toothpaste, soap, and hair shampoo
because these products are very different in their use and appeals.

A fourth alternative is to establish divisions around the major company products or product groups and use functional arrangements within
divisions. Pearson and Wilson feel that a functional marketing organization "is
the oldest, simplest and, in many respects, the soundest form of organization
for marketing."[5]

The product manager position is undoubtedly undergoing important
change. Two particular trends have been accelerated by company experiences
with shortages, rapid inflation, and recession. The first is the greater assumption
of profit responsibility by product managers. Cost inflation has led companies
to be less satisfied with the sheer volume they sell and more concerned with the
profits they make. The product manager is becoming more of a profit center
and must put a profit test to the various items in his line and to his various
marketing expenditures. Some companies are even holding their product managers responsible for the costs of inventory and receivables. The second tendency
is the heightened need for improved communication and cooperation between
product managers and various resource managers to find ways of securing
scarce supplies, developing substitute ingredients, engineering product economy, smoothing production, and so on.

---

[4]Andrall E. Pearson and Thomas W. Wilson, Jr., *Making Your Organization Work* (New York:
Association of National Advertisers, 1967), pp. 8–13.

[5]*Ibid.*, p. 5. Also see "The Brand Manager: No Longer King," *Business Week*, June 9, 1973.

Market management organization

Many companies will sell a product line to a highly diverse set of markets. For example, a paint firm will sell to the consumer, industrial, and government markets. A steel fabricator will sell to the railroad industry, construction industry, and public utilities. A soft-drink company will sell to retail and institutional markets. Where the company sells to customers who fall into distinct groups in terms of buying practices or product preferences, some market specialization is desirable in the marketing organization.

The general structure of a market management organization is illustrated in Figure 18-3. Along with functional managers, there is a markets manager who supervises several market managers. Each market manager draws functional services as needed from the rest of the department. Occasionally, the market manager responsible for an important market may have some functional specialists under him, including at times his own sales force.

The market manager's duties are very similar to those of a product manager. He must develop long-range and annual plans for the sales and profits in his market. He must coax assistance from the various resource managers in the organization. This system produces some of the same advantages and disadvantages as the product management system. Its strongest advantage is that the marketing activity is organized to meet the needs of distinct customer groups rather than focusing on marketing functions, products, or regions per se.

An increasing number of companies are reorganizing their management systems along market lines. Xerox has converted from geographical selling to vertical selling by industry. Mead is clustering its marketing activities around home building and furnishings, education, and leisure markets. Hanan calls these *marketcentered organizations* and argues that "the only way to ensure being market-oriented is to put a company's organizational structure together so that its major markets become the centers around which its divisions are built."[6]

Product/market organization

Companies that produce multiple products that flow into multiple markets face a real dilemma. They could utilize a product-management system, which

---

[6]Mack Hanan, "Reorganize Your Company around Its Markets," *Harvard Business Review*, November–December 1974, pp. 63–74.

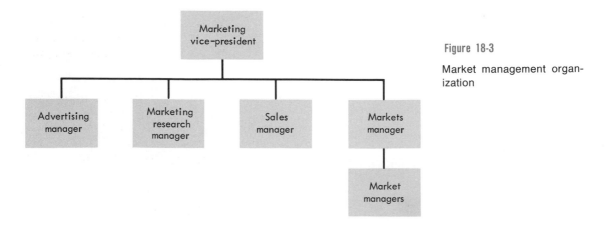

Figure 18-3

Market management organization

requires product managers to be familiar with highly divergent markets. Or they could utilize a market-management system, which means that market managers would have to be familiar with highly divergent products bought by their markets. Or they could install both product and market managers, that is, a product/market organization.

Du Pont is an example of a company that has done the latter. Its textile fibers department consists of separate product managers for rayon, acetate, nylon, orlon, and dacron; and also separate market managers for men's wear, women's wear, home furnishings, and industrial markets. The product managers have responsibility for planning the sales and profits of their respective fibers. They are primarily focused on short-run performance and uses of their fiber. The market managers have responsibility for developing profitable markets for existing and potential Du Pont fibers. They take a long view of market needs and care more about evolving the right products for their market than pushing any specific fibers.

It would seem that a product/market organization would be desirable in a multiple-product, multiple-market company. The rub, however, is that this system is both costly and conflictual. There is the cost of supporting a three-dimensional matrix organization (i.e., two layers of program management in addition to one level of resource management). There are also serious questions as to where authority and responsibility should reside. Here are two of the many dilemmas:

1 How should the sales force be organized? In the Du Pont example, should there be separate sales forces for rayon, nylon, and each of the other fibers? Or should the sales forces be organized according to men's wear, women's wear, and other markets? Or should the sales force not be specialized?

2 Who should set the prices for a particular product/market? In the Du Pont example, should the nylon product manager have final authority for setting nylon prices in all markets? What happens if the men's wear market manager feels that nylon will lose out in this market unless special price concessions are made on nylon?

Some companies are adapting a product/market organization, and others using this organization are having second thoughts. Most agree that only the more important products and markets would justify separate managers. Some observers are not upset about the conflicts in this system on the argument that it provides the company with the benefit of both the short-run and the long-run view and the conflict is healthy.[7]

Corporate-divisional organization

As multiproduct companies grow in size, they have a tendency to turn their larger product groups into separate divisions. The larger divisions often set up their own marketing departments on the ground that this will give them more knowledgeable and controllable marketing resources. This poses the question as to what marketing services and activities should be retained at the corporate headquarters level.

---

[7]See B. Charles Ames, "Dilemma of Product/Market Management," *Harvard Business Review,* March–April 1971, pp. 66–74.

Divisionalized companies have reached different answers to this question. Corporate marketing staffs seem to follow any of four models:[8]

1   Some companies do without a corporate marketing staff.
2   Other companies have a small corporate marketing staff with minimal functions, such as assisting top management with overall opportunity evaluation and providing divisions with consulting assistance on request.
3   Still other companies have a corporate marketing staff that manages certain marketing services for the company as a whole where economies require this.
4   Finally, some companies have a corporate marketing staff with strong involvement in planning, counseling, and controlling relative to divisional marketing policy.

The model used in any particular multidivision company is influenced by a number of factors, such as the capabilities of the corporate marketing staff, the management style of the chief executive, and the extent to which the company is highly diversified into completely different types of businesses. A corporate staff generally has two justifications. The first is to serve as a corporate focus for review and leadership of overall company marketing activities and opportunities. The second is to offer certain marketing services that could be provided more economically on a centralized basis than by being duplicated in the different divisions, such as media buying, corporate-wide promotions, advanced marketing research techniques, and long-range marketing planning.

MARKETING'S INTERFACE WITH OTHER DEPARTMENTS

In principle, business functions should mesh harmoniously to achieve the overall objectives of the firm. In practice, departmental interfaces are often characterized by deep rivalries and misunderstandings that profoundly impede the realization of the company's objectives. Some interdepartmental conflict stems from differences of opinion as to what lies in the best interests of the firm; some from real trade-offs between departmental well-being and company well-being; and some from unfortunate departmental stereotypes and prejudices.

Types of interdepartmental conflict

In the typical organization, made up of specialized departments charged with carrying out different company tasks, each department directly or indirectly has an impact on customer satisfaction through its own activities and decisions. Typically these impacts are uncoordinated. Under the marketing concept, it is desirable to coordinate them, because the satisfaction gained by the customer is a function of the *totality* of stimuli, not simply of the stimuli managed by the marketing department.

The marketing department is glad to accept this responsibility. But there is little unanimity on how much authority marketing should have over other departments to bring about coordinated marketing.

---

[8]See Watson Snyder, Jr., and Frank B. Gray, *The Corporate Marketing Staff: Its Role and Effectiveness in Multi-Division Companies* (working paper published by the Marketing Science Institute, Cambridge, Mass., April 1971).

Other departments naturally resent having to bend their efforts to the will of the marketing department. Just as marketing stresses the customer's point of view, other departments wish to stress the importance of their tasks. Inevitably, departments and individuals define company problems and goals in terms slanted by self-interest. The reason is that each deals continuously with problems in a local portion of the overall system. The major departmental differences in point of view—or organizational conflicts—between marketing and other departments are summarized in Table 18-1. Using this table, we can briefly examine the typical concerns of each department:

Table 18-1

Summary of organizational conflicts between marketing and other departments

Other departments	Their emphasis	Marketing emphasis
Engineering	Long design lead time	Short design lead time
	Functional features	Sales features
	Few models	Many models
	Standard components	Custom components
Purchasing	Standard parts	Nonstandard parts
	Price of material	Quality of material
	Economical lot sizes	Large lot sizes to avoid stockouts
	Purchasing at infrequent intervals	Immediate purchasing for customer needs
Production	Long production lead time	Short production lead time
	Long runs with few models	Short runs with many models
	No model changes	Frequent model changes
	Standard orders	Custom orders
	Ease of fabrication	Aesthetic appearance
	Average quality control	Tight quality control
Inventory	Fast-moving items, narrow product line	Broad product line
	Economical levels of stock	High levels of stock
Finance	Strict rationales for spending	Intuitive arguments for spending
	Hard and fast budgets	Flexible budgets to meet changing needs
	Pricing to cover costs	Pricing to further market development
Accounting	Standard transactions	Special terms and discounts
	Few reports	Many reports
Credit	Full financial disclosures by customers	Minimum credit examination of customers
	Low credit risks	Medium credit risks
	Tough credit terms	Easy credit terms
	Tough collection procedures	Easy collection procedures

Product engineering. The product engineer is interested in designing a product that meets engineering standards of simplicity and economy. Often he concentrates on these attributes at the expense of those that would increase the product's marketability.

Purchasing. The purchasing agent's main concern is to keep down the costs of acquiring the company's required inputs. Often his material and design recommendations conflict with qualities that marketing would like to build into the product.

Production. The production officer is interested in keeping down manufacturing costs. But manufacturing economies are achieved in ways often incompatible with the goal of high customer satisfaction.

Inventory management. The executive responsible for inventory management wants to keep down inventory costs. He is typically more concerned with holding down carrying costs than with the less-tangible costs of stockout.

Finance. The financial officer likes to keep a tight rein on company expenditures and wants to see profit on each transaction. This often conflicts with the need to take initial losses in order to develop loyal customers.

Accounting. The accountant's natural interest in keeping down the costs of the company's reporting operation usually leads him to resent nonstandard marketing transactions and to resist requests by the marketing department for a multitude of sales and cost analyses.

Credit. The credit officer looks on the bad debt as a blot on his record. To minimize credit losses he tends to set higher standards for customer credit than seems reasonable to the salesman who is working so hard to find customers.

It is no wonder that many departments resent the marketing concept. Marketing, in trying to mobilize the company's resources to develop customer satisfaction, often causes other departments to do a poorer job *in their terms.* Requests and pressures by the marketing department can increase product design and material purchasing costs, disrupt production schedules, increase accounting costs, and create budget headaches.

Role of the marketing concept

The office of marketing vice-president can play a decisive role in mitigating or aggravating these conflicts. The reason for creating a marketing vice-president is twofold: (1) to bring about an integration and coordination of the formal marketing activities of the company, such as sales forecasting, marketing research, advertising, sales force, promotion, and customer service; and (2) to deal with the vice-presidents of finance, operations, and so on, on a regular basis to try to develop a deeper appreciation by them of the value and benefits of a customer orientation.

Whether the other departments cooperate to follow the marketing concept depends upon the marketing vice-president's personal effectiveness and on the president's backing. In one of the large railroads, operations for a long time held the dominant power. The needs of freight customers were less important than scheduling efficiency. The marketing vice-president was not personally effective in convincing operations of the shortsightedness of placing operations ahead of marketing imperatives. One day a new company president came upon the scene, and along with him, a new company marketing vice-president. They made the point strongly that all freight railway services were to be shaped to meet the needs and interests of customers. The power of operations was finally broken, and the operations vice-president was heard to say at the end of a year: "I guess I work for marketing."

The job of implementing a marketing orientation throughout the company is an uphill and never-ending battle. It calls for a commitment by the president, preplanning on how to sell the concept to others, and a continuous program of training and education.[9] The purpose is not to resolve every issue in favor of the customer, no matter what the cost; but rather to remind others that customers are the foundation of the company's business.

SUMMARY

The modern marketing department evolved through several stages to reach its contemporary form. It started as a simple sales department consisting of only a sales force. Later the sales department took on some ancillary functions, such as advertising and marketing research. As the ancillary functions grew in importance, many companies created a marketing department separate from the sales department to manage these other marketing activities. But the heads of sales and marketing often disagreed on company marketing policy, and eventually the two departments were merged into a modern marketing department headed by the marketing vice-president. A modern marketing department, however, does not automatically create a modern marketing company unless the other officers accept marketing as the hub of the enterprise.

Modern marketing departments are organized in a number of ways. The most common form is the functional marketing organization in which the various marketing functions are headed by separate managers who report to the marketing vice-president. Another common form is the product management organization in which major products are the responsibility of product managers who work with the various functional specialists in the company to develop and achieve their plans for the product. Another, less common, form is the market management organization in which major markets are the responsibility of market managers who work with the various functional specialists to develop and achieve their plans for the market. Some large companies use a product/market organization, which combines both systems of management. Finally, multidivision companies normally develop a corporate marketing staff and separate marketing departments at the divisions, with some variations as to the division and authority for different services.

Marketing must work smoothly with the other functions in a company. In its pursuit of the customers' interests, marketing frequently comes into conflict with purchasing, manufacturing, finance, and other functions that stress a cost minimization logic. These conflicts can be reduced when the company president commits himself and the company to a market orientation and when the marketing vice-president learns to work effectively with the other officers.

**QUESTIONS
AND PROBLEMS**

1 In order to carry out a proposed national sales promotion, describe some of the departments whose efforts must be coordinated with those of the marketing department. Through what kind of planning device might these efforts be integrated?

---

[9]An excellent discussion on problems and methods of installing the marketing concept in organizations is found in Edward S. McKay, *The Marketing Mystique* (New York: American Management Association, 1972), pp. 22–30.

2   What are some of the major tensions between company engineer-scientists and company marketing executives?

3   Does it make organizational sense to combine the company's marketing department and public relations department under one vice-president?

4   A major airline's marketing department is presently organized on a functional basis: advertising, field sales, customer services, and so on. The airline is considering setting up a route manager organization, with a manager assigned to each major route. He would be to a route what a brand manager is to a brand. Do you think this is a good idea?

5   "In 1945 he had been brought back to Millburgh and made Vice-President of sales. At fifty-three, J. Walter Dudley was probably the best-known man in the entire furniture industry. His memory for names and faces was phenomenal. At one Chicago Market . . . two bystanding salesmen had actually kept a count and heard him greet two hundred and eighteen furniture store owners and buyers by name before he was confronted by an individual whose name he did not know. There were hundreds of furniture merchants who would not have thought a market visit complete without having had the opportunity to shake hands with good old Walt Dudley."—Cameron Hawley, *Executive Suite* (Boston: Houghton Mifflin Company, 1952), pp. 133–34. Does J. Walter Dudley sound like the ideal vice-president of marketing?

6   You are being interviewed for the position of brand manager at the Blogg's Blotting Paper Company. Sales of blotters have been declining for several years. Develop a list of questions and suggestions that would reflect well on your qualifications for this position.

19
MARKETING RESEARCH
AND INFORMATION SYSTEM

To manage a business well is to manage its future;
and to manage its future is to manage information.

MARION HARPER, JR.

Modern marketing executives depend upon a deep and continuous flow of information in order to make decisions. Three trends, in particular, render the need for marketing information stronger than at any time in the past.

The first is the shift from local to national and international marketing. This means that marketing executives are physically removed from their markets and are highly dependent on information flows in making their decisions. *The second is the transition from buyer needs to buyer wants.* This means that sellers require more information on how buyers will spend their discretionary incomes. *The third is the transition from price to nonprice competition.* As sellers increase their reliance on competitive weapons such as branding, product differentiation, advertising, and sales promotion, they require great quantities of information on the effectiveness of these marketing tools.

The explosive information requirements have been met on the supply side by impressive new information technologies. The last thirty years have witnessed the emergence of the computer, microfilming, closed-circuit television, copy machines, tape recorders, and many other devices that have created a veritable revolution in information-handling capacity.

Most business firms, however, do not operate at a high level of information sophistication. Many firms do not have a marketing research department. Many other firms have small marketing research departments whose work is

419

limited to routine forecasting, sales analysis, and occasional surveys. Only a few firms have developed advanced marketing information systems that provide company management with up-to-date marketing information and analysis.

CONCEPT AND COMPONENTS OF A MARKETING INFORMATION SYSTEM

Every firm is the scene of several information flows affecting marketing management. Each firm has made some arrangements to tap these flows. These arrangements constitute the firm's *marketing information system:*

> A structured, interacting complex of persons, machines, and procedures designed to generate an orderly flow of pertinent information, collected from both intra- and extra-firm sources, for use as the basis for decision making in specified responsibility areas of marketing management.[1]

Figure 19-1 presents a picture of the main components of a total marketing information system. The *marketing information system* is shown to stand between the *environment* and the *marketing executive-user.* There is a *marketing data flow* from the environment to the marketing information system of the company. The marketing information system turns this data flow into a *marketing information flow* that goes to its executives. On the basis of this information, the executives develop plans and programs, which enter a *marketing communication flow* that goes back to the environment.

We now turn to the main components of the marketing information system.

INTERNAL ACCOUNTING SYSTEM

The earliest and most basic information system used by the marketing executive is the internal accounting system. It is the system that reports orders, sales, inventory levels, receivables, payables, and so on. Through this information the executives can spot opportunities and problems and can compare actual and expected levels of performance.

The order-shipping-billing cycle

The heart of the accounting system is the order-shipping-billing cycle. Salesmen, dealers, and customers dispatch orders to the firm. The order department prepares multicopy invoices and dispatches them to various departments. Items that are out of stock are back-ordered. Items that are shipped are accompanied by shipping and billing documents that are also multi-copied and go to various departments.

The company has a strong interest in carrying out these steps as quickly and accurately as possible. Salesmen are supposed to send in their orders every evening, in some cases to phone them in when they are obtained. The order department should process these quickly. The warehouse should send the goods out as soon as possible. And bills should go out as soon as possible. The com-

[1]Samuel V. Smith, Richard H. Brien, and James E. Stafford, eds., *Readings in Marketing Information Systems* (Boston: Houghton Mifflin Company, 1968), p. 7.

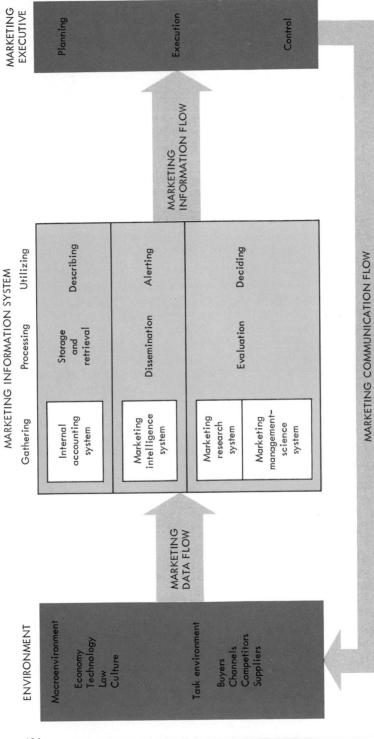

Figure 19-1
Components of the marketing information system

puter should be harnessed to expedite the order-shipping-billing cycle. Ringer and Howell reported a study of one company's order routine, which resulted in cutting down the elapsed time between the receipt and issuance of an order from sixty-two hours to thirty hours without any change in costs.[2]

**Improving the timeliness
of sales reports**

Marketing executives in many companies receive sales reports some time after the sales have taken place. In consumer food companies, warehouse withdrawal reports are issued with fair regularity, but actual retail purchase reports take about two months, based on special store or consumer panel audits. In the auto industry, executives wait with bated breath for a sales report that comes out every ten days; if sales are down, they can expect ten sleepless nights. Most marketing executives complain that they don't get the sales report fast enough, no matter how often they get it.

Here are three companies that have designed sophisticated sales-reporting systems to increase the value of sales information:

General Mills. The executives at General Mills receive their information daily. Every zone, regional, and district sales manager in the Grocery Products Division starts his day with a teletype report on orders and shipments in his area the day before. The report also contains progress percentages to compare with target percentages and last year's progress percentages.

Schenley. Schenley's system allows its key executives to retrieve within seconds, via video-display desk consoles and printers, current and past sales and inventory figures for any brand and package size for each of four hundred distributors; an executive can determine within seconds all areas where sales are lagging behind expectations.

Mead Paper. Mead Paper's system permits its salesmen in buyers' offices to obtain on-the-spot answers to customers' queries about paper availability. The salesman dials Mead Paper's computer center. The computer determines whether paper is available at the nearest warehouse and when it can be shipped; if it is not in stock, the computer checks the inventory at other nearby warehouses until one is located. If the paper is nowhere in stock, the computer program goes through a production-scheduling routine to determine where and when the paper can be produced and shipped. The salesman gets his answer in seconds, and this places him in an advantageous position in relation to competitors.

**Designing a
user-oriented
reports system**

In designing an advanced sales information system, the company should avoid certain pitfalls. First, it is possible to create a system that delivers too much information to the executives. They arrive at their office each morning to face voluminous sales statistics. Second, it is possible to create a system that delivers information that is too current! The executive may end up reacting to sales movements that are essentially random; and his actions may in fact destabilize the market. Third, it is possible that the cost of supplying all of this information at some point will exceed its value.

The company's marketing information system should represent a cross between (a) what executives think they need, (b) what executives really need, and (c) what is economically feasible. A cross section of marketing executives—product managers, sales executives, salesmen, and so on—should be interviewed

---

[2]Jurgen F. Ringer and Charles D. Howell, "The Industrial Engineer and Marketing," in *Industrial Engineering Handbook,* 2nd ed., ed. Harold Bright Maynard (New York: McGraw-Hill Book Company, 1963), pp. 10, 102–3.

to find out their information wants. A useful set of questions is shown in Table 19-1. The information-planning committee will want to pay special attention to strong desires and complaints. At the same time, the planning committee will wisely discount some of the alleged information needs. Executives who have an appetite for information will list a great deal, failing to distinguish between *what is nice to know* and *what they need to know.* Other executives will be too busy to give the questionnaire serious thought and will omit many things they ought to know. This is why the information-planning committee must take another step, that of determining what executives *should know* to be able to make responsible decisions. For example, what should a brand manager know in order to make a truly informed decision on the size of the advertising budget? He should know something about the degree of market saturation, the rate of sales decay in the absence of advertising, and the spending plans of competitors. The information system should be designed around models for making the key marketing decisions.

Table 19-1
Questionnaire for determining marketing information
needs of executives

1. What types of decisions are you regularly called upon to make?
2. What types of information do you need to make these decisions?
3. What types of information do you regularly get?
4. What types of special studies do you periodically request?
5. What types of information would you like to get that you are not now getting?
6. What information would you want daily? weekly? monthly? yearly?
7. What magazines and trade reports would you like to see routed to you on a regular basis?
8. What specific topics would you like to be kept informed of?
9. What types of data-analysis programs would you like to see made available?
10. What do you think would be the four most helpful improvements that could be made in the present marketing information system?

MARKETING INTELLIGENCE SYSTEM

Whereas the internal accounting system supplies executives with *results data,* the marketing intelligence system supplies executives with *happenings data.* We shall define the *marketing intelligence system as the way in which company executives are kept current and informed about changing conditions in the macroenvironment and task environment.*

All executives engage at different times in four modes of scanning the environment:[3]

1   *Undirected viewing:* general exposure to information where the viewer has no specific purpose in mind.

---

[3]Francis Joseph Aguilar, *Scanning the Business Environment* (New York: The Macmillan Company, 1967).

2   *Conditioned viewing:* directed exposure, not involving active search, to a more or less clearly identified area or type of information.

3   *Informal search:* a relatively limited and unstructured effort to obtain specific information or information for a specific purpose.

4   *Formal search:* a deliberate effort—usually following a preestablished plan, procedure, or methodology—to secure specific information or information relating to a specific issue.

The marketing executive carries on marketing intelligence mostly on his own, being most interested in market news, keeping abreast by reading newspapers and trade material, relying on subordinates for search information, and getting some unsolicited information from outside sources. To the extent that his intelligence work is casual, valuable information will often come in too little or too late. Executives may learn of a competitive move, a new customer need, or a dealer problem too late to make the best response.

**Improving
intelligence-gathering
activity**

A company can take three steps to improve the executives' intelligence system: (1) improve the salesmen's intelligence activity, (2) utilize additional intelligence resources, and (3) buy information from special marketing research services.

Salesmen as intelligence agents   Salesmen have correctly been called the company's "eyes and ears to the marketplace." They meet the buyers, dealers, and occasionally the competitors. They are in a good position to pick up significant bits of information that would never appear in the usual summary statistics of company sales activity. When these bits and pieces of information are correlated at headquarters, they often yield a revealing picture.

The critical question is whether a company's salesmen feel motivated to *look* for information and to *pass it on* to their superiors. In a telling experiment, Albaum arranged with a sample of company customers to pass on six fabricated pieces of market information to company salesmen.[4] Of the six pieces of market information, only two were ever passed on by salesmen to their superiors. One arrived in three days but was seriously distorted; the other arrived in about ten days in fairly accurate form. Albaum concluded that there was not a free flow of market intelligence within this company; that, in general, most unmanaged intelligence systems are characterized by information disappearance, delay, and distortion.

The solution requires training the salesman in his role as an intelligence agent for the firm. Call reports should be designed for maximum convenience in filling out. The salesman should be told who in the company can use various types of information, so that information does not always have to travel through a dozen relay points before reaching the person who needs it. An intelligence office might be established to receive and disseminate intelligence. The salesman's superior should make a point of reviewing the salesman's information performance and making it a factor in pay raises.

Other means of gathering competitive intelligence   Similar attempts should be made to incentivize sales managers, dealers, the advertising agency, and others to pay more attention to gathering and passing along intelligence. It is

---

[4]Gerald S. Albaum, "Horizontal Information Flow: An Exploratory Study," *Journal of the Academy of Management,* March 1964, pp. 21-33.

sometimes desirable to hire one or more full-time specialists in marketing intelligence gathering. This does not necessarily mean industrial espionage agents. Many companies send out comparison shoppers to learn how various brands are selling and how helpful retail sales personnel are. Interviewing customers and dealers to learn about new opportunities and problems is a legitimate intelligence activity. Much can be learned about competitors' activities through such overt means as (1) pricing or purchasing competitors' products; (2) attending "open houses" and trade shows; (3) reading competitors' reports and attending stockholders' meetings; (4) talking to competitors' former employees and present employees, dealers, distributors, suppliers, and freight agents; (5) hiring a clipping service; and (6) reading the *Wall Street Journal, New York Times,* and trade-association papers.

Purchase of special marketing intelligence services   Many companies purchase information from outside suppliers. The A. C. Nielsen Company sells bimonthly data (based on a sample of sixteen hundred stores) on major brand shares, retail prices, percentage of stores stocking item, and percentage of stockout stores. The Market Research Corporation of America sells reports (based on the purchase diaries of a representative panel of seventy-five hundred households scattered throughout the country) on weekly movements of brand shares, sizes, prices, and deals. Clipping services may be hired to report on competitive advertising expenditures, media mixes, and advertising appeals.

**Improving
intelligence-processing
activity**

The usefulness of gathered intelligence depends on its accuracy, retrievability, and speed in moving to higher management levels where it can be used. A centralized marketing intelligence center can offer several services to improve the processing and dissemination of intelligence.

The first service is intelligence *evaluation.* An analyst trained in data evaluation would be available to examine any information and render a technical opinion as to how much confidence can be placed in it. A second important service is intelligence *abstraction.* Trained abstracters can condense and edit incoming information to make it more useful for executives. *Dissemination* is a third important intelligence-processing service. Dissemination involves getting information to the right people in the right form in the shortest feasible time. Among the devices used are periodic newsletters, telephone calls, cassettes, teletype services, and interconnected company computers. The fourth service is *storage and retrieval.* Each company must develop an *indexing system* and organize all the existing information into easily accessible files. It is also necessary to establish rules for the periodic purging of information that has exceeded its useful life.

MARKETING RESEARCH SYSTEM

Beside internal accounting information and marketing intelligence, the executive needs specific studies of problem and opportunity areas. He may need a market survey, a product-preference test, a sales forecast by region, or an advertising-effectiveness study. These studies require the talents of skilled researchers who can apply principles of sample size, sample design, and questionnaire construction to the task. These researchers usually make up the marketing research department of the company.

Since its humble beginnings nearly seventy years ago, marketing research has steadily expanded.[5] About 60 percent of all companies have formal marketing research departments; in firms with annual sales over $500 million, 80 percent have formal marketing research departments. Such departments tend to be most common among consumer companies (70 percent), followed by publishers and broadcasters (66 percent), industrial companies (59 percent), retailers and wholesalers (54 percent), and advertising agencies (53 percent).

The median size of the marketing research budget, as a percentage of company sales, was largest in advertising and media companies (varying between .29 and 1.30 percent of sales), next largest among consumer products companies (.07 to .60 percent of sales), followed by industrial-products companies (.04 to .50 percent of sales). In 1973 companies spent between one-quarter and one-half of their marketing research budget on outside services. Bradford lists over 350 marketing research firms, including full-line marketing research firms, specialty-line marketing research firms, and information selling firms.[6]

The scope of marketing research   Marketing research departments have been steadily expanding their activities and techniques. Table 19-2 lists thirty-one different marketing research activities along with the percentage of firms carrying on each. The nine most common activities are determination of market characteristics, measurement of market potentials, market-share analysis, sales analysis, competitive-product studies, new-product acceptance and potential, short-range forecasting, long-range forecasting, and studies of business trends. Less than half of the firms do their own advertising research or carry out any marketing operations research.

These studies have benefited over the years from increasingly sophisticated techniques. Table 19-3 shows the approximate decade when various techniques began to be substantially considered or used in marketing research. Many of them—such as questionnaire construction and area sampling—came along naturally and were quickly and widely accepted as belonging in the corpus of marketing research practice. Others—such as motivation research and mathematical methods—came in uneasily, with prolonged and heated debates among practitioners over their practical usefulness. But they, too, settled in the corpus of marketing research methodology—or at least the parts that stood the test of time.

Management's use of marketing research   The growth in the number of marketing research departments suggests extremely rapid acceptance of marketing research by American business. Yet this impression must be qualified. About 40 percent of all companies have no formal marketing research department. Many companies with marketing research departments give them inadequate budgets for carrying out their work. Operating executives often resist or ignore marketing research findings. Too often they view this research as a narrow fact-finding operation or as too abstruse. Clearly there is a continuing need to

---

[5]For the status of marketing research in the United States, see Dik Warren Twedt, ed., *1973 Survey of Marketing Research: Organization, Functions, Budget, Compensation* (Chicago: American Marketing Association, 1973). Statistics in the text are drawn from this report.

[6]Ernest S. Bradford, *Bradford's Directory of Marketing Research Agencies and Management Consultants in the United States and the World*, 15th ed., 1973–1974 (Middlebury, Vt.: Bradford Co.).

Table 19-2
Research activities of 1,322 companies in 1973

Type of research	Percent doing
Advertising research:	
Motivation research	33
Copy research	37
Media research	44
Studies of ad effectiveness	49
Other	7
Business economics and corporate research:	
Short-range forecasting (up to 1 year)	63
Long-range forecasting (over 1 year)	61
Studies of business trends	61
Pricing studies	56
Plant and warehouse location studies	47
Product mix studies	51
Acquisition studies	53
Export and international studies	41
Internal company employees studies	45
Other	4
Corporate responsibility research:	
Consumers "right to know" studies	18
Ecological impact studies	27
Studies of legal constraints on advertising and promotion	38
Social values and policies studies	25
Other	2
Product research:	
New-product acceptance and potential	63
Competitive-product studies	64
Testing of existing products	57
Packaging research—design or physical characteristics	44
Other	3
Sales and market research:	
Measurement of market potentials	68
Market-share analysis	67
Determination of market characteristics	68
Sales analysis	65
Establishment of sales quotas, territories	57
Distribution channels studies	48
Test markets, store audits	38
Consumer-panel operations	33
Sales compensation studies	45
Promotional studies of premiums, coupons, sampling, deals, etc.	39
Other	2

Source: Dik Warren Twedt, ed., *1973 Survey of Marketing Research: Organization, Functions, Budget, Compensation* (Chicago: American Marketing Association, 1973), p. 41.

Table 19-3

Evolving techniques in marketing research

Decade	Technique
Prior to 1910	Firsthand observation Elementary surveys
1910–20	Sales analysis Operating-cost analysis
1920–30	Questionnaire construction Survey technique
1930–40	Quota sampling Simple correlation analysis Distribution-cost analysis Store auditing techniques
1940–50	Probability sampling Regression methods Advanced statistical inference Consumer and store panels
1950–60	Motivation research Operations research Multiple regression and correlation Experimental design Attitude-measuring instruments
1960–70	Factor analysis and discriminant analysis Mathematical models Bayesian statistical analysis and decision theory Scaling theory Computer data processing and analysis Marketing simulation Information storage and retrieval
1970–	Nonmetric multidimensional scaling Econometric models Comprehensive marketing planning models Test-marketing laboratories Multiattribute attitude models

educate management about the vital role of competent marketing research in carrying out the marketing concept.

Marketing research procedure

Marketing research is undertaken in the effort to learn something reliable about a marketing problem facing management. The value of the results depends upon the skill with which the marketing research project is designed and implemented. The investment of money and time can all be wasted or even be positively misleading if the marketing research project is ill designed.

Effective marketing research involves the following five steps: *problem definition, research design, fieldwork, data analysis,* and *report preparation.*

Problem definition The first step in the conduct of research calls for a careful definition of the problem. If the problem is stated vaguely, if the wrong problem is defined, or if the uses of the research are not made clear, then the research results may prove useless to the manager.

The poor definition of the problem is often the fault of the manager requesting the study. Thus a top administrator in the U.S. Postal System might ask the marketing research manager to find out everything he can about public attitudes toward the postal system. The marketing research manager has a right to feel uneasy about the assignment. It is too general. It is not clear how much interviewing should be done of light users and heavy users of the postal system, of home users and business users. It is not clear what aspects of the postal system they should comment on: personnel, postage cost, delivery reliability, speed, and so on. While all of this information would be interesting, none of it may help management come any closer to making good policy decisions. There is something sterile about facts that are not made part of a larger model of decision-making alternatives that themselves come out of a definition of the real problem.

The kind of research assignment just mentioned is called exploratory research, and this is mostly warranted in situations where the organization's ignorance of the marketplace is substantial, and it may uncover much that is interesting. Yet the research effort is generally more efficient when the problem and the alternatives are well defined—the cost of research is generally related to the total amount of information gathered, while the value of research is associated only with the proportion of information that is useful.

Research design   The problem definition stage should lead to the development of a clear set of research objectives stated in writing if possible. The marketing research manager faces a choice among many alternative ways to collect the information that will satisfy the research objectives. He must decide on the *data collection method, research instrument,* and *sampling plan.*

DATA COLLECTION METHODS   In simple cases the data needed already exist in an accessible form and merely have to be found. This is called *secondary data.* They might be present in the organization's internal records; in advertising agencies or professional associations; in government, commercial, or trade publications; or purchasable from marketing research firms. If the data are found in existing sources, the researcher has saved time and expense. However, he must be careful to evaluate secondary data, since they were collected for a variety of purposes and under a variety of conditions that may limit their usefulness. Marketing researchers should check these data for impartiality, validity, and reliability.

When satisfactory secondary data are not available, the researcher must collect *primary data.* The data can be gathered from customers, middlemen, salesmen, competitors, or other information sources. There are three basic primary data collection methods.

The first is *observation*, in which case the researcher attempts to learn about the problem by observing the relevant actors. The observational method can be used to study sales techniques, customer movements, and customer responses. Its main advantage is that it generally leads to a more objective picture of overt behavior than can be expected from relying on people's accounts of how they behave. On the other hand, this method yields no information about the state of mind, buying motives, or brand images of those being observed.

At the other extreme is *experimentation* as a method of gathering primary data. The experimental method consists of introducing selected stimuli into a controlled environment and systematically varying them. To the extent that extraneous factors are eliminated or controlled, the observed effects can be related to the variations in the stimuli. The purpose of control is to eliminate competing hypotheses that might also explain the observed phenomena. Marketers have applied this data collection method to such marketing problems as finding the best sales-training method, the best incentive scheme, the best price level, and the best ad campaign.[7]

A third method of generating primary data, and the most common, is through *surveys*. Compared with either direct observation or experimentation, surveys yield a broader range of information and are effective for a greater number of research problems. Surveys can produce information on socio-economic characteristics, attitudes, opinions, motives, and overt behavior. Surveys are an effective way of gathering information for planning product features, advertising copy, advertising media, sales promotions, channels of distribution, and other marketing variables.

RESEARCH INSTRUMENT   The researcher has to use or design a reliable research instrument to gather the information he is seeking. The observational method makes use of such instruments as tape recorders, cameras, and tally sheets. The experimental method might involve similar instruments if the subjects are put through a task. The survey method, and to some extent the experimental method, commonly rely on questionnaires.

The construction of good questionnaires calls for considerable skill. Every questionnaire should be pretested on a pilot sample of persons before being used on a large scale. A professional marketing researcher can usually spot several errors in a casually prepared questionnaire.

A common type of error occurs in the *types of questions asked:* the inclusion of questions that cannot be answered, or would not be answered, or need not be answered, and the omission of other questions that should be answered. Each question should be checked to determine whether it is necessary in terms of the research objectives. The form should avoid questions that are just interesting (except for one or two to start the interview on a good basis) because they lengthen the time required and try the respondent's patience.

The *form and wording of questions* can make a substantial difference to the response. An open-ended question is one in which the respondent is free to answer in his own words. A close-ended question is one in which the possible answers are supplied. The respondent may be asked to respond in one or two ways (dichotomous questions), to check one of several answers (multiple-choice questions), to place marks along a scale (scaling questions), and so forth. The choice between open-ended and close-ended questions affects the thoughtfulness of responses, the costs of interviewing, and the quality of the subsequent analysis.

The *choice of words* calls for considerable care. The designer should strive for simple, direct, unambiguous, and unbiased wording. A good rule is always to pretest the questions on a sample of respondents before they are used on a wide scale.

Other "dos" and "don'ts" arise in connection with the *sequencing of questions* in the questionnaire. The lead questions should create interest, if possible. Open questions are usually better here. Difficult questions or personal questions

---

[7] See Seymour Banks, *Experimentation in Marketing* (New York: McGraw-Hill Book Company, 1965).

should be used toward the end of the interview, in order not to create an emotional reaction that may affect subsequent answers or cause the respondent to
break off the interview. The body of questions should be asked in as logical an
order as possible in order to avoid confusing the respondent. Classificatory data
on the respondent are usually asked for last, because they tend to be less interesting and are on the personal side.

SAMPLING PLAN   The third element of research design is a sampling plan.
The sampling plan answers four questions: who is to be surveyed? (sampling
unit); how many are to be surveyed? (sample size); how are they to be selected?
(sampling procedure); and how are they to be reached? (sampling media).

Perhaps the basic issue is: who is to be surveyed? The proper *sampling unit*
is not always obvious from the nature of the information sought. In a survey
designed to uncover attitudes toward breakfast cereals, should the primary
sampling unit be the housewife, the husband, the children, or some combination of the three? Where the roles of instigators, influencers, deciders, users,
and/or purchasers are not combined in the same person, the researcher must
determine not only what information is needed but also who is most likely to
have it.

The next issue is *sample size.* Large samples obviously give more reliable
results than small samples. However, it is not necessary to sample the entire
universe or even a substantial part of it to achieve satisfactory precision. Samples
amounting to less than 1 percent of the entire population can often provide
good reliability, given a creditable sample procedure. In exploratory research,
very small samples suffice. Much insight about marketing processes and attitudes can be gained from a sample of fewer than one hundred persons. In
motivation-research studies, fewer than thirty depth interviews usually suffice
to uncover significant attitudes.

Sampling procedure depends upon the research objective. For exploratory
research, nonprobability sampling procedure may be adequate. However, to
make an accurate estimate of population characteristics, a random (probability)
sample of the population should be drawn. Random sampling allows the calculation of confidence limits for sampling error. One could say "the chances are
ninety-five in a hundred that the interval '5 to 7 bottles' contains the true
number of bottles purchased annually by the typical user of brand X." But
random sampling is almost always more costly than nonrandom sampling.
Some marketing researchers feel that the extra expenditure for probability
sampling could be put to better use. Specifically, more of the money of a fixed
research budget could be spent in designing better questionnaires and hiring
better interviewers to reduce response and nonsampling errors, which can be
just as fatal as sampling errors. This is a real issue, one that the marketing
researcher and marketing executives must carefully weigh.

The final issue is *sampling method,* whether the target population should be
reached by telephone, mail, or personal interviews. *Telephone interviewing* stands
out as the best method for gathering information quickly. It permits the interviewer to clarify his questions if they are not understood. The two main drawbacks of telephone interviewing are that only people with telephones can be
interviewed, and only short, not too personal, interviews can be carried out.
The *mail questionnaire* may be the best way to reach persons who would not give
personal interviews or who might be biased by interviewers. On the other hand,
mail questionnaires require simple and clearly worded questions, and the return
rate is usually low and/or slow. *Personal interviewing* is the most versatile of the

three methods. The personal interviewer can ask more questions and can supplement the interview with personal observations. Personal interviewing is the most expensive method and requires much more technical and administrative planning and supervision.

Fieldwork   After the research design has been finalized, the research department must supervise, or subcontract, the task of collecting the data. This phase is generally the most expensive and the most liable to error. Four major problems arise:

1   *Not-at-homes.* When an interviewer does not find anyone at home, he can either call back later or substitute the household next door. The latter is the less expensive alternative because the interviewer will not have to travel back to the same block. The only problem is that there is no easy way to learn whether the adjacent household resembles the original one precisely, because no data were collected on the original. The substitution may be biasing.
2   *Refusal to cooperate.* After finding the designated individual at home, the interviewer must interest the person in cooperating. If the time is inconvenient or if the survey appears phony, the designated person may not cooperate.
3   *Respondent bias.* The interviewer must encourage accurate and thoughtful answers. Some respondents may give inaccurate or biased answers in order to finish quickly or for other reasons.
4   *Interviewer bias.* Interviewers are capable of introducing a variety of biases into the interviewing process, through the mere fact of their age, sex, manner, or intonation. In addition, there is the problem of conscious interviewer bias or dishonesty. Interviewers face a great temptation to fill their quota of interviews as quickly or as cheaply as possible. This can be done by not making the required number of call-backs, or by claiming refusals to cooperate, or, in extreme cases, by actually falsifying an interview.

Data analysis   The fourth step in marketing research procedure is to attempt to extract meaningful information from the data. Anyone who has had the experience of amassing data knows that further work has to be done to reveal underlying magnitudes and patterns of association or causality. The first step is to calculate relevant averages and measures of dispersion. The second step is to cross-tabulate the data to produce useful relationships. The third step is to measure correlation coefficients and perform goodness-of-fit tests. The fourth step is to attempt multivariate analysis of the data, using such statistical techniques as multiple-regression analysis, discriminant analysis, factor analysis, and cluster analysis.[8]

Report preparation   The last step is the preparation of a managerially oriented report presenting the major findings and recommendations coming from the study. The report should begin with a short statement of the problem and the major findings. This should be followed by an elaboration of the findings. A brief description of the research method should then be given, with the more technical details being saved for an appendix. Many of the data should also be appendixes. The last section should discuss the major reservations and

[8]See David A. Aaker, ed., *Multivariate Analysis in Marketing: Theory and Applications* (Belmont, Calif.: Wadsworth Publishing Co., 1971).

qualifications. In general, the report should be written to facilita[
standing and interest of the marketing executives and their abil[
actionable information.

**Characteristics of good
marketing research**

Having examined marketing research procedure, we can now a[
earmarks of good marketing research.

Scientific method Competent marketing research is characterized by an
attempt to follow the scientific method: careful observation, formulation of
hypotheses, prediction, and testing. An example follows:

> A small mail-order house was suffering from a high rate (30 percent) of merchan-
> dise return. Management asked the marketing research manager to uncover
> the causes of the high return. The research manager proceeded to analyze various
> characteristics of the returned orders, such as the geographical locations of the
> customers, the sizes of the returned orders, and the type of merchandise. One
> hypothesis he formulated was that the longer the customer waited for ordered
> merchandise, the greater the probability of its return. His regression analysis
> confirmed this hypothesis. He ventured the prediction that the return rate would
> fall if the company speeded up its delivery time. The company did this, and his
> prediction proved correct.[9]

Research creativity At its best, marketing research develops innovative
ways to solve a problem. A classic example of research creativity is described
below:

> When instant coffee was first introduced, housewives complained that it did
> not taste like real coffee. Yet in blindfold tests, many of these same housewives
> could not distinguish between a cup of instant coffee and real coffee. This indi-
> cated that much of their resistance was psychological. The researcher decided
> to design two almost identical shopping lists, the only difference being that
> regular coffee was on one list and instant coffee on the other. The regular coffee
> list was given to one group of housewives and the instant coffee list was given
> to a different, but comparable, group. Both groups were asked to guess the social
> and personal characteristics of the woman whose shopping list they saw. The
> comments were pretty much the same with one significant difference; a higher
> proportion of the housewives whose list contained instant coffee described the
> subject as "lazy, a spendthrift, a poor wife, and failing to plan well for her
> family." These women obviously were imputing to the fictional housewife their
> own anxieties and negative images about the use of instant coffee. The instant-
> coffee company now knew the nature of the resistance and could develop a
> campaign to change the image of the housewife who serves instant coffee.[10]

Multiple methods Competent marketing researchers shy away from
overreliance on any one method, preferring to adapt the method to the problem
rather than the other way around. They also recognize the desirability of the
simultaneous gathering of information in different ways to give greater confidence than any one method would provide.

---

[9]Horace C. Levinson, "Experiences in Commercial Operations Research," *Operations Research*,
August 1953, pp. 220–39.

[10]Mason Haire, "Projective Techniques in Marketing Research," *Journal of Marketing*, April
1950, pp. 649–56.

Interdependence of models and data Competent marketing researchers recognize that the facts do not speak for themselves but rather derive their meaning from models of the problem. They attempt to guide their search for information on the basis of a useful decision model to help the executive.

Value and cost of information Competent marketing researchers show concern for measuring the value of information against its cost. Value/cost is a consideration when the department chooses which research projects to conduct; when it is trying to decide between different research designs; when the evidence is in and a decision must be made between immediate action and further information; and when the contribution of the research department as a whole is to be evaluated.[11]

MARKETING MANAGEMENT-SCIENCE SYSTEM

An increasing number of organizations have been adding a fourth information service to help their marketing executives—management science (also called operations research). A management scientist applies scientific methodology to organizational problems in the search for improved understanding, prediction, and control. Management scientists are often called model builders, and quite appropriately, because "model" is one of the central defining concepts in their field. *A model is the specification of a set of variables and their interrelationships designed to represent some real system or process, in whole or in part.*

Although management science is a relative latecomer in marketing, it has already yielded useful insights and decision models in such areas as new-product development, competitive pricing, advertising budgeting and media selection, sales call time allocation, and marketing-mix planning. Beginning in the late 1950s, marketing management scientists have produced a rich harvest of models on almost every conceivable quantifiable marketing problem or process. Unfortunately, usage has lagged substantially behind model development, in some cases due to the inappropriateness of the models, in other cases due to the lack of empirical data, and in a large number of cases due to marketing management's widespread lack of understanding and sympathy for quantitative approaches to marketing. Today some models are fully established and running in some larger companies, but they are the exception. The vast majority of marketing decisions are still made intuitively in spite of the availability of more rigorous decision procedures borne out of years of patient management-science work.

The marketing management scientist is found only in the larger companies. He is located in the company's management-science department or sometimes in the marketing department. If the latter, he may report to the marketing vice-president or to the marketing research manager. His influence in the company depends upon the level of management's appreciation of fundamental notions such as "models," "decision theory," and "optimization" and the fundamentals of certain important solution techniques. Lacking basic understandings, marketing managers tend to avoid his services. The management scientist can do three things to improve the interest and involvement of company executives:

---

[11]See James H. Myers and A. Coskun Samli, "Management Control of Marketing Research," *Journal of Marketing Research*, August 1969, pp. 267–77.

1   He can sponsor company seminars to explain the leading concepts and techniques along with real case examples.

2   He can identify a few company problem areas where early and substantial payout could be effected by these techniques and use his successes to increase his credibility in the eyes of others.

3   He can involve managers in defining the problem and helping build the model. This is a better strategy than going off to his office, designing a complex problem statement and solution, and handing it over cold to the executive.

Basic types of models in management science

The marketing executive is in a much better position to understand and evaluate marketing management-science projects when he is aware of the major types of models. A description of model types is provided in Table 19-4.

Table 19-4

A classification of models

I. According to Purpose	II. According to Techniques
A. Descriptive Models 　1. Markov-process model 　2. Queuing model 　3. Simulation B. Decision Models 　1. Differential calculus 　2. Mathematical programming 　3. Statistical decision theory 　4. Game theory	A. Verbal Models B. Graphical Models 　1. Logical-flow model 　2. Network-planning model 　3. Causal model 　4. Decision-tree model 　5. Functional-relationship model 　6. Feedback-systems model C. Mathematical Models 　1. Linear vs. nonlinear model 　2. Static vs. dynamic model 　3. Deterministic vs. 　　stochastic model

---

Descriptive models   Descriptive models are designed to communicate, explain, or predict. They can be built at three different levels of detail. A *macro-model* postulates only a few variables and a set of gross relationships among them. An example would be a sales model consisting of a single equation with total sales as the dependent variable and national income, average price, and company advertising expenditures as the independent variables. These have been also called "black-box models," because they link two or more variables in a gross way without explaining the specific mechanisms operating within the box. They are achieved by simply fitting the "best" equation that can be found between the set of variables.

A *microanalytic model* postulates more detailed links between a dependent variable and its determinants. A good example is the DEMON model, in which the effect of total advertising expenditures on total sales is explained through the successive linking of total advertising expenditure, gross number of exposures, reach and frequency, advertising awareness, consumer trial, usage, and usage rate.[12]

---

[12]See Chapter 16, pp. 354–55.

A *microbehavioral model* creates hypothetical entities (consumers, dealers, and so on) who interact and produce a record of behavior, which is then analyzed. A good example is a consumer model built by Amstutz, in which a population of potential purchasers are exposed to weekly marketing stimuli, and some fraction of them purchase the product.[13] Microbehavioral models are very costly to design. They usually make an important contribution to understanding the phenomenon and may (though this is less certain) emerge as a useful predictive tool.

Two descriptive models in the operations research literature have turned out to be particularly germane to marketing-type problems. The first is the *Markov-process model*, which is useful in describing systems whose next state is influenced by the current state and a set of transitional probabilities. Suppose there are three coffee brands, A, B, and C. Of those consumers who bought brand A last time, suppose 70 percent bought it again, 20 percent bought B, and 10 percent bought C. This information is represented in row one of Figure 19-2, along with further transitional probabilities associated with brands B and C. The brand-switching matrix provides information about:

> The *repeat-purchase rate* for each brand, indicated by the numbers in the diagonal starting at the upper left. Under certain assumptions, the repeat-purchase rate can be interpreted as a measure of brand loyalty.
>
> The *switching-in and switching-out rate* for each brand, represented by the off-diagonal numbers.

If the switching rates are likely to remain constant, at least for the short run, the matrix becomes a useful tool in forecasting both the magnitude and the speed of change in future market shares on the basis of present market shares.[14]

A second descriptive model of relevance to many marketing situations is a *queuing model*. Queuing models are designed to represent waiting-line situations and answer two specific questions: What amount of waiting time may be expected in a particular system? How will this waiting time change as a result of given alterations in the facilities? These questions can be of particular importance to retailing institutions such as supermarkets, gasoline stations, and airline

---

[13]Arnold E. Amstutz, *Computer Simulation of Competitive Market Response* (Cambridge: The M.I.T. Press, 1967).

[14]See John U. Farley and Alfred A. Kuehn, "Stochastic Models of Brand Switching," in *Science in Marketing*, ed. George Schwartz (New York: John Wiley & Sons, Inc., 1965), pp. 446–64.

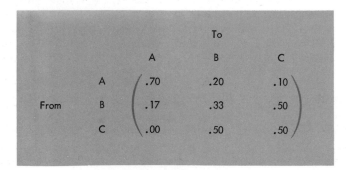

Figure 19-2
A brand-switching matrix

ticket offices. Wherever customers wait, there is the danger that waiting time will become excessive, leading to the loss of these customers to competitors.

If the existing system breeds long queues, the decision maker can simulate the effects of different changes. In the case of a supermarket with a serious queuing problem on Saturdays, four possible attacks are indicated by the dimensions. The supermarket can try to influence its customers to do their shopping on other days. The supermarket can decrease the service time, by employing baggers to aid the cashiers. More service channels can be added. Or some of the channels can be specialized to handle smaller orders.

Decision models   Decision models are designed to evaluate alternative outcomes associated with different decisions, and to find the "best" decision. Decision models are subclassified into *optimization* and *heuristic* models. An *optimization model* is one for which computational routines exist for finding the best solution to the problem as stated. A *heuristic model* is one for which computational routines are not available for finding the best solution, but that offers other advantages. The model may be a much more flexible and complex statement of the problem. To use this model, the analyst applies *heuristics*, defined as rules of thumb that tend to shorten the time required to find a reasonably good solution. For example, in a model to determine good warehouse locations, a heuristic used may be "Only consider locations in large cities." This may exclude a perfectly good location in a small city, but the savings in having to check far fewer cities is expected to compensate for the omission.

The field of decision models contains four standard models that are of particular relevance to marketing-type problems. The first is *differential calculus*, a mathematical technique that can be applied to well-defined mathematical functions to determine whether the dependent variable has a maximum and/ or minimum value(s), and if so, corresponding to which value(s) of the dependent variable(s). Suppose a marketing analyst has determined the profit equation shown in Figure 19-3(a). The task is to find the best price—that is, the value of P that will maximize the value of Z. One approach is to draw a picture of the equation and examine it for the profit-maximizing price, here $150. A quicker, more reliable procedure is to apply differential calculus to this equation without bothering to draw a graph.[15]

The second type of decision model is known as *mathematical programming*. Mathematical programming calls for expressing a decision maker's objective(s) in the form of a mathematical function whose value is to be optimized. Various constraints are also introduced in the form of equations and/or inequalities. Consider, for example, the problem in Figure 19-3(b). Suppose the marketing analyst has found a profit function relating profits to the amount of funds spent

---

[15]The calculus reader will know that the slope of a tangent to the curve is given by the first derivative of the equation:

$$\frac{dZ}{dP} = 1,200 - 8P$$

But the maximum (or minimum) takes place where the slope is zero:

$$1,200 - 8P = 0$$

Therefore profits are a maximum when $P = \$150$. (The sign of the second derivative must be checked to be sure that $P = \$150$ establishes a maximum and not a minimum.)

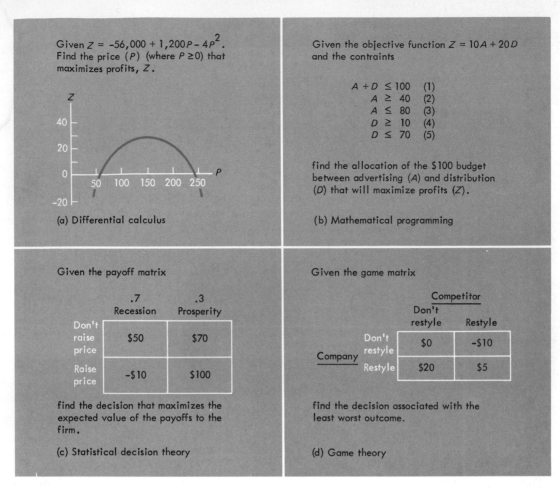

Given $Z = -56,000 + 1,200P - 4P^2$. Find the price (P) (where $P \geq 0$) that maximizes profits, Z.

(a) Differential calculus

Given the objective function $Z = 10A + 20D$ and the constraints

$$
\begin{array}{ll}
A + D \leq 100 & (1) \\
A \geq 40 & (2) \\
A \leq 80 & (3) \\
D \geq 10 & (4) \\
D \leq 70 & (5)
\end{array}
$$

find the allocation of the $100 budget between advertising (A) and distribution (D) that will maximize profits (Z).

(b) Mathematical programming

Given the payoff matrix

	.7 Recession	.3 Prosperity
Don't raise price	$50	$70
Raise price	-$10	$100

find the decision that maximizes the expected value of the payoffs to the firm.

(c) Statistical decision theory

Given the game matrix

		Competitor Don't restyle	Restyle
Company	Don't restyle	$0	-$10
	Restyle	$20	$5

find the decision associated with the least worst outcome.

(d) Game theory

Figure 19-3
Four decision models

on advertising and distribution. Note that a dollar of advertising appears to contribute $10 profit and a dollar of distribution appears to contribute $20. A set of policy constraints is also introduced. First the total marketing budget, as divided between advertising and distribution, should not exceed $100 (constraint 1). Of this, advertising should receive at least $40 (constraint 2) and no more than $80 (constraint 3); and distribution should receive at least $10 (constraint 4) and no more than $70 (constraint 5). Because of the simplicity of this problem, it is possible to find the best marketing program without invoking an advanced solution technique. Since distribution dollars are twice as effective as advertising dollars, it would make sense to spend all that is permitted within the constraints on distribution. This would appear to be $70, leaving $30 for advertising. However, advertising must receive at least $40 according to constraint 2. Therefore, the optimal marketing-mix allocation would be $40 for advertising and $60 for distribution; and with this solution, profits will be $10($40) + $20($60) = $1,600. In larger problems, the analyst would have to resort to specific solution techniques.

The third type of decision model is called *statistical decision theory*. This model calls for (1) distinguishing major decision alternatives facing the firm, (2) distinguishing the events (states of nature) that might, in conjunction with each possible decision, bring about a distinct outcome, (3) estimating the probability of each possible state of nature, (4) estimating the value (payoff) of each possible outcome to the firm, (5) determining the expected value of each decision, and (6) choosing the decision with the highest expected value. Consider this in the context of the problem in Figure 19-3(c). Suppose the product manager is trying to decide between raising the price on a product or leaving it alone. The outcome will be significantly affected by whether the economy moves into a recession, of which the product manager believes there is a .7 chance. If there is a recession and he has left prices alone, he estimates that profits will be $50; but if he has raised prices, he estimates a loss of $10. On the other hand, if the economy is prosperous in the coming year, he estimates that leaving prices alone would yield $70 and raising prices would yield $100. These estimates are summarized conveniently in the payoff matrix.

Statistical decision theory calls for the product manager to estimate the *expected value* of each decision. Expected value is the weighted mean of the payoffs, with the probabilities serving as the weights. The expected value associated with not raising the price is .7($50) + .3($70) = $56, while the expected value of raising the price is .7(−$10) + .3($100) = $23. Clearly the extra gain with the best thing happening (a raised price and prosperity) is not worth the risk, and he is better off leaving the price alone. This conclusion assumes that expected value is a satisfactory criterion for the firm to maximize. This criterion is a sensible one for the large firm that makes repeated decisions of this kind and is not going to go out of business with one or two adverse developments. It makes less sense for a smaller firm facing a major one-shot decision that could ruin it if things go wrong.

Game theory is a fourth approach to evaluating decision alternatives. Like statistical decision theory, it calls for an identification of the decision alternatives, uncertain variables, and the value of different outcomes. It differs from statistical decision theory in that the major uncertain variable is assumed to be a competitor, nature, or some other force that is malevolent. The probability is 1.00 that each actor will do what is in his best interest. Consider the example in Figure 19-3(d). An auto manufacturer is trying to decide whether to restyle its car or leave it alone. It knows that the competitor is also trying to make the same decision. The company estimates that if neither restyles, neither would gain anything over the normal rate of profit. If the company restyles and the competitor does not, the company will gain $20 over the competitor. (We will assume the competitor loses $20—that is, the gain to one company is a loss to the other.) If the company does not restyle and the competitor does, the company loses $10. (By the same token, the competitor gains $10.) Finally, if they both restyle, the company gains $5, and the competitor loses $5, because the company is assumed to be better at restyling.

A solution is possible if we assume that both opponents will want to take the course of action that will leave them *least worst off*. Called the minimax criterion (minimizing the maximum loss), it assumes that both opponents are conservative rather than adventurous. This criterion would lead the company to prefer the restyling alternative. If it does not restyle, it might lose as much as $10; if it does restyle, it will make at least $5. The competitor would also prefer to restyle. If it did not restyle, it might lose as much as $20; if it does restyle, it cannot lose more than $5. Hence, both opponents will decide in favor of restyling, which leads to a $5 gain for the company and a $5 loss for the competitor. Neither opponent can gain by switching unilaterally to a different strategy.

Verbal models   Models in which the variables and their relationships are described in prose are *verbal models*. Most of the great theories of individual, social, and societal behavior are cast in verbal terms—theories such as those of Freud, Darwin, and Marx. Many models of consumer behavior are essentially in the verbal-model stage. Consider

> . . . advertising should move people from *awareness* . . . to *knowledge* . . . to *liking* . . . to *preference* . . . to *conviction* . . . to *purchase*.[16]

Graphical models   Graphical models represent a useful next step in the process of symbolizing a verbal model. Six different graphical models can be distinguished.

Figure 19-4(a) shows a *logical-flow diagram*. A logical-flow diagram is a visual representation of a logical process or operation. The various boxes of such a diagram are connected in a sequential flow pattern and are related to each other through two fundamental operations. One of these is *branching*. Branching takes place when a question is posed at a certain step of the process and its possible answers are expressed as alternative branches leading away from the box. The other operation is *looping*. Looping takes place if certain answers return the flow to an earlier stage. The flow diagram in Figure 19-4(a) describes a firm's efforts to determine how many competitors will cut their prices. The firm first considers competitor i and asks whether he is likely to cut his price. If the answer is yes, this result is tabulated, and then the firm asks whether there are any additional competitors to consider. If the answer is no, the firm goes directly to the next question. If there are more competitors to consider, the logical flow returns to the first box (that is, it loops back); otherwise, the flow ends. Logical-flow diagrams are coming into increasing use in marketing because of the clarity with which they illustrate a logical process.

Figure 19-4(b) shows a *network-planning diagram* (also called a critical-path diagram), which is used to portray the events that must occur to complete a project. The events, shown as circles, are connected by arrows indicating precedent relationships. In Figure 19-4(b) event 6 cannot occur until events 4 and 5 are completed; event 5 cannot occur until event 2 is completed; event 4 cannot occur until events 2 and 3 are completed; and so on. After going on to estimate the completion time of each task (and sometimes the optimistic and pessimistic completion times), the analyst can find the earliest date to completion of the entire project. Somewhere in the network there is a critical path that defines the earliest possible completion time: here it is fifteen weeks. Unless this critical path is shortened, there is no way to complete the project earlier. This diagram is the basis of planning, scheduling, and controlling projects.

---

[16]Robert J. Lavidge and Gary A. Steiner, "A Model for Predictive Measurements of Advertising Effectiveness," *Journal of Marketing*, October 1961, pp. 59–62.

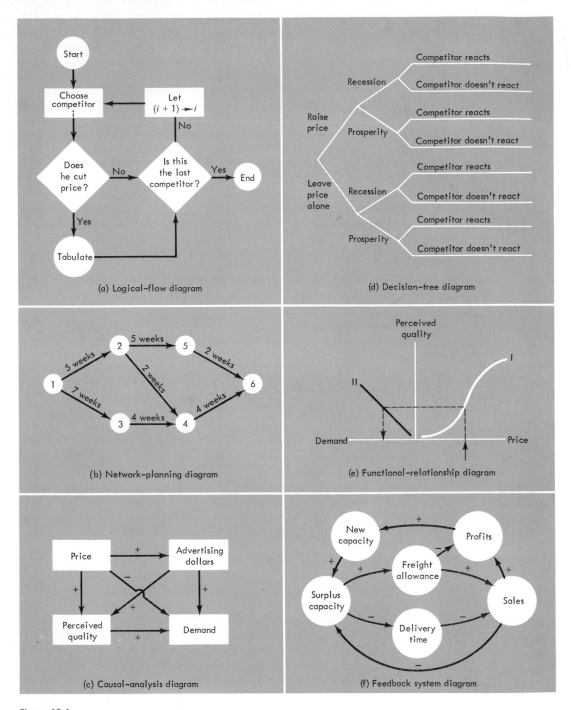

(a) Logical-flow diagram

(d) Decision-tree diagram

(b) Network-planning diagram

(e) Functional-relationship diagram

(c) Causal-analysis diagram

(f) Feedback system diagram

Figure 19-4
Six graphical models for marketing analysis

441

Figure 19-4(c) shows a *causal-analysis diagram*, which is used to portray the directions of influence of various variables on each other. This diagram shows that price has a direct (negative) influence on demand, and an indirect influence also through its positive effects on advertising dollars and perceived quality. A high price leads to high perceived quality and leads the company to spend more on advertising. Both of these in turn have a positive effect on demand. (Not shown is the fact that the level of resulting demand will have a feedback influence on the level of advertising expenditures as well as on the perceived quality.) The value of causal-analysis diagrams is in exposing the complex relationships that the analyst should take into account. They remind us that single-equation relationships between variables may fail to capture the true structure of the phenomena.

Figure 19-4(d) shows a *decision-tree diagram*, which is used to portray the various decision alternatives and consequences found in a decision situation. The firm is trying to decide between raising its price and leaving it alone. The outcome will be influenced by whether the economy moves toward recession or prosperity, and further by whether or not competitors react. The tree could be extended still further to show other contingencies related to buyer reactions, inventory situations, and so on. By adding payoffs and probabilities to the various branches of the tree, the best decision can be found by using statistical decision theory.

Figure 19-4(e) is a *functional-relationship diagram*, which is used to portray functional relationship(s) between two or more variables. Quadrant I shows a positive relationship between price and perceived quality. Quadrant II shows a positive relationship between perceived quality and demand. The two quadrants enable the analyst to trace the effect of a *particular* price, through perceived quality, on a *particular* demand level. Thus one can generate a demand function from knowledge of two other functions. Functional graphs can be used to portray sales-response functions, probability distributions, and many other relationships.

Figure 19-4(f) shows a *feedback-system diagram*, which is used to portray any system that yields outputs that return to earlier inputs and act as an influence. This process should not be confused with looping in logical-flow diagrams, which merely returns the procedure to an earlier point without implying any influence on that point. The example given here shows the interactions among sales, profits, capacity, and marketing variables. Surplus capacity leads the company to offer higher freight allowances to customers and reduced delivery time. These lead to higher sales. Increased sales lead to increased profits while drawing down surplus capacity. In the meantime the higher freight allowances reduce profits. If the net effect is a gain in profits, this leads to additional investment in capacity, which increases surplus capacity, and the cycle continues. Thus feedback-system diagrams are useful devices for representing variables that have interactive properties and feedbacks.

Graphical models, in general, have all the virtues that are found in "pictures." A graph strips the phenomenon of inessentials; it allows a viewer to grasp the whole and follow particular relationships according to his interests. For marketing analysts, graphs improve exposition, facilitate discussion, and guide analysis.

Mathematical models Mathematical models can be subclassified in many ways. A first distinction can be drawn between *linear* and *nonlinear models*. In a *linear model* all the relationships between variables are expressed as straight lines. This means that a unit change in one variable has a *constant* marginal impact on a related variable. The advertising-sales relationship would be linear if every $100 increase in advertising created a $1,000 increase in sales, no matter how much had already been spent. This, of course, is dubious, because increasing or diminishing returns to advertising are likely to be found at different points in the relationship. It is also likely that other marketing inputs, such as price and sales-call time, do not relate to sales in a thoroughly linear way. The assumption of linearity is generally useful only as a first approximation for mathematical convenience.

A second distinction can be drawn between *static* and *dynamic models*. A *static model* centers on the ultimate state (or solution) of a system, independent of time. A *dynamic model* brings time explicitly into its framework and allows the observation of the movement of the state (or solution) of the system over time. The elementary demand-supply diagram in beginning economics courses represents a static model of price determination in that it indicates where price and output will be in equilibrium without indicating the path of adjustment through time. Brand-switching models are dynamic in that they predict period-to-period changes in customer states.

A third distinction can be drawn between *deterministic* and *stochastic models*. A *deterministic model* is one in which chance plays no role. The solution is determined by a set of exact relationships. The linear-programming model for determining blends (oils, animal feeds, candies) is deterministic, because the relationships are exact and the cost data are known. A *stochastic model*, on the other hand, is one where chance or random variables are introduced explicitly. Brand-switching models are stochastic in that customer's brand choices are regulated by probabilities.

Marketing management-science system

As the marketing management scientist works his craft in the firm, various data, statistical procedures, and models will be developed. These can offer maximum value to the marketing executive if they are organized and made easily available. This can be accomplished by viewing the task as one of building and integrating a data bank, statistical bank, and model bank. The *data bank* is an organized collection of the company's internal and external data. The *statistical bank* is a readily accessible set of statistical routines for summarizing and analyzing specific data banks. The *model bank* is a computerized set of programs to help the manager explore "what if" and "which is best" questions. The key need is to make the various programs and services of the marketing management scientist as available as possible to the various marketing executives.

SUMMARY

Marketing information has become the critical input into effective marketing as a result of the trend toward national and international marketing, the transition from buyer needs to buyer wants, and the transition from price to non-price competition. All firms have a marketing information system connecting the external environment with its executives, but the systems vary greatly in sophistication and the number and quality of services they provide.

Marketing information systems consist of four components. The internal accounting system reports orders, sales, inventory levels, receivables, payables, and so on. Several companies have made large investments in improving the speed, accuracy, and reporting potentials of their order-shipping-billing cycle.

The marketing intelligence system provides executives with current information about developments and changing conditions in the macro and task environments. Executives gather intelligence on their own, but their effectiveness can be augmented by improved training of salesmen in their intelligence responsibilities, the development of a marketing-intelligence center, and the purchase of information when appropriate from specialized intelligence services.

Marketing research provides specific studies of market opportunities, marketing effectiveness, and marketing problems. Marketing research procedure consists of five steps: problem definition, research design, fieldwork, data analysis, and report preparation. Good marketing research is characterized by the scientific method, creativity, multiple methodologies, model building, and cost/benefit measures of the value of information.

The marketing management-science system is responsible for building models to explain, predict, or improve marketing processes. Marketing management scientists may build or use descriptive or decision models and verbal, graphical, or mathematical models to come to grips with marketing problems.

**QUESTIONS
AND PROBLEMS**

1 List six major complaints that marketing executives typically make about the quality and quantity of marketing information.

2 (a) Suggest how a liquor company might estimate the amount of liquor consumed in a legally dry town. (b) Suggest how a research organization might estimate the number of people who read given magazines in a doctor's office. (c) Suggest six different ways in which a sample of men can be gathered to be interviewed on their usage of hair tonics.

3 What is the major issue (impartiality, validity, reliability) that is likely to come up in the following use of secondary data: (a) using a time series of disposable personal income (in current dollars) to indicate the historical trend in consumer purchasing power; (b) using a local chamber of commerce study on the average income of the community; (c) using a man-in-the-street sample to estimate the proportion of men who own dinner jackets.

4 "A manufacturer of automobiles is testing a new direct-mail approach B versus a standard approach A. An experiment is conducted in which each of the two approaches is tried out on random samples of size n (sample size $2n$ in total) from a large national mailing list. Suppose that $n = 100,000$ so that 200,000 is the total sample size of the experiment. During a three-month period, approach B has 761 sales and A has 753." What decision should be made? List the alternatives and the rationale of each.

5 Evaluate the following questions to be asked in a consumer survey: (a) What is your husband's favorite brand of golf balls? (b) What TV programs did you watch a week ago Monday? (c) How many pancakes did you make for your family last year? (d) Tell me your exact income. (e) Can you supply me with a list of your grocery purchases this month?

6 Although marketing research is indispensable to practicing the marketing concept, resistance to it is still found in some quarters. What factors have retarded the greater acceptance of marketing research?

7 In obtaining estimates from company salesmen, product managers, and other personnel, one must discourage their supplying estimates that are self-serving. Give some examples of self-serving estimates by company personnel and suggest what might be done to discourage this.

8 The text mentioned the following three tools for analyzing multivariate data: (a) multiple regression analysis, (b) discriminant analysis, and (c) factor analysis. Describe the basic idea behind each tool and illustrate a marketing application for each.

9 List and discuss the major criteria for judging the usefulness of a mathematical marketing model.

10 Some marketing men view the emergence of mathematical model building in marketing with hostility. They will make the following statements: (a) we don't use models; (b) models are typically unrealistic; (c) anyone can build a model; (d) a model is of no help unless you can get the data. How would you answer these objections?

11 With the emergence of operations research in marketing, large companies are trying to determine the proper organizational relationship between marketing research activities (MR) and marketing operations research (MOR). Describe five alternative conceptions.

20
MARKETING CONTROL

Having lost sight of our objective, we redoubled our efforts.

OLD ADAGE

Marketing planning means little unless accompanied by vigorous systems of marketing control. Even if all plans were sound, they could undergo poor implementation or meet with unexpected developments in the economy. Management must therefore provide for continuous monitoring of the results against the objectives. Disappointing performance must be met by swift steps to investigate the causes and institute remedial action.

Marketing control has become a major concern of marketing management in recent years. One reason is the accelerated pace of economic change. In a relatively short period the economy plunged from surpluses into shortages, then into substantial inflation, and then into recession. No amount of careful planning could anticipate these changes, and therefore more of the burden is placed upon management control. Second, the substantial inflation has made management much more conscious of costs. Management is seeking better ways of determining the marketing effectiveness of different marketing expenditures. There has been a distinct shift of marketing management from a concentration on sales volume to profitability. This means that costs must be carefully measured to learn the real profitability of marketing action.

Marketing control, like marketing planning, is far from being a single process. Three different levels of marketing control can be distinguished. They are shown in Table 20-1 and described in the remainder of this chapter.

Table 20-1

Types of control

Type of control	Prime responsibility	Purpose of control	Tools
I. Strategic control	Top management	To examine whether the company is pursuing its best opportunities with respect to markets, products, and channels	Marketing audit
II. Annual plan control	Top management Middle management	To examine whether the planned results are being achieved	Sales analysis Market-share analysis Sales-to-expense ratios Other ratios Attitude tracking
III. Profitability control	Marketing controller	To examine where the company is making and losing money	Profitability by: product territory market segment trade channel order size

STRATEGIC CONTROL

Every organization needs to review its basic operations from time to time to make sure they are attuned to the changing environment and opportunities. Marketing is one of the major areas where rapid obsolescence of objectives, policies, and programs is a constant possibility. First, the marketing environment tends to undergo continuous and rapid change. Second, organizational slack creeps in and afflicts all departments and renders them less than optimally efficient.

This has led to the call for a formal *marketing audit* that all companies should periodically carry out in order to keep the company's marketing under strategic control. The original model is the financial audit which companies carry out to assure stockholders and creditors that the company's financial reporting is adequate and accurate. The financial audit is performed on a periodic basis with a standard set of procedures. It is argued that a marketing audit should be developed that follows a standard set of procedures. Several marketing consulting organizations list a marketing audit as one of the services they provide to clients.

Unfortunately, the marketing audit has not yet developed into a standard tool comparable to the financial audit. In some circles it is used to suggest any marketing review of a sick company designed to unearth its problems and help it get back on its feet. Others use it to mean any intensive examination of a specific marketing activity for the sake of improving the activity—examples would be a sales-force audit, an advertising audit, and so on.

We would like to propose a concept of the marketing audit that has a more formal and standardized character. It would rest on four pillars.

1 *Periodic.* The marketing audit would be carried out on an annual or other calendar basis and not only when there is a crisis. It promises benefits for the company that is seemingly successful as well as the company that is in deep trouble. "No marketing operation is ever so good that it cannot be improved. Even the best can be made better. In fact, even the best *must* be better, for few if any marketing operations can remain successful over the years by maintaining the status quo."[1]

2 *Comprehensive.* The marketing audit would cover all of the marketing operations and not just focus on one or a few marketing activities that seem to be in trouble. Focusing on only the troubled marketing activities may blind management as to their real cause and location. Excessive sales-force turnover, for example, may be a symptom not of poor sales-force training but of poor company products and promotion. Only a comprehensive marketing audit will reveal the basic sources of the observed symptoms of marketing ineffectiveness.

3 *Systematic.* The marketing audit would involve a standard sequence of diagnostic steps covering the organization's marketing environment, internal marketing system, and specific marketing activities. The diagnosis would be followed by the design of a corrective action plan involving both short-run and long-run remedial actions to improve the organization's overall marketing effectiveness.

4 *Independent.* The marketing audit would be conducted by a party who has sufficient independence from the marketing department to attain top management's confidence and the needed objectivity. An outside party is recommended who has broad experience in auditing many companies and sufficient familiarity with this industry.

We are now ready to summarize the nature of a marketing audit.

A **marketing audit** is a periodic, comprehensive, systematic, and independent examination of the organization's marketing environment, internal marketing system, and specific marketing activities with a view to determining problem areas and recommending a corrective action plan to improve the organization's overall marketing effectiveness.

Marketing audit procedure

The marketing audit should utilize a systematic set of questions that takes the auditor into the main areas of the company's marketing operations. A proposed marketing audit form is contained in Table 20-2 and consists of three diagnostic steps:[2]

1 *Marketing Environment Review.* The first step is to profile the current and expected marketing environment of the organization. This breaks down into examining the markets, customers, competitors, and macroenvironment.

[1]Abe Shuchman, "The Marketing Audit: Its Nature, Purposes, and Problems," in *Analyzing and Improving Marketing Performance,* Report No. 32 (New York: American Management Association, 1959), pp. 16–17.

[2]The general framework, though not the specific questions, is adapted from the excellent article by Ernst A. Tirmann, "Should Your Marketing Be Audited?" *European Business,* Autumn 1971, pp. 49–56.

2 *Marketing System Review.* The second step is to review the internal marketing system in terms of its suitability to the emerging marketing environment. This step takes a look at the organization's objectives, program, implementation, and organization.

3 *Detailed Marketing Activity Review.* The third step is to review the main components of the company's marketing mix, specifically its products, prices, distribution, personal selling, advertising, publicity, and sales promotion.

On the basis of this review, the marketing auditor now prepares a list of findings describing the major problems facing the organization. Here is an example:

> Beginning in 1962 the A. C. Gilbert Company, manufacturer of Erector sets, electric trains, chemistry sets, and microscopes, suffered mounting losses each year. In 1966 a marketing audit uncovered the following faults in the company's marketing system: (1) insufficient use of television advertising, which was becoming the most powerful medium for selling toys; (2) failure to move heavily into discount stores and supermarkets, which were assuming dominance over traditional toy outlets; (3) deterioration in quality control standards, which was leading to bad word of mouth; and (4) poor timing in the introduction of new toys, sometimes right after the Christmas season.[3]

Findings such as these call for a corrective action plan by the auditor. The plan is divided into steps that should be implemented immediately and steps to be taken in the long run. Some short-run corrective steps for the A. C. Gilbert Company would include (1) revising the media plan to shift 75 percent of the advertising budget into television and (2) immediate improvement in quality control. Some long-run corrective steps would include (1) developing a missionary sales force to penetrate the discount store and supermarket industry and (2) revamping the new-product development program to do a better job of spotting new-product opportunities and timing their development.

ANNUAL PLAN CONTROL

Companies must also establish a regular pattern of control procedures to ensure the realization of the annual plan goals. The realization of these goals is constantly threatened by faulty implementation and by rapidly changing market conditions.

The heart of annual plan control is the establishment within each annual plan of *management-by-objectives.* The overall sales and profit goals in the plan must be elaborated into specific objectives for every actor in the company. Each person knows what he and his subordinates are supposed to achieve (*objectives*). His results are checked by his superior on a weekly, monthly, or quarterly basis (*performance measurement*). Below-normal performances trigger an analysis of the causes (*causal analysis*). The findings lead to a corrective plan to close the gap between expectations and performance (*corrective action plan*).

Managers use five performance tools to check on the progress of the annual plan.

---

[3]See "A. C. Gilbert: A Victim of Poor Quality, Timing, Product Planning," *Marketing Insights,* March 6, 1967, pp. 10–11.

Table 20-2

A systematic marketing audit

Part I. The Marketing Environment Review

A. *Markets*

1. What are the organization's major markets and publics?
2. What are the major market segments in each market?
3. What are the present and expected future size and characteristics of each market or market segment?

B. *Customers*

4. How do the customers and publics see and feel toward the organization?
5. How do customers make their purchase or adoption decisions?
6. What is the present and expected future state of customer needs and satisfaction?

C. *Competitors*

7. Who are the organization's major competitors?
8. What trends can be foreseen in competition?

D. *Macroenvironment*

9. What are the main relevant developments with respect to demography, economy, technology, government, and culture that will affect the organization's situation?

Part II. The Marketing System Review

A. *Objectives*

10. What are the organization's long-run and short-run overall objectives and marketing objectives?
11. Are the objectives stated in a clear hierarchical order and in a form that permits planning and measurement of achievement?
12. Are the marketing objectives reasonable for the organization, given its competitive position, resources, and opportunities?

B. *Program*

13. What is the organization's core strategy for achieving its objectives and is it likely to succeed?
14. Is the organization allocating enough resources (or too much resources) to accomplish the marketing tasks?
15. Are the marketing resources allocated optimally to the various markets, territories, and products of the organization?
16. Are the marketing resources allocated optimally to the major elements of the marketing mix, i.e., product quality, personal contact, promotion, and distribution?

C. *Implementation*

17. Does the organization develop an annual marketing plan? Is the planning procedure effective?
18. Does the organization implement control procedures (monthly, quarterly, etc.) to ensure that its annual plan objectives are being achieved?
19. Does the organization carry out periodic studies to determine the contribution and effectiveness of various marketing activities?
20. Does the organization have an adequate marketing information system to service the needs of managers for planning and controlling operations in various markets?

Table 20-2 (continued)

D. *Organization*

21. Does the organization have a high-level marketing officer to analyze, plan, and implement the marketing work of the organization?
22. Are the other persons directly involved in marketing activity able people? Is there a need for more training, incentives, supervision, or evaluation?
23. Are the marketing responsibilities optimally structured to serve the needs of different marketing activities, products, markets, and territories?
24. Do the organization's personnel understand and practice the marketing concept?

Part III. Detailed Marketing Activity Review

A. *Products*

25. What are the main products of the organization? What are the generic products?
26. Should any products in the line be phased out?
27. Should any products be added to the line?
28. What is the general state of health of each product and the product mix as a whole?

B. *Prices*

29. To what extent are prices set on cost, demand, and/or competitive criteria?
30. What would the likely response of demand be to higher or lower prices?
31. How do customers psychologically interpret the price level?
32. Does the organization use temporary price promotions and, if so, how effective are they?

C. *Distribution*

33. Are there alternative methods of distributing the product that would result in more service or less cost?
34. Does the organization render adequate service, along with the product, to its customers?

D. *Personal Selling*

35. Is the sales force large enough to accomplish the organization's objectives?
36. Is the sales force organized along the best lines of specialization (territory, market, product)?
37. Does the sales force show high morale, ability, and effectiveness? Are they sufficiently trained and incentivized?
38. Are the procedures adequate for setting quotas and evaluating performance?

E. *Advertising*

39. Does the organization adequately state its advertising objectives?
40. Does the organization spend the right amount on advertising?
41. Are the themes and copy effective?
42. Are the media well chosen?

F. *Publicity*

43. Does the organization have a carefully formulated program of publicity?

G. *Sales Promotion*

44. Are sales promotions used by the organization and, if so, are they well conceived?

The first performance tool used by managers is sales analysis. Sales analysis is an effort to examine the actual sales being achieved in relation to expected sales in different parts of the system. There are two specific tools in this connection.

Sales variance analysis is an attempt to determine the relative contribution of different factors to a gap in sales performance. Suppose the annual plan called for selling 4,000 widgets in the first quarter at $1 a widget, or $4,000. At quarter's end, only 3,000 widgets were sold at $.80 a widget, or $2,400. The sales performance variance is −$1,600, or −40 percent of expected sales. The question arises, How much of this underperformance is due to the price decline and how much is due to the volume decline? The following calculation answers this question:

$$\text{Variance due to price decline} = (\$1 - .80)\,(3,000) = \$\,600 \quad 37.5\%$$
$$\text{Variance due to volume decline} = (\$1)\,(4,000 - 3,000) = \underline{\$1,000} \quad \underline{62.5\%}$$
$$\$1,600 \quad 100.0\%$$

Accordingly, almost two-thirds of the sales variance is due to a failure to realize the volume target. Since this may be under more control normally than the price, the company should look closely into why its expected sales volume was not achieved.

Micro-sales analysis may provide the answer. Micro-sales analysis is an attempt to determine the specific products, territories, and so forth, that failed to produce their expected share of sales. Suppose the company sells in three territories and expected sales were 1,500, 500, and 2,000 units, respectively, adding up to 4,000 widgets. The actual sales volume was 1,400, 525, and 1,075, respectively. Thus territory one showed a 7 percent shortfall in terms of expected sales; territory two, a 5 percent surplus; and territory three, a 46 percent shortfall! It is now clear that territory three is causing most of the trouble. The sales vice-president can check into territory three to see which, if any, of the following hypotheses explains the poor performance: (1) territory three's salesman is loafing or he has a personal problem; (2) a major competitor has entered this territory; (3) GNP is depressed in this territory.

A company's sales performance fails to reveal whether it is gaining or losing ground relative to its competitors. The key statistic in this connection is its *market share.*

There are at least two reasons for management's interest in market-share measurement.[4] In the first place, it suggests whether changes in company sales were due to uncontrollable outside forces or weaknesses in the company's marketing program. If a company's sales fall but its market share remains constant, this implies that the whole industry was affected by similar environmental forces. In the second place, the market-share standard implies a comparison of the company's performance with the average performance of the other companies in the industry. If management could not maintain its share of the market, the implication is that the company's marketing mix or its execution is seriously at fault.

---

[4]See Alfred R. Oxenfeldt, "How to Use Market-Share Measurement," *Harvard Business Review,* January–February 1959, pp. 59–68.

At the same time, several qualifications should be kept in mind to avoid drawing the wrong conclusions from market-share measurements:

The assumption that outside forces affect all companies in the same way is often not true. The surgeon general's report on the harmful sequences of cigarette smoking caused total cigarette sales to falter but not equally for all companies. The companies that had established a reputation for a better filter were hit less hard.

The assumption that a company's performance should be judged against the average performance of all companies also is not always valid. A company with greater than average opportunities should register a growing market share. If its market share remains constant, this may imply deficient rather than average management.

If a new firm enters the industry, then every existing firm's market share may fall (again, not necessarily equally). Here is a case where a fall in the company's market share does not mean that the company is performing below the average of the industry.

Sometimes the decline in a company's market share is the result of a deliberate policy to improve profits. Management, for example, may drop unprofitable customers or products, with resulting decline in market share.

Market share fluctuates for many reasons. For example, the market share in a particular period can be affected by whether a large sale is made on the last day of the period or at the beginning of the following period. A current shift in market share does not always have a significant marketing implication.

Market-share analysis, like sales analysis, increases in value when the data are disaggregated along various dimensions. The company might watch the progress of its market share by product line, customer type, region, or other breakdowns.

Market-share analysis requires, of course, periodic information on total industry sales and, hopefully, individual competitors' sales. In some industries, these data are made available through industry trade associations or governmental agencies. For example, automakers' sales are available from official statistics on new-car registration. In the food and drug industry, brand shares are measured through store or consumer panels such as those run by A. C. Nielsen or the Market Research Corporation of America. In other industries, total industry sales and competitors' sales require some conjecture on the basis of indirect indicators.

Expense-to-sales ratios

Annual plan control also requires checking on actual expenses in relation to sales to make sure that the company is not overspending to achieve its sales goals. One key ratio is *gross-profit-to-sales.* A fall in this ratio signals an unexpected increase in expenses. Management can then examine particular *expense-to-sales ratios* to see which ones are growing out of control. Among the key ratios to check are advertising expense-to-sales and sales-force expense-to-sales.

These ratios will experience some random fluctuations that could well be ignored. Only fluctuations beyond some normal level are a cause for concern. In this connection, the period-to-period fluctuations in each ratio can be charted on a *control chart* such as the one shown in Figure 20-1. This chart shows that the advertising expense-to-sales ratio normally fluctuates between 8 and 12 percent, say ninety-nine out of one hundred times. In the fifteenth period, however, the ratio exceeded the upper control limit. One of two opposing hypotheses can explain this occurrence:

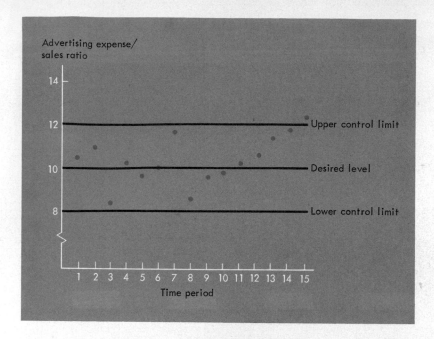

Figure 20-1
The control chart model

Hypothesis A: The company still has good control over sales, and this represents one of those rare chance events.

Hypothesis B: The company has lost control over this cost as a result of some assignable cause.

If hypothesis A is accepted, no investigation is made to determine whether the environment has changed. The risk in doing this is that some real change has occurred and the company will fall behind. If hypothesis B is accepted, the environment is investigated at the risk that the investigation will uncover nothing and be a waste of time and effort.

The behavior of successive observations even within the control limits should also be watched for patterns that seem difficult to explain by chance. In Figure 20-1 it should be noted that the level of the expense-to-sales ratio rose steadily from the ninth period onward. The probability of encountering a pattern of six successive increases in what should be a random and independent process is only one out of sixty-four.[5] This unusual pattern should have led to an investigation sometime before the fifteenth observation.

When an expense-to-sales ratio gets out of control, disaggregative data may be needed to track down the source of the problem. An *expense-to-sales deviation chart* can be used in this connection. Figure 20-2 shows the performances of different sales districts in terms of their quota attainment and expense attainment (in percentages). For example, district D has accomplished its quota nearly at the expected expense level. District B has exceeded its quota and its expenses are proportionately higher. The most troubling districts are in the second quad-

---

[5]There is a chance of $\frac{1}{2}$ that any succeeding observation will be higher and the same chance that it will be lower (excluding the possibility that two successive values are identical). Therefore the probability of finding six successively higher values is given by $(\frac{1}{2})^6 = \frac{1}{64}$.

Other ratios

rant. For example, district J has accomplished less than 80 percent of its quota and its expenses are disproportionately high. The next step is to prepare a similar chart for each deviant district that shows salesmen standings on percentage of quota attainment and expense attainment. Within district J, for example, it may turn out that the poor performance is associated with a few salesmen.

Various managers will track other ratios that bear on the efficiency with which the marketing resources under their control are being used to achieve the annual plan goals. A *sales manager*, for example, will pay close attention to:

1 Premise contacts per salesman per day
2 Average sales-call time per contact
3 Revenue per contact hour
4 Percentage of closures per contact
5 Entertainment expense as a percentage of total sales

An *advertising manager* will pay close attention to:

1 Cost per thousand consumers reached by the ad
2 Cost per thousand consumers reached with each media category and vehicle

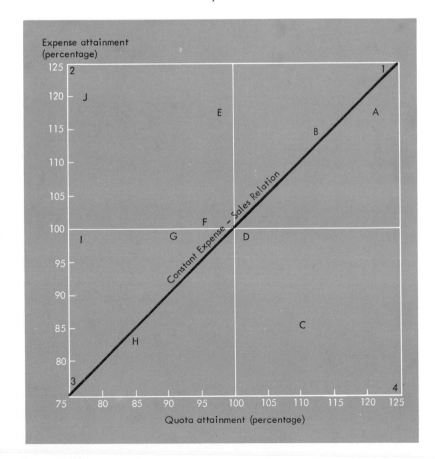

Figure 20-2

Comparison of expense and revenue deviations by district

SOURCE: Adapted from D. M. Phelps and J. H. Westing, *Marketing Management,* 3rd ed. (Homewood, Ill.: Richard D. Irwin, Inc., 1968), p. 754

3 Percentage of a media vehicle's audience who saw the ad

4 Number of inquiries stimulated by the ad

5 Change in share-of-favorable attitude following the ad

A *sales promotion manager* will heed:

1 Percentage of goods sold on deal

2 Display costs per customer

3 Percentage of coupons redeemed

4 Number of inquiries resulting from a demonstration

A *marketing administration manager* will heed:

1 Administrative expenses as a percentage of sales

2 Dollars profits per manager

3 Ratio of management to nonmanagement personnel

Aside from checking into these ratios periodically, various managers will commission special studies to determine how to increase marketing resource efficiency. Sales managers often conduct *time-and-duty studies* to find ways to increase the ratios of productive to idle sales force time. Merchandise managers try to analyze the causes behind the *percentage of returned merchandise* to reduce this problem. Distribution managers carry out *logistical studies* to bring down inventory, warehousing, and transportation costs without reducing the level of customer service.

Attitude tracking

Some organizations monitor customer attitudes toward their products on a regular basis. Sears, for example, conducts a telephone survey every quarter to measure customer attitudes toward Sears and particular product lines. If Sear's share-of-favorable attitude starts falling, this indicates that a sales decline may shortly ensue. Attitude tracking serves to indicate the need for early action to avert a potential downturn in sales.

Corrective action

We have mentioned corrective action several times. When actual performance deviates too much from the annual plan goals, companies go through a well-known cycle of defensive maneuvers to correct the situation. Consider the following case:

> A large fertilizer producer found itself falling behind in its sales goals for the year. This was happening to its competitors as well, all of whom had built excess capacity. Some of the competitors were beginning to cut prices in order to achieve their planned sales volume.

In attempting to save and reverse the situation, this company was observed to go through several increasingly drastic steps:

1 *Price cutting.* The company began to soften its own prices (higher discounts, freight allowances, and so on) to meet competition and retain its share of market.

2 *Increased pressure on sales force.* The company applied more pressure on its salesmen to meet their quotas. The salesmen in turn started "beating down" doors, pres-

suring customers to buy more or buy before the end of the year to improve the performance picture.

3 *Fringe expenditure cutting*. The company proceeded to cut the budgets for personnel hiring and training, advertising, public relations, charities, and research and development.

4 *Manpower cuts*. The previous steps were inadequate and the company began to lay off, retire, or fire personnel in various departments, particularly in staff services such as public relations, marketing research, and operations research.

5 *Bookkeeping adjustments*. The company undertook some fancy bookkeeping to bring about a better picture of profits. One step was to change the depreciation and thus improve the profit picture. Another step was to record purchases wherever possible as capital items rather than as expenses. A third step was to sell some company assets for leaseback in order to increase cash resources. Another step was to record sales to phantom buyers, revising them as returned merchandise in the following year.

6 *Investment cutting*. The company began to cut back on its investment in plant and equipment.

7 *Selling property*. The company started to consider selling some of its product lines or divisions to other companies.

8 *Selling the company*. The ultimate step this company considered was selling out or merging with another company that had good finances or some complementarities with this firm.

PROFITABILITY CONTROL

Besides long-range control and annual plan control, companies carry on periodic research to determine the actual profitability of their different products, territories, customer groups, trade channels, and order sizes. This task requires an ability to assign marketing and other costs to specific marketing entities and activities.

Methodology of marketing cost analysis

Marketing cost analysis is a tool for helping the marketing executive determine whether any current marketing activities should be eliminated, added, or altered in scale.[6] The starting point for marketing cost analysis is the company's profit and loss statement. A simplified profit and loss statement is shown in Table 20-3. Profits are arrived at by subtracting cost of goods sold and other expenses from sales. The marketing executive's interest would be in developing analogous profit statements by functional marketing breakdowns, such as products, customers, or territories. To do this, the "natural" expense designation (such as salaries, rent, supplies) would have to be reclassified into "functional" expense designations. Consider the following example:

> The marketing vice-president of a lawn-mower firm wishes to determine the costs and profits of selling through three different types of retail channels: hardware stores, garden supply shops, and department stores. The company produces only one model of lawn mower. Its profit and loss statement is shown in Table 20-3.

---

[6]For a basic text, see Donald R. Longman and Michael Schiff, *Practical Distribution Cost Analysis* (Homewood, Ill.: Richard D. Irwin, Inc., 1955).

Table 20-3

A simplified profit and loss statement

Sales		$60,000
Cost of goods sold		39,000
Gross margin		$21,000
Expenses		
Salaries	$9,300	
Rent	3,000	
Supplies	3,500	
		15,800
Net profit		$ 5,200

Step 1: Identifying the functional expenses. Assume that the expenses listed in Table 20-3 are incurred to carry out the activities of selling the product, advertising the product, packing and delivering the product, and billing and collecting. The first task is to show how much of each natural expense was incurred in each of these activities.

Suppose that most of the salaries went to salesmen and the rest went to an advertising manager, packing and delivery help, and an office accountant. Let the breakdown of the $9,300 be $5,100, $1,200, $1,400, and $1,600, respectively. Table 20-4 shows allocation of the salary expense to these four activities.

Table 20-4 also shows the rent account of $3,000 as allocated to the four activities. Since the salesmen work away from the office, none of the building's rent expense is assigned to the selling activity. Most of the floor space and rental of equipment arises in connection with packing and delivery. A small portion of the floor space is taken up by the activities of the advertising manager and the office accountant.

Finally, the supplies account lumps together promotional materials, packing materials, fuel purchases for delivery, and home-office stationery. The $3,500 in this account should be reassigned to the functional uses made of the supplies. The result of this and the previous breakdowns is that the total expenses of $15,800 are reclassified from a natural basis into a functional activity basis.

Table 20-4

Mapping natural expenses into functional expenses

Natural accounts	Total	Selling	Advertising	Packing and delivery	Billing and collecting
Salaries	$ 9,300	$5,100	$1,200	$1,400	$1,600
Rent	3,000	—	400	2,000	600
Supplies	3,500	400	1,500	1,400	200
	$15,800	$5,500	$3,100	$4,800	$2,400

Step 2: Assigning the functional expenses to the marketing entities. The next task is to determine how much of each activity has gone into serving each type of channel. Consider the selling effort. The selling effort devoted to each channel is approximated by the number of sales calls made in each channel. This is given in the first column of Table 20-5. Altogether 275 sales calls were made during the period. Since the total selling expense amounted to $5,500 (see Table 20-4), then the selling expense per call averaged $20.

As for the advertising expense, Table 20-5 shows this allocated on the basis of the number of advertisements addressed to the different trade channels. Since there were 100 advertisements altogether, the advertising expense of $3,100 means that the average advertisement cost $31.

The basis chosen for allocating the packing and delivery expense was the number of orders placed by each type of channel; this same basis also was used for allocating the expense of billing and collections.

Step 3: Preparing a profit and loss statement for each marketing entity. It is now possible to prepare a profit and loss statement for each type of channel. The results are shown in Table 20-6. Since hardware stores accounted for one-half of total sales ($30,000 out of $60,000), this channel is charged with half of the cost of goods sold ($19,500 out of $39,000). This leaves a gross margin from hardware stores of $10,500. From this must be deducted the proportions of the functional expenses that hardware stores consumed. According to Table 20-5 hardware stores received 200 out of 275 total sales calls. At an imputed value of $20 a call, hardware stores have to be charged with $4,000 of the selling expense. Table 20-5 also shows that hardware stores were the target of 50 advertisements. At $31 an advertisement, the hardware stores are charged with $1,550 of the advertising activity. The same reasoning applies in computing the share of the other functional expenses to charge to hardware stores. The result is that hardware stores gave rise to $10,050 of the total expenses. Subtracting this from the gross margin, the profit from the activities of selling to hardware stores is small ($450).

Table 20-5

Bases for allocating functional expenses to channels

Channel type		Selling No. of sales calls in period	Advertising No. of advertise-ments	Packing and delivery No. of orders placed in period	Billing and collecting No. of orders placed in period
Hardware		200	50	50	50
Garden supply		65	20	21	21
Department stores		10	30	9	9
		275	100	80	80
Functional expense	=	$5,500	$3,100	$4,800	$2,400
No. of units		275	100	80	80
	=	$20	$31	$60	$30

Table 20-6

Profit and loss statements for channels

	Hardware	Garden supply	Dept. stores	Whole company
Sales	$30,000	$10,000	$20,000	$60,000
Cost of goods sold	19,500	6,500	13,000	39,000
Gross margin	$10,500	$ 3,500	$ 7,000	$21,000
Expenses				
Selling ($20 per call)	$ 4,000	$ 1,300	$ 200	$ 5,500
Advertising ($31 per advertisement)	1,550	620	930	3,100
Packing and delivery ($60 per order)	3,000	1,260	540	4,800
Billing ($30 per order)	1,500	630	270	2,400
Total expenses	$10,050	$ 3,810	$ 1,940	$15,800
Net Profit (or loss)	$ 450	$ (310)	$ 5,060	$ 5,200

The same analysis is repeated for the other channels. It turns out that the company is losing money in selling through garden supply shops and makes virtually all of its profits from sales to department stores. Clearly, gross sales through each channel is not a reliable indicator of the net profits being made in each channel.

Determining the best corrective actions

The results of a marketing cost analysis do not constitute an adequate informational basis for deciding on corrective action. It would be naive to conclude that garden supply shops (and possibly hardware stores) should be dropped as channels in order to concentrate on department stores. Such information as the following would be needed first on each question:

To what extent do buyers buy on the basis of the type of retail outlet versus the brand? Would they seek out the brand in those channels that are not eliminated?

What are the future market trends with respect to the importance of these three channels?

Have marketing efforts and policies directed at the three channels been optimal?

On the basis of this and other information, marketing management will want to define the major alternatives open to them:

Establish a special charge for handling smaller orders to encourage larger orders. This move is based on the assumption that small orders are the ultimate cause of the relative unprofitability of dealing with garden supply shops and hardware stores.

Give more aid to garden supply shops and hardware stores. This is based on the assumption that the managers of these stores could increase their sales with more coaching or promotional materials.

Reduce the number of sales calls and the amount of advertising going to garden supply shops and hardware stores. This is based on the assumption that some of these costs can be saved without reducing proportionately the level of sales to these channels.

Do nothing. This is based on the assumption that current marketing efforts are optimal and that either future marketing trends point to an imminent improvement in the profitability of the weaker channels or dropping any type of channel would reduce rather than improve profits because of repercussions on production costs or on demand.

Don't abandon any channel as a whole but only the weakest retail units in each channel. This is based on the assumption that a more detailed cost study would reveal many profitable garden shops and hardware stores whose profits are concealed by the poor performance of other stores in these categories.

To evaluate these alternatives, each would have to be spelled out in greater detail. In general, marketing cost analysis provides information on the relative profitability of different channels, products, territories, or other marketing entities. It does not imply that the best course of action is to drop the unprofitable marketing entities, nor does it actually measure the likely profit improvement if these marginal marketing entities are dropped.

Direct versus full costing

Like all information tools, marketing cost analysis is capable of leading or misleading the marketing executive, depending upon the degree to which he understands its processes and limitations. The example showed some arbitrariness in the choice of bases for allocating the functional expenses to the marketing entities being evaluated. Thus the "number of sales calls" was used to allocate selling expenses, when in principle "number of sales man-hours" would have been a more accurate indicator of cost. The former base was used because it generally involves less record keeping and computation. Such approximations may not involve the loss of too much accuracy, but the marketing executive should be cognizant of this judgmental element in determining distribution costs.[7]

Far more serious may be another judgmental element affecting the computation of marketing costs. This is the matter of whether to allocate *full costs* or only *direct and traceable costs*. The example sidestepped this problem by assuming only simple costs that seemed to fit in with marketing activities. But it cannot be avoided in an actual analysis of marketing costs. Three classes of costs have to be distinguished:

Direct costs. These are costs that can be assigned directly to the marketing entities that give rise to them. For example, sales commissions are a direct cost in a cost analysis of sales territories, salesmen, or customers. Advertising expenditures are a direct cost in a cost analysis of products to the extent that each advertisement promotes only one company product. Other costs that are direct for some purposes are salesmen salaries, supplies, and traveling expenses.

Traceable common costs. These are costs that can be assigned only indirectly, but on a plausible basis, to the marketing entities. In the example, rent was analyzed in this way. The company's floor space reflected the need to carry on three different marketing activities, and it was possible to estimate how much floor space supported each activity.

Nontraceable common costs. These are costs whose allocation to the marketing entities is necessarily arbitrary. Consider "corporate image" expenditures. It would be arbitrary to allocate them equally among all products, since all products do not benefit equally from corporate image making. It would be arbitrary to

---

[7]For common bases of allocation, see Charles H. Sevin, *Marketing Productivity Analysis* (New York: McGraw-Hill Book Company, 1965).

allocate them proportionately to the sales of the various products, since relative product sales reflect many factors besides corporate image making. Other typical examples of common costs that are difficult to assign are management salaries, taxes, interest, and other types of overhead.

There is no controversy concerning the inclusion of direct costs in the marketing cost analysis. There is a small amount of controversy concerning the inclusion of traceable common costs. Traceable common costs lump together costs that would change with the scale of the marketing activity and costs that probably would not change in the near future. If the lawn-mower manufacturer drops garden supply shops, he is likely to continue to pay the same rent, for contractual reasons or through inertia. In this event his profits would not rise immediately by the amount of the present loss in selling to garden supply shops ($310). The profit figures are more meaningful when fixed traceable costs can be liquidated.

The major controversy concerns whether the nontraceable common costs should be allocated to the marketing entities. This is called the *full-cost approach*, and its advocates defend it on the grounds that all costs ultimately must be imputed in order to determine true profitability. But this argument tends to confuse the use of accounting for financial reporting with the use of accounting to provide a quantitative basis for decision making and profit planning. Full costing has three major weaknesses:

> The relative profitability of different marketing entities can shift quite radically when one highly arbitrary way to allocate nontraceable common costs is replaced by another. This tends to weaken confidence in the tool.
>
> The arbitrariness leads to argument and demoralization, especially by those who feel that their performance or interest is being judged adversely as a result.
>
> The inclusion of nontraceable common costs may weaken efforts at real cost control. Operating management is most effective in controlling direct costs and traceable common costs. Arbitrary assignments of nontraceable common costs may lead them to spend their time fighting the arbitrary allocations or may altogether discourage them in meeting their cost responsibility.

THE MARKETING CONTROLLER CONCEPT

Some companies are beginning to think about the possible advantages of creating the position of marketing controller, with an occupant who understands marketing thinking and yet can bring sharp financial analysis to bear on the profitability of contemplated and past marketing actions. A survey by Goodman showed that

> large sophisticated companies, such as General Foods, Du Pont, Johnson & Johnson, Trans World Airlines, and American Cyanamid, have all instituted financial control positions which directly oversee advertising and, in some selected cases, merchandising policies. The major functions of these individuals are to verify advertising bills, ensure the optimization of agency rates, negotiate agency contracts, and perform an audit function regarding the client's agency and certain of the suppliers.[8]

---

[8]Sam R. Goodman, *Techniques of Profitability Analysis* (New York: John Wiley & Sons, Inc., 1970), p. 2. Chapter 1 is devoted to the marketing controller concept.

Goodman feels that this is a step in the right direction and advocates even a fuller role for the marketing controller. Based on his discussions of the idea with various marketing executives, he sees a lineup of the following primary duties for the marketing controller:

> Maintain record of adherence to profit plans.
> Maintain close control of media expense.
> Prepare brand manager's budgets.
> Advise on optimum timing for strategies.
> Measure the efficiency of promotions.
> Analyze media production costs.
> Evaluate customer and geographic profitability.
> Present sales-oriented financial reports.
> Assist direct accounts in optimizing purchasing and inventory policies.
> Educate the marketing area to financial implications of decisions.[9]

The Nestlé Company took a step in this direction in 1965 when a specific segment of the controller operation was made available for marketing planning and control. Marketing service analysts were assigned to each of Nestlé's six marketing divisions to work for the marketing head. They carried out diverse assignments designed to improve marketing efficiency and performance. Their reports proved helpful, and the position has served as a valuable training ground for future general managers because of their exposure to marketing, production, and finance.

The marketing controller concept is an intriguing one, particularly in organizations where marketing is still practiced with a primary eye toward sales rather than profits. As future marketing managers come on the scene with a greater training in financial concepts, they can be expected to do more of this work themselves, with the possible assistance of marketing-staff financial specialists to help in data gathering and analysis.

SUMMARY

Marketing control is the natural sequel to marketing planning. Organizations need to exercise at least three types of marketing control. Strategic control is attempted through a tool known as the marketing audit, which is a periodic, comprehensive, systematic, and independent examination of the organization's marketing environment, internal marketing system, and specific marketing activities. The purpose of the marketing audit is to determine marketing problem areas and recommend a corrective action plan to improve the organization's overall marketing effectiveness.

Annual plan control is the task of monitoring the current marketing effort and results to be sure that the annual sales and profit goals will be achieved. The main tools are sales analysis, market-share analysis, expense-to-sales ratios, other ratios, and attitude tracking.

Profitability control is the task of determining the actual profitability of different marketing entities, such as the firm's products, territories, market segments, and trade channels. The main tool is marketing cost analysis.

---

[9]*Ibid.*, pp. 17–18.

1 Do you foresee a professional marketing auditing association which licenses practitioners, on the model of professional certified public accountants? Why or why not? Do you think it is a good idea?

2 What are the main problems an outside marketing auditor is likely to encounter on a first-time assignment in a company?

3 What are the alternative groups that might perform a company marketing audit?

4 A sales manager examined his company's sales by region and noted that the East Coast sales were about 2 percent below the quota. To probe this further, the sales manager examined district sales figures. He discovered that the Boston sales district within the East Coast region was responsible for most of the underachievement. He then examined the individual sales of the four salesmen in the Boston district. This examination revealed that the top salesman, Roberts, had filled only 69 percent of his quota for the period. Is it safe to conclude that Roberts is loafing or having personal problems?

5 Suppose a company's market share falls for a couple of periods. The marketing vice-president, however, refuses to take any action, calling it a "random walk." What does he mean? Is he justified?

6 Company XYZ produces five products, and its salesmen represent the full product line on each sales call. In order to determine the profit contribution of each product, salesmen costs (salary, commission, and expenses) have to be allocated among the five products. How should this be done?

7 A large manufacturer of industrial equipment has a salesman assigned to each major industrial city. Regional sales managers supervise the salesmen in several cities. The chief marketing officer wants to evaluate the profit contribution of the different cities. How might each of the following costs be allocated to the cities? (a) billing; (b) district sales manager's expenses; (c) national magazine advertising; (d) marketing research.

8 A company conducts a marketing cost study to determine the minimum size order for breaking even. After finding this size, should the company refuse to accept orders below this size? What issues and alternatives should be considered?

9 *Wholesale bakers* face increased competition from chain bakers. They are especially at a disadvantage in the physical distribution of bread. The wholesale bakers must make more stops than the chain bakers and deliver a smaller average volume. Furthermore, the driver typically loads the store's shelf while the chain bakery leaves the bread at the chain's unloading platform to be placed on the shelf by store personnel. Can you recommend some ways in which wholesale bakers can reduce their distribution costs?

10 The idea of treating the marketing department as a profit center raises several difficult problems. Name them and suggest possible solutions.

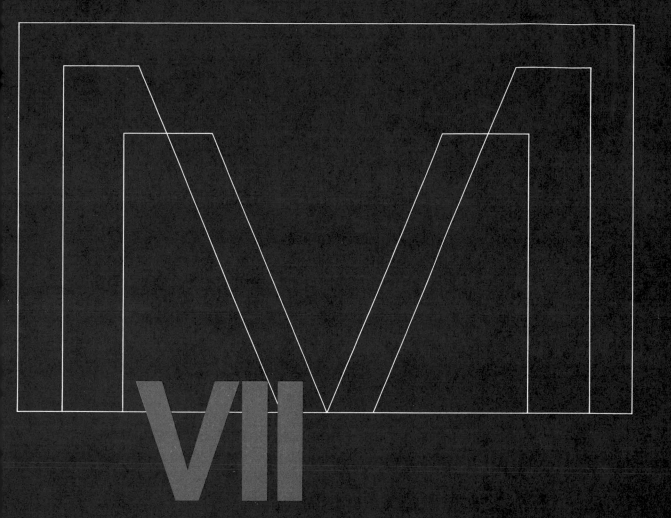

VII

BROADENING MARKETING

21
INTERNATIONAL MARKETING

A traveller without knowledge is a bird without wings.

SA'DI, GULISTAN (1258)

Most company executives—at least in the United States—still think of their market as consumers and business firms located in the United States. American exports, after all, account for only 6 percent of the U.S. gross national product. The American home market has been so large that American thinking has traditionally been directed inward.

A Belgian business executive, on the other hand, when he thinks of selling his goods thinks largely of foreign markets. Thirty-six percent of the Belgian national output is sold abroad. In other economies, such as the Netherlands, Denmark, Sweden, and Venezuela, marketing also largely means international marketing.

Ordinarily, most firms would prefer home marketing to foreign marketing. Home marketing is generally simpler and safer. The businessmen do not have to learn another language, deal with a different currency, face political and legal uncertainties, adapt the product to a different set of needs and expectations, and so on. There are, in fact, only two factors that might draw a businessman into international marketing. First, he might be *pushed* into it by the general lack of opportunity in the home market. The gross national product of his country may be low or growing very slowly, or his own government may be antibusiness or tax him heavily. Second, he might be *pulled* into it by great and inviting opportunities for his product in other countries. Without necessarily

467

abandoning his home market, he may find other markets an attractive place to make a profit even after discounting the extra encumbrances and irritations he might face in operating abroad.

One may ask whether international marketing involves any new principles that have not been examined as part of effective marketing management in general. After all, a foreign market consists of consumers, producers, resellers, and governments buying products and services. These buyers have to be researched, and products, prices, promotion, and distribution adapted to their needs. International marketing would seem to pose no new problems not faced by the seller who is trying to market successfully in different regions *within* his country. Our justification for a separate treatment lies not in propounding any new principles. The steps, concepts, and techniques for effective marketing management are the same. The justification lies in the fact that differences between nations are typically more striking than regional differences within one country. The international marketer must master special environmental factors and institutions and be prepared to drop some of his most basic assumptions about market operations and even "human nature." The discussion that follows is designed to sensitize him to the special factors and problems faced in taking his product abroad.

THE INTERNATIONAL MARKETING ENVIRONMENT

The hundred-odd nations of the world differ greatly in the kinds of goods and services they are ready to use. It would be as much a mistake for an American manufacturer of electric rotisseries to seek a market in Nigeria as for Nigerians to seek a market for loincloths here. On the other hand, American bicycles fetch a premium in Nigeria, and Nigerian palm oil is imported in large quantities into the United States. A nation's readiness for different products and services, and its general attractiveness as a market to foreign firms, depends on its economic, political-legal, cultural, and business environment.

Economic environment The nations of the world exhibit great variation in *industrial structure* and *national income,* both of which critically influence the goods and services they are likely to need and their ability to buy.

Economies classified according to industrial structure It is useful to distinguish among four types of industrial structure that a nation can have:

1 *Subsistence economies.* In a subsistence economy the vast majority of people are engaged in simple agriculture. They consume most of their output and barter the rest for simple goods and services. For obvious reasons, they offer few opportunities for exporters.

2 *Raw-material exporting economies.* These economies are rich in one or more natural resources but poor in other respects. Much of their revenue comes from exporting these resources. Examples are Chile (tin and copper), Congo (rubber), and Saudi Arabia (oil). These countries are good markets for extractive equipment, tools and supplies, materials-handling equipment, and trucks. Depending on the number of foreign businessmen and wealthy native rulers and landholders, they are also a market for Western-style commodities and luxury goods.

3 *Industrializing economies.* In an industrializing economy, manufacturing is beginning to play a role of some importance, probably accounting for somewhere between 10 and 20 percent of the country's gross national product. Examples include Egypt, the Philippines, India, and Brazil. As manufacturing increases, the country relies more on imports of textile raw materials, steel, and heavy machinery, and less on imports of finished textiles, paper products, and automobiles. The industrialization tends to create a new rich class and a small but growing middle class, both demanding new types of goods, some of which can be satisfied only by imports.

4 *Industrial economies.* Industrial economies have built up their industrial base to the extent that they become exporters of manufactured goods and investment funds. They trade manufactured goods among themselves and also export them to other types of economies in exchange for raw materials and semifinished goods. The large and varied manufacturing activities of these industrial nations and their sizable middle class make them rich markets for all sorts of goods.

Economies classified according to national incomes   The products and services consumed by a nation are also affected by its level and distribution of national income. These goods can be distinguished for five different national income profiles:

1 *Very low family incomes.* Subsistence economies tend to be characterized by very low family incomes. The families spend long hours at hard work eking out a bare living from the soil. Homegrown food and homemade clothing and simple services constitute the bulk of consumer goods and services.

2 *Mostly low family incomes.* Economies that are seeking industrialization along Marxist lines are characterized by low family incomes to allow as much as possible for capital formation. Most consumer goods are produced domestically by state-owned enterprises. These nations present some opportunities for trade.

3 *Very low, very high family incomes.* Several countries of the world are characterized by extremes of income, where most of the population is very poor and a small minority is very rich. This makes the market for consumer goods very bizarre. The masses live on subsistence farming, supplemented by the import of needed foodstuffs and textiles, and the rich live on the import of expensive cars, appliances, and Western amenities.

4 *Low, medium, high family incomes.* Industrialization tends to be accompanied by the rise of a middle class. The very low and very high income classes tend to persist along with their distinct consumption patterns. The middle class is able to afford basic necessities and have something left over to purchase amenities.

5 *Mostly medium family incomes.* The advanced industrial nations tend to develop institutions that reduce the extremes of income. The result is a large and comfortable middle class confronted with a wide array of branded products, able to own automobiles and major appliances, as well as to enjoy leisure and take vacations.

Political-legal environment

Nations differ greatly in the favorableness of their political-legal environment for imports and foreign investment. At least four factors should be considered by the prospective marketer who is evaluating whether to do business in another country.

1 *Attitudes toward international buying.* Some nations are very receptive, indeed encouraging, to foreign firms, and others are very hostile. As an example of the former, Mexico for a number of years has been attracting foreign investment by

offering investment incentives, site-location services, and a stable currency. On the other hand, India has required the exporter to deal with import quotas, blocked currencies, stipulations that a high percentage of the management team be nationals, and so on.

2 *Political stability.* One must consider not only the host country's present political climate but also its future stability. Governments change hands, sometimes quite violently. Even without a change in government, a regime may decide to respond to new popular feelings. At worst, the foreign company's property may be expropriated; or its currency holdings may be blocked; or import quotas or new duties may be imposed. Where political instability is high, the international marketer may still find it profitable to do business with the host country, but the situation will affect his mode of entry. He will favor export marketing to direct foreign investment. He will keep his foreign stocks low. He will convert his currency rapidly. As a result, the people in the host country end up paying higher prices, have fewer jobs, and get less satisfactory products.

3 *Monetary regulations.* The marketer wants to realize profits in a currency of value to him. In the best situation, the foreign buyer can pay him either in the seller's currency or in hard world currencies. Short of this, the marketer might accept a blocked currency if he can buy other goods in that country that he needs in his operation or that he can sell elsewhere for a currency he needs. In the worst case he has to take his money out of the host country in the form of relatively unmarketable products that he can sell elsewhere only at a loss. Besides currency restrictions, a fluctuating exchange rate also leads to unusual risks for the exporter.

4 *Government bureaucracy.* A fourth factor is the extent to which the host government runs an efficient system for assisting foreign businessmen: efficient customs-handling procedures, market information, and other factors conducive to doing business. Perhaps the most common shock to American businessmen is the extent to which various impediments appear to stand in their way, all of which disappear if a suitable payment (bribe) is made to some official(s).

Cultural environment

Perhaps the most difficult aspect of international marketing is to grasp the host country's cultural nuances. Businessmen abroad have different buying and selling styles:

> South Americans are accustomed to talking business in close physical proximity with other persons, in fact almost nose to nose. The American businessman retreats, but the South American pursues. And both end up being offended.

> In face-to-face communication Japanese businessmen rarely say "No" to an American businessman. The American is frustrated, he doesn't know where he stands. Also, Americans tend to come to their point quickly and directly in business dealings. Japanese businessmen tend to find this offensive.

> In France, wholesalers just don't care to promote a product. They simply ask the retailer what he wants today, and they deliver it. If any American company builds its strategy around the French wholesaler, it is almost bound to fail.

Consumers also offer many surprises:

> The average Frenchman uses almost twice as many cosmetics and beauty aids as does his wife.

> The Germans and the French eat more spaghetti than the Italians.

French and Italian housewives are not as interested in cooking as their counterparts in Luxembourg and Belgium.[1]

Each country (and even regional groups within each country) has cultural traditions, preferences, and taboos that must be carefully studied by the marketer.

THE INTERNATIONAL MARKETING DECISION

In considering international marketing a company faces five major types of decisions. (1) The *international marketing decision* determines whether the foreign opportunities and the firm's resources are attractive enough to justify a general interest in marketing abroad. (2) The *market-selection decision* determines *which* foreign markets to enter. (3) The *entry and operating decision* determines the best way to enter and operate in an attractive foreign market. (4) The *marketing-mix decision* develops an appropriate product, price, distribution, and promotion program for that market. (5) The *marketing-organization decision* determines the best way for the firm to achieve and maintain control over its international business operations.

As for the international marketing decision, firms get involved in international marketing in two ways. In some cases the firm is approached by someone—a domestic exporter, a foreign importer, a foreign government. Or the firm may start to think on its own about overseas marketing. Perhaps it faces overcapacity; or perhaps it forecasts better opportunities abroad than at home.

It must then determine two basic questions. The first is whether overseas *opportunities* are sufficiently attractive to justify further investigation. The second is whether the company has, or can obtain, the resources and capabilities to market abroad. Assuming these two conditions are satisfied, the firm has to define its *international marketing objectives and policies.* Will foreign marketing be a minor or major part of its business? Will the firm seek to market in a few countries or many countries? Will it simply sell its present products abroad or will it try to create new and appropriate products needed by these other countries? Will it prefer medium-return, medium-risk situations or high-return, high-risk situations?

MARKET-SELECTION DECISION

The company should have some orderly procedure for ranking the various markets it might enter. Consider how this was done by Computer Machinery Corporation, a small American company that decided in the late sixties to go abroad—first, because of fierce competition at home, and second, to get a foothold before its competitors did:

> CMC's market research in the computer field revealed that England, France, West Germany, and Italy offer us significant markets. England, France, and Germany are about equal-size markets, while Italy represents about two thirds

---

[1]Robert L. Brown, "The Common Market: What Its New Consumer Is Like," *Printer's Ink,* May 31, 1963, pp. 23–25.

the potential of any one of those countries. . . . Taking everything into consideration, we decided to set up first in England because its market for our products is as large as any and its language and laws are similar to ours. England is different enough to get your feet wet, yet similar enough to the familiar U.S. business environment so that you do not get in over your head.[2]

The market choice seems relatively simple and straightforward. Yet one can question whether the reason given for selecting England—the compatibility of its language and culture—should have been given this prominence. We propose that market selection should utilize a rate of return on investment framework. Five steps are involved:[3]

1 *Estimate of current market potential.* The first step is to estimate current market potential in each candidate market. This *marketing research task* calls for using existing published data supplemented by primary data collection through company surveys and studies of various kinds. The rub is that foreign marketing research is more difficult, as a general rule, than domestic market research, for at least four reasons. (1) Published census and market data are usually scarce and somewhat unreliable in several countries, especially the poorer ones. (2) Many trade associations do not make their data public. (3) Marketing research firms are not always of high quality. (4) Buyers in other countries are less used to cooperating in interviews. Yet there are some signs of improvement. The U.S. Department of Commerce and several large banks are increasing the amount of information available about foreign markets. The United Nations publishes statistical data and market information. Foreign governments, banks, chambers of commerce, and private companies are increasingly responding to the problem of better market information.

2 *Forecast of future market potential.* The firm also needs a forecast of future market potential. This is complicated because the market analyst is usually insufficiently versed in the economic, political, cultural, and business currents of another country. Many foreign countries do not show the stability of government, currency, or law that his own country may show.

3 *Forecast of market share.* The normal difficulties of forecasting market shares are compounded in a foreign marketing environment. The foreign marketer will find himself competing against other foreign marketers as well as against home-country firms. He has to estimate how the buyers will feel about the relative merits of his product, selling methods, and company. Even if the buyers are impartial, their government may put up barriers in the form of quotas, tariffs, taxes, specifications, or even outright boycotts.

4 *Forecast of costs and profits.* Costs will depend on the marketer's contemplated entry strategy. If he resorts to exporting or licensing, his costs will be spelled out in the contracts. If he decides to locate manufacturing facilities abroad, his cost estimation will require an understanding of local labor conditions, taxes, trade practices, and stipulations regarding the hiring of nationals as key employees. After estimating future costs, he subtracts them from estimated company sales to find company profits for each year of the planning horizon.

5 *Estimate of rate of return on investment.* The forecasted income stream must be related to the investment stream to derive an implicit rate of return. The estimated rate

---

[2]James K. Sweeney, "A Small Company Enters the European Market," *Harvard Business Review,* September–October 1970, pp. 127–28.

[3]See David S. R. Leighton, "Deciding When to Enter International Markets," in *Handbook of Modern Marketing,* ed. Victor P. Buell (New York: McGraw-Hill Book Company, 1970), Section 20, pp. 23–28.

of return should be high enough to cover (1) the company's normal target return on its investment and (2) the risk and uncertainty of marketing in that country. The risk premium has to cover not only the chance that the basic estimates of sales and costs may be wrong but also the chance that unanticipated monetary changes (devaluation, blocked currency) and political changes (future discrimination against foreign business firms, or even expropriation) may occur.

ENTRY AND OPERATING DECISION

Once a company decides that a particular foreign market represents an attractive opportunity, its task is to determine the best mode of entering that market. Here it has three major options: exporting (home production and selling abroad), joint venturing (joining with foreign companies in some way), or direct investment abroad.[4]

Export

The simplest way for a manufacturer to get involved in a foreign market is to arrange to sell some of his present output abroad. His manufacturing facilities remain located in his own country. He may or may not modify his product for the foreign market. Exporting allows him to enter foreign markets with a minimum of change in his product line, company organization, investment, or company mission.

Indirect export The seller can enter the exporting field in two broad ways. He can hire independent international marketing middlemen (the indirect method), or he can assume direct responsibility for selling to the foreign buyers or importers (the direct method).

The indirect method is the more popular for the firm that is just beginning its international exporting activity. First, it involves less investment. The firm does not have to develop an overseas sales force or set of contacts. Second, it involves less risk. International marketing middlemen presumably bring know-how and services to the relationship, and the seller should make fewer mistakes.

Three types of domestic middlemen arrangements are available to the exporter. He may engage a *domestic-based export merchant.* This middleman buys the manufacturer's product and sells it abroad on his own account. The manufacturer is relieved of all aspects of the international marketing task because he makes his sales simply to the export merchant. Or he may engage in a *domestic-based export agent.* In this case the manufacturer retains some of the chores and all the risk, because the agent simply agrees to seek overseas buyers for a commission.[5] Finally, he may join a *cooperative organization* that carries on exporting activities on behalf of several producers and is partly under the administrative control of the manufacturers. This form is often used by producers of primary

---

[4]The discussion of entry channels in this section is indebted to the discussion in Gordon E. Miracle and Gerald S. Albaum, *International Marketing Management* (Homewood, Ill.: Richard D. Irwin, Inc., 1970), Chaps. 14–16.

[5]Within the agent class, there are several variants: *export buying agents* reside in the manufacturer's country, represent foreign buyers, place orders with the manufacturer, take care of shipments, and make payment; *brokers* exist to find buyers, are paid a commission, and do not handle the products; *manufacturers' export agents* represent several exporters whose interests are noncompeting and carry out selling and other services.

products—fruits, nuts, and so on—for overseas selling. Another form consists in piggyback arrangements between two or more domestic manufacturers trying to develop a complementary overseas product line.

Direct export Sellers who are approached by foreign buyers will most likely undertake direct export instead of paying service charges to middlemen. So will larger sellers or those whose market has grown to sufficient size to justify undertaking their own export activity. The investment and risk are somewhat greater, but so is the potential return.

Here, too, there are several ways in which the company can carry on direct exporting activity. It may set up a *domestic-based export department* or division consisting of an export sales manager with some clerical assistants. This department does the actual selling and draws on the regular company departments for marketing assistance in advertising, credit, logistics, and so on. Or it may graduate to a self-contained export department or sales subsidiary carrying out all the activities involved in export, and possibly having distinct profit responsibility. The company might set up an *overseas sales branch (or subsidiary)* in addition to, or instead of, a domestic export department. An overseas sales branch allows the manufacturer to achieve greater presence and supervision in the foreign market. The sales branch handles sales distribution, and it may handle warehousing and promotion as well. It often serves as a display center and customer service center. Still another alternative is the use of *traveling export salesmen.* The company can decide to have one or more home-based salesmen travel abroad at certain times to take orders or find business. Or direct exporting may involve contracting with *foreign-based distributors or agents* to sell the company's goods. Distributors would buy his goods; agents would sell in his behalf. In either case they may be given exclusive rights to represent the manufacturer: that is, they act as the sole importer. Or they may be given general rights.

Joint venturing

A second broad method of entering a foreign market is to join with nationals in the foreign country to set up production and marketing facilities. Joint venturing differs from exporting in that a partnership is formed that leads to some production facilities abroad, and it differs from direct investment in that an association is formed with someone in that country. Four types of joint venture can be distinguished.

Licensing Licensing represents a comparatively simple way for a manufacturer to become involved in international marketing. The licensor enters an agreement with a licensee in the foreign market, offering him the right to use a manufacturing process, trademark, patent, trade secret, or other item of value for a fee or royalty. The licensor gains entry into the market at little risk; the licensee gains production expertise, or a well-known product or name, without having to start from scratch. Gerber entered its baby foods in the Japanese market through a licensing arrangement. It did not have the staff to develop and operate its own production facility, nor did it want to risk the capital loss if the Japanese were not receptive to its products. Coca-Cola has carried out its international marketing activities by licensing bottlers around the world—or, more technically, *franchising* bottlers, because it supplies the syrup needed to produce the product.

Licensing has potential disadvantages in that the firm has less control over the licensee than if it had set up its own production facilities. Furthermore, if the licensee is very successful, the firm has forgone these profits, and if and when the contract ends, it may find it has set up a competitor. To avoid these dangers the licensor must establish a mutual advantage in working together, and a key to doing this is to remain innovative so that the licensee continues to depend upon him.

Contract manufacturing Instead of licensing a foreign company to manufacture and market its products, the firm may wish to retain the marketing responsibility. But it may not be ready to invest in its own foreign production facilities. Under these conditions, an excellent option is to contract with local manufacturers to produce the product. Sears has used this method in opening up department stores abroad, as in Mexico and Spain. Sears enters into contracts with qualified local manufacturers to produce many of the products it sells. Procter & Gamble resorted to contract manufacturing of soap in entering the Italian market, where it faced Colgate and Unilever, who were both longer entrenched and owned their production facilities. This allowed it to move in fast and get the feel of the market.

Contract manufacturing has the drawback of less control over the manufacturing process and the loss of potential profits on manufacturing. On the other hand, it offers the manufacturer a chance to get started faster, with less risk, and with the opportunity to possibly form a partnership or buy out the local manufacturer if his facility operates efficiently.

Management contracting Here the domestic firm agrees to supply the management know-how to a foreign company that is willing to supply the capital. Thus, the domestic firm is really exporting management services rather than its own products. This arrangement is used by the Hilton hotel system in undertaking to manage hotels throughout the world.

Management contracting is a low-risk method of getting into a foreign market, and it starts yielding income right from the beginning. The arrangement is especially attractive if the contracting firm is given an option to purchase some share in the managed company within a stated period. On the other hand, the arrangement is not sensible if the company can put its scarce management talent to better uses or if there are greater profits to be made by undertaking the whole venture. Management contracting prevents the company from setting up its own operations for a period of time.

Joint-ownership ventures An increasingly popular arrangement is for foreign investors to join with local investors to create a local business in which they share joint ownership and control. The foreign investor may buy an interest in a local company, a local company may buy an interest in an existing operation of a foreign company, or the two parties may form a new business venture.

From the point of view of the foreign investor, a joint venture may be necessary or desirable for economic or political reasons. Economically, the firm may find it lacks the financial, physical, or managerial resources to undertake the venture alone. Or the foreign government may require joint ownership with local companies as a condition for entry.

Joint ownership can have certain drawbacks for the foreign firm. The partners may disagree over investment, marketing, or other policies. Whereas many American firms like to reinvest earnings for growth, local firms often like to pay out these earnings. Whereas American firms tend to accord a large role to marketing, local investors may see marketing as simply selling. If the American firm has only a minority interest, then its views are overruled in these disagreements. Furthermore, joint venturing can hamper the plans of a multinational company seeking to carry out specific manufacturing and marketing policies on a worldwide basis. The agreement may also make it difficult for the foreign firm to enter other markets where its partner already operates.

Direct investment

The ultimate form of involvement in a foreign market is investment in foreign-based assembly or manufacturing facilities. Companies just starting out in the market would be well advised to avoid this scale of participation at the outset. However, as experience is gained through export channels, and if the foreign market appears large enough, foreign production facilities offer distinct advantages. The company may secure these advantages partially through licensing or joint-ownership ventures, but if it wants full control (and profits), it may give serious consideration to direct investment.

The advantages of direct investment are several. First, the firm may secure real cost economies in the form of cheaper labor or raw materials, foreign government investment incentives, freight savings, and so on. Second, the firm will gain a better image in the host country because it demonstrates its concern with that country's future. Third, the firm develops a deeper relationship with government, customers, local suppliers, and distributors, enabling it to make a better adaptation of its products to the local marketing environment. Fourth, the firm retains full control over the investment and therefore can develop manufacturing and marketing policies that serve its long-term international objectives.

The main disadvantage is that the firm has exposed a large investment to certain risks, such as blocked or devalued currencies, worsening markets, or expropriation. In some cases, however, the firm has no choice but to accept these risks if it wants to operate effectively in the host country.

Multinational marketing

We have been examining the nature, advantages, and disadvantages of different modes of entry into a particular foreign market that appears attractive. If the company eventually gets involved in several foreign markets, it will want to begin thinking about its entire system for operating abroad rather than making ad hoc adaptations in each individual market. In fact, it may stop thinking of itself as a national marketer who ventures abroad and instead as a *global marketer* who operates in many countries, including the "home" country. At this point the company begins to think about developing a worldwide network of production facilities and serving a plurality of markets through a global marketing strategy. Such companies are called multinational corporations. According to Baker:

> The multinational corporation is defined as a company which has a direct investment base in several countries, which generally derives from 20–50 percent or more of its net profits from foreign operations, and whose management makes

policy decisions based on the alternatives available anywhere in the world. Approximately 300 such companies are operating and most of these are American.[6]

Multinational corporations include such giants as Unilever, Philips Electric, the Beecham Group, Nestlé, Olivetti, IBM, and Massey-Ferguson. Such corporations must decide very carefully how uniform their marketing strategy should be. For example, Nestlé strives for uniform quality, branding, labeling, and packaging of its chocolate products; however, its advertising policy is largely decentralized. Beecham, on the other hand, tries to make its advertising policy uniform: if a campaign or idea works well in one country, it will be used elsewhere.

MARKETING-MIX DECISION

Companies that operate in one or more foreign markets must decide how much, if at all, to adapt their product and marketing mix to local conditions.

Product and promotion

Keegan has distinguished five possible strategies involving the adaptation of product and marketing communications to a foreign market (Figure 21-1).[7]

The first strategy, *straight extension,* means introducing the product in the foreign market in the same form and with the same communications that the company uses at home. It has been used successfully by Pepsi-Cola to introduce its soft drinks everywhere in the world, but it has failed for some other producers such as Philip Morris in the Canadian market and Campbell's tomato soup in the British market. The strategy is a tempting one because it involves no additional expense of research and development, manufacturing retooling or setup, inventory control or marketing communication reprogramming.

[6]James C. Baker, "Multinational Marketing: A Comparative Case Study," in *Marketing in a Changing World,* ed. Bernard A. Morin (Chicago: American Marketing Association, 1969), p. 61.

[7]This section relies heavily on Warren J. Keegan, "Multinational Product Planning: Strategic Alternatives," *Journal of Marketing,* January 1969, pp. 58–62.

Figure 21-1
Five multinational product marketing strategies

		PRODUCT		
		Don't change product	Adapt product	Develop new product
COMMUNICATIONS	Don't change communications	1. Straight extension	3. Product adaptation	5. Product invention
	Adapt communications	2. Communication adaptation	4. Dual adaptation	

In the second strategy, *communication adaptation*, the company introduces its unchanged product but modifies its communications. For example, American bikes are advertised abroad for their transportation rather than pleasure qualities, since bikes are a basic mode of transportation in many other countries. Logic rather than fancy is used in advertising copy in Scandinavia; big colored illustrations and terse copy in Spain; sex appeal is avoided in Pakistan; and a hundred other communication adaptations are made. The appeal of a communication-adaptation strategy is its relatively low cost of implementation.

The third strategy, *product adaptation*, involves altering the product to meet local conditions or preferences without altering the marketing communications. Thus, Exxon changed the formulation of its gasoline in different countries but still advertised "Put a Tiger in Your Tank." Many manufacturers vary the size or contents of their foods, fertilizers, clothing, or appliances to meet local conditions. This strategy involves extra engineering and production cost but may be better than introducing an unaltered product possessing less appeal.

The fourth strategy, *dual adaptation*, involves altering both the product and the communications to increase the product's acceptability. For example, the National Cash Register company took an innovative step backward by developing and advertising a crank-operated cash register that could sell at half the cost of a modern cash register. This unit caught on greatly in the Philippines, the Orient, Latin America, and Spain. Dual adaptation is an expensive strategy but is worthwhile if the target markets are large enough.

The last strategy, *product invention*, involves creating a new product to meet a need in another country. For example, there is an enormous need in less-developed countries for low-cost high-protein foods. Companies such as Pillsbury, Swift, and Monsanto are researching the food needs of these countries, formulating new foods, and developing mass-communication programs to gain product trial and acceptance. Product invention would appear to be the costliest of all strategies, but the payoffs to the successful firm also appear to be the greatest.

Distribution channels

The international marketer must take a *whole-channel* view of the problem of getting his products to the final users or consumers. He must see the channel of distribution as an integrated whole, from the manufacturer on one end to the final user or buyer on the other end.[8] Figure 21-2 shows the three major links between the seller and ultimate buyer. The first link, *seller's headquarters organization*, supervises the channels and is part of the channel itself. The second link, *channels between nations*, does the job of getting the products to the overseas markets. The third link, *channels within nations*, is extremely pertinent. Too many American manufacturers think of their channels as ending with the channels between nations, and they fail to observe what happens to their product once it

---

[8]See Miracle and Albaum, *op. cit.*, pp. 317–19.

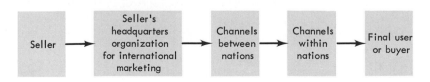

Figure 21-2
Whole-channel concept for international marketing

arrives in the foreign market. If the channels within the foreign market are weak or inefficient, then the target customers fail to achieve satisfaction and the company fails to achieve its international objectives.

With respect to consumer goods, within-country channels of distribution vary considerably from country to country. There are striking differences in the *size distribution of retailing units.* For example, food channels in the United States are dominated by the large supermarket chain; in France, supermarkets are progressing but food retailing is still dominated by small merchants with modest stores; in India, food is sold mainly through thousands of individual tradesmen squatting in open markets or selling in tiny shops. Second, the *services offered* by retailers vary considerably, with much more personal attention and bargaining in countries such as India as compared with the United States. Third, there tends to be greater specialization in the *assortment of goods* handled by retailers in the lower-income economies. Fourth, the retailing system in other countries tends to be more *stratified* according to class structure; thus selecting the retailer is tantamount to selecting the social class the product will reach.[9]

With respect to industrial goods, within-country channels in advanced countries resemble those found in the United States. In the less-developed countries, importers are strong and the foreign manufacturer must often leave his products in their hands. If he seeks his own distributors, he must carefully sort out the good ones from the poor ones. Often he has to offer exclusive distribution to a local distributor, and his fate in this market is tied up with how well he makes his choice.

Pricing

Manufacturers often price their products lower for the foreign market than for the domestic market. This may be a response to lower incomes abroad, keener competition, or the use of the foreign market as a dumping ground for surpluses. Although the price quoted to merchants abroad may be lower, these merchants may not lower the retail price. Foreign middlemen often prefer high unit margins, even though this leads to a smaller volume. They also like to buy on credit, although this increases the manufacturer's cost and risk.

INTERNATIONAL MARKETING-ORGANIZATION DECISION

Firms manage their international marketing activities in many different ways. The different organizational arrangements often parallel their degree of involvement and experience in international marketing and their international marketing objectives.

Export department

A firm normally gets started in international marketing by responding to a few orders that come in over its transom. At first it simply ships out the goods. If its international sales expand, the company usually organizes an export department consisting of a sales manager and a few clerical assistants. As sales increase further, the staff of the export department is expanded to include various marketing services so that it can go after business more aggressively and

---

[9]These retailing variations are discussed in John Fayerweather, *International Marketing* (Englewood Cliffs, N.J.: Prentice-Hall, Inc., 1965), p. 63.

not depend on the domestic staff. If the firm moves beyond exports into a program of joint ventures or direct investment, the export department will no longer serve these purposes.

International division

Many companies eventually become involved in a number of different international markets and ventures. A company may export to one country, license to another, have a joint-ownership venture in a third, and own a subsidiary in a fourth, and it may eventually create an international division or subsidiary with responsibility for all of its international activity. The international division is headed by a president (who usually ranks as one of the corporation's divisional vice-presidents). The president has goals and budgets and is given total responsibility for the company's growth in the international market.

International divisions, like domestic divisions, are organized in a variety of ways. Usually the international division's corporate staff consists of functional specialists in marketing, manufacturing, research, finance, planning, and personnel. This staff will plan for, and provide services to, various operating units. The operating units may be organized according to one or more of three principles. First, the operating units may be *geographical organizations.* For example, reporting to the international division president (in addition to the division staff) may be vice-presidents for different areas such as North America, Latin America, Europe, Africa, and the Far East. Each area vice-president is responsible for a sales force, sales branches, distributors, and licensees in his area. Or the operating units may be *product-group organizations,* with a vice-president responsible for worldwide sales of each product group. He may draw on corporate staff area specialists for expertise on different areas. Finally, the operating units may be *international subsidiaries,* each headed by a president. The various subsidiary presidents report to the president of the international division.

A major disadvantage of the international-division concept is that the corporation's top management may think of it as just another division and never really get involved enough to fully appreciate and plan for global marketing. Top management may not give the division the attention it deserves, and in difficult times may deprive it of adequate supplies or budget.

Multinational organization

Several firms have passed beyond the international-division organization into a truly multinational organization. This means the top corporate management and staff are involved in the worldwide planning of manufacturing facilities, marketing policies, financial flows, and logistical systems. The various operating units around the world report directly to the chief executive or executive committee, not to the head of an international division. The company trains its executives in worldwide operations, not just domestic *or* international. Management talent is recruited from many countries; components and supplies are purchased where they can be obtained at the least cost; and investments are made where the anticipated returns are greatest.

SUMMARY

International marketing does not involve any new principles not found in domestic marketing, but nevertheless it deserves special attention because of (1) its growing importance as an area of marketing opportunity and (2) its greater level of risk and uncertainty stemming from the marketer's unfamiliarity with other cultures. Doing business abroad requires learning about quite different economic, political, and cultural environments. The marketer should make a decision in favor of international marketing only when both the opportunities appear attractive relative to those at home and the resources are available for carrying out overseas marketing.

In entering overseas marketing, the first step is to compare the various foreign markets and make market selections on the basis of a hard evaluation of the probable rate of return on investment. Given an attractive market, it can be entered in three ways: export, joint venturing, and direct investment. Many companies start as exporters, move to joint venturing, and finally undertake direct investment as their overseas business expands. A few become multinational corporations with worldwide markets and operating strategies. Companies must also decide on the extent to which their products, communications, distribution, and pricing should be adapted and individuated to individual foreign markets. Finally, they must develop an effective organization for pursuing international marketing. Most firms start with an export department and graduate to an international division. A few pass this stage and move to a multinational organization, which means that worldwide marketing is planned and managed by the top officers of the corporation.

QUESTIONS AND PROBLEMS

1   Develop a list of American products that might have a good reception in Greece. Select one of these and discuss the major problems you anticipate.

2   Pepsi Cola has used the advertising theme "Now It's Pepsi for Those Who Think Young" quite successfully in the United States. Do you think the same theme makes sense in the Netherlands? Liberia? Hong Kong?

3   A U.S. heavy equipment manufacturer operating in Western Europe has been using Americans as salesmen. The company feels that it could reduce its costs by hiring and training nationals for salesmen. What are the advantages and disadvantages of using Americans versus nationals for selling abroad?

4   A large American tire company decided to enter the French tire market some years ago. The company produced tires for medium-size trucks designed to meet the official rear-axle weights. Its subsequent experience was bad, many of its tires blowing out. The company acquired a poor image in France as a result. What went wrong?

5   Select one of the following nations—Italy, Japan, or U.S.S.R.—and describe its marketing institutions and practices.

22
MARKETING IN THE CONTEMPORARY ENVIRONMENT

"Cheshire Puss," she [Alice] began . . . "would you
please tell me which way I ought to go from here?"
"That depends on where you want to get to," said
the cat.

LEWIS CARROLL

Marketing is a constantly evolving craft and discipline. As society changes, so do our ideas of what constitutes effective and socially responsible marketing. Recent years have produced such great changes that it behooves us in this last chapter to examine the major changes and their implications for marketing management in the 1970s and 1980s.

The great body of modern marketing principles received their shaping in the 1950s and early 1960s. This was a period of rapid economic growth throughout the world. Important new inventions—television, computers, xerography, wonder drugs, and so on—provided great frontiers for investment and employment. There was growing affluence to buy the rapidly expanding goods that were being made available. More and more people adopted the expectation of steadily rising incomes and living standards.

Marketing played three major roles during this period. First, it monitored the character of the emerging wants of consumers and translated them into appropriate products. Second, it contributed to the growth of consumption values through massive expenditures in advertising and promotion. Third, it created new forms of mass distribution to ensure that goods and services would be available and affordable to large groups of people.

So rapid was the growth of productive capacity during this period that industries often found themselves with excess inventories and capacity. These industries needed solutions to the problem of underdemand. This problem was turned over to marketing. In time, marketing became coidentified with the problem of *building demand*. In the public mind, marketers spent their time trying to persuade customers to buy their products.

In spite of the "hard-selling" orientation of modern marketing, there was a general feeling that marketing worked in everyone's interests. Firms made profits and offered employment; consumers improved their incomes and standards of living. The marketing concept offered the ultimate justification by arguing that the firms that succeeded best were those that served the consumers' interests best. Thus the principles of modern marketing were felt to be in harmony with the principles of consumer welfare.

Starting in the mid-1960s and continuing to this day, a new set of factors arose to challenge some of the major premises of marketing practice. These factors constitute a new marketing environment and pose challenging questions about the appropriate character of effective and socially responsible marketing in the years ahead. In this chapter we shall consider six of these new factors: consumerism, environmentalism, shortages, inflation, recession, and public sector needs.

CONSUMERISM

In this century American business firms found themselves the target of an organized consumer movement on three different occasions.[1] The first consumer movement took place in the early 1900s and was fueled by such factors as rising prices, Upton Sinclair's exposés of conditions in the meat industry, and ethical drug scandals. The second wave of consumerism took place in the mid-1930s and was fanned by such factors as an upturn in consumer prices in the midst of the depression and another drug scandal. The third movement began in the 1960s as a result of a complex set of developments. Consumers had become better educated; products had become increasingly complex and hazardous; discontent with American institutions was widespread; influential writings by John Kenneth Galbraith, Vance Packard, and Rachel Carson accused big business of wasteful and manipulative practices; presidential messages of Kennedy and Johnson discussed consumer rights; congressional investigations of certain industries proved embarrassing; and finally Ralph Nader appeared on the scene to crystallize many of the issues.

Since these early stirrings, many private consumer organizations have emerged, several pieces of consumer legislation have been passed, and several state and local offices of consumer affairs have been created. Furthermore, the consumer movement has taken on an international character with much strength in Scandinavia and the Low Countries, a growing presence in France, Germany, Austria, and Japan, and signs of new efforts in a number of other countries.

But what is this movement? Put simply, *consumerism is an organized movement of concerned citizens and government to enhance the rights and power of buyers in relation to sellers*. The traditional sellers' rights include:

---

[1]The discussion in this section is adapted from the author's "What Consumerism Means for Marketers," *Harvard Business Review*, May–June 1972, pp. 48–57.

1   The right to introduce any product in any size and style, provided it is not hazardous to personal health or safety; or, if it is, to introduce it with the proper warnings and controls

2   The right to price the product at any level, provided there is no discrimination among similar classes of buyers

3   The right to spend any amount of money to promote the product, provided it is not defined as unfair competition

4   The right to formulate any product message, provided it is not misleading or dishonest in content or execution

5   The right to introduce any buying incentive schemes they wish

The traditional buyers' rights include:

1   The right not to buy a product that is offered for sale
2   The right to expect the product to be safe
3   The right to expect the product to be what is claimed

Comparing these rights, many believe that the balance of power lies on the sellers' side. It is true that the buyer can refuse to buy any product. But it is generally felt that the buyer is really without sufficient information, education, and protection to make wise decisions in the face of highly sophisticated sellers. Consumer advocates therefore call for the following additional consumer rights:

4   The right to be adequately informed about the more important aspects of the product

5   The right to be protected against questionable products and marketing practices

6   The right to influence products and marketing practices in directions that will enhance the "quality of life"

Each of these proposed rights leads to a whole series of specific proposals by consumerists. The right to be informed includes such things as the right to know the true interest cost of a loan (*truth-in-lending*), the true cost per standard unit of competing brands (*unit pricing*), the basic ingredients in a product (*ingredient labeling*), the nutritional quality of foods (*nutritional labeling*), the freshness of products (*open dating*), and the true benefits of a product (*truth-in-advertising*).

The proposals related to additional *consumer protection* include the strengthening of consumers' position in cases of business fraud, the requiring of more safety to be designed into products, and the issuing of greater powers to existing government agencies.

The proposals relating to *quality-of-life* considerations include regulating the ingredients that go into certain products (detergents, gasoline) and packaging (soft-drink containers), reducing the level of advertising and promotional "noise," and creating consumer representation on company boards to introduce consumer welfare considerations in business decision making.

Implications for marketing management

A number of business firms at first balked at the consumer movement. They resented the power of strong consumer leaders to point an accusing finger at their products and send their sales plummeting. This happened when Ralph

Nader called the Corvair automobile unsafe, when Robert Choate accused breakfast cereals of "empty calories," and when Herbert S. Denenberg published a list showing the wide variation in premiums different insurance companies were charging for the same protection. Businessmen also resented consumer proposals that appeared to increase business costs more than helping the consumer. They felt that most consumers would not pay attention to unit pricing or ingredient labeling and that the doctrines of advertising substantiation, corrective advertising, and counter advertising would stifle advertising creativity. They felt that the consumer was better off than ever, that large companies were very careful in developing safe products and promoting them honestly, and that new consumer laws would only lead to new constraints and higher seller costs that would be passed on to the consumer in higher prices. Thus many companies opposed the consumer movement and lobbied vigorously against new legislation.

Many other companies took no stand and simply went about their business. A few companies undertook a series of bold initiatives to show their endorsement of consumer aims. They introduced unit pricing, informative labeling, stronger product warranties, and easier access to top management when there was product dissatisfaction.

In adopting a "we-care" leadership role, these companies increased their market shares and profits substantially. Others were forced to emulate them, without, however, achieving the same impact enjoyed by the leader.

At the present time most companies have come around to accepting the new consumer rights in principle. They might oppose certain pieces of legislation on the ground that such measures are not the best way to solve a particular consumer problem. But they recognize the consumers' right to information and protection. Those who take a leadership role recognize that business consumerism involves more than public relations or a few isolated new products or services that meet neglected consumer needs. Consumerism involves a total commitment by top management, middle-management education and participation, new policy guidelines, marketing research, and company investment. All of these steps should improve customer satisfaction and company sales and profits.

The product manager, who has to propose specific marketing programs, will find his role changing as a result of consumerism. In many ways, his job will be more difficult. He will have to spend more time checking product ingredients and product design for safety, preparing safe packaging and informative labeling, substantiating his advertising claims, reviewing his sales promotion, developing clear and adequate product warranties, and so on. He will have to check many decisions with company lawyers. He will have to develop a sixth sense about what the consumers really want and may feel about the product and various marketing practices.

On the other hand, consumerism is actually, in a profound way, the ultimate expression of the marketing concept. It will compel the product manager to consider things from the consumers' point of view. It will suggest needs and wants that may have been overlooked by all the firms in the industry. The resourceful manager will look for the positive opportunities implicit in the doctrine of consumerism rather than brood over its restraints.

ENVIRONMENTALISM

Whereas consumerists focus on whether the marketing system is efficiently serving consumer needs and wants, environmentalists focus on the impact of modern marketing on the surrounding environment and the costs that are extracted in serving these consumer needs and wants. Throughout most of American history, people and industry have shown a careless, if not exploitative, attitude toward natural resources. The country was blessed with such a wealth of resources that no one worried about running out of them. Early Americans burned and cut down forests, killed wildlife, almost destroyed the buffalo, and extracted minerals from mines hastily and inefficiently.

A few voices were heard to protest, but not until Theodore Roosevelt's term as president did the American conservation movement make much progress. This was the beginning of a national forest and wildlife policy and the creating of several state commissions on conservation. In the 1930s and early 1940s conservation received renewed public attention under President Franklin D. Roosevelt in the form of various work projects to reclaim the soil and harness the waterways.

In 1962 the conservation movement was again revived by the publication of Rachel Carson's *Silent Spring,* with its devastating and documented criticism of pesticidal pollution of the environment. It was no longer a matter of wasted resources but a matter of human survival. In 1969 Paul Ehrlich coined the term "eco-catastrophe" to symbolize the harmful impact of certain American business practices on the environment. And in early 1970 the Meadowses published *The Limits to Growth,* which warned mankind, through the evidence of systems simulation, that the quality of life would eventually decline in the face of unchecked population growth, spreading pollution, and continued exploitation of natural resources.

These concerns underpin the movement known as environmentalism. *Evnironmentalism is an organized movement of concerned citizens and government to protect and enhance man's living environment against those who would run it down.* Environmentalists are concerned with aesthetics as a neglected cost; they see the landscape uglified by strip mining, forest depletion, factory smoke, billboards, and litter. They are concerned with the destruction of recreational opportunity and increase in health problems due to bad air, water, and chemically sprayed food. They are fearful of profound and irreversible ecological disturbances through mankind's callous treatment of its environment.

Environmentalists are not against marketing and consumption; they simply want them to operate on more sensible principles. They do not think the goal of the marketing system should be the maximization of *consumption,* or *consumer choice,* or *consumer satisfaction* as such. The goal of the marketing system should be the maximization of *life quality.* And life quality means not only the quantity and quality of the consumer's goods and services but also the quality of his environment.

Since environmental costs have traditionally been neglected by the marketing system, environmentalists want to see these costs formally introduced into the decision calculus of the producers and consumers. They favor the use of tax mechanisms and regulations to impose the true social costs of antienvironmental business and consumption activity. Requiring business to invest in antipollution devices, taxing nonreturnable bottles, prohibiting detergent soap, and other measures are seen as necessary to lead businessmen and consumers to move in directions that are environmentally sound.

Environmentalists go beyond these simple proposals to question a whole range of marketing practices. They complain that there is too much packaging in the United States, resulting in more forest depletion and chemical activity than necessary. Consumerists, on the other hand, like the convenience offered by modern packaging. Environmentalists feel that the scale of advertising leads people to buy more than they need, which drives the business system to plunder the planet of precious resources. Consumerists, on the other hand, worry more about deception in advertising. Environmentalists dislike the continuous encroachment of the city on the country, creating instant suburbs, shopping areas, and traffic jams. Consumerists welcome the values provided by more stores and more competition.

In contrast to consumerism, environmentalism is, therefore, a radical challenge to current marketing philosophy. It does not accept the sacredness of consumer sovereignty and satisfaction. Environmentalists are ready to question consumer needs and wants and intervene to prevent environmental abuse. Consumption is not, in their minds, the be-all and end-all of human existence.

Implications for marketing management

As a movement, environmentalism has hit industries hard. Steel companies and public utilities have been forced to invest billions of dollars in pollution control equipment and costlier fuels. The auto industry has had to introduce expensive emission-control devices in cars. The soap industry has had to research and develop low-phosphate detergents. The packaging industry has been required to develop ways to reduce litter and increase biodegradability in its products. The gasoline industry has had to formulate new low-lead and no-lead gasolines. Naturally, these industries are inclined to resent environmental regulations, especially when formulated and imposed too rapidly to allow the companies to make the proper adjustments. These companies have had to absorb large costs and pass them on to buyers.

Companies that did not experience direct environmental regulation found themselves paying more for their fuels and materials. Thus environmentalism touches everyone and reflects itself in higher costs. As a result, many business firms have attacked these regulations, using inflation, the energy crisis, and declining profits as their argument for a slower rate of implementation.

At the same time, many companies have taken positive steps to respond to the spirit and implications of environmentalism:

1 Companies have appointed plant-wide committees to review methods of production with an eye toward spotting wasteful procedures and identifying sources of pollution that critics or government agencies may point out.

2 Companies are introducing environmental criteria in their decision making on product ingredients, design, and packaging. They try to design their products in a way that will minimize damage to the environment. Some companies direct their R&D toward finding ecologically superior products as the major selling point of the product.

3 Some companies moved directly into the rapidly expanding market for environmental products, such as pollution control equipment and recycling plants.

4   Marketing managers are improving their information gathering on buyer interest in and attitudes toward environmental issues to help in deciding in which ways to respond.

From the viewpoint of the product manager, his job has been made more difficult as a result of environmentalism. He has to check more carefully into the ecological properties of his product and packaging. He has to raise prices to cover environmental costs, knowing that this will hurt some of the demand.

It does not seem likely that the product manager can return to the golden days of the 1950s and 1960s when no one worried about the effect of product and marketing decisions on the quality of the air, water, and physical terrain. Nor should he. He and his company are arriving at a larger sense of social responsibility which, if practiced earlier, might have averted many current problems. His only consolations are that his competitors face the same environmental responsibilities and that these steps will pave the way for improved life quality.[2]

SHORTAGES

The gloomy predictions of the environmentalists that man would exhaust his natural resources took on an air of frightening reality in 1973 when suddenly the world was plunged into alarming shortages of oil, various minerals, and even food. Business firms found themselves facing marked shortages of oil, chemicals, electricity, natural gas, cement, aluminum, copper, textiles, paper, glass, and furniture. Ironically, as late as 1972 most of these firms were spending the greater part of their time trying to dispose of surpluses. They were searching for markets, studying customer needs, cultivating and servicing customers, and practicing the marketing concept or the sales concept as energetically as they could. Now they were plunged into a new and unexpected overdemand situation that left them perplexed and frantic.

One business columnist saw in shortages the possible end of marketing:

> There is little doubt that the energy crisis will force an alteration in the role of the marketing man. In some industries, it may alter him out of existence. . . . When demand exceeds supply marketing men can be replaced by order-takers. The art of selling is unnecessary. There also is no need for advertising, sales promotion, incentives, sweepstakes, trading stamps, free road maps or even windshield cleaning.[3]

What is the proper marketing response of companies to widening shortages? The two most common responses to periods of shortage are both shortsighted.

---

[2]For further reading on the implications of environmentalism for marketing, see George Fisk, "Criteria for a Theory of Responsible Consumption," *Journal of Marketing,* April 1973, pp. 24–31; and Norman Kangun, "Environmental Problems and Marketing: Saint or Sinner?" in *Marketing Analysis for Societal Problems,* ed. J. N. Sheth and P. L. Wright (Urbana, Ill.: University of Illinois, 1974), pp. 250–70.

[3]Joe Cappo, "Will Marketing Run Out of Energy?" *Chicago Daily News,* November 27, 1973, p. 34. Unfortunately, the columnist makes the mistake of identifying marketing with the demand stimulation problem rather than the total problem of managing demand.

The first is an *"aggressive-demarketing" response.* The company rushes to buy supplies wherever it can get them, at any cost. It raises its own prices sharply, shaves product quality and new-product development, eliminates weaker customers, reduces customer services, allocates to the remaining customers according to ability to pay, cuts marketing budgets for research, advertising, and sales calls, and drops low-profit items. All of these steps have the positive effect of creating instant profits for the company. At the same time, the company is playing dangerously with its only asset, its customers. Their goodwill is sorely taxed, and when normal times return, many of them will have found other vendors and other ways to meet their needs.

The second is a *"marketing-as-usual" approach.* Here the company expects shortages to be temporary. The company continues to buy its supplies carefully. It maintains the same product line and sells to the same customers. It raises prices a little to keep up with cost increases, but not excessively. It maintains the same expenditures on advertising, sales force, and marketing research, with minor changes in its messages. These steps at best maintain the company's profit margins and customer goodwill. On the other hand, they smack too much of "Nero fiddling while Rome burns" and do not implement certain steps to improve the company's position in the long run.

A period of deep shortages calls for a third response, which can be characterized as *strategic remarketing.* It calls for the appointment of a top-management committee to review the company's basic policies on its *customer mix, product mix,* and *marketing mix,* and to make a set of recommendations. This committee studies the following questions:

1 Which markets will be the most profitable in the coming years?
2 Which customers in these markets will be the best ones to serve?
3 What principle should be used to allocate scarce supplies to existing customers?
4 How many new customers can be cultivated without diluting the interest of present customers in receiving adequate supplies?
5 What products might the company drop from its line and what products should the company try to add to its line?
6 How much price increase can the company take and justify to its customers?
7 What should the company be communicating to its customers and what will this require in the way of an advertising and public relations budget?
8 How many salesmen does the company need and what kind of retraining should they receive?
9 What can be done to bring down costs to customers and assist them in solving their problems?

Although the answers to these questions will vary from company to company, the guiding principle should be one of customer orientation. The major asset that a firm has in the long run is its loyal customers. Loyal customers are not created by serving them royally during good times and charging what the traffic will bear during bad times. Loyal customers are created by companies that are considerate of their customers at all times. During a shortage period, the market-oriented company strives to help its customers solve their problems.

This philosophy can be translated into specific marketing tasks and activities:

1   *Salesmen* will find their selling role diminished but their other roles increased. Their *customer-counseling role* becomes crucial. They should be able to suggest other sources of supply to customers or substitutes for the scarce material. Their *communication role* increases because they must explain and justify company allocations and price increases to customers. Their *intelligence role* increases because they must carefully monitor and report back to management regarding customer and competitive adjustments to the shortages. Their *order-expediting role* is increased because customers will phone more often to find out about deliveries. Even their *selling role* has not entirely vanished because they must turn some attention to selling slower-moving company products that are in adequate supply.

2   *Advertising* should probably be reduced somewhat but by no means abandoned. It has several important roles to play. The company can redirect some of its advertising budget to build up demand for company products that are in oversupply. Some of this budget must be used to create awareness and interest in new products and product modifications. Some of it should be used to educate buyers in more economical uses of the scarce product. Finally, some of this budget should be used to keep customers apprised of steps the company is taking to solve the shortages.

3   *Marketing research* should be maintained at a level that permits the monitoring of competitive market changes and interpretation of evolving buyer practices and needs.

4   *Product development* should be alert to new-product opportunities created by the shortage. To a resourceful firm, a shortage means a need for substitute products. A shortage of gasoline expands the market for bikes and mass transportation; a shortage of heating oil expands the market for sweaters, fireplaces, and electric blankets.

5   *Purchasing* must be considerably strengthened as a company function. It must do a better job of finding alternative sources of supply and arranging long-term contracts. Purchasing departments have a need to utilize marketing principles, now that they must "sell" the company's needs to vendor salesmen. Some companies have transferred salesmen into the purchasing department to improve their effectiveness in attracting suppliers and supplies.[4]

INFLATION

Another major event in recent years has been worldwide double-digit inflation. Prices in the United States rose over 11 percent in 1974; prices in Japan, 22 percent; in Brazil, 27 percent; and in many European countries, 15–25 percent.

Many causes contributed to the rampant level of inflation. The Mideast War of 1973 led to severe oil shortages and heightened oil prices, which affected the prices of virtually everything else—clothing, furniture, food, appliances—because of their direct or indirect dependence on petroleum and petroleum derivatives. Countries exporting other raw materials followed their example and raised their prices. Companies rushed for substitutes, and in the process, pushed up the prices of these substitutes. They also raised their own prices to cover their rising costs. Customers accepted the higher prices because they were more concerned with shortages than costs. Labor unions demanded higher wages and got them. In the face of these factors, government took some mea-

---

[4]For additional steps, see the author's "Marketing during Periods of Shortage," *Journal of Marketing*, July 1974, pp. 20–29.

sures to discourage excessive price increases and to encourage conservation steps by consumers. But it avoided taking stronger measures because of their political unpopularity either with business or with consumers.

High inflation poses a number of new problems for marketing management that, like shortages, have no easy answers. Again, the company would be wise to form a high-level management committee to wrestle with the following questions calling for policy guidelines:

1   How much price increase should be passed on to customers?
2   How can the price increase be made plausible to the customers?
3   Should prices be set at time of shipment instead of time of order?
4   How much product simplification and service elimination should be introduced to bring down costs?
5   What other steps can the company take to bring down its manufacturing and marketing costs?

Companies face a strong temptation to make no basic changes and simply pass on cost increases in the form of higher prices. Some try to pass on price increases that exceed the cost increases (called "price pyramiding"). The practice is explained on the ground that some of the price increase anticipates future cost increases and will obviate the need to change prices later. Yet, some of it is just charging what the traffic will bear. Companies were able to do this easily in 1974 because of the shortages and the rush to buy. Passing on high price increases is more difficult when demand softens. Companies find themselves less and less able to simply levy higher prices and have to find better means of offsetting the cost increases.

A major solution is product simplification. Buyers are very apt to favor product versions that feature economy and durability. Once again, market-oriented management will try to find ways to help the customer, and in terms of inflation, this translates into introducing more economic products that hold down customer costs.

RECESSION

The American consumer of the 1950s and 1960s believed in the American dream: continuous rising real income, a home in the suburbs, two cars, and money to travel. In the early 1970s this dream was shaken. The American consumer confronted shortages, then inflation, and then recession. His real income deteriorated.

The typical consumer exposed to income deterioration goes through a number of stages in adjusting to the new economic realities:

1   At first he maintains his old spending patterns, refusing to take his loss in real income seriously.
2   As things get worse, he starts to cut certain things from his budget and search for less expensive goods.
3   At a further point, he gets angry at certain forces that he thinks are behind the economic downturn: big business, unions, government. If he could, he would vote the culprits out of power.

4   Still later, he shows signs of despair because the situation continues to get worse and no one is able to do anything about it.

5   Finally, the consumer begins to take stock of his new situation and adopts a new set of consumer values matched to his economic realities.

Not all consumers pass through all these stages, but many of them make several adjustments of great importance to sellers. The dominant goal of consumers is to find ways to economize. This takes a number of forms:

1   Increased preference for *store brands* over manufacturer brands because of their lower prices, similar quality, and prominent display.

2   Increased *multiple shopping* and *discount store patronage* to find lower prices.

3   Increased *trading down* toward substitute products. Consumers go from steak to chicken to tuna fish to rice and beans.

4   Increased *do-it-yourself* in the area of home repair services, clothing, and food production.

5   Increased patronage of *secondhand markets* (used-clothing stores, flea markets, garage sales).

6   Increased interest in *functional product features* and *durability* and less in product aesthetics and convenience.

7   Increased elimination of *impulse buying* and *nonnecessities.*[5]

These changes result in the emergence of three distinct consumer life-style groups. The majority group, the *intense consumers,* still retain the consumption values of the 1950s and 1960s and do their best to continue purchasing on the old scale and with attention to product style, convenience features, and status. They want to spend freely, drive a large car, live high, and not worry about waste. The second group, the *sensible consumers,* concentrate on functional product values and economy. They buy smaller cars, the more practical clothes, the simpler appliances. The third and smallest group, the *austere consumers,* have voluntarily turned against material values and started deconsuming. They have given up their cars and reduced the number of their appliances, and they wear simple clothes on all occasions, make their own furniture, grow some of their own food, and eat less. Many of them are convinced that they will be healthier and happier and live longer this way.

Implications for marketing management

Many of these consumer changes call for a substantial redirection in marketing thinking. Traditional marketing projected the consumer philosophy that "more is better" and that happiness lay in owning a large home, driving a Cadillac, having a hundred appliances, wearing expensive clothes, and eating steak four times a week. The majority of Americans still want this, and many companies are doing their best to sustain this want structure and supply it. At the same time, there is a growing market for goods that are less extravagant and conspicuous and more durable and economical. This market segment constitutes

---

[5]Industrial buyers go through similar changes in the face of rising costs and declining profits. They seek ways to achieve economy and long-term supplier commitment. Their steps include (1) search for additional suppliers, (2) search for new terms, (3) movement toward self-production, (4) search for cheaper materials, and (5) product simplification. The industrial seller must take these evolving values into account in formulating his marketing program.

a growing market opportunity for manufacturers and retailers. It calls for a different emphasis in product design, distribution, pricing, and marketing communication. Companies may bemoan the decline of the old values which were based on insatiable demand and never-ending product elaboration and replacement. But the alert marketer knows that there is always work to do as long as there are people, and it is only a question of finding out and offering what they need and want.

PUBLIC SECTOR NEEDS

The evolving needs of the public sector lead to a final new direction for marketing. The private marketing economy has managed to produce an extraordinary level of goods and services to satisfy man's material appetites. For a price, a person can obtain the most elegant cars, clothes, houses, furniture, foods, and so on. But the growth in private goods has not been matched by a corresponding growth in public goods. Galbraith calls this the *social imbalance:*

> An increase in the consumption of automobiles requires a facilitating supply of streets, highways, traffic control, and parking space. The protective services of the police and the highway patrols must also be available, as must those of the hospitals. Although the need for balance here is extraordinarily clear, our use of privately produced vehicles has, on occasion, got far out of line with the supply of the related public services. The result has been hideous road congestion, an annual massacre of impressive proportions, and chronic colitis in the cities.[6]

Because the issue of what to produce in capitalist economies is left mainly to be determined in the marketplace, public services tend to be underfinanced and neglected. Public education is so bad that those who can afford private schools send their children to them. Medical services and facilities are in short supply and inequitably distributed. Social services for the poor and the aged are so inadequate as to be scandalous. Police services are inferior in quantity and quality. Symphonies and museums are in constant danger of going bankrupt. Many public library systems are underhoused and underbudgeted. Many parks and zoos show signs of neglect. Most large cities must cope with an alarming rate of crime and physical deterioration.

The irony is that as the society increasingly accumulates private goods, it increasingly yearns for public goods: clean air, clean beaches, adequate parks, safe streets, fast roads, and good schools. *Quality of life* overtakes *quantity of goods* as a major concern.

Two factors lie at the root of the gross social imbalance. One is *public attitudes.* Although the public wants more public services, it is unwilling to vote sufficient tax money for them. People prefer a lower tax rate and more private spending choice to a higher tax rate and more public services.

The second factor is the *backward character of management* in many nonprofit institutions. These organizations operate under archaic administrative philosophies that lead them to rapidly lose touch with their publics. They start out at first with a clear mandate and intent to serve a certain class of human needs.

---

[6]John Kenneth Galbraith, *The Affluent Society* (Boston: Houghton Mifflin Company, 1958), p. 255.

Over time, they become inward-oriented and self-serving. An officialdom emerges; the organization grows rule-bound and impersonal; and it concentrates on producing the same old services in the same old way. The organization becomes increasingly removed from, and unresponsive to, the emerging needs of its clients. There is no mechanism of competition and market votes, as in the private sector, to tie the organization's survival to client satisfaction.

It soon becomes apparent that what is missing from many of these non-profit organizations is a *marketing orientation* toward their publics and tasks. These organizations are mostly in the *product orientation* stage that characterized business firms many years ago. They focus on their products and services, not on their markets. They have great belief in the value of these products and the traditional way they are offered. Thus a college believes that students should want the kind of education that has always been provided; a church believes that members should want traditional religious services; and a police force believes that citizens should accept the way in which police services have been delivered in the past. There is little research into their clients' evolving needs. There is little effort to create new products, services, and delivery systems adapted to the changing market needs.

Organizational unresponsiveness ultimately engenders client apathy or hostility that throws the organization into a crisis. Colleges find that they cannot attract enough students. Public school administrators cannot attract enough citizen support to pass a bond referendum. Police departments fail to get enough citizen cooperation and respect. Churches face falling membership. Symphonies cannot raise enough money. The U.S. Army cannot attract enough recruits.

At this point these organizations are finally ready to reexamine their mission and client relations. As they do so, some begin to recognize their problems as marketing problems. They look at business firms and their effectiveness in using marketing to develop demand for their output. They begin to conjecture that the solution to their problems may lie in a marketing orientation.

Unfortunately, these organizations do not at first understand marketing and what it entails. They confuse the marketing concept with the selling concept. A good illustration is provided by many colleges facing declining enrollments. These colleges begin to believe that the problem and the solution lie in the college admissions office (sales department). The admissions office is failing to attract enough students. It needs to do a better job of "marketing." The administration takes the following steps: (1) it gives the admissions director more money to hire more staff; (2) it increases the admission office's budget for advertising; (3) it puts more money into preparing an attractive college catalog. Some colleges go further and place commercials on rock radio stations, pass out promotional Frisbees on Fort Lauderdale beaches, and send letters to qualified high school graduates saying "Congratulations, you have been accepted to our program." One college started to pay a finder's fee to its present students for every new student they recruited.[7]

These colleges are discovering not marketing so much as one small part of it, selling. And the increased investment in selling works for a while. The admissions office reverses the enrollment decline. Essentially, the first colleges

---

[7]"Colleges Beat Bushes to Lure New Students, Up Enrollment," *Chicago Tribune*, April 14, 1974, Sec. 1, p. 33.

that turn to hard selling start pulling in more students than those who still re-main product-oriented. But whether the gain lasts depends on how long the other schools remain passive and how much real program satisfaction the new students find at the college.

This is the rub. The new students often find that the college experience does not match the image that they got at the admissions office. In their dis-appointment with boring classes and an indifferent administration, they bad-mouth the college to their high school friends. And the admissions department has to work harder and harder to attract more students.

Hopefully, at this point the college begins to grasp the difference between a selling approach and a marketing approach. It begins to realize that it must modify its product as well as its promotion. It begins to ask the proper questions: What is happening in the marketing environment? How is the college seen by different groups? What are its marketing opportunities? How should it position itself among colleges? How can it communicate to inside and outside publics a clear identity and mission? And, how can it organize to do more effective marketing?

Implications for marketing management

A wide range of nonprofit organizations are beginning to see marketing as a major answer to their problems. Many trained marketers are beginning to consult with, or work for, these organizations. Hopefully, they will bring to these organizations a full marketing concept and not just a selling concept. Here we will briefly describe what this means.[8]

Every organization is surrounded by a set of publics with whom it has exchanges of various kinds. The organization will have goals with respect to what it would like to obtain from each of its publics. In turn, it will have to think through what it will have to offer to each public in order to elicit what it wants. *Marketing is a systematic approach to planning the benefits to offer to a distinct public in order to elicit the resources or support that the organization wants in return.*

Nonprofit organizations have at the very least three kinds of publics. There are publics who consume its services, publics who supply the necessary resources, and miscellaneous publics whose goodwill is important to the organi-zation. The nonprofit organization, therefore, uses marketing to develop the right services for its clients, to attract the resources that it needs, and to com-municate and win the goodwill of third-party publics.

Marketing can be used to bring *products, services, organizations, persons, places,* or *social causes* to the attention of a market. An increasing number of organiza-tions are getting involved in the last type of marketing, that of trying to win support for a social cause, such as population, energy conservation, environ-mental protection, and cigarette and drug control. These efforts go under the name of social marketing:

> **Social marketing** is the design, implementation, and control of programs seeking to increase the acceptability of a social idea, cause, or practice in a target group(s). It utilizes market segmentation, consumer research, concept development, communication, facilitation, incentives, and ex-change theory to maximize target group response.

---

[8]See the author's *Marketing for Nonprofit Organizations* (Englewood Cliffs, N.J.: Prentice-Hall, Inc., 1975).

Social marketing is one of the promising new developments expected to increase the effectiveness of social change agents in bringing about desired social changes.[9]

The marketing principles for nonprofit organizations are the same as those for profit organizations. The organizational marketer must identify the key markets and publics, employ segmentation, analyze consumer behavior, determine market positioning, develop products and a marketing mix, implement marketing action, monitor results, and take corrective steps.

Ultimately, nonprofit organizations that want to be market-oriented will need to create a position equivalent to that of marketing vice-presidents in commercial organizations. The job of the person in this position is twofold. First, he undertakes to coordinate all the marketing functions to achieve a balanced marketing mix. Second, he educates nonmarketing officers about the fundamental importance of the marketing concept. The marketing concept is not readily accepted by other officers in an organization. It takes a great deal of work to convince them that the organization begins and ends with the customer.

SUMMARY

Marketing is an evolving discipline that must develop new answers as new problems arise. The marketing principles of the 1950s and 1960s are being challenged by new factors in the marketing environment—consumerism, environmentalism, shortages, inflation, recession, and public sector needs.

Consumerism calls for a strengthening of consumers' rights and power in relation to sellers. Resourceful marketers will recognize it as an opportunity to serve consumers better through providing more information, education, and protection. *Environmentalism* calls for minimizing the harm done by marketing practices to the environment and quality of life. It calls for intervening in consumer wants when their satisfaction would create too much environmental cost. *Shortages* have made real the possibility of running out of resources in the absence of their wise use. Marketers must avoid responding to shortages with either aggressive demarketing or marketing-as-usual. Shortages call for strategic reprogramming of the customer mix, product mix, and marketing mix. *Inflation* raises the producer's costs and he has to determine how much to pass on to the buyer. Resourceful marketers will not simply pass on higher costs but will seek ways to offset them to hold customer costs down. *Recession* and the preceding developments lead to changing consumer life style, characterized by more sensible or austere consumption. Some firms recognize a marketing opportunity to serve the needs of the growing segment of sensible consumers. Finally, *public sector services* are generally poor in quantity and quality. Nonprofit organizations have a great opportunity to improve their services by adopting the same marketing orientation that has worked so effectively in the commercial sector.

QUESTIONS AND PROBLEMS

1 Consumerists have suggested that public schools should train students in how to view television commercials critically. Students should be taught to recognize objectively what the advertising is trying to do. As a businessman, would you support this proposal? Why or why not?

---

[9]See Philip Kotler and Gerald Zaltman, "Social Marketing: An Approach to Planned Social Change," *Journal of Marketing,* July 1971, pp. 3–12.

2 The following products satisfy individual wants but at the same time have certain undesirable societal consequences: (a) detergents, (b) automobiles, (c) disposable paper diapers. Discuss what the manufacturers can or ought to do about each product.

3 Develop a social marketing campaign to influence people to buy two-way bottles instead of the convenient throwaway bottles. What appeals would you use? What pricing mechanism? How much funding would you need? Do you think the campaign has much chance of success?

4 Distinguish four alternative advertising strategies by an oil company in the event of another major fuel shortage.

5 Two companies, A and B, account for virtually 100 percent of the sales in a certain industry. Company A is the high price, high quality company and company B is the low price, low quality company. During the period of rising real incomes, company A enjoyed a 60 percent market share and company B had the rest. In the subsequent period of high inflation and recession, several buyers switched to company B because of their need to economize. What are some of the strategies available to company A to avoid losing further market share?

6 What are some of the responsibilities that might be assumed by a vice-president of marketing who works for a hospital?

7 The New York Metropolitan Museum of Art is seeking to increase its membership, which begins at $15 a year. It believes that persons would respond more to selfish reasons for joining the museum than to broad social appeals. In this connection, the Met is trying to develop at least five tangible benefits that would go with museum membership. Can you suggest five benefits and prepare an ad that displays them?

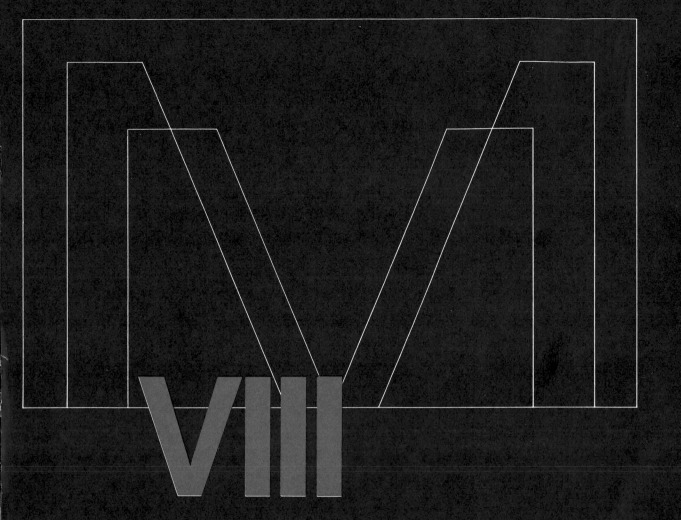

VIII

CASES IN MARKETING

1. Green Packing Company—competing with private brands

The Green Packing Company is a leading food processor with sales of around $300 million annually. Its brand name is found on canned fruits and vegetables and a variety of frozen foods. It has distribution in all leading chains. Green spends around $8 million a year in direct consumer advertising to maintain consumer preference for its brands. It spends another $5 million in consumer deals and promotions (cents-off, premiums, etc.) and another $2 million in trade deals (discounts, allowances, premiums).

Although its brand name is highly regarded by consumers, Green's management has become concerned about the growth of private brands. Large food chains are increasingly selling products under their own label, often at several cents less than national brands. The product is often identical, in many cases coming from a national brand producer under contract. The lower store price of the private brand shows that chain-store distribution is efficient, and chains spend little on advertising or promoting their own brands. Consumers seem to be turning to private brands as they become more educated and interested in saving money. Even when the private brand is not exactly of the same quality as a national brand, many consumers do not find the slight quality difference worth paying for.

One of the large food chains recently solicited Green Packing to produce some of its output for the chain's private label. The proposal and price were attractive, especially since Green was operating with excess capacity because recent sales were down. Management had not produced for private label before, and its opposition to private label did not reduce the tempting quality of the offer. Its chief executives realized they were facing a major policy decision.

To compound the problem, another large chain approached Green with a plea for lower prices on its national brands. This second chain had stayed out of the private label business and was hurting because its prices were somewhat higher than those of competing food chains. It felt that the larger food processors, including Green, had an obligation to hold down prices. It told Green's management that Green's high level of spending on consumer advertising raised prices to the retailer and the consumer. It felt that Green's total promotional budget, especially the amount spent on consumer advertising, was excessive and that a larger part of it should go into trade deals to incentivize the retailers. This would bring down costs on national brands, and they would then be able to compete better against private brands.

What alternatives face the Green Packing Company? Which seem most attractive? What does Green need in the way of further information? Present a well-reasoned set of recommendations.

Reliable Foundry is a medium-sized firm that produces metal castings for customers in a variety of industries. Ralph Fox, the president, has headed the company for the last thirty years and is near retirement. He has run the company along lines fairly traditional for foundries. Reliable is operated on a job-shop basis with a high labor input. The company takes all the business it can find, with the exception of very large or very fine metal-casting work. It gets customers in two ways. Some castings buyers phone Reliable on a recommendation or after seeing its name in the telephone directory. They describe the job and invite Reliable to submit a price bid. These unsolicited calls account for about 40 percent of Reliable's business. The remaining business is generated by its sales force of ten men. They have their territories and look up the names of metalworking firms that might use castings in their production. In the nation as a whole, there are over ninety thousand plants in metalworking, making the prospecting problem quite complex. The salesmen make cold calls on prospects to learn about their operations, in the hope of uncovering some part or assembly that Reliable might cast. This is an expensive method, and Ralph Fox would like to find better ways to locate prospects.

Most of Reliable's castings are done for such end-use industries as automobiles, farm equipment, machine tools, electric motors, and air conditioning. These industries have different rates of growth, although Reliable welcomes work from all of them. About 20 percent of Reliable's customers yield 70 percent of its revenues, and Reliable goes all out to treat its large customers right.

As far as Reliable can determine, castings customers choose vendors on the basis of price, quality, and service. Reliable sets prices a little higher than competitors but offers more quality. Producing higher-quality castings means, according to Reliable, fewer imperfections, fewer tolerance variations, and therefore less machining, all of which saves the customer money. Furthermore, Reliable has a better record of meeting its delivery schedules. Still, there are many price-cutting competitors around. A lot of purchasing agents look only at price. Sometimes the customer's controller is at fault because he criticizes the purchasing agent for not taking the lowest bid, not realizing that the total cost is more than the price.

Reliable is concerned about its future position in the industry. The number of foundry firms has decreased from thirty-eight hundred in the late 1940s to eighteen hundred today. Smaller firms are closing down because of poor economics and poor marketing. A new factor has been the enforcement of the Occupational Safety and Hazard Act. Foundries—which are normally places of high temperature, pollution, and safety problems—have been required recently to spend a lot of money to control these problems, money that does not increase productivity. Some foundries prefer to go out of business rather than bear these costs.

Ralph Fox is having basic doubts about Reliable's continuing to be a general job shop. Some of the larger foundries have been specializing and increasing their capital intensity. He also is troubled about Reliable's methods of generating business. He has lately heard of the distinction between a sales orientation and a marketing orientation. He would like to review Reliable's marketing objectives and marketing operations in the search for a strategy for growth in the coming decade.

3. Sears, Roebuck—developing a product concept

Many companies are hard at work attempting to design a practical electric car. This includes, of course, such a major automaker as General Motors. It also includes, according to rumor, such firms as General Electric and Sears.

Offhand, General Motors would enjoy the greatest *differential advantage* in this market, since it possesses all the *distinctive competences* that match the *success requirements* of the product:

1 Good relations with suppliers of metal, rubber, plastic, glass, and other materials needed to produce an automobile
2 Skill at mass production and mass assembly of complicated pieces of equipment
3 Great distribution capacity to store, show, and deliver automobiles to the American public
4 Good reputation with buyers as to its ability to produce and service a good auto product

A company like General Electric possesses distinctive competences in numbers 1 and 2 but not in numbers 3 and 4. It also has superb know-how in electrical technology, although General Motors is probably as knowledgeable. Sears's major distinctive competence is its extensive distribution and retailing system, but it would have to acquire the other needed competences.

An independent inventor has approached Sears with an excellent electric-car design with a capability of a one-hundred-mile range on a full charge and the ability to reach and cruise at a top speed of sixty miles per hour. Recharging of the power source would take eight hours (usually overnight) and would cost about $1.50 for a slow charge using ordinary household current.

Sears's management shows a strong interest in this car. It believes that the company would have a tremendous distribution advantage by ultimately setting up showrooms next to its auto service centers. Initially, it would display the car in its high-traffic retail stores and set up a sales operation next to the Allstate car insurance and financing operations. Sears might also set up Sears Rent-A-Car in its stores featuring the electric car. The car would be maintained and repaired through the Sears Service Centers.

Sears would face many difficult decisions, such as used-car policy, new-car options, warranty policy and options, inventory location and shipment policies, and promotion policy. Let us assume that these issues can be resolved.

Let us turn to the basic question of what the car should be. People don't buy cars; they buy utilities. A car is simply a packaging of a service. It is a tool for solving a consumer problem. At this stage Sears only has a *product idea*, not a *product concept*. You are asked to prepare the following points for discussion:

1 Generate three alternative *product concepts* for the new electric car. (A product concept expresses the car's meaning in consumer terms; for example, "a car that is good for the environment.")

2 Develop *a set of criteria* for making a choice among the alternative product concepts. Choose one of the basic product concepts, using these criteria.

3 Describe the *product positioning* of the chosen product concept. (Product positioning shows the consumer's concept of the product's relationship to (a) competing products and (b) important dimensions of consumer choice.)

4 Discuss the questions that would be put to potential buyers to determine whether the positioned product concept would appeal to them and motivate purchase. (*Concept testing*)

5 What features should be designed into the car to convincingly communicate the product concept to the potential buyer? (*Attribute cues*)

4. General Products. Inc.—screening new-product ideas

General Products is a large multidivision firm manufacturing a variety of consumer products—canned and frozen foods, drugs, cosmetics, toys, and sporting goods. The company has experienced a sustained and high rate of growth over the last several years. New products have been a key element in the company's success. All six divisions of General Products have had vigorous new-product development programs.

New-product ideas went through several stages of screening, concept testing, economic analysis, prototype design, product testing, consumer testing, and market testing before they were ready for full-scale introduction. The early stages of the new-product process, especially screening, involved rather informal procedures. For example, the Food Products Division submitted all new-product ideas to a screening committee, which made the first "go–no go" decision. Many executives felt that not enough effort was devoted to these early stages, and some even suggested that the "success ratio" of new introductions was beginning to decline for this reason.

Corporate management had been aware for some time of the need to systematize the process of new-product development. In September 1974 it made the decision to form a New Products Analysis group as a part of the corporate staff. The purpose of the New Products Analysis group was "to coordinate the new-product development efforts of the various divisions and to provide a mechanism for screening of new-product ideas at the corporate level." The group had a staff of five people with special skills in marketing research, operations research, and economic analysis. One of the first tasks undertaken by the NPA group was an extensive analysis of the criteria suitable for new-product screening. A list of criteria to be employed for corporate-level screening was developed and is shown in Exhibit I. The committee felt that the criteria had differential importance and were complexly interrelated. It wanted to design a screening procedure that would indicate how various new-product proposals fared relative to each other on the basis of the criteria in Exhibit I.

In 1975 the various divisions of General Products submitted eight new-product proposals for evaluation to the NPA group. The descriptions of these eight proposals are given in Exhibit II. The NPA group prepared detailed economic projections for each proposal based on reasonable assumptions derived from past experience and executive judgments. Projections of investment requirements and profit contribution potentials are shown in Exhibit III.

I am indebted to Nikhilesh Dholakia for permission to use Case 4.

Exhibit I

New-product screening criteria

Criterion No.	Criterion	Criterion category	Description
1.	Newness	Product criterion	Novelty and communicable differentiating features
2.	Technical feasibility	Product criterion	Compatibility with current technology and extent of development required
3.	Market size and share	Market criterion	Market size, expected growth in market, and expected share of proposed product
4.	Competitive position	Market criterion	Direct and indirect competition likely to be encountered by proposed product
5.	Profit contribution	Financial criterion	Average present value of contribution flow expected from the product during its estimated life span
6.	Investment requirement	Financial criterion	New plant and equipment, start-up costs, and working capital requirements
7.	Organizational support	Organizational criterion	Extent of top-level executive support for the product idea
8.	Strategic fit	Organizational criterion	Compatibility with existing product lines, production capabilities, marketing organization
9.	Ecological compatibility	Environmental criterion	Compatibility of proposed product, package, and production process with environment
10.	Consumer welfare	Environmental criterion	Impact of proposed product on consumer health, safety, and general well-being

Exhibit II

New-product proposals to be screened

A *Nutrisnack* originated due to the joint efforts of the Food Products and Drugs divisions. In several consumer studies, it has been established that mothers are very concerned about the nutritive value of the snacks their children eat. This gave birth to the idea of a high-protein, nutritious snack, but it became feasible only after the Drug Division came up with a flourlike protein supplement. Exploratory laboratory studies still indicate a problem of unpleasant medicinal aftertaste in food products prepared with this protein supplement. The plant manufacturing the protein has a non-degradable hydrocarbon discharge. R&D is working on a decomposition method that would lead to reduction of hydrocarbon content to acceptable level. Assuming that a potato-chip-like consistency and crispiness could be achieved, Nutrisnack is expected to gain wide consumer acceptance.

Market growth is expected to be very rapid, with virtually unchallenged market position for eighteen to thirty months.

B *Standup Alphabets* is similar to competitive product just introduced. Tubular plastic construction makes handling by child safer. Very little retooling is required in existing Toy Division facilities. The distributors are willing to take on the product, but market penetration would require extensive trade promotion and consumer advertising. In any case, a maximum market share of 10 percent is expected, and the novelty value of the product is likely to wear off in ten to fourteen months.

C *Jellywhip* will provide entry in growing but highly competitive ready-to-eat dessert market. The packaging concept needs considerable improvement in order to be both attractive and convenient. Apprehensions about effective disposability of package persist, although R & D is working on two promising ideas. The existing food brokers that we deal with are unwilling to take on this line at the anticipated sales volume. Consumer preference relative to leading brand is moderate but significant, although concern has been expressed regarding high-calorie value of whipped cream.

D *PX-20C* attempts to combine advantages of popular menthol-eucalyptus-type cold formulations with vitamin C. Product concept is novel enough to gain shelf space in drugstores, but competitive entry can be expected within six months. Laboratory formulations using orange-flavored base have been successful, but scale-up problems are anticipated in large-scale manufacture. FDA approval is assured, but vitamin C appeal cannot be over-stressed awaiting conclusive evidence of cold-resisting properties of this vitamin. A fairly large market with moderate growth is expected, but product life span is contingent on possible breakthroughs in cold cures.

E *Bikeviewer* is a proposed extension of the Bicycle Accessory line of the Outdoor Recreation Division. Existing products in market are of poor quality and mounting requires special effort. All trends indicate a steady spread of the "pedal power" movement and therefore an expanding market for all bicycle accessories. However, competition from Italian and Japanese manufacturers is intense, and only a marginal market position can be expected for our product. Dealer acceptance is assured because the dealer organization has been pressing for a product whose shatter-resistance properties lead to increased safety.

F *Milkubes* attempts to develop a nonsticky formulation that can withstand 100°F. temperatures have been only partially successful. Although Coffee-mate and Cremora positions are unassailable, market structure analysis reveals a sizable convenience segment, which could be tapped if an appropriate product is offered. New plant would have to be commissioned, although existing marketing organization can handle the product with little change. Novelty of concept is likely to aid in gaining consumer and dealer acceptance.

G *Signature F-G Rackets* offers a strong entry in the growing tennis equipment market. Fiberglass construction is expected to be popular in the high-price serious amateur segment. Technology of fiberglass frame-drawing is still in early experimental stage. Developmental expenses are expected to be high, partially justified by a long product life span. Competitive position is not assured for any extended period. Problems of occasional "micro-splintering" of fiberglass frames could be possible cause for palm irritation for some users. Balance and swing characteristics are expected to be superior to those of most existing rackets.

H *Frozen Shortcakes* would offer a new brand in the frozen dessert market. Market growth is moderate, and competitive brands have dominant positions. However, "precut serving" convenience offers a somewhat novel product concept. Consumer tests indicate good acceptance of the concept, but [tests] also indicate slightly unfavorable attitude toward the more elaborate package. It would be difficult to obtain adequate distribution without extensive promotion and advertising.

Exhibit III

Investment requirements and contribution potentials

Proposal code	Investment requirement* (in thousands of dollars)	Contribution potential†
A	12,500	3,700
B	470	82
C	5,700	1,300
D	10,000	2,350
E	520	120
F	8,800	2,000
G	27,200	8,100
H	11,300	2,900

*Includes plant and equipment, start-up costs, working capital requirements, but not R&D expenses.
†Expected present value of total contribution over product life span divided by the life span.

Question

Propose a systematic method of rating these product proposals and develop actual ratings.

5. Star Chemical Company—evaluating alternative distribution strategies

The Star Chemical Company is an old-line manufacturer of chemicals with annual sales of $100 million. In recent years it has experienced a profit slump, mainly because of excess capacity and severe price competition. Industrial buyers choose their chemical suppliers chiefly on price. They pay some attention to delivery reliability and service, but generally they show little loyalty. Star was more profitable in the past because of superior production efficiency, but competitors had built newer plants and were enjoying equal or lower costs than Star.

A number of stockholders were critical of Star's management for not getting into consumer products. Other chemical companies had integrated forward into making and branding some of the final products that were sold to consumers, thereby capturing the value added and sheltering these products from strict price competition. Star Chemical had not done this, primarily because of its lack of experience in consumer marketing and the lack of any specific product opportunities.

Star's research and development department recently developed a new line of chlorinated organic chemicals that functioned as bleaches, germicides, and oxidants. Ralph Hemstead, the R&D director, suggested that one of the uses of the line could be a germicidal chemical developed for the swimming pool market. He believed that the new chemical would have qualities superior to those of existing swimming pool chemicals. Top management was interested because this offered an opportunity to enter the consumer market on a small scale and gain experience.

A new-products committee consisting of the research director, sales manager, marketing research manager, and advertising manager met to discuss what to do with this new consumer product opportunity. They knew that there were a great number of swimming pools in the United States (residential pools, motel pools, public pools, school pools, etc.). Most of the private residential pools were found in warmer-climate states, although some were found in all big cities. Pools required periodical chemical treatment to keep them safe in use. Pool owners and managers bought their supplies through department stores, hardware stores, garden supply stores, pool specialty supply houses, pool service firms, and so on.

Star Chemical's sales force had no experience selling to wholesale or retail firms in the consumer area. However, the sales manager felt that his sales force should be given a chance to sell the new product to the appropriate channels of distribution. Otherwise the company's salesmen would feel bypassed and demoralized at losing a chance to make commissions on the new product. The other managers, however, felt that the company's sales force should not be diverted from its regular job and that a new sales force or distributor could handle the new task more efficiently.

The new-product committee faced some additional decisions. It had to decide whether to brand the product or sell it in bulk form for private labeling. It had to decide whether to cover a large number of distribution channels and markets or concentrate on certain channels and markets. It had to decide whether to push the brand through with good sales-force effort or pull the brand through with heavy advertising.

The members of the new-product committee realized that there were many alternative approaches to the marketing of this germicidal chemical. They recognized the need for clear criteria to make a choice among distribution alternatives. The members agreed to judge alternative proposals against the following criteria (percentages show the criterion's rated importance):

1 Effectiveness in reaching swimming pool owners (15 percent)
2 Amont of profit if this alternative works well (25 percent)
3 Experience company will gain in consumer marketing (10 percent)
4 Amount of investment involved (lower investment considered preferable) (30 percent)
5 Ability of company to cut short its losses (20 percent)

Star Chemical has called you in to consult on this problem. Management would like to receive a clear picture of its major distribution alternatives. It would also like you to propose a method for evaluating the major distribution alternatives on a quantitative basis.

Louis A. Weiss Memorial Hospital, a medium-sized 350-bed institution serving the Near North section of Chicago, was opened in 1953 and named after the late Chicago philanthropist and industrialist. Since its inception, the hospital has gradually expanded its services by carefully planning and implementing an extensive program: providing more ambulatory, out-patient services; enlarging the medical library; adding a new floor to the professional wing that houses doctors' offices; establishing a Cardiac Physiology Laboratory; increasing bed capacity; and so forth.

While planning is one key to Weiss Hospital's steady growth, a concerted effort to market the hospital has also been employed in order to maintain the superior image of the institution, to keep the public aware of the services the hospital has to offer, and to acquire both large and small charitable donations from interested citizens.

The hospital's board of trustees goes about acquiring funds for Weiss in a number of ways. Each year they sponsor a members' night at a major cultural event (theater, ballet, etc.), to raise money. Donors who make significant contributions to the hospital might have their name placed on a plaque and installed in a room, a laboratory, or a wing. Prominent citizens who show an interest in the hospital may be considered for membership on the board of trustees. Each member of the board is asked to contribute one thousand dollars annually. Possible donors are also suggested by individual board members in the form of lists and are sent personalized letters asking for contributions.

Weiss Hospital employs a full-time public relations man plus an assistant whose many jobs include seeing that the hospital receives newspaper coverage when a major hospital-connected event occurs, such as a large charity affair for Weiss or the opening of a new wing. However, the hospital does not rely exclusively on outside media to relay its news. *Word from Weiss,* published quarterly by Friends of Louis A. Weiss Hospital, is a fifteen- to twenty-page magazine that covers events and items of interest to those who are connected with the hospital. There is also a movie, fifteen to twenty minutes in length, which describes the hospital and its history. The film is used for any interested public gathering.

Also important in fund raising is the Women's Auxiliary, which provides an extremely valuable service to the hospital through its running of the gift shop. One of the largest gift shops of its kind in the United States, its profits go to various hospital needs. Not only is this gift shop a significant marketing effort, but the women's board helps arrange benefits, charity affairs, and awards and tributes ceremonies.

Thus we can see that Weiss Hospital has engaged in a thoughtful and extensive marketing program to raise money to support its many services to the community.

What further improvements can Weiss Hospital make in its fund raising efforts? What other publics might Weiss Hospital relate to through organized marketing programs?

7. Lever Brothers—
strengthening the profit
accountability of the
brand manager

Donald Johnson, assistant to the vice-president of marketing at Lever Brothers, had just been given a major assignment by his boss. Top management was expressing increasing concern with the product management system at Lever's. It

---

I am indebted to Louis W. Hirschmann for Case 6.

felt that the system needed a major overhaul in objectives and procedures. Several problems were involved:

1 Brand managers were still heavily volume and market-share oriented. To build volume, they often took steps that could never recover the costs of building that volume. They were loath to raise price to absorb increasing costs because this would reduce their market share.

2 There were increasing conflicts between brand managers, plant managers, and purchasing managers. A brand manager would have his sales and profit plans wrecked because the purchasing department had failed to order enough material or anticipate the right cost, or because a plant manager had failed to meet his production schedule or deliver good quality.

3 Brand managers did not seem sufficiently attentive to consumerist criticism. Their advertising claims continued to exaggerate their product's virtues and led to a Federal Trade Commission investigation on more than one occasion. The packaging sometimes suggested an exaggerated weight content. The ingredients were not always checked with consumer health and safety in mind. This neglect was due to brand managers' (1) being billed for their use of corporate legal services and R&D, and (2) being under pressure to maximize short term sales.

Don decided to interview a sample of brand managers to get their reactions to these criticisms. Here are some reactions:

Robert Dale: I think our first task is to maintain market share. Profits will follow. Suppose I have a 20 percent share and my cost of ingredients, packaging, and promotion go up. To maintain my profitability, I ought to raise prices. If I do that and my competitors stand still, I will lose some customers. I have maintained my profits at the loss of a little market share. But it is often more than a little. Suddenly I notice that I didn't lose 1 percent market share but 2, 3, or 4 percent. Then I desperately try to rebuild market share to where it was. But this costs a lot of money, especially in these days of soaring promotion costs. I think my job is to maintain market share, not to simply turn in a current profit of so many dollars at the expense of my market share.

Harold Fry: I would like more control over the factors that affect my brand's profitability. As far as I'm concerned, you can hold me accountable for gross profit contribution or even variable profit contribution. But how can I be a profit center when I have to beg for every little bit of cooperation? Last week I asked the plant manager to sharply increase the production of my brand in preparation for a sampling campaign I wanted to run to support a product improvement. The product improvement would shortly be matched by competitors and I had to act fast. But he refused. He said that the sharp increase in production for a limited period of time would require hiring and training several new workers. He would have to lay them off after the job was completed. He would have to answer to the union. Furthermore, he has been plagued with quality control problems recently because of new workers. He answers not to me but to the manufacturing vice-president, who judges him on his ability to produce cheaply, to maintain quality standards, and to avoid labor trouble. So he told me that he would be willing to get additional production out over a six-month period, rather than in the two-month period I need. You can see that profit accountability makes no sense unless I can call the shots.

Larry Evans: I try to be careful about consumerism in developing my marketing plans, but one has to take some risk. For example, our shampoo doesn't really eliminate dandruff in all cases. We only say that "it controls dandruff when used at least as frequently as recommended on the label." I can't help it if some customers think that it promises to eliminate their dandruff problem. As for the statement "Use as often as you want," we do not wish to imply that it would be harmless to do so. It is possible to overuse the product, which would result in more hair breakage. But on the whole, we are helping more people than hurting; just look at the number who buy our product again. I don't use much legal counsel because the guys in legal don't know anything. They are so conservative that any exaggeration is taboo. They don't want to lose their jobs by going out on a limb. The result is they would leave me no room for a significant claim if they had their way.

Donald Johnson pondered these comments and realized the complexity of the issues. His vice-president was expecting a report calling for bold revisions in the brand management system. His recommendations had to promise more profit-mindedness by the brand managers, less friction between brand managers and other managers, and more social concern or at least caution.

8. Transnational Pharmaceutical Company—organizing the marketing function

The Transnational Pharmaceutical Company is a major international drug company with worldwide sales of $200 million annually. The company's major markets are the United States, Europe (particularly England, France, and Germany), and South America.

Transnational Pharmaceutical produces two major product lines, *antibiotics* and *multivitamins.* To sell the antibiotics, the company has to contact physicians to build brand preference. It uses a combination of detail-men visits, samples, direct mail, and journal advertising. The same detail men visit the pharmacies to make sure they carry stock so they can fill physicians' prescriptions.

The multivitamins are sold through major retail stores, such as drug stores, food chains, department stores, and discount stores. To sell the multivitamins, the company spends a great sum of money on marketing research, consumer advertising, sales promotion, and salesmen activities at retail.

At present the marketing function is organized as follows. Marketing policies are developed in the United States, and international marketing activities are carried on by the International Division. The International Division uses a regional management structure. Corporate marketing is handled by a single marketing staff that does marketing research, advertising, and marketing planning for the two product lines. Each product line is divisionally organized and has its own domestic sales force. Both product divisions have to work through the International Division to get their policies implemented. The International Division uses a single sales force to sell both antibiotics and multivitamins.

In recent years the product divisions have been complaining about their lack of control over marketing planning and functions as well as over international activities. Each product division would like to run its own marketing functions and do away with the corporate marketing staff. Furthermore, each product division would like to have worldwide authority for operations and do away with the International Division.

According to top management, these organizational changes would increase management costs, with fewer assured benefits. The company, however, has called you in as a consultant. Your assignment is to recommend an organizational structure that accommodates the management of different products (antibiotics, multivitamins), geographic regions (U.S., Europe, South America), marketing functions (marketing research, advertising, sales force), and customer type (doctors, pharmacies, retail stores). You recognize that the organization must be designed to be competitively efficient where it counts—at the customer level. Propose an organization and defend it against alternative organization designs.

9. O'Brien Candy Company—applying a marketing audit

O'Brien Candy Company is a medium-sized chocolate manufacturer located in the Midwest. In the last two years its sales and profits have barely held their own. Top management feels that the trouble lies with the sales force; somehow they don't "work hard or smart enough." To correct this, management is planning to introduce a new incentive compensation system and is planning to hire a high-powered specialist to train the salesmen in modern merchandising and selling techniques.

The company's product line consists primarily of eighteen products, mostly candy bars. Its two leading brands are in the mature stage of their life cycles and account for 76 percent of total sales. The company has looked at the fast-developing markets of chocolate snacks and candies but has not made any moves yet.

The company recently researched its customer profile. Its products appeal especially to lower-income and older people. Respondents who were asked to assess O'Brien's chocolate products in relation to competitors' products described them as "average quality and a bit old-fashioned."

O'Brien sells its products to candy jobbers and large chains. Its salesmen call on many of the small retailers reached by the candy jobbers to fortify displays and provide ideas; its salesmen also call on many small retailers not covered by jobbers. O'Brien enjoys good penetration of small retailing, although not in all segments, such as the fast-growing restaurant area. Its major approach to middlemen is a "sell-in" strategy: discounts, exclusivity contracts, and stock financing. At the same time, O'Brien does not do too well in penetrating the various chains. Some of its competitors rely much more heavily on mass-consumer advertising and store merchandising and are more successful with the large chains.

O'Brien's marketing budget amounts to about 15 percent of its total sales, compared with competitors' budgets of close to 20 percent. Most of the marketing budget supports the sales force and the remainder supports advertising; consumer promotions are very limited. The advertising budget is spent primarily in reminder advertising for the company's two leading products. New products are not developed often, and when they are, they are introduced to retailers by using a "push" strategy.

Case 9 is adapted from a paper by Dr. Ernst A. Tirmann.

The marketing organization is headed by a sales vice-president. Reporting to him is the sales-force manager, the marketing research manager, and the advertising manager. Having come up from the ranks, the sales vice-president is partial to sales-force activities and pays less attention to the other marketing functions. The sales force is organized by territorial responsibilities headed by area managers.

The company has called you in as a marketing auditor to review its imminent plans to "give the sales force a shot in the arm" by introducing a new incentive compensation plan and sales training program.

Questions

Do you think this will turn the tide? If not, what do you think the company ought to do? Develop a short-term and a long-term action plan.

10. Charles Lamb & Sons—analyzing customer profitability

Charles Lamb & Sons, a New England tobacco wholesaler, has a policy of "total distribution." It seeks to reach every potential independent retail customer in its area and to get at least a portion of his business. Robert Lamb, the marketing vice-president, recently heard a talk by a marketing controller to the effect that customers differ vastly in profitability and that going after all potential customers does not make sense. The marketing controller said that many of the accounts of any established company lose money for that company on a direct cost basis. Unless account profitability is analyzed, the company will not know where to concentrate its marketing effort.

Robert Lamb returned to his office determined to check on this allegation. He knew that his larger accounts were generally more profitable than his smaller accounts; in fact, two hundred of his four thousand accounts provided 50 percent of his total sales and a high percentage of his profits. He decided to examine a typical small-customer account, the Easy Rider Company, to determine its profitability. The following facts describe this account:

1 The Easy Rider Company places one order a week for $300.
2 A company salesman makes one call a week on the Easy Rider Company.
3 The Easy Rider Company pays its bill forty days after receiving its shipment.

Robert Lamb proceeded to determine various costs and ratios for customer account analysis:
1 The cost of the merchandise sold is 80 percent of sales.
2 A sales call costs the company $30.
3 Packing, billing, and delivery expense is approximately $15 per order sent to an average customer at an average distance.
4 The company estimates its advertising and promotion cost to be 3 percent of sales.
5 The inventory stockturn is eighteen times a year. That is, goods are held an average of twenty days. The company estimates its inventory holding cost at 18 percent of sales per year, or .05 percent per day.
6 The company estimates that its accounts receivables opportunity cost is 18 percent of sales per year, or .05 percent per day.

Question

Is this customer profitable? What steps might make this account more profitable? Develop a method by which the profitability of accounts can be regularly determined.

The Commonwealth Edison Company of Chicago supplies the Greater Chicago area with the electric power its citizens and industries need to run their homes and businesses. Like other power utilities, Commonwealth's traditional policy has been to build up demand for electricity. Commonwealth encouraged home-owners to buy as many electric appliances as possible because "electrical living is better living." Commonwealth also engaged in intense competition with coal, oil, and natural gas suppliers every time a new high-rise apartment or office building was erected in Chicago.

The eruption of the worldwide energy crisis in the early seventies completely changed the picture. Energy suppliers found themselves in short supply and had to put their customers on allocation. They had to slow down or stop efforts to expand demand for their energy. This created all sorts of ironies. One executive observed: "It is interesting sport to convert salesmen of long standing from avid 'sellers' of our product to avid 'discouragers' of the use of our product. We've reached the ludicrous situation where the more effective the selling job we do, the lower our net revenues will be."

Top management at Commonwealth appointed a special committee to look into its alternatives for future marketing and come up with a recommendation. This committee's first step was to look at what other public utilities were doing. Committee members found a wide range of responses by leading power firms. At one extreme were a few utilities following "marketing-as-usual." They were better situated with fuels, relying more on nuclear-generated energy. They took a long-run view that the use of electric energy should be built up in relation to other types of energy.

At the other extreme, many utilities with inadequate capacity resorted to an aggressive demarketing policy. They put customers on allocation, rewarded customers who shifted their use of energy to off-peak hours, and waged public conservation campaigns calling upon customers to use less electricity. An example was Con Ed's campaign in New York called Save-A-Watt:

> The energy crisis has struck home. Your home and my home. What do I mean? Those lights we use. The television set. The radio. Other appliances. Maybe even an air conditioner. They're big watt-users. To keep them running takes electricity and that takes a lot of fuel. And supplies are short. So Con Edison urges you to Save-A-Watt. Because when you save watts, you save the fuel that's used to make electricity.

Commonwealth Edison's executives felt that neither "marketing-as-usual" nor aggressive demarketing was the answer. The company had to take some drastic steps because it could not supply its customers with all their needs at peak demand. It had redundant salesmen. On the other hand, it worried about the consequences of selling conservation too successfully. A public utility in a western state had so successfully got customers to cut down their energy use that the utility found itself with excess capacity. It was in the ironic position of trying to restimulate demand and finding this hard to do. General demarketing may be a one-way street.

The company's committee began to feel that the answer might lie in selling customers on the *wise use* of electricity rather than its *nonuse*. The marketing vice-president summarized this point of view:

We should not ask our customers to stop using electric power. Instead, we should call on them to use the available electric power more wisely. For example, they should be encouraged to buy air conditioners with energy efficiency ratings (EER) of 8 or more, not stop buying air conditioners. If air conditioners with an EER of 8 were sold from now until 1980, peak demand for energy would be reduced by two million kilowatts. People should be encouraged to insulate their homes better, clean their furnace filters, run their dishwashers and clothes washers at full loads, and in general use their appliances more wisely. Those who advocate a no-growth policy or drastic cutback in energy use should be aware of the adverse impact such moves will have on our living and working habits, the national economy, and our profitability. Wise use, not conservation, is the answer.

The committee had to come up with a recommendation for a revised marketing policy. It needed to propose short- and intermediate-run marketing objectives. It had to recommend what to do with rates, with the redundant sales force, and with advertising. It had to do this in the light of the company's relatively fortunate position in having seven nuclear plants which generated 30 percent of its power, making it less dependent on fossil fuels than many of its eastern utility counterparts.

INDICES

NAME INDEX

SUBJECT INDEX